DATE DUE

~~Mar 31~~			
~~Apr 14~~			

DEMCO 38-296

Risk Management and Insurance

Scott E. Harrington
University of South Carolina

Gregory R. Niehaus
University of South Carolina

Boston • Burr Ridge, IL • Dubuque, IA • Madison, WI
New York • San Francisco • St. Louis • Bangkok • Bogotá
Caracas • Lisbon • London • Madrid • Mexico City
Milan • New Delhi • Seoul • Singapore • Sydney
Taipei • Toronto

For Marcia and Liz and our parents

Irwin/McGraw-Hill

A Division of The McGraw-Hill Companies

RISK MANAGEMENT AND INSURANCE

Copyright © 1999 by The McGraw-Hill Companies, Inc. All rights reserved. Printed in the United States of America. Except as permitted under the United States Copyright Act of 1976, no part of this publication may be reproduced or distributed in any form or by any means, or stored in a data base or retrieval system, without the prior written permission of the publisher.

This book is printed on acid-free paper.

   3 4 5 6 7 8 9 0 DOC/DOC   3 2 1

ISBN 0-256-21018-7

Vice-president/Editor-in-chief: *Michael W. Junior*
Publisher: *Craig S. Beytien*
Developmental editor: *Michele Janicek*
Senior marketing manager: *Katie Rose Matthews*
Project manager: *Carrie Sestak*
Production associate: *Debra R. Benson*
Cover design: *Gino Cieslik*
Supplement coordinator: *Cathy L. Tepper*
Compositor: *ElectraGraphics, Inc.*
Typeface: *10/12 Times Roman*
Printer: *R. R. Donnelley & Sons Company*

Library of Congress Cataloging-in-Publication Data

Harrington, Scott E.
    Risk management and insurance / Scott E. Harrington, Gregory R.
Niehaus.
        p.   cm. -- (Irwin/McGraw-Hill series in finance, insurance,
and real estate)
    Includes index.
    ISBN 0-256-21018-7
    1. Risk (Insurance)   2. Risk management.   I. Niehaus, Greg.
II. Title.   III. Series.
HG8054.5.H37   1999
368--dc21   98-36318

http://www.mhhe.com

THE IRWIN/MCGRAW-HILL SERIES
IN FINANCE, INSURANCE AND REAL ESTATE

Stephen A. Ross
Franco Modigliani Professor of Financial Economics
Sloan School of Management
Massachusetts Institute of Technology
Consulting Editor

FINANCIAL MANAGEMENT

Benninga and Sarig
Corporate Finance: A Valuation Approach

Block and Hirt
Foundations of Financial Management
Eighth Edition

Brealey and Myers
Principles of Corporate Finance
Fifth Edition

Brealey, Myers, and Marcus
Fundamentals of Corporate Finance
Second Edition

Brooks
PC FinGame: The Financial Management Decision Game
Version 2.0—DOS and Windows

Bruner
Case Studies in Finance: Managing for Corporate Value Creation
Third Edition

Chew
The New Corporate Finance: Where Theory Meets Practice
Second Edition

Grinblatt and Titman
Financial Markets and Corporate Strategy

Helfert
Techniques of Financial Analysis: A Modern Approach
Ninth Edition

Higgins
Analysis for Financial Management
Fifth Edition

Hite
A Programmed Learning Guide to Finance

Kester, Fruhan, Piper, and Ruback
Case Problems in Finance
Eleventh Edition

Nunnally and Plath
Cases in Finance
Second Edition

Parker and Beaver
Risk Management: Challenges and Solutions

Ross, Westerfield, and Jaffe
Corporate Finance
Fifth Edition

Ross, Westerfield, and Jordan
Essentials of Corporate Finance
Second Edition

Ross, Westerfield and Jordan
Fundamentals of Corporate Finance
Fourth Edition

Schall and Haley
Introduction to Financial Management
Sixth Edition

Smith
The Modern Theory of Corporate Finance
Second Edition

White
Financial Analysis with an Electronic Calculator
Third Edition

INVESTMENTS

Ball and Kothari
Financial Statement Analysis

Bodie, Kane, and Marcus
Essentials of Investments
Third Edition

Bodie, Kane, and Marcus
Investments
Fourth Edition

Cohen, Zinbarg, and Zeikel
Investment Analysis and Portfolio Management
Fifth Edition

Farrell
Portfolio Management: Theory and Applications
Second Edition

Hirt and Block
Fundamentals of Investment Management
Sixth Edition

Jarrow
Modelling Fixed Income Securities and Interest Rate Options

Morningstar, Inc., and Remaley
U.S. Equities OnFloppy Educational Version
Annual Edition

Shimko
The Innovative Investor
Excel Version

FINANCIAL INSTITUTIONS AND MARKETS

Cornett and Saunders
Fundamentals of Financial Institutions Management

Flannery and Flood
Flannery and Flood's ProBanker: A Financial Services Simulation

Johnson
Financial Institutions and Markets: A Global Perspective

Rose
Commercial Bank Management
Third Edition

Rose
Money and Capital Markets: Financial Institutions and Instruments in a Global Marketplace
Sixth Edition

Rose and Kolari
Financial Institutions: Understanding and Managing Financial Services
Fifth Edition

Santomero and Babbel
Financial Markets, Instruments, and Institutions

Preface

Introduction

The types of risk, risk analysis tools, and methods used to manage risk are always changing. To illustrate, consider the following brief sampling of events that occurred during the 1990s:

- Large catastrophe losses disrupt property insurance markets and lead to innovative approaches to their financing.
- Legal liability for environmental damage expands.
- Rising costs of medical care lead to the widespread adoption of managed care systems by employers and health insurers.
- Corporations take a holistic approach to risk management.
- Eighty percent of Fortune 1000 companies use Monte Carlo simulation software to analyze and manage risk.
- Hedging price risk using derivatives continues to grow at high rates.

A course in risk management and insurance therefore requires that students be taught a framework for understanding the effects of risk, the tools and methods used to measure and manage risk, and the process of making risk management decisions. We believe that this new book accomplishes these tasks.

Background

Current risk management and insurance textbooks do an excellent job of describing the varied and complex institutional and contractual details of the insurance industry. While detailed institutional knowledge is important for those who currently work or plan to work in the insurance industry, the vast majority of business students do not plan to enter the insurance field. They are being trained to be general managers or specialists in other fields. Business students therefore need a general framework for thinking about the effects of risk and a broad knowledge of risk management and insurance. In addition, they need to be aware of the many important public policy issues related to risk, including legal liability and economic security issues. Students who seek careers in risk management and insurance also need a strong conceptual foundation for understanding institutional details. Because institutional details are constantly changing, it is very important for students to learn general concepts that can be applied to new sets of problems, new types of risk, and new institutional structures. In addition, introductory courses in risk management and insurance should stimulate critical thinking and promote the development of problem solving skills to better prepare students for meaningful careers in an information-intensive global economy.

Philosophy and Objectives

We believe that the overall philosophy of this book reflects an innovative approach to teaching risk management and insurance. We have attempted to achieve four major objectives:

1. Provide students with a broad perspective of risk management that, while emphasizing traditional risk management and insurance, introduces other types of risk management and stresses that the same general framework can be used to manage all types of risk.

2. Provide students with a conceptual framework for (*a*) making risk management and insurance decisions to increase business value and individual welfare; (*b*) understanding insurance contracts and institutional features of the insurance industry, including their relationship to contracts used to manage other types of risks; and (*c*) understanding the effects of and the rationale for public policies that affect risk and the allocation of risk among businesses and individuals.

3. Acquaint students with the essential details of insurance contracts and insurance markets without providing extensive descriptions of numerous types of insurance contracts, emphasizing how and why insurance contracts are designed as they are and how insurance markets function.

4. Enhance the ability of students to think critically and analytically and solve problems in order to better prepare them to confront the myriad opportunities and problems that confront business managers and individuals.

Examples of questions and issues that are examined in this book and receive much less coverage or no coverage in most existing texts include: (1) What are the economic functions of particular features of insurance contracts and insurer operations? (2) How does risk management affect the value of businesses with diversified shareholders, and why do these firms buy substantial amounts of insurance and use hedging instruments to reduce risk? (3) What decision rules are appropriate for loss control and the choice among loss financing methods, and how can these methods be applied? (4) Why are some types of risk insured, while other types of risk are hedged with financial contracts, such as futures and options contracts? (5) What are the causes and consequences of government policies to protect citizens from risk?

The objective of providing a broader perspective than other risk management and insurance texts reflects several influences. Because most contracts allocate risk among the contracting parties, many of the concepts and tools that we discuss are drawn from and apply to a wide variety of contracts, not just insurance contracts. In addition, there obviously are many important types of risk besides the risks covered in traditional risk management and insurance courses. These risks often can be successfully hedged using tools that are in many respects similar to insurance. We introduce these risks and associated hedging methods, again emphasizing that the same general framework is applicable to all types of risk. Given the increased importance of overall risk management in business management in recent years, this broader perspective is important for students who are being trained as general managers or specialists in other fields. It also has become increasingly important for specialists in traditional risk management and insurance to be familiar with other types of business risk and the tools used to manage these risks.

Finally, we believe that the issues associated with the allocation of risk in society are of fundamental importance and are inherently interesting. Without losing sight of our main task of studying risk management and insurance, we have tried to convey our enthusiasm for the topics and the wide applicability of the concepts and tools.

Intended Audience

This book is designed for use in introductory risk management and insurance courses at the undergraduate and MBA levels and in second level risk management courses. We have designed the book to be as flexible as possible. In particular, the structure and content allow instructors who do not wish to emphasize corporate risk management and financial issues in an introductory class to omit selected chapters or parts of chapters without loss of continuity. The main sections of each chapter are numbered to facilitate selective coverage. Moreover, while we frequently relate the material to concepts to which most business students will be exposed in basic economics, finance, and statistics classes, we have developed all of the key ideas assuming little or no student background in these subjects. Appendixes to several chapters provide more in-depth treatment of selected subjects. Instructors who feel that their students could profit from more discussion can assign these appendixes.

Organization

This book has seven main parts. Part I (Overview of Risk Management) contains two chapters that introduce the types of risk that are covered in the book, the risk management process, risk management methods, and objectives of risk management. This material will likely be covered whether the book is used for an introductory or a second level course.

Part II (Risk Reduction through Insurance Markets) includes six chapters that provide students with a foundation for understanding risk and insurance markets. Chapter 3 covers tools for measuring risk and shows how and why risk is reduced through pooling (diversification). Chapters 4 through 8 then discuss (1) risk pooling and insurance institutions; (2) insurer insolvency risk, solvency ratings, and regulation; (3) insurance pricing and price regulation; (4) basic aspects of the demand for risk reduction by individuals and businesses; and (5) factors that influence the insurability of risk, as well as insurance contract provisions and legal doctrines that enhance the insurability of risk. Most or all of this material normally will be covered in an introductory course, and it provides the foundation for discussion of specific types of risk and insurance in later chapters. Depending on students' background, several of these chapters also will likely be appropriate as a foundation for a second level course on risk management.

Part III (Fundamentals of Corporate Risk Management) contains five chapters with detailed discussion of how risk management affects business value, why large firms hedge risk and purchase insurance, loss financing methods, risk management decision making, and how insurance compares with hedging risk via financial derivatives. This material generally will be an integral part of a second level course on business risk management.

Part IV (Legal Liability and Worker Injury Risk) begins with a chapter on the economics of liability risk and the legal liability system. The other three chapters cover key business liability risk exposures and insurance for these exposures, workers' compensation, and issues in liability risk management. An introductory course commonly will cover much of this material, with the possible exception of one or more parts of Chapter 15 that deal with specific business liability risk exposures and coverage in Chapter 17 regarding issues in liability risk management. A second level course on risk management will likely cover Chapter 14 (the economics of liability risk and the legal liability system), Chapter 15 (specific business liability exposures), and Chapter 17 (issues in liability risk management). Depending on the treatment in a prior course, some instructors of second level courses on risk management also may choose to cover some or all of the material in Chapter 16 on worker injuries.

Part V (Benefit Plans and Social Security) provides an overview of employee benefit plans (Chapter 18), the issues related to group medical expense plans (Chapter 18), retirement plans (Chapter 19), and Social Security (Chapter 20). We expect that many instructors would include much of the material in these chapters.

Part VI (Personal Insurance) introduces personal insurance contracts and markets and discusses key public policy issues concerning personal insurance. The three chapters in this part deal with automobile insurance, homeowners insurance, and life insurance and annuities, respectively. We expect that many instructors will choose to cover much of this material in an introductory course.

Part VII (Government Regulation of Insurance Markets) contains a concluding chapter that summarizes key aspects of insurance regulation, including regulatory goals and the possible effects of political pressure on regulatory behavior. This chapter supplements the discussion of specific facets of regulation in earlier chapters, such as the discussion of solvency regulation in Chapter 5, price regulation in Chapter 6, and regulatory issues associated with particular types of insurance in a number of other chapters. Our discussion of regulation in these earlier chapters is based on our classroom experience, which suggests that it is both helpful and more interesting to students to cover selected aspects of regulation as issues arise.

Pedagogy

To further support the objectives of this text—that is, to present a broad perspective of risk management, provide a conceptual framework, and enhance critical and analytical thinking—the following features have been included:

Chapter Objectives. Each chapter begins with a list of key objectives, which provide students with an overview of the material they will learn in reading the chapter.

Concept Checks. Strategically placed throughout each chapter, these self-test questions enable the student to determine whether he or she has understood the preceding material and enhance critical thinking skills. Answers to these questions are found at the end of each chapter.

Key Terms. Key terms are found in bold throughout the text and are listed at the end of each chapter with page references for easy review.

Examples. The examples in the narrative of the text emphasize real-world applications of the material being covered. Students will recognize the currency of the examples and therefore will be able to more easily apply concepts learned from this text to future situations.

Current Events and Concepts Boxes. Boxes containing recent business press and journal articles are included in various chapters to provide an additional view of current risk management issues. Also, concepts and issues that are more specialized or advanced are set off in a separate boxed feature. This enables the discussion to be easily skipped if it is not integral to the course, but it also provides a good summary if the instructor chooses to cover it.

Exhibits. Tables, figures, and diagrams are included to help illustrate the topics in each chapter.

Summaries. This bulleted feature expands on the learning objectives by revisiting the important points in the chapter, providing an extra study aid for students at the end of the chapter.

Questions and Problems. This section includes both numerical problems and conceptual questions that build on the material learned in the chapter. Solutions are included in the Instructor's Manual.

References. Key articles are included at the end of each chapter, along with one-sentence descriptions.

Supplements

Instructor's Manual. Prepared by the authors, this teaching tool includes lecture outlines for each chapter, transparency masters, and solutions to the end-of-chapter questions and problems.

PowerPoint Presentation Software. Also prepared by the authors, the PowerPoint slides include the transparency masters in an electronic format. If you have PowerPoint installed on your PC, you have the ability to edit, print, or rearrange the complete presentation to meet your needs.

Test Bank. Prepared by Vickie Bajtelsmit, Colorado State University, the Test Bank includes multiple-choice questions, fill-ins, and problems and short-answers. Each question is coded as a "knowledge-based" or an "application-based" question. There are 15–20 questions per chapter.

ACKNOWLEDGMENTS

We wish to thank the reviewers and class testers for their valuable comments, many of which had a material impact on the finished product. They include:

Tom Aiuppa, *University of Wisconsin—La Crosse*

Vickie Bajtelsmit, *Colorado State University*

Mark Browne, *University of Wisconsin—Madison*

Ann Butler, *University of Illinois at Urbana-Champaign*

James Carson, *Illinois State University*

David Cather, *University of Pennsylvania, The Wharton School of Business*

Lisa Gardner, *Bradley University*

Jim Garven, *Louisiana State University*

Martin F. Grace, *Georgia State University*

Anne Kleffner, *University of Calgary*

Joan Lamm-Tennant, *Villanova University, and vice president, General Reinsurance Corporation*

Craig Merrill, *Brigham Young University*

Laureen Regan, *Temple University*

Allen Seward, *Baylor University*

David Shaheen, *Michigan State University*

David Sommer, *University of Georgia*

Sharon Tennyson, *Cornell University*

Special thanks are due to David Cather and Sharon Tennyson for taking the time and trouble to survey their Wharton students concerning the effectiveness of the first and second drafts of the manuscript. Additional thanks are due to Sharon for her suggestions throughout our development process. Two of our doctoral students, Karen Epermanis and Tong Yu, also provided useful input.

The editorial and production staff at McGraw-Hill were a delight to work with. We are grateful for the smooth transition following the merger of McGraw-Hill and Richard D. Irwin after this project was well under way. Special thanks are due to Carrie Sestak, project manager; Katie Rose Matthews, marketing manager; and especially Michele Janicek, development editor. Mike Junior, vice president/editor-in-chief, and Gina Huck were instrumental in getting this project off the ground.

The concepts and ideas developed in this book reflect our years of reading, thinking, and teaching about these subjects. Because this is a textbook and not a treatise, we did not attempt to cite a material fraction of the dozens of articles that have influenced us, apart from including a small number of end-of-chapter references that are likely to be appropriate for our target audience. Our intellectual debt is nonetheless very large. We also wish to acknowledge the late Robert I. Mehr of the University of Illinois at Urbana-Champaign, who had a defining influence on the career path of the first-named author. Finally and most of all, we wish to thank our wives and children for their encouragement and patience during the long process of completing this first edition.

Scott Harrington and Greg Niehaus
Columbia, South Carolina
June 1998

Contents

PART III

Fundamentals of Corporate Risk Management

9 Risk Management and Shareholder Wealth— A Financial Exposition   189

PART IV

Legal Liability and Worker Injury Risk

PART VII

Government Regulation of Insurance Markets

24   Insurance Regulation   635

Overview of Risk Management

Risk and Its Management

Chapter Objectives

- Discuss different meanings of the term *risk.*
- Describe major types of business risk.
- Explain and compare pure risk to other types of risk.
- Outline the risk management process and describe major risk management methods.
- Discuss organization of the risk management function within business.

1.1 Risk

Different Meanings of Risk

The term *risk* has a variety of meanings in business and everyday life. At its most general level, risk is used to describe any situation where there is uncertainty about what outcome will occur. Life is obviously very risky. Even the short-term future is often highly uncertain. In probability and statistics, financial management, and investment management, risk is often used in a more specific sense to indicate possible variability in outcomes around some expected value.

We will develop the ideas of expected value and risk as reflecting variability around the expected value in Chapter 3. For now it is sufficient for you to think of the expected value as the outcome that would occur on average over time if a person or business were repeatedly exposed to the same type of risk. If you have not yet encountered these concepts in statistics or finance classes, the following example from the sports world might help. Michael Jordan has averaged about 30 points per game in his career in the National Basketball Association. As we write this, he shows little sign of slowing down. It is therefore reasonable to assume that the expected value of his total points in any given game is about 30 points. Risk, in the sense of variability around the expected value, is clearly present. He might score 50 points or even higher in a particular game, or he might score as few as 10 points (e.g., if he were to break a leg early in the second quarter).

In other situations, the term risk may refer to the expected value of the outcome (or, sometimes, the probability of a particular outcome). In insurance markets, for example, it is common to refer to high-risk policyholders. The meaning of risk in this context is that the expected value of losses to be paid by the insurer (the expected loss) is high. As another example, California often is described as having a high risk of earthquake. While this statement might encompass the notion of variability around the expected value, it usually simply means that California's expected loss from earthquakes is high relative to other states.

Thus, the term risk refers broadly to situations where outcomes are uncertain. It is sometimes used in a specific sense to describe variability around the expected or average value, and other times to describe the expected value. We employ each of these meanings in this book because it is customary to do so in certain types of risk management and in the insurance business. The particular meaning usually will be obvious from the context.

Business Risk

While we introduce and analyze major risks that individuals face in their non-business pursuits, this book emphasizes business risk and its management. Broadly defined, business risk management is concerned with possible reductions in business value from any source. Business value to shareholders, as reflected in the value of the firm's common stock, depends fundamentally on the expected size, timing, and risk (variability) associated with the firm's future net cash flows (cash inflows less cash outflows). Unexpected changes in expected future net cash flows are a major source of fluctuations in business value. In particular, unexpected reductions in cash inflows or increases in cash outflows can significantly reduce business value. The major business risks that give rise to variation in cash flows and business value are price risk, credit risk, and pure risk.

Price Risk.   **Price risk** refers to uncertainty over the magnitude of cash flows due to possible changes in output and input prices. Output price risk refers to the risk of changes in the prices that a firm can demand for its goods and services. Input price risk refers to the risk of changes in the prices that a firm must pay for labor, materials, and other inputs to its production process. Analysis of price risk associated with the sale and production of existing and future products and services plays a central role in strategic management.[1]

Three specific types of price risk are *commodity price risk, exchange rate risk,* and *interest rate risk.* Commodity price risk arises from fluctuations in the prices of commodities, such as coal, copper, oil, gas, and electricity, that are inputs for some firms and outputs for others. Given the globalization of economic

---

[1] Thus, most strategic risks can be viewed as particular examples of price risk.

FIGURE 1–1

Major types of business risk

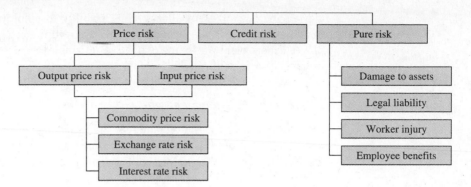

activity, output and input prices for many firms also are affected by fluctuations in foreign exchange rates. Output and input prices also can fluctuate due to changes in interest rates. For example, increases in interest rates may alter a firm's revenues by affecting both the terms of credit allowed and the speed with which customers pay for products purchased on credit. Changes in interest rates also affect the firm's cost of borrowing funds to finance its operations.[2]

Credit Risk.   The risk that a firm's customers and the parties to which it has lent money will fail to make promised payments is known as **credit risk.** Most firms face some credit risk for account receivables. The exposure to credit risk is particularly large for financial institutions, such as commercial banks, that routinely make loans that are subject to risk of default by the borrower. When firms borrow money, they in turn expose lenders to credit risk (i.e., the risk that the firm will default on its promised payments). As a consequence, borrowing exposes the firm's owners to the risk that the firm will be unable to pay its debts and thus be forced into bankruptcy, and the firm generally will have to pay more to borrow money because of credit risk.

Pure Risk.   The risk management function in medium-to-large corporations (and the term "risk management") has traditionally focused on the management of what is known as **pure risk.** As summarized in Figure 1–1, the major types of pure risk that affect businesses include:

   1. The risk of reduction in value of business assets due to physical damage, theft, and expropriation (i.e., seizure of assets by foreign governments).
   2. The risk of legal liability for damages for harm to customers, suppliers, shareholders, and other parties.
   3. The risk associated with paying benefits to injured workers under workers' compensation laws and the risk of legal liability for injuries or other harms to employees that are not governed by workers' compensation laws.

---

[2] More generally, changes in interest rates affect value through their effect on the present value of the firm's net cash flows, as reflected in the value of the firm's assets and liabilities.

4. The risk of death, illness, and disability to employees (and sometimes family members) for which businesses have agreed to make payments under employee benefit plans, including obligations to employees under pension and other retirement savings plans.

Comparison of Pure Risk and Its Management with Other Types of Risk

Much of this book focuses on pure risk and its management, including the use of insurance as a tool to reduce risk and finance losses for businesses and individuals. The framework that we present for managing risk, however, is very general. It can be applied with little or no modification to other types of risk. In addition, our detailed discussion of insurance markets and comparison of insurance contracts to the tools used to reduce other types of business risk will help you understand the rich variety of risk reduction methods available in modern risk management.

Common (but not necessarily distinctive) features of pure risk include the following.

1. Losses from destruction of property, legal liability, and employee injuries or illness often have the potential to be very large relative to a business's resources. While business value can increase if losses from pure risk turn out to be lower than expected, the maximum possible gain in these cases is usually relatively small. In contrast, the potential reduction in business value from losses greater than the expected value can be very large and even threaten the firm's viability.[3]

2. The underlying causes of losses associated with pure risk, such as the destruction of a plant by the explosion of a steam boiler or product liability suits from consumers injured by a particular product, are often largely specific to a particular firm and depend on the firm's actions. As a result, the underlying causes of these losses are often subject to a significant degree of control by businesses; that is, firms can reduce the frequency and severity of losses through actions that alter the underlying causes (e.g., by taking steps to reduce the probability of fire or lawsuit). In comparison, while firms can take a variety of steps to reduce their exposure or vulnerability to price risk, the underlying causes of some important types of price changes are largely beyond the control of individual firms (e.g., economic factors that cause changes in foreign exchange rates, marketwide changes in interest rates, or aggregate consumer demand).

3. Businesses commonly reduce uncertainty and finance losses associated with pure risk by purchasing contracts from insurance companies that specialize

---

[3] Pure risk sometimes is defined as risk where the random outcome can only result in loss (produce a cash outflow); that is, no outcome involving a gain (cash inflow) is possible. But this is also true for other uncertain cash outflows faced by firms (e.g., the cost of raw materials). This definition also ignores the fact that businesses or individuals gain financially whenever losses from pure risk are less than expected. The gain is no different in substance from the gain that would occur if the price of raw materials dropped so that the firm could buy them more cheaply.

in evaluating and bearing pure risk. The prevalence of insurance in part reflects the firm-specific nature of losses caused by pure risk. The fact that events that cause large losses to a given firm commonly have little effect on losses experienced by other firms facilitates risk reduction by diversification, which is accomplished with insurance contracts (see Chapters 3 and 4). Insurance contracts generally are not used to reduce uncertainty and finance losses associated with price risk (and many types of credit risk). Price risks that can simultaneously produce gains for many firms and losses for many others are commonly reduced with *financial derivatives,* such as forward and futures contracts, option contracts, and swaps (see Chapter 13). With these contracts, much of the risk of loss is often shifted to parties that have an opposite exposure to the particular risk.

4. Losses from pure risk usually are not associated with offsetting gains for other parties. In contrast, losses to businesses that arise from other types of risk often are associated with gains to other parties. For example, an increase in input prices harms the purchaser of the inputs but benefits the seller. Likewise, a decline in the dollar's value against foreign currencies can harm domestic importers but benefit domestic exporters and foreign importers of US goods.[4] One implication of this difference between pure risk and price risk is that losses from pure risk reduce the total wealth in society, whereas fluctuations in output and input prices need not reduce total wealth. In addition, and as we hinted above, the fact that price changes often produce losses for some firms and gains for others in many cases allows these firms to reduce risk by taking opposite positions in derivative contracts.

While many of the details concerning pure risk and its management differ from other types of risk, it is nonetheless important for you to understand that pure risk and its management are conceptually similar, if not identical, to other types of risk and their management. To make this concrete, consider the case of a manufacturer that uses oil in the production of consumer products. Such a firm faces the risk of large losses from product liability lawsuits if its products harm consumers, but it also faces the risk of potentially large losses from oil price increases. The business can manage the expected cost of product liability settlements or judgments by making the product's design safer or by providing safety instructions and warnings. While the business might not be able to do anything to reduce the likelihood or size of increases in oil prices, it might be able to reduce its exposure to losses from oil price increases by adopting a flexible technology that allows low cost conversion to other sources of energy. The business might purchase product liability insurance to reduce its liability risk; it might hedge its risk of loss from oil price increases using oil futures contracts.

While the concepts and broad risk management strategies are the same for pure risk and other types of business risk, the specific characteristics of pure risk and the significant reliance on insurance contracts as a method of managing these

---

[4] With respect to credit risk, one party's loss also is often associated with the other party's gain in the sense that the party that defaults on its obligation does not make payment.

risks generally lead to their management by personnel with specialized expertise. Major areas of expertise needed for pure risk management include risk analysis, safety management, insurance contracts, and other methods of reducing pure risk, as well as broad financial and managerial skills. The insurance business, with its principal function of reducing pure risk for businesses and individuals, employs millions of people and is one of the largest industries in the United States (and other developed countries). In addition, pure risk management and insurance have a major effect on many other sectors of the economy, such as the legal sector, medical care, real estate lending, and consumer credit.

Increases in business risk of all types and dramatic growth in the use of financial derivatives for hedging price risks in recent years have stimulated substantial growth in the scope and efforts devoted to overall business risk management. It has become increasingly important for managers that focus on pure risk to understand the management of other types of business risk. Similarly, general managers and managers of other types of risk need to understand how pure risk affects specific areas of activity and the business as a whole.

1.2 Risk Management

The Risk Management Process

Regardless of the type of risk being considered, the risk management process involves several key steps:

1. Identify all significant risks that can reduce business value (cause loss).
2. Evaluate the potential frequency and severity of losses.[5]
3. Develop and select methods for managing risk in order to increase business value to shareholders.
4. Implement the risk management methods chosen.
5. Monitor the performance and suitability of the firm's risk management methods and strategies on an ongoing basis.

The same general framework applies to individual risk management. You will learn more about major exposures to losses from pure risk, risk evaluation, and the selection and implementation of risk management methods in subsequent chapters. Chapter 2 discusses the objective of maximizing business value to shareholders in detail. It also discusses risk management objectives for nonprofit businesses, government entities, and individuals. It is useful in this introductory chapter to further acquaint you with basic aspects of risk management by briefly identifying the major types of losses that can arise from pure risk and then summarizing the major methods used to manage risk.

---

[5] If possible, this includes an estimation of the maximum loss that can reasonably be expected to occur in a given period with a relatively high level of confidence. This value is known in pure risk management as the *maximum probable loss* and in financial risk management as *value at risk* (see Chapter 12).

Losses from Pure Risk

Figure 1–2 summarizes the major types of direct and indirect losses that can arise from pure risk. Major examples of *direct losses* include losses from damage, destruction, or expropriation of assets; payments made to injured or ill employees; and the cost of paying and defending against liability claims.

Indirect losses arise as a consequence of direct losses. For example, damage to productive assets can produce an indirect loss by reducing or eliminating the normal profit (net cash flow) that the asset would have generated if the damage had not occurred. Large direct losses also can lead to indirect losses if they threaten the viability of the business and thereby reduce the willingness of customers and suppliers to deal with the business or change the terms (prices) at which they transact.

Moreover, if sales or production are reduced in response to direct losses, certain types of normal operating expenses (known as continuing expenses) may not decline in proportion to the reduction in revenues, thus increasing indirect losses. If a long interruption in production would cause many customers to switch suppliers, or if a firm has binding contractual commitments to supply products, it also may be desirable for the firm to increase operating costs above normal levels following direct losses. For example, some businesses might find it desirable to maintain production by leasing replacement equipment at a higher cost so as to avoid loss of sales. The increased operating cost would create an indirect loss. Similarly, a business that decides to recall defective products that have produced liability claims will incur product recall expenses and perhaps increased advertising costs to reduce damage to the firm's reputation.

Other forms of indirect losses include the possibility that the business will face a higher cost of obtaining funds from lenders or from new equity issues following large direct losses. In some cases, the higher costs of raising capital will cause the firm to forego making otherwise profitable investments. Finally, in the case of severe direct and indirect losses, the firm might have to reorganize or be liquidated through costly legal proceedings under bankruptcy law. Chapters 7 and

FIGURE 1–2

Types of losses from pure risk

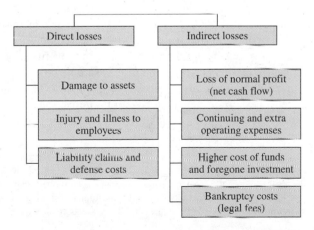

FIGURE 1–3

Major risk management methods

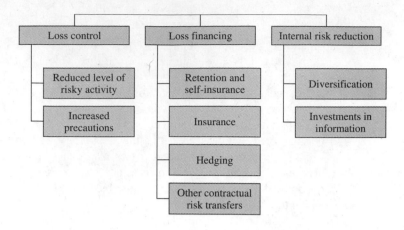

9 have more to say about these types of indirect losses and their potentially important influence on decisions to purchase insurance for direct losses and to hedge other types of risk.

Risk Management Methods

Figure 1–3 summarizes the major methods of managing risk. These methods, which are not mutually exclusive, can be broadly classified as (1) loss control, (2) loss financing, and (3) internal risk reduction. Loss control and internal risk reduction commonly involve decisions by firms to invest (or forego investing) resources in order to increase business value. They are conceptually equivalent to other investment decisions made by firms, such as the decision to buy a new plant. Loss financing activities reflect financing decisions that are conceptually similar to the firm's other financing decisions, such as deciding whether to finance investment in a new plant using debt or equity.

Loss Control. Actions that reduce the expected cost of losses by reducing the frequency of losses and/or the severity (size) of losses that occur are known as **loss control.** Loss control also is sometimes known as risk control.[6] Actions that primarily affect the frequency of losses are commonly called *loss prevention* methods. Actions that primarily influence the severity of losses that do occur are often called *loss reduction* methods. An example of loss prevention would be routine inspection of aircraft for mechanical problems. These inspections help reduce the frequency of crashes; they have little impact on the magnitude of losses for crashes that occur. An example of loss reduction is the installation of heat- or

---

[6] Use of the term *loss control* as opposed to *risk control* helps avoid confusion between activities that reduce the expected cost of losses and activities that reduce risk (variability), such as internal risk reduction. Terminology aside, the most important thing for you to understand is how these activities work and can be used to increase business value.

smoke-activated sprinkler systems that are designed to minimize fire damage in the event of a fire.

Many types of loss control influence both the frequency and severity of losses and cannot be readily classified as either loss prevention or loss reduction. For example, thorough safety testing of consumer products will likely reduce the number of injuries, but it also could affect the severity of injuries. Similarly, equipping automobiles with airbags in most cases should reduce the severity of injuries, but airbags also might influence the frequency of injuries. Whether injuries increase or decrease depends on whether the number of injuries that are completely prevented for accidents that occur exceeds the number of injuries that might be caused by airbags inflating at the wrong time or too forcefully, as well as any increase in accidents and injuries that could occur if protection by airbags causes some drivers to drive less safely.

Viewed from another perspective, there are two general approaches to loss control: (1) reducing the level of risky activity, and (2) increasing precautions against loss for activities that are undertaken. First, businesses can reduce their exposure to loss by reducing the level of their risky activities, for example, by cutting back production of risky products or shifting attention to less risky product lines. Limiting the level of risky activity will primarily affect the frequency of losses. The main cost of this strategy is that it foregoes any benefits of the risky activity that would have been achieved apart from the risk involved. In the limit, exposure to losses can be completely eliminated by reducing the level of activity to zero; that is, by not engaging in the activity at all. This strategy is called *risk avoidance.*

As a specific example of limiting the level of risky activity, consider a trucking firm that hauls toxic chemicals that might harm people or the environment in the case of an accident and thereby produce claims for damages. This firm could reduce the frequency of liability claims by cutting back on the number of shipments that it hauls. Alternatively, it could avoid the risk completely by not hauling toxic chemicals and instead hauling nontoxic substances (such as clothing or, apart from cholesterol, cheese). An example from personal risk management would be a person who flies less frequently in order to reduce the probability of dying in a plane crash. This risk could be completely avoided by never flying. Of course, alternative transportation methods might be much riskier (e.g., driving down Interstate 95 from New York to Miami the day before Thanksgiving—along with many long-haul trucks, including those transporting toxic chemicals).

The second major approach to loss control is to increase the amount of precautions (level of care) for a given level of risky activity. The goal here is to make the activity safer and thus reduce the frequency and/or severity of losses. Thorough testing for safety and installation of safety equipment are examples of increased precautions. The trucking firm in the example above could give its drivers extensive training in safety, limit the number of hours driven by a driver in a day, and reinforce containers to reduce the likelihood of leakage. Increased precautions usually involve direct expenditures or other costs (e.g., the increased time and attention required to drive an automobile more safely).

Concept Checks

1. Explain how the two major approaches to loss control (reducing risky activity and increasing precautions) could be used to reduce the risk of injury to construction firm employees.
2. How could these two approaches be used to reduce the risk of contracting a sexually transmitted disease?

Loss Financing.   Methods used to obtain funds to pay for or offset losses that occur are known as **loss financing** (sometimes called risk financing). There are four broad methods of financing losses: (1) retention, (2) insurance, (3) hedging, and (4) other contractual risk transfers. These approaches are not mutually exclusive; that is, they often are used in combination.

With **retention,** a business retains the obligation to pay for part or all of the losses. When coupled with a formal plan to fund losses for medium-to-large businesses, retention often is called *self-insurance.* In addition, many large businesses have established *captive insurance companies,* which in some cases can be viewed as a special type of self-insurance (see Chapter 11).

Internal sources of funds to pay retained losses include cash flows from ongoing activities, general working capital (the excess of the firm's liquid assets over its short-term liabilities), and investments in liquid assets that are dedicated to financing losses. Firms also may obtain funds by selling other business assets. External sources of funds to finance retained losses include borrowing and issuing new stock, but these approaches may be very costly following large losses (see Chapters 7 and 9). Note that these approaches still involve retention even though they employ external sources of funds. For example, the firm must pay back any funds borrowed to finance losses. When new stock is issued, the firm must share future profits with new stockholders.

The second major method of financing losses is the purchase of insurance contracts. As you most likely already know, the typical insurance contract requires the insurer to provide funds to pay for specified losses (thus financing these losses) in exchange for receiving a premium from the purchaser at the inception of the contract. Insurance contracts reduce risk for the buyer by transferring some of the risk of loss to the insurer. Insurers in turn reduce risk through diversification. For example, they sell large numbers of contracts that provide coverages for a variety of different losses (see Chapter 4).

The third broad method of loss financing is **hedging.** As noted above, financial derivatives, such as forwards, futures, options, and swaps, are used extensively to manage various types of risk, most notably price risk. These contracts can be used to hedge risk; that is, they may be used to offset losses that can occur from changes in interest rates, commodity prices, foreign exchange rates, and the like. Some derivatives have begun to be used in the management of pure risk, and it is possible that their use in pure risk management will expand in the future.

We discuss derivatives, their use in hedging risk, and how they compare to insurance in Chapter 13. At this point, it is useful to illustrate hedging with a very simple example (which we elaborate in Chapter 13). Firms that use oil in the production process are subject to loss from unexpected increases in oil prices; oil producers are subject to loss from unexpected decreases in oil prices. Both types of firms can hedge their risk by entering into a *forward contract* that requires the oil producer to provide the oil user with a specified amount of oil on a specified future delivery date at a predetermined price (known as the *forward price*), regardless of the market price of oil on that date. Because the forward price is agreed upon when the contract is written, the oil user and the oil producer both reduce their price risk.

The fourth major method of loss financing is to use one or more of a variety of **other contractual risk transfers** that allow businesses to transfer risk to another party. Like insurance contracts and derivatives, the use of these contracts also is pervasive in risk management. For example, businesses that engage independent contractors to perform some task routinely enter into contracts, commonly known as *hold harmless* and *indemnity agreements,* that require the contractor to protect the business from losing money from lawsuits that might arise if persons are injured by the contractor (see Chapter 17).

Internal Risk Reduction.   In addition to loss financing methods that allow businesses and individuals to reduce risk by transferring it to another entity, businesses can reduce risk internally. There are two major forms of **internal risk reduction:** (1) *diversification,* and (2) *investment in information.* Regarding the first of these, firms can reduce risk internally by diversifying their activities (i.e., not "putting all of their eggs in one basket"). You will learn the basics of how diversification reduces risk in Chapter 3. The main benefits and costs of firm diversification as a risk management method are explored in Chapter 13. In addition, the ability of shareholders to reduce risk through portfolio diversification is an important factor affecting insurance and hedging decisions (see Chapters 7 and 9).

The second major method of reducing risk internally is to invest in information to obtain superior forecasts of expected losses. Investing in information can produce more accurate estimates or forecasts of future cash flows, thus reducing variability of cash flows around the predicted value. Examples abound, including estimates of the frequency and severity of losses from pure risk, marketing research on the potential demand for different products to reduce output price risk, and forecasting future commodity prices or interest rates. One way that insurance companies reduce risk is by specializing in the analysis of data to obtain accurate forecasts of losses. Medium-to-large businesses often find it advantageous to reduce pure risk in this manner as well. Given the large demand for accurate forecasts of key variables that affect business value and determine the price of contracts that can be used to reduce risk (such as insurance and derivatives), many firms specialize in providing information and forecasts to other firms and parties.

Selecting Risk Management Methods to Increase Firm Value

We devote substantial discussion in later chapters to factors that affect the choice of risk management methods. When the objective of risk management is to maximize the value of the business to shareholders, the methods selected will depend upon the cost of each method and its effect on the expected cost and variability of losses, including its effect on employees, lenders, customers, and suppliers, as well as the amount of additional return that is necessary to compensate shareholders for bearing risk.

This choice often involves tradeoffs in costs that will be highlighted in later chapters. For example, by increasing expenditures on safety precautions, a firm can reduce the expected cost of direct and indirect losses. By increasing insurance costs and retaining less risk, the firm can reduce the expected cost of certain indirect losses and reduce the variability in its net cash flows and costs associated with variability. As we suggested above in the discussion of internal risk reduction, an important factor influencing risk reduction decisions is the extent to which the benefits of risk reduction to shareholders are significantly reduced by the ability of shareholders to reduce risk on their own through portfolio diversification.

1.3 Risk Management Organization

Where does the risk management function fit within the overall organizational structure of businesses? In general, the views of senior management concerning the need for, scope, and importance of risk management and possible administrative efficiencies determine how the risk management function is structured and the exact responsibilities of units devoted to risk management. Most large companies have a specific department responsible for managing pure risk that is headed by the *risk manager* (or director of risk management). However, given that losses can arise from numerous sources, the overall risk management process ideally reflects a coordinated effort between all of the corporation's major departments and business units, including production, marketing, finance, and human resources.

Depending on a company's size, a typical risk management department includes various staff specializing in areas such as property–liability insurance, workers' compensation, safety and environmental hazards, claims management, and, in many cases, employee benefits. Given the complexity of modern risk management, most firms with significant exposure to price risk related to the cost of raw materials, interest rate changes, or changes in foreign exchange rates have separate departments or staff members that deal with these risks. Whether there will be more movement in the future toward combining the management of these risks with pure risk management within a unified risk management department is uncertain.

In most firms, the risk management function is subordinate to and thus reports to the finance (treasury) department. This is because of the close relationships between protecting assets from loss, financing losses, and the finance function. However, some firms with substantial liability exposures have the risk management department report to the legal department. A smaller proportion of firms have the risk management unit report to the human resources department.

Firms also vary in the extent to which the risk management function is centralized, as opposed to having responsibility spread among the operating units. Centralization may achieve possible economies of scale in arranging loss financing. Moreover, many risk management decisions are strategic in nature, and centralization facilitates effective interaction between the risk manager and senior management.

A possible limitation of a centralized risk management function is that it can reduce concern for risk management among the managers and employees of a firm's various operating units. However, allocating the cost of risk or losses to particular units often can improve incentives for unit managers to control costs even if the overall risk management function is centralized (see Chapter 11). On the other hand, there are advantages to decentralizing certain risk management activities, such as routine safety and environmental issues. In these cases, operating managers are close to the risk and can deal effectively and directly with many issues.

1.4 Summary

- The term *risk* broadly refers to situations where outcomes are uncertain. Risk often refers specifically to variability in outcomes around the expected value. In other cases, it refers to the expected value (e.g., the expected value of losses).
- Major types of business risk that produce fluctuations in business value include price risk, credit risk, and pure risk.
- Pure risk encompasses risk of loss from (1) damage to and theft or expropriation of business assets, (2) legal liability for injuries to customers and other parties, (3) workplace injuries to employees, and (4) obligations assumed by businesses under employee benefit plans. Pure risk frequently is managed in part by the purchase of insurance to finance losses and reduce risk.
- Risk management involves (1) identification of potential direct and indirect losses, (2) evaluation of their potential frequency and severity, (3) development and selection of

  methods for managing risk to maximize business value, (4) implementation of these methods, and (5) ongoing monitoring.
- Major risk management methods include loss control, loss financing, and internal risk reduction.
- Loss control reduces expected losses by lowering the level of risky activity and/or increasing precautions against loss for any given level of risky activity.
- Loss financing methods include retention (self-insurance), insurance, hedging, and other contractual risk transfers.
- Many businesses achieve internal risk reduction through diversification and through investments in information to improve forecasts of expected cash flows.
- Most large corporations have a specific department, headed by the risk manager, that is devoted to the management of pure risk and, in some cases, other types of risk.

Key Terms

price risk   4
credit risk   5
pure risk   5
loss control   10
loss financing   12

retention   12
hedging   12
other contractual risk transfers   13
internal risk reduction   13

Questions and Problems

1. Explain the ways in which the risk of loss from a major fire at a hotel differs from the risk of loss to a manufacturer due to an increase in wages needed to attract and retain workers.

2. Describe possible direct and indirect losses to a business from: (*a*) an explosion that produces major damage to a manufacturing plant, and (*b*) lawsuits arising from the business's release of toxic chemicals that damage the environment.

3. Explain how a business could reduce the risk of loss from lawsuits by consumers injured by the business's products.

4. Describe loss control measures that you could take to reduce your risk of being injured in an automobile accident.

5. What major methods are used to finance losses? How does loss financing differ from internal risk reduction?

Answers to Concept Checks

1. Taking on less hazardous projects and/or reducing the total number of projects would reduce the level of risky activity. Examples of increasing precautions for a given level of risky activity include giving employees safety instruction and making them wear protective devices (such as hard hats).

2. The level of risky activity could be reduced by abstinence (complete or partial). An example of increasing precautions for a given level of risk activity (number of contacts) would be the regular use of protective devices (such as condoms).

CHAPTER 2

Objectives of Risk Management

Chapter Objectives

- Define and explain business value maximization as the overall objective of risk management.
- Explain the cost of risk and how minimizing the cost of risk maximizes business value.
- Explain the overall objective of risk management for individuals and society and discuss possible conflicts between business and societal objectives.

2.1 Risk, Value, and Value Maximization

In the first chapter you learned that risk refers to either variability of cash flows (or other outcomes) around the expected value or, in other contexts, the expected value of losses. Holding all else equal, both types of risk—cash flow variability and expected losses—generally reduce business value and the value to individuals of engaging in various activities. Risk management seeks to mitigate this reduction in value and thus increase business value and individual welfare. Two simple examples should help illustrate how risk reduces value and how risk management can increase value: (1) the risk of product liability claims against a pharmaceutical company, and (2) the risk to individuals associated with automobile accidents.

Consider first a pharmaceutical company that is developing a new prescription drug for the treatment of rheumatoid arthritis, a crippling disease of the joints. The risk of adverse health reactions to the drug and thus legal liability claims by injured users could be substantial. The possibility of injuries, which cause the firm (and/or its liability insurer) to defend lawsuits and pay damages, will increase the business's expected costs. Loss control, such as expenditures on product development and safety testing that reduce expected legal defense costs and expected damage payments, also will be costly.

If the firm purchases liability insurance to finance part of the potential losses, the premium paid will include a "loading" to cover the insurer's administrative costs and provide a reasonable expected return on the insurer's capital (see Chapter 6). The possibility of uninsured damage claims (self-insured losses or losses in excess of liability insurance coverage limits) will create uncertainty about the amount of costs that will be incurred in any given period.

Most and perhaps all of these factors can increase the price that the firm will need to charge for the drug, thus reducing demand. For a given price, the risk of injury also might discourage some doctors from prescribing the drug. The risk of injury also might cause the firm and the medical profession to distribute the drug only to the most severe cases of the disease, or the firm might even decide not to introduce the drug. As a result, from the company's perspective, the risk of consumer injury could have a significant effect on the value of introducing the drug.

Now consider the risk that you will be involved in an auto accident, which could cause physical harm to you and your vehicle, as well as exposing you to the risk of a lawsuit for harming someone else. The possibility of being involved in an accident reduces the value of driving. Other things being equal, people obviously would prefer to have a lower likelihood of accident. But other things are not equal. Safety equipment included in vehicles usually increases their price. Attempting to reduce the likelihood of injury by driving less also can be costly. You either must stay home or take alternative transportation that may not be as attractive as driving (apart from the risk of accident). Driving more safely usually means taking more time to get places, or it requires greater concentration, which means you cannot think as much about other things while you are behind the wheel.

In addition to the component needed to pay losses, auto and health insurance premiums must again include a loading for the insurer's administrative costs and to provide a reasonable expected return on the insurer's capital. Even with insurance, you face some uncertainty about the cost of losses that are less than your deductible (or for liability losses greater than policy limits). You also are exposed to uninsured indirect losses that arise from accidents, such as the time lost in getting your car repaired and submitting a claim to your insurer.

Along with the discussion in Chapter 1, you should be thoroughly convinced by now that risk is costly. Given these costs, what is the overall objective of risk management? With respect to business risk and its management, we assume throughout the book that the overall objective of risk management for "for-profit" businesses is **value maximization.** This objective is a basic tenet of modern financial theory, which generally assumes that businesses make decisions to maximize the value of the firm's stock price, thus maximizing the wealth of shareholders. The value maximization assumption is grounded in reality because a number of factors provide strong incentives for managers to pursue this goal (see Box 2–1).[1]

---

[1] We take it as given that a market economy with an emphasis on private property and individual freedom to pursue profits—subject to appropriate legal constraints to protect other parties from harm and social programs to aid disadvantaged persons—is the best achievable method of enhancing economic welfare. Thus, firm value maximization also has an ethical foundation.

Box 2–1

Will Managers Maximize Value?

Owner-managers (e.g., sole proprietors, managing partners, and owner-managers of corporations without publicly traded common stock) have a clear incentive to operate their businesses to achieve their own interests. This generally will involve value maximization provided that value is appropriately defined to reflect the owners' attitude toward risk and their ability to diversify their risk of ownership.

One of the longest and most thoroughly debated subjects in business economics and finance is whether managers of large corporations with widely held common stock (i.e., with large numbers of shareholders that are not involved in management) will diligently strive to maximize value to shareholders. The ownership and management functions are separated in businesses with widely held common stock. Managers can be viewed as agents of shareholders. Managers may have incentives to take actions that benefit themselves at a cost to shareholders, thus failing to maximize shareholder wealth. The costs associated with these actions, including the costs incurred by shareholders in monitoring managerial behavior, are broadly referred to as *agency costs.*

Agency costs reduce business value. In the context of risk management, agency costs might be manifested by managers being excessively cautious. Because managers could be seriously harmed by financial distress of the firm, they might spend more money than is needed on insurance, loss control, or other methods of reducing the likelihood of financial distress.

From a normative perspective (i.e., from the perspective of how people or businesses *should* behave), managers are agents of shareholders and therefore should seek to maximize value. As a practical matter, a number of factors give managers strong incentives not to deviate too much from value maximization, thus reducing agency costs:

1. Managers often are compensated in part with bonuses linked to the firm's profitability (and thus indirectly to its stock price), or with stock or stock options that directly increase managers' personal wealth when the firm's stock price increases. These performance-based compensation systems provide a direct incentive for value maximization. Poor performance by managers also can reduce their prospects for achieving employment with other firms (it can reduce their value in the managerial labor market).

2. Failing to maximize the value of the firm's stock makes it more likely that the firm will be acquired by another firm or parties that can then replace current top management with managers that will take actions to increase firm value.

3. If failure by managers to control costs, including the cost of risk, increases the price or reduces the quality of the firm's products, the firm will lose sales to firms with managers who are more inclined to control costs and increase value. This outcome makes it more likely that managers will be replaced and/or that the managers' salaries will be lower than if they maximized value.

4. Many firms have stockholders with large stakes and other stakeholders (such as lenders) that routinely monitor managerial performance.

5. State laws and the legal liability system impose fiduciary duties on managers. Failing to act in the interest of shareholders can give rise to lawsuits against managers and potential legal liability.

2.2 Value Maximization and the Cost of Risk

Determinants of Value

As we noted in Chapter 1, a business's value to shareholders depends fundamentally on the expected magnitude, timing, and risk (variability) associated with future net cash flows (cash inflows minus cash outflows) that will be available to provide shareholders with a return on their investment. If these concepts are new to you, you might be thinking, I thought that stock prices depended on profits. Your thinking is correct, but fundamentally, economic value depends on flows of money that can be used for consumption and investment rather than on accounting rules for reporting business profits (income).

Business value and the effects of risk on value reflect an ex ante perspective: Value depends on expected future net cash flows and risk associated with these cash flows. Cash inflows primarily result from sales of goods and services. Cash outflows primarily arise from the production of goods and services (e.g., wages and salaries, the cost of raw materials, interest on borrowed funds, and liability losses). Increases in the expected size of net cash flows increase business value; decreases in expected net cash flows reduce value. The timing of cash flows affects value because a dollar received today is worth more than a dollar received in the future. The reason for this is that a dollar received today can be spent immediately or invested to accumulate more dollars to spend in the future.[2]

Unexpected changes in a firm's cash flows cause fluctuations in its stock price. Because most investors are risk averse, the resulting risk reduces the price that they are willing to pay for the firm's stock and thus its value (provided that this risk cannot be eliminated by investors holding a diversified portfolio of investments, which we discuss in more detail in Chapter 7). For a given level of expected net cash flows, this reduction in the firm's stock price due to risk increases the expected return from buying the stock. In other words, the variation in net cash flows causes investors to pay less for the rights to future cash flows, which increases the expected return on the amount that they invest. Thus, a fundamental principle of business valuation is that risk reduces value and increases the expected return required by investors. The actual return to investors in any given period will depend on realizations of net cash flows during the period and new information about the expected future net cash flows and risk.

Maximizing Value by Minimizing the Cost of Risk

Unexpected increases in losses from pure risk or other types of risk that are not offset by cash inflows from insurance contracts, hedging arrangements, or other contractual risk transfers (see Chapter 1) increase cash outflows and often reduce cash inflows, thus reducing the value of a firm's stock. The effects of risk and risk management on firm value before losses are known reflect their influence on (1) the expected value of net cash flows and (2) the compensation required by shareholders to bear risk. Much of basic financial theory deals with the kind of risk for which investors demand compensation and the amount of compensation required. We will have more to say about how risk affects expected cash flows, risk, and required compensation in later chapters. For now, it is sufficient for you to under-

---

[2] As a result, value depends on what is called the *present value* of expected net cash flows. We discuss how to calculate present value when we introduce insurance pricing in Chapter 6, and we use this concept in a number of later chapters.

stand that making risk management decisions to maximize business value requires an understanding of how risk and risk management methods affect (1) expected net cash flows and (2) the compensation for risk that is required by shareholders.

The reduction in business value that arises from risk is known as the **cost of risk.** The cost of risk is a general concept that applies to all types of risks. However, it is helpful to explain this somewhat abstract concept by focusing first on pure risk and the **cost of pure risk.** We illustrate the cost of risk concept for price risk later in the chapter.

If the cost of pure risk is defined to include all pure risk-related costs from the perspective of shareholders, *a business can maximize its value to shareholders by minimizing the cost of pure risk.* To see this, note first that an appropriate definition of the cost of pure risk is the reduction in value to shareholders that occurs due to the presence of pure risk. This definition implies:

$$\text{Cost of pure risk} = \text{Value without pure risk} - \text{Value with pure risk} \quad (2.1)$$

Writing this expression in terms of the firm's value to shareholders in the presence of pure risk gives:

$$\text{Value with pure risk} = \text{Value without pure risk} - \text{Cost of pure risk} \quad (2.2)$$

The value of the firm without pure risk is a hypothetical and abstract concept that is nonetheless very useful. It equals the hypothetical value of the business in a world in which losses and uncertainty associated with losses could be eliminated at zero cost. This hypothetical value reflects the magnitude and timing of future net cash flows that would occur without pure risk and pure risk–related costs. We emphasize that this value is entirely hypothetical because pure risk is inherent in real-world business activities.

To illustrate the cost of pure risk, consider the product liability example introduced earlier. For the pharmaceutical company, the value of the firm without pure risk is the hypothetical value that would arise if (1) it were impossible for the drug to hurt consumers and thus produce lawsuits and (2) the firm did not have to incur any cost to achieve this state of riskless bliss. The reality of injury risk and the costs of loss control give rise to risk-related costs, thus reducing the value of the business.

Equation 2.2 implies that if the firm seeks to maximize value, it can do so by minimizing the cost of pure risk. It accomplishes this by making the reduction in value due to risk as small as possible. Thus, *as long as costs are defined to include all the effects on value of risk and risk management,* minimizing the cost of pure risk is the same thing as maximizing value. More generally, minimizing the firm's cost of risk for all risks that it faces maximizes its value.

Why bother introducing the cost of risk instead of just talking about value maximization? First, the cost of risk concept helps focus attention on and facilitates categorization of the major ways that risk reduces value. Second, the concept is used extensively in practice (although its breadth is sometimes narrower, as is noted below). Third, the cost of risk concept is frequently used in discussions of public policy issues and societal goals related to pure risk and its management, and it applies with some modification to individual risk management. In these contexts, it is more succinct and less abstract to talk about the cost of risk than about reductions in the "value of society's scarce resources" or reductions in the "expected utility" of individuals (concepts that are introduced later in this chapter).

2.3 Understanding the Cost of Risk

Recall from Chapter 1 that most risk management decisions must be made before losses are known. The magnitude of actual losses during a given time period can be determined after the fact (i.e., after the number and severity of accidents are known). Before losses occur, the cost of direct and indirect losses reflects the predicted or expected value of losses during an upcoming time period. Thus, the cost of losses can be determined ex post (after the fact) and estimated ex ante (before the fact). Most risk management decisions must be based on ex ante estimates of the cost of losses and thus the cost of risk.

Components of the Cost of Risk

Regardless of the type of risk being considered, the cost of risk has five main components. However, it is again useful to discuss these components for the case of pure risk. Using the ex ante perspective, the cost of pure risk includes: (1) the expected cost of losses, (2) the cost of loss control, (3) the cost of loss financing, (4) the cost of internal risk reduction, and (5) the cost of any residual uncertainty that remains after loss control, loss financing, and internal risk reduction methods have been implemented. Figure 2–1 summarizes these five components.

FIGURE 2–1

Components of the cost of risk

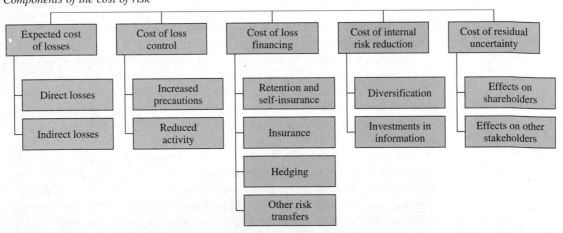

Expected Cost of Losses.   The **expected cost of losses** includes the expected cost of both direct and indirect losses. As you learned in the last chapter, major types of direct losses include the cost of repairing or replacing damaged assets, the cost of paying workers' compensation claims to injured workers, and the cost of defending against and settling liability claims. Indirect losses include reductions in net profits that occur as a consequence of direct losses, such as the loss of normal profits and continuing and extra expense when production is curtailed or stopped due to direct damage to physical assets. In the case of large losses, indirect losses can include loss of profits from foregone investment and, in the event of bankruptcy, legal expenses and other costs associated with reorganizing or liquidating a business.

In the case of the pharmaceutical company discussed earlier, the expected cost of direct losses would include the expected cost of liability settlements and defense. The expected cost of indirect losses would include items such as (1) the expected cost of lost profit if sales had to be reduced due to adverse liability experience, (2) the expected cost of product recall expenses, and (3) the expected loss in profit on any investments that would not be undertaken if large liability losses were to deplete the firm's internal funds available for investment and increase the cost of borrowing or raising new equity.

Cost of Loss Control.   The **cost of loss control** reflects the cost of increased precautions and limits on risk activity designed to reduce the frequency and severity of accidents. For example, the cost of loss control for the pharmaceutical company would include the cost of testing the product for safety prior to its introduction and any lost profit from limiting distribution of the product in order to reduce exposure to lawsuits.

Cost of Loss Financing.   The **cost of loss financing** includes the cost of self-insurance, the loading in insurance premiums, and the transaction costs in arranging, negotiating, and enforcing hedging arrangements and other contractual risk transfers. The cost of self-insurance includes the cost of maintaining reserve funds to pay losses. This cost in turn includes taxes on income from investing these funds, as well as the possible opportunity cost that can occur if maintaining reserve funds reduces the ability of a business to undertake profitable investment opportunities (see Chapter 11).

Note that when losses are insured, the cost of loss financing through insurance only reflects the loading in the policy's premium for the insurer's administrative expenses and required expected profit. The amount of premium required for the expected value of insured losses is included in the firm's expected cost of losses.

Cost of Internal Risk Reduction Methods.   Insurance, hedging, other contractual risk transfers, and certain types of loss control can reduce the uncertainty associated with losses; that is, these risk management methods can make the cost of losses more predictable. You learned in Chapter 1 that uncertainty also can be reduced through diversification and investing in information to obtain better forecasts of losses. The **cost of internal risk reduction** includes transaction costs associated with achieving diversification and the cost associated with managing a diversified set of activities (see Chapter 13). It also includes the cost of obtaining and analyzing data and other types of information to obtain more accurate cost forecasts. In some cases this may involve paying another firm for this information; for example, the pharmaceutical company may pay a risk management consultant to estimate the firm's expected liability costs.

Cost of Residual Uncertainty.   Uncertainty about the magnitude of losses seldom will be completely eliminated through loss control, insurance, hedging, other contractual risk transfers, and internal risk reduction. The cost of uncertainty that remains (that is "left over") once the firm has selected and implemented loss control, loss financing, and internal risk reduction is called the **cost of residual uncertainty.** This cost arises because uncertainty generally is costly to risk-averse individuals and investors. For example, residual uncertainty can affect the amount of compensation that investors require to hold a firm's stock.

Residual uncertainty also can reduce value through its effects on expected net cash flows. For example, residual uncertainty might reduce the price that customers are willing to pay for the firm's products or cause managers or employees to require higher wages (e.g., the top managers of the pharmaceutical company could require higher pay to compensate them for uncertainty associated with product liability claims).[3] We provide detailed discussion of how residual uncertainty affects individuals and shareholders of large corporations in Chapters 7 and 9.

Cost Tradeoffs

A number of tradeoffs exist among the components of the cost of risk. The three most important cost tradeoffs are those between: (1) the expected cost of direct/indirect losses and loss control costs, (2) the cost of loss financing/internal risk reduction and the expected cost of indirect losses, and (3) the cost of loss financing/internal risk reduction and the cost of residual uncertainty.

First, recall from Chapter 1 that a tradeoff normally exists between expected losses (both direct and indirect) and loss control costs. Increasing loss control costs should reduce expected losses. In the case of the pharmaceutical company, for example, expenditures on developing a safer drug will reduce the expected cost of liability suits. Ignoring for simplicity the possible effects of loss control on other components of the cost of risk (such as the cost of residual uncertainty),

---

[3] Note that these managers also may require higher pay because of the expected cost of indirect losses to them from, for example, lost pay and the costs of seeking new employment if large losses cause them to lose their jobs. The cost of residual uncertainty in this case reflects the increase in pay above the amount needed to compensate managers for the expected cost of these indirect losses. That is, the cost of residual uncertainty arises because of the uncertainty about whether these costs will be incurred.

minimizing the cost of risk requires the firm to invest in loss control until the marginal benefit—in the form of lower expected costs resulting from direct and indirect losses—equals the marginal cost of loss control (see Chapters 12 and 14).

The amount of loss control that minimizes the cost of risk generally will not involve eliminating the risk of loss. (We touched on this point in Chapter 1.) It will not produce a world in which buildings never burn, workers are never hurt, and products never harm customers because *reducing the probability of loss to zero would be too costly.* Beyond some point, the cost of additional loss control exceeds the reduction in the expected cost of losses (that is, the marginal cost exceeds the marginal benefit) so that additional loss control will increase the cost of risk. Eliminating the risk of loss will not minimize the cost of risk for either businesses or society.

Even if it were technologically feasible to eliminate the risk of harm, people would not want to live in such a world. It simply would be too expensive. To use an absurd example to prove this point, injuries from automobile accidents might be virtually eliminated if automobiles were simply tanks without weapons. But very few people could afford to drive a tank, and those who could would rather risk injury and get to their destination more quickly with a pickup or luxury sports sedan. Because loss control is costly, a point is reached where people prefer some risk of harm to paying more for goods and services or incurring other costs to reduce risk.

The second major tradeoff among the components of the cost of risk is the tradeoff between the costs of loss financing/internal risk reduction and the expected cost of indirect losses. As more money is spent on loss financing/internal risk reduction, variability in the firm's cash flows declines. Lower variability reduces the probability of costly bankruptcy and the probability that the firm will forego profitable investments as a result of large uninsured losses. As a result, the expected cost of these indirect losses declines. This tradeoff between the costs of loss financing/internal risk reduction and the expected cost of indirect losses is of central importance in understanding when firms with diversified shareholders will purchase insurance or hedge (see Chapters 7 and 9).

The third major tradeoff is that which often occurs between the costs of loss financing/internal risk reduction and the cost of residual uncertainty. For example, if the firm incurs higher loss financing costs by purchasing insurance, residual uncertainty declines. Greater and more costly internal risk reduction also reduces residual uncertainty.

Concept Checks

1. For an airline, describe the most important components of the cost of risk that arise from the risk of plane crashes.

2. How might the risk of crashes be eliminated by the airline, if at all?

3. Assume that you want to fly across the country and that for a price of $400 the probability of a fatal crash is one in a million trips. In order to reduce this probability to one in 1.5 million trips, the price of a ticket would increase to $800. Would you be willing to pay the extra $400?

Measuring the Cost of Pure Risk

In order to maximize business value by minimizing the cost of pure risk, businesses ideally will estimate the size of the various components of the cost of pure risk and consider how these costs will be affected by the firm's operating and risk management decisions. However, in practice, the necessary analysis is costly. Moreover, some of the components are particularly difficult to measure. Examples include the estimated cost of foregone activity (e.g., profits that would have been achieved but for risk and the reduction in activity), the impact of decisions on customers or suppliers, and the cost of residual uncertainty.

As a result of these practical limitations, businesses often will not attempt to quantify all of their costs precisely. Small businesses especially are unlikely to measure costs with much precision because the·cost of analysis is usually large compared to the potential benefit in the form of improved decisions. However, even when quantifying the various components of the cost of risk is not cost-effective, managers need to understand these components and the general ways in which their magnitude will be affected by risk management. This understanding is necessary for making informed decisions using intuitive and subjective assessments of the effects of decisions on costs.[4]

Cost of Other Types of Risk

The cost of risk is a general concept. With some modification, our discussion of the cost of pure risk is applicable to other types of risk. To illustrate, we will briefly discuss the risk of input price changes, using the specific example of a manufacturer that uses oil in its production process. In this case, the prices charged for the firm's products generally will not immediately adjust to reflect changes in the price of oil so that the firm's profits will be affected by oil price changes. Oil price increases will cause the firm's profits (or net cash flows) to decline in the short run, and oil price decreases will lead to a short-run increase in profits.

From an ex ante perspective, the expected cost of oil is analogous to the expected cost of direct losses from pure risk, such as those associated with product liability claims against the pharmaceutical company. Ex post, the actual cost of oil price changes can differ from what was expected, just as the actual costs from product liability claims can differ from those expected. If costs are greater than expected, then profits will be lower than expected in both cases. However, because oil is an integral input to the production process for which ongoing expen-

---

[4] Some survey evidence exists on the magnitude of the cost of pure risk for large corporations (see *Cost of Risk Survey,* Risk and Insurance Management Society, New York, NY). Corporate respondents provide estimates of amounts spent on property–liability insurance, uninsured losses, and loss control and loss financing programs. While still valuable to managers, these estimates of the total cost of risk will underestimate the true cost (perhaps substantially in many cases) because information on the cost of loss control that arises from reducing the level of risky activity and many indirect costs of losses are not included, presumably due to the difficulty of estimating these costs.

ditures are routinely expected, the expected cost of oil normally would not be considered as part of the cost of risk. (Similarly, while wages paid to employees can differ from what is expected, the expected cost of wages normally would not be considered as part of the cost of risk.)

Large increases in the price of oil could cause indirect costs if, for example, production is reduced, alternative sources of energy need to be arranged, or profitable investment is curtailed. The possibility of indirect costs increases the expected cost of using oil in the production process. Expenditures on loss control, such as redesigning the production process to allow for the substitution of other sources of energy, would decrease the expected cost of oil use and indirect losses.

With regard to loss financing, the manufacturer might choose to reduce its exposure to the risk of oil price changes with futures contracts. As we explain in Chapter 13, the appropriate use of futures will produce a profit if oil prices increase, thus offsetting all or part of the loss to the firm. (If oil prices drop, all or part of the gain that the firm otherwise would experience will be offset by a loss on its futures contracts.) However, the use of futures contracts involves transaction costs that are analogous to the loading in insurance premiums. The firm also might engage in internal risk reduction by diversifying its activities to reduce the sensitivity of its profits to oil price changes or by investing in information to obtain better forecasts of oil prices.

You can see from this simple example that the cost of risk concept illustrated in Figure 2–1 is quite general. This concept provides a useful way of thinking about and evaluating all types of risk management decisions.

2.4 Other Goals of Business Risk Management

Subsidiary Goals

While the overall objective of risk management is to maximize business value to shareholders by minimizing the cost of risk, a variety of subsidiary goals are used to guide day-to-day decision making. Examples of these subsidiary goals include making insurance decisions to keep the realized cost of uninsured losses below a specified percent of revenues, purchasing insurance against any loss that could be large enough to seriously disrupt operations, making decisions to comply with stipulations in loan contracts on the types and amounts of insurance that must be purchased, and spending money on loss control when the savings on insurance premiums are sufficient to outweigh the costs. These types of rules generally can be viewed as a means to an end (i.e., as practical guides to increasing business value). However, in each case, there should be a reasonably clear link between the particular goal and the increase in value.

Objectives for Nonprofit Firms and Government Entities

How does the overall objective of risk management differ for nonprofit or government entities that do not have shareholders? Nonprofit firms can be viewed as attempting to maximize the value of products or services provided to various customers and constituents (e.g., taxpayers or persons that donate money to finance the firm's operations), where value depends on the preferences of these parties. If the cost of risk is defined as the reduction in value of the nonprofit firm's activities due to risk, the appropriate goal of risk management remains minimization of the cost of risk to those constituents.

Minimizing the cost of risk for a nonprofit firm may involve giving greater weight to certain factors than would be true for a for-profit firm. A nonprofit hospital, for example, might place greater emphasis on the adverse effects of large losses on its customers than would a for-profit firm. As another example, state and federal government agencies and county and municipal governments pay close attention to their ability to obtain additional funds on a temporary basis through borrowing or tax revenues when making insurance and other loss financing decisions. Exemption from income taxes, to which government entities and many nonprofit firms are entitled, also can influence risk management decisions, as compared to for-profit firms.

However, while the details may differ, the overall objective of risk management and the key decisions that must be made by nonprofit firms are similar to those for for-profit firms. Nonprofit firms and government entities need to identify how risk reduces the net value of services provided and make decisions with the goal of minimizing the cost of risk. They have to consider the same basic components of the cost of risk as for-profit firms. It is not clear whether the absence of shareholders and the possibly fewer penalties for failing to minimize costs make agency costs (see Box 2–1) greater for nonprofit firms or government entities than for for-profit firms, or, if so, whether this affects risk management.

2.5 Risk Management and Societal Welfare

Risk Management Objectives for Individuals and Society

What are the appropriate objectives of risk management for individuals and for society at large? While the details vary, the basic idea is the same as that for businesses. The objective of risk management for individuals is to maximize their well-being (welfare) given their attitudes toward risk. This issue is discussed more fully in Chapter 7, where we discuss how risk management decisions might be made to maximize a person's *expected utility of wealth,* where the utility or satisfaction associated with different amounts of wealth reflects attitudes toward risk. If the cost of risk is defined as the reduction in welfare (expected utility) that arises from risk, the objective of risk management again is to minimize the cost of risk.

From a societal perspective, the key question is how risky activities and risk management by individuals and businesses can best be arranged to minimize the total cost of risk for society. This cost is the aggregate—for all members of society—of the costs of losses, loss control, loss financing, internal risk reduction, and residual uncertainty. Minimizing the total cost of risk in society would maximize the value of societal resources.

Minimizing the total cost of risk for society produces an **efficient level of risk.** Efficiency requires individuals and businesses to pursue activities until the marginal benefit equals the marginal cost, including risk-related costs. Expressed in terms of the cost of pure risk, *efficiency requires that loss control, loss financing, and internal risk reduction be pursued until the marginal reduction in the expected cost of losses and residual uncertainty equals the marginal cost of these risk management methods.* As was discussed earlier, however, achieving the efficiency goal does not eliminate losses because it is simply too costly to do so.

While the efficiency concept is abstract and the benefits and costs of risk management are often difficult to measure, the efficiency goal is nonetheless viewed as appropriate by many people (especially economists). The main reason for this is that maximizing the value of resources by minimizing the cost of risk makes the total size of the economic "pie" as large as possible. Other things being equal, this permits the greatest number of economic needs to be met.

Greater total wealth allows greater opportunity for governments to transfer income from parties that are able to pay taxes to parties that need assistance. A fundamental problem that affects these transfers, however, is that the size of the economic pie is not invariant to how it is sliced (i.e., divided among the population). High marginal tax rates, for example, discourage work effort beyond some point, thus tending to reduce the size of the economic pie. Thus, attempts to produce a more equal distribution of income generally involve some reduction in economic value. The goal is to achieve the right balance between the amount of total wealth and how it is distributed.

Similar issues arise within the context of pure risk. An important example (discussed in Chapters 6 and 24) is the effect of government regulations that cause insurance premium rates for some buyers to differ from the expected costs of providing them coverage. By changing how the total cost of risk is divided (or how the total cost pie is sliced), these regulations can alter incentives in ways that increase the total cost of risk (e.g., by encouraging too much risky activity by individuals whose insurance premiums are subsidized). While many persons might argue that these regulations produce a fairer distribution of costs, they nonetheless involve some increase in cost.

Conflict between Business and Societal Objectives

Businesses that seek to maximize value to shareholders will make risk management decisions to minimize the cost of risk to the business. The question arises: Will minimizing the cost of risk to the business minimize the cost of risk to society?

Note first that maximizing business value by minimizing the cost of risk generally will involve some consideration of the effects of risk management decisions on other major stakeholders in the firm. As suggested above and explained in detail in Chapters 7 and 9, the firm's value to shareholders and the reduction in value due to the cost of risk will depend in part on how risk and risk management affect employees, customers, suppliers, and lenders. The basic reason is that risk and its management affect the terms at which these parties are willing to contract with the business. For example, other things being equal, businesses that expose employees to obvious safety hazards will have to pay higher wages to attract employees. This provides some incentive for the firm to improve safety conditions in order to save on wages (apart from any legal requirement for the firm to pay for injuries).

Unfortunately, because we do not live in a perfect world, the goal of making money for shareholders can lead to risk management decisions that may not necessarily minimize the total cost of risk to society. In order for business value maximization to minimize the total cost of risk to society, the business must consider all societal costs in its decisions. In other words, all social costs should be internalized by the business so that its private costs equal social costs. If the **private cost of risk** (the cost to the business) differs from the **social cost of risk** (the total cost to society), business value maximization generally will not minimize the total cost of risk to society.

A few simple examples should help to illustrate the increase in the social cost of risk that can arise when the private cost is less than the social cost. To illustrate the point simply, assume that there is no government regulation of safety, no workers' compensation law, and no legal liability system that allows persons to recover damages from businesses that cause them harm. Under this assumption, businesses that seek to maximize value to shareholders may not consider possible harm to persons from risky activity. It would be very likely that many businesses would make decisions without fully reflecting upon their possible harm to "strangers" (persons with no connection to the business).

In addition, businesses would tend to produce products that are too risky and expose workers to an excessive risk of workplace injury given the social cost if consumers and workers underestimate the risk of injury. Note in contrast that if consumers and workers can accurately assess the risk of injury, they can influence the business to consider the risk of harm by reducing the price they are willing to pay for products and increasing the wages demanded in view of the risk of injury.

You will learn more about these issues in chapters that address the legal liability system and workers' compensation law. For now, it is sufficient to note that a major function of liability and workplace injury law is to get businesses to reflect more upon the risk of harm to consumers, workers, and other parties in making their decisions. If legal rules are designed so that private costs are approximately equal to social costs, then value maximizing decisions by businesses will help to minimize the total cost of risk in society. Efficient legal rules are those that achieve this goal.[5]

---

[5] In concluding this chapter, we note that some of this material might seem fairly abstract to you at this point. If so, these ideas will become clearer to you as you progress further along in the course. It also might be helpful for you to reread parts of this chapter after covering the related material that comes later.

2.6 Summary

- The overall objective of business risk management for for-profit firms is to maximize the business's value to its shareholders. Managers have substantial incentives to maximize business value.

- In the context of risk management, maximizing business value is equivalent to minimizing the cost of risk, where the cost of risk is defined as the reduction in business value that arises in the presence of risk.

- Components of the cost of pure risk include: (1) the expected cost of losses, (2) the cost of loss control, (3) the cost of loss financing, (4) the cost of internal risk reduction, and (5) the cost of any residual uncertainty that remains after loss control, loss financing, and internal risk reduction methods have been implemented.

- Loss control reduces the expected cost of losses. Beyond some point, the cost of additional loss control will exceed the reduction in the expected cost of losses. As a result, minimizing the cost of pure risk will not eliminate completely the risk of loss. If it were feasible, eliminating the risk of loss would be excessively costly to businesses and consumers alike.

- Loss financing and internal risk reduction reduce risk and therefore can reduce both the expected cost of indirect losses and the cost of residual uncertainty.

- The overall objective of risk management for nonprofit firms and government entities also should be to minimize the cost of risk, provided that the special objectives and circumstances of these firms are incorporated into the cost of risk.

- The overall objective of risk management for individuals and society as a whole can be viewed as minimizing the cost of risk and thus maximizing the welfare of individuals and the value of societal resources. Achieving this objective produces an efficient level of risk in society.

- If businesses do not bear the full costs of their risky activities (that is, if the private cost of risk is less than the social cost), the total cost of risk in society will not be minimized when businesses maximize value. A major function of business liability and workplace injury law is to align private costs with social costs so that business value maximization will minimize the social cost of risk.

Key Terms

value maximization   18
cost of risk   21
cost of pure risk   21
expected cost of losses   23
cost of loss control   23
cost of loss financing   23

cost of internal risk reduction   24
cost of residual uncertainty   24
efficient level of risk   29
private cost of risk   30
social cost of risk   30

Questions and Problems

1. Mr. Fatcat manages a large corporation. Given his preferences, he would like to take expensive and frivolous trips in the company jet, receive a large salary, decorate his office with ancient artifacts, and throw corporate money at projects with borderline prospects for making any significant returns. What motivating influences can help Mr. Fatcat

resist these temptations and maximize firm value?

2. Describe specific factors included in the cost of risk for: (*a*) the risk that workers in a manufacturing plant will be injured by machines and equipment, (*b*) the risk that an international business will suffer loss from the expropriation of its investments by a foreign government, and (*c*) the risk that the price that a beer manufacturer can charge will decline due to a change in consumer preferences toward wine and soda.

3. Some people argue that *any* risk of injury from toxic chemicals and environmental pollutants is too high. Explain why this "zero risk" goal would not lead to an efficient level of risk in society.

4. Ignoring incentives from the legal system, what incentives do businesses have to: (*a*)

make safe products, (*b*) reduce worker injury risk, and (*c*) avoid polluting the environment?

5. Describe how the risk of injury to consumers and "bystanders" could affect the design, production, distribution, and pricing of jet skis if the manufacturer seeks to maximize firm value (assuming no safety regulations and that the producer cannot be held liable for harm to consumers or bystanders). Will value maximization cause the manufacturer to consider the effects of noise on the tranquillity of beaches and inland waterways?

6. We-Dump-It is in the business of disposing of toxic chemicals. Explain why a legal system might be necessary to increase the private cost of risk for We-Dump-It in order to better align its goal of maximizing firm value with the goal of achieving an efficient level of risk in society.

References

Mishan, E. J. *What Political Economy Is All About.* New York, NY: Cambridge University Press, 1982. (*Part One provides a very readable introduction to the nature and rationale of the efficiency criterion used by economists. Reading this material will help you understand economic efficiency and the efficient level of risk in society.*)

Risk and Insurance Management Society. *Cost of Risk Survey.* New York, NY: Risk and Insurance Management Society. (*Annual report on the cost of insurance, uninsured losses, and loss control based on a survey of medium-to-large corporations.*)

Answers to Concept Checks

1. The most important components of the cost of risk for the airline are: (*a*) the expected cost of damage to aircraft and liability claims and defense costs for injured people; (*b*) the expected cost of indirect losses, such as a reduction in profits and continuing and extra expenses if a major crash harms the airline's reputation for safety; and (*c*) the costs of retention and of premium loadings for aircraft property and liability insurance.

2. While enormous sums of money could be

spent on precautions such as design changes that improve safety and more comprehensive maintenance between flights, it almost certainly would be impossible to eliminate the risk of crashes completely without shutting down the airline ("stuff happens").

3. Your answer will be no unless you are extremely risk averse or suffer from a pathological fear of flying, in which case we encourage you to take the bus. You also might answer yes if you are extremely rich.

Risk Reduction through Insurance Markets

Risk Measurement and Risk Pooling

Chapter Objectives

- Define and measure risk.
- Review basic concepts from probability and statistics that are important in risk measurement and risk management.
- Illustrate how and when pooling arrangements reduce risk.

3.1 The Pervasiveness of Risk

This chapter develops some of the basic tools needed for measuring risk and applies these tools to demonstrate how people can reduce risk by participating in risk pooling arrangements. In order to help motivate this discussion, we first illustrate the pervasiveness of risk by considering a few examples that amplify the discussion in the first two chapters.

Risks Faced by an Automobile Manufacturer

Consider some of the major risks faced by an automobile manufacturer during the coming year. In order to produce automobiles, the firm must purchase steel; therefore, it is subject to risk due to uncertain future steel prices. The price of steel can change due to a number of factors, including government policy with respect to steel imports, technological changes, labor union negotiations, and fuel prices. Risk also exists because demand for automobiles is uncertain. Employees can injure themselves on the job. Customers can be injured using the product and sue for damages. We could, of course, go on and on identifying risks that the automaker faces. How should the firm manage these risks? Should it purchase insurance in some cases and retain the risk in others? Should it undertake loss control? To answer these questions, the firm needs to measure risk and identify the costs and benefits of reducing risk.

Risks Faced by Students

Consider some of the risks that you face during a semester as a student. The obvious risks are that you could become ill or injured, you could have an automobile accident, your residence could burn down, your vehicle could be stolen, and so on. A common aspect of these risks is that insurance contracts generally exist to help you manage the risk. In addition, you could reduce your exposure to the risk by taking additional precautions or by avoiding the activity that gives rise to the risk.

Consider some other risks that you face: You could buy food that is contaminated, you could purchase a product that causes an accident, and your bank could fail. A common aspect of these risks is that some type of government or social policy exists to help you deal with the consequences. Notice that the existence of these social policies lessens the extent to which you will deal with them privately, either by purchasing insurance or by taking additional precautions.

You also are exposed to many other risks where neither insurance contracts nor public programs exist to help you. For example, a sibling could die, causing you emotional distress. Your teacher could give a very difficult exam, or you could forget a fundamental concept—so that in either case you bomb the exam, causing your grade point average to suffer. Alternatively, your best friend could decide to avoid you forever. Generally, the only way to deal with these risks is to engage in some loss control activity (e.g., studying more often) that will reduce either the chance of the loss occurring or the size of the loss if it does occur.

The pervasiveness of risk is apparent. The optimal response to risk from a business's or an individual's perspective is one of the central issues addressed in this book. In addition, we will provide answers to other interesting and important questions, such as: Why do insurance contracts exist for some, but not all risks? Why do we have government programs to lessen some types of risk? What are the effects of these programs on individual behavior? Answers to these questions and many others require a framework in which to analyze risky situations. The framework we use is based on a few fundamental concepts from probability and statistics.

3.2 Basic Concepts from Probability and Statistics

Random Variables and Probability Distributions

The starting point for our framework is the idea of a random variable. A **random variable** is a variable whose outcome is uncertain. For example, suppose a coin is to be flipped and the variable X is defined to be equal to $1 if heads appears and $-$1 if tails appears. Then prior to the coin flip, the value of X is unknown; that is, X is a random variable. Once the coin has been flipped and the outcome revealed, the uncertainty about X is resolved, because the value of X is then known.

Information about a random variable is summarized by the random variable's probability distribution. In particular, a **probability distribution** identifies all the possible outcomes for the random variable and the probability of the outcomes. For the coin flipping example, Table 3–1 gives the probability distribution for X.

TABLE 3–1   Probability Distribution for Coin Flipping Example

Possible Outcomes for X	Probability
$1	0.5 or 50%
–$1	0.5 or 50%

In addition to describing a probability distribution by listing the outcomes and probabilities, we also can describe probability distributions graphically. Figure 3–1 illustrates the probability distribution for the coin flipping example. On the horizontal axis, we graph the possible outcomes. On the vertical axis, we graph the probability of a particular outcome. There are only two possible outcomes in this very simple example: $1 and –$1, and the probability of each is 0.5. When discussing random variables, we will use the term *actual* or *observed* outcome (or, sometimes *realized* outcome) to refer to the outcome observed (realized) in a particular case, as opposed to the *possible* outcomes that could have occurred. In the coin flipping example, once the coin has been tossed we can observe the actual outcome, which either must be $1 or –$1.

As emphasized in the first two chapters, risk management decisions need to be made prior to knowing what the actual (realized) outcomes of key variables will be. A manager does not know beforehand which outcomes of the random variables affecting the firm's profits will occur. Nevertheless, he or she must make decisions. Once the outcomes are observed, it usually is easy to say what would have been the best decision. However, we cannot evaluate decisions from this perspective, which is why probability distributions are so important. Probability distributions tell us all of the possible outcomes and the probability of those outcomes. Information about probability distributions is needed to make good risk management decisions.

As a second example of a probability distribution, we can approximate the probability distribution for the dollar amount of damages to your car during the coming year. For simplicity, our approximation will assume only five possible levels of damages: $0; $200; $1,000; $5,000; and $10,000. The probabilities of each of these outcomes are listed in Table 3–2. The most likely outcome is zero

FIGURE 3–1

Probability distribution for coin flipping example

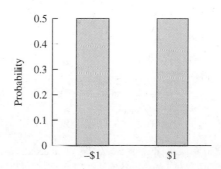

TABLE 3–2   Probability Distribution for Automobile Damages

Possible Outcomes for Damages	Probability
$ 0	0.50
$ 200	0.30
$ 1,000	0.10
$ 5,000	0.06
$ 10,000	0.04

damages, and the least likely outcome is that damages equal $10,000. Note that the sum of the probabilities equals 1; this must always be the case. An alternative way of describing the probability distribution is provided by Figure 3–2, where the height of each bar gives the probability of each possible outcome.

As a final example, let's return to the automaker introduced earlier. We identified a number of reasons why profits are uncertain (e.g., steel price changes and labor conditions). In the language just introduced, the automaker's profits are a random variable. There are numerous possible outcomes for the automaker's profits. For example, steel prices could increase so much that profits could be negative. On the other hand, favorable outcomes for steel prices and the economy could cause very high profits.

What is the probability distribution for the automaker's profits? Recall that a probability distribution identifies all of the possible outcomes and associates a probability with each outcome. In the coin flipping example, there were only two possible outcomes and so listing the probabilities was simple. In the automaker example, however, we could spend hours listing all the possible outcomes for profits and still not be finished, due to the large number of possible outcomes. In these situations, it is useful to assume that the possible outcomes can be *any* number between two extremes (the minimum possible outcome and the maximum possible outcome) and that the probability of the outcomes between the extremes is represented by a specific mathematical function.[1] For example, assume that

FIGURE 3–2

Probability distribution for automobile damages

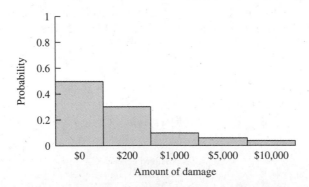

---

[1] This is equivalent to assuming that the probability of outcomes below the assumed minimum or above the assumed maximum is so small that these outcomes can be ignored.

FIGURE 3–3

*Probability
distribution for
automaker's profits*

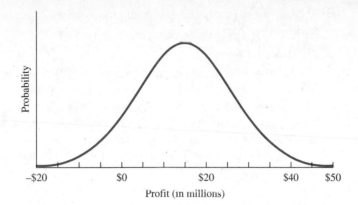

profits for the automaker could be any number between –$20 million and $50 million. Just as with the earlier graphs, we can identify the possible outcomes for profits between these amounts on the horizontal axis of Figure 3–3, which illustrates the probability distribution for the automaker's profits. Analogous to the earlier graphs, the vertical axis will measure the probability of the possible outcomes.[2] The probabilities of the outcomes are illustrated in Figure 3–3 by a bell-shaped curve, which might appear familiar to you.

Recall that the sum of the probabilities of all the possible outcomes must equal 1 (some outcome must occur). In the coin flipping example and the automobile damage example, this property is easy to verify because the number of possible outcomes is small. Stating that the probabilities sum to 1 in these examples is equivalent to stating that the heights of the bars in Figures 3–1 and 3–2 sum to 1. This is a useful observation because it helps to illustrate the analogous property in the automaker example, where any outcome between –$20 million and $50 million is possible. You can think of the curve in Figure 3–3 as a curve that connects the tops of many thousands of bars that have very small widths, and the sum of the heights of all these bars is equivalent to the area under the curve.[3] Thus, stating that the probabilities must sum to 1 is equivalent to stating that the area under the curve must equal 1.

Since the area under the curve in Figure 3–3 equals 1, we can graphically identify the probability that profits are within a certain interval. For example, the probability that profits are greater than $40 million is the area under the curve to the right of $40 million. The probability that profits are less than $0 is the area under the curve to the left of $0. The probability that profits are between $10 and $30 million is the area under the curve between $10 and $30 million. Thus, the bell-shaped curve in Figure 3–3 tells us that for the automaker, there is a relatively high probability that profits will be between $10 and $30 million. In contrast,

---

[2] Given that any outcome is possible between –$20 million and $50 million, the vertical axis measures what technically is known as the "probability density," rather than the probability. However, the basic idea is the same, and you can think of it as the probability in order to understand the essential ideas of this book.

[3] Adding up the heights of these bars is a problem in calculus, which is not needed for understanding the material in this book.

while very low profits and very high profits are possible, they do not have a high probability of happening.

Concept Checks

1. What information is given by a probability distribution? What are the two ways of describing a probability distribution?
2. Property damage from earthquakes is rare, but it can be very large when it occurs. Illustrate these features by drawing a probability distribution for property losses due to an earthquake for a business that has property valued at $50 million. Identify on your graph the probability that losses will exceed $30 million.

Characteristics of Probability Distributions

In many applications, it is necessary to compare probability distributions of different random variables. Indeed, most of the material in this book is concerned with how decisions (e.g., whether to purchase insurance) change probability distributions. Understanding how decisions affect probability distributions will lead to better decisions. The problem is that most probability distributions have many different outcomes and are difficult to compare. It is therefore common to compare certain key characteristics of probability distributions: the expected value, variance or standard deviation, skewness, and correlation.

Expected Value.   The **expected value** of a probability distribution provides information about where the outcomes tend to occur, on average. For example, if the expected value of the automaker's profits is $10 million, then profits should average about $10 million. Thus, a distribution with a higher expected value will tend to have a higher outcome, on average.

To calculate the expected value, you multiply each possible outcome by its probability and then add up the results. In the coin flipping example there are two possible outcomes for X, either $1 or –$1. The probability of each outcome is 0.5. Therefore, the expected value of X is $0:

$$\text{Expected value of } X = (0.5)\ (\$1) + (0.5)\ (-\$1) = \$0$$

If one were to play the coin flipping game *many* times, the *average* outcome would be approximately $0. This does not imply that the actual value of X on any single toss will be $0; indeed, the actual outcome for one toss is never $0.

To define expected value in general terms, let the possible outcomes of a random variable, X, be denoted by $x_1, x_2, x_3, \ldots, x_M$ (these correspond to –$1 and $1 in the coin flipping example) and let the probability of the respective outcomes be denoted by $p_1, p_2, p_3, \ldots, p_M$ (these correspond to the 0.5's in the coin flipping example). Then, the expected value is defined mathematically as:

$$\text{Expected value} = x_1\, p_1 + x_2\, p_2 + \ldots + x_M\, p_M = \sum_{i=1}^{M} x_i p_i \qquad (3.1)$$

Figure 3–4

Comparing the expected values of two distributions (distribution A has a higher expected value than distribution B)

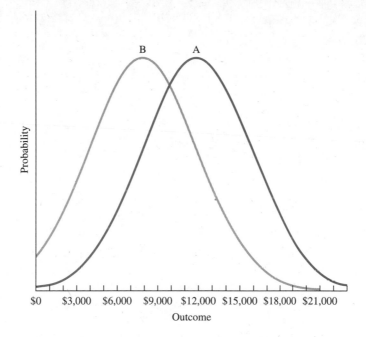

If we examine a probability distribution graphically, we often can learn something about the expected value of the distribution. For example, Figure 3–4 illustrates two probability distributions. Since the distribution for A is shifted to the right compared with B, distribution A has a higher expected value than distribution B.

When distributions are symmetric, as in Figure 3–4, identifying the expected value is relatively easy. When the probability distributions are not symmetric, identifying the expected value by examining a diagram sometimes can be difficult. Nevertheless, you often can compare the expected values of different distributions visually. Consider, for example, the two distributions illustrated in Figure 3–5. Distribution C has a higher expected value than distribution D. Intuitively, the high outcomes are more likely with distribution C than with D, and the low outcomes are less likely with C than with D.

Many risk management decisions depend on the probability distribution of losses that can arise from lawsuits, worker injuries, damage to property, and the like. When a probability distribution is for possible losses that can occur, the distribution is called a **loss distribution.** The expected value of the distribution is called the **expected loss.**

Concept Check

3. What is the expected value of damages for the distribution listed in Table 3–2?

Variance and Standard Deviation.   The **variance** of a probability distribution provides information about the likelihood and magnitude by which a particular

FIGURE 3–5

Comparing expected values of distributions (distribution C has a higher expected value than distribution D)

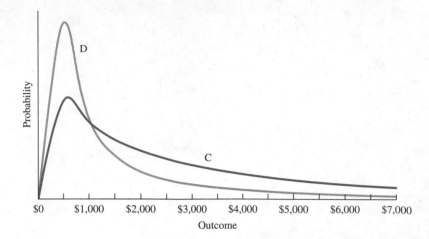

outcome from the distribution will differ from the expected value. In other words, variance measures the probable variation in outcomes around the expected value. If a distribution has low variance, then the actual outcome is likely to be close to the expected value. Conversely, if the distribution has high variance, then it is more likely that the actual (realized) outcome from the distribution will be far from the expected value. A high variance therefore implies that outcomes are difficult to predict. For this reason, variance is a commonly used measure of risk. In some instances, however, it is more convenient to work with the square root of the variance, which is known as the **standard deviation.**

To illustrate variance and standard deviation, consider three possible probability distributions for accident losses. Each distribution has three possible outcomes, but the outcomes and the probabilities differ. The three probability distributions are shown in Table 3–3.

For each of the loss distributions in Table 3–3, the expected value is $500 (you should verify this for yourself), but the variances of the three distributions differ. Loss distribution 2 has a larger variance than distribution 1, because the extreme outcomes for distribution 2 are farther from the expected value than they are for distribution 1. Distribution 3 has a larger variance than distribution 2, because even though the outcomes are the same for distributions 2 and 3, the ex-

TABLE 3–3   Comparing Standard Deviations of Three Distributions
(distribution 1 has the lowest standard deviation and
distribution 3 has the highest)

Distribution 1		Distribution 2		Distribution 3	
Loss Outcome	*Probability*	*Loss Outcome*	*Probability*	*Loss Outcome*	*Probability*
$250	0.33	$ 0	0.33	$ 0	0.4
$500	0.34	$ 500	0.34	$ 500	0.2
$750	0.33	$ 1,000	0.33	$ 1,000	0.4

treme outcomes are more likely with distribution 3 than with distribution 2. That is, the probability of having a loss far from the expected value ($500) is greater with distribution 3 than with distribution 2. The comparison of distributions 2 and 3 illustrates that the variance depends not only on the dispersion of the possible outcomes but also on the probability of the possible outcomes.

The mathematical definitions of variance and standard deviation show precisely how the probabilities of the different outcomes and the deviation of each outcome from the expected value affect these measures of risk. The definitions are:

$$\text{Variance} = \sum_{i=1}^{N} p_i \, (x_i - \mu)^2 \tag{3.2}$$

and

$$\text{Standard deviation} = \sqrt{\sum_{i=1}^{N} p_i \, (x_i - \mu)^2} \tag{3.3}$$

where

μ (mu) = the expected value;
x_i = the possible outcome; and
p_i = the probability of the outcome.

Notice that the quantity in parentheses measures the deviation of each outcome from the expected value. This difference is squared so that positive differences do not offset negative differences. Each squared difference is then multiplied by the probability of the particular outcome so those outcomes that are more likely to occur receive greater weight in the final sum than those outcomes that have a low probability of occurrence.

Additional insights about these measures of risk can be gained by going step-by-step through the calculations for distribution 1 introduced above. Table 3–4 provides this analysis. It indicates that distribution 1 has a standard deviation equal to $204. Similar calculations for distributions 2 and 3 (not shown) indicate that their standard deviations equal $408 and $447, respectively.

As noted earlier, variance and standard deviation measure the likelihood that and magnitude by which an outcome from the probability distribution will deviate from the expected value. They thus measure the predictability of the out-

TABLE 3–4   Calculating Variance and Standard Deviation for Distribution 1 from Table 3–3

Step 1: Take difference between each outcome and the expected value ($500)	Step 2: Square the results of step 1.	Step 3: Multiply the results of step 2 by the respective probabilities.
$250 – $500 = –$250	(–$250)² = $62,500	0.33 ($62,500) = $20,833
$500 – $500 = $0	($0)² = $0	0.34 ($0) = $0
$750 – $500 = $250	($250)² = $62,500	0.33 ($ 62,500) = $20,833

Step 4: Sum the results of step 3 to find the variance. $41,666
Step 5: Calculate the square root of the result of step 4 to find the standard deviation. $204

FIGURE 3–6

Comparing the standard deviations of two distributions (distribution B has a larger standard deviation)

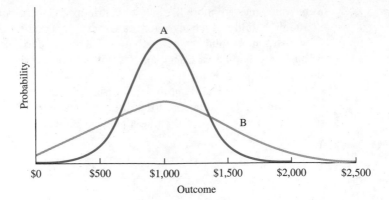

comes. As a consequence, when referring to risk as variability around the expected value, *we generally will measure risk using variance or standard deviation*.[4]

Like expected values, standard deviations of distributions often can be compared by visually inspecting the probability distributions. For example, Figure 3–6 illustrates two distributions for accident losses. Both have an expected value of $1,000, but they differ in their standard deviations. There is a greater chance that an outcome from distribution A will be close to the expected value of $1,000 than with distribution B.

Concept Checks

4. Explain why variance and standard deviation are useful measures of risk.

5. Without doing any calculations, compare the standard deviations of the following distributions:

Distribution 1		Distribution 2		Distribution 3	
Loss Outcome	*Probability*	*Loss Outcome*	*Probability*	*Loss Outcome*	*Probability*
$ 5,000	0.33	$ 5,000	0.00	$ 0	0.2
$ 10,000	0.34	$ 10,000	1.00	$ 10,000	0.6
$ 15,000	0.33	$ 15,000	0.00	$ 20,000	0.2

6. Compare the expected values and standard deviations of distributions A and B illustrated in the following figure:

---

[4] Other measures of risk sometimes are used. For example, in some situations it is useful to measure risk as the probability of an extreme outcome (e.g., a large loss). Another commonly used measure of risk is the maximum probable loss or value at risk, both of which identify the loss amount that will not be exceeded with some confidence, say 95 percent of the time. We define and utilize these risk concepts in Chapter 12.

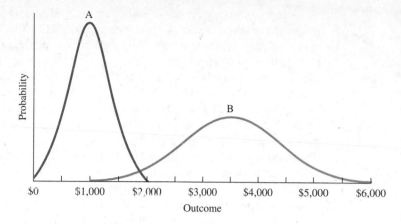

Sample Mean and Sample Standard Deviation.   Sometimes the expected value is called the *mean of the distribution.* We will avoid using this term because it leads to confusion with another concept: the average value from a sample of outcomes from a distribution, which also is known as the **sample mean.** A simple illustration will help you understand the difference between the average outcome from a sample (the sample mean) and the expected value of the probability distribution. The probability distribution of the sex of children is well known. There is a 0.5 probability that the fertilization of an egg will produce a female, and there is a 0.5 probability that the fertilization will produce a male.[5] The group of babies born this month in the town where you live can be viewed as a sample from this distribution. The sample mean proportion of females is the number of females in the sample divided by the total number of newborns in the sample. The sample mean proportion generally will differ from the expected value of 0.5 due to random fluctuations (unless there are lots and lots of babies in the sample). Similarly, if the expected loss from accidents for a large group of people is $500, the sample mean loss or **average loss** during a given time period for a sample of these people will differ from the expected value due to random fluctuations.

The **sample standard deviation** (or, similarly, the sample variance) reflects the variation in outcomes of a particular sample from a distribution. It is calculated with the same formula that we used above for the standard deviation but with three differences. First, only the outcomes that occur in the sample are used. Second, the sample mean is used instead of the expected value, which usually is not known. Third, the squared deviations between the outcomes and the sample mean are multiplied by the proportion of times that the particular outcome actually occurs in the sample—rather than by the proportion of times that the outcome is likely to occur, according to the probability distribution.[6]

---

[5] Actually, the probability that a female will be conceived is very slightly greater than 0.5.

[6] This calculation is equivalent to adding the squared deviations, dividing by the sample size, and then taking the square root. (In many cases, statisticians divide by the sample size minus one instead. This adjustment causes the sample standard deviation to be a better [unbiased] estimator of the true standard deviation.)

It is useful to introduce the sample mean and sample standard deviation at this point for several reasons. First, the probability distributions for random variables that concern managers generally are not known. The sample mean and sample standard deviation sometimes can be used to estimate the unknown expected value and standard deviation of a probability distribution. Thus, estimation of the expected value and standard deviation of losses is often very important in risk management (see Chapter 12). In addition, the concept of the average loss for a group of people that pools its risk (i.e., the sample mean loss for the group) and the standard deviation of the average loss for the group (i.e., the sample standard deviation) are used below to explain how pooling can reduce risk. Finally, you will no doubt calculate sample means and sample standard deviations if you take a statistics course. We don't want you to confuse the expected value and standard deviation of the underlying probability distribution with the sample mean and sample standard deviation for a particular sample.

Concept Check

7. Recall the coin flipping game discussed earlier in the chapter where you win $1 if heads appears and lose $1 if tails appears. What is the expected value of the outcome from the game if it is played only one time? Calculate the sample mean and sample standard deviation if the game is played five times with the following results: T, T, H, T, H.

Skewness.   Another statistical concept that is important in the practice of risk management is the **skewness** of a probability distribution. Skewness measures the symmetry of the distribution. If the distribution is symmetric, it has no skewness. For example, consider the two distributions for accident losses illustrated in Figure 3–7. The distribution at the top of Figure 3–7 is symmetric; it has zero skewness. However, the distribution at the bottom is not symmetric; it has positive skewness.

Note how the skewed distribution has a higher probability of very low losses and a higher probability of very high losses when compared to the symmetric distribution. While this will not always be true, it is true for many loss distributions that are relevant to risk management. Recognizing this characteristic of skewed distributions is important when assessing the likelihood of large losses. If you incorrectly assume that the loss distribution is symmetric (you think that losses have distribution 1 when they really have distribution 2 in Figure 3–7), you will underestimate the likelihood of very large losses. As you will see in later chapters, large losses usually are the most harmful.

Concept Check

8. Draw a distribution that might describe your automobile liability losses for the coming year (i.e., the losses that you could cause to other people for which you could be sued and held liable).

Correlation.   To this point, we have limited our discussion to probability distributions of a single random variable. Because businesses and individuals are exposed to many types of risk, it is important to identify the relationships among

FIGURE 3–7

*Skewness in
probability
distributions
(top distribution is
symmetric; bottom
distribution is skewed)*

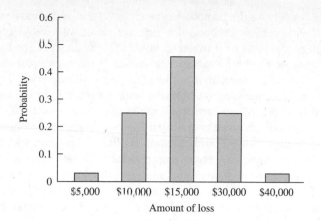

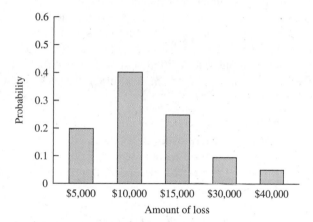

random variables. The **correlation** between random variables measures how random variables are related.

If the correlation between two random variables is zero, then the random variables are not related. Intuitively, if two random variables have zero correlation, then knowing the outcome of one random variable will not give you information about the outcome of the other random variable. For example, an automaker has risk due to an uncertain number of product liability claims for autos previously sold and also due to uncertain steel prices. There is no reason to believe that these two variables will be related. Knowing that steel prices are high will not imply anything about the frequency or severity of liability claims for autos already sold. Similarly, knowing that a large liability claim for damages has occurred will not imply anything about steel prices. Thus, the correlation between steel prices and product liability costs (for past sales) is zero. When the correlation between random variables is zero, we will say that the random variables are *independent* or *uncorrelated.* These terms are used because they suggest that the outcome observed for one distribution is unrelated to the outcome observed for the other distribution.

In many cases random variables will be correlated. For example, a recession may decrease the demand for new cars and also decrease steel prices. Thus, the demand for new cars and steel prices both are affected by general economic conditions, and, as a result, the demand for new cars and steel prices are correlated. When demand for new cars is high, steel prices also tend to be high.[7]

Positive correlation implies that the random variables tend to move in the same direction. For example, the returns on common stocks of different companies are positively correlated—the return on one stock tends to be high when the returns on other stocks are high. Random variables can be negatively correlated as well. Negative correlation implies that the random variables tend to move in opposite directions. For example, sales of sunglasses and sales of umbrellas on any given day in a given city are likely to be negatively correlated.

You should keep in mind that positive (negative) correlation does not imply that the random variables will always move in the same (opposite) direction. Positive correlation simply implies that when the outcome of one random variable— for example, the demand for cars—is above (below) its expected value, the other random variable—for example, steel costs—tends to be above (below) its expected value. Similarly, negative correlation implies that when one random variable—for example, sales of sunglasses—is above (below) its expected value, the other random variable—for example, umbrella sales—tends to be below (above) its expected value.

Concept Check

9. For each scenario below, explain whether the correlation between random variable 1 and random variable 2 is likely to be zero (the random variables are uncorrelated), positive, or negative.

   (*a*) Random variable 1: Your automobile accident costs for the coming year.
   Random variable 2: The automobile accident costs of a student in another city for the coming year.

   (*b*) Random variable 1: The property damage due to hurricanes in Miami, Florida, in September.
   Random variable 2: The property damage due to hurricanes in Ft. Lauderdale, Florida, in September.

   (*c*) Random variable 1: The property damage due to hurricanes in Miami, Florida, in September 1999.
   Random variable 2: The property damage due to hurricanes in Miami, Florida, in September 2000.

   (*d*) Random variable 1: The number of people in New York who die from AIDS in the year 2005.
   Random variable 2: The number of people in London who die from AIDS in the year 2005.

---

[7] Note also that lower sales of new cars could produce fewer product liability claims in the future. Thus, while steel prices and the number of liability claims for autos previously sold will likely be uncorrelated, liability claims arising from new sales and steel prices will likely be correlated.

3.3 Risk Reduction through Pooling Independent Losses

With the concepts from probability and statistics we have just reviewed, we can now explain one of the most important concepts in risk management: Pooling arrangements reduce risk when losses are independent (uncorrelated). We will use the following example to illustrate.

Suppose that Emily and Samantha each are exposed to the possibility of an accident in the coming year. In particular, assume that each person has a 20 percent chance of an accident that will cause a loss of $2,500 and an 80 percent chance of no accident. The probability distribution for accident losses for each woman is summarized in Table 3–5. Also assume that Emily's and Samantha's accident losses are uncorrelated.

We want to examine what will happen if Emily and Samantha agree to *split evenly any accident costs that the two might incur.* That is, they agree to share losses equally, each paying the average loss. This arrangement often is called a **pooling arrangement** (or risk pooling arrangement), because Emily and Samantha are pooling their resources to pay the accident costs that may occur.

Because Emily and Samantha each have a 20 percent chance of having an accident that causes $2,500 in losses, the expected costs and the standard deviation for each person without a pooling arrangement are as follows:

$$\text{Expected cost} = (0.80)\,(\$0) + (0.20)\,(\$2,500) = \$500$$

$$\text{Standard deviation} = \sqrt{0.8\,(\$0 - \$500)^2 + 0.2\,(\$2,500 - \$500)^2} = \$1,000$$

Our goal is to determine how the pooling arrangement will affect the expected cost and standard deviation for each person.

Note that the pooling arrangement changes the distribution of costs paid by each person in Table 3–5; this is because the costs paid by Emily now depend on the accident losses incurred by Samantha, and vice versa. Specifically, with pooling, the cost paid by each person is the average loss of the two people.

The first column of Table 3–6 lists the possible outcomes for Emily and Samantha with pooling. If neither woman has an accident, total accident costs are zero and each woman pays zero. If either of the women has an accident, total accident costs are $2,500 and each woman pays $1,250. If both women have an accident, total accident costs equal $5,000 and each pays $2,500.

TABLE 3–5   Probability Distribution of Accident Losses for Each Person (Emily and Samantha) without Pooling

Outcomes	Probability
$ 0	0.80
$ 2,500	0.20

TABLE 3–6   **Probability Distribution of Accident Costs Paid by Each Woman with Pooling**

Possible Outcomes	Total Cost	Cost Paid by Each Woman (Average Loss)	Probability
1. Neither Samantha nor Emily has an accident	$ 0	$ 0	(0.8)(0.8) = 0.64
2. Samantha has an accident, but Emily does not	$ 2,500	$ 1,250	(0.2)(0.8) = 0.16
3. Emily has an accident, but Samantha does not	$ 2,500	$ 1,250	(0.2)(0.8) = 0.16
4. Both Samantha and Emily have an accident	$ 5,000	$ 2,500	(0.2)(0.2) = 0.04

Now let's find the probabilities of each of these outcomes (the last column of Table 3–6). Since the losses incurred by Emily are independent of the losses incurred by Samantha, the probability that neither woman has an accident is simply the probability that Emily does not have an accident times the probability that Samantha does not have an accident. Thus, the probability of the first outcome is (0.8)(0.8) = 0.64. An analogy might help reinforce this result. Consider flipping a coin twice. The result of the second coin flip is independent of the result of the first coin flip. The probability of obtaining two heads is the probability of heads on the first coin flip times the probability of heads on the second coin flip, or (0.5)(0.5) = 0.25. You can convince yourself that this is true by noting that there are four possible outcomes: heads–heads, heads–tails, tails–heads, and tails–tails. Each of these outcomes has a 0.25 probability of occurring.

Returning to the accident costs example, let's find the probability of the second and third outcomes shown in Table 3–6 (in which only one of the two women has an accident). The probability that Samantha has an accident, but Emily does not equals (0.2)(0.8) = 0.16. The probability that Emily has an accident, but Samantha does not is also 0.16. Thus, the probability that only one of the women has an accident equals 0.16 + 0.16 = 0.32. The probability of the fourth outcome (both Emily and Samantha have an accident) is (0.2)(0.2) = 0.04.[8]

As can be seen clearly from this example, *the pooling arrangement changes the probability distribution of accident costs facing each person.* The probability that Emily will have accident costs equal to $2,500 is reduced from 0.20 to 0.04. This is because in order for Emily to pay $2,500, both Emily and Samantha must experience an accident. Given that accidents are independent, the probability that both Emily and Samantha will have an accident is lower than the probability that only Emily (or only Samantha) will have an accident.

Because the pooling arrangement reduces the probabilities of the extreme outcomes, the standard deviation (risk) of accident costs paid by both Emily and Samantha is reduced. Recall that, without pooling, the standard deviation of accident costs in this example is $1,000. With pooling, the standard deviation of accident costs declines to $707:

---

[8] As another example, suppose that the probability that Michael Jordan makes a free throw is 0.8. Then, assuming that the outcome of each free throw is independent of the other free throws, the probability that Jordan will make two in a row is (0.8) (0.8) = 0.64, the probability that he will make one of two is (0.8) (0.2) + (0.2) (0.8) = 0.32, and the probability that he will make neither is (0.2) (0.2) = 0.04.

Standard deviation = $\sqrt{0.64 \times (\$0 - \$500)^2 + 0.32 \times (\$1,250 - \$500)^2 + 0.04 \times (\$2,500 - \$500)^2} = \$707$

While both Samantha's and Emily's risk is reduced by pooling, each person's expected accident cost is unchanged by pooling. It still equals $500:

$$\text{Expected cost} = (0.64)\,(\$0) + (0.32)\,(\$1,250) + (0.04)\,(\$2,500) = \$500$$

In summary, the pooling arrangement does not change either person's expected cost, but it reduces the standard deviation of costs from $1,000 to $707. Accident costs have become more predictable. The pooling arrangement reduces risk (uncertainty) for each individual.

Additional risk reduction can be obtained from pooling by adding additional people to the arrangement. To illustrate, suppose that Anne, who has the same probability distribution for accident costs as Samantha and Emily, joins the pooling arrangement. At the end of the year, each woman will pay one-third of the total losses (the average loss). The addition of a third person whose losses are independent of the other two causes an additional reduction in the probability of the extreme outcomes. For example, in order for Samantha to pay $2,500 in accident costs, all three individuals must experience a $2,500 loss. The probability of this occurring is (0.02) (0.02) (0.02) = 0.008. As a consequence, the standard deviation for each individual decreases with the addition of another participant. While risk (standard deviation) decreases, each individual's expected accident cost again remains constant at $500.

The probability distribution of each person's accident cost will continue to change as more people are added. Figure 3–8 compares the probability distribution for average accident costs when there are 4 and 20 participants in the pooling arrangement. Note that as the number of participants in the pooling arrangement increases (1) the probability of the extreme outcomes (very high average losses and very low average losses) goes down. Stated differently, the probability that average losses (the amount paid by each participant) will be close to $500, the expected loss, increases. Also, as the number of participants increases, the probability distribution of each person's cost (the average loss) becomes more bell shaped. In summary, pooling makes the amount of accident losses that each person must pay less risky (more predictable), because pooling reduces the standard deviation of the average loss for all the participants and thus the standard deviation of the payment by each participant. Thus, the pooling arrangement reduces risk for each participant.[9] As even more participants are added, the probability distribution would become more and more bell shaped.

As a more realistic illustration, consider the case of a large number of small businesses. The dashed line in Figure 3–9 presents the probability distribution for

---

[9] Note that in the simple example shown in Figure 3–8, where there are only two discrete outcomes for each individual, the height of the bars generally decreases as the number of participants increases. This is because additional outcomes become possible as the number of participants increases. This feature would not carry over to more realistic examples, where each individual's loss lies on a continuum. That is, when individual losses can assume any value within a range, the probability of outcomes near the expected value generally increases as participants are added.

FIGURE 3–8

Distribution of average losses with 4 and 20 participants in a pooling arrangement when each individual has a 0.2 probability of incurring a loss of $2,500 (pooling with 20 participants results in a lower probability of extreme losses and a lower standard deviation of losses)

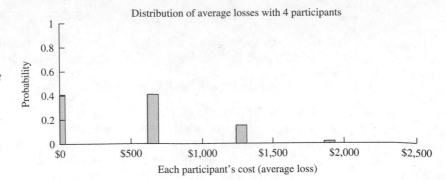

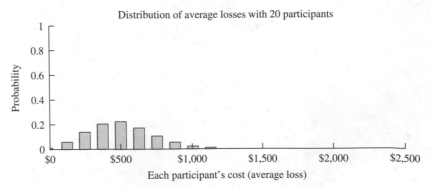

each business's property losses without a pooling arrangement. Each business's property losses could be any number between $0 and $100,000, and, although not obvious from the graph, the expected loss is $20,000. Without pooling, the distribution for each business is skewed and has a relatively high standard deviation. By entering into a pooling arrangement, the distribution of property losses for each business changes to that shown by the dashed line in Figure 3–9. The diagram highlights the two important effects of pooling arrangements on the probability distributions facing each participant. First, the standard deviation of property losses is lower. Second, the distribution of property losses becomes less skewed and more bell shaped around the expected loss.

Notice in all of these examples that each participant is *not* simply transferring risk to someone else. Instead, there is a reduction in risk for each individual. This is the beauty of risk pooling arrangements: *Risk can be reduced substantially for the participants.* This point is extremely important and often is not fully appreciated by students. Pooling arrangements reduce the amount of risk that *each* participant has to bear.[10]

To summarize, when losses are independent, pooling arrangements have two

---

[10] While the standard deviation of average loss declines as the number of participants grows, the standard deviation of the sum of losses for the group grows. The latter result does not alter the fact that each participant's risk is lower.

FIGURE 3–9

The effect of pooling arrangements on probability distributions for a large number of small businesses

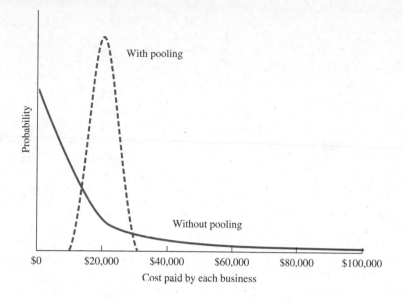

important effects on the probability distribution of the accident cost paid by each participant. First, the standard deviation of the average loss is reduced. As a consequence, the probability of extreme outcomes for participants—both high and low—is reduced. Second, the distribution of average losses becomes more bell shaped.

In the extreme (i.e., as the number of people in the pooling arrangement becomes very large), the standard deviation of each participant's cost becomes very close to zero and the risk thus becomes negligible for each participant. This result reflects what is known as the **law of large numbers** (see Box 3–1). In addition, as the number of participants grows, the probability distribution of the average loss (each participant's cost) becomes more and more bell shaped until it eventually equals the **normal distribution,** the most famous distribution in all of statistics. This result reflects what is known as the **central limit theorem** (which we discuss in Box 3–1).

Finally, our examples of risk reduction through pooling arrangements have assumed that all participants have the same probability distribution. This assumption is not essential. The standard deviation of average loss also tends to decline when more and more participants with different loss distributions are added to a pooling arrangement.[11] Furthermore, risk in principle still becomes negligible as the number of participants becomes infinitely large.

---

[11] An exception can occur if a participant with a very high standard deviation of losses is added to the pool. Also, participants with different expected losses may be unwilling to share losses equally in a pooling arrangement (e.g., would Emily and Samantha want to share losses with someone whose probability of an accident is twice the size of theirs?). For related reasons, insurers charge people with different expected losses different premiums (see Chapter 6).

Box 3–1

The Law of Large Numbers and the Central Limit Theorem

The effects of pooling arrangements on probability distributions are derived from two important theorems from probability theory: the law of large numbers and the central limit theorem.

The Law of Large Numbers

Let X_i equal a random variable (the loss for one participant in a pooling arrangement), where $i = 1, \ldots, N$ (where N equals the number of participants—not the number of possible outcomes for each participant's loss). Assume that the expected value of $X_i = \mu$ and that the standard deviation of $X_i = \sigma$ for all i (each participant has the same expected loss and standard deviation). Then, for any small number $\varepsilon > 0$

$$\text{Prob}\left(\left| \frac{\sum_{i=1}^{N} X_i}{N} - \mu \right| > \varepsilon \right) \to 0 \quad \text{as} \quad N \to \infty$$

The quantity within the straight brackets is the absolute value of the average loss for the pool minus the expected loss for each participant. In words, this formula states that the probability that the average outcome (the loss each participant in the pooling arrangement must pay) differs from the expected

value by more than a small number ε approaches zero as N approaches infinity. Simply stated, as N gets large, the average outcome is likely to get very close to the expected value.

The Central Limit Theorem

Given the same assumptions and notation as the law of large numbers, according to the central limit theorem the distribution of the average outcome approaches a normal distribution with mean μ and standard deviation $\sigma / \sqrt{N}$ as N get very large. Thus, as N gets large, the distribution of the average outcome becomes more symmetric and bell shaped. Since the distribution of the average outcome will be approximately normal for large N, it also is possible to use probability values from the normal distribution to estimate the probability that the average outcome will exceed any given value. Note that, consistent with the law of large numbers, the standard deviation decreases as N increases. For example, if the standard deviation of losses for each participant in a pooling arrangement is initially $5,000 and there are 10,000 participants, then the standard deviation of losses after entering the pooling arrangement equals $5,000/100 = $50. See the appendix at the end of this chapter for further discussion.

Concept Checks

10. Explain how a pooling arrangement reduces risk for each participant when losses are uncorrelated. Does pooling reduce the expected cost paid by each participant? Explain.

11. Suppose that each participant in a pooling arrangement has potential losses ranging from $0 to $4,000 and that each participant's expected loss is $1,000. Using Figure 3–9 as a guide, sketch the probability distribution of average losses if the losses across participants are independent and if:

    (*a*) there is one participant (i.e., no pooling)

(*b*) there are 100 participants

(*c*) there are 1,000 participants

3.4 Pooling Arrangements with Correlated Losses

Since in many instances losses will be positively correlated, we need to examine risk reduction through pooling in this case. We will demonstrate that the essential point—that pooling arrangements reduce risk for each participant—continues to hold provided losses are not perfectly positively correlated. However, *the magnitude of risk reduction is lower when losses are positively correlated than when they are independent (uncorrelated).*

Losses across many different businesses or individuals may be positively correlated for a number of reasons. The occurrence of a loss is often due to events that are common to many people. Catastrophes, such as hurricanes and earthquakes, are examples of events that cause property losses to increase for many individuals at the same time. Consequently, losses in certain geographical regions during a given time period are positively correlated. Similarly, since epidemics can cause medical costs to increase for many people during a given time period, the medical costs across people can be positively correlated.

The severity or magnitude of losses also is often influenced by common factors. For example, unexpected inflation can cause everyone who needs health care to pay more than expected. The probability of receiving medical care may be independent across people (in contrast to the epidemic example), but the magnitude of the medical costs incurred by different people is related to a common underlying factor—inflation.

How do positively correlated losses affect pooling arrangements? Intuitively, positively correlated losses imply that when one person (or business) has a loss that is greater than the expected loss, then other people (or businesses) also will tend to have losses that are above the expected loss. Similarly, when one person has a loss that is less than the expected loss (e.g., no loss), then other people also will tend to have losses below the expected value. Thus, when losses are positively correlated, there is a greater chance that lots of people will have high losses and a greater chance that lots of people will have low losses, relative to the case of uncorrelated losses. Consequently, pooling arrangements do not decrease the standard deviation of average losses as much when losses are positively correlated. Stated differently, average losses are more difficult to predict when losses are positively correlated.

To reinforce this idea, with uncorrelated losses, there is a relatively high probability that unexpectedly high losses experienced by one person will be offset by the unexpectedly low losses of other participants. Thus, the average loss becomes very predictable. When losses are positively correlated, similar losses are incurred by more participants, and one person's unexpectedly high losses are less likely to be offset by another person's unexpectedly low losses.

To illustrate, consider the effect of introducing positive correlation between

Emily's and Samantha's losses. Positive correlation does not change Emily's or Samantha's initial probability distribution for accident costs. We start the year knowing that the probability of an accident is 0.2 for both Emily and Samantha. Now suppose you hear later that Emily has had an accident, but you do not know whether Samantha has had an accident. What is your assessment of the probability that Samantha will have an accident? If the accidents are assumed to be independent, then your assessment will not change; the probability of Samantha having an accident still will be 0.2. However, if the accidents are assumed to be positively correlated, then knowing Emily has had an accident will raise your assessment of Samantha's accident probability above 0.2.

Positive correlation between Emily's and Samantha's accident costs implies that the probability of both women having an accident is greater than 0.04. Similarly, positive correlation implies that the probability of neither woman having an accident is greater than 0.64. Unless we make more assumptions, we cannot specify the exact probabilities of the various outcomes. The critical point, however, is that positive correlation between Emily's and Samantha's accident costs implies that the probability of the extreme outcomes (i.e., that either both or neither will have an accident) is higher than if accident costs were independent.

The maximum degree of positive correlation is *perfect positive correlation.* In this case, if Emily has an accident, so will Samantha, and if Emily does not have an accident, neither will Samantha. Perfect positive correlation implies that whatever happens to Emily also happens to Samantha. As a result, the probability of both women having an accident is the same as the probability that either one of them will have an accident (0.2), and the probability that neither woman will have an accident is the same as the probability that one of them will not have an accident (0.8).

The effect of positively correlated losses on the distribution of average losses is summarized in Figure 3–10. Two cases are presented. In both cases, there are 1,000 participants in the pooling arrangement and each participant has an ex-

FIGURE 3–10

Distribution of average losses with and without positive correlation (positive correlation increases the standard deviation)

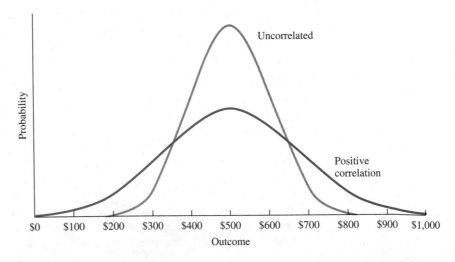

FIGURE 3–11

Effect of positive correlation in losses on risk reduction in pooling arrangements (risk is not reduced when losses are perfectly positively correlated; risk is reduced when there is less than perfect positive correlation, but not as much as when losses are uncorrelated)

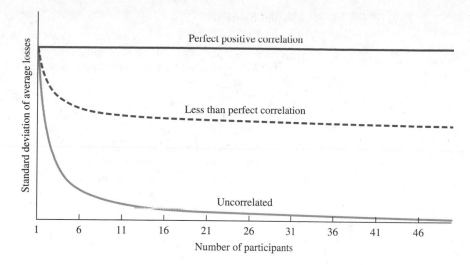

pected loss of $500. In one case, the losses of each participant are uncorrelated; in the other case, they are positively correlated. As illustrated, when losses are positively correlated, the distribution of average losses has a higher standard deviation so that average losses are less predictable.

Figure 3–11 further illustrates the effect of correlated losses on pooling arrangements by examining how the standard deviation of average losses changes as the number of participants increases. The vertical axis measures the standard deviation of average losses. The horizontal axis measures the number of participants in the sharing arrangement. When losses are uncorrelated, the standard deviation approaches zero as the number of participants gets large (recall the law of large numbers). When losses are perfectly positively correlated, the standard deviation of average losses does not change as the number of participants increases. Intuitively, when losses are perfectly positively correlated, there can be no risk reduction from pooling, because whatever happens to one participant happens to all other participants.

Figure 3–11 also illustrates the intermediate case, where losses are characterized by less than perfect positive correlation. As can be seen, the standard deviation of average losses decreases as the number of participants increases, but the standard deviation does not approach zero. The amount of risk (standard deviation) cannot be reduced as much by adding participants when losses are positively correlated; the greater the degree of correlation, the less is the reduction in risk.

Later chapters will show that correlation in losses has very important implications for risk management and insurance. You will learn, for example, how positive correlation in losses affects business risk, insurance pricing, the types of provisions included in insurance contracts, and insurer operations (e.g., reinsurance transactions and insurer capital structure).

Concept Check

12. Sketch the probability distribution for average losses in a pooling arrangement in each of the following cases:

    (*a*) The expected loss for each participant is $500, and losses for the 100 participants are independent.

    (*b*) The expected loss for each participant is $500, and losses for the 100 participants are positively correlated.

    (*c*) The expected loss for each participant is $1,500, and losses for the 100 participants are independent.

    (*d*) The expected loss for each participant is $1,500, and losses for the 100 participants are positively correlated.

Other Examples of Diversification

Pooling arrangements provide a major example of how risk is reduced through diversification. Simply stated, diversification means that you do not "put all your eggs in one basket." By entering into a pooling arrangement, Emily and Samantha made their accident costs for the year equal the average loss for the participants. If they had not entered into the pooling arrangement, their accident costs would equal their own losses. The key point is that the average loss is much more predictable than each individual's loss. Applying the egg analogy to the pooling arrangement, (1) each woman puts half of her eggs into one basket and half into another basket, and (2) Emily carries one basket and Samantha carries the other. After reaching their destination, they divide the surviving eggs equally.

There are many ways that people diversify risk in addition to pooling arrangements. For example, most investors do not put all of their wealth into one stock; instead, they invest relatively small amounts of their wealth in many different stocks. In this way, their wealth at the end of their investment horizon is not totally dependent on the fortunes of just one company. Portfolio diversification reduces the investor's risk without necessarily sacrificing expected return. As you will see in Chapters 7 and 9, the ability of individual investors to eliminate risk through portfolio diversification raises an important issue for corporations. In particular, why should corporations reduce risk—for example, by diversifying their own operations or by purchasing insurance—when their stockholders can diversify risk on their own?

The main message from the discussion of pooling arrangements with correlated losses is that positive correlation limits the amount of risk that can be eliminated through pooling arrangements. An analogous result holds for stock portfolio (investment) diversification. Returns on different stocks are positively correlated, because all firms are affected to some degree by common factors, such as general economic conditions and interest rates. Consequently, some of the risk associated with holding stocks cannot be diversified away. That is, the positive correlation in stock returns limits the amount of risk that can be eliminated through portfolio diversification. The risk that cannot be eliminated usually is called systematic risk or sometimes nondiversifiable or market risk.

3.5 Summary

- A probability distribution describes the possible outcomes and the probabilities of those outcomes for a random variable.
- The expected value of a probability distribution is the weighted average of the possible outcomes, where the weights are the probabilities.
- Standard deviation or variance is a measure of probable variation around the expected value of a probability distribution for a random variable and, thus, of the risk (unpredictability) of the variable.
- Pooling arrangements reduce risk (standard deviation) for each participant, provided losses are not perfectly positively correlated.
- The amount of risk that can be reduced through pooling arrangements increases as the number of participants increases, all other factors being held constant.
- In the special case where losses are uncorrelated across participants, risk can be virtually eliminated with a very large number of participants in a pooling arrangement.
- The amount of risk that can be reduced through pooling arrangements decreases as the correlation in losses across participants increases, all other factors being held constant.

Key Terms

random variable   36
probability distribution   36
expected value   40
loss distribution   41
expected loss   41
variance   41
standard deviation   42
sample mean   45

average loss   45
sample standard deviation   45
skewness   46
correlation   47
pooling arrangement   49
law of large numbers   53
normal distribution   53
central limit theorem   53

Questions and Problems

1. Suppose that L is a random variable equal to property losses from a hurricane and that L has the following probability distribution:

    $$L = \begin{array}{ll} \$90,000 & \text{with probability } 0.01 \\ \$10,000 & \text{with probability } 0.05 \\ \$\quad 0 & \text{with probability } 0.94 \end{array}$$

    What is the expected value of hurricane losses (i.e., the expected loss)?

2. Suppose that P is a random variable equal to profits from an ice cream stand at the beach and that P has the following probability distribution:

    $$P = \begin{array}{ll} \$70,000 & \text{with probability } 0.05 \\ \$50,000 & \text{with probability } 0.20 \\ \$30,000 & \text{with probability } 0.40 \\ \$10,000 & \text{with probability } 0.25 \\ -\$10,000 & \text{with probability } 0.10 \end{array}$$

    What is the expected value of profits?

3. Assume that property losses for Buckeye Brewery have the following distribution:

    $$\text{Loss} = \begin{array}{ll} \$3,000,000 & \text{with probability } 0.005 \\ \$1,500,000 & \text{with probability } 0.010 \\ \$\quad 800,000 & \text{with probability } 0.025 \\ \$\qquad\quad 0 & \text{with probability } 0.96 \end{array}$$

What is the expected value of property losses (i.e., the expected loss)?

4. Assume that Buckeye Brewery determines that its liability losses have the following distribution:

$$\text{Loss} = \begin{array}{ll} \$\,5,000,000 & \text{with probability } 0.002 \\ \$\,1,500,000 & \text{with probability } 0.015 \\ \$\ \ \ \ 500,000 & \text{with probability } 0.040 \\ \$\ \ \ \ \ \ \ \ \ \ \ 0 & \text{with probability } 0.943 \end{array}$$

What is the expected value of liability losses?

5. Do you think that Buckeye Brewery's property losses are independent, positively correlated, or negatively correlated with its liability losses?

6. Company Blue is located in Toronto and has property valued at $5 million. Sketch a reasonable probability distribution of Company Blue's property losses.

7. Company Red is located in Cincinnati, Ohio, and has property valued at $5 million. Sketch a reasonable probability distribution for Company Red's property losses.

8. Suppose that Company Blue buys Company Red and the new firm is called Big Red (not to be confused with Big Blue). Sketch a

reasonable probability distribution for Big Red's property losses.

9. Suppose that Kate and Anne enter into a pooling arrangement. Assume that both women have the following loss distributions and that losses are independent.

$$\text{Loss} = \begin{array}{ll} \$\,50,000 & \text{with probability } 0.005 \\ \$\,20,000 & \text{with probability } 0.01 \\ \$\,10,000 & \text{with probability } 0.02 \\ \$\ \ \ \ \ \ \ 0 & \text{with probability } 0.965 \end{array}$$

(*a*) Write out the possible outcomes and the probability of each outcome for Kate and Anne after they enter into a pooling arrangement. That is, write out the probability distribution for each of the women after they enter into a pooling arrangement.

(*b*) Calculate the expected loss to each person prior to and subsequent to entering into a pooling arrangement.

(*c*) What happens to the standard deviation of the distribution of losses to each individual subsequent to the pooling arrangement?

References

Cummins, J. David. "Statistical and Financial Models of Insurance Pricing and the Insurance Firm." *Journal of Risk and Insurance,* June 1991, pp. 261–302. (*The first part of this article provides a more advanced treatment of the material presented in this chapter.*)

Answers to Concept Checks

1. A probability distribution identifies all the possible outcomes and the probabilities of those outcomes for a particular random variable. Simple probability distributions can be described by listing the possible outcomes and the corresponding probabilities. Probability distributions also can be described graphically, with the possible outcomes listed on the horizontal axis and the probabilities

of these outcomes measured on the vertical axis.

2. The following probability distribution indicates that the probability of low losses is relatively high, but that the probability of very high losses is relatively low. The maximum loss (ignoring indirect losses) is $50 million. The shaded area is the probability that losses exceed $30 million.

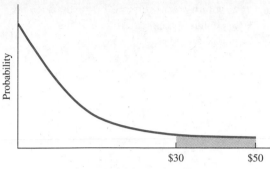

Property losses (in millions)

3. Expected loss = ($0 × 0.7) + ($200 × 0.2)
   + ($1,000 × 0.06) + ($5,000
   × 0.03) + ($10,000 × 0.01)
   = $0 + $40 + $60 + $150
   + $100 = $250

4. Variance (standard deviation) is a measure of risk, because variance measures the predictability of outcomes. The greater the variance, the more likely it is that a realization from the distribution will deviate materially from the expected value.

5. First, note that the expected value of each distribution is $10,000. Distribution 2 has zero standard deviation; the $10,000 outcome occurs all the time. Thus, there is no variation around the expected value. The standard deviation of distribution 1 is difficult to compare to that of distribution 3 without doing the calculations, because the probability of an outcome other than $10,000 is greater with distribution 1, but the deviation of the outcomes from the expected value is greater with distribution 3.

6. Distribution A has a lower expected value and a lower standard deviation than distribution B.

7. The expected value of the game is $0, as our earlier calculation demonstrated (see page 40). The sample mean equals (2/5) ($1) + (3/5) (–$1) = –$0.20. The point is that the sample mean can and usually will differ from the expected value.

8. The distribution would be expected to be highly skewed (i.e., you most likely would have a relatively high probability of no liability losses and a very low probability of extremely high liability losses). The following distribution is consistent with this description.

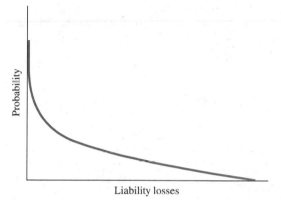

Liability losses

9. (a) Uncorrelated.

   (b) Given the proximity of Miami and Ft. Lauderdale, if Miami experiences hurricane losses greater than the expected value, then Ft. Lauderdale also is likely to experience hurricane losses greater than the expected value. Thus, these random variables would be positively correlated.

   (c) Given that the weather in one year is likely to be independent of the weather in the subsequent year, hurricane losses in one year are likely to be independent of the hurricane losses in the same location in another year.

   (d) Since the number of people who die from AIDS in a given year (regardless of where they live) will be affected by the development of drugs to treat or possibly cure AIDs, these random variables would likely be positively correlated.

10.   By entering a pooling arrangement, a person pays the average loss of the members of the group as opposed to his

or her own loss. The average loss is more predictable (that is, has a lower standard deviation) than an individual's loss. The pooling arrangement, however, does not change the expected loss of the participants.

11.

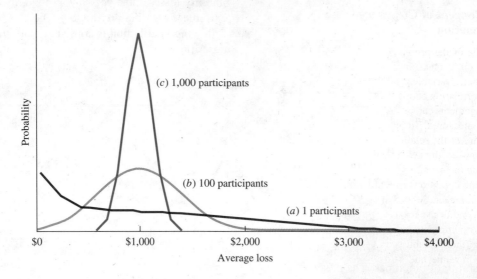

12.

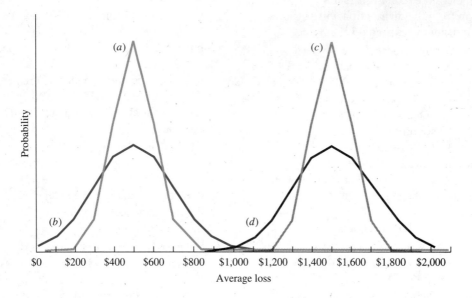

APPENDIX 3A
MORE ON RISK MEASUREMENT AND RISK REDUCTION

3A.1 The Concept of Covariance and More about Correlation

Although none of the problems or analysis in this book will require you to measure or calculate the correlation between random variables, additional insight into the meaning of correlation and its effect on risk reduction in pooling arrangements can be obtained by explaining how correlation is measured. To begin, it helps to introduce a related measure of the relationship between two random variables, known as the **covariance.**

To illustrate the meaning of covariance, consider how macroeconomic conditions might affect the revenue and costs of an automaker. Suppose that there are three types of economic conditions: strong growth, weak growth, or no growth. For simplicity, assume that each outcome is equally likely (the probability is one-third) and that the outcomes for revenue and costs under each economic outcome are those presented in Table 3A–1. Under these assumptions, the expected values of revenue and costs equal $717 and $650, respectively.

We want to find the covariance between the random variables: revenue and costs. First, notice that when revenue is above its expected value (as in the strong and weak growth conditions), costs are either above or equal to their expected value, and when revenue is below its expected value (as in the no growth condition), costs are below their expected value. Thus, revenue and costs tend to move in the same direction, relative to their respective expected values. Based on our earlier discussion of correlation, we therefore know that revenue and costs are positively correlated.

The mathematical definition of covariance is:

$$Cov(X,Y) = \sum_{i=1}^{N} p_i(x_i - \mu_x)(y_i - \mu_y) \qquad (3A.1)$$

where

N = the number of possible outcomes ($N = 3$ in the example);

X = one random variable (revenue) with possible outcomes $x_1, \ldots, x_N$;

Y = the other random variable (costs) with possible outcomes $y_1, \ldots, y_N$;

$p_1, \ldots, p_N$ = the probabilities of each joint outcome (one-third in the example);

μ_x = the expected value of X ($717); and

μ_y = the expected value of Y ($650).

Note that this formula implies that if X has outcomes that are greater than its expected value when Y has outcomes that are greater than its expected value, then the terms in parentheses will both be positive and their product also will be positive. Similarly, if X has outcomes that are less than its expected value when Y has outcomes that are less than its expected value, then the terms in parentheses both will be negative and again their product will be positive. Thus, when X and Y tend to move in the same direction, the terms being summed in the formula will be positive, so that the covariance between X and Y will be positive.

In contrast, if X and Y tend to move in opposite directions (high outcomes for X occur when Y has low outcomes), then the terms in parentheses will have opposite signs and their product will be negative. Consequently, the terms being summed will be negative, and the covariance will be negative. Notice that this discussion of covariance sounds very much like our discussion of correlation. In fact, covariance has the same sign as correlation. Returning to the revenue and costs example, if revenue is high when costs are high, then revenue and costs have positive covariance and positive correlation.[1]

TABLE 3A–1

Economic Condition	Probability	Revenue	Costs
Strong growth	1/3	$850	$700
Weak growth	1/3	800	650
No growth	1/3	500	600
Expected value		$717	650

---

[1] You may have noticed that the formula for covariance is very similar to the formula for variance presented earlier in the chapter. Indeed, you can view them as the same formula, because the variance of a random variable is the covariance of that random variable with itself. You can see this by substituting X and its expected value for Y and its expected value in the covariance formula.

Applying the formula for covariance to the auto-maker's revenue and costs, we find

$$\begin{aligned}\text{Cov(Revenue, Costs)} = 1/3 \, [(\$850 - \$717)(\$700 \\ - \$650) + (\$800 - \$717)(\$650 \\ - \$650) + (\$500 - \$717)(\$600 \\ - \$650)] = 1/3 \, [(\$133)(\$50) \\ + (\$83)(\$0) + (-\$217)(-\$50)] \\ = \$3,617\end{aligned}$$

While the sign of covariance tells us whether the two random variables tend to move together, the magnitude of the covariance measure has little intuitive meaning by itself. For this reason, the covariance often is scaled to obtain the **correlation coefficient.** The correlation coefficient, usually denoted by the Greek letter ρ (rho), equals the covariance divided by the product of the standard deviations. Mathematically, the correlation coefficient between X and Y is defined as:

$$\rho(X, Y) = \frac{\text{Cov}(X, Y)}{\text{Std}(X)\text{Std}(Y)} \qquad (3A.2)$$

where

Std(X) = the standard deviation of X, and
Std(Y) = the standard deviation of Y.

A nice feature of the correlation coefficient is that it is always between -1 and 1. The greater the correlation coefficient in absolute value, the more strongly related are the two random variables. If the correlation coefficient is 1, then the two random variables are perfectly positively correlated. If the correlation coefficient is -1, then the two random variables are perfectly negatively correlated. Perfect correlation implies that if you were to plot the outcomes of X and Y on a two-dimensional graph, the outcomes would lie along a straight line (i.e., X and Y would be perfectly linearly related). If the correlation coefficient is 0 between two random variables, then they are uncorrelated or independent.[2] Intuitively, a correlation coefficient of 0 implies that the outcomes for X are unrelated to the outcomes for Y.

To calculate the correlation coefficient in our example, we must first find the standard deviations of revenue and costs:

---

[2] There is actually a subtle distinction between random variables that are uncorrelated and random variables that are independent. Independent random variables always are uncorrelated, but some uncorrelated random variables do not satisfy the technical definition of independence. It is not important for you to know the distinction to understand the ideas in this book.

$$\begin{aligned}\text{Std(Revenue)} = \{1/3 \, [(\$850 - \$717)^2 + (\$800 - \$717)^2 \\ + (\$500 - \$717)^2 \,]\}^{1/2} = \$154.6\end{aligned}$$

$$\begin{aligned}\text{Std(Costs)} = \{1/3 \, [(\$700 - \$650)^2 + (\$650 - \$650)^2 \\ + (\$550 - \$650)^2 \,]\}^{1/2} = \$40.8\end{aligned}$$

Dividing the covariance by the product of the standard deviations gives:

$$\begin{aligned}\rho\text{(Revenue, Costs)} = \$8,333/(\$154.6)(\$40.8) \\ = \$3,617/\$6,306 = 0.57\end{aligned}$$

That is, the correlation coefficient between revenue and costs is positive, but the two random variables are not perfectly correlated.

3A.2 Expected Value and Standard Deviation of Combinations of Random Variables

We now can illustrate how distributions of random variables change when they are combined in certain ways. These results are important in measuring the amount of risk (standard deviation) that is eliminated by pooling arrangements.

Expected Value of a Constant Times a Random Variable. Suppose that X is a random variable equal to Samantha's auto accident costs for the coming year and that X equals $2,500 with probability 0.8 and $0 with probability 0.2 (as in our earlier example). The expected value of X is:

$$E(X) = (0.2) \, (\$2,500) + (0.8) \, (\$0) = \$500$$

Now suppose that Samantha's father, because he is so nice, agrees to pay one-half of her accident losses. Thus, there is a difference between Samantha's accident losses and the costs she must pay. Samantha's accident costs for the year will equal $\frac{1}{2}X$, which is a constant (one-half) times the original random variable. The expected value of the new random variable is simply the constant times the expected value of the original random variable:

$$E(\tfrac{1}{2}X) = \tfrac{1}{2} \, E(X) = \tfrac{1}{2}(\$500) = \$250$$

In general, the expected value of a constant times a random variable equals the constant times the expected value of the random variable.

Standard Deviation and Variance of a Constant Times a Random Variable. What is the standard deviation of Samantha's accident costs after her father agrees to pay one-half of her accident costs? Once again, the standard deviation of a constant times a random variable equals the constant (½) times the standard deviation of the random variable. That is

$$\text{Std}(\tfrac{1}{2}X) = \tfrac{1}{2}\,\text{Std}(X)$$

Samantha's total accident costs (without the subsidy from her father) have a standard deviation equal to

$$\text{Std}(X) = \sqrt{0.8\,(\$0 - \$500)^2 + 0.2\,(\$2{,}500 - \$500)^2}$$
$$= \$1{,}000$$

Therefore, the standard deviation of Samantha's accident costs after her father agrees to pay 50 percent is ½ ($1,000) = $500. (This result can be shown to hold by plugging in one-half of the accident costs and one-half of the original expected value in the standard deviation formula; that is, by calculating the standard deviation of ½X directly.)

Recall that the variance of a random variable is the square of the standard deviation. Therefore, the variance of a constant times a random variable is the *constant squared* times the variance of the random variable. Algebraically

$$\text{Var}(\tfrac{1}{2}X) = [\text{Std}(\tfrac{1}{2}X)]^2 = [\tfrac{1}{2}\text{Std}(X)]^2 = (\tfrac{1}{2})^2\,\text{Var}(X)$$

In Samantha's case, the variance of accident costs was originally $1,000². After her father agreed to pay one-half of her accident costs, the variance decreased to (¼)($1,000)².

Expected Value of a Sum of Random Variables. The expected value of a sum of random variables is the sum of the expected values. To illustrate this result, consider the Emily–Samantha example. Both Emily and Samantha have expected accident costs equal to $500. The expected value of Emily's costs plus Samantha's costs is therefore $500 + $500 = $1,000. This is true no matter what the correlation coefficient is between Emily's and Samantha's costs. In general

$$E(X + Y) = E(X) + E(Y)$$

One combination of random variables that plays a particularly important role in statistics, insurance, and investments is the average of random variables. Remember the pooling arrangement between Emily and Samantha. By entering the pooling arrangement, each woman basically trades her personal loss for the average loss. That is, if X = Emily's personal loss and Y = Samantha's personal loss, then by entering the pooling arrangement Emily pays $(X + Y)/2$ instead of X and Samantha pays $(X + Y)/2$ instead of Y. Applying the results just derived (that the expected value of a sum equals the sum of the

expected values and that the expected value of a constant times a random variable is the constant times the expected value), we find that the expected cost to Emily and Samantha after entering the pooling arrangement is:

$$E[(X + Y)/2] = \tfrac{1}{2}\,E(X) + \tfrac{1}{2}\,E(Y) = \$250 + \$250 = \$500$$

That is, the pooling arrangement does not change either woman's expected cost.

Variance and Standard Deviation of a Sum of Random Variables. Algebraically, the variance of a sum of random variables X and Y is given by the following equation:

$$\text{Var}(X + Y) = \text{Var}(X) + \text{Var}(Y) + 2\text{Cov}(X,\ Y)$$

If the covariance is 0, the variance of the sum equals the sum of the variances.

The standard deviation of the sum is:

$$\text{Std}(X + Y) = \sqrt{\text{Var}(X) + \text{Var}(Y) + 2\text{Cov}(X,Y)}$$

Often it is more convenient to use this formula by first substituting the relation between the covariance and the correlation coefficient. Recall $\rho(X,Y) = \text{Cov}(X,Y)/[\text{Std}(X)\,\text{Std}(Y)]$. Therefore

$$\text{Std}(X + Y) = \sqrt{\text{Var}(X) + \text{Var}(Y) + 2\rho(X,Y)\text{Std}(X)\text{Std}(Y)}$$

The standard deviation of a sum of random variables is the sum of the standard deviations in one special case— perfect positive correlation. (To see this, set $\rho = 1$ and note that the expression under the square root sign equals $\text{Std}(X)$ plus $\text{Std}(Y)$ squared.) In all other cases, the standard deviation of a sum of random variables is less than the sum of the standard deviations.

Variance and Standard Deviation of the Average of Homogeneous Random Variables. Recall that the average of random variables plays a particularly important role in insurance because participants in pooling arrangements pay the average loss of the group. Using the results already presented, the variance of an average of random variables is:

$$\text{Var}\!\left[\frac{X+Y}{2}\right] = \text{Var}\!\left[\frac{X}{2}\right] + \text{Var}\!\left[\frac{Y}{2}\right] + 2\rho(X,Y)\text{Std}\!\left[\frac{X}{2}\right]\text{Std}\!\left[\frac{Y}{2}\right]$$

If the random variables X and Y have the same variance (standard deviation), then the formula can be simplified as follows (recalling that $\text{Var}\!\left[\frac{X}{2}\right] = \frac{1}{4}\text{Var}(X)$):

$$\text{Var}\!\left[\frac{X+Y}{2}\right] = \tfrac{1}{4}\text{Var}(X) + \tfrac{1}{4}\text{Var}(X) + 2\rho(X,Y)\tfrac{1}{4}\text{Var}(X)$$

Combining terms yields the following equation:

$$\text{Var}\left[\frac{X+Y}{2}\right] = \frac{1}{2}\text{Var}(X)[1 + \rho(X,Y)]$$

If the correlation coefficient is 0 (X and Y are uncorrelated), then the variance of the average loss is one-half of the original variance. This indicates that averaging uncorrelated losses reduces variance (risk). This is the fundamental result that was presented, in less technical terms, in the text.

In general, if losses are uncorrelated and have the same variance, then the variance of the average loss is the original variance divided by the number of participants in the pooling arrangement. Thus, if N people each having a variance of losses equal to Var decide to create a pooling arrangement, then the variance of losses paid by each individual changes from Var to Var/N (assuming losses are uncorrelated). As N gets large, the variance approaches 0.

The effect of pooling arrangements on the standard deviation of losses paid by each participant is found by taking the square root of the variances. If each participant has a variance of losses equal to Var and a standard deviation of losses equal to Std ($= \sqrt{\text{Var}}$), then a pooling arrangement with N participants and uncorrelated losses changes the standard deviation of the amount paid by each person to Std/$\sqrt{N}$.

To apply these results to the accident costs paid by Emily and Samantha after they enter the pooling arrangement, let X equal Samantha's accident costs and Y equal Emily's accident costs. Recall that the standard deviations of Emily's and Samantha's accident costs are $1,000, since Std($X$) = Std($Y$) = $1,000. What is the standard deviation of accident costs for each woman after entering the pooling arrangement?

If Emily's and Samantha's accident costs are uncorrelated ($\rho = 0$), then the standard deviation after entering the pooling arrangement (using the above expression for the variance of ($X + Y$)/2 with $\rho = 0$) equals:

$$\text{Std}\left[\frac{X+Y}{2}\right] = \frac{\text{Std}(X)}{\sqrt{2}} = \frac{\$1{,}000}{\sqrt{2}} = \$707$$

The standard deviation is reduced from $1,000 to $707, indicating that losses for Emily and Samantha are more predictable.

If Emily's and Samantha's accident costs are perfectly positively correlated ($\rho = 1$), then the standard deviation after entering the pooling arrangement (using the expression for the variance of ($X + Y$)2 with $\rho = 1$) equals the average standard deviation of the random variables:

$$\text{Std}\left[\frac{X+Y}{2}\right] = \frac{1}{\sqrt{2}}(\$1{,}000)\sqrt{1+1} = \$1{,}000$$

The standard deviation is unchanged by the pooling arrangement when losses are perfectly positively correlated. These results highlight that the effect of a pooling arrangement on the standard deviation depends on the correlation between losses. The greater the correlation, the less that risk is reduced by the pooling arrangement.

Key Terms

covariance   63
correlation coefficient   64

Risk Pooling and Insurance Institutions

Chapter Objectives

- Explain why insurance organizations exist by introducing their main economic functions.
- Describe different types of insurance company ownership.
- Discuss the role of insurer capital and factors that affect insurer capital decisions.
- Describe how insurers reduce insolvency risk through diversification of underwriting risk, reinsurance, and investment choices.

4.1 Contracting Costs for Risk Pooling Arrangements

As we learned in the previous chapter, individuals can reduce their risk by forming a pooling arrangement. As a result, risk-averse individuals would have strong incentives to participate in pooling arrangements if they could be organized at zero cost. However, risk pooling arrangements obviously are not costless to operate. Indeed, the cost of organizing and operating pooling arrangements is the main reason why insurance companies exist and why most pooling arrangements take place indirectly through insurance contracts. In essence, insurance contracts are a way of lowering the costs of operating pooling arrangements.

This chapter introduces the key factors that affect the cost and effectiveness of risk pooling through insurance contracts. An important issue with insurance contracts is insolvency risk, that is, the risk that the insurer will not fulfill its promises to pay losses. We therefore discuss the roles of insurer capital, diversification, and reinsurance in reducing insolvency risk. The next chapter then describes insurance company insolvency experience, insurer solvency ratings, and solvency regulation.

Types of Contracting Costs

Consider a risk pooling arrangement like the one introduced in Chapter 3, in which Emily and Samantha agree to share losses equally. We showed how this type of pooling arrangement reduces each participant's risk, as measured by the standard deviation of his or her payment, provided that losses are not perfectly positively correlated. The greater the number of people who participate in a pooling arrangement, the greater is the reduction in risk. There are, however, several important costs associated with writing and enforcing contracts among participants, which in general are referred to as contracting costs. To illustrate how insurance companies economize on these costs, this section describes the major types of contracting costs associated with pooling arrangements.

Consider first the costs associated with adding participants to risk pools. In practice, risk pooling arrangements incur substantial costs in marketing and in specifying the terms of agreement. These costs often are called **distribution costs.** As discussed in Box 4–1, insurers employ a variety of distribution systems, including exclusive agents and independent agents and brokers. Once a potential participant in a pooling arrangement has been identified, it must be decided whether to allow the individual to participate. For example, suppose that existing participants in a pooling arrangement all have expected losses of $200. Then those participants will be reluctant to allow a person with an expected loss of $400 to join on the same terms. Thus, the pool members will want to evaluate each potential participant's expected loss. The process of identifying (estimating) a potential participant's expected loss is known as **underwriting,** and the costs of doing so are called *underwriting expenses.*[1]

When a participant in a pooling arrangement experiences a loss, the person must inform and seek payment from the other members. To prevent people from fraudulently claiming that a loss has occurred or exaggerating loss amounts, the pooling arrangement must monitor claims. The costs associated with this process usually are called **loss adjustment expenses** (or *claims settlement expenses*). Pooling arrangements also involve collection costs. If, for example, a particular member has a valid claim of $10,000, each participant will ultimately have to be assessed the specified share of the $10,000 loss (e.g., $10 each if there are 1,000 members that agree to share losses equally). Alternatively, each member will have to be billed periodically for his or her share of total claim costs since the last payment. In either case, the collection of funds will involve costs in sending a bill to each member and attempting to ensure that each member pays his or her assessment.

---

[1] In practice, the term *underwriting expenses* often encompasses both underwriting expenses and distribution costs or even all costs apart from claim and capital costs.

Box 4–1

Insurance Distribution

The three principal means of distributing insurance are: (1) independent agents and brokers, (2) exclusive (captive) agents and/or insurance company employees, and (3) direct response methods, such as telemarketing, mail order systems, and on line marketing. A large majority of insurance contracts are sold through the first two methods. On-line marketing is in its infancy; it is not clear how significant it may become. Insurers that rely on exclusive agents, employees, or direct response methods are known as *direct writers.*

Independent agencies and brokerages are independent organizations that have agency and/or brokerage relationships with multiple insurers. Technically, a *broker* represents the insurance buyer for the purpose of arranging insurance coverage with one or more insurers, while an *agent* represents the insurer for the purpose of selling coverage to buyers. This distinction can be important in the event of disputes between the buyer, agent or broker, and insurer.

These firms range in size from those with only a few personnel specializing in personal lines and small business insurance, up to the large international insurance brokerage firms that employ thousands of people in order to provide a wide range of risk management, insurance, and employee benefit services, primarily to medium-to-large businesses. Many businesses enter into a brokerage arrangement with a specific firm (the *broker of record*), but it also is common for larger firms to utilize more than one broker.

Insurers that use independent agents/brokers traditionally have been dominant in property–liability insurance sold to businesses (commercial lines). However, the market share of these insurers has been declining, largely due to the growth of direct writers in the small business market. According to the A.M. Best Company, insurers that use independent agents

and brokers wrote 72 percent of US commercial lines premiums in 1996. The remainder was written by direct writers (most commonly through exclusive agents). The large commercial lines market share of insurers that use independent agents and brokers reflects their important function of matching business buyers with widely varying risk characteristics to insurers with different areas of specialization. In contrast, direct writers wrote 68 percent of personal lines premiums (auto and homeowners insurance). Direct writers generally emphasize careful underwriting and achieve a large volume of sales per agent by targeting consumers with well-defined risk characteristics and coverage needs. For both commercial and personal lines, direct writers have lower distribution/underwriting expenses as a proportion of premiums than insurers that use independent agents and brokers.

Direct writers and insurers that use independent agents and brokers both have a major presence in the market for employee benefit plan services (group life–health insurance and retirement plans). Direct writers dominate the market for individual life–health insurance, where the most common distribution method is through exclusive agents (known as career agents). However, the amount of individual life and health insurance and annuity products purchased through independent agents and brokers increased significantly in the 1980s and 1990s. A significant proportion of annuities is marketed by life–health insurers through banks and securities firms (especially banks). The market penetration of banks and other noninsurance firms into insurance distribution (and possibly underwriting) could expand significantly if Congress adopts proposed legislation that would substantially eliminate the complex set of government regulations that have historically discouraged the distribution and underwriting of insurance by banks.

You can think of insurance companies as organizations that have emerged to reduce the costs of operating pooling arrangements. For example, without a central organization to recruit new members and distribute contracts (marketing and distribution), screen applicants (underwriting), monitor claims (loss adjustment), and collect assessments, each member of a pooling arrangement would need to contract with each of the other members. With 1,000 members, 499,500 separate contracts would be needed (1,000 members × 999 contracts per member ÷ 2, since only one contract per pair is needed). With a central organization, only 1,000 contracts between the organization and the members are needed.

In addition, without a central organization, each member would have to (1) become involved in underwriting each of the other members, (2) investigate each claim, and (3) individually collect assessments. These activities involve expertise that most people do not have and require considerable amounts of time. The existence of insurance companies that specialize in these activities typically is efficient (i.e., it lowers costs).[2]

Ex Ante Premium Payments versus Ex Post Assessments

In contrast to pure pooling arrangements, insurance companies seldom have the legal right to assess members of the pooling arrangement (policyholders) for losses that have occurred. Instead, policyholders pay an ex ante premium—that is, prior to knowing the magnitude of losses—without giving the insurer the right of assessment if more money is ultimately needed to pay claims (ex post). One explanation for having fixed ex ante premiums as opposed to ex post assessments is that collecting assessments from people who do not have losses is costly. Some people will attempt to delay and in some cases avoid paying assessments.

Moreover, with a pure assessment system, funds might not be available to pay losses quickly. The resulting delay in claim payments would be costly to those participants that have experienced losses. Finally, assessments impose risk on participants: They do not know in advance how much they will have to contribute (although the risk still is lower than if they were not members). For these reasons, insurers commonly charge policyholders a fixed, advance premium without having the right to assess policyholders for losses during the coverage period if realized losses for the insured group turn out to be higher than expected.[3]

Fixed ex ante premiums imply that the insurer obtains revenue (premium payments) prior to paying claims. As we elaborate later in the chapter, insurers typically invest these funds in a variety of financial assets. The resulting investment earnings can be used to help pay claims when they come due. As you will see in Chapter 6, the insurer's expected investment earnings reduce the premium that needs to be charged to cover the insurer's expected costs, all else being equal.

---

[2] Some pooling arrangements are organized without the involvement of insurance companies. As you would expect given the previous discussion, these pooling arrangements typically involve relatively small numbers of business participants with similar exposures to loss, which helps to reduce underwriting and collection costs.

[3] Commercial insurance contracts with retrospective experience rating make the premium payment depend on the insured's loss experience during the contract period. The reasons for these types of contracts are discussed in Chapter 11.

4.2 Insurer Insolvency Risk and the Role of Capital

With a typical insurance policy, the policyholder pays a fixed premium to the insurer and the insurer promises to pay losses that are covered under the terms of the policy. This arrangement raises the question: If the premiums and investment income are insufficient to pay administrative costs and claim costs, who (if anyone) is obligated to pay the shortfall? Conversely, if premium revenue and investment income exceed the insurer's costs, who receives the excess? The short answer to these questions is that the owners of the insurer are responsible for any shortfall (subject to limited liability and contractual limits on assessments of owners) and the owners have rights to any excess. In this section, we describe and analyze how owners generally fulfill their obligation to pay policyholders' claims. We then discuss the various types of ownership arrangements for insurance companies in the next section.

Most insurance companies hold substantial capital that is available to pay claims in the event that premiums and investment income from premiums are insufficient. **Economic capital** is defined as the difference between the market value of assets and the market value of liabilities. The market value of assets reflects the market value of the insurer's stocks, bonds, real estate, cash, and the like. The market value of liabilities equals the present value of the payments the insurer has promised to make in the future for policies already sold. Note that the economic value of assets, liabilities, and capital does not correspond to the way accountants measure these items. We will briefly comment on some of these accounting issues later.

To clarify these concepts using a simple example, suppose that Drennan Capital Corporation (DCC) sells policies to 10,000 homogeneous policyholders at the beginning of the year. DCC will cease operations after the claims on the policies have been paid at the end of the year. The expected claim cost for each policyholder is $500. The actual claim cost for any given policyholder, of course, could be much different from $500. Suppose that DCC charges each policyholder a premium of $525. To keep things simple, we will ignore the distribution, underwriting, and claims processing costs and the investment income from investing premiums and capital mentioned earlier.

Immediately after receiving the premium payments, DCC has assets of $525 × 10,000 = $5.25 million. DCC's (economic) liabilities equal the expected value of its obligations to pay policyholders' claims, which equals $5 million (10,000 policyholders × $500 expected cost per policyholder). Thus, immediately after selling the policies, DCC has $5.25 million in assets and $5 million in liabilities, giving it $0.25 million in (economic) capital.

Now let's look at DCC's capital after paying losses at the end of the year. Suppose that policyholders had fewer losses than were expected, so that the average loss was $450. Then, DCC would pay claims of $450 × 10,000 = $4.5 million. Assets would be diminished by $4.5 million and liabilities would be eliminated. At this point, DCC would have assets of $0.75 million and no liabilities, and its capital would be $0.75 million. This capital belongs to the owners of DCC.

Suppose, however, that claim costs at the end of the year exceeded the amount expected so that the average loss was $550. In this case, DCC's assets of $5.25 million would be insufficient to pay all of the $5.5 million in claim costs (10,000 policyholders × $550 average claim cost). We could say that the insurer in this case has negative capital, or, more commonly, that the insurer is *insolvent*—it cannot meet all of its obligations.

As discussed in the next chapter, the frequency of insurer insolvencies generally is relatively low and, historically, most insolvent insurers have been relatively small companies. One reason the insolvency probability is very small for most insurers is that they hold enough capital to cover unexpectedly high claim costs. We will discuss the incentives for insurers to hold capital after describing who owns insurance companies.

Concept Checks

1. Why do insurance companies exist? What are the major functions undertaken by insurers?

2. Why might insurer capital sometimes be referred to as a cushion?

4.3 Ownership and Sources of Capital

Who owns insurance company capital? That is, (1) who commits the capital to provide a cushion from which unexpectedly high claims costs are paid, and (2) who has rights to excess funds when claim costs are lower than expected? There are two broad approaches to insurance company ownership. One approach is to make the policyholders the owners; the other is to make investors the owners. Each approach has several variations.

Mutual Insurers

The most common form of policyholder-owned insurer is called a **mutual insurer.** Mutual insurers are incorporated insurance companies that usually charge fixed, advance premiums to policyholders. Because policyholders usually cannot be assessed to pay unexpectedly high claim costs, their liability for the insurer's claim costs is limited to what they originally paid in premiums.

The capital needed to start a mutual insurer and to provide an initial cushion from which unexpectedly high claim costs could be paid usually is obtained by borrowing money from investors. The loan then is repaid from operating profits over time.[4] In addition, when a mutual insurer retains operating profits (earnings), it accumulates additional assets, which are used as a cushion (capital) for future liabilities. If the managers of a mutual insurer determine that all the additional capital is not needed, they can pay out profits to policyholders as policyholder

---

[4] The securities that mutual insurers issue to obtain capital generally are called *surplus notes.* They are similar to corporate bonds, but the repayment of principal usually must be approved by state insurance regulators.

dividends. Policyholder dividends are low in property–liability insurance compared to life insurance. One explanation is that many life insurance products bundle insurance with investment products, and a portion of the investment return is paid as dividends. A fuller discussion of life insurance contracts and policy dividends is provided in Chapter 23.

Another type of insurer with policyholder ownership is called a **reciprocal.** In practice, mutuals and reciprocals operate similarly. One technical difference is that a reciprocal is not incorporated but is instead managed by an entity known as an *attorney in fact,* which is in essence a management company.

Stock Insurers

Stock insurers are incorporated insurance companies that are owned by investors who have purchased the stock (equity) of the company. At its inception, a stock insurer issues shares of stock. Thereafter, capital is accumulated through retained earnings and through additional stock or bond issues.[5] Stockholders can suffer losses from unexpectedly high claim costs (or low returns on the insurer's assets). However, as is true for stockholders of corporations in general, their maximum loss is limited to the amount of money that they have invested in the stock, according to the legal doctrine of *limited liability.* Stockholders have the right to any profits that the insurer earns. If managers decide that the firm has accumulated enough capital, dividends can be paid to the stockholders (or stock can be repurchased). Like mutual insurers, stock insurers sometimes pay dividends to policyholders. In workers' compensation insurance, for example, price regulation sometimes holds insurance rates above the competitive market level for some employers. As a result, both stock and mutual insurers often compete by offering policyholder dividends if claims experience is favorable.

There are large numbers of both mutual and stock insurers in the property–liability and life–health insurance industries. In order to achieve greater access to capital (i.e., by issuing stock), a number of mutual insurers have converted to stock insurers and hybrid stock-mutual structures in recent years (see Box 4–2). Figure 4–1 provides information on the 1996 premiums written by all stock and mutual insurance groups in the United States for both the property–liability and life–health insurance industries. Mutual insurers wrote 25 percent of property–liability insurance premiums in 1996; stock insurers wrote 69 percent. Reciprocals accounted for approximately 6 percent of premiums. Approximately one-half of this amount was written by one reciprocal organization (Farmers Insurance Group, a leading writer of automobile and homeowners' insurance in the West and Southwest).

---

[5] From the policyholder's perspective, debt obligations of the insurer provide additional capital because policyholders' claims generally must be paid prior to interest and principal on debt contracts. Shareholders, however, would not view funds provided by debt as additional capital, because shareholders have the residual claim; that is, they only get paid after policyholders and debtholders.

Box 4–2

Mutual Insurers Consider New Means of Going Public
Shift Reflects Need for Capital to Stay Competitive, Changes in State Laws

Mutual insurance companies, the industry's stodgy veterans, may soon be changing their stripes.

After thriving for decades on policyholders' premiums and retained earnings, many mutual insurers are discovering the limits of not having shareholders. As the insurance industry consolidates and becomes more competitive, mutuals find they are in danger of being left behind by bigger and better-capitalized publicly owned insurers. As a result, some of the nation's biggest mutuals are considering going public themselves.

Most of these mutuals are successful operations and "aren't undercapitalized companies with cash flow problems," says David Spuria, a lawyer with Weil, Gotshal & Manges in New York. "Many are interested in this for the flexibility, so when they do land an acquisition, they can strike when the iron is hot."

Converting from a mutual to a shareholder-owned company is both cumbersome and costly, however. To make the process easier, mutuals are pushing states to adopt legislation allowing them to create special operating units that could issue stock, while the present company remains under the ownership of policyholders.

Push for Hybrid Structure
So far, about 10 states have approved this hybrid-type of company, and about a dozen others—including Massachusetts and New York—are debating it. Although states traditionally have discouraged conversions by mutuals out of concern for policyholder interests, many have been swayed recently by the mutuals' argument that shareholder-owned companies have a big competitive advantage because they can raise capital more easily.

For policyholders, one benefit of such a conversion is that their policies would in most instances be backed by a bigger, stronger company that would be less likely to suffer a ratings downgrade because it is losing competitive ground. But consumer activists fret that mutual policyholders would be gaining some things they won't like, such as competing demands for capital within the company. For example, policyholders who desire higher dividends to be paid on policies or improved claims service would be up

Table 4–1 illustrates that some of the largest property–liability and life–health insurers are mutuals. It lists the 1996 premium volume and ownership form for the 10 largest US insurance organizations in each industry based on 1996 premiums. Note that some groups rank in the top 10 for both industries.

Lloyd's of London

Lloyd's of London provides another example of investor ownership of insurers. Strictly speaking, Lloyd's of London is not an insurance company; it is an organization that provides a location and, more importantly, a set of rules and procedures under which insurance business is transacted. Also, contrary to what many people often think, Lloyd's of London does not provide unusual insurance coverage alone. Instead, the vast majority of business conducted at Lloyd's of London is commercial insurance, reinsurance, and auto insurance.

The owners of the insurance organizations that conduct business at Lloyd's are called **names.** Until the early 1990s, all names were individuals with rela-

against shareholders who favor higher stock dividends and earnings.

Still, to mutual-insurance management, the hybrid structure "is a happy medium," says Mr. Spuria, the lawyer. "Mutual companies love it, and more of them will push their legislators to adopt it," he adds.

Mutuals have long had the option of converting to stock ownership through a process known as "demutualization." But it is a costly, cumbersome and controversial route because many state laws require mutuals converting to shareholder ownership to compensate their policyholders, who, by long tradition, have been defined as the owners. Demonstrating to regulators that policyholders are equitably compensated—with cash, stock or policy enhancements—leads to big bills for consultants, actuaries, accountants, and lawyers. But no such demonstration is generally necessary under the hybrid form, analysts say.

Policyholders' Interests

The concept is borrowed from the savings-and-loan industry, says Moody's Investors Service analyst Joel Salomon. It involves creation of a "mutual holding company." Many historical rights of mutual policyholders—such as the right to vote for board members—are transferred to the holding company from the long-standing mutual operating business. Policy-

holders' contractual rights—matters related to premiums and benefits, for instance—continue with the operating unit. It is this operating unit, or an intermediate holding company above it, that has the ability to sell a public stake.

To be sure, the hybrid company form isn't without controversy of its own. Jason Adkins, executive director of the Center for Insurance Research, a policyholder rights organization based in Cambridge, Mass., calls much of the legislation—both approved and proposed—"grossly anticonsumer." He argues that some versions "substantially alter the legal rights and protections formerly available to mutual policyholders" and introduce "obvious conflicts of interest." For example, directors of a mutual holding company, he says, would no longer owe a fiduciary duty solely to policyholders, as they have historically.

But Stephen Brown, John Hancock's chairman, says the criticism "is not valid." He contends that ample regulatory and other safeguards exist to protect policyholders' interests, and he believes policyholders, who must approve the conversions, gain by becoming part of a "stronger and sounder" company.

tively large amounts of wealth. At Lloyd's, insurance policies are sold through syndicates (groups) of names. Each syndicate has a lead underwriter who usually specializes in a particular type of business (e.g., aviation risks) and who makes decisions about what policies to sell and the terms of those policies. When joining Lloyd's and each year thereafter, a name decides which syndicates to participate in and the extent of participation. For example, a name with $150,000 of capital to commit to Lloyd's may allocate $50,000 each to three different syndicates. Essentially, the name has invested in three different insurance companies.

The investment by an individual name, however, differs from investment in a stock insurance company, because an individual name has **unlimited liability.** If the syndicate does not have sufficient funds to pay all the claims on its policies from its premium revenue, its investment income, and the capital contributed by the names, then the names can be assessed for the shortfall. As noted earlier, an investor in a stock insurance company cannot be assessed; the investor's loss is limited to the amount invested in the stock.

FIGURE 4–1

Property–liability and life–health insurance industry premiums written for mutual insurers, stock insurers, and total industry in 1996

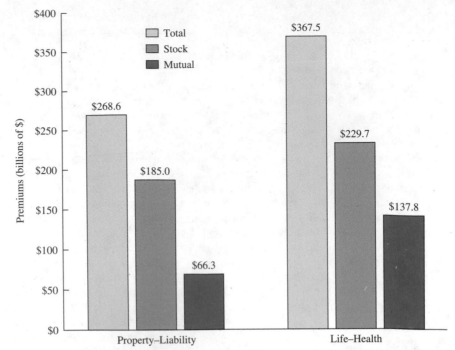

Source: Data obtained from *Best's Aggregates and Averages, 1987,* Property–Liability and Life–Health editions.

While the unlimited liability feature of Lloyd's of London would appear to enhance its ability to pay claims, this organizational form was severely tested during the 1990s. Large losses from catastrophes, environmental liability claims, and asbestos liability claims forced a number of syndicates to assess names. As we discussed in general terms earlier, the collection of assessments turned out to be difficult and very costly for Lloyd's. Many names refused to pay their assessments, alleging that they were misled about the risks involved and that the agents they hired to allocate their capital to various syndicates breached their duty. At one time, more than 19,000 names were involved in lawsuits related to these circumstances (the number of names reached its peak in 1989, when there were approximately 30,000 names). The failure of names to pay assessments pushed Lloyd's to the brink of financial distress and forced it to reorganize—a process that included the introduction of corporate names, with limited liability, in the early 1990s. Lloyd's now operates with both individual names (with unlimited liability) and corporate names.

4.4 Factors Affecting Insurer Capital Decisions

An important decision facing all insurers is how much capital to hold, given underwriting and investment decisions. This section analyzes the key factors that affect this decision in the absence of regulation. Capital regulation is discussed in

TABLE 4–1   **Ownership Form and Premium Volume for the 10 Largest Writers of US Property–Liability and Life–Health Insurance in 1996**

Property–Liability	Ownership	Net Premiums Written ($ millions)
State Farm Insurance Group	Mutual	$34,559
Allstate Insurance Group	Stock	17,773
CNA Insurance Group	Stock	9,993
American International Group	Stock	9,270
Farmers Insurance Group	Reciprocal	8,555
Nationwide Insurance Group	Mutual	8,243
Travelers Property & Casualty Group	Stock	7,436
Hartford Insurance Group	Stock	5,744
Liberty Mutual Insurance Companies	Mutual	5,142
Zurich Insurance Group–US	Stock	5,096
Life–Health		
Metropolitan Insurance Group	Mutual	$21,482
Prudential Insurance Group	Mutual	21,158
CIGNA Group	Stock	13,498
New York Life	Mutual	12,307
Principal Mutual	Mutual	12,156
Aetna Life & Casualty Group	Stock	11,237
Nationwide Insurance Group	Mutual	9,661
ITT Hartford Insurance Group	Stock	9,521
Lincoln National Group	Stock	9,029
John Hancock Group	Mutual	8,824

Note: Rankings based on 1996 premiums. Data are for insurer groups, which include affiliated companies under common ownership. Data obtained from *Best's Aggregates and Averages, 1987,* Property–Liability and Life–Health editions.

Chapter 5. To make the ideas in this chapter concrete, we consider a hypothetical stock insurer, Tennant-Lamm Corporation (TLC). TLC came into existence when it issued stock to investors for $5 million. Some of this start-up capital was used to develop a corporate plan, conduct marketing research, and train employees. The remainder was used to acquire office facilities, computer equipment, and the like. TLC intends to write automobile liability insurance policies during its first year, with total expected claim costs equal to $20 million. For simplicity, it is assumed that all claim costs will be paid at the end of the year. While expected claim costs equal $20 million, actual claim costs could be higher or lower than $20 million. Figure 4–2 presents the probability distribution for TLC's claim costs.

The issue to be addressed is: How much more capital, if any, should TLC raise by issuing additional stock before it begins operations? The additional capital that TLC raises, along with the premium revenue remaining after paying underwriting and distribution costs, will be invested in bonds and stocks until year-end. The accumulated funds from the new capital and premium revenue then will

FIGURE 4–2

Probability distribution for TLC's claim costs

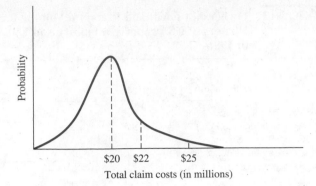

Total claim costs (in millions)

be available to pay claim costs. Assuming that TLC sells its policies at prices that cover its expected costs, any new capital that TLC raises should provide an extra cushion from which unexpectedly high claim costs could be paid. Our objective is to identify the main factors that influence the capital decision rather than to provide a numerical answer for the amount of new capital to raise.

Benefits of Increasing Capital

The most important effect of issuing more stock is that the additional capital obtained will decrease the likelihood that claim costs will exceed TLC's assets at the end of the year; in other words, additional capital reduces the likelihood of insolvency. The more money that TLC raises from issuing stock, the more money it will have to pay claim costs at year-end (holding all other factors constant). This effect of new capital can be illustrated using Figure 4–2.

Assume that if TLC issues no stock, year-end assets from investing the premiums received (less the underwriting and distribution costs paid) will equal $22 million. Thus, the probability that claim costs will exceed the value of assets (the probability of insolvency) is the area under the probability distribution (see Chapter 3) to the right of $22 million. However, if TLC raises additional capital, then the assets available at year-end to pay claim costs will increase beyond $22 million, and the probability of insolvency will decrease accordingly. For example, if TLC issues enough additional stock so that the value of assets at year-end is $25 million, the probability of insolvency decreases to the area under the curve to the right of $25 million.

Why would the stockholders of TLC care about decreasing the probability of insolvency? There are two main answers: (1) to achieve higher premium revenues, and (2) to protect against the loss of the insurer's specific assets, known as its franchise value.

Higher Premium Revenue.   If policyholders are well-informed about the risk of insolvency, they will be reluctant to purchase insurance from TLC if it does not issue additional stock because the insurer will have a relatively high probability of insolvency.[6] The more stock that TLC issues, the greater the likelihood that policyholders will receive what they are promised. Since informed policyholders generally are willing to pay higher prices for policies from insurers that are more likely to fulfill their promises, TLC can increase its premium revenue by raising additional capital.

You may question the importance of this effect if you have purchased auto insurance without giving any thought to your insurer's probability of insolvency. In fact, your behavior may not be that unusual. One explanation is that insurance solvency regulation helps to ensure that most insurers hold sufficient capital so that some people feel that they do not need to go to the trouble of monitoring insurer solvency. Also, all states in the United States have guaranty funds that pay much (and for many policyholders all) of the claim costs of policyholders should their insurer become insolvent. These guaranty funds can reduce incentives for people to monitor insurer insolvency risk and to pay a higher premium to obtain coverage from an insurer with lower insolvency risk, as we discuss in Chapter 5.

In contrast, business risk managers who buy commercial insurance usually are very concerned about the ability of their insurers to pay claims as promised. The magnitude of potential claim costs for businesses is often much larger than for individuals, and guaranty funds typically provide relatively less protection to businesses against insurer insolvencies. Consequently, risk managers (or their brokers) investigate the probability of insurer insolvency and generally are willing to pay higher prices for insurance from companies that have more capital. We will discuss the insurer solvency ratings routinely used by many business insurance buyers (and some personal insurance buyers) in Chapter 5.[7]

In summary, consumers of insurance, especially commercial customers, generally are willing to pay higher premiums to insurers that have a lower probability of insolvency. As a result, insurers are motivated to hold capital. The magnitude by which additional capital will increase premium revenue will likely decline as more and more capital is added (i.e., there are likely to be diminishing returns to additional capital).

Protect the Value of Specific Assets (Franchise Value).   Recall that the stockholders of TLC have already invested $5 million to set up operations. Some of these funds were used for activities such as training employees and obtaining market research, which have zero salvage value—that is, they cannot be sold to someone else. TLC made these investments with the expectation that they would

---

[6] An exception to this includes policyholders who are forced to buy compulsory liability insurance, but who have little or no wealth that could be lost from lawsuits by persons they might harm.

[7] Just as consumers of insurance will pay higher premiums to insurers that have a lower likelihood of insolvency, insurer employees and other suppliers may demand lower compensation from insurers that are more likely to remain in business. Thus, reducing the probability of insolvency by holding more capital can reduce the costs of contracting with employees and other suppliers. We discuss this issue as applied to corporate risk management in general in Chapters 7 and 9.

help generate returns (profits) over time. Thus, the return on this investment occurs only if TLC continues to operate. If TLC becomes insolvent, then the future returns on the investment are lost. TLC also invested in physical property like land, buildings, and computer equipment. These assets would have positive salvage value. However, if TLC experiences financial difficulty in paying claims, it may lose some or even most of the value of these assets if it cannot readily find buyers. Finally, over the course of its operations, TLC will make considerable investments to develop a "book of business"—a pool of policyholders likely to renew policies year after year. The value of an insurer's book of business is an important asset that is created by investments in sales forces, marketing, and high quality service. While its book of business could be sold to another insurer if TLC were to experience financial difficulty, part of its value again could be lost.

In summary, TLC (as is true with most insurers) has assets whose entire value can not be recouped if TLC experiences financial difficulties. That is, TLC has assets whose value is greater to TLC as an ongoing enterprise than if TLC ceases operations. When assets have greater value to one firm than to other firms, the assets are said to be **specific assets.** A major reason for an insurer to hold capital is to protect the value of its specific assets, which commonly is called the insurer's **franchise value.** The key point is that an insurer could lose its franchise value if it were to experience financial distress due to unexpectedly high claim costs or a reduction in the value of its investment portfolio. Holding more capital reduces the likelihood that franchise value will be lost.

Costs of Increasing Capital

Given the benefits of raising additional capital, why doesn't TLC necessarily increase its capital to the point where the probability of insolvency is infinitesimal (or virtually zero)? The reason is that there are also costs of holding more capital. Investors who contribute capital to TLC (buy stock) forego the opportunity to invest their money in other ventures. Thus, there is an *opportunity cost* associated with investing in TLC. This opportunity cost depends on the differences between an investment in TLC and an alternative investment.

To identify these opportunity costs, it is helpful to compare an investment in TLC with an investment in a mutual fund. When investing in a mutual fund, an individual gives the mutual fund some money and the mutual fund managers invest that money in financial assets such as stocks and bonds. Notice that this is similar to investing in TLC. Someone who buys stock in TLC gives the managers of TLC some money, and the managers invest that money in financial assets. Moreover, an individual could find a mutual fund (or a portfolio of mutual funds) that invests in the same mix of securities as TLC. Thus, the relevant benchmark to assess the opportunity cost of investing in TLC is an investment in a mutual fund with the same portfolio of securities as TLC. What are the differences between an investment in an insurer like TLC and an investment in such a mutual fund?

One difference between a mutual fund investment and an investment in an insurer like TLC is that the mutual fund investor does not face the possibility that part of his or her investment could be used to pay unexpectedly high insurance claims costs. At first, this might seem like a disadvantage to investing in TLC. However, insurance claim costs are a two-edged sword. An investment in TLC also creates the possibility that the return from investing in an insurer will be higher than the return on the mutual fund investment, because insurance claim costs could be lower than expected. It can be shown that an insurer's potential claim costs (liabilities) do not create a net advantage or disadvantage for an investor relative to an investment in a mutual fund if the claim costs are uncorrelated with the rest of the investor's wealth and if there are no greater tax, agency, or issuance costs for investing with insurers.[8] Thus, the opportunity costs of investing in an insurer like TLC arise because of potential correlation between insurer claim costs and investors' other assets and because of potentially greater tax, agency, and issuance costs compared to investing in a mutual fund with the same asset portfolio.

Correlation of Insurer Liabilities with Investors' Other Assets.   Suppose that TLC's claim costs tend to be high when the value of investors' other wealth tends to be low (i.e., there is negative correlation between the insurer's liabilities and the value of investors' other assets). This negative correlation implies that TLC's profits will tend to be low when the returns on other assets are low. Thus, investors will tend to receive low returns from investing in TLC when they would want low returns the least—when other assets have performed poorly. Conversely, negative correlation implies that TLC's profits will tend to be high when the returns on other assets are high. But again, investors would be receiving high returns from investing in TLC when they would want them the least—when other assets have performed well. As a result, investors will require additional compensation to invest in TLC because of the correlation of its stock return with their other assets. The additional expected return required by investors if there is a negative correlation between insurer liabilities and the value of investors' other assets is a cost of raising additional capital for insurers.

If, on the other hand, insurer claim costs are positively correlated with the value of investors' other assets (i.e., claim costs tend to be high when the returns on other assets are high and claim costs tend to be low when the returns on other assets are low), then investors would view an investment in TLC as a partial hedge for the uncertainty associated with the investors' other assets. That is, when other assets have low returns, TLC will tend to have high returns because its claim costs will tend to be low. In this case (positive correlation between claim costs and the value of other assets), investors would require less expected return for investing in TLC than from a mutual fund that held the same asset portfolio as TLC.

---

[8] An insurer's liabilities (claim costs) create what is called *financial leverage.* For students with a finance background, the irrelevance of financial leverage in the absence of tax, agency, and issuance costs is an application of the famous Modigliani and Miller theorem, which was noted by the Nobel committee when both Franco Modigliani and Merton Miller were awarded their Nobel prizes.

In summary, uncertain claim costs increase (decrease) the expected return required by investors in an insurer, compared to an investment in a mutual fund with the same assets, if claim costs are negatively (positively) correlated with the value of investors' other assets. Although studies have been conducted to examine the correlation between insurer claim costs and the value of other assets, the evidence generally is inconclusive regarding the sign and magnitude of the correlation. Thus, subsequent discussions of insurer capital costs usually will focus on the tax, agency, and issuance costs of capital, to which we now turn. The implications of possible correlation between claim costs and returns on investors' other assets for insurance prices are discussed briefly in Chapter 6.

Double Taxation of Investment Returns.   The US tax code presents another important difference between investing in TLC and investing in a mutual fund with the same portfolio of stocks and bonds. When an individual invests directly in a mutual fund, the fund managers invest the money in financial assets. The returns on these securities then are distributed to the individual through dividends and capital gains. The investor has to pay tax on the returns, but the mutual fund does not. In contrast, when an individual buys stock in an insurance company, the managers invest the money in financial assets, but the insurer has to pay corporate income tax on the investment returns. When the insurer pays dividends to the stockholders or they sell their stock and realize a capital gain, the stockholders have to pay tax on the investment returns again. Thus, by investing in an insurance company's stock, investment returns are taxed first at the corporate level and then again at the personal level. This double taxation of investment returns imposes a cost on insurer capital.

Because of the double taxation of investment returns, an insurer must earn a higher before-tax rate of return on its capital in order to give investors the same after-tax return they could receive by investing in a mutual fund. This higher before-tax return must be generated from selling insurance policies at a price that exceeds expected claim costs and administrative costs (see Chapter 6). That is, insurance premiums must be large enough to compensate investors for the double taxation of investment returns on capital.[9]

Agency Costs.   When investors buy stock, they give some discretion to managers as to how to use those funds. In essence, stockholders make managers their agents. As discussed in Chapter 2, managers sometimes use the firm's assets to further their own interests as opposed to the interests of the stockholders. The reduction in firm value due to managers not acting in the stockholders' interest is called an **agency cost.** Likewise, any costs incurred in monitoring and motivating

---

[9] Note that the focus here is on the double taxation of investment returns on capital. Any taxes on investment returns of assets backing liabilities and any profits from underwriting exclusive of investment returns also will increase insurance prices. However, these taxes do not increase the cost of holding capital as a cushion, and they are reduced substantially by the tax deductibility of claim costs.

managers to act in the stockholders' interest are additional agency costs. If agency costs are greater for an insurance company than for a mutual fund company, then investors will view agency costs as a disadvantage of investing in the insurance company. Thus, agency costs represent another cost of holding capital in an insurer. With agency costs, the insurer must sell insurance at prices above expected claim costs and administrative costs in order to give investors a return which, net of agency costs, is equal to the return investors can receive by investing in a mutual fund.

Issuance and Underpricing Costs.   Insurers also may limit the amount of capital that they raise through equity issues because of equity issuance and underpricing costs. When an insurer issues new stock, it usually employs investment bankers to help sell the new stock. The fees charged by investment bankers are a cost associated with raising additional capital.

In addition, whenever a firm issues new stock, it faces the possibility that the price received for the new shares will be less than the true value of the shares. This problem is worse when investors are not as well informed about the firm's prospects as the firm's managers and when investors know that they are not as well informed. Before purchasing the new stock, these investors will ask themselves: Why do the better-informed managers want to sell additional shares? If the investors decide it is because the stock is worth less than what the managers say it is, then the investors may lower the price that they are willing to pay below the true value of the stock. In other words, the stock may then be underpriced. This underpricing limits the extent to which insurers will raise new capital and leads to greater reliance on retained earnings to accumulate capital.

Summary and Relationship to Business Risk Management

Additional capital reduces the probability of insolvency, which can both increase the price consumers will pay for insurance and protect the insurer's franchise value that could be lost in the event of insolvency. Additional capital, however, is costly. Investors require compensation for (1) any additional risk arising from the correlation between insurer liabilities and investors' other assets, (2) the double taxation of investment returns, (3) agency costs, and (4) issuance and underpricing costs.

In Chapters 7 and 9, where we discuss business risk management, many of these arguments will be revisited. In essence, insurer capital decisions are business risk management decisions. Therefore, the factors affecting insurer capital decisions are similar to the factors affecting business risk management in general.

Amount of Capital Held by Insurers

The amount of capital held by insurers varies across companies and across lines of business. Figure 4–3 gives the total industry assets, liabilities, and capital for property–liability insurers compared to life–health insurers for 1996. The numbers reported in Figure 4–3 reflect accounting numbers from financial statements filed with insurance regulators, not economic (market) values. (Accounting values equal market values for common and preferred stock but not for most other investments and liabilities.)

Property–liability insurers had 1996 year-end assets of $802 billion, liabilities of $547 billion, and capital (assets minus liabilities) of $256 billion, producing an aggregate ratio of capital to assets of 32 percent. The capital-to-asset ratio varies considerably across individual insurers, depending on product mix, assets, and reinsurance (see below). The principal assets of property–liability insurers are described later in this chapter. The principal liabilities are: (1) the *loss reserve,* which equals the liability for claims that have occurred but have not yet been paid, and (2) the *unearned premium reserve,* which equals the liability for premiums that have been paid but not yet earned by insurers because the entire coverage period has not elapsed.

Life–health insurers' assets totaled $2,303 billion at year-end 1996, which is much greater than property–liability insurers. This difference reflects, in part, that many of the products sold by life–health insurers are investment products bundled with insurance products. Life–health insurance liabilities, which primarily reflect insurer obligations for policyholder savings under life insurance and annuity con-

FIGURE 4–3

Insurer assets, liabilities, and capital in 1996

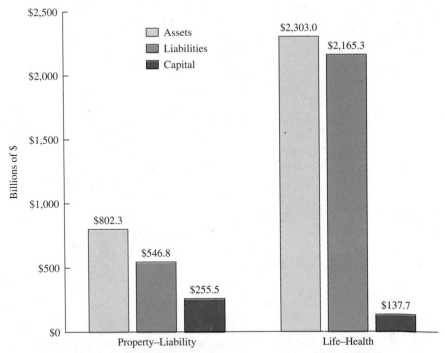

Source: Data obtained from *Best's Aggregates and Averages, 1987,* Property–Liability and Life–Health editions.

tracts (known as *policy reserves*), were $2,165 billion, resulting in total capital of $138 billion and an aggregate capital-to-asset ratio of 6 percent.[10]

The much lower aggregate capital-to-asset ratio for life–health insurers as compared to property–liability insurers (6 percent versus 32 percent) in part reflects differences in risk for the products that the groups sell. Variability of claim costs generally is lower for life and health insurance than for property–liability insurance, with life insurance generally having the lowest variability in claim costs. In addition, some of the variability in the value of life insurer investment products usually is borne by policyholders. As a result, a smaller cushion (or amount of capital per dollar of assets) is needed to achieve a given probability of insolvency.

Concept Check

3. Which of the following statements are true? Explain.
    (*a*) The US tax code decreases the amount of capital that insurers hold.
    (*b*) If policyholders are uninformed or don't care about insolvency, then owners of insurers do not care about reducing the probability of insolvency.

4.5 Insurer Operations, Reinsurance, and Insolvency Risk

Diversification of Underwriting Risk

You learned in Chapter 3 that the standard deviation of average claim costs in a risk pooling arrangement declines as the number of participants increases, provided that claim costs are not perfectly correlated across participants. The standard deviation also decreases as the correlation between claim costs across participants declines. As a result, insurers generally can reduce **underwriting risk**—the risk that average claim costs will differ from the amount expected when policies are sold—by selling large numbers of policies across different types of insurance coverage in different areas. Lower underwriting risk reduces the amount of capital needed for a given level of insolvency risk.

To elaborate, many insurers routinely reduce underwriting risk by selling policies in different geographic regions. Geographic diversification reduces the correlation in claim costs across policies that arises from factors such as catas-

---

[10] The life–health insurance data in Figure 4–3 include "separate account" assets and liabilities associated with some pension and other retirement plans (see Chapter 19). The risk of separate account asset returns is borne by the retirement plan rather than the insurer. Separate account assets and liabilities equaled $572.4 and $569.5 billion, respectively, in 1996. Excluding separate account assets and liabilities, the ratio of capital to assets for life–health insurers was 7.8 percent. Also, the data reported in this chapter for life–health insurers do not include data from Blue Cross/Blue Shield organizations and health maintenance organizations (HMOs).

trophes and other weather-related claims (as well as from state legislation, court decisions, and regulations that affect claim costs). Insurers also reduce underwriting risk by selling multiple types of policies, for example, by selling a variety of commercial and personal lines coverages, and sometimes both property–liability and life–health insurance. Other things equal, risk reduction through geographic and product line diversification reduces the amount of capital that the insurer must hold in relation to its liabilities to achieve a given level of insolvency risk. A potential disadvantage of diversification is less focus on "core" coverages or geographic regions. Moreover, insurers that specialize more narrowly can often achieve the benefits of diversification indirectly by transferring underwriting risk to other insurers by buying reinsurance.

Reinsurance

Primary Function of Reinsurance.   Just as businesses and individuals purchase insurance, insurers also purchase insurance. **Reinsurance** is the purchase of insurance by an insurer. In addition to reducing underwriting risk (and the amount of capital needed to achieve a given level of insolvency risk) by diversifying across geographic areas and lines of business, insurers can reduce underwriting risk by purchasing reinsurance. As a result, the purchase of reinsurance can substitute for capital and allow an insurer to hold less capital without increasing its insolvency probability.

To illustrate this major function of reinsurance, suppose that Southeast Property & Transportation Insurance Company (SEPTIC) has written property insurance on the coast of Florida with expected claim costs equal to $100 million. The probability distribution of claim costs is shown in Figure 4–4. Midwest Insurance Company (MIC) also has written property insurance in the Midwest with expected claim costs equal to $100 million and a probability distribution of claim costs that is identical to SEPTIC's. Since specific events that cause variability in claim costs in the Southeast are different from those in the Midwest, the claim

FIGURE 4–4

Probability distribution for SEPTIC's and MIC's claim costs with and without reinsurance

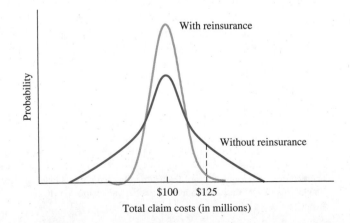

costs of the two insurers are assumed to be independent (which also simplifies the example).

Suppose that the two insurers agree to pay one-half of each other's claim costs; that is, they enter into a pooling arrangement similar to the one formed by Emily and Samantha in Chapter 3. This pooling arrangement will reduce risk (the standard deviation of claim costs for each insurer). As depicted in Figure 4–4, the new distribution of claim costs facing each insurer will become tighter around the expected value of $100 million. The lower standard deviation implies that each insurer reduces its probability of insolvency for a given amount of capital. For example, if each insurer initially had assets equal to $125 million and hence capital equal to $25 million, then the pooling arrangement would change the probability of insolvency from the area under the "without reinsurance" curve in Figure 4–4 to the area under the "with reinsurance" curve.

In this example, reinsurance allows SEPTIC and MIC to diversify without marketing their policies and establishing sales and claims facilities in another geographic area. In addition, reinsurance can allow insurers specializing in particular lines of business to diversify across lines. For example, SEPTIC could enter into a reinsurance arrangement with an environmental liability insurer. In this way, both SEPTIC and the liability insurer could change their books of business from a single line to two lines of insurance.

This discussion illustrates the primary benefit of reinsurance: It allows greater diversification of claim costs, which in turn reduces the probability of insurer insolvency for a given amount of total capital held by all insurers/reinsurers or, equivalently, reduces the total capital needed for a given insolvency probability. Of course, reinsurance also involves costs. The distribution, underwriting, and loss adjustment costs associated with primary insurance also apply to reinsurance contracts. Reinsurers also must hold capital (which is costly) to make their promises to insurers credible (recall our earlier discussion of the costs of insurer capital). The key point is that reinsurance reduces the total amount of capital that must be held by all insurers and reinsurers combined in order to achieve a given level of insolvency risk in the industry.

Types of Reinsurance.   While reinsurance transactions sometimes take the form of the simple pooling arrangement described between SEPTIC and MIC, most reinsurance transactions are more like typical insurance transactions. The reinsurance contract specifies the conditions under which the reinsurer will pay some of the buyer's claim costs and the amount that the reinsurer will pay. In exchange, the buyer, known as the **ceding insurer** or **primary insurer,** pays the reinsurer a premium.

With respect to the way in which risk is shared, property–liability reinsurance arrangements can be categorized broadly as either *proportional contracts* (also called pro-rata reinsurance) and *nonproportional contracts* (also called excess-of-loss reinsurance). Similar risk-sharing arrangements between ceding insurers and reinsurers are used in life–health insurance. With proportional reinsurance, the ceding company pays a proportion of its premium on a pool of policies to a reinsurer. In exchange, the reinsurer pays the same proportion of the claim costs on those policies. The contract also requires the reinsurer to pay a commission to the ceding insurer as compensation for the ceding insurer's distribution, underwriting, and loss adjustment expenses.[11]

With nonproportional contracts, the reinsurer pays part of the ceding insurer's claims only if a particular threshold (or attachment point) is reached. The attachment point is analogous to a deductible amount in many insurance contracts (see Chapter 8). While reinsurance contracts can be tailored to the needs of the two insurers, several types of thresholds are common. Often the threshold will be based on the claim costs from a single policy written by the ceding insurer (known as *per risk excess reinsurance*). For example, a property insurer may reinsure claim costs in excess of $25 million arising from a policy that the ceding insurer sold to a large manufacturer covering its plant and equipment (either during a year or from a single event). Another common type of nonproportional contract, known as *catastrophe reinsurance,* specifies that the reinsurer will start paying claim costs on a pool of policies written by the ceding insurer if total claims costs arising from a single event, such as a hurricane, exceed some dollar amount (the attachment point). Other nonproportional reinsurance contracts require the reinsurer to pay claim costs in excess of a specified threshold if total claim costs on a pool of policies exceed the threshold during a specified time period, such as one year.

A **reinsurance treaty** covers multiple policies written by the ceding insurer. For example, at the beginning of the year, a workers' compensation insurer may engage in a reinsurance treaty whereby the reinsurer agrees to accept, without the right to refuse, a portion of each policy that the primary insurer wishes to cede during the year. In contrast, with *facultative reinsurance,* the reinsurer evaluates each risk (policy) that the primary insurer would like to cede and decides whether to accept it on a case-by-case basis.

The reinsurance market is global in scope. Some organizations that sell reinsurance (known as "professional" reinsurers) specialize exclusively in reinsurance and do not offer primary insurance. Some insurers that sell primary insurance have subsidiaries or divisions that sell reinsurance. The international flavor of the reinsurance market is illustrated by the largest reinsurers in the world listed in Table 4–2. Although the table does not list Lloyd's of London, when considered as a group the syndicates at Lloyd's represent one of the largest writers of reinsurance.

---

[11] The pooling arrangement described between SEPTIC and MIC could be replicated by two proportional reinsurance contracts. For example, suppose (1) SEPTIC buys proportional reinsurance from MIC that requires MIC to pay 50 percent of the claim costs on the policies SEPTIC has written, and (2) SEPTIC sells proportional reinsurance to MIC that requires SEPTIC to pay 50 percent of the claim costs on the policies MIC has written. If the premiums on the two reinsurance contracts are equal, then the two transactions have the same effect as the pooling arrangement.

TABLE 4–2   Five Largest Reinsurers in Terms of 1996 Premiums

Reinsurer	Location	Net Premiums Written ($ millions)
Munich Reinsurance Company	Germany	$13,188
Swiss Re Group	Switzerland	10,794
General Re/Cologne Re Group	US	6,661
Generali	Italy	5,950
Employers Re	US	5,910

Source: *Business Insurance,* September 1, 1997.

Asset Choice and Investment Risk

The asset choices made by insurers also have a major effect on insurer risk and the need to hold capital. In order to maximize insurer value and compete successfully with other insurers, insurer investment decisions need to balance higher expected returns from holding riskier investments against the increased **investment risk** and need for capital. Insurer investment decisions also are strongly influenced by the tax treatment of investment returns.

Figure 4–5 shows the percentage distribution of invested assets at year-end 1996 for both property–liability and life–health insurers (as reported in financial statements filed with regulators).[12] As a group, insurers invest heavily in medium- to long-term fixed income securities, such as US government bonds, municipal bonds, corporate bonds, and mortgages. The average risk of default on the specific securities held is very low. Life–health insurers invest more heavily in corporate bonds and mortgages (largely on commercial properties) than do property–liability insurers, in part due to the long-term nature of many life insurance and annuity products. Property–liability insurers invest more heavily in tax exempt municipal bonds than do life–health insurers, in large part to reduce taxes on investment income associated with their larger amount of capital in relation to assets and liabilities. The comparatively greater investment in common stocks by property–liability insurers also is due in part to taxes (since dividends received by corporate owners of common stock are largely exempt from income tax).

Asset choices by insurers also affect their vulnerability to *interest rate risk* (i.e., changes in the economic or market value of capital due to changes in interest rates). A majority of both property–liability and life–health insurers are ex-

---

[12] The life–health data exclude investments in separate accounts because the necessary breakdown by type of investments was not available. Separate account assets are invested much more heavily in common stocks than are insurer "general account" assets. Figure 4–5 also understates the extent to which life–health insurers (and, to a lesser extent, property–liability insurers) invest in assets with returns that depend on mortgages because mortgage and other asset-backed securities (including collateralized mortgage obligations) are included in the corporate and municipal bond categories.

FIGURE 4–5

Insurer invested assets in 1996

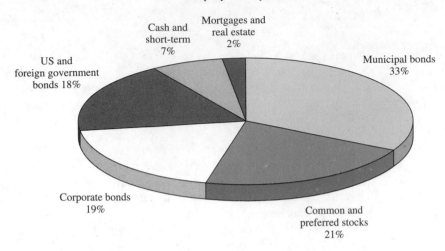

Property–liability insurers

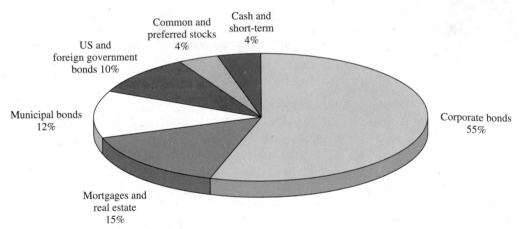

Life–health insurers

Source: Data obtained from *Best's Aggregates and Averages, 1987,* Property–Liability and Life–Health editions.

posed to reductions in the value of assets when interest rates increase. The reason is that they invest heavily in long-term fixed income securities that decline in value when interest rates increase. The economic value of insurer liabilities also declines when interest rates increase, because the present value of cash outflows for contracts sold declines, other factors being held constant. However, the decline in the value of liabilities for a majority of insurers does not completely offset the decline in asset values, so that the value of capital declines when interest rates rise.

Many insurers could reduce their exposure to interest rate risk by investing in shorter-term fixed income securities, which are less sensitive to interest rate changes. This strategy might allow insurers to hold less capital to achieve a given level of insolvency risk. On average, however, it would reduce investment yields because long-term fixed income securities have higher yields on average than short-term investments. Many insurers reduce their interest rate risk by hedging with a variety of financial derivatives that increase in value when interest rates rise. However, insurers often do not fully hedge interest rate risk because hedging involves transaction costs and can reduce expected yields.

4.6 Summary

- Insurance companies are institutions that economize on the contracting costs associated with pooling arrangements, including distribution, underwriting, and loss adjustment expenses.

- Because few insurers have the right to assess policyholders for losses during the coverage period (in addition to the premium paid), they must hold capital to serve as a cushion in the event of adverse experience.

- With respect to who owns insurer capital, insurers are commonly organized as either stock insurers, which are owned by stockholders, or as mutual insurers, which are owned by policyholders.

- Benefits that encourage insurers to hold more capital to reduce insolvency risk include the ability to (1) obtain higher premiums from policyholders and (2) better protect against loss of the insurer's franchise value. Costs to insurers of increasing capital include the double taxation of investment returns on capital, agency costs, and issuance and underpricing costs.

- Insurers commonly reduce insolvency risk and/or the amount of capital needed to achieve a given level of insolvency risk by (1) diversifying underwriting risk across geographic regions and different types of coverage, (2) entering into reinsurance contracts that help achieve better diversification of risk among insurers, and (3) investing heavily in fixed income securities with low default risk.

Key Terms

distribution costs   68
underwriting   68
loss adjustment expenses   68
economic capital   71
mutual insurer   72
reciprocal   73
stock insurer   73
Lloyd's of London   74
names   74

unlimited liability   75
specific assets   80
franchise value   80
agency costs   82
underwriting risk   85
reinsurance   86
ceding or primary insurer   87
reinsurance treaty   88
investment risk   89

Questions and Problems

1. What is economic capital for an insurer with assets of $200 million and liabilities of $150 million?

2. Is your (or your family's) automobile insurer a mutual, stock, or reciprocal insurer?

3. How do mutual insurers accumulate capital? How does this differ for stock insurers?

4. Draw a graph of an insurer's probability distribution for total claim costs, assuming that it has expected claim costs of $500 million. Identify the probability of insolvency if the insurer has assets equal to $700 million.

5. Explain the principal ways in which insurance companies can reduce risk through diversification.

6. Identify on your graph how the probability of insolvency for the insurer described in question 4 changes if:
   (a) The insurer raises $100 million of new capital.
   (b) The insurer cedes a proportion of its liabilities to a reinsurer and simultaneously reinsures a similar amount of business from another insurer with a similar, but uncorrelated book of business.

7. Describe the major investments held by property–liability insurers and life–health insurers.

References

Brockett, Patrick; Robert Witt; and Paul Aird. "An Overview of Reinsurance and the Reinsurance Markets." *Journal of Insurance Regulation* 9, no. 3 (March 1991), pp. 432–54. (*Provides additional discussion of reinsurance.*)

Hansmann, Henry. "The Organization of Insurance Companies: Mutual versus Stock." *Journal of Law, Economics, and Organization* 1 (1985), pp. 125–53. (*Discusses the evolution and functions of mutual insurers compared to stock insurers.*)

Answers to Concept Checks

1. First note that pooling arrangements reduce risk for those that participate in the arrangement. Risk-averse people will therefore want to participate in pooling arrangements as long as the operating costs are not too high.

   Insurance companies exist because generally they can operate pooling arrangements at lower costs than individuals and businesses. In particular, insurance companies are able to economize on distribution, underwriting, and loss adjustment expenses.

2. Insurer capital is referred to as a cushion because it is the amount of funds available to pay unexpected claim costs. If economic capital equals $50 million, then the insurer can withstand $50 million of unexpected claim costs without becoming insolvent.

3. (a) This is true, because the US tax code creates a disincentive to hold capital.
   (b) This is false, because owners still will want to protect the firm's franchise value.

CHAPTER 5

Insolvencies, Solvency Ratings, and Regulation

Chapter Objectives

- Summarize the historical record of insurance company insolvencies.
- Describe the insurance company solvency ratings provided by financial rating agencies and how they are used.
- Introduce the main features and functions of solvency regulation, including solvency monitoring, capital requirements, and insurance guaranty funds.

5.1 Insurer Insolvencies

In order for insurance contracts and other loss financing devices to be effective in reducing risk, the party that agrees to provide funds following a loss must honor its promise. As a result, an important issue in risk management is the credit risk associated with loss financing arrangements such as insurance and hedging. In the last chapter we discussed how insurer capital, diversification of underwriting risk, reinsurance, and investment decisions affect insolvency risk. We also discussed the major factors influencing the amount of capital held by an insurer to reduce insolvency risk given its underwriting and investment decisions.

In this chapter we review the historical record of insurer insolvencies to acquaint you with the magnitude of insolvency risk and the reasons why insurers become insolvent. We describe solvency ratings of insurers that are provided by several financial rating agencies and used widely by business risk managers, insurance agents and brokers, and many individuals. We then introduce the objectives and major features of solvency regulation.

Frequency and Severity of Insurance Company Insolvencies

Figure 5–1 shows the number of property–liability insurers and life–health insurers declared insolvent each year during the period 1981–1996. It also shows assessments by state insurance guaranty funds against surviving insurers (in constant 1996 dollar amounts) to pay some of the claims against insolvent insurers.[1] (We discuss guaranty funds in section 5.5.) We noted in the last chapter that insolvency rates for insurers generally have been low and that most insolvent companies have been small. Nonetheless, beginning in the mid-1980s, the number of insurer insolvencies increased significantly compared to historical norms. Since the mid-1980s approximately 1 percent of both property–liability insurers and life–health insurers have failed on average each year. The increase in the number of insolvencies and an increase in the average size of insolvent insurers have substantially increased guaranty fund assessments.

The largest insolvent property–liability insurer to date (Mission Insurance Group in 1987) ranked among the top 50 insurers in total premiums and among the top 10 in workers' compensation insurance premiums prior to its insolvency. The Mission insolvency required guaranty fund assessments of nearly $500 million. Several other insolvent property–liability insurers have required assessments of $250 million or more. Several relatively large life insurers failed in 1991, including two insurer groups that ranked in the top 25 in terms of assets (Executive Life and Mutual Benefit Life). Executive Life invested heavily in high yield (junk) bonds that later experienced sharp declines in value. Guaranty fund assessments for Executive Life totaled $2.1 billion, over five times greater than for any other life–health insurer insolvency. Assessments for Mutual Benefit Life totaled $81 million.

The increase in the frequency and severity of insurer insolvencies generated concern about the quality of state solvency regulation and the performance of financial rating agencies. It also led to proposals for federal solvency regulation and to the adoption of significant changes in state solvency regulation, such as risk-based capital requirements (see section 5.3). When considering insurer insolvency experience, you should keep in perspective that preventing insolvencies is costly, whether by insurers voluntarily reducing risk or increasing capital or through solvency regulation. Recall from Chapter 4, for example, that holding additional capital increases insurer tax costs and thus the amount of premiums needed to provide a given amount of coverage. Like our earlier discussion of loss control in general, beyond some point, the marginal costs of reducing insolvency risk will exceed the benefits. As a result, the total costs of an "insolvency proof" insurance system would be unattractive to consumers.

---

[1] The assessment data are for new assessments during the year, except for life–health insurers prior to 1988, where the available data subtract any refunds during the year for assessments made in prior years that exceeded the amount ultimately needed to pay claims covered by the guaranty funds. Annual data on assessment refunds are available for property–liability insurers. These data indicate that refunds averaged 10–15 percent of new assessments until 1995–1996, when refunds equaled 75 percent of new assessments in 1995 and 55 percent of new assessments in 1996.

FIGURE 5–1

Number of insurer insolvencies and guaranty fund assessments (in constant 1996 dollar amounts), 1981–1996

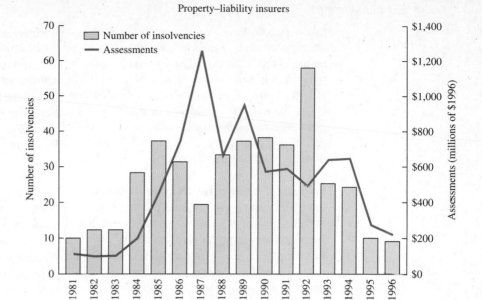

Property–liability insurers

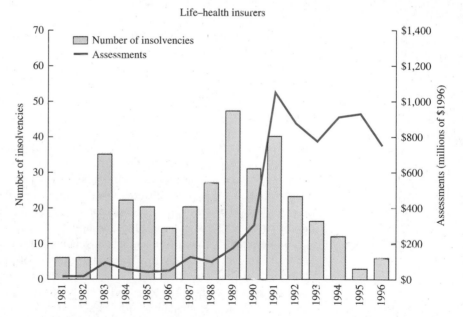

Life–health insurers

Note. Assessments for life–health insurers prior to 1988 are net of any refunds for prior years' assessments during the year. Number of insolvencies obtained from the National Association of Insurance Commissioners. Property–liability assessments obtained from the National Conference of Insurance Guaranty Funds; life–health assessments obtained from the National Organization of Life and Health Insurance Guaranty Association. Constant 1996 dollar amounts calculated by the authors using the US consumer price index.

Causes of Insolvencies

Many factors have contributed to insurer insolvencies, including inadequate prices, excessive growth in business written compared to capital, excessive investment risk, catastrophe losses, and declines in asset values. Management fraud sometimes has played a role, and many insolvent insurers appear to have deliberately understated claim liabilities and overstated asset values prior to insolvency. Unless there is clear evidence of fraud, however, it usually is difficult to distinguish whether an insolvency has been caused primarily by inadequate capitalization or risk management prior to the adverse events, as opposed to large, unpredictable reductions in capital.

Property–Liability Insurer Insolvencies.   Many property–liability insurers that failed during the 1980s wrote large amounts of business liability insurance, including products liability, environmental liability, and professional liability insurance (e.g., for physicians, architects, and engineers). These insolvencies were associated with much higher claim costs than the insurers originally reported on their financial statements. Evidence suggests that a large component of the increase in claim costs was probably unexpected in many cases; in other words, the actual costs were significantly higher than could reasonably have been expected when the insurers wrote the business and initially reported estimates of claim costs.

Conversely, it has been argued that some of these insurers deliberately wrote large amounts of business at prices that they knew to be too low in comparison to expected claim costs, either because they had inadequate incentives to be safe or in an attempt to generate cash and buy time after they began to experience difficulty. These insurers also are alleged to have hidden their inadequate prices and capital by deliberately understating their estimated liabilities and using questionable (if not completely phony) reinsurance arrangements. Whether fraudulent or not, the reinsurance mechanism often broke down. Many reinsurers failed to pay because they became insolvent. Other reinsurers denied payment, alleging that the now insolvent primary insurer had deliberately failed to report material information about the business reinsured. The resulting disputes produced extensive litigation between some reinsurers and the state insurance departments responsible for settling the estates of insolvent insurers.[2]

Some property–liability insurer insolvencies during the mid- to late 1980s probably were influenced by low prices during the "soft market" for business liability insurance during the early 1980s (see Chapter 6). A large increase in market interest rates in the late 1970s and early 1980s also may have contributed to some insolvencies. Higher interest rates substantially reduced the market value of bonds held by many insurers. Some companies might have been weakened to

---

[2] As was true for a number of large insolvencies in the savings and loan industry, insurance departments sometimes sued and obtained settlements from the accounting firms responsible for auditing the books of the insolvent insurer.

the point that they engaged in excessively risky behavior in the hope of getting lucky and avoiding insolvency. (This behavior sometimes is known as "going-for-broke" or "gambling for resurrection.")

Life–Health Insurer Insolvencies.   The increase in the frequency of life–health insurer insolvencies that began in the mid-1980s (see Figure 5–1) was due in large part to small health insurers that experienced large claim costs in relation to premiums and the claim liabilities that they originally reported. The insolvency of several large life insurance companies in 1991 was more consequential and accounted for much of the increase in guaranty fund assessments shown in Figure 5–1. The large life insurer insolvencies primarily reflected reductions in the value of assets held; these insolvencies received enormous attention in the national media. The most highly publicized insolvencies were those of a few insurers, such as Executive Life, that invested heavily in high yield bonds. More widespread financial problems were caused by depressed commercial real estate values, which reduced the value of real estate and mortgage holdings for hundreds of life insurers. Problem real estate precipitated the insolvency of Mutual Benefit Life.

The insolvencies of Executive Life, Mutual Benefit Life, and a few other insurers were preceded by substantial cash withdrawals by life insurance and annuity policyholders who had accumulated savings with these insurers and who had become concerned with the safety of their funds. Following concerns expressed by some state regulators about its financial condition, Mutual Benefit Life asked to be taken over by New Jersey insurance regulators when confronted with massive demands for funds by its policyholders.

There was significant concern during the spring and summer of 1991 that large numbers of life insurance and annuity policyholders might panic and attempt to withdraw funds from other insurers that were not experiencing significant financial problems. If this had happened, it could have created severe stress for many companies, forcing them to sell assets at a time when asset values were already depressed. These sales would have created additional downward pressure on asset prices in the short run, further weakening the life–health insurance industry and possibly causing more insurers to fail.

No other large insurer failed in 1991, however, and asset values subsequently rebounded in many cases, which significantly strengthened the capital of the industry. Some evidence suggests that because of the rebound in high yield bond prices that occurred in 1991, Executive Life might have remained solvent if it could have survived until year-end. In addition, the corporation that succeeded Mutual Benefit Life and was supervised by New Jersey regulators was in good enough financial shape to be offered for sale to the private sector in 1997 (see Box 5–1). Whether some regulators took action against some insurers prematurely or made statements that unduly frightened policyholders and contributed to the insolvency of others is subject to debate.

Following the events of 1991, many life insurers raised new capital and improved the quality of their assets. Evidence suggests that policyholder withdrawals of funds during 1990 and 1991 primarily occurred for weak companies,

Box 5–1

Old Mutual Benefit Is Putting Itself Up for Sale as Financial Shape Improves

The Old Mutual Benefit Life Insurance Company, an insurer once largely given up for dead as the nation's biggest life insurance failure, is putting itself up for sale in better financial shape than ever expected.

With the blessing of the New Jersey insurance regulators who are still its overseers, the Newark, NJ, company will announce today that it has hired Goldman, Sachs & Company to identify potential bidders, Alan J. Bowers, its president and chief executive officer, said in an interview Friday. Since its seizure in 1991, the company now known as MBL Life Assurance Corporation, has continued to pay policyholders and annuitants under terms of its contracts but hasn't made new sales.

Analysts said the company could well fetch its book value, or net worth, of approximately $600 million, and may possibly bring more given feverish insurance industry merger and acquisition activity.

Mutual Benefit, which was a mutual owned by policyholders rather than shareholders, collapsed under a mountain of poorly performing real estate holdings, including ill-fated Florida luxury condominium developments. The company was one of several high profile insurance failures in the early 1990s.

Real Estate Assets

MBL's improved financial condition—an eightfold increase in book value since 1994—stems largely from a rebound in the market that caused its biggest problems. Over the past two years, the company has sold more than $1 billion of real estate assets at higher than anticipated prices.

The insurer's board opted to explore a sale after concluding the company had "created a lot of value," while trying to become a sales operation again would be "risky" given competitive industry conditions, said Mr. Bowers, a former Coopers & Lybrand managing partner who joined MBL in 1995. He noted that an important factor in MBL's decision is the current frenzied consolidation activity.

"We thought we should at least explore the opportunity to take advantage of what's happening" in that arena, he said.

Any proceeds would be split between the insurer's 450,000 remaining customers, who have received below-market interest rates on their investments since the seizure, among other penalties, and a group of creditors, including numerous big banks, with claims totaling $625 million, according to Mr. Bowers. For creditors, a sale represents their only source of payment. A steep sales price could make them whole, while a book value one wouldn't.

The takeover of Mutual Benefit, whose $14 billion in assets made it one of the nation's 25 biggest life insurers, came after the company searched unsuccessfully for a merger partner or investors to boost its capital. In the weeks leading up to the seizure, redemptions by Mutual Benefit policyholders tallied $1 billion. The insurer then had about 400,000 policyholders and 200,000 workers whose pension plans had bought annuities from it.

as opposed to reflecting irrational panic and contagion that adversely affected all insurers. Many policyholders appear to have become more concerned with insurer safety during this time. The resulting *flight to quality* provided additional incentives for insurers to increase their capital and reduce risk.

5.2 Solvency Ratings

A number of financial **rating agencies** provide **solvency ratings** of insurance companies. The leading rating agencies include the A. M. Best Company, Moody's, Standard and Poor's, and Duff and Phelps. Solvency ratings are used extensively by corporate risk managers and independent insurance agents and brokers when deciding on an insurer. Many corporate risk managers restrict their attention to highly rated insurers. In addition, risk managers routinely enter into hold harmless and indemnity agreements that require another entity to protect their firm against loss under specified circumstances (see Chapter 17). In order to reduce the credit risk of these agreements, the party required to respond in the event of loss commonly backs its promise with an insurance contract from a highly rated insurer. Given the widespread uses of solvency ratings, an insurer could experience a significant reduction in sales to business policyholders if it were to lose a high rating. Insurer solvency ratings also are used, albeit to a lesser extent, by individual insurance buyers.

Rating agencies provide valuable summary information about insurer financial strength at a relatively low cost. These firms are compensated by sales of publications that include ratings and updates of rating changes and by fees from rated insurers. The willingness of insurers to pay to be rated indicates the importance of receiving a financial rating by one or more rating agencies.

The A. M. Best Company is the oldest and largest insurance rating agency. It reviews a large majority of US insurers and many international insurers. Companies are placed in two broad categories: (1) some insurers receive an A. M. Best "letter" rating based on a statistical and qualitative analysis of financial information and management interviews, and (2) other insurers are placed in the "rating not assigned" category. Table 5–1 provides a description of A. M. Best letter ratings as of 1996. Roughly 75 percent of insurers with over 90 percent of insurer

TABLE 5–1 A. M. Best Company Rating Categories and Associated Letter Ratings

Major Category	Subcategory	Letter Ratings
Secure	Superior	A++, A+
	Excellent	A, A–
	Very good	B++, B+
Vulnerable	Adequate	B, B–
	Fair	C++, C+
	Marginal	C, C–
	Very vulnerable	D
	Regulatory supervision	E
	Liquidation	F

Source: Descriptions obtained from *Best's Insurance Reports*, 1996 edition.

assets receive letter ratings. The remaining companies are included in the "rating not assigned" category because, for example, the insurer is very small, has too little data or experience, or buys extensive reinsurance from an unrated reinsurer. Insurers also can request that a rating not be assigned. Best's provides a numerical "financial performance rating" for many insurers that are not assigned a letter rating. The financial performance rating is based on a less extensive analysis than the letter ratings.

Apart from using "++" grades and basing ratings on current and future prospects as opposed to past performance only, Best ratings look a lot like the grades you receive in school. Most insurers rated by Best and most other rating agencies receive high marks. (Different agencies have different rating definitions and do not rank insurers the same.) In the mid-1990s, for example, approximately 85–90 percent of property–liability insurance companies with an A. M. Best letter rating had a rating of A– or better. About one-third of rated insurers (with about one-half of total industry assets) received grades of A+ or, much less frequently, A++. Less than 5 percent of insurers (with less than 1 percent of industry assets) received ratings lower than B+. Very few insurers received ratings below B–. To keep these numbers in perspective, however, recall that roughly 25 percent of insurers do not receive a letter rating. The main reason that ratings are high on average is that the majority of insurers with the bulk of total industry assets are reasonably secure.

Statistical analysis indicates that solvency ratings help predict insurer insolvencies. Lower rated or unrated insurers are more likely to become insolvent than higher rated insurers. However, the ability of ratings to distinguish between weak and strong insurers on average does not mean that a high rating ensures solvency. Some of the larger insurers that failed in the late 1980s and early 1990s received high solvency ratings until a year or two before they were declared insolvent.

Some people argue that insurer solvency ratings are of questionable accuracy and could be biased upward due to pressure from insurers, which are a significant source of revenue for rating agencies. Evaluating these criticisms is problematic because of the difficulty in determining whether many insolvencies are caused by severe but unpredictable adverse events, as opposed to poor ex ante capitalization and risk management. Demand for accurate ratings by risk managers, insurance agents and brokers, and financially strong insurers should provide a substantial incentive for accuracy. The leading rating agencies have made many changes designed to increase the accuracy and timeliness of their ratings since the late 1980s. During and following the events of 1991, ratings were downgraded for many life insurers. Some observers have suggested that the rating agencies may have been overreacting to criticism that they had been too slow to downgrade some insurers that failed.

5.3 Overview of Solvency Regulation

Solvency regulation has three main parts: (1) regulatory monitoring of insurer insolvency risk, (2) restrictions on insurers' capital and assets, and (3) the guaranty fund system, which pays some of the claims of insolvent insurers. The primary authority for insurance regulation rests with the states (see Chapter 24); solvency regulation is no exception. Primary responsibility for regulating a specific insurer's solvency lies with the insurance department in the state where the insurer is domiciled (where it has its corporate charter). Nevertheless, most state insurance departments provide some level of monitoring for all insurers that write business in their states. Regulation by the different states is loosely coordinated by the National Association of Insurance Commissioners (NAIC). Among other activities, the NAIC proposes "model" legislation regarding solvency and other forms of regulation for consideration by state legislatures.[3]

Objectives of Solvency Regulation

Consumers generally desire two things from solvency regulation: (1) the reduction of insolvency risk, through monitoring and controls, and (2) protection against loss if insurers fail. Because reducing risk and providing protection against loss are costly, solvency regulation must examine both the benefits and the costs of each approach if it is to minimize the total cost of risk in society.

To elaborate, recall that a tradeoff exists between the benefits of lower insolvency risk and the price of insurance because increasing insurer capital to reduce insolvency risk is costly. In addition, regulatory monitoring and controls to reduce insolvency risk involve direct costs, such as the salaries of regulators and the cost of data collection and processing. Moreover, regulatory monitoring and controls might produce indirect costs, for example, if they distort the decisions of some financially sound insurers in ways that increase their costs.

A tradeoff also exists between protecting people against loss when insurers fail and incentives for insurers to be safe.[4] The reason is that protection against loss reduces consumers' demand for lower insolvency risk and the incentive to seek a safe insurer, thus dulling one of the major influences that encourages insurers to hold more capital. The tradeoff between protection against loss and incentives to reduce loss is a general phenomenon, known as the *moral hazard* problem, which we discuss in detail in Chapter 8.

Minimizing the total cost of risk basically requires that the sum of the expected cost of insolvencies, the cost of solvency regulation, and the cost of residual uncertainty concerning insolvencies be made as small as possible. The optimal mix of monitoring, controls, and protection is not known with precision. It is clear, however, that neither zero insolvency risk nor complete protection of all policyholders against loss when insurers fail is optimal, given the costs that either solution would impose on consumers. It also is clear that regulation should try to

---

[3] The NAIC established an accreditation program for state solvency regulation in the early 1990s. This program allows states that meet minimum standards for solvency regulation to become accredited by the NAIC. Many states passed legislation and took other actions to meet the minimum standards and become accredited.

[4] A large degree of protection against bank insolvencies often is justified by the need to avoid financial panics and bank runs that could have a large effect on the economy. As suggested earlier, these concerns might have some relevance to insurance, especially with respect to providers of savings-oriented life insurance and annuity products.

(1) target those insurers that have little incentive to be safe without regulation (e.g., insurers with little franchise value or with a majority of policyholders fully protected by guaranty funds), and (2) avoid distorting the decisions of insurers that have strong safety incentives without regulation.

Concept Checks

1. Why would complete protection of consumers against loss from insurer insolvency tend to increase the frequency of insolvencies?

2. Assuming that complete elimination of insolvency risk through regulation is feasible, why would achieving this goal increase the total cost of risk in society?

Regulatory Monitoring

In effect, consumers that would find it very costly to evaluate and monitor insurer insolvency risk (or who might have little incentive to do so) delegate the major responsibility for such monitoring to state solvency regulators. Regulatory monitoring of insolvency risk, including the early detection of financially weak insurers, thus can be viewed as a form of **delegated monitoring.** Regulatory monitoring sometimes can detect insurer financial problems early enough to prevent insolvency. In other cases, monitoring can help regulators intervene before the deficit between an insolvent insurer's assets and liabilities gets any larger.

The practice of solvency monitoring focuses on financial ratios and other insurer characteristics that presumably are correlated with factors that affect insurer incentives for safety (e.g., policyholder desires for safety, insurer franchise value, and capital costs). Some states have their own systems for screening insurers that may need more in-depth scrutiny by regulators, but most states rely to some extent on screening or "early warning" systems developed through the NAIC. These systems rely heavily on regulatory financial statements that must be filed by every insurer. Early warning system results are used to prioritize insurers for in-depth analysis and on-site examinations by regulators. Otherwise, each insurer normally receives a detailed financial examination every three to five years.

IRIS.   The NAIC's Insurance Regulatory Information System **(IRIS)** is a basic solvency screening system that has been used by the NAIC and state regulators since the mid-1970s. Separate but similar systems are used for property–liability insurers and life–health insurers. IRIS involves calculating 11 financial ratios for each insurer with subsequent review and analysis by a team of examiners. A "usual range" is established for each IRIS ratio based on historical comparisons of ratio values for insurers that later failed to insurers that remained solvent. Insurers are initially selected for more in-depth review by the examiner team based on several criteria, including having four or more unusual ratio values (values that fall outside the usual ranges). The examiners then conduct a more in-depth review of the financial statements of these insurers to determine whether further analysis by their domiciliary (home-state) regulators is warranted. Insurers are placed into one of five priority categories for further analysis and/or action by regulators.

Several of the IRIS ratios for property–liability insurers and their usual ranges are shown in Table 5–2.

FAST.   The NAIC developed a new solvency screening system for nationally significant insurers in the early 1990s. Known as **FAST** (short for Financial Analysis Tracking System), this system employs separate screening models for property–liability, life, and health insurers. FAST employs an expanded set of financial ratios compared to IRIS (two examples for property–liability insurers are shown in Table 5–2). In contrast to IRIS, FAST assigns different point values for different ranges of ratio results, and the point values are summed to produce a total *FAST score* for each insurer. The point values and total FAST score are not released to the public.

The FAST score is used by an NAIC committee to classify companies as those requiring immediate attention, priority attention, or routine monitoring. For immediate and priority attention insurers, the committee follows up on actions taken by the insurer and regulators in the insurer's state of domicile, and the committee can recommend additional corrective action to the domiciliary state. If the domiciliary regulators fail to follow these recommendations, the committee alerts regulators in other states, which might then take action against the insurer.

Statistical analysis indicates that both IRIS and FAST help predict insurer insolvencies and that the FAST score is a better predictor of insolvencies than the IRIS ratios. However, the effectiveness of these systems has been debated (especially for IRIS, which has been around a lot longer than FAST). Some persons argue that better systems could be developed to identify a greater proportion of "weak" insurers without incorrectly classifying any more "strong" insurers. This argument usually is based on a finding that one or more financial ratios not used in the existing systems could have predicted more insolvencies based on historical data. Whether these additional ratios are correlated with insolvency risk for insurers that have yet to fail is more difficult to establish.

Similar to the criticisms of the rating agencies we discussed earlier, some people argue that regulators often wait too long to take action against weak companies. Unjustified *regulatory forbearance* generally is regarded as a major con-

---

TABLE 5–2   Examples of IRIS and FAST Variables for Property–Liability Insurers

Variable	System	Rationale for Variable	IRIS Usual Range
Net premiums written ÷ surplus (capital)	IRIS & FAST	Higher values increase vulnerability to underwriting risk.	Less than 300%
Percent change in net premiums written	IRIS & FAST	High premium growth could indicate inadequate prices; low values could indicate constrained resources.	Between −25% and +25%
Loss and unearned premium reserves ÷ surplus	FAST	Higher values increase vulnerability to underwriting risk.	Not applicable
Reinsurance recoverable on unpaid losses ÷ surplus	FAST	Large amounts due from reinsurers increase vulnerability to credit risk.	Not applicable

tributor to the large insolvency costs for the savings and loan industry during the 1980s and early 1990s. Factors that might lead to unjustified forbearance against troubled insurers include: (1) weak insurers might exert substantial pressure for forbearance; (2) insolvencies might make regulators appear incompetent, so that they delay taking action with the hope that the insurer's condition will improve; or (3) some regulators might indeed be incompetent.

On the other hand, regulators have to be concerned about premature intervention. Premature action against a weak but still solvent insurer might cause it to become insolvent. This result could occur if the news of intervention spreads and inappropriately damages the insurer's ability to operate and take steps to improve its condition. As suggested earlier, some observers suggest that regulatory action may have been premature against one or more of the large life insurers that failed in the early 1990s. Balancing the risks of acting too soon (premature intervention) and waiting too long (excessive forbearance) can be difficult in practice.

Regulatory Controls and Risk-Based Capital Requirements

Regulations also limit an insurer's ability to take on risk. Most states have complex investment regulations that constrain an insurer's ability to invest in risky assets. For example, regulation often limits total investments in "risky" investments (such as common stocks and, since the early 1990s, high yield bonds) and investments in a single issuer's securities to specified percentages of either the insurer's capital or assets.

Historically, insurers also have had to meet **fixed minimum capital requirements** to establish and continue operations in a state. These requirements, which usually vary depending on the type of insurer (stock or mutual) and the broad type of business written (e.g., property–liability versus life–health insurance), average around $2 million, varying from $100,000 in a few states up to $5 million or more in a few others. Fixed minimum capital requirements are more appropriate for start-up operations than for established insurers with significant liabilities and premiums. Because insurers vary substantially in size, underwriting risk, and investment risk, fixed minimum capital requirements are of little relevance for many insurers.

In a major development in insurance solvency regulation during 1991–1995, which paralleled developments in bank solvency regulation, the NAIC developed **risk-based capital requirements** for adoption by the states. In contrast to the historical system of fixed minimum capital requirements, risk-based capital (RBC) requirements vary in relation to the specific amounts and types of an insurer's assets, liabilities, and premiums. The basic idea is that insurers with riskier activities need to hold more capital to meet the minimum RBC requirements.

The NAIC's property–liability RBC formula encompasses four major risk categories: (1) asset risk (the risk of issuer default and market value declines); (2) credit risk (e.g., the risk that reinsurance and other receivables will prove to be uncollectible); (3) underwriting risk (the risk that prices and reported claim liabilities will be inadequate compared to realized claim costs); and (4) miscellaneous "off-balance sheet" risks, such as the risk associated with rapid premium

TABLE 5–3   **Required Actions If Insurer Capital Falls below Specified RBC Thresholds**

Insurer Capital Level	Action
Between 150 and 200% of formula RBC	Company must file plan with insurance commissioner explaining cause of deficiency and how it will be corrected.
Between 100 and 150% of formula RBC	Commissioner must examine insurer and take corrective action as necessary.
Between 70 and 100% of formula RBC	Commissioner has legal grounds to rehabilitate or liquidate the company.
Less than 70% of formula RBC	Commissioner must take over the company.

growth. The life–health insurer formula also includes four major risk categories: (1) asset risk; (2) insurance risk (underwriting risk associated with sickness and mortality); (3) interest rate risk (which focuses on the risk that policyholders will withdraw funds and invest them elsewhere if market interest rates increase); and (4) miscellaneous business risks, such as the risk of guaranty fund assessments.

The specific RBC formulas and calculations are complicated. Section 5.4 provides a simple example that illustrates the basic procedure. The important point is that in states that have adopted the NAIC's model RBC law, each insurer must calculate a dollar figure called its RBC. This figure is higher for insurers that take on more risk. An insurer's actual capital is then compared to its RBC. If the insurer's actual capital falls below specified percentages of its RBC, regulators can take the actions shown in Table 5–3.

Most insurers were able to easily meet the RBC requirements when they were adopted by the NAIC, especially in the property–liability insurance industry, where the median property–liability insurer had actual capital equal to 400–500 percent of its RBC. The RBC requirements nevertheless may significantly affect the insurance industry and solvency regulation. Specifically, they should (1) encourage some weak insurers to limit their risk or increase their capital; (2) encourage faster corrective action by regulators in some cases and thus discourage unjustified forbearance; and (3) perhaps help regulators and other parties identify insurers with too little capital to produce a reasonably low level of insolvency risk.[5]

---

[5] The NAIC's RBC requirements have been criticized for a variety of reasons, including the crudity of some of the risk factors and omission of some types of risk (e.g., the property–liability formula does not consider interest rate risk or fully reflect the risk of catastrophe losses). Some people have argued that the relatively low levels of total RBC compared to total industry capital indicate that the formulas on average do not require enough capital to keep many insurers from operating with excessive insolvency risk. However, given that a substantial proportion of insurers has strong incentives to be reasonably safe without risk-based capital requirements, this conclusion does not necessarily follow. Moreover, a drawback to increasing the overall level of RBC relative to actual capital is that more decisions of sound insurers probably would be distorted, which could lead to a reduced willingness among these insurers to provide coverage, less efficient investment strategies, and/or higher prices.

5.4 Illustration of Risk-Based Capital

Given the complexity of insurer operations and the RBC formulas, our purpose here is not to provide a detailed description of the property–liability and life–health insurer RBC formulas. We will, however, illustrate the main ideas underlying RBC for a property–liability insurer using an expanded version of the TLC Insurance Company example introduced in Chapter 4.

Assume that:

1. TLC wrote personal auto liability policies during the year with expected claim costs equal to $20 million.

2. TLC received premiums of $30 million, of which $15 million was earned during the year for accounting purposes with the remaining $15 million reported as its year-end liability for unearned premiums (known as the *unearned premium reserve*).[6]

3. TLC paid underwriting and distribution expenses of $10 million.

4. TLC estimated that claim costs (including loss adjustment expenses) for accidents that had occurred by year-end equaled $10 million, of which $5 million had been paid by year-end and $5 million was unpaid and reported as its year-end liability for unpaid claim costs (known as the *loss reserve*).

5. TLC had assets at year-end of $25 million, with $7.5 million invested in US government bonds, $15 million in municipal and corporate bonds in the highest NAIC quality category (i.e., with the lowest default risk), and $2.5 million in common stocks.

Under the RBC system, TLC's accounting capital (known as *surplus*) is compared to its RBC. (To focus on the main ideas, this discussion ignores a number of adjustments to capital required by the RBC system before conducting this comparison.) TLC's accounting capital equals its assets minus its accounting liabilities for unearned premiums and unpaid claims. That is, its accounting capital equals assets ($25 million) minus the unearned premium reserve ($15 million) minus the loss reserve ($5 million), so that its capital equals $5 million.

Ignoring (again for simplicity) credit risk and off–balance sheet risk, TLC's required RBC will reflect its asset risk and underwriting risk. The asset and underwriting risk factors and charges for TLC as of 1996 are shown in Table 5–4. The risk factors for asset risk are the same for each insurer, and they will not vary over time unless changed by the NAIC. The calculations of the underwriting risk factors depend on several variables, including (in part) an average of industry and individual company experience using the worst underwriting profit (loss) experi-

---

[6] Accounting rules require insurers to recognize premiums as earned evenly over the coverage period. For example, for a one-year policy sold on July 1, one-half of the annual premium would be earned by December 31. The remaining one-half would be unearned and thus included in the unearned premium reserve liability. The term *reserve* is potentially confusing. Keep in mind that the unearned premium reserve and loss reserve are liabilities, not earmarked asset accounts as might be implied by the term reserve.

TABLE 5–4   RBC Charges for TLC at Year-End (in thousands)

Risk Category	Description	Amount for TLC (a)	RBC Factor (b)	Required RBC (a) × (b)
Assets	US government bonds	$ 7,500	0.0	$ 0
	Highest quality bonds	15,000	0.003	45
	Common stocks	2,500	0.15	375
Underwriting	Loss reserve	5,000	0.155	775
	Premiums written during year	30,000	0.172	5,160

ence during the preceding decade. The underwriting risk factors vary across insurers and over time.

The total RBC for TLC is obtained using the charges shown in Table 5–4 by (1) summing the squares of each charge, (2) taking the square root of this sum, and (3) multiplying the result by 0.5. Taking the square root of the sum of squared charges adjusts for the less than perfect correlation across risk categories.[7] The purpose of multiplying by 0.5 is to reduce the amount of RBC produced by the formula so as not to produce an excessive level of RBC in relation to industry capital when the formula was adopted.

This calculation produces total RBC for TLC equal to $2,615,764. The ratio of TLC's accounting capital ($5 million) to its total RBC is 191.1 percent. How would TLC look to regulators and other parties interested in whether its capital was adequate? The answer would be, not very good, even though TLC's $5 million in capital would exceed the fixed minimum capital requirement in almost all states. Specifically, TLC's ratio of capital to RBC would require the insurer to file a plan with regulators explaining why its ratio of capital to RBC was less than 200 percent and describing its plan to correct the deficiency (see Table 5–3).

TLC could increase its ratio of capital to RBC by raising more capital or by altering its investment policy. However, if TLC sold its common stock investments and invested the proceeds in US government bonds, its total RBC would only decline from $2,615,764 to $2,609,035. Its ratio of capital to RBC would only increase from 191.1 percent to 191.6 percent. The increase is negligible because (1) TLC has written a relatively large amount of premiums in relation to its capital, and (2) the property–liability insurer RBC formula gives more weight to underwriting risk than asset risk. The greater weight for underwriting risk in the property–liability insurer RBC formula is based on the historical evidence that underwriting risk generally plays a greater role than asset risk in property–liability insurer insolvencies. The life–health insurer RBC formula gives more weight to asset risk, given that changes in asset values have led to more insolvencies for life–health insurers.

---

[7] This procedure is theoretically appropriate if the risks associated with each item are uncorrelated.

TLC's basic problem is that it has too little capital compared to the amount of business it has written. (The typical insurer with this amount of business would have two to three times as much capital.) In order for TLC to reduce its ratio of capital to RBC significantly, it would have to raise more capital, write less coverage, and/or reinsure more of its business. If TLC did this, its ratio of RBC to capital would be dominated less by the RBC charge for underwriting risk; the ratio thus would become more sensitive to changes in TLC's investment mix.

5.5 State Guaranty Systems

All states have guaranty systems, known as **guaranty funds,** that provide substantial protection to consumers that have coverage with an insolvent insurer. The basic function of these systems is to pay part of the claims that exceed the assets of insolvent insurers. While only a few states had guaranty funds in 1970, most states had guaranty funds for both property–liability and life–health insurance by 1980. All states had funds for both industries by the early 1990s.

Coverage

Property–Liability Insurance.   Each state's property–liability insurance guaranty fund covers all of the major types of coverage sold by the primary insurers licensed in the state (reinsurance is excluded). Coverage limits vary across states. Claims in excess of a small deductible, typically $100, commonly are covered up to a maximum limit of $300,000 per claim (or, if lower, the limit in the policyholder's insurance contract). A significant majority of guaranty funds do not have a maximum limit for workers' compensation insurance claims. Most states also provide some protection against the loss of premiums paid for unexpired coverage at the time of insolvency. Some states exclude or further limit coverage for large business insurance buyers in order to encourage them to search for coverage from safe insurers.

Life-Health Insurance.   Like the property–liability systems, life–health guaranty funds exclude reinsurance. They also exclude coverage for savings accumulations in contracts where the investment risk is borne by the policyholder (e.g., variable life insurance and annuities, which are discussed in Chapter 23, and certain pension plans). They commonly pay up to $300,000 for death and illness claims and $100,000 for life insurance policyholder savings and annuity accumulations (see Chapter 23 for descriptions of these products). Some states provide coverage from $1 million to $5 million for group annuity contracts (e.g., for groups of employees) where accumulations are not allocated to individual participants. Other states exclude coverage for these "unallocated" annuities.

Most states have interest rate adjustment clauses ("haircut" provisions), which limit coverage of investment income for policies that involve savings accumulation. The typical guaranty fund guarantees a rate of interest that is 2 percentage points less than the average yield for the Moody's corporate bond index during a three to four year period prior to the insurer's insolvency. To prevent undue hardship that would occur to some policyholders if their contracts were terminated at insolvency (for example, if a life insurance policyholder had become uninsurable since purchasing the policy), policyholders generally are allowed to keep their contracts in force by continuing to pay premiums to a successor insurer established or chosen by state regulators and the guaranty association. However, the future rate of interest credited for savings accumulations will be relatively low (e.g., 2–3 percent less than the Moody's corporate bond yield).

Funding

State guaranty funds obtain money to pay claims by levying **post-insolvency assessments** on surviving insurers. (An exception is New York, which assesses insurers before insolvencies occur to build up a fund to pay covered claims.) Following an insolvency, the state guaranty association, which is composed of industry and regulatory representatives, estimates how much money is needed to pay covered claims in excess of the assets of the insolvent insurer. Each surviving insurer that writes business in the state is then assessed a pro rata share of the total assessment based on its market share of premiums in the state.[8] In order to reduce the risk of a domino effect from large assessments (i.e., large assessments that could push other insurers into insolvency), annual assessments typically are capped at 1 or 2 percent of premiums in a state. If the cap is hit, which is uncommon, the guaranty association can temporarily borrow funds. Insurers then are assessed in subsequent years to pay back the loan.

The countrywide guaranty fund assessments shown in Figure 5–1 might seem large to you in absolute terms. However, assessments have averaged a very small percentage of premiums. For example, in 1987, the worst year for assessments (in 1996 dollars) for either the property–liability or life–health insurance industries, countrywide property–liability insurer assessments were less than one-half of 1 percent of countrywide property–liability insurance premiums.

Depending on the state, the cost of assessments generally is shared by policyholders, insurers, and the government (taxpayers). Some states allow insurers to offset 50 to 100 percent of assessments against future state premium taxes over a 5 to 10 year period. (State premium taxes commonly equal about 2 percent of premiums.) An offset against premium taxes is more prevalent for life–health insurance guaranty funds. Assessments also are deductible when calculating insurer state and federal taxable income. Most states specify that insurers can increase

---

[8] Again, separate systems are used for property–liability insurance and life–health insurance. For both property–liability and life–health insurance, many states have two or three separate guaranty fund accounts for broad classes of coverage. Separate assessments are made for each account (e.g., the auto insurance account) based on the insurer's share of total premiums for each account. If the amounts originally assessed turn out to exceed the amount needed to pay claims, the excess is refunded to insurers.

premiums to reflect the cost of assessments. In a competitive market, however, premiums generally will reflect the expected cost of assessments for the period of coverage as opposed to being continually adjusted to reflect assessments in the prior year. (The next chapter discusses how insurance prices usually reflect expected costs rather than past experience.) As a result, the risk of year-to-year changes in the after-tax cost of assessments is borne primarily by insurance company owners.

Design Issues

The design of guaranty funds was the subject of considerable controversy during the early 1990s. This controversy will resume if one or more large insurers fails in the future. Three of the most important issues are: (1) the level of coverage, (2) pre-insolvency versus post-insolvency assessments, and (3) the potential advantages of risk-based assessments.

Level of Coverage.   Some people argue that guaranty fund limits are too low, especially in the few states that cover only $100,000 per claim. As discussed in section 5.3, however, a problem with increasing protection for policyholders is that the resulting reduction in policyholder concern with safety weakens incentives for insurers to be safe.[9] Because of this problem, other observers believe instead that guaranty fund protection is too generous and suggest that it should be restricted. They support adoption by more states of limits on protection for large commercial property–liability insurance buyers with safeguards to protect injured employees and third-party liability claimants against these businesses. The argument is that large businesses are better able to monitor and bear insolvency risk than personal insurance buyers and that restricting their guaranty fund protection will provide greater incentives for insurer safety.

Risk managers of large firms generally have opposed the elimination of guaranty fund protection for commercial insurance, in large part because premiums for large businesses reflect guaranty fund assessments. They argue that their firms should not be excluded from guaranty fund coverage as long as they have to pay more for insurance over time to cover at least part of the cost of assessments.

Pre-Insolvency versus Post-Insolvency Funding.   It has frequently been argued that the system of post-insolvency assessments provides inadequate capacity to handle potentially large insolvencies. Pre-insolvency funding could increase capacity by creating a large pool of assets that would be available to finance covered claims. Counterarguments include: (1) by reducing risk to insurers, pre-insolvency assessments might reduce incentives for safe insurers to press

---

[9] This effect is probably less severe for life insurance and annuity products that provide savings accumulation because policyholders may still be very concerned about access to their funds and haircut provisions may reduce the insured yield on savings below what the insurer had promised.

for effective regulatory solvency monitoring and for state governments to monitor effectively; (2) pre-insolvency assessments might tempt state legislatures to use the accumulated funds for other purposes; and (3) pre-insolvency assessments are not needed to enhance capacity in view of the guaranty funds' ability to borrow money if assessment caps are reached in a given year.

The question of pre- versus post-insolvency assessments also is related to the discussion of risk pooling arrangements in the last chapter that pointed out the disadvantages of assessing policyholders after losses. Collection and enforcement costs are relatively low for guaranty funds, however, because the entities that are assessed are insurers subject to state insurance law. Other things being equal, this weakens the case for pre-insolvency assessments.

Risk-based Assessments.   Another issue is whether better incentives for safety could be achieved with risk-based assessments, whether on a post-insolvency or a pre-insolvency basis. Similar to risk-based capital requirements, either pre- or post-insolvency assessments could be varied across insurers in relation to measures of insolvency risk. In principle, risk-based assessments could help deter excessive insolvency risk, because higher risk behavior would require an insurer to pay higher assessments. In practice, however, risk-based assessments might reflect only a few broad risk categories (as is true in banking), which would reduce any beneficial effect on incentives. Risk-based assessments also are at least partially redundant in principle as a means to reduce insolvency risk given the existence of risk-based capital requirements.

The risk-based assessment issue is related to pre- versus post-insolvency funding. Post-insolvency risk-based assessments, which would allocate a greater share of total post-insolvency assessments to higher risk insurers than to lower risk insurers, would probably have less effect on incentives for safety than pre-insolvency risk-based assessments. The reason is that higher risk insurers are more likely to become insolvent and thus less likely to have to pay post-insolvency risk-based assessments following an increase in insolvencies. In contrast, pre-insolvency risk-based assessments require insurers to pay in advance in order to operate with higher risk (i.e., they have to pay in order to play). Post-insolvency risk-based assessments also could further harm companies that have been weakened by an industry shock, such as a major catastrophe, thus increasing their likelihood of insolvency.

As a result of these influences, risk-based guaranty fund assessments might need to be prefunded. As noted above, risk associated with unexpected changes in pro rata (nonrisk-based) post-insolvency assessments gives safe insurers more incentive to exert pressure for effective regulation that will reduce the likelihood of large assessments. A combination of some pre-insolvency funding with risk-based assessments that vary over time in relation to the average cost of paying claims of insolvent insurers might provide safe insurers with similar incentives to press for effective regulation. The reason is that insurers still would be exposed to increased assessments in the event of adverse insolvency experience.

5.6 Summary

- The frequency and severity of insurer insolvencies increased beginning in the mid-1980s in conjunction with unexpected increases in claim costs and reductions in asset values. It is difficult to determine the extent to which the increase in insolvencies reflected inadequate ex ante capitalization and risk management by some insurers, as opposed to large, unexpected shocks that reduced insurer capital.

- A number of financial rating agencies rate insurer insolvency risk. These solvency ratings are widely used by business insurance buyers, insurance agents and brokers, and some personal insurance buyers.

- State regulation of insurer solvency includes: (1) regulatory monitoring of insurer insolvency risk, (2) controls on insurer assets and capital, and (3) guaranty funds that pay part of the claims of insolvent insurers.

- Solvency screening systems, such as IRIS and

FAST, are used by regulators to help identify insurers that have high insolvency risk.

- Risk-based capital requirements link required capital to an insurer's exposure to risk, including asset risk and the risk that claims will be higher than expected. If an insurer's ratio of capital to its risk-based capital requirement falls below one or more specified thresholds, the insurer is subject to specific regulatory actions.

- Insurance guaranty funds provide substantial protection against loss to consumers when insurers fail. Guaranty fund payments generally are financed by post-insolvency assessments on surviving insurers.

- Guaranty fund protection of consumers against losses from insurer insolvency reduces the incentive for consumers to seek coverage from safe insurers. As a result, increases in guaranty fund protection can increase insurer insolvency risk.

Key Terms

rating agencies   99
solvency ratings   99
delegated monitoring   102
IRIS   102
FAST   103

fixed minimum capital requirements   104
risk-based capital requirements   104
guaranty funds   108
post-insolvency assessments   109

Questions and Problems

1. Does the insolvency of an insurance company necessarily imply that the insurer had too little capital before insolvency, thus leading to a high risk of insolvency?

2. Does the insolvency of an insurance company necessarily imply that solvency regulators either engaged in unjustified forbearance or

were "asleep at the switch" and thereby failed to intervene in time to prevent insolvency?

3. Why are solvency ratings more likely to be used by business insurance buyers than by personal insurance buyers?

4. Would risk-based capital be desirable in a world in which each insurer's insolvency risk

was known to consumers? Would guaranty funds be desirable in such a world?

5. Explain why (*a*) and (*b*) might be related. (*a*) Insolvency problems have been much worse in the banking and savings and loan industries than in the insurance industry. (*b*) Federal deposit insurance and other guarantees of banks and savings and loan obligations provide broader and more comprehensive protection to bank depositors than guaranty funds provide to insurance consumers.

6. Why might some insurers be reluctant to reduce their capital if guaranty fund coverage was increased and the incentives of insurance buyers to deal with safe insurers were therefore reduced?

References

Best's Insolvency Study—Life/Health Insurers, 1976–1991. Oldwick, NJ: A. M. Best Company, 1991. (*Comprehensive discussion of the frequency, severity, and causes of life–health insurer insolvencies.*)

Best's Insolvency Study—Property/Casualty Insurers, 1969–1990. Oldwick, NJ: A. M. Best Company, 1991. (*Comprehensive discussion of the frequency, severity, and causes of property–liability insurer insolvencies.*)

Cummins, J. David; Scott Harrington; and Greg Niehaus. "Risk-Based Capital Requirements for Property–Liability Insurers: A Financial Analysis." In *The Financial Dynamics of the Insurance Industry,* eds. Edward I. Altman and Irwin T. Vanderhoof. New York: New York University Salomon Center, 1995. (*Analyzes risk-based capital, including the NAIC system.*)

Harrington, Scott. "Policyholder Runs, Life Insurance Company Failures, and Insurance Solvency Regulation." *Regulation: Cato Review of Business and Government,* Spring 1992. (*Reviews insolvency problems in the life insurance industry and discusses guaranty funds and possible changes in regulation.*)

Klein, Robert W. "Solvency Monitoring of Insurance Companies: Regulators' Role and Future Direction." In *The Financial Dynamics of the Insurance Industry,* eds. Edward I. Altman and Irwin T. Vanderhoof. New York: New York University Salomon Center, 1995. (*Detailed introduction to regulatory solvency monitoring and screening systems.*)

Answers to Concept Checks

1. Complete guaranty fund protection would substantially eliminate consumers' incentive to buy coverage from safe insurers. As a result, insurers would have less incentive to hold capital and take other actions to reduce insolvency risk, thus increasing the probability of insolvency for many insurers.

2. The large amount of capital required and the regulatory costs of making every insurer hold enough capital would exceed what most consumers would be willing to pay to eliminate insolvency risk. (Note the similarity of this question and response to concept checks 2 and 3 in Chapter 2, on the willingness of consumers to pay more for airline safety.)

Insurance Pricing

Chapter Objectives

- Explain the fundamental determinants of insurance premiums.
- Explain why and how insurers classify buyers into different groups based on estimates of their expected claim cost, and describe the effects of this classification on societal welfare.
- Explain how insurance premiums may be affected by shocks to insurer capital.
- Summarize the evidence and explanations for the insurance underwriting cycle.
- Discuss reasons for and consequences of government regulation of insurance prices.

6.1 Insurance Costs and Fair Premiums

This chapter provides a general introduction to insurance pricing. Later chapters contain more details on pricing particular types of coverage, such as workers' compensation insurance, automobile insurance, and life insurance. A fundamental principle of insurance pricing is that if insurers are to sell coverage willingly, they must receive premiums that (1) are sufficient to fund their expected claim costs and administrative costs and (2) provide an expected profit to compensate for the cost of obtaining the capital necessary to support the sale of coverage. The premium level that is just sufficient to fund the insurer's expected costs and provide insurance company owners with a fair return on their invested capital is known as the **fair premium.** The fair premium is the premium that would be charged in a perfectly competitive insurance market; its major determinants are summarized in Figure 6–1.

FIGURE 6–1

*Major determinants of
fair insurance
premiums*

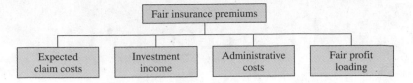

6.2 Expected Claim Costs

In this section we ignore investment income, administrative costs, and any required profit and focus on the expected cost of claims—known as the **expected claim cost**—that must be paid by the insurer for a contract or group of contracts. The expected claim cost represents the largest component of the fair premium for most types of insurance.

Homogeneous Buyers

Suppose that within a large group of insurance buyers each has the following loss distribution: Each buyer has a 0.15 probability of suffering a loss of $1,000 and a 0.85 probability of having no loss. Since each buyer has the same loss distribution, the buyers are said to be *homogenous.* Also assume that each buyer's loss is independent of (uncorrelated with) the loss of other buyers.

How much would an insurer need to charge each buyer to cover its claim costs if it insures a large group of these buyers, agreeing to pay the amount of each buyer's loss if a loss occurs? Since the policy pays the full loss of the buyer, the expected claim cost for each buyer equals the buyer's expected loss, which equals $150 (that is, 0.15[$1,000] + 0.85[$0]).[1] The actual claim cost could differ from the expected claim cost. Nevertheless, from the law of large numbers, the insurer knows that the distribution of average losses will be tightly concentrated around the expected value of $150, because losses are uncorrelated and there are large numbers of policyholders. In practice, an insurer will always have some uncertainty about its claim costs. For now we will ignore this complexity and assume that there are enough policyholders so that average claim costs will equal $150. (The effects of uncertainty in claim costs are introduced in section 6.5.)

Thus, if the insurer charges each buyer $150, it will collect enough money to pay claim costs given that the expected claim cost for each buyer is $150 and average claim costs are assumed to equal expected claim costs. If the probability of loss for each buyer increased from 0.15 to 0.20, then the average claim cost would increase to $200, and the insurer would need to increase premiums from $150 to $200 in order to pay its claim costs.

As can be seen in this simple example of a large number of independent homogeneous insurance buyers, an insurer can charge a premium equal to the expected claim cost and be able to cover all of its claim costs. Thus, a fundamental

---

[1] If insurance contracts do not cover the entire loss (see Chapter 8), using the term expected claim cost helps distinguish expected claim costs to be paid by the insurer from the policyholder's full expected loss. Other terms that are used to indicate the expected claim cost in the insurance business are *pure premium* and *actuarially fair premium.*

determinant of insurance premiums is the expected claim cost. If the insurer charged less than the expected claim cost, average claim costs would exceed average revenues. On the other hand, competition keeps the insurer from charging more than the expected claim cost.

Heterogeneous Buyers

Consider next what happens when there are two groups of consumers—bookworms and skateboarders—with different loss distributions as described in Table 6–1. The expected loss equals $100 for each buyer classified as a bookworm and equals $200 for each buyer classified as a skateboarder. Assume for simplicity that there are equal numbers of buyers in each group and that the number of buyers is large enough for the law of large numbers to imply that the average loss is equal to the expected loss for each group.

Now let's examine how the insurance market might operate when faced with this situation. Suppose Equal Treatment Insurance Company charged $150 to consumers in both groups and sold equal numbers of policies to both groups. It would expect to lose $50 on policies sold to skateboarders, but it would expect to make a profit of $50 on policies sold to bookworms. On average, it would break even.

Consider what would happen, however, if Careful Selection Insurance Company discovered how to identify the bookworms at zero cost. Careful Selection could then charge the bookworms a premium less than $150 and not offer any coverage to the skateboarders (or offer coverage at $200 or higher) and make a large profit. For example, suppose Careful Selection sold policies only to bookworms at a price of $130. Careful Selection's claim costs would be very close to $100 per policyholder, but it would receive $130 in revenue from each policyholder. The expected profit therefore would be $30 on each policy sold.

What will happen to Equal Treatment Insurance Company? When Careful Selection charges a lower premium to bookworms, Equal Treatment will lose the bookworms as policyholders and end up only with skateboarders. As a result, Equal Treatment will experience **adverse selection,** which is defined as the tendency of buyers with high expected losses to buy more coverage than buyers with low expected losses when charged the same premium. The term adverse selection is derived from the fact that, from the insurer's perspective (that is, from Equal Treatment's perspective), it receives an adverse selection of policyholders. The adverse selection is caused by the bookworms being attracted to Careful Selection Company.

TABLE 6–1   Loss Distributions for Bookworms and Skateboarders

Group	Probability of Loss	Probability of No Loss	Size of Loss	Expected Loss
Bookworms	0.10	0.90	$1,000	$100
Skateboarders	0.20	0.80	$1,000	$200

As a result of the adverse selection, Equal Treatment Company will lose money if it continues to charge $150 to all policyholders, because the only policyholders that it will attract are the policyholders with an expected claim cost of $200 (the skateboarders). Thus, Equal Treatment Company either has to increase premiums or classify policyholders in the same way as Careful Selection Company.

The story of Equal Treatment and Careful Selection illustrates the following points:

1. Identifying low and high risk buyers has the potential to produce large profits (at least in the short run) for an insurer.
2. An insurer that fails to base premiums on information that is known to explain differences in expected claim cost across buyers will lose money due to adverse selection.

These points lead to a fundamental principle of insurance pricing: In a competitive market, differences in expected claim cost across consumers will produce differences in premiums across consumers as long as three conditions hold:

1. Insurance companies want to make money or at least avoid losing money.
2. Insurance buyers generally look for policies with low premiums for a given amount and quality of coverage.
3. One or more insurers can predict differences in expected claim costs across consumers at a sufficiently low cost.

By now you should be convinced that when differences in expected claim costs are known, competition, profit-seeking, and consumer desire for low premiums give rise to **cost-based prices**—that is, premiums that are commensurate with the expected claim cost of each buyer. In practice, insurers incur costs gathering and processing information in order to estimate differences in expected claim costs across buyers. These information costs and intrinsic uncertainty about the expected claim cost for different buyers make it infeasible in practice to have each buyer pay a premium based on the buyer's true but unknown expected claim cost. Instead, insurers estimate buyers' expected claim costs using all of the information that can help predict differences in expected claim costs as long as the information can be obtained at reasonable cost. The process by which insurers estimate the expected claim cost for different buyers and charge premiums that vary according to expected claim costs is known as **risk classification** (or *categorization*). Note that in the classification context, a "high risk" policyholder has high expected claim costs.[2]

---

[2] As we explained in Chapter 1, the term *risk* refers to expected claim costs in some contexts and variability around the expected value in other contexts. Although we use risk to indicate variability around the expected value in Chapter 3 and throughout most of the book, it is important for you to stop and make sure that you understand how the term is being used in a given context.

Concept Checks

1. Innovative Collision Insurance Company has discovered that the weight of cars and "light" trucks helps to predict collision claim costs for its policyholders (heavier vehicles have lower collision claim costs). Explain how Innovative can maximize profits with this information and the likely effect of this on the firm's competitors.

2. Will Innovative's customers be happy that it has discovered this new factor that predicts claim costs?

Competition, Risk Classification, and Societal Welfare

The previous section demonstrated that risk classification naturally results from competition among insurers. In this section, we consider an important and often controversial issue: Is risk classification good for society? We will discuss this issue by considering a situation in which risk classification is not allowed and then examine the effects of introducing risk classification. In the context of the previous example, we start with the bookworms and the skateboarders all being charged the same price ($150) and examine the effects of allowing bookworms to be charged a different price than skateboarders. We will see that there are three general effects of allowing classification: (1) a redistribution of wealth (bookworms will benefit from lower premiums and skateboarders will have to pay higher premiums); (2) a change in behavior (more people might become bookworms); and (3) the introduction of classification costs (insurers' efforts to identify bookworms might be costly). When deciding whether classification is "good for society," all three factors must be considered.

Redistributive Effects of Classification.   When low risk (low expected claim cost) and high risk (high expected claim cost) buyers are forced to pay the same rate, a **cross-subsidy** takes place in that low risk buyers pay more than their expected claim cost and high risk buyers pay less. The high risk buyers typically like this cross-subsidy and the low risk buyers do not. If risk classification is then introduced, the price paid by the high risk buyers will increase and the price paid by the low risk buyers will decrease, thereby reducing cross-subsidies. In our previous example, classification caused a premium reduction for each bookworm and a premium increase for each skateboarder and thereby reduced the cross-subsidy from bookworms to skateboarders. Thus, one effect of classification is to redistribute wealth: bookworms benefit and skateboarders lose.

As noted earlier, it would be too costly and ultimately impossible to have each buyer pay a rate based on the buyer's true but unknown expected cost. Thus, introducing risk classification is not likely to eliminate cross-subsidies completely. Nevertheless, allowing classification will shift or redistribute wealth from high risk to low risk buyers. Viewed from the opposite perspective, if insurers are prevented by regulation from using certain types of information to classify buyers that helps predict claim costs, wealth is shifted from low risk buyers to high risk buyers. As we discuss later in this chapter and in the chapters that follow, this sometimes has occurred in auto, workers' compensation, health, and other insurance markets.

Note that by itself the redistribution effect from classification does not provide much guidance concerning whether classification is good or bad for society. This is because some buyers will benefit from classification and others will not. A value judgment must be made as to which buyers should receive greater weight when making the public policy decision. If the skateboarders were in charge of public policy, they would most likely say that classification should not be allowed, but the bookworms would likely disagree.

We showed in the last section that allowing insurers to compete based on price would lead bookworms to be charged less and skateboarders to be charged more if bookworms could be identified at low cost. Thus, allowing insurers to compete in this way would reflect a value judgment that buyers with higher estimated expected claim cost should pay more for coverage. Such a value judgment often is based on the notion that buyers with higher expected claim costs should pay more because they are expected to receive more money in claim payments from the insurer. On the other hand, some people feel that they should not have to pay more when their higher expected claim costs are due to circumstances largely outside of their control (e.g., due to their genes or the location of their residence). In contrast to the redistributive effects of classification, the next two effects to be discussed—behavioral changes and classification costs—in principle provide a more objective basis on which to decide whether classification is good for society.

Behavioral Effects of Classification.   If changes in insurance prices affect behavior, classification can increase societal wealth by reducing the cost of risk, a concept that you learned about in Chapter 2. Before explaining this idea in general terms, we can convey some basic intuition using the skateboarders as an example. Note first that being a skateboarder results in an additional $100 in expected claim costs. That is, each person who decides to be a skateboarder, as opposed to a bookworm, increases the expected claim costs in society by $100. With classification, skateboarders have to pay all these additional costs, because their insurance premiums reflect the fact that they are skateboarders. Consequently, the only people who will choose to be skateboarders are those that value that activity more than the costs associated with the activity. Without classification (when everyone pays $150), however, part of the cost associated with being a skateboarder is paid by the bookworms. Since skateboarders do not pay all the costs associated with their activity, *too many people may choose to be skateboarders.* As a consequence, there may be too much skateboarding in society without classification and the cost of risk may increase.

These points can be stated in general terms. Recall from Chapter 2 that individuals and businesses generally make economic decisions based on the *private* benefits and costs that will accrue to the individual or business. Activities are undertaken until the marginal private cost equals the marginal private benefit. This type of decision making minimizes the cost of risk in society provided that decision makers pay all the costs associated with their actions and receive all the benefits. Thus, charging higher premiums to insurance buyers with higher expected claim costs provides higher risk individuals and businesses with more incentive to take actions to reduce the cost of risk through increased precautions and reduced levels of risky activity. Lowering their premiums below expected costs would reduce their incentive to reduce the cost of risk.

The magnitude of the reduction in the cost of risk due to the incentive effects of cost-based insurance pricing depends on how much behavior is affected by insurance prices. For example, charging higher premiums for workers' compensation insurance to businesses that have more frequent or severe worker injuries has been shown to reduce the number of injuries. Charging higher premiums for life and health insurance to people with genetic conditions that cause a higher incidence of sickness or illness may have much less, if any, effect on behavior.

Behavioral responses to insurance prices are complex and often cannot be measured accurately. In many cases, however, intuition suggests that cost-based prices can have a significant effect on risky behavior. In addition, cost-based insurance prices also affect the amount of insurance purchased, which in turn can affect incentives to avoid loss.[3] If, for example, the price of insurance is reduced (increased) to high (low) risk people or businesses because of government restrictions on classification (see section 6.7), then high (low) risk people or businesses will buy more (less) insurance coverage. This change in the amount of insurance coverage can increase the cost of risk by (1) increasing the cost of residual uncertainty for low risk people or businesses that purchase less coverage in response to the restrictions, and by (2) further reducing incentives for high risk people or businesses to undertake loss control.

Concept Check

3. Other things being equal, 20-year-old males in most states face significantly higher rates for auto insurance than 20-year-old females because young males are involved in more accidents. Explain how charging 20-year-old males and females an equal rate based on their average expected loss might affect behavior. Would total losses from accidents increase for males?

Classification Costs.   Consider next the effects of classification costs; that is, the money spent by insurers on the collection and evaluation of information to classify applicants based on estimates of their expected claim costs. These costs obviously reduce the economic advantages of classification. In some cases, classification costs might cause classification to increase the total cost of risk because classification costs are greater than any savings due to changes in behavior. To see why, let's modify the Careful Selection Insurance Company example. Recall that Equal Treatment is charging everyone $150. Now Careful Selection enters the market and is able to identify bookworms by spending $25 for each policy sold to a bookworm (e.g., they administer a test on literature, history, and insurance).

---

[3] We discuss how increases in the amount of coverage can reduce incentives to engage in loss control in detail when we explain the concept of moral hazard in Chapter 8.

Careful Selection charges $135 for applicants classified as bookworms and $200 to applicants classified as skateboarders. Since skateboarders can buy coverage from Equal Treatment at a price of $150, only bookworms will buy Careful Selection's policies. At a premium of $135, Careful Selection has an expected profit of $10 per policy ($135 in revenue, $100 in expected claim costs, and $25 in classification costs).

Other insurers eventually will copy Careful Selection and also classify policyholders. Competition will cause the price for bookworms to fall to $125 and skateboarders eventually will have to pay $200. If behavior is not affected, the $50 loss to high risk persons from classification ($200 − $150) will substantially exceed the $25 gain to low risk persons ($150 − $125), and this type of classification will increase total costs, including classification costs. If classification costs money, but if it does not affect behavior, there is no reduction in the cost of losses (and the cost of loss control, including the value of foregone activity) that would offset the cost of classification. The total cost of risk is more likely to decline from classification when classification costs are small or the effects of premiums on behavior (in the way of precautions, a reduced amount of risky activity, or a greater amount of insurance purchased) are large.

When considering the possibility that classification might increase the total cost of risk, you should consider at least two other issues. First, disincentives for insurers to spend money on classification sometimes might lead to too little classification. For example, if competing insurers can quickly discover and copy new methods that better predict claim costs and lead to significant reductions in the cost of risk, insurers will have less incentive to develop these methods. This is one major advantage of insurers making underwriting decisions (decisions to accept or reject an applicant in a given rate class, which we discuss below) using information that is not disclosed to competitors. Second, any attempt to prevent classification by regulating insurance company classification processes will involve some cost. Regulation also will be less than completely effective, and it could have unexpected and unintended effects. You will learn about the types of regulations that restrict the use of information and their consequences later in this chapter and in subsequent chapters on automobile and workers' compensation insurance.

Risk Classification Practices

When allowed by law, insurers generally use elaborate risk classification systems. This section describes some of the common classification methods used by insurers. Subsequent chapters provide more detail on the classification methods used in specific lines of business.

Classification involves grouping together consumers with similar characteristics and charging them a premium or *rate* that differs from consumers with different characteristics. The term "rate" often is used synonymously with "premium" in the insurance business. In other cases, it refers to the price per unit of coverage (e.g., $1,000 of life insurance), with the total premium equal to the rate per unit of coverage times the amount of coverage purchased. These risk classes and the rates charged to each risk class are based on analysis performed by actuaries who examine historical data and estimate expected claim costs. They also are affected by competition and, in many states, regulation. Insurers then employ selection standards to determine whether an applicant in a given class will be offered coverage at the **class rate.**

As was introduced in Chapter 4, the overall process of assessing the expected claim costs for buyers, determining the applicable rate, and deciding whether to offer coverage is known as **underwriting.** Class rates and associated underwriting standards generally differ across insurers. Insurers with more stringent standards generally offer lower premiums in any given class. For many types of business insurance, the underwriter also has substantial flexibility to modify the class rate to reflect the underwriter's evaluation of additional characteristics of the business applicant, such as the condition of business premises or property, the existence of safety programs, and so on. This procedure is commonly known as *schedule rating.*

Class rates and underwriting standards are based on a variety of characteristics of the buyer. For many types of insurance, class rates are modified to reflect the prior loss experience of the applicant. These modifications are known as **experience rating,** or *merit rating.* Medium-to-large businesses also may have their premiums for a given coverage period modified based on loss experience during the same period. This is known as *retrospective experience rating.*

For example, workers' compensation insurance rates are routinely based on the buyer's prior loss experience, except for very small businesses where the prior loss experience has little ability to predict future claim costs (see below). Rates for larger firms also often reflect their claims experience during the coverage period. Personal auto insurance rates generally will be increased for drivers involved in an accident, at least when the driver is at fault. The simple reason is that the driver's past auto accident experience helps to predict future claim costs. People that cause accidents in a given year on average have more accidents during the next three to five years than people who do not.

However, a fundamental feature of insurance pricing for individuals and small- and medium-sized businesses is that factors besides prior loss experience of the buyer (or other direct evidence of risky activity, such as traffic citations for automobile insurance or safety regulation violations for a business) have a major effect on prices. The reason for this is that the use of nonexperience factors leads to substantially improved estimates of future loss experience. As noted above for the case of workers' compensation insurance for very small businesses, experience rating sometimes is not used at all because a buyer's prior loss experience does not reliably predict future claim costs. In the language of actuaries, the loss experience has insufficient *credibility* for use in rating.

6.3 Investment Income and the Timing of Claim Payments

The timing of claim payments and the ability of the insurer to earn investment income before claims are paid also affect the fair premium. In the simplest insurance contracts, the full premium is paid in a lump sum when the policy is issued, whereas claim payments are made over time. In some contracts, such as business liability insurance, a significant proportion of total claim costs are paid over a period of years after the coverage period has ended. Payments occur slowly over time as the insurer negotiates and settles known claims against its policyholders and is notified of additional injuries that occurred during the period of coverage. The lag between the time that coverage is sold and claims are paid is known as the *claims tail.*

Liability and workers' compensation insurance are "long-tailed" lines; that is, a large proportion of claims are paid a number of years after the coverage period. Property insurance coverage and coverage for employee medical costs under group health insurance contracts are examples of "short-tailed" lines; that is, most claims are paid during the year of coverage or the year after. Figure 6–2 illustrates the claims tail for several types of property–liability insurance. (In this figure, "other liability" insurance consists of business liability insurance other than auto liability, product liability, and medical malpractice liability.)

The fair premium reflects the ability of the insurer to invest premium dollars and earn interest until claims are paid. As interest rates rise, the amount of premium that needs to be charged to fund claim payments declines because the insurer can earn more interest. Similarly, as the claims tail gets longer (i.e., as a given total value of claims is paid over a longer period of time), the amount of money that the insurer needs to fund claims payments declines because more investment income will be earned before claims are paid. Thus, a fundamental principle of insurance pricing is that *fair premiums reflect the ability of the insurer to earn interest on premium dollars before it has to pay claims.* In other words, the fair premium reflects the time value of money. The fair premium is negatively related to both the level of interest rates and the length of the claims tail. The fol-

FIGURE 6–2

Cumulative percentage of total losses paid over time for accidents in year t

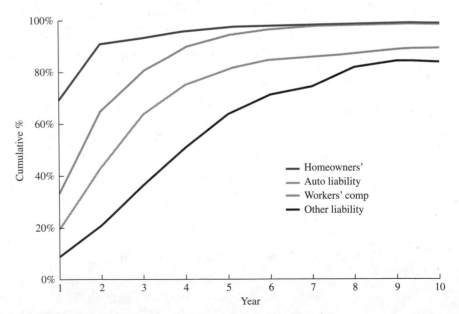

lowing two examples will help you understand the relationship between premiums, interest rates, and the speed with which claims are paid.

All Claims Paid at the End of One Year

An insurer sells a policy that will produce $100 in claim payments at the end of one year. The timing of premium and claim payments is illustrated below:

Ignoring administrative costs and the fair profit loading, how much money does the insurer need to collect at the beginning of the year to pay the $100? Let P denote this amount of money and let r denote the annual interest rate. The interest earned by investing P for one year equals rP (i.e., it equals the interest rate times the amount invested). At the end of the year, the insurer will have $P + rP = P(1 + r)$. This sum must equal $100, the amount of claims to be paid at the end of the year. Thus,

$$P(1 + r) = 100$$

Solving this expression for P by dividing both sides by $(1 + r)$ gives:

$$P = 100/(1 + r)$$

If $r = 0.10$ (10%), then $P = \$90.91$. If $r = 0.05$ (5%), then $P = \$95.24$. Note that P is lower for the higher interest rate.

All Claims Paid at the End of Two Years

Let's go one step further and consider what happens if the $100 is paid in a lump sum at the end of two years rather than at the end of one year. The timing of premium and claim payments is illustrated below.

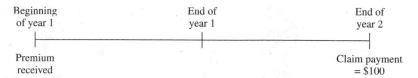

Again we will let P indicate the money collected at the time the contract is sold and r denote the interest rate. As we explained above, the insurer will have $P(1 + r)$ at the end of one year. If it reinvests this amount. it will earn interest equal to $rP(1 + r)$ the second year (i.e., the interest rate times the amount invested during the second year). At the end of the second year, its total amount of funds will equal *P,* plus the interest earned the first year, plus the interest earned the second year, or $P(1 + r) + rP(1 + r)$. This amount must equal $100:

$$P(1+ r) + rP(1 + r) = 100$$

Dividing both sides by $(1 + r)$ gives:

$$P + rP = 100/(1 + r)$$

Solving for *P* (by dividing by $[1 + r]$ again) gives:

$$P = 100/(1 + r)^2$$

If $r = 0.10$, then $P = \$82.64$. If $r = 0.05$, then $P = \$90.71$. Note that these values are lower than when claims are paid at the end of one year.

The amount of money needed to fund expected claim costs taking into consideration the insurer's ability to earn investment income is called the **discounted expected claim cost;** that is, the expected claim cost times a discount factor (or *present value* factor) to reflect the time value of money. The discount factors in the preceding examples were $1/(1 + r)$ for the one-year case and $1/(1 + r)^2$ for the two-year case. When claims are paid gradually over time, the discount factors are more complicated.

Figure 6–3 shows the discounted expected claim cost for $100 of undiscounted expected claim cost for several different types of coverage (based on historic claim cost payment patterns) and two interest rates. As can be seen, the discounted expected claim cost is materially lower using the 10 percent interest rate

FIGURE 6–3

Discounted expected claim cost per $100 of undiscounted expected claim cost using 5 percent and 10 percent interest rates

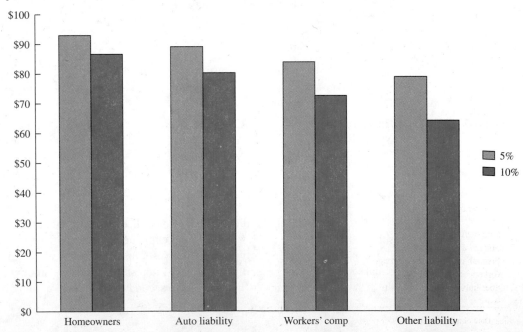

than the 5 percent interest rate for each type of coverage. In addition, the discounted expected claim cost declines with the length of the claims tail (compare Figure 6–2). For example, $87 would be needed to fund the payment of $100 of expected claim cost for homeowners coverage when the interest rate is 10 percent; only $65 would be needed for other liability coverage due to its much longer claims tail.

In more complicated cases, premiums for coverage during a given period are made in installments (e.g., quarterly premiums for a one-year homeowners policy), or coverage lasts for multiple years with premiums due annually, quarterly, or monthly (e.g., most types of life insurance). In these cases, the sum of the periodic premium must be higher than when the premium is paid in a single sum at the beginning of the coverage period because the insurer will earn less investment income.

Concept Checks

4. Other factors being held constant, why do long-tailed lines of insurance have lower fair premiums than short-tailed lines?

5. An insurer sells a policy for which it expects to pay $500 at the end of one year. It can invest funds at 6 percent per year. What is the expected claim cost? What is the discounted expected claim cost? What is the discounted expected claim cost if the $500 is expected to be paid after two years rather than one?

6.4 Administrative Costs

Insurers incur significant administrative costs for pricing/underwriting and distributing policies. As noted in Chapter 4, these costs commonly are called underwriting expenses. You also have learned about insurer costs associated with processing claims, known as loss adjustment expenses. The fair premium must include an **expense loading** to cover both underwriting and loss adjustment expenses.

Table 6–2 illustrates the magnitude of total underwriting expenses and the

TABLE 6–2   **Underwriting Expenses and Loss Adjustment Expenses as a Percent of Premiums for Selected Types of Insurance: 1987–1996**

Type of Insurance	Underwriting Expenses			Loss Adjustment Expenses
	Commissions	General Expenses	Total Underwriting Expenses	
Homeowners	15.8%	15.0%	30.8%	11.5%
Personal auto liability	8.5	14.0	22.5	13.0
Personal auto physical damage	8.5	13.9	22.4	8.6
Workers' compensation	5.6	14.3	19.9	12.0
Other liability	11.0	15.1	26.1	28.1

Source: Data obtained from *Best's Aggregates & Averages, Property–Casualty,* 1997 edition.

two major categories of underwriting expenses—commissions to agents and general expenses—as a percent of premiums for four types of property–liability insurance. General expenses include expenditures for pricing/underwriting, marketing, and issuing policies not written by agents. Table 6–2 also shows loss adjustment expenses as a percent of premiums. Loss adjustment expenses for liability insurance coverage are greater than for property coverage because of defense costs (e.g., attorney fees) involved in negotiating settlement or taking a case to trial.

The total expense loading for underwriting and loss adjustment expenses ranges from about 30 percent for personal auto physical damage insurance to about 50 percent for other liability coverage. It should be kept in perspective that some of these expenses are incurred to provide valuable ancillary services to insurance buyers (e.g., defense costs for liability coverage, much of the cost of settling workers' compensation claims, and general expenses that are incurred to provide business insurance buyers with advice on loss control).

Many types of insurance require significantly higher underwriting expenses when an insurer first sells coverage to a particular buyer than when the coverage is renewed. In these cases, only part of the first year's expense usually will be recovered in the first year's premium. The remainder of the expense is expected to be recovered over the duration of the relationship with the policyholder. Other factors held constant, this implies that fair premium rates will be lower the longer the buyer is expected to renew coverage, because the insurer then needs a lower periodic charge to recover its initial expenditure. The amount of renewal premiums that is available to recover first-year expenses constitutes a significant source of franchise value for many insurers and thus provides additional incentive for these insurers to hold capital to reduce the probability of insolvency (see Chapter 4).

6.5 Profit Loading

We now eliminate the unrealistic assumption made at the beginning of the chapter that an insurer's average claim costs equal its expected claim costs. You learned in Chapter 4 that when claim costs are uncertain, fixed premium insurance contracts make it necessary for the insurer to hold capital—that is, to hold assets in excess of expected claim costs—in order to increase the likelihood that it can pay all claims. In order to obtain capital, an insurer must offer investors an expected after-tax return equal to what they could earn elsewhere on an investment of similar risk.

We also explained in Chapter 4 that a disadvantage of investing in an insurance company is the double taxation on the investment income earned on the financial capital held by the insurer.[4] To offset this disadvantage, an insurer must

---

[4] If the insurer invests in tax-exempt bonds to reduce this cost, there is still a cost due to lower returns on these bonds. In addition to the tax disadvantage, Chapter 4 also identified that an investment in an insurance company might suffer from greater agency costs and greater risk compared to an investment in a mutual fund that holds the same portfolio of assets as the insurer.

find an additional source of income for capital providers; otherwise, investors will not provide capital. The additional income is obtained by charging premiums in excess of the discounted value of expected claim costs and administrative costs. Stated differently, policyholders must compensate investors for the disadvantages of investing in an insurance company. The extra amount that policyholders must pay to compensate investors for providing capital is called the fair **profit loading.** Since the underlying reason that the profit loading exists is uncertainty in claim costs, the profit loading also is sometimes called the *risk loading.*

As we explained in Chapter 4, the greater the risk that claim costs could be substantially higher than expected, the more capital an insurer needs to achieve a given probability of solvency. As a result, when claim costs are more variable (less predictable), greater amounts of capital will be required and thus a higher profit loading will be needed by insurers. Recall from Chapter 3 that variability in average claim costs increases as the correlation in claim costs across policyholders increases. Thus, other things being equal, the fair profit loading typically will be higher in lines of insurance that cover correlated losses (such as homeowners insurance, which covers windstorm damage).[5]

Concept Check

6. Assume that (*a*) the discounted expected claim cost for windstorm (hurricane) insurance is $100, (*b*) the discounted expected claim cost for fire insurance is $100, and (*c*) administrative costs are the same for both types of insurance. Which type of coverage will have the higher fair premium? Why?

Summary

To summarize the material on the determinants of fair premiums, we will work through a simple numerical example that will incorporate each of the four determinants. Suppose that you wanted to find the fair premium for a group of insurance policies each having the following loss distribution:

$$\text{Loss} = \begin{array}{l} \$10,000 \text{ with probability } 0.1 \\ \$\qquad 0 \text{ with probability } 0.9 \end{array}$$

Assume that all claim payments will be made at the end of one year, the interest rate is 10 percent, and administrative expenses, which are paid immediately, equal

---

[5] Note that this discussion has focused on a basic economic model of insurance pricing that emphasizes the need to achieve profits to compensate insurers for the cost of holding capital to back their policies. Actuarial models of insurance prices usually describe the profit loading as a risk loading that is necessary due to the unpredictability of claim costs, with less predictability (higher standard deviation) leading to a higher risk charge. The economic model instead focuses on how higher standard deviation increases the capital required, which in turn increases the required profit loading necessary to cover tax and other costs of holding capital. While the details vary, both approaches have the same implication: Greater variability in claim costs increases the premium needed to sell coverage.

20 percent of the expected claim cost. Some administrative costs in practice are proportional to premiums rather than proportional to expected claim costs (e.g., commissions to agents). In addition, some administrative costs are fixed (i.e., they are approximately the same for each policy of a given type). We ignore these complications, which are readily handled, to focus on the main ideas. Finally, assume that this type of policy requires a profit loading (due when policies are sold) equal to 5 percent of the expected claim cost.

To calculate the fair premium, we separately measure each of the four factors affecting fair premiums and then add them together.

Step 1 (Expected claim cost): The expected claim cost equals $(0.1)(\$10,000) = \$1,000$.

Step 2 (Discounted expected claim cost): The discounted expected claim cost equals $\$1,000/1.1 = \$909.09$.

Step 3 (Expense loading): Administrative expenses equal $(0.20)(\$1,000) = \$200$.

Step 4 (Profit loading): The required profit loading is $(0.05)(\$1,000) = \$50$.

Step 5 (Fair premium): The fair premium therefore must equal $\$909.09 + \$200 + \$50 = \$1,159.09$.

Now, let's see what happens if policies are sold at the fair premium and actual claim payments average $1,000 per policy. Each policyholder pays a premium of $1,159.09, from which administrative expenses of $200 are paid immediately. After deducting this amount and the amount of premium necessary to provide the desired profit loading ($50), the insurer will have $909.09 to invest for one year at a 10 percent interest rate in order to pay claims. At the end of the year, the insurer will have $1,000, which equals the actual claim cost per policy. Thus, the fair premium is just sufficient to pay claim costs and administrative costs and produce the required profit loading.

6.6 Capital Shocks and Underwriting Cycles

Two related phenomena have been difficult to explain with the basic theory of fair premiums. First, some insurance markets have experienced dramatic increases in premiums following large industrywide reductions in capital caused by adverse loss or investment experience. We refer to these large reductions in capital as **capital shocks.** The magnitude of the premium increases cannot readily be explained by probable changes in fair premiums (i.e., by changes in the discounted value of expected claim costs, expenses, and normal profits). Instead, it appears that the adverse experience and the corresponding decrease in capital causes actual premiums to rise above fair premiums. Second, most analysts of the property–liability insurance industry believe that historically many lines of business have been characterized by a cycle in premium rates and profits. These cyclical price movements also suggest that actual premiums depend on past profitability. Before discussing these two influences on premiums, it is first important to review a basic implication of fair premiums.

Fair Premiums Are Forward Looking

As you learned earlier in this chapter, fair premiums depend on expected future claim costs and underwriting expenses, as opposed to depending on whether the insurer made more or less money than expected last year. Thus, *fair premiums are forward looking.* This point sometimes is subject to some confusion. Our goal is to help you clearly understand what "forward looking" means.

Consider an insurer that has completed operations in year one and that is writing policies in year two. Year one's results are presented in Table 6–3, along with the expected claim cost and fair premium for year two. The example ignores investment income and expense and profit loadings to keep things simple.

Because the actual claim cost for year one exceeds the expected claim cost, the insurer experiences an operating loss (negative profit). The expected claim cost for year two grows to $115, so the fair premium also increases to $115. The higher expected claim cost perhaps is partially due to the information that the insurer received from year one's results. That is, because claim costs were higher than expected in year one, the insurer's estimate of expected claim costs for year 2 may have increased. The actual claim cost and profit for year two is not known at the beginning of the year, but the expected profit is $0.

A common belief is that an insurer will routinely increase prices in order to make up for any bad experience in the prior year. However, this example illustrates that a price increase following a bad year need not indicate that an insurer is increasing rates to make up for unexpectedly high prior claim costs. The fair premium generally will increase following unexpected growth in claim costs because this often leads to upward revisions in insurer estimates of future expected claim costs.

Competition normally should keep an insurer from raising its rates in order to replenish its capital after a bad year. If an insurer with the experience shown for year one tried to raise the premium to $125 to cover the $115 expected claim cost for year two and recover the $10 loss for year one, other insurers could attract some of its customers by charging less than $125 and still have enough premium to cover the expected cost of selling the coverage. More generally, since insurance buyers usually prefer greater price stability, insurers that insulate buyers from fluctuations in premium rates due to random fluctuations in losses will tend to dominate those who do not (as is implied by our discussion of the advantages of fixed premium insurance in Chapter 4). Given this background, you are ready to examine situations in which insurance prices may depend on past underwriting profitability or investment performance.

TABLE 6–3   **Insurer Operating Results in Years One and Two**

Year	Expected Claim Cost	Fair Premium	Actual Claim Cost	Profit
One (past)	$100	$100	$110	$ –10
Two (future)	$115	$115	$?	$?

Large Losses and Capital Shocks

Extensions to the theory of insurance prices and some empirical evidence suggest that insurance premiums sometimes increase by more than the discounted value of expected claim costs, expenses, and normal profits if *most insurers in a given market simultaneously experience very large losses* on insurance contracts or investments. Many observers, for example, believe that this happened following large unexpected growth in business liability insurance claim costs in the mid-1980s.

Large unexpected losses that affect most insurers at once substantially reduce industry capital. Thus, there is a depletion in the funds insurers hold to make sure that claims will be paid. In order for insurers to renew policies without increasing the likelihood of insolvency following large losses on previously issued policies, they would need to raise large amounts of capital in a short time period. However, the cost of raising capital is likely to be especially high following large losses due do uncertainty about the magnitude of losses and insurers' financial conditions. If capital cannot be obtained quickly at a reasonable cost, insurers have the choice of either increasing the probability of insolvency or reducing the amount of coverage they are willing to sell at a given price. To the extent that insurers reduce the amount of coverage they are willing to sell at a given price, there will be a reduction in the supply of coverage. As in any market, if industry supply is reduced, prices will increase (holding demand fixed).

The possible effects of capital shocks are illustrated in Figure 6–4 using the simplifying assumption that the demand curve for coverage does not change over time. The demand curve slopes downward: As price falls, more coverage is demanded. The industry (short-run) supply curves slope upward: A higher price increases supply. Now consider what happens if large losses occur in year zero. For example, assume that an earthquake destroys major parts of San Francisco and Los Angeles and that a hurricane wipes out Miami. Two effects are illustrated in Figure 6–4.

FIGURE 6–4

Effect of large losses on industry supply

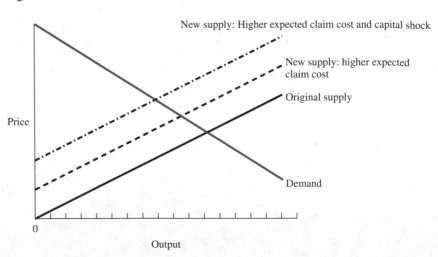

First, the large loss may increase the expected claim cost for new policies. For example, following unexpected growth in business liability claim costs in the mid-1980s, insurers revised their expectations of losses on new business. In the earthquake/hurricane example, the magnitude of the losses might indicate that property is more vulnerable to damage than previously believed. The higher expected claim cost on new business causes the industry supply curve to shift back (up) because a higher price is needed to cover the higher expected claim cost. This effect on prices is consistent with the basic theory of fair premiums: higher expected claim costs imply higher insurance premiums.

Second, the large loss in year zero depletes insurer capital, and, given the costs of raising new capital quickly and the reluctance to substantially increase the likelihood of insolvency, insurers reduce the amount of coverage they are willing to sell. Thus, there is an additional shift in supply, leading to an additional increase in price (and an additional reduction in total quantity of coverage sold). This second effect appears inconsistent with the theory of fair premiums, because premiums are increasing by more than the discounted value of expected claim costs, expenses, and normal profits.

The higher premiums imply that short-run profits will exceed the long-run fair return to suppliers of capital. This high return is not due to a lack of competition among insurers. Instead, the explanation is that large losses deplete capital and, given that capital is costly to replenish, existing insurer capital becomes a scarce factor of production. Given its scarcity, it is not surprising that it will earn higher returns. However, this situation is not likely to last long. Prices higher than implied by changes in expected claim costs will help restore insurer capital. In addition, over time, the sale of new stock and borrowing by insurers will restore capital. As capital accumulates, insurers will expand supply (the supply curve will shift out), thus putting downward pressure on price. Note that if price increases help replenish insurer capital, then policyholders are sharing the risk of very large, industrywide losses with insurers.

The Underwriting Cycle

Many lines of property–liability insurance, especially business insurance, historically have exhibited a cycle in premiums and insurer operating profits known as the **underwriting cycle.** The underwriting cycle can be described in terms of periodic soft and hard markets. Soft markets are characterized by numerous insurers seeking to write new coverage and by stable or even falling prices. Hard markets consist of reductions in the supply of coverage and sharp price increases. Many observers believe and some evidence suggests that the underwriting cycle causes actual premiums to fluctuate in a cyclical fashion around fair premium levels. Figure 6–5 illustrates a hypothetical cycle in the ratio of actual premiums to fair premiums.

Uncertainty associated with cyclical movements in insurance prices is a major concern to insurance consumers, especially business risk managers. We will discuss the ramifications and response to this uncertainty in Chapter 11. For now, we simply will describe the basic evidence on the underwriting cycle and discuss some possible explanations.

The underwriting cycle does not appear to be strongly related to the general business cycle. Until the 1980s, the insurance cycle appeared to regularly last about six years between hard markets. However, the last hard market, which primarily affected business liability insurance, occurred in 1985–1986. The preceding hard market occurred in 1974–1975. The long period between these hard markets and the lack of a hard market since 1986 has led some "cycle watchers" to proclaim that the underwriting cycle is dead.

One explanation for the underwriting cycle begins with the capital shock theory presented above. Large losses might cause capital to be depleted, which in turn causes premiums to rise above fair premiums and coverage to be reduced (the hard market). Subsequently, high prices during the hard market help to restore capital and new capital is raised. Both sources of capital increase industry supply and lower premiums (the soft market). If competition among insurers causes premiums to decline below fair premium levels, operating losses and reductions in capital will occur again, thus contributing to price increases and another hard market.

This explanation, however, does not make clear why competition would produce a persistent tendency for premiums to fall below fair premium levels (discounted expected claim costs, expenses, and normal profit levels) in soft markets. Some observers suggest that prices repeatedly tend to fall too low because of the difficulty in accurately forecasting claim costs for some types of insurance. One possible explanation is that some insurers charge inadequate prices due to overly optimistic forecasts of expected claim costs. Difficulty in accurately forecasting claim costs and thus in knowing whether an insurer's prices are adequate also makes it difficult for buyers and regulators to identify financially weak insurers. Some weak insurers could offer coverage at inadequate prices to generate cash to pay claims on previously sold policies and thereby delay being discovered and

FIGURE 6–5

Illustration of cycle in ratio of actual premiums to fair premiums

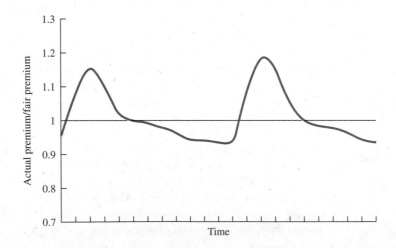

shut down by regulators. In either of these cases, inadequate prices by some companies could contribute to price cuts by other companies that wish to avoid losing their customers and the return on their investments in building a customer base.

In summary, there are various explanations for the underwriting cycle, but there is no consensus regarding why it has occurred or whether it still exists. Regardless of its explanation, corporate risk managers generally view the underwriting cycle as a disadvantage of purchasing insurance. The reason is that the cycle causes undesirable fluctuations in the availability and price of coverage from year to year.

6.7 Price Regulation

Government regulation of insurance prices assumes two major forms. First, many state governments regulate the size of changes in premium rates. Second, some state governments significantly restrict the type of information that can be used in risk classification. The first form of regulation governs changes in rate levels over time; the second form affects the magnitude of differences in rates across buyers within a given time period. There is a long history of both types of regulation in property–liability insurance. More recently, many states have begun to regulate rate changes and risk classification for health insurance sold to individuals and small businesses. The remainder of this chapter provides a broad overview of these types of regulation. Additional details are provided in later chapters that deal with particular types of insurance.

Regulation of Rate Changes

Until the 1960s, most property–liability insurers were essentially required to charge rates developed by insurer-controlled rating organizations (formerly known as rating bureaus). (The activities of these organizations and the insurance industry's limited antitrust exemption are discussed in Chapter 24.) These rates were subject to **prior approval laws,** which require regulators to approve rate changes proposed by the industry before new rates can be used. Beginning in the late 1960s, many states began to replace their prior approval laws with **competitive rating laws.** These laws generally require insurers to file rate changes with state insurance departments, but they do not require rate changes to be approved by regulators. Today, about one-half of the states have competitive rating laws for most types of property–liability insurance. An exception is workers' compensation insurance, for which a significant majority of states continue to make rate changes subject to prior approval. A number of states also require prior approval of some health insurance rates.

Why Regulate Rate Changes?   While it might surprise some of you, economists generally agree that the economic case for prior approval regulation of insurance rate changes is very weak. Most insurance markets have many insurers, the market shares of the major firms are relatively low compared to many major industries, and there has been ongoing entry by new firms in many states. These features and other evidence suggest substantial price competition and no danger of excessive profits due to monopoly power, although insurance industry critics often argue otherwise.

Most insurers supported the regulation of property–liability insurance rates (and rate classes) into the 1960s, ostensibly to foster stability and availability of coverage. Consumer pressure for rate regulation was modest at that time. Today, most insurers oppose rate regulation—at least when it creates a significant risk of inadequate rates. Periods of rapid growth in claim costs and associated increases in premiums for auto, workers' compensation, and health insurance since the 1960s often created strong consumer pressure for rate regulation to reduce and delay rate increases (also see Box 6–1). Rapid growth in both costs and premiums appears to make relying on market competition to keep rates in line with costs politically untenable.

Because insurance markets are competitive, efforts to lower overall rates through price regulation in response to consumer pressure are ultimately self-defeating. Unless prices would be higher than costs in the absence of regulation, the only way in which regulation can persistently lower rates without causing insurers to leave a market is by inducing insurers to restrict supply or to reduce quality in ways that lower the cost of providing coverage. Temporary suppression of rates with rate regulation can cause insurers to (1) suffer operating losses, (2) reduce supply, and (3) curtail investments that are necessary to support the sale of quality coverage. In addition, a significant risk that prior approval regulation might produce inadequate rates can increase the price needed by insurers to make investments in building their operations and meeting demand for coverage in a given state.

Effects of Regulating Rate Changes.   With the exception of workers' compensation, proposals for changes in business property–liability rates commonly are approved without modification. In contrast, regulators in a number of states frequently have not approved proposed rate increases for personal auto insurance, workers' compensation, and, to a lesser extent, homeowners insurance. When their requests are not approved, insurers often will submit a subsequent request for a lower increase that will be approved. In cases where agreement with regulators is not reached, insurers sometimes have challenged state regulators in court.

Numerous studies have estimated the effect of rate regulation on rate levels. This research suggests wide variation in its effect across states, types of insurance, and over time. Focusing on the last two decades, rate regulation appears to have had little effect on rate levels in some states and lines of insurance. In other states, regulation of auto and workers' compensation insurance rates has reduced, at least temporarily, the margin between premiums and claim costs. A few states (e.g., Massachusetts and New Jersey for auto insurance and Maine and Massachusetts for workers' compensation) were characterized by chronic suppression

------

Box 6–1

King Canute's Revenge? California's Proposition 103

The mythical King Canute commanded the tides to go back—without much success. A slight majority of California voters commanded property–liability insurance rates to be rolled back by enacting Proposition 103 in 1988, following a period of rapid growth in business liability and personal auto insurance claim costs and premiums. Among other features, Proposition 103 called for a mandatory 20 percent reduction in property–liability insurance rates and prior approval of subsequent rate increases. The California Supreme Court later held that the 20 percent rate cut was unconstitutional to the extent that it would deprive insurers of a fair rate of return on capital.

Were California voters more successful than King Canute? Following extensive hearings, court rulings, California Department of Insurance rulings, and more

hearings, a few insurers agreed to make refunds in the mid-1990s, based on insurance department rulings that their rates of return in 1988 exceeded the level deemed as fair by the department. Other insurers still are fighting rollback orders, arguing that the insurance department's methodology overstates their rates of return and understates fair rates of return.

In late 1997, a California consumer group that had advocated Proposition 103 and that was involved in much of the subsequent litigation filed suit against leading California auto insurers. The suit alleged that the insurers had achieved profits in the 1990s in excess of the amounts permitted by Proposition 103. Although the saga continues in California, the rate rollback movement never really caught on in other states.

---

of rate increases relative to growth in claim costs during much of the 1970s and 1980s. Significant numbers of insurers stopped selling auto or workers' compensation insurance in these states during this time.

Regulation of Rating Factors

Earlier in this chapter we discussed the effects of risk classification and noted that classification is often a controversial issue. We now discuss in more detail the debate over whether insurers should be allowed to charge higher premiums to those buyers perceived as having high expected claim costs. This debate has focused primarily on personal auto insurance and, in recent years, workers' compensation and personal and small business health insurance. Current issues include whether auto and health insurers should be able to base rates on age, sex, geographic region, health status or diagnostic tests for conditions such as AIDs (for health insurance), and credit history (for auto insurance). Some states have restricted either the types of information that personal auto insurers can use, or the right of insurers to reject applicants, or both. For example, a number of states do not allow personal auto insurers to base rates on the sex of the driver, and a few states require each insurer to accept almost all applicants for coverage. Several states have adopted community rating programs for health insurance that require insurers to offer coverage using risk classification plans that significantly limit differences in rates based on the applicant's age, sex, or health status. Some of the pressure for restricting risk classification undoubtedly arises because classification often produces high premiums that create significant affordability problems for some buyers.

The participants in the debate over insurance risk classification find it difficult to agree on much of anything, including whether competitive risk classification actually produces cost-based prices. It is nonetheless possible to provide an overview of the key issues.

Incentives for Risk Control.   As you learned earlier, charging higher premiums to insurance buyers with higher expected claim costs often helps reduce the cost of risk by providing higher risk individuals and businesses with a greater incentive to reduce losses. Lowering their premiums below expected costs would reduce this incentive and thereby increase the cost of risk. While it is generally difficult to measure how much the cost of risk changes due to cost-based insurance pricing, an important argument for allowing classification is that it does provide incentives to reduce the cost of risk.

Fairness, Imperfect Classification, and Control/Causality Issues.   Many people regard cost-based insurance prices as fundamentally fair; people with higher expected claim costs on average should pay higher premiums. Other people argue that the imperfections in cost-based pricing justify government intervention to improve fairness.

You learned earlier that, due to the costs associated with classifying policyholders, classification systems will not be perfect; that is, policyholders with different expected claim costs will be placed in the same risk class. Consequently, low risk buyers in a given rating class who cannot be identified at reasonable cost pay premiums that are too large given their unobservable but lower expected claim costs. High risk buyers in a given rating class who cannot be identified get subsidized. For example, the very safest teenage drivers must pay high rates because most teenage drivers have high expected claim costs even if they have clean driving records to date. The problem is that the safe teenage drivers cannot be distinguished (at low cost) from other teenagers and consequently these safe teenage drivers subsidize the other teenage drivers.

Some persons argue that it would be fairer to prevent classification based on age and instead spread the burden of the subsidy to high risk teenage drivers broadly across all age groups, rather than making the safe teenage drivers bear the entire burden. For example, suppose that the expected claim cost for teenage drivers with clean driving records as a group is $500, but that 20 percent of the individuals in this group (who cannot be identified) have an expected claim cost of $100 and 80 percent have an expected claim cost of $600 ($0.2 \times \$100 + 0.8 \times \$600 = \$500$). The argument against using age as a classification factor is that it is unfair to the teenagers with expected claim costs of $100 to pay $500 and thereby fully subsidize the high risk teenage drivers. Note that similar arguments can be used for other rating factors and types of insurance.

The counterargument is that preventing the use of a rating characteristic can increase the total subsidy to high risk buyers. Continuing with the example, suppose that the expected claim cost for drivers of other ages with clean driving records is $100 and that 10 percent of all drivers with clean records are teenage drivers. Then, if age cannot be used as a rating factor, all drivers with clean driving records would be charged $140, the average expected claim cost of all such drivers ($140 = 0.10 × $500 + 0.9 × $100). As a result, safe teenage drivers pay a much smaller subsidy to high risk teenage drivers, and drivers of other ages now pay an equal subsidy ($40). Notice, however, that the subsidy to high risk teenage drivers increases. Instead of being subsidized by only $100 ($600 − $500) with age as a rating factor, high risk teenage drivers receive a subsidy of $460 ($600 − $140) without age as a rating factor. Any adverse consequences on the behavior of high risk teenage drivers (see above) from not paying the premiums commensurate with their expected claim costs are likely to worsen.

Some people also argue that it is unfair to base rates on factors that are largely or completely beyond the control of the individual, such as age and sex, or, as sometimes is argued, where a person lives. Moreover, they object to these variables as only being proxies for higher expected claim costs, as opposed to measuring risky behavior directly. In addition, the use of uncontrollable factors in pricing often will have less impact on safety than basing rates on controllable factors. For example, auto insurance experience rating surcharges for accidents and tickets will likely do more to motivate young drivers to slow down than will basing premiums on age and sex. On the other hand, basing rates on uncontrollable factors still may help to significantly reduce the cost of risk by providing incentives to alter the level of risky activity or to reduce the value of property exposed to damage. For example, when young males pay higher rates in conjunction with their greater likelihood of accident involvement, fewer young males may buy cars, and those that do might on average buy less expensive vehicles. Both responses reduce the cost of risk.

Excessive Classification and Use of Subjective Assessments.   The possibility that classification costs could cause some forms of risk classification to increase the cost of risk implies that government restrictions on classification could improve societal welfare in some cases. However, much of the debate over rating factors has focused on factors that can be observed at low cost (e.g., age, sex, and geographic region). Classification using low cost information is likely to reduce the cost of risk.

A related issue is whether insurers use too much subjective judgment in underwriting and, if so, whether this use should be prohibited. No consensus exists as to what constitutes subjective judgment. Some people feel that basing rates on geographic region is subjective. Others would not go this far, but they would argue that employing information about factors such as a person's credit history or personal life (e.g., a recent divorce) is subjective and undesirable. The basic theory of competitive risk classification suggests that use of subjective judgment by an insurer will not be rewarded and could easily cause an insurer to lose money—

unless the judgment helps predict future losses, administrative costs, or the expected length of time that the policyholder will renew. Thus, insurers have no economic incentive to use information that does not improve predictions. There is substantial evidence that the major classification factors used by insurers help predict expected claim costs.

Concept Check

7. Subjective Life Insurance Company has a hunch that brown-eyed 25-year-old males are less likely to die young than blue-eyed 25-year-old males. The company decides to (a) lower rates to the brown-eyed buyers by an amount that will attract more of them but still produce a profit, and (b) raise rates to the blue-eyed group to cover the higher number of expected death claims. What will happen to Subjective Life if its hunch is wrong (i.e., if there is no difference in expected death rates based on eye color)?

Ensuring Availability When Regulation Depresses Rates

When the regulation of rate changes or risk classification lowers rates for some buyers below the levels needed to cover expected costs and produce a reasonable profit, insurers will not voluntarily sell coverage. Severe supply shortages under these circumstances are prevented by state **residual market** systems. These systems force insurers that write a given type of coverage in a state to collectively supply coverage to most if not all applicants. An insurer must participate in the residual market if it wants to sell coverage in the voluntary market.

All states have residual markets for auto insurance and workers' compensation insurance. Some states also have residual markets for other types of insurance, such as homeowners and health insurance. While residual market policies usually are issued and serviced by private insurers, the prices for these policies are regulated by the state. The prices often are regulated to be below the cost of supplying the coverage (i.e., below the fair premium). As a consequence, residual market business generally produces operating losses. Residual markets usually are designed so that these operating losses are divided among insurers writing the given coverage in proportion to their market share in the voluntary insurance market.

Residual markets originally developed as a market of last resort; that is, to make coverage available to small numbers of high risk applicants that otherwise would be uninsurable or face prohibitively high premiums. However, residual markets for auto and workers' compensation insurance periodically have become very large in some states during the past three decades. The major reason is that regulation of rate changes or risk classification has caused rates for many buyers to fall below levels needed by insurers to provide coverage voluntarily. You will learn more about residual markets for different types of insurance in later chapters.

6.8 Summary

- The fair premium is the premium that is just sufficient to fund an insurer's expected costs and provide insurance company owners with a fair return on their invested capital. The fair premium depends on (1) expected claim costs; (2) investment income that can be earned on premiums prior to the payment of claims and administrative costs; (3) administrative costs; and (4) the fair profit loading.

- Risk classification by insurers involves grouping together buyers with similar expected claim costs and charging them the same premium rate. Buyers in risk classes with higher expected claim costs are charged higher rates. Insurers have strong incentives to classify buyers based on all information that helps predict differences in claim costs across buyers, provided that the information can be obtained at a sufficiently low cost.

- Risk classification generally helps reduce the total cost of risk by providing insurance buyers with incentives to alter their behavior (in terms of precautions, amount of risky activity, and amount of insurance purchased) in ways that reduce the cost of risk.

- Given the ability of insurers to earn investment income on premiums prior to the payment of claims, the fair premium reflects the discounted value of expected claim costs. As a result, the fair premium is inversely related to the level of interest rates and to the length of the claims tail (i.e., the average lag between the time that coverage is sold and the time that claims are paid).

- The fair premium includes an expense loading to cover the insurer's administrative costs, including both underwriting expenses and loss adjustment expenses.

- The fair premium includes a profit loading to compensate investors for the disadvantages (e.g., double taxation of investment returns) of investing in an insurance company. Other things being equal, the fair profit loading is higher for lines of insurance with more uncertainty concerning future claim costs because the insurer needs to hold more capital to achieve a given probability of insolvency.

- Fair premiums are forward looking: They depend on expected future claim costs and administrative costs, as opposed to depending on whether the insurer made more or less money than expected in the past.

- If most insurers in a given market simultaneously experience very large capital shocks in the form of either losses on insurance contracts or investments, insurance premiums may increase temporarily by more than any increase in the discounted value of expected claim costs, administrative costs, and the normal fair profit loading. To the extent that this occurs, policyholders share the risk of very large, industrywide losses with insurers.

- Many lines of property–liability insurance have historically exhibited a cycle in premiums and insurer operating profits known as the underwriting cycle. Coverage is readily available and prices are stable and falling during soft market periods; coverage is comparatively scarce and prices increase sharply during hard market periods.

- Some states have prior approval laws that require insurers to obtain prior regulatory approval of rate changes for one or more lines of insurance; other states have competitive rating laws that allow insurers to change rates without prior approval. Some states have restricted the types of information that insurers can use in rate classification based on arguments that use of the information would either be unfair or make coverage unaffordable for some buyers.

- If regulation of rate changes or risk

classification lowers the premium that can be charged to some buyers below the fair premium, state residual markets for some types of

coverage prevent supply shortages by requiring insurers to collectively supply coverage to most if not all applicants.

Key Terms

fair premium   115
expected claim cost 116
adverse selection   117
cost-based prices   118
risk classification   118
cross-subsidy   119
class rate   123
underwriting   123
experience rating   123

discounted expected claim cost   126
expense loading   127
profit loading   129
capital shocks   130
underwriting cycle   133
prior approval laws   135
competitive rating laws   135
residual market   140

Questions and Problems

1. An insurer sells a very large number of policies to people with the following loss distribution:

$$\text{Loss} = \begin{array}{ll} \$\,50{,}000 & \text{with probability } 0.005 \\ \$\,30{,}000 & \text{with probability } 0.010 \\ \$\,10{,}000 & \text{with probability } 0.020 \\ \$\,\;5{,}000 & \text{with probability } 0.05 \\ \$\,\qquad 0 & \text{with probability } 0.915 \end{array}$$

(a) Calculate the expected claim cost per policy.

(b) Assume claims are paid one year after premiums are received and that the interest rate is 8 percent. Calculate the discounted expected claim cost per policy.

(c) Assume that the only administrative cost is the cost of processing an application (which equals $200 per policy) and that the fair profit loading is $100. What is the fair premium?

2. Redo problem 1, but include the expected cost of loss adjustment expenses (the cost of processing claims) assuming that loss

adjustment expenses equal 10 percent of losses and are paid at the same time that claims are paid.

3. Redo problem 1 with the following loss distribution:

$$\text{Loss} = \begin{array}{ll} \$1{,}000{,}000 & \text{with probability } 0.001 \\ \$\;\;500{,}000 & \text{with probability } 0.005 \\ \$\;\;100{,}000 & \text{with probability } 0.010 \\ \$\;\;\;\,50{,}000 & \text{with probability } 0.020 \\ \$\qquad\quad 0 & \text{with probability } 0.964 \end{array}$$

4. Suppose an insurer estimates that an exposure has the following loss distribution:

$$\text{Loss} = \begin{array}{ll} \$500{,}000 & \text{with probability } 0.01 \\ \$100{,}000 & \text{with probability } 0.02 \\ \$\;\,20{,}000 & \text{with probability } 0.03 \\ \$\qquad 0 & \text{with probability } 0.94 \end{array}$$

Claim payments are not expected to be paid until one year after the premium is received. If the interest rate is 10 percent, what is the discounted expected claim cost?

5. Redo problem 4 assuming a 12 percent interest rate.

6. Redo problem 4 assuming claim payments are not made until two years after the premium is received.

7. Based on your answers to problems 4 through 6, make general statements about the effect of interest rates and the claims tail on insurance premiums.

8. You have been hired to prepare a report examining whether gender should be outlawed as a rating factor for all insurance. Summarize your main arguments for and against.

9. Chapter 4 explained how fixed premium insurance contracts cause insurers to bear the risk that losses will be greater than expected. Explain why this might not be true if capital shocks affect insurance prices.

10. Given the existence of an underwriting cycle, when is the best time for individuals or businesses to have to buy insurance? When is the worst time?

References

Abraham, Kenneth. "Efficiency and Fairness in Insurance Risk Classification." *Virginia Law Review* 71 (1985), pp. 403–51. (*Provides a clear summary of fairness issues.*)

Cummins, J. David; Scott Harrington; and Robert Klein. "Cycles and Crises in Property/Casualty Insurance: A Background Discussion." *Journal of Insurance Regulation* 10 (Fall 1991), pp. 50–93. (*Summarizes theory and empirical evidence on capital shocks and the underwriting cycle.*)

D'Arcy, Stephen; and Neil Doherty. *The Financial Theory of Pricing Property–Liability Insurance Contracts.* S.S. Huebner Foundation Monograph No. 15. Homewood, IL: Richard D. Irwin, 1988. (*Provides an in-depth treatment of the theory of fair premiums.*)

Harrington, Scott; and Helen Doerpinghaus. "The Economics and Politics of Automobile Insurance Rate Classification." *Journal of Risk and Insurance* 60 (March 1993), pp. 59–84. (*Discusses possible effects on behavior, political pressure for restrictions on classification, and consequences of restrictions.*)

Answers to Concept Checks

1. Innovative could profit by reducing collision premiums for owners of heavier vehicles below levels offered by competitors in order to attract more of these owners and provide a substantial profit to the insurer. Innovative probably would increase premiums for owners of other types of vehicles to reflect their higher expected claim costs. Some of these other owners would switch to other insurers. Other insurers would experience a reduction in the proportion of their customers that own heavier vehicles and experience losses from adverse selection. (Note: Some recent data indicate that heavier vehicles cause more harm to drivers of other vehicles than do lighter vehicles. As a result, some insurers are raising *liability insurance* rates for owners of heavier vehicles and lowering liability insurance rates for owners of other vehicles. Thus, owners of heavier vehicles may pay lower collision insurance rates but higher liability insurance rates than owners of other vehicles.)

2. Innovative's customers that own heavier vehicles will be pleased; those that own other vehicles will not be happy if their rates are increased. Some of them will switch to other insurers unless other insurers also begin to base collision insurance premiums on vehicle weight.

3. Because their rates would decline, some 20-year-old males would be more likely to (a) buy a car, (b) buy a more expensive car, (c) buy an auto insurance policy with a lower deductible, and (d) reduce precautions while driving if they have lower deductibles or if experience rating charges for accidents and tickets are lower because of unisex rating. Total accident losses would increase because of (a), (b), and (d).

4. Other factors held constant, long-tailed lines will have lower premiums than short-tailed lines because the insurer will have more time to invest premiums before claims are paid (the discounted expected value of claim costs is lower).

5. The expected claim cost is $500. The discounted expected claim cost if claims are paid at the end of one year is $471.70 = $500/1.06. The discounted expected claim cost if claims are paid at the end of two years is $445 = $500/1.06^2.

6. Higher correlation for windstorm insurance claim costs across policyholders—as opposed to fire insurance claim costs—will require the insurer to hold more capital to achieve a given probability of solvency. Thus, the fair premium for windstorm insurance will be higher to compensate the insurer's investors for providing the higher amount of capital needed for windstorm coverage. (Note: In practice most property insurance policies that cover fire losses also cover windstorm losses. Fair premiums for policies that cover both fire and windstorm losses will be higher in geographic areas that are more prone to large windstorm losses because of (a) the higher expected claim costs from windstorms, and (b) the higher amount of capital needed to sell coverage in these areas.)

7. If the hunch that brown-eyed males are less likely to die young is wrong, Subjective Life will lose money. The insurer will attract brown-eyed males at premium rates that are inadequate to cover costs given that the insurer's hunch is incorrect; it will insure fewer blue-eyed males because of the higher premium rates charged to these buyers. As a result, Subjective Life's customer base will consist of a disproportionate number of brown-eyed males with inadequate premiums. Any profits on its blue-eyed customers will be insufficient to offset losses on its brown-eyed customers.

Risk Aversion and Risk Management by Individuals and Corporations

Chapter Objectives

- Describe what it means to be risk averse and why risk-averse individuals buy insurance.
- Explain the main factors affecting individuals' demand for insurance.
- Explain how business risk management differs from individual risk management.
- Explain how business risk reduction can benefit shareholders even when shareholders hold diversified portfolios of investments.

7.1 Risk Aversion and Demand for Insurance by Individuals

One objective of this section is to explain why individuals take actions to reduce risk, where risk is defined as uncertainty in the outcomes facing an individual. This objective may sound trivial. You may be thinking: People reduce risk because they do not like risk; that is, they are risk averse—end of discussion! While this reasoning is essentially correct, this section provides additional insight into risk aversion and explains why individuals may purchase insurance in some circumstances and not others. Many of these insights about individual demand for insurance are important in later chapters where we discuss public policy issues related to insurance.

The Effects of Insurance on Wealth

To show why people often take actions to reduce risk (e.g., by buying insurance), we first describe an insurance transaction from an individual's point of view. This perspective probably will differ from the way that you have previously thought about insurance (assuming you have thought about it at all). Suppose that Mr.

145

Grace is faced with the possibility of being sued and held liable for damages this coming year as a result of a car accident. Assume that the probability of being sued successfully by a plaintiff is 0.5. (Mr. Grace probably is a more reckless driver than you are.) For simplicity, assume that the payment to a successful plaintiff is $20,000 and ignore defense costs. Finally, assume that Mr. Grace will have $100,000 at the end of the year if he is not sued.

Without insurance, Mr. Grace's wealth at the end of the year is uncertain: It either will be $100,000 or $80,000, depending on whether he loses a lawsuit. Using different terminology, Mr. Grace is faced with two possible outcomes for his wealth, and he does not know which outcome will occur. Given that the probability of a loss is 0.5, Mr. Grace's expected level of wealth at the end of the year is $90,000 ($100,000 × 0.5 + $80,000 × 0.5). His actual wealth will be either $10,000 above the expected outcome or $10,000 below the expected outcome. Thus, there is variability around the expected value.

Consider what happens if Mr. Grace purchases $10,000 of liability insurance coverage at a price of $5,000, where the premium is paid at the end of the year so that we can ignore the time value of money and thereby simplify the calculations. Note that the premium is equal to the insurer's expected claim costs ($5,000 = 0.5 × $10,000). Thus, we also are ignoring for simplicity the other factors (administrative costs and capital costs) discussed in Chapter 6 that affect the fair premium.

With insurance, if Mr. Grace does not have a loss, his wealth will be $95,000 ($100,000 minus the premium). On the other hand, if Mr. Grace has a loss, his wealth will be $85,000 ($80,000 minus the premium of $5,000 plus the $10,000 reimbursement from the insurer). Figure 7–1 illustrates the key point that the purchase of insurance reduces wealth when no losses occur, but increases wealth when losses do occur. By purchasing this insurance contract, Mr. Grace narrows the range of possible wealth outcomes; he reduces the variability (standard deviation) of wealth around the expected level of wealth.

Suppose instead that Mr. Grace purchases $20,000 of coverage, which is full insurance coverage since the severity of the loss equals $20,000. As before, we assume that the premium equals expected claim costs, or $10,000. With this higher level of coverage and higher premium, if a loss does not occur, Mr. Grace has wealth of $90,000 ($100,000 minus the $10,000 premium). If a loss does occur, he also has wealth of $90,000 ($80,000 minus the insurance premium of

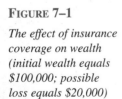

FIGURE 7–1

The effect of insurance coverage on wealth (initial wealth equals $100,000; possible loss equals $20,000)

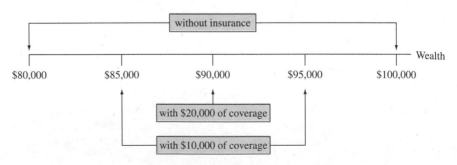

$10,000 plus the reimbursement from the insurer of $20,000). Full coverage implies that wealth is the same regardless of whether the loss occurs. Assuming that there are no uncompensated losses associated with the lawsuit, such as time away from work or aggravation, Mr. Grace would not care whether he is sued or not. His risk has been eliminated.

In summary, this example demonstrates that by purchasing insurance Mr. Grace increases his wealth if a loss occurs and reduces his wealth if a loss does not occur. The increase in wealth if a loss occurs can be viewed as the *benefit* of insurance and the reduction in wealth if a loss does not occur can be viewed as the *cost* of insurance. This perspective is a useful way to think about insurance decisions. By purchasing auto insurance, for example, you reduce your wealth if you do not have an accident over the policy period, but you increase your wealth if you do have a serious accident. If a parent purchases life insurance on a child's life, the parent reduces the amount of money available when the child is alive but increases the amount of money available if the child dies.[1]

While the amount of insurance coverage that people purchase depends on several factors to be discussed below (e.g., the price of coverage and the buyer's income), this discussion indicates that one of the factors affecting insurance purchases is a person's preference for when he or she would rather have more money. Does a person prefer more money following a loss, or does a person prefer to have more money when the loss does not occur? Although people would prefer more money in both cases, this is not possible. To receive additional money following a loss, a person must decrease wealth when a loss does not occur. Most people are willing to give up some money when a loss does not occur (pay an insurance premium) in order to receive additional money from the insurer after a financial loss. In essence, the payment of the premium when a loss does not occur hurts individuals less than the benefit that individuals receive from having the insurer pay part of the loss. The reason is that money is more valuable to a person when the person has less of it and a monetary loss causes people to have less money.

Risk Aversion

The issue of when money is more valuable to a person is related to the concept of risk aversion. Technically, a person who is **risk averse** prefers a certain amount of wealth to a risky situation that yields the same expected wealth. For example, suppose that Mr. Grace is asked whether he would accept a 50–50 chance of winning $1,000 and losing $1,000. The expected value of the gamble is $0 (0.5 × $1,000 + 0.5 × –$1,000); thus, the gamble does not change his expected wealth. If Mr. Grace were risk averse he would not accept the gamble, because the risk

---

[1] While the perspective that purchasing insurance reduces wealth when a loss does not occur and increases wealth when a loss does occur is useful for many purposes, this perspective does not apply to situations when insurance covers losses that can be less than the premium, because it is then possible for insurance to reduce wealth if there is a small loss.

(uncertainty) created by the gamble makes him worse off. Note that Mr. Grace's aversion to risk implies that the possible loss of $1,000 hurts him more than the possible gain of $1,000 benefits him. This is the essence of risk aversion. People are averse to risk because a loss of $X hurts them more than a gain of $X benefits them.

In order for Mr. Grace to accept the gamble he would need to be compensated for the risk created by the gamble. Suppose that he would only accept the gamble if the odds were changed so that there was a 60 percent chance of winning $1,000 and a 40 percent chance of losing $1,000. Then, the gamble would increase his expected wealth by $200 ($1,000 × 0.6 – $1,000 × 0.4). The $200 in additional expected wealth is the *risk premium* required to induce Mr. Grace to accept the gamble. All else being equal, people who are more risk averse will require a higher risk premium to induce them to accept risk.

In contrast, if Mr. Grace were risk neutral, he would be indifferent between accepting the original gamble and rejecting the gamble. The reason is that the gamble does not change his expected wealth and the uncertainty created by the gamble does not bother him. In other words, a person who is **risk neutral** cares only about expected wealth. A risk-neutral person therefore would not require a risk premium to accept risk.

These examples illustrate that risk-averse people require a risk premium to accept risk. Similarly, risk-averse people are willing to pay a risk premium to reduce risk. Suppose for example that Mr. Phillips has a 2 percent chance of losing $10,000. Then his expected loss is $200 (0.02 × $10,000). If Mr. Phillips were risk averse, he would be willing to pay more than $200 to eliminate the risk. However, if Mr. Phillips is risk neutral, the most he would pay to eliminate the risk is $200.

Risk aversion appears to be a characteristic of most people as evidenced by their behavior when faced with risky scenarios. Most people are willing to pay insurance premiums in excess of expected claim costs for insurance; that is, they are willing to pay a risk premium. Also, most people require additional compensation to induce them to accept or take on risk. For example, people require higher expected returns to induce them to invest in common stocks rather than government bonds, because stocks have greater risk. The appendix to this chapter provides additional analysis relating to risk aversion.

Other Factors Affecting an Individual's Demand for Insurance

The previous section showed that risk aversion is the fundamental force that induces people to purchase insurance. This section expands on the analysis of individual demand for insurance by explaining some of the other factors that influence people's decisions about insurance purchases.

Premium Loading.   Although risk-averse people generally desire insurance, the extent to which they will purchase insurance depends on the policy's premium loading. Recall from Chapter 6 that the premium on an insurance policy equals expected claim costs plus a loading for administrative and capital costs.[2] If the loading is zero, then purchasing insurance does not change a person's expected wealth, because the premium equals the expected payments from the insurer. Since insurance with a zero loading does not change expected wealth but reduces the variability of wealth, a risk-averse person will purchase full insurance coverage if the policy has a zero loading.

Unfortunately, the premium loading is rarely zero because insurers must be compensated for their costs. A positive loading implies that the policyholder pays a premium in excess of the expected payments from the insurer. As discussed in the previous section, a risk-averse person may be willing to pay this additional amount (the positive loading) because insurance reduces risk. However, the amount of coverage that risk-averse people will purchase generally will decline as the loading on the policy increases. That is, the demand for insurance follows the fundamental economic principle that the quantity demanded decreases as the price increases. (Price in this context refers to the policy's loading.) In the extreme, if the loading on an insurance policy is too high, then people will not purchase insurance.

Income and Wealth.   Income and wealth can influence a person's demand for insurance for at least four reasons. First, having more wealth usually is associated with having more assets subject to loss, which typically will increase the total amount of insurance purchased. Second, some people simply do not have sufficient income to afford large amounts of insurance coverage. The necessities of life (food and shelter) may exhaust a person's income. Consequently, very poor people are likely to bear more risk (insure less). Third, the degree of risk aversion may decline as a person's wealth increases. For example, a person with $20,000 of wealth is likely to be more willing to insure against the possibility of losing $10,000 than a person with $1 million in wealth. Fourth, limited liability often induces people with little wealth to purchase relatively little insurance against liability risk. Most legal systems give individuals the ability to declare bankruptcy and thus be shielded from debts that cannot be paid from their existing wealth. This feature, known as limited liability, can reduce the demand for liability insurance by people with low levels of wealth, because it limits the loss a person can suffer from a liability suit.

An example helps illustrate the effect of limited liability. Suppose that Ms. Ambrose has wealth of $5,000 and a 0.005 probability of causing $100,000 of damages to another person as a result of driving an automobile. If Ms. Ambrose purchased insurance to cover the entire loss to potential victims, she would need to purchase $100,000 of coverage. Ignoring any loading and investment income, the fair premium would be $500 (0.005 × $100,000). The benefit received by Ms. Ambrose from this policy is the protection of her wealth. Since she has only $5,000, she perceives the expected benefit as $5,000 × 0.005, which is only $25.

---

[2] For simplicity, we ignore the time value of money in this discussion—that is, that the premium depends on the discounted value of expected costs.

From Ms. Ambrose's perspective, this insurance policy is extremely high priced; she has to pay $500 to cover an expected loss of $25, which she is unlikely to do voluntarily. The failure of individuals to buy auto liability coverage has influenced the adoption of compulsory insurance laws in most states. You will learn more about this issue in Chapter 21. We discuss the implications of limited liability for business risk management in detail in Chapter 17.

Information.   The demand for insurance will depend on the information that the individual has about the loss distribution. For example, if an individual does not perceive that a loss is possible, the person will not purchase insurance unless forced to do so. More generally, if an individual perceives that the expected loss is lower than the amount perceived by the insurer, the individual will demand less insurance than a person who has the same probability assessment as the insurer. The reason is simple. As you learned in previous chapters, the insurer will price the policy based on its expectation of claim costs. If an individual has a lower estimate of expected claim costs than the insurer, the policy will appear to have a high loading, and the individual will demand less insurance. The opposite situation also can occur. Overestimation of expected claim costs compared to the insurer will induce the individual to purchase more coverage.

This discussion of the effect of information on the demand for insurance assumes that both the policyholder and the insurer view their information as correct and place no weight on the other party's information. The implications of different information are more complicated when one party (e.g., the policyholder) is better informed about expected losses than the other party (the insurer) and the other party knows that its information is inferior. These situations lead to adverse selection problems, which were discussed in Chapter 6 and will play an important role in subsequent chapters.

Other Sources of Indemnity.   When deciding whether to purchase insurance, a person will consider whether there are other sources of payment (indemnity). Consider the decision to purchase property insurance that will cover windstorm damage from hurricanes. An individual may expect that if a catastrophe occurs the government (society) will provide some compensation for losses that are suffered (e.g., through disaster relief). The availability of these payments in essence constitutes implicit insurance, which can reduce the demand for explicit coverage. The individual is not charged directly for this implicit insurance (taxpayers will foot the bill), but the person has to pay the premium for explicit insurance. A similar situation can arise with respect to the purchase of health insurance—if a person thinks that society will pay some of his or her medical costs, then the demand for health insurance will be reduced. We discuss these issues in more detail in Chapters 18 and 22.

Nonmonetary Losses.   Most of our discussion has been concerned with situations where people suffer monetary losses. However, people can experience **non-**

monetary losses as well as monetary losses (e.g., pain and suffering from physical injuries and grief when a loved one dies). People generally do not purchase insurance against nonmonetary losses for reasons discussed below. However, insurance against nonmonetary losses often is provided implicitly by the court system (and by liability insurance) when injured parties receive compensation for pain and suffering. For example, by forcing lawnmower manufacturers to compensate people who are injured using their products, the court system essentially makes lawnmower manufacturers provide insurance to their customers. Customers pay for this insurance in the form of higher lawnmower prices. If the court system makes lawnmower manufacturers compensate customers for pain and suffering, then the court system makes customers purchase this type of insurance. Thus, it is useful to consider whether people really would want to purchase insurance against nonmonetary losses, such as pain and suffering.

The demand for insurance coverage against nonmonetary losses differs fundamentally from the demand for insurance against monetary losses. To provide some intuition for why this is true, recall why people buy insurance against monetary losses: They demand insurance against monetary losses because the payment from the insurer following a loss benefits them more than they are hurt by the foregone income from paying the insurance premium when a loss does not occur. This is because money is more valuable to risk-averse people when they have less of it. In contrast, a purely nonmonetary loss (e.g., pain) does not lower a person's wealth. Thus, the fundamental reason why people buy insurance to cover monetary losses—money means more to them when they have less of it—does not apply to purely nonmonetary losses.

Wealth is not lower when a purely nonmonetary loss occurs or when the person has been compensated for any monetary loss associated with the nonmonetary loss. As a result, the demand for insurance against nonmonetary losses depends on different factors, such as whether the person values money more following a purely nonmonetary loss than without such a loss. The key point is that many people probably would not be willing to pay even the expected claim cost for insurance against some types nonmonetary losses, even though they would be willing to pay a risk premium to insure against monetary losses.[3] Thus, it would be incorrect to assume that people automatically would want to insure against nonmonetary losses.

One example of when private insurance could be purchased against nonmonetary losses is life insurance on a child. Ignoring the cost of funerals, the loss of a child typically does not cause a monetary loss, but it does cause a huge non-

---

[3] Specifically, the basic theory of insurance demand predicts that a purely nonmonetary loss only will be insured if the person values money more following a purely nonmonetary loss. In this case, insuring the loss produces an increase in income when money is more valuable and decreases income (because of the premium) when money is less valuable. In contrast, many persons argue and some evidence suggests that money often is less valuable after a purely nonmonetary loss so that these losses will not be insured. We return to this issue in Chapter 14.

monetary loss (for most parents). Ignoring tax reasons for purchasing life insurance on children, most parents do not voluntarily purchase insurance to compensate them for nonmonetary loss if a child would die. This is because the parents prefer not to give up money when their children are alive to receive additional money if they should die. Note, however, that even if people do not purchase insurance against nonmonetary losses, they often will engage in loss control to reduce expected nonmonetary losses. For example, parents who do not purchase life insurance on their children often will spend considerable resources to reduce the probability of them dying (e.g., putting a fence in the backyard to prevent them from falling into a neighbor's unfenced swimming pool, and buying safer cars).

Concept Checks

1. Using the following scenario, describe why a risk-averse person would purchase insurance.

   Loss = $5,000 with probability 0.1 and $0 with probability 0.9.

   Premium for full coverage = $500

2. Why might we observe wealthier people purchasing more insurance?

3. Why might we observe wealthier people purchasing less insurance?

7.2 Business Risk Management and Demand for Insurance

Even though businesses are owned by individuals, business risk management may differ in fundamental ways from individual risk management. The reason is that businesses often are organized in a way that allows business owners to diversify business risk on their own. This section explains when and why this distinction between individual and business risk management is relevant.

Shareholder Diversification

Recall from Chapter 3 how diversification reduces risk to individuals. Because risk reduction through diversification is desirable to risk-averse individuals, many institutions have developed to reduce the cost of diversification. Chapter 4 explained how insurance companies allow individuals to diversify risk at low cost. The stock market is another institution that allows individuals to diversify risk.

To see how stock markets can diversify risk, consider the risk that Ms. Butler would bear if she started her own business, called Butler Incorporated. Suppose that $100,000 is needed to begin operations and that Ms. Butler has just enough savings to pay the start-up costs. The problem with Ms. Butler using all of her savings for this new business is that she bears substantial risk. She might make a lot of money, or she could lose her entire wealth. Specifically, assume for simplicity that at the end of the year there is a 95 percent chance that Ms. Butler's business will be worth $150,000 and a 5 percent chance that it will be worth $0, where the latter outcome would occur if her facility blows up.

An alternative way for Ms. Butler to pay the start-up costs would be to issue stock to investors. By issuing stock, many individuals could contribute small amounts of money to start the business. Ms. Butler also could contribute a small portion of her wealth to the new business. For example, if 20 investors (including Ms. Butler) each contributed $5,000, then sufficient funds would be generated to start the business. Ms. Butler would have to share the returns from the business with the other investors. Each investor (including Ms. Butler) would receive 1/20th of the firm's profits.[4] The benefit of issuing stock, however, is that Ms. Butler shares the risk associated with her business with the other 19 investors. If the plant blows up, then all 20 investors share in the loss.

By issuing the stock, Ms. Butler can take the $95,000 not invested in her company and invest it in other companies, which will reduce her risk relative to the case where she invested all her wealth in Butler Inc. To illustrate how Ms. Butler reduces her risk by investing her wealth in a number of different companies, suppose there are 20 new businesses that are going to be created and that each one requires an initial investment of $100,000. Also assume that each business has the same probability distribution for value as Butler Inc. Further assume that the outcome for each business is independent of the outcomes for the other businesses.

If Ms. Butler (and the other entrepreneurs) invest $5,000 in each of the 20 businesses, then each one will own 1/20th of the stock of each business. In essence, each entrepreneur has entered into a pooling arrangement with the other entrepreneurs that involves equal sharing of profits and losses. This pooling arrangement is similar to the pooling arrangements discussed in Chapter 3 between Emily, Samantha, and their friends, where each person had the potential for a loss and all members of the pooling arrangement agreed to pay an equal share of the total losses. Recall that because losses were independent, risk was reduced for each member of the pooling arrangement relative to the situation where each paid his or her own loss. Similarly, each entrepreneur's risk is reduced by holding 1/20th of the stock of each company, as opposed to being a sole owner.

This example illustrates that stock markets allow business risk to be pooled, just as insurance companies allow certain types of risk to be pooled. Corporate insurance contracts and shareholder diversification are alternative mechanisms for diversifying pure risk for shareholders. That is, both mechanisms reduce the variability (risk) in shareholders' returns that arises because of pure risk.[5] More generally, any corporate activities that reduce the variability of corporate cash

---

[4] Not being the sole owner, we would expect Ms. Butler also to receive a salary as manager of the business.

[5] The effect of stock portfolio diversification on risk is just like the effect of pooling arrangements. As discussed in Chapter 4, fixed premium insurance contracts can reduce risk more than pooling arrangements. Similarly, fixed premium corporate insurance purchases can reduce risk more than investors can achieve through portfolio diversification. This technical point does not diminish the importance of portfolio diversification as a means of reducing the risk borne by the owners of corporations.

flows will not necessarily reduce shareholders' risk, because shareholders already may have diversified away the risk.

Since individual portfolio diversification and corporate insurance purchases are close substitutes for the purpose of reducing shareholders' risk, it is necessary to consider which mechanism has lower expected cost. The cost of diversifying through the stock market is the cost to shareholders of obtaining a diversified portfolio. With mutual funds, it is easy for an individual to spread even a modest amount of money across many stocks. The cost of buying into a mutual fund typically is not higher than the transaction cost of buying just one stock. In other words, the marginal cost to hold a diversified portfolio typically is close to zero.[6]

Recall that insurance contracts must be priced to include a loading for insurers' administrative and capital costs. Typical loadings range from about 10 percent to 50 percent of the premium, depending on the line of insurance and the amount of coverage. Why would diversified owners be willing to pay a positive loading for insurance (pay more than expected claim costs) when the insurance does not materially reduce their risk? We will answer this question shortly; for now simply note that corporate purchases of insurance often will increase a firm's value even when shareholders are diversified.

Concept Checks

4. True or false: Business insurance purchases do not reduce shareholders' risk significantly if shareholders hold diversified portfolios.

5. True or false: Shareholder diversification implies that business insurance purchases are contrary to shareholders' interests.

Closely Held Businesses

Even though stock markets allow business risk to be diversified, it is important to emphasize that the risk borne by a particular individual investing in the stock market depends on the proportion of his or her wealth that is invested in each stock. As we discussed above, if Ms. Butler invests all of her wealth ($100,000) in Butler Incorporated, she bears significant risk. On the other hand, she could invest $5,000 in Butler Incorporated and $95,000 in other businesses, thus spreading her wealth across many firms and creating a diversified portfolio. By holding a diversified portfolio, she reduces her risk without necessarily sacrificing expected return.

If the owners of a business are not well diversified, business insurance purchases will reduce the owners' risk. This reduction in risk is potentially an im-

---

[6] There are, however, other potential costs of diversifying through the stock market. For example, if Ms. Butler diversifies, then she has less incentive to operate her business to the best of her ability. Similarly, she will be concerned that the managers of the other businesses in which she invested will not manage efficiently. These moral hazard problems are an additional cost of diversification through stock markets. Note, however, that insurance markets also have moral hazard problems, the implications of which will be discussed in Chapter 8.

portant benefit of business insurance. Just as our discussion of individual risk management indicated that individual insurance is beneficial to risk-averse people, business insurance is beneficial to risk-averse owners that are not diversified. Thus, most small businesses and most privately held businesses will find that business insurance is beneficial because it reduces the owners' risk.

Why Purchase Insurance When Shareholders Are Diversified?[7]

The previous sections highlighted the fact that corporate activities that reduce the variability of the firm's cash flows (such as purchasing insurance) do not necessarily reduce shareholders' risk, because shareholders already may have diversified away the risk by holding a diversified portfolio. We noted, however, that corporate insurance purchases can nonetheless be beneficial to shareholders. These benefits arise because insurance has indirect effects that cause a firm's expected cash flows to increase. In particular, this section briefly and intuitively explains how business insurance purchases can (1) provide an efficient method of purchasing claims processing and loss control services; (2) reduce the expected cost of financing losses; (3) reduce the likelihood that the firm will have to raise costly external capital for new investment projects and thereby increase the likelihood that it will adopt good investment projects; (4) reduce the likelihood of financial distress and thereby improve the terms at which the firm will be able to contract with other claimants, such as employees, suppliers, lenders, and customers; and (5) reduce expected tax payments. Chapter 9 provides a more in-depth analysis of these effects.

Insurer Services.   A portion of an insurance policy's loading covers the insurer's cost of providing services to policyholders, such as claims processing and loss control, that a firm would have to undertake or purchase elsewhere if it did not purchase insurance. If the loading were less than the firm's cost of obtaining comparable services, then purchasing insurance would benefit shareholders even if they were diversified. In this case, however, the firm would not be purchasing insurance to reduce risk for shareholders but to obtain claims processing and loss control services at the lowest cost.[8]

---

[7] Although this section focuses on corporate insurance, the arguments generally apply to other corporate activities that reduce risk, with the exception of the services provided by insurers.

[8] In some cases it may be more efficient (lower cost) to bundle claims processing and loss control services with the financial responsibility of paying losses, because by doing so, the service provider has greater incentive to provide high quality service. For example, a firm that provides loss control services that also must pay losses has an additional incentive to identify and undertake cost-effective loss control measures. A firm that provides claims processing services that also must pay losses has an additional incentive to identify fraudulent claims. If the service and financial responsibility are not bundled, then a firm must expend some resources monitoring the service providers or alternatively design a contract that provides proper incentives. When monitoring is too costly and contract design efforts ineffective, bundling the services with financial responsibility for paying losses can be the least costly method of obtaining services.

Reducing the Expected Cost of Financing Losses.   The failure to reduce risk implies that there is a greater likelihood of large losses that must be paid either from the firm's internal funds or, if internal funds are not available, by raising new funds through borrowing or issuing new securities. Significant costs can be incurred if new securities have to be issued.[9] Thus, firms that are not likely to have the internal funds to finance losses might prefer to purchase insurance to reduce the likelihood of incurring the costs associated with issuing new securities to pay for losses.

Reducing Financing Costs for New Investment Opportunities.   Another reason for reducing risk (e.g., by purchasing insurance) is to increase the likelihood that the firm will have sufficient internal funds to adopt new investment projects. Without insurance, the firm's internal funds could be used to pay losses that occur, in which case the firm will have to raise new funds to pay for new investment projects. But since external funds generally are more costly than internal funds (see footnote 9), their use reduces the profitability of new investment projects net of financing costs. In some cases, the additional costs from raising external funds can cause the firm to pass up new investment projects that would have been profitable had the firm had the internal resources to pay for the project. By purchasing insurance to cover losses, a firm can reduce the likelihood that costly external capital will be needed for new investment opportunities and thereby increase the profitability of new projects (net of financing costs).

Reducing the Likelihood of Financial Distress and Improving Contractual Terms.   If a firm does not have the internal funds to pay losses that occur and cannot convince banks or investors to provide new funds, then it will be forced into bankruptcy. When this occurs, the firm either must liquidate or reorganize so that it can continue to operate. Reorganization can take place under Chapter 11 of the federal bankruptcy code or outside of bankruptcy in what commonly is called a "workout." Substantial legal costs can be incurred when a firm liquidates or reorganizes. By reducing the probability of bankruptcy, a firm reduces the likelihood of incurring these costs. Thus, risk reduction that protects a firm from large losses and therefore reduces the likelihood of bankruptcy can benefit shareholders by reducing the likelihood of incurring these bankruptcy costs.

When a firm is in financial distress (either in bankruptcy or close to bankruptcy), other claimants besides shareholders typically are harmed. To illustrate, consider the plight of banks and investors who have lent money to a firm that now finds itself in financial distress. In an effort to receive the money that they were

---

[9] Raising capital by issuing new securities is costly for several reasons. First, there are explicit costs, such as investment banker fees, associated with issuing new securities. Second, there are legal and regulatory costs associated with filing appropriate documents. Finally, there are implicit costs associated with selling new securities if the new securities are priced below their true value. Underpricing is more likely to occur if investors view themselves as having less information about the true value of the new securities than managers have. To protect themselves from paying too high a price, investors may lower the price they are willing to pay for new issues.

promised, these lenders will incur legal costs.[10] As a result of these costs, lenders will demand compensation for investing in a firm with a high probability of financial distress. Consequently, if a firm can reduce its risk, say through insurance, lenders will be willing to contract with the firm at better terms. One benefit of risk reduction from the shareholders' perspective therefore is that it can improve the terms at which the firm can borrow money.

Employees, suppliers, and customers also incur costs when their relationships with a firm are interrupted due to financial distress. For example, employees who are laid off incur costs while being out of work and customers incur costs if their products are not serviced. In addition, risk-averse individuals and closely held suppliers will require compensation (a risk premium) for the uncertainty associated with receiving their promised payments. As a result, employees, suppliers, and customers will demand compensation when contracting with a firm with a high probability of financial distress. Employees, for example, will demand higher compensation from a firm that has a greater likelihood of distress. Similarly, customers will pay lower prices to a firm with a higher probability of not being around to service its products. When product prices and input prices reflect the expected costs imposed by financial distress, then the firm's shareholders can benefit by reducing the probability of distress because doing so increases product prices and decreases input prices.

Reducing Expected Tax Payments.   Another reason risk reduction can benefit diversified shareholders is that it can reduce expected tax payments when corporate tax rates are progressive. Progressivity in tax rates implies that tax rates increase as a firm makes higher profits. For example, if profits up to $100,000 were taxed at a 20 percent tax rate and profits above $100,000 were taxed at a 30 percent tax rate, then tax rates would be progressive. Although the details of the corporate tax code in practice are complex, corporate taxes are in effect progressive. Operating profits generally are taxed at a 34 percent rate; operating losses (negative profits) may not be fully deductible against past and future profits. It can be shown that with progressivity in tax rates firms can lower the expected value of taxes paid by reducing variability in their profits (see Chapter 10). The advantage of insurance when taxes are progressive is analogous to our earlier discussion of insurance demand by risk-averse individuals. Insurance allows risk-averse individuals to obtain money following a loss, when money is more valuable because they have less of it. Likewise, insurance allows businesses to obtain money following a loss, when money is more valuable (in part) because it is subject to a lower effective tax rate.

Insurance purchases also can reduce expected tax payments for three other reasons, which are analyzed in some detail in Chapter 10. One tax benefit arises because insurance companies are taxed differently than noninsurance companies.

---

[10] Also, if managers are acting in the shareholders' interests, managers will have incentives either to adopt bad investment projects or fail to adopt some good investment projects, which would reduce the expected payments to lenders (see Chapter 9).

The difference allows insurers to deduct loss payments earlier than noninsurance firms, which lowers the present value of expected tax payments. Assuming that part of the value of this benefit is passed on to the policyholder, firms will have an incentive to purchase insurance. Another tax benefit arises from the tax treatment of depreciated property. Finally, reducing risk through insurance can allow a firm to borrow more than otherwise would be possible, which increases the tax shield from interest payments.

7.3 Summary

- Risk aversion is the major underlying force that motivates most individuals to purchase insurance even though insurance premiums exceed expected claim costs.

- Individuals' demand for insurance depends on (1) the premium loading; (2) a person's income and wealth; (3) an individual's information about expected losses relative to the insurer's information; (4) the availability of other sources of indemnity, such as government assistance; and (5) the nature of losses (monetary versus nonmonetary).

- One of the fundamental functions of the stock market is to allow investors in corporations to diversify risk. Thus, stock markets and insurance companies are similar in this regard.

- When shareholders are well diversified, corporate activities to reduce the variability in cash flows due to pure risk are largely redundant from the perspective of the shareholders, who already have reduced their risk by diversification.

- When shareholders are well diversified, corporate insurance still can benefit shareholders by (1) reducing the costs of purchasing claims processing and loss control services; (2) reducing the expected cost of financing losses; (3) reducing the likelihood that the firm will have to raise costly external capital for new investment projects and thereby increasing the likelihood that it will adopt good investment projects; (4) reducing the likelihood of incurring bankruptcy costs and thereby improving the terms at which the firm contracts with other claimants, such as employees, suppliers, lenders, and customers; and (5) reducing expected tax payments.

Key Terms

risk averse   147
risk neutral   148

nonmonetary losses   150

Questions and Problems

1. What are the possible wealth outcomes for a person with $10,000 in wealth who faces a 5 percent chance of losing $5,000 under each of the following insurance policies?

   (*a*) $2,500 of coverage; premium = $125.
   (*b*) $2,500 of coverage; premium = $175.
   (*c*) $5,000 of coverage; premium = $250.
   (*d*) $5,000 of coverage; premium = $325.

2. Would a risk-averse person necessarily purchase policy (*c*) in the previous question? Would a risk-averse person necessarily purchase policy (*d*)?

3. Poor people often do not purchase liability insurance. What are some of the explanations?

4. Suppose that a liability insurance policy with a coverage limit of $100,000 (i.e., the insurer will pay liability claims up to $100,000) has a premium of $500. For each of the following people, what is the premium per dollar of personal wealth protected if the policy were purchased?

Person	Person's Wealth
Mary	$ 5,000
Curly	$ 50,000
Moe	$ 100,000
Alice	$ 150,000
Nancy	$ 200,000

5. Suppose that Skipper's insurer views him as having the following distribution for the present value of losses:

$$\text{Loss} = \begin{array}{l} \$\,20,000 \text{ with probability } 0.01 \\ \$\ \ 5,000 \text{ with probability } 0.05 \\ \$\ \ 1,000 \text{ with probability } 0.10 \\ \$\ \ \ \ \ \ \ 0 \text{ with probability } 0.84 \end{array}$$

(*a*) What is the fair premium for full coverage if the competitive loading (administrative costs and capital costs) equals 15 percent of expected claim costs?

(*b*) Suppose that Skipper believes his probabilities of losses are one-half of what the insurer believes. What is the loading on the policy from Skipper's perspective?

6. Intuitively explain why corporate actions to reduce variability in cash flows may be redundant from the perspective of diversified shareholders.

7. Intuitively explain how the absence of insurance can cause a firm to forego good investment projects.

8. Suppose that a business expects to have profits of $100,000 if it is not sued over the coming year. The probability of a suit is 0.05 and the loss if a suit occurs is $200,000. The firm's tax rate if it earns positive profits is 30 percent. If it makes negative profits, it pays a 0 percent rate.

(*a*) What is the firm's before-tax expected profit without insurance? What is its after-tax expected profit without insurance?

(*b*) Suppose the firm can purchase a liability insurance policy with full coverage for a premium of $11,000. From the insurer's point of view, does this policy have a positive loading?

(*c*) What is the firm's expected before- and after-tax profit if it purchases the insurance policy (assume that the premium is a tax-deductible expense)?

(*d*) Does the insurance policy have a positive loading from the firm's point of view after taxes are considered?

Answers to Concept Checks

1. A risk-averse person would purchase full insurance coverage because the premium equals the expected claim cost. This would eliminate risk without reducing the person's expected wealth.

2. Wealthier people are likely to purchase higher property and liability insurance coverage limits because the values of assets owned are likely to be higher. Wealthier people are likely to purchase more life insurance

coverage in order to maintain a high standard of living for their dependents after their death. Also, very poor people might purchase very little insurance coverage because their resources are used for more basic necessities.

3. Wealthier people might purchase less insurance in some cases (e.g.,they may buy policies with higher deductibles) because risk aversion might decrease as wealth

increases.

4. True. The type of risk that business insurance eliminates generally can be eliminated by investors through holding a diversified portfolio.

5. False. Business insurance purchases still can increase shareholder wealth even when shareholders are diversified.

APPENDIX 7A
EXPECTED UTILITY

7A.1 Risk Aversion and Utility

Additional insights about what it means to be risk averse can be gained by introducing the concept of *utility,* which is a measure of a person's well-being associated with different amounts of wealth. Suppose that people prefer more wealth to less. Then a person's utility increases with wealth. This relationship is illustrated in Figure 7A–1, where utility is measured on the vertical axis and wealth is measured on the horizontal axis. Since people prefer more wealth to less, the function relating utility to wealth is positively sloped. In Figure 7A–1, the utility associated with $80,000 of wealth is given by the point labeled $U(80,000)$, and the utility of $100,000 is given by the point labeled $U(100,000)$. The units of utility are not important for our purposes.

Risk aversion implies that utility does not increase

linearly with wealth; instead, utility increases at a decreasing rate as wealth increases (the utility function is thus concave in shape). This feature is called *diminishing marginal utility,* because the additional utility received from an increment in wealth (the marginal utility) diminishes as wealth increases. An increment to wealth of $1,000 raises utility more when a person has $80,000 than when the same person has $100,000. Since the curve relating utility to wealth in Figure 7A–1 is concave, the utility function is for a risk-averse person.

Using Figure 7A–1, we can gain additional insight into a person's decision to purchase insurance. Recall the example used in the text where Mr. Grace has wealth of $100,000 and a 0.5 chance of losing $20,000. Assuming that Mr. Grace's utility is given by Figure 7A–1, let's analyze the effect on his utility of purchasing full insurance coverage for a premium of $10,000. If the loss

FIGURE 7A–1

Relationship between utility and wealth

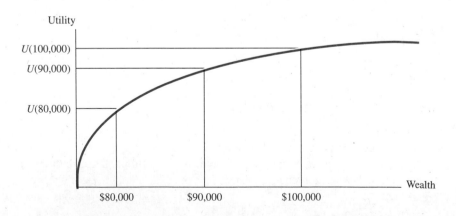

occurs, the insurance policy will increase his wealth from $80,000 to $90,000. Using utility as a measure of his well-being, the gain in utility from having insurance is

$$U(90,000) - U(80,000) \qquad (7A.1)$$

which is depicted on the vertical axis in Figure 7A–1. If the loss does not occur, the insurance policy reduces his wealth from $100,000 to $90,000. The cost in terms of utility is

$$U(100,000) - U(90,000) \qquad (7A.2)$$

which also is depicted in Figure 7A–1.

Of course, Mr. Grace has to make a decision about whether to purchase insurance before he knows whether a loss will occur. That is, he does not know whether insurance will increase utility by the amount given by expression 7A.1 or decrease utility by the amount given by expression 7A.2. Therefore, he has to weigh the benefit of insurance (expression 7A.1) and the cost of insurance (expression 7A.2) by their respective probabilities. In this example, the two outcomes are equally likely; therefore, both possible outcomes receive equal weight and the decision to purchase insurance entails comparing expression 7A.1 to expression 7A.2.

Figure 7A–1 indicates that expression 7A.1 is greater than 7A.2. The reason is the concavity of the utility function. Diminishing marginal utility implies that the loss in utility of having less wealth when a loss does not occur is less than the gain in utility of having more wealth when a loss does occur. Therefore, anyone who has diminishing marginal utility will want to purchase this insurance policy. This example illustrates that diminishing marginal utility implies that a person is risk averse. A

loss of $X hurts Mr. Grace more than a gain of $X benefits him.

The assumptions of equal probabilities and only two possible outcomes in the previous example are used to simplify the discussion; the results do not depend on these simplifying assumptions. Intuitively, the purchase of insurance implies that an individual gives up wealth if a loss does not occur (when wealth is relatively high) so that additional wealth may be received if a loss occurs (when wealth is relatively low). Diminishing marginal utility (risk aversion) implies that an increment to wealth means more to individuals when they have less of it. Therefore, a person with diminishing marginal utility will be willing to give up wealth if a loss does not occur so that additional wealth can be received if a loss does occur.

7A.2 Cost of Uncertainty and the Total Cost of Risk

The utility function introduced in the previous section can be used to conceptually identify the cost of uncertainty and the total cost of risk for an uninsured individual. Consider, for example, Mr. Grace's situation when he is uninsured. He has a 50 percent chance of having wealth equal to $100,000 and a 50 percent chance of losing the lawsuit and having wealth equal to $80,000. Figure 7A–2 illustrates the utility levels associated with these possible outcomes.

Now consider the question: How much would Mr. Grace be willing to pay for full insurance coverage? To answer this question, we must calculate Mr. Grace's expected utility without insurance. Without insurance, Mr. Grace has a 50 percent chance of receiving utility of

FIGURE 7A–2

Relationship between the utility function, the cost of uncertainty, and the total cost of risk

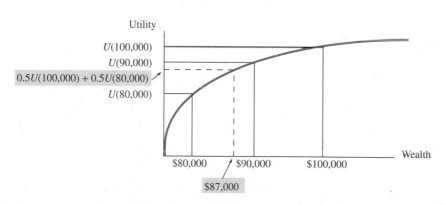

$U(100,000)$ and a 50 percent chance of receiving $U(80,000)$. Because the probability of each outcome is 0.5, Mr. Grace's expected utility without insurance is equal to $[0.5 \times U(100,000) + 0.5 \times U(80,000)]$. This number is illustrated on the vertical axis in Figure 7A–2 as the midpoint between $U(100,000)$ and $U(80,000)$.

Now we can find the amount of wealth that Mr. Grace would accept if he could eliminate the uncertainty. By following the horizontal dotted line from the expected utility level until it reaches the utility curve and then following the vertical dotted line down to the wealth axis, we find $87,000. If Mr. Grace had wealth of $87,000 for certain, then he would have the same expected utility as he has without insurance. In other words, Mr. Grace is indifferent between having $87,000 for certain and having a 50–50 chance of either $80,000 or $100,000. Thus, Mr. Grace would be willing to pay $13,000 ($100,000 minus $87,000) for full insurance coverage.

Notice that the amount that Mr. Grace would be willing to pay exceeds the expected claim cost, which is $10,000 (0.5 × $20,000). That is, when faced with expected losses of $10,000, Mr. Grace is willing to spend more than $10,000 to eliminate the uncertainty as to whether the losses will occur. The amount that Mr. Grace is willing to spend in excess of the expected loss ($3,000) measures Mr. Grace's cost of uncertainty due to

his risk aversion. In total, Mr. Grace is willing to spend $13,000 to eliminate risk—$10,000 of which would be spent by a risk–neutral person (this is the expected loss) and $3,000 because Mr. Grace is risk averse. Thus, $13,000 is the total cost of risk for Mr. Grace if he is uninsured or if he insures for a premium equal to $13,000.

In this chapter, we intuitively argued that if the loading on insurance contracts is too high, then consumers will not purchase insurance. This analysis provides some justification. If the loading for a full coverage policy exceeded $3,000 (e.g., if the total premium equaled $13,500), then Mr. Grace would not purchase the policy. His cost of risk would be greater with insurance than without. On the other hand, if the loading were less than $3,000, Mr. Grace could reduce his cost of risk by buying insurance.

Utility functions are not commonly used to help make risk management decisions. Nevertheless, the conceptual framework provided by utility functions helps us understand individual decision making. That is, utility functions provide a model to help us understand and predict individual decisions. We do not suggest that individuals actually use utility functions or calculate expected utility, rather we are simply pointing out that individuals often behave *as if* they calculate expected utility.

Questions and Problems

1. A person who is risk neutral has a linear utility function, as opposed to a risk-averse person, who has a concave utility function. Redraw Figure 7A–1 assuming Mr. Grace is risk neutral.

2. Redraw Figure 7A–2 and calculate the cost of uncertainty and the total cost of risk for a risk-neutral person who is uninsured.

3. Suppose that an individual has wealth of $20,000 and utility function $U(W) = ln(W)$, where $ln(W)$ indicates the natural logarithm of wealth. What is the maximum amount this individual would pay for full insurance to cover a loss of $5,000 with probability 0.10?

Insurability of Risk, Contractual Provisions, and Legal Doctrines

Chapter Objectives

- Identify and explain factors that can limit the insurability of risk.
- Describe and explain the major provisions that limit coverage in insurance contracts.
- Explain the fundamental legal doctrines underlying insurance contracts.

8.1 Factors That Limit the Insurability of Risk

Chapters 3 and 4 explained how insurance reduces risk. The discussion of risk aversion in Chapter 7 indicated that most people are risk averse and therefore prefer to have less risk. It might therefore seem to follow that insurance would be provided against most risks. This conclusion, however, is incorrect because it ignores the costs of providing insurance. These costs cause people to demand less than full coverage against most risks and no insurance against some risks.

The first part of this chapter summarizes the three major factors that increase costs and thereby limit the insurability of risk in private insurance markets. As highlighted in Figure 8–1, the three factors are: (1) premium loadings, which re-

FIGURE 8–1

Factors limiting the insurability of risk

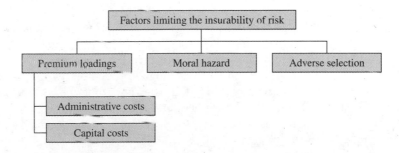

163

flect insurer administrative and capital costs; (2) moral hazard that arises because insurance changes a person's incentive to take precautions; and (3) adverse selection that arises when policyholders are better informed about expected claim costs than insurers. While these factors can lead to no insurance coverage for some types of risk, more typically these factors lead to partial, rather than full, insurance coverage. The second part of the chapter therefore describes contractual provisions in insurance contracts, such as deductibles and coinsurance, which limit insurance coverage. The third part discusses legal doctrines that affect insurance coverage. A major function of these contractual provisions and legal doctrines is to reduce the contracting costs associated with insurance and thus facilitate the insurability of risk.

Premium Loadings

As discussed in Chapter 7, if an insurance contract's premium equals the present value of expected claim costs, a risk-averse person will likely demand full insurance coverage for monetary losses that otherwise would be paid by the person. Because premiums almost always have a positive loading, however, risk-averse people will demand less than full coverage. As the loading increases, the quantity of coverage demanded is likely to decrease. Thus, any factor that increases administrative or capital costs (and thus the loading on a policy) will limit the amount of private market insurance coverage. Simply stated, higher premium loadings generally imply less coverage.

In addition, insurance coverage for some risk exposures is likely to be extremely limited or even nonexistent because of administrative and capital costs. As we now explain, this can be true for exposures with low severity, high frequency, correlated losses across people or businesses, and unknown loss distributions (parameter uncertainty).

Exposures with Low Severity.   Exposures with low severity of losses are not likely to be insured on an individual basis because the fixed costs associated with underwriting and distributing a policy make the loading very high compared to expected losses. For example, the paperwork involved in processing an application is essentially the same whether the applicant is trying to obtain coverage for a diamond-studded, gold Rolex watch (high expected claim costs) or an inexpensive Casio watch (low expected claim costs). These fixed administrative costs imply that exposures with very small severity will have a high loading relative to expected claim costs, making the cost of insuring small losses on an individual basis unattractive to most people.

To illustrate, consider two bicycles: one worth $200 and the other worth $6,000. Assume that the probability of each bike being stolen is 0.05. Then the expected claim costs for full insurance would be $10 ($200 × 0.05) and $300 ($6,000 × 0.05), respectively. Assume that the fixed costs of paying employees to market, underwrite, and process an application for bike insurance are $100, that these are the only administrative costs, and that capital costs are $0. Then, ignoring investment income, the fair premiums would be $110 for the $200 bike and $400 for the $6,000 bike. The loading as a proportion of expected claim costs would be $100/$10 = 1,000 percent for the policy on the $200 bike and $100/$300 = 33.3 percent for the policy on the $6,000 bike. Very few people, if any, would be sufficiently risk averse to be willing to pay a 1,000 percent loading (the $110 premium) to insure a $200 bike. More people would be willing to pay the 33.3 percent loading (the $400 premium) to insure the $6,000 bike.

Items with small value and thus low severity are more likely to be insured if they are bundled together with other exposures. For example, a homeowners policy routinely covers most types of property with low values. By bundling, the fixed administrative costs are spread over many items and consequently the cost per item falls.

Exposures with High Frequency.   When the probability of a loss is high, insurance is less likely to be observed. With a high probability of loss, expected claim costs are high, which in turn causes administrative costs, which are proportional to expected claim costs, to be high.[1] Consequently, the fair premium is close to the potential loss and, in some cases, can exceed the potential loss. The demand for insurance in such a situation is low, because the high insurance premium reduces a person's wealth almost as much as the contingency being insured. For example, suppose that the probability of a $10,000 loss is 0.75 and administrative costs equal 20 percent of expected losses. Then the fair premium would equal $9,000, or $(0.75 \times \$10,000) + (0.20 \times 0.75 \times \$10,000)$.

Correlated Exposures.   When losses are highly correlated across potential policyholders, the variance of the distribution of average losses also will be high (see Chapter 3). Examples of highly correlated losses are losses from major earthquakes, hurricanes, and other storms, war, and contagious diseases. The problem with insuring highly correlated losses is that there is a relatively high probability that average losses will exceed what was expected. In order to make the probability of insolvency relatively low, insurers therefore will need to hold a large amount of capital. The costs of raising and holding this capital imply that insurance against highly correlated losses will have a high premium loading. As a re-

---

[1] While some of an insurer's administrative costs are fixed, most administrative costs increase at a proportional or approximately proportional rate with expected claim costs. For example, underwriters are likely to spend more time learning about an exposure when expected claim costs are high. Sales commissions typically are a percentage of premiums, which increase with expected claim costs. Finally, the extent to which claims are investigated and litigated increases with the size of the claim. For all these reasons and others, the bulk of an insurer's administrative costs associated with a particular policy are likely to increase at a roughly proportional rate as expected claim costs increase.

sult, the amount of coverage purchased is likely to be limited and in some cases private insurance coverage will not exist.[2]

Exposures with Parameter Uncertainty (Uncertain Expected Losses). When insurers are uncertain about the true expected losses of insureds, **parameter uncertainty** is said to exist.[3] From the insurer's perspective, parameter uncertainty has an effect that is similar to positively correlated losses. A high level of parameter uncertainty about expected losses can limit the insurability of losses.

The effect of parameter uncertainty can be illustrated using a simple example. Suppose that losses are uncorrelated across policyholders and that there are a huge number of policyholders, each having the same probability of losing $50,000. The law of large numbers would then imply that the insurer could predict average losses very accurately if the insurer knew the probability of a loss. Suppose, however, that nobody (including the insurer) knows the true probability of a loss (there is parameter uncertainty), but that everyone knows that the true loss probability for all policyholders is either 0.02 or 0.04. Since all the consumers have a probability of 0.02 or all the consumers have a probability of 0.04, the average loss either will be very close to $1,000 ($50,000 loss × 0.02) or very close to $2,000 ($50,000 × 0.04). If we assume that the insurer believes that the two possible probabilities are equally likely, then the insurer's prediction of expected claim costs per policyholder is $1,500. However, average losses are likely to differ from $1,500, because average losses are likely to be either very close to $1,000 or very close to $2,000, depending on whether the true probability is 0.02 or 0.04. The insurer therefore perceives that there is a large variance in the distribution of average losses around the expected value of $1,500.

Thus, parameter uncertainty causes the distribution of average losses around the insurer's estimate of expected loss per policyholder to have greater variance, which is the same effect as having high correlation in losses. The analogy to a high correlation in losses is reinforced by noting that parameter uncertainty implies that the insurer's estimate of expected loss could be wrong. In the exam-

---

[2] In situations where losses are highly correlated across insureds for a particular type of exposure, an insurer can diversify across exposures by selling insurance in different lines of business or through reinsurance (see Chapter 4). Also, when losses are highly correlated across insureds during a given time period, losses tend to be uncorrelated over time. For example, the occurrence of a major earthquake in one year is likely to be uncorrelated with major earthquakes in subsequent years. This observation suggests the possibility that risk pooling could work through time. That is, an insurer could pool correlated exposures over many time periods. As a result of pooling through time, the variance of average losses over the many time periods would be reduced relative to the variance of average losses during one time period. Note, however, that to pool over time, long-term contracts are needed as well as financing arrangements to pay unexpected losses should they occur early during the contractual period. Enforcement costs often make private insurance contracts ineffective in these situations. The ability of government to tax may overcome some of these enforcement problems, although possibly at the expense of introducing other problems associated with government allocation of resources.

[3] Some authors also refer to this situation as *ambiguity.*

ple above, the insurer's estimate is $1,500, and the true expected loss is either $1,000 or $2,000. Any error in the estimate of expected loss will apply to all policyholders. Thus, there is correlation in the insurer's estimation errors across policyholders.

Some parameter uncertainty always exists; insurers simply cannot know the true expected losses of a group of insureds. Just as when losses are highly correlated, an insurer faced with a high level of parameter uncertainty must hold large amounts of capital to achieve a low probability of insolvency. In our example where the insurer's estimate of expected loss is $1,500 but the true expected loss could be $2,000, the insurer would have to hold more than $500 of capital per policyholder to have a low insolvency probability. The costs of holding larger amounts of capital imply that when it is more difficult to estimate expected losses (i.e., when there is a high level of parameter uncertainty), insurance coverage will be limited.

Moral Hazard

Moral hazard refers to the effect of insurance on the insured's incentives to reduce expected losses. For example, once Bob Puelz purchases theft insurance, his incentive to take precautions to reduce the likelihood of theft is reduced. This is because, once insured, Bob bears all the cost of additional precautions, but he does not receive all the benefits of additional precautions. Since losses are insured, a portion of the benefits accrues to the insurer in the form of lower expected claim costs.

To illustrate in more detail, suppose that Bob is at home and ready to go to bed when he realizes that he forgot to lock the door to his office, which is five miles away, and that he has left his personal computer in the office. He must decide whether to go to his office to reduce the likelihood that his computer is stolen. Bob incurs all the costs (the hassle) associated with reducing the probability of his computer being stolen. However, if his insurer pays for theft losses, then some of the benefits of going to his office do not accrue to Bob. Instead, the insurer receives the benefits. In contrast, if he were not insured, the entire benefit from protecting his computer would accrue to him in the form of lower expected theft losses. Consequently, Bob is less likely to go to his office if he is insured.

Insurers understand that insurance reduces policyholders' incentive to prevent losses. The insurance market responds to this moral hazard problem in several ways, which we elaborate below. A central point is that, as a result of moral hazard, insurance contracts are not likely to offer full coverage. Instead, part of the losses will have to be paid by the insured. Thus, moral hazard implies that policyholders will have to bear risk (i.e., moral hazard limits the insurability of risk). In addition, because moral hazard is seldom if ever completely eliminated, moral hazard increases the cost of coverage that is provided by increasing expected claim costs.

Conditions for Moral Hazard.   Two conditions are required for moral hazard to arise. First, expected losses must depend on the insured's behavior after having obtained insurance. Second, it must be costly for the insurer to observe precautions by policyholders and measure their impact on expected claim costs.

Examples where expected losses depend on the insured's behavior are numerous. With automobile insurance, expected claim costs depend on the speed at which the car is driven, when the car is driven, and where the car is parked. With life insurance, the expected claim cost (the probability of death) depends on the insured's eating and drinking habits, leisure activities, and exercise routine. Expected claim costs for workers' compensation insurance depend on the implementation of safety programs and the treatment of employees following an injury. Medical insurance losses depend on how much medical care the policyholder seeks and the doctor prescribes (e.g., the number of tests or the number of office visits).

In all of these situations, expected losses depend on the insured's behavior after being insured. Since insurance pays losses, insurance can affect the incentive to take precautions. As noted above, the basic problem is that once someone is insured, some of the benefits of additional precautions accrue to the insurer rather than the policyholder and therefore the insured does not take these benefits into account when deciding whether to take additional precautions.

One potential solution to the moral hazard problem is to make the premium or coverage contingent on the insured's behavior during the policy period. For example, if a driver increases expected claim costs by driving fast, then the premium could be increased immediately or coverage reduced. This solution requires that the insurer monitor quite closely the insured's behavior, which is costly and sometimes impossible. This gives rise to the second condition that is required for moral hazard problems to arise: that it is costly to observe and measure the impact of people's behavior on expected claim costs.

To illustrate these points, consider an automobile insurance policy for Dave Appel, who enjoys driving fast. Holding other factors constant, expected claim costs increase with driving speed, but the relationship between driving speed and expected claim costs also depends on other factors, such as traffic congestion and road conditions. Suppose that the insurer could put a device in Dave's car that (1) accurately measures driving speed, road conditions, and traffic congestion, as well as their effects on expected claim costs, and (2) instantly incorporates that information into a visual display telling Dave how much additional premium he must pay if he decides to go faster. If this device were costless, there would be no moral hazard problem. Even though Dave's driving speed affects expected claim costs (a necessary condition for moral hazard), Dave would take the appropriate level of precautions, because his premiums would decline if additional precautions were taken (or would increase if fewer precautions were taken). In other words, if the measuring device were both perfectly accurate and costless, Dave would consider the effect of driving speed on expected claim costs when making decisions about how fast to drive and consequently there would be no moral hazard problem.

Monitoring insureds' behavior and incorporating this behavior into the premium obviously is costly. Consequently, monitoring will be used only if it is cost-effective (i.e., if the reduction in expected claim costs from monitoring exceeds the monitoring costs). Monitoring is common after a claim is filed. Insurers routinely investigate claims to identify if the insured has purposely caused the loss or if the claim has been exaggerated. In recent years, insurance fraud (an extreme form of moral hazard) has increased, which in turn has led to additional investigation of claims by insurers. Note as well that since insurance fraud is usually a violation of criminal law, governments also expend resources investigating and punishing insurance fraud, which helps to control extreme forms of moral hazard.

When it is not cost-effective to eliminate moral hazard by monitoring, it may appear that Dave does not pay for the expected cost of his driving behavior. However, an insurer usually will incorporate a person's expected behavior when setting the premium. In our example, the premium would not vary with Dave's *actual* driving speed, but the premium in effect would incorporate Dave's *expected* driving speed. Since the premium Dave pays reflects the insurer's expectations about Dave's behavior after being insured, Dave has an incentive to accept contracts that give him incentives to take precautions. It is better for Dave to have a contract that induces him to take cost-justified precautions and therefore have a lower premium than to have a contract that does not induce him to take cost-justified precautions and therefore have a higher premium.

Reducing Moral Hazard.   Experience rating and limited coverage are the two major methods of reducing moral hazard. Both approaches provide incentives for insureds to take precautions after policies are issued by placing some risk on the insured.[4]

Experience rating makes the premium charged contingent on the claims in prior periods. As described in Chapter 6, one reason for experience rating is to incorporate new information about future expected claim costs into the premium. Another reason for experience rating is to reduce moral hazard. An insured, knowing that future premiums depend on his or her behavior, is more likely to take precautions.

Limiting the amount of insurance coverage through deductibles and other provisions that require the insured to bear part of any loss (see below) also reduces moral hazard. The general point is that, when moral hazard problems exist (which to some extent is always the case), insurance contracts will likely offer incomplete coverage. The intuition is simple: Since insurance creates moral hazard, providing less of it reduces moral hazard.

Moral Hazard in Other Contexts.   Our discussion of moral hazard illustrates a very important concept. A tradeoff exists between risk shifting (e.g., insurance coverage) and incentives: More risk shifting implies less incentive to reduce ex-

---

[4] Note that premium credits for safety devices (e.g., airbags, antilock brakes, and antitheft devices) encourage precautions before coverage begins.

pected costs. The application of this concept is not limited to insurance contracts. The tradeoff between risk shifting and incentives in contracts is pervasive because most contracts shift risk in some way, and whenever risk is shifted, incentives are altered. For example, you probably do not like having uncertainty associated with your grade in this course. Your instructor could "insure" you by guaranteeing a B in the course. The problem with this response and the reason that your instructor will not offer such insurance (we hope) is that your incentive to learn the material would be greatly reduced. That is, eliminating your risk of a low grade creates a moral hazard problem.

Employment contracts provide a more important example. An employer could eliminate risk for employees by offering guaranteed employment for life at a fixed wage that is indexed to inflation (assuming that the employer could credibly make this promise). This type of contract is rare. One reason is moral hazard. Once this contract is offered, the employee's incentive to be productive is greatly reduced. Thus, employment contracts almost always impose some risk on employees. As another example, once society guarantees a certain standard of living for everyone through social programs, some people will have less incentive to work. Again this is a moral hazard problem—reducing risk causes some people to work less. As noted above, moral hazard is mitigated by limiting the extent of insurance coverage. Politicians and public policymakers constantly debate what the optimal balance is between social insurance and providing incentives for people to work hard and be productive.

In summary, moral hazard implies that there is a tradeoff between risk shifting and incentives. Since people designing contracts typically understand this tradeoff, private contracts (insurance contracts being one example) usually will involve incomplete risk shifting so that moral hazard limits the insurability of risk.

A potential impression from this discussion is that the changes in behavior induced by insurance are necessarily undesirable because insurance encourages people to take fewer precautions. However, one of the primary benefits of insurance is that it encourages risk-averse people to engage in productive, yet risky, activities. Without insurance, risk-averse people would take excessive precautions by avoiding certain risky activities, thus increasing the total cost of risk. For example, without the ability to purchase liability insurance, people with considerable wealth would likely take excessive precautions to avoid being sued. The key point is that a balance is needed. A complete lack of insurance coverage is likely to lead to too many precautions and full insurance is likely to lead to too few precautions. Consequently, the optimal level of insurance coverage typically is partial coverage, which takes both effects into account.

Adverse Selection

Another factor that limits the insurability of risk is adverse selection. Recall from Chapter 6 that **adverse selection** refers to situations in which consumers have different expected losses (e.g., bookworms versus skateboarders), but the insurer is unable to distinguish between the two types of consumers and charge them different premiums. If an insurer offers insurance at the same price to heterogeneous consumers and consumers know their expected losses, then the higher expected loss consumers (skateboarders) will tend to purchase more insurance coverage relative to the case where insureds are charged premiums based on their expected losses. Conversely, the lower expected loss consumers (bookworms) will tend to purchase less insurance coverage. When this scenario occurs, adverse selection takes place.

As described in Chapter 6, classification (basing premiums on expected claim costs) reduces adverse selection. Thus, adverse selection arises because it is too costly to classify insureds perfectly. Indeed, if each consumer's expected claim costs could be observed costlessly, then insurance premiums (barring government restrictions) would vary exactly with expected claim costs and there would be no adverse selection.

Classification is costly in practice and thus insurers will only classify to the extent that it is cost-effective to do so. When consumers know more about their expected losses than insurers, adverse selection occurs. Insurers understand adverse selection, and they design and price policies taking it into account. For example, if insurers believed there would be adverse selection with a particular policy, then premiums would be increased to reflect the expected adverse selection. The net result of adverse selection is that consumers with low expected losses (bookworms) purchase less coverage than they would if classification were costless. Thus, adverse selection limits the insurability of risk for consumers with low expected losses.

Example of Adverse Selection.   For the sake of argument, suppose that it is prohibitively costly for insurers to classify bookworms and skateboarders. Suppose also that (1) there are an equal number of bookworms and skateboarders; (2) both bookworms and skateboarders can lose $1,000 in an accident; and (3) bookworms have an accident probability equal to 0.1 and skateboarders have an accident probability of 0.2. Ignoring administrative/capital costs and the time value of money, insurers need to charge rates (premiums per dollar of coverage) that are sufficient to cover expected claim costs. Assume that insurers consider charging a rate equal to the average accident probability for bookworms and skateboarders (i.e., premiums equal 0.15 times the amount of coverage). At this rate, skateboarders would view the insurance as having a negative loading (the expected claim cost for skateboarders equals 0.2 times the amount of coverage) and bookworms would view the insurance as having a high loading (the expected claim cost for bookworms equals 0.1 times the amount of coverage). Consequently, skateboarders would be likely to purchase more insurance coverage than bookworms; that is, adverse selection would occur.

Assume specifically that each bookworm purchases $500 of coverage and each skateboarder purchases $1,000 of coverage. Then, the insurer's premium revenue per policyholder equals

$$[\$500\ (0.15) + \$1,000\ (0.15)]/2 = \$112.50$$

However, the expected claim cost per policyholder equals

$$[\$500\ (0.1) + \$1,000\ (0.2)]/2 = \$125.00$$

Thus, the insurer cannot charge \$0.15 per dollar of coverage and expect to break even.

Understanding this adverse selection problem, insurers will not charge \$0.15 per dollar of coverage, but instead will charge a higher rate that reflects the fact that they are providing more coverage to skateboarders than bookworms. Assume, for example, that insurers charge \$0.18 per dollar of coverage. At this higher rate, bookworms will purchase even less coverage. If bookworms purchase \$250 of coverage and skateboarders continue to purchase \$1,000 of coverage, the insurer's premium revenue per policyholder equals

$$[\$250\ (0.18) + \$1,000\ (0.18)]/2 = \$112.50$$

The expected claim cost per policyholder equals

$$[\$250\ (0.1) + \$1,000\ (0.2)]/2 = \$112.50$$

In this example, a rate of \$0.18 per dollar of coverage allows the insurer to break even, and both bookworms and skateboarders purchase some insurance. Nevertheless, the inability to classify implies that bookworms are not fully insured (i.e., costly classification limits the insurability of their risk).

Another possibility is that an insurer will not be able to find a price that allows it to break even and induces bookworms to purchase insurance. In this extreme case, the insurer will have to charge such a high price that all bookworms will stop buying insurance and only skateboarders will purchase insurance.[5] Examples of this extreme outcome are difficult to find in practice. One possible reason is that insurers can design policies to help sort out the high expected loss consumers (skateboarders) from the low expected loss consumers (bookworms). We will discuss how deductibles and coinsurance can serve this purpose in the next section.

Concept Check

1. What are the major reasons that insurance contracts rarely provide full coverage?

8.2 Contractual Provisions That Limit Coverage

The central theme of the previous section is that a number of factors (administrative and capital costs, correlated losses, parameter uncertainty, moral hazard, and adverse selection) limit the extent to which risk exposures are insured. In extreme

---

[5] Furthermore, if skateboarders were for some reason unwilling to buy coverage at a premium that reflects their expected claim costs (e.g., due to the possible effects of limited liability on the demand for liability insurance discussed in the last chapter), the market for coverage would break down completely.

cases, these factors can eliminate the market for insurance coverage. In most cases, however, the amount of coverage is limited by contractual provisions that are discussed in this section.

Deductibles

A common way to limit the amount of coverage is through **deductibles,** which eliminate coverage for relatively small losses. To illustrate, suppose that Annie buys a six-month automobile insurance policy that covers damage to her car from events other than collisions (for more details on this type of coverage, see Chapter 21) and that her policy has a $250 deductible per occurrence. Then Annie will pay up to $250 of the loss each time her car is damaged. If the loss is less than $250, then Annie will pay the entire loss. If the loss is $1,000, Annie will pay $250 and the insurer will pay $750.

As discussed earlier, risk-averse people are likely to desire less than full coverage when policies have a positive loading. Thus, deductibles chosen by policyholders are likely to increase in size as premium loadings increase. There are other important effects of deductibles that also help to explain why they are so prevalent in insurance contracts. In particular, deductibles reduce claims processing costs, reduce moral hazard problems, and mitigate adverse selection.

Deductibles and Claims Processing Costs.   One reason that policies have deductibles is to reduce the costs of processing small claims that occur relatively frequently. Some claims processing costs are unrelated to the size of the claim. For example, regardless of the claim severity, the insurer must pay a claims adjuster to process the claim and issue a check. These fixed claim processing costs make insuring small claims that occur relatively frequently very expensive (i.e., they have a high loading). To illustrate, if there is a 0.1 probability of a $50 loss and the fixed cost of processing a claim is $100, the required loading to cover the expected fixed cost associated with insuring the $50 loss is $10 (0.1 × $100), which is twice as large as the expected claim cost if the loss is covered (0.1 × $50). This is one reason that consumers prefer not to purchase insurance for small losses; that is, they prefer to bear a modest amount of risk with a deductible, as opposed to paying a relatively large loading.

Deductibles and Moral Hazard.   As noted earlier, another important function of deductibles is to reduce moral hazard. For example, with the $250 deductible, Annie has greater incentive to park her car in safe places where the likelihood of damage is lower. Without the deductible, the insurer would be forced to charge Annie a higher price, not only because a larger amount of coverage is being offered (coverage of losses below $250) and higher transaction costs exist, but also because the expected loss for a given amount of coverage would be greater due to the higher likelihood of a claim. In other words, deductibles change people's behavior in a way that reduces the likelihood and severity of losses, which in turn lowers premiums.

Deductibles and Adverse Selection.   Recall that adverse selection arises when it is too costly for insurers to classify perfectly and when consumers have superior information about their expected losses. In our previous discussion of this situation, we assumed that the insurer simply charged all consumers the same rate per unit of coverage. This resulted in the low expected loss consumers in our example (the bookworms) purchasing less coverage than the high expected loss consumers (the skateboarders).

However, insurers also may be able to use deductibles to induce (1) high expected loss consumers to choose a policy that is priced to reflect their expected claim costs, and (2) low expected loss consumers to choose a policy with a larger deductible that is priced to reflect their lower expected claim costs. Thus, even though insurers cannot distinguish skateboarders from bookworms, in theory, contracts might be designed to induce consumers to reveal their expected loss by their choice of deductible so that the bookworms and the skateboarders are separated into two classes and charged different prices.

The key to understanding how deductibles might separate consumers is to recognize that people with a higher probability of a loss (skateboarders) usually will be willing to pay more for a given amount of coverage than will people with a lower probability of a loss (bookworms). With this in mind, consider what happens if an insurer offers the following two contracts to skateboarders and bookworms, where each has a potential loss of $1,000.

Contract 1:   Deductible = $500   Coverage = $500
                Premium = $50 $\rightarrow$ Premium per $ of coverage (rate) = $50/$500 = $0.10

Contract 2:   Deductible = $250   Coverage = $750
                Premium = $150 $\rightarrow$ Premium per $ of coverage (rate) = $150/$750 = $0.20

Notice that to obtain an additional $250 of coverage (move from the $500 deductible to the $250 deductible), the consumer must pay $100 more in premiums. Also notice that the premium per dollar of coverage (the rate) for the higher amount of coverage is 20 cents, compared to 10 cents for the lower amount of coverage. Because of their higher loss probability, skateboarders will be more willing to pay the higher rate to obtain the additional coverage. Thus, it is possible that the skateboarders will choose contract 2 and that the bookworms will choose contract 1. If so, the two types have separated themselves, and they are being charged different prices per unit of coverage to reflect their different accident probabilities. The separation of bookworms and skateboarders is not costless, however. Bookworms have to accept less insurance—a higher deductible—in order to separate themselves from skateboarders. In essence, bookworms reveal themselves by their willingness to bear more risk.

The extent to which insurers actually are able to design policies to induce consumers to separate themselves into distinct risk classes is uncertain. It is likely in many cases, however, that relatively more low expected loss buyers choose policies with high rather than low deductibles. Since the price of coverage will reflect the average expected claim costs for buyers that choose a particular deductible, it is likely that some degree of separation is therefore achieved in practice. To the extent that separation occurs, the degree to which low expected loss buyers subsidize high expected loss buyers is reduced.

Coinsurance

A **coinsurance** provision requires an insured to pay a specified proportion of the loss (e.g., 20 percent).[6] Medical expense insurance policies often have a coinsurance requirement. Coinsurance reduces coverage below full coverage, just as risk-averse consumers would demand when policies have a positive loading. Coinsurance also reduces moral hazard. Since the insured pays part of any loss with a coinsurance provision, the insured has a greater incentive to reduce losses with the coinsurance provision.[7]

The following anecdote helps illustrate how coinsurance can reduce moral hazard. When Liz had a new baby in 1996, her medical insurance paid all the costs of doctor visits; that is, there was no coinsurance and no deductible. Whenever the infant was grouchy, Liz thought that the baby might have an ear infection and therefore took the baby to the doctor, who was only a short distance away. These happy days were short-lived. When the baby was six months old, Liz's medical insurance plan changed. She had to pay a coinsurance charge every time she visited the doctor's office. Although the baby's disposition remained the same, Liz seldom visited the doctor.

Policy Limits

Insurance policies often limit the amount of coverage by placing an upper limit, known as a **policy limit,** on the amount that the insurer will pay for any loss. Policy limits always are used in liability insurance policies. For example, an automobile liability insurance policy may state that the insurer will pay up to $20,000 in physical damage to another person's car and up to $100,000 in bodily injury damages to a driver or passenger of another car. As discussed in Chapter 7, the demand for liability insurance depends on a person's wealth. Thus, one explanation for liability policy limits below the level of potential damages is that people have a limited amount of wealth that they want to protect from liability suits. They therefore have little incentive to purchase insurance for the entire amount of damage that they potentially can cause other people.

Policy limits in property insurance keep people from paying for coverage in excess of the amount of loss that they could sustain. Policy limits also can reduce classification costs when consumers have information that is relevant for classifi-

---

[6] As discussed later in the section, insurance-to-value provisions in property insurance contracts, which also are known as coinsurance clauses, differ in their operation and purpose.

[7] Coinsurance also can be used to reduce adverse selection in a manner similar to that described for deductibles.

cation but which is costly for insurers to obtain. Suppose, for example, that the vast majority of homeowners have jewelry that has value less than $2,500, but that some homeowners have jewelry that has value greater than $2,500. The loss severity of the latter group obviously is higher than that of the former group. The problem is that insurers cannot distinguish people with expensive jewelry from those without expensive jewelry without incurring some costs (by evaluating each homeowner's jewelry prior to selling a policy). However, individuals are likely to know whether they have expensive jewelry. By limiting coverage for jewelry losses to $2,500 and offering special coverage for jewelry valued greater than $2,500 (through what is called an *endorsement* to the policy or with a separate policy), the insurer induces the homeowners with valuable jewelry to reveal themselves.

Pro Rata and Excess Coverage Clauses

Insureds sometimes will have multiple insurance policies that apply to the same loss. Coverage of a loss under multiple policies potentially could allow an insured to receive more from insurance than the loss suffered, which would require the insured to pay more for coverage and also increase moral hazard. For these reasons, insurers commonly prevent recovery in excess of the amount of the loss by including a clause, known as a **pro rata clause,** that specifies that each policy will pay a proportion of the loss. Alternatively, the policy may include an **excess clause** that specifies that the insurer will pay only losses in excess of the coverage provided by another policy.

Exclusions

You no doubt already are aware that insurance policies often contain **exclusions** —that is, they exclude coverage for specific types of losses. For example, homeowners policies exclude coverage for losses arising from flood, normal wear and tear, war, and a variety of other causes. Life insurance policies usually have exclusions for suicide within two years of policy purchase. Other examples of exclusions are presented in later chapters that deal with specific types of insurance. There are several reasons for exclusions. One reason is that the capital costs of insuring some types of losses are high due to the correlation in losses. This explains why losses from war, nuclear accidents, and perhaps flood often are excluded. Moral hazard also helps to explain why losses from some events, such as suicide in the case of life insurance, are excluded. Nonfortuitous losses, such as losses from normal wear and tear, are excluded because they involve little or no risk.

Another function of exclusions is similar to that described above for coverage limits for particular types of coverage. Exclusions often are designed to eliminate coverage that is not needed by the typical buyer. Policyholders thus do not have to pay for coverage that they do not need, and persons or businesses that need the coverage are induced to reveal themselves through purchasing an endorsement or a separate policy. In fact, many exclusions can in effect be removed for a price, especially in business insurance policies.

Indemnity versus Valued Contracts

Insurance policies can be classified into two types: indemnity contracts and valued contracts. With an **indemnity contract,** the amount that the insurer pays is determined after a loss, and the amount paid equals the value of the loss (as defined in the policy and subject to deductibles, coinsurance, limits, and exclusions). Depending on the policy, the insurer agrees to pay the cost of replacing the property (e.g., in homeowners insurance), the actual cash value (replacement cost minus depreciation), or repair cost up to the actual cash value (e.g., in auto insurance). We discuss these policy terms further in the chapters on auto and homeowners insurance. In any case, the amount that the insurer pays under an indemnity contract depends on the amount of damage. In contrast to indemnity contracts, **valued contracts** establish the amount that the insurer pays at the time the contract is initiated without regard to the amount of loss caused by the insured event. For example, the life insurance benefit paid following someone's death is fixed in the contract. The insurer does not determine the death benefit based on the circumstances of the beneficiaries at the time of death.

The choice between indemnity and valued contracts can be explained largely by the costs of assessing value and moral hazard. In many situations, the size of the loss can be determined at low cost after a loss has occurred; for example, an auto mechanic can estimate repair costs following a car accident. In these circumstances, indemnity contracts have the advantage that the amount paid by the insurer is related to the size of the loss and does not exceed the loss suffered, thus reducing moral hazard. The policyholder does not have an incentive to cause a loss (or to take fewer precautions), because the indemnity payment from the insurer will not exceed the value of the loss.

In other situations, however, the occurrence of a loss can make it costly (if not impossible) to determine the size of the loss. If expensive artwork is stolen, for example, its value cannot be readily assessed. This can lead to a moral hazard problem: Policyholders may overstate the value of the property, and, if they think they can do so with impunity, even might have an incentive to arrange for the property to be stolen. In these circumstances, contracts which assess the value and establish the insured value of the property when the contract is initiated are more likely.

Other losses can be costly or impossible to value either before a loss or after a loss. For example, the value of a person's life, including the present value of future earnings, is costly to estimate and subject to considerable uncertainty regardless of whether the person is alive or dead. In order to avoid costly haggling following a loss in these circumstances, insurance contracts are likely to be valued contracts. Moral hazard problems associated with valued contracts in life insurance are reduced by insurer underwriting standards that limit the amount of coverage in relation to the buyer's income, by suicide clauses (discussed earlier), and by the inherent value people place on their life. People purchasing life insurance also usually choose beneficiaries carefully, and criminal penalties for murder help deter murder for profit by beneficiaries.[8]

---

[8] As we discuss later, insurable interest requirements also reduce moral hazard.

Insurance-to-Value (Coinsurance) in Property Insurance

Property insurance contracts for homeowners and business owners often have an insurance-to-value clause. This clause commonly is called a *coinsurance provision,* although it differs from the coinsurance requirement discussed above. The **insurance-to-value (coinsurance) clause** in property contracts specifies the percentage of the property's value that the insurer requires the insured to purchase to receive full reimbursement (above any deductible and up to the policy limit) following a loss. A typical coinsurance percentage is 80 percent, with percentages for commercial property insurance varying from 50 to 100 percent. These clauses are much less important than they used to be, especially in residential property insurance, given that many insurers have underwriting standards that essentially require a policy limit that is approximately equal to the value of the property. It is nonetheless useful to briefly describe the basic operation and purpose of these clauses.[9]

If the policy limit is less than the coinsurance percentage times the value of the property at the time of a loss, then the insurer will reduce the reimbursement for losses using the following formula:

$$\begin{matrix} \text{Maximum} \\ \text{proportion of} \\ \text{loss paid by} \\ \text{insurer} \end{matrix} = \left[\frac{\text{Amount of insurance purchased}}{\text{Value of property at time of loss}} \right] \frac{1}{\text{Coinsurance percentage}}$$

If the ratio in brackets is less than the coinsurance percentage, then the maximum proportion of the loss paid by the insurer is less than one. For example, if the policy limit is $150,000, the property's value is $200,000, and the coinsurance percentage is 80 percent, then the maximum proportion of the loss paid by the insurer is

$$\left[\frac{\$150,000}{\$200,000} \right] \frac{1}{0.80} = \frac{0.75}{0.80} = 93.75\%$$

Regardless of whether the insured purchased the required amount of coverage, the insurer will neither pay more than the amount of insurance purchased nor more than the actual loss. Thus, the amount paid by the insurer is the lesser of (1) the maximum proportion of the loss times the actual loss, (2) the amount of insurance coverage purchased, and (3) the actual loss.

Why did insurers develop a formula to impose a penalty on insureds who fail to maintain coverage equal to the coinsurance percentage? The explanation lies, in part, on industry practice that establishes premiums by multiplying the policy limit (the amount of coverage purchased) times a rate that does not vary with the policy limit. Thus, the premium charged is proportional to the limit chosen by the policyholder. The straight line in Figure 8–2 illustrates this relationship. However, the probability that a small proportion of the property is damaged is higher than

---

[9] The specific coinsurance clause in homeowners insurance is described briefly in Chapter 22.

FIGURE 8–2

Explanation for coinsurance provision in property contracts (industry practice is to charge premiums that are proportional to coverage, but fair premiums increase less than proportionally)

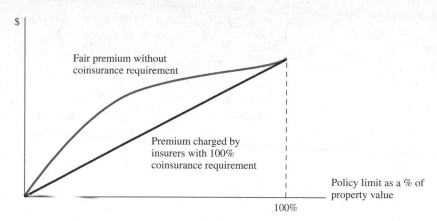

the probability that a large proportion of the property is damaged (small fires are more likely than large fires). This implies that the fair premium for a policy without a coinsurance clause would increase at a less than proportional rate as more coverage is purchased. This relationship is depicted by the curve in Figure 8–2. Thus, without a coinsurance penalty, policyholders who insure property for less than the coinsurance percentage assumed in the flat rate premium structure would pay less than the fair premium. The coinsurance penalty reduces the amount of coverage so that the premium charged in these cases is closer to the fair premium.

Instead of the existing practice of charging a constant rate regardless of the amount of coverage, insurers could alter the rate based on the amount of coverage purchased relative to the market value of the property. This would be more complicated, and there would be a greater need for insurers to assess the value of property accurately every time a policy is written or renewed to determine more precisely how much coverage is being purchased relative to the market value of the property. Because in some cases the property owner is likely to incur lower costs obtaining information about the market value of the property, it can be less costly to place the ultimate burden on the owner by including a coinsurance provision. As noted earlier, however, modern underwriting criteria and property valuation methods used by insurers often require property insurance policyholders to insure property for at least 80 percent of its estimated value, so that the coinsurance clause is much less important than in the past. This in part reflects the development of lower cost methods of estimating the approximate value of property when coverage is issued. It also reflects increasing insurer concern that imposing coinsurance penalties could lead to litigation by policyholders against insurers and agents.

8.3 Legal Doctrines

Before discussing legal doctrines affecting insurance contracts, it is useful to discuss briefly how the legal system potentially can improve private insurance contracts. The issue is: Why not let people contract with each other without the legal system imposing restrictions on the nature of contracts? One role of the legal system is to reduce contracting costs by establishing legal rules or fundamental doctrines that apply to all insurance contracts. With fundamental legal doctrines, participants in the insurance market begin with a mutual understanding of how insurance contracts will be interpreted under some unforeseen circumstances. This mutual understanding can reduce contracting costs. A second role of the legal system is to enforce private contracts and to resolve disputes at a lower cost than could be achieved through private contracts.

Reducing Contracting Costs through Fundamental Legal Doctrines

As discussed earlier in this chapter, one problem with insurance is moral hazard—once someone is insured, the incentive to take precautions and to lower claim costs is reduced. Another problem is information disclosure; that is, consumers often have information that is relevant to the pricing of insurance. As we discussed earlier, it is mutually beneficial for the insurer and the insured to have contracts that mitigate moral hazard and that induce people to reveal information truthfully that otherwise would be costly for insurers to gather. As a result, legal principles that mitigate moral hazard and promote information disclosure have developed over time.

Mitigating Moral Hazard.   Moral hazard problems become particularly severe if a policyholder can benefit from the occurrence of an insured event. For example, if an event causes $10,000 of damage, but a policyholder can collect $20,000 from the insurer, then the policyholder has some incentive to see that the insured event occurs. The **indemnity principle** states that an insurance policy cannot pay more than the financial loss suffered. Most property and liability insurance policies are indemnity contracts. The financial loss is measured after the loss has occurred and payment is limited to the amount of the loss as defined in the contract (e.g., replacement cost or actual cash value).[10] As we discussed earlier, when it is costly or impossible to measure the loss subsequent to its occurrence, valued policies are used. The indemnity principle does not apply to valued contracts.

Another legal doctrine related to the indemnity principle is the requirement that the insurance policyholder have an **insurable interest.** This generally means that the policyholder must suffer adverse financial consequences if the event that causes the insurance company to pay a claim occurs. A policy can be voided if insurable interest is found to be nonexistent. To illustrate the moral hazard problems that could arise without an insurable interest rule, suppose that Anne and Carol are not related and that Anne can buy an insurance policy that pays her 80 percent of Carol's medical expenses over the coming year. Then Anne would have an incentive to see that Carol needs medical care.

---

[10] Note that the indemnity principle could be seriously violated with replacement cost coverage if the property's replacement cost greatly exceeds its market value. As we discuss in Chapter 22, some homeowners policies limit payment to the actual cash value or market value for this reason.

For property and liability insurance, an insurable interest must exist at the time of the loss, and a person cannot receive more than his or her insurable interest from the insurer. In this case, the insurable interest rule is essentially the same as the indemnity principle. With life insurance contracts, the owner of the policy must have an insurable interest in the subject (the person whose death triggers payment) at the time the policy is purchased. The insurable interest rule is not applied to immediate family members. In addition, a person can insure his or her own life and name a beneficiary who does not have an insurable interest in the person's life. As noted earlier, several other factors help mitigate moral hazard in life insurance. For example, social norms and criminal penalties reduce the likelihood of murder, and a policyholder whose life is insured usually chooses the beneficiary with care.[11]

Moral hazard problems also would arise if people could collect compensation from multiple sources following an event that causes a loss. Earlier we discussed how pro rata and excess clauses prevent an insured from recovering more than the loss from multiple insurance policies. People also might potentially collect twice for the same loss when their insurance covers the loss and another party is legally liable. For example, if a neighbor's negligence destroys Joe's property, he might seek compensation by suing his neighbor. In these circumstances, if Joe files a claim with his insurer, then the insurer receives the legal right to obtain compensation from the party who caused the loss. The transfer of Joe's right to seek compensation through the courts to his insurer is called **subrogation;** it prevents Joe from recovering twice for his loss and thus mitigates moral hazard.[12]

Information Disclosure.   Insurance contracts require that both the policyholder and the insurer disclose all relevant information; that is, the two parties must negotiate with **utmost good faith.** This doctrine implies that policyholders must respond truthfully to questions that the insurer asks. For example, if an insurer asks whether you smoke, your answer is called a *representation,* and it must be truthful. If incorrect, it is known as a **misrepresentation.** The doctrine also applies to any information that the policyholder knows to be relevant to the decision to insure, but about which the insurer does not directly ask. For example, seeking property insurance without telling the agent that a forest fire is raging one-half mile from your business would be considered **concealment** of relevant information.

Although the specific rules vary across states and types of insurance, the le-

---

[11] As an additional safeguard against moral hazard, the person on whose life the policy is written typically must also sign the application if the policy is purchased by someone else.

[12] Subrogation also allows a victim to receive compensation immediately from his or her insurer, who may then receive reimbursement from the other party at a later date. Subrogation also reduces the price of property insurance; people do not have to pay for the right of double recovery. Insurance policies often include subrogation clauses (even though it is a legal doctrine) to clarify the conditions of subrogation.

gal remedy for misrepresentation or concealment of a material fact is that the insurer can void the contract. *Material* means that the information is relevant to the insurer's decision to sell or price the policy. The contract usually can be voided even if the nondisclosed or incorrect information is unrelated to the cause of the accident. For example, if a life insurance policyholder lies about smoking and later dies in an automobile accident (unrelated to smoking) within two years of buying the policy, then the life insurer may be able to void the contract. After two years, life insurance policies (but not property–liability insurance contracts) are generally *incontestable.* This means that the insurer cannot deny coverage for misrepresentation or concealment.

Voiding the contract for misrepresentation and/or concealment can be justified by the importance of information for risk classification (underwriting) and the fact that the policyholder often is the lowest cost provider of information. If the courts instead pursued the less stringent resolution of simply making the beneficiary reimburse the insurer for the higher premium that should have been paid, policyholders would have stronger incentives to misrepresent and conceal information.[13] If caught, which usually occurs when a claim is filed, the policyholder simply could pay the higher premiums that should have been paid initially. Thus, there would be little or no cost to misrepresentation or concealment and people would misrepresent and conceal information more often. Insurers also would expend greater resources trying to gather information. To the extent that such efforts are unsuccessful, other policyholders who have lower expected claim costs would be charged higher prices in order to cover those who have higher expected claim costs but who fail to truthfully reveal the information.

Resolving Coverage Disputes

When coverage disputes arise between a policyholder and an insurer, the courts generally apply several legal principles in interpreting insurance contracts. Insurance contracts generally are **contracts of adhesion,** which means that the insurer has written and offered the contract to the policyholder for acceptance or rejection. Since the insurer writes the contract and has expertise in anticipating conditions that could cause disputes, the courts generally interpret any ambiguous policy language in favor of the policyholder. However, this practice is not followed for some large business insurance policies where the terms are mutually negotiated between the insurer and the insured.

In addition, some courts have adopted the **doctrine of reasonable expectations.** This doctrine holds that policies will be interpreted according to how a reasonable person who is not trained in the law would expect. For example, if a reasonable person would expect a policy to cover a certain loss, the courts might

---

[13] In fact, life insurance policies usually contain a provision that specifies this less stringent remedy (paying the extra premium) in the event of misrepresentation of a person's age or sex. In these cases, the insurer should be able to obtain the information at low cost.

require the insurer to pay even if the contract language clearly excludes coverage. To illustrate, in one instance a liability claim was brought against a tavern owner for negligently serving alcohol to a person who later caused an auto accident. The tavern owner had been sold a standard business liability insurance contract that clearly excluded coverage for all claims arising out of the sale of alcoholic beverages. The insurer claimed that the policyholder knowingly chose this policy to receive a lower premium. However, the courts ruled that the insurer had to pay the liability claim because a tavern owner would reasonably expect that the claim would be covered.

The general point is that the courts usually place the burden of anticipating events and writing explicit contracts to handle events on insurers. The placement of this burden on insurers usually makes sense given the information, experience, and expertise that insurers develop as a result of dealing with many contracts. On the other hand, it sometimes is argued that some courts have gone too far in ignoring contract language in order to compensate policyholders or the victims of policyholders' actions, because insurers are viewed as having "deep pockets." A controversial example involves environmental liability insurance coverage. As discussed in more detail in Chapter 15, over the past 30 years, some courts' interpretation of business liability insurance policies has expanded coverage for environmental damage beyond the circumstances originally envisioned by insurers. The insurance market has responded with policies that contain more explicit and more restrictive exclusions.

A related issue concerns the general legal duty of the insurer to negotiate in good faith with claimants. Based on the rationale that market incentives and normal judicial remedies for breach of contract may be insufficient to prevent some insurers from behaving opportunistically by refusing to pay claim costs or by offering to pay too little for claims, some courts have allowed policyholders (or third-party claimants) to sue an insurer for bad faith. These **bad-faith suits** allege that insurers have acted in a manner inconsistent with what a reasonable policyholder would have expected and therefore have failed to act in good faith. In some cases, courts have awarded damages to claimants many times over the disputed amount. The number of these lawsuits has increased substantially in recent years. These cases sometimes have been quite controversial, with some observers suggesting that courts often have found bad faith on the part of insurers even when their dispute with claimants over the existence or amount of coverage was reasonable. To the extent that courts find insurers liable in bad-faith suits when the disputes are reasonable, premium rates for all policyholders must increase.

8.4 Summary

- Because of administrative costs, capital costs, moral hazard, and adverse selection, individuals and businesses generally do not demand full insurance coverage for their loss exposures.

- Low severity losses generally are not insured on a stand-alone basis (i.e., unless bundled with other losses) because of fixed administrative costs.

- High frequency losses generally are not insured because the fair premium is close to or exceeds the potential loss.

- Insurance for highly correlated losses generally is limited due to the costs of holding the capital needed to achieve a low probability of insolvency.

- Insurance for losses with high parameter uncertainty (uncertain loss distributions) generally is limited because of the costs of holding the capital needed to achieve a low probability of insolvency.

- Moral hazard limits the extent to which risk is insured.

- Adverse selection limits the insurance coverage purchased by low expected loss consumers who are pooled with higher expected loss consumers.

- Insurance coverage is limited through contractual provisions like deductibles, coinsurance, policy limits, exclusions, and pro rata and excess coverage provisions.

- Legal doctrines have been developed that reduce the cost of coverage by (1) mitigating moral hazard, (2) providing incentives for insureds to disclose relevant information to insurers, and (3) reducing the costs of resolving disputes.

- The indemnity principle and insurable interest rule help to reduce moral hazard.

- Voiding insurance contracts when policyholders make misrepresentations or conceal material information helps to promote low cost information disclosure.

- When resolving contract disputes, courts generally interpret any ambiguous policy terms in favor of the insured. Some courts go farther and interpret the policy in terms of the insured's reasonable expectations even if contract language clearly specifies a different outcome.

Key Terms

parameter uncertainty   166
moral hazard   167
adverse selection   170
deductibles   173
coinsurance   175
policy limit   175
pro rata clause   176
excess clause   176
exclusions   176
indemnity contract   177
valued contracts   177

insurance-to-value (coinsurance) clause   178
indemnity principle   180
insurable interest   180
subrogation   181
utmost good faith   181
misrepresentation   181
concealment   181
contracts of adhesion   182
doctrine of reasonable expectations   182
bad-faith suits   183

Questions and Problems

1. Explain how the amount of insurance coverage purchased by a risk-averse person is likely to change in response to each of the following:

(*a*) The legal costs associated with processing claims increase.

(*b*) Regulatory compliance costs decrease.

(c) The tax on insurer investment earnings increases.

(d) The variability of claim costs increases.

(e) The criminal penalties for fraud increase.

2. Explain why a business property insurance policy may have an exclusion for damages due to a nuclear accident.

3. A friend says "Insurance policies are a rip-off; they always have provisions that limit how much you can be compensated." You enlighten your friend by saying . . .

4. For each of the following risk exposures, explain why the amount of private market insurance coverage may be significantly limited through contractual provisions (exclusions, limits, coinsurance, and deductibles) or in extreme cases nonexistent:
   (a) A pet's life
   (b) Pain from injuries
   (c) Earthquakes
   (d) Unemployment

5. Suppose that Annie's loss distribution is as follows:

$$\text{Loss} = \begin{array}{l} \$5,000 \text{ with probability } 0.005 \\ \$1,000 \text{ with probability } 0.010 \\ \$ \ \ 250 \text{ with probability } 0.050 \\ \$ \ \ \ \ \ 0 \text{ with probability } 0.935 \end{array}$$

Assume that the only administrative cost is the cost of processing a claim, which equals $500 regardless of the claim size. Ignoring moral hazard, adverse selection, the time value of money, and capital costs, the cost of providing insurance is the sum of expected claim costs and expected claim processing costs. Fill in the table below for a policy with

a $250 deductible and a policy without a deductible. What does the table illustrate about the marginal cost of insuring small losses and the desirability of deductibles?

6. A lawnmower manufacturer has the following loss distribution for its annual products liability costs:

$$\text{Loss} = \begin{array}{l} \$ \ \ \ \ \ \ \ 0 \text{ with probability } 0.984 \\ \$ \ \ 50,000 \text{ with probability } 0.010 \\ \$ 250,000 \text{ with probability } 0.005 \\ \$ 750,000 \text{ with probability } 0.001 \end{array}$$

Determine the expected claim costs for each of the following policies:
(a) Full insurance.
(b) $50,000 deductible and a $500,000 limit.
(c) No deductible and a $700,000 limit.

7. Captain Mack's, a seafood restaurant, offers medical cost coverage for its employees. Its probability distribution for medical costs for the coming year is as follows:

$$\text{Medical costs} = \begin{array}{l} \$ \ \ \ \ \ \ \ 0 \text{ with probability } 0.9335 \\ \$ \ \ \ \ 2,000 \text{ with probability } 0.0500 \\ \$ \ \ \ \ 5,000 \text{ with probability } 0.0100 \\ \$ \ \ 10,000 \text{ with probability } 0.0050 \\ \$ \ \ 50,000 \text{ with probability } 0.0010 \\ \$ 500,000 \text{ with probability } 0.0005 \end{array}$$

Calculate Captain Mack's expected claim costs for each of the following policies:
(a) Full insurance.
(b) $5,000 deductible and a $250,000 limit.
(c) 20 percent coinsurance and a $250,000 limit.
(d) $5,000 deductible, 20 percent coinsurance, and a $250,000 limit.

	Policy with Full Coverage (1)	*Policy with a $250 Deductible* (2)	*Implicit Cost of Coverage for $250 Loss* (1) – (2)
(a) Expected claim costs			
(b) Expected claim processing costs			
(a) + (b) Fair premium			
(b)/(a) Percent loading			

8. What is the maximum percentage that a property insurer would pay under a property insurance policy with coverage equal to $1.5 million and an insurance-to-value (coinsurance) requirement of 80 percent if the market value of the property at the time of a loss is
   (a) $1.5 million
   (b) $1.75 million
   (c) $2 million

   For each of the three scenarios, what is the recovery from the property insurer if the property owner experiences a $1 million fire loss?

9. Lawrence lives in California but buys his automobile insurance from a Colorado insurer, which violates California law. He says he lives in Colorado and uses a friend's Colorado address when filling out the application in order to pay the lower Colorado premium rates. What is likely to happen if Lawrence is involved in an accident?

10. Mary buys a woodburning stove for her cabin in the mountains. She remembers that when she originally purchased homeowners insurance for the cabin, the insurance agent asked if she had a woodburning stove, because woodburning stoves increase the risk of fire. At that time, she correctly answered no. Now, she must decide whether to inform her insurance agent about the new stove. Would you advise her to inform the insurance agent? Explain.

References

Arrow, Kenneth. "Insurance, Risk, and Resource Allocation." In *Essays in the Theory of Risk Bearing*. Chicago: Marham Press, 1971. (*Explains how moral hazard and adverse selection limit the insurability of risk.*)

Mayers, David; and Clifford Smith. *Toward a Positive Theory of Insurance*. New York, NY: Salomon Center, New York University, 1982. (*Explains many insurance contract provisions as well as other institutional arrangements in insurance.*)

Rea, Samuel A., Jr. "The Economics of Insurance Law." *International Review of Law and Economics* 13 (1993), pp. 145–62. (*Provides historical and economic background on the important doctrines in insurance law.*)

Answer to Concept Check

1. Insurance contracts rarely provide full coverage because (a) people prefer less than full coverage when premiums exceed expected claim costs (i.e., have positive premium loadings) due to administrative and capital costs; (b) less than full coverage reduces moral hazard; and (c) adverse selection causes low expected loss consumers to have less than full coverage.

Fundamentals of Corporate Risk Management

Risk Management and Shareholder Wealth— A Financial Exposition

---

Chapter Objectives

- Analyze corporate risk management using the concepts and tools of modern financial management.
- Explain the fundamental determinants of firm value: (1) expected cash flows and (2) the opportunity cost of capital.
- Describe how shareholder diversification affects the opportunity cost of capital.
- Explain why corporate risk reduction often does not affect the opportunity cost of capital.
- Analyze how corporate risk reduction affects expected cash flows.

9.1 Principles of Business Valuation

In Chapter 2 we stated that the objective of business risk management is to increase the value of the business to its owners. In this chapter, we first explain the fundamental determinants of business value and then analyze how corporate risk management affects value.

Valuation Formula

A business's value is defined as the present (discounted) value of its expected net cash flows, where net cash flows equal cash inflows minus cash outflows. Thus, to calculate firm value you must first estimate the firm's expected cash flows and then discount the expected cash flows using the appropriate discount rate.

A simple example will illustrate how to calculate a firm's value. Schmit Enterprises is a corporation that will exist for one year. It has no outstanding debt, and the net cash flows per share of its common stock at the end of the year are

TABLE 9–1   **Probability Distribution of Cash Flows per Share for Schmit Enterprises**

Outcome	Probability	End-of-Year Cash Flow per Share
No lawsuit	0.9	$100
Lawsuit	0.1	$100 – $30 = $70

Expected cash flow = (0.9 × $100) + (0.1 × $70) = $97

forecasted to be $100 if it does not lose a lawsuit. However, there is a 10 percent chance that it will lose a lawsuit that will cost $30 per share. We ignore taxes for simplicity. These assumptions imply that the probability distribution for the firm's cash flows is as given in Table 9–1.

The expected cash flow per share at the end of the year is $97 (see Table 9–1). To find the value of Schmit Enterprises today, we discount the end-of-year expected cash flow back to the present. Assuming that the appropriate discount rate is 13.5 percent, the value of one share of stock in Schmit Enterprises today is

$$\text{Value} = \frac{\$97}{1 + 0.135} = \$85.46 \tag{9.1}$$

This is the value of Schmit Enterprises without undertaking any risk management activities. In the subsequent sections we will examine how various risk management activities might affect the probability distribution of cash flows, the discount rate, and thus the stock value of Schmit Enterprises.

It is important to emphasize that we are interested in the value of Schmit Enterprises *today*—that is, prior to knowing what the actual cash flows at the end of the year will be. If you bought one share of Schmit Enterprises today, it would cost $85.46. At the end of the year, you would expect the value of your share to be greater than $85.46. Specifically, you would expect it to be worth 13.5 percent more than $85.46, since 13.5 percent is the discount rate used to value the firm. Your actual return for the year, however, would depend on the firm's actual cash flows at the end of the year. If the firm's actual cash flows equal $100 (no lawsuit), then each share of stock will be worth $100 at the end of the year. This will produce a rate of return on your investment equal to 17.01 percent [(100 – 85.46)/85.46]. If Schmit Enterprises's cash flow per share at the end of the year is $70, then each share of stock will be worth $70 at the end of the year, and your realized rate of return will be –18.09 percent [(70 – 85.46)/85.46]. Thus, your realized rate of return will be either 17.01 percent or –18.09 percent, which implies an expected rate of return equal to 13.5 percent [(17.01 × 0.9) – (18.09 × 0.1)].

This example illustrates the two fundamental determinants of value: (1) the level and timing of expected cash flows, and (2) the interest rate used to discount each cash flow. More complicated examples that increase the number of years considered or that have more complicated cash flow distributions do not change these basic determinants of value. When examining the effects of risk management on value, we must examine how risk management affects each of these fundamental determinants.

In general, the value of a firm can be written as follows:

$$\text{Value} = \sum_{t=1}^{\infty} \frac{\text{Expected net cash flow in year } t}{(1 + r)^t} \tag{9.2}$$

where r is the appropriate discount rate. The appropriate discount rate is the rate of return an investor could expect to earn on an alternative investment with the same risk as the firm's cash flows. It is important to emphasize that the appropriate discount rate depends on the risk of the cash flows. Because of risk aversion, cash flows that are more uncertain should have a higher discount rate. The appropriate rate is called the **opportunity cost of capital,** because it is the expected return an investor could have received had the person invested in a similar risk investment.

Concept Checks

1. Assume Schmit Enterprises's end-of-year cash flow is as described by Table 9–1, but suppose that the price of a share of stock is $90 today.
   (*a*) What are the possible rates of return for the coming year?
   (*b*) What is the expected rate of return?
2. Compare your answer to part (*b*) of question 1 to the example in the text where the stock price today is $85.46 and the expected rate of return is 13.5 percent. What does this example illustrate about the relationship between the expected rate of return on a share of stock and its price, holding the expected cash flows constant?

Components of the Opportunity Cost of Capital

The opportunity cost of capital has two basic components. The first component is the return needed to compensate investors for the time value of money. The second component is the expected return needed to compensate investors for risk. Since the first component only reflects the time value of money and does not consider risk, it is equal to the return an investor could earn on a risk free asset, such as US government bonds. This return usually is called the **risk-free rate** of return. The second component is the additional compensation (premium) over the risk-free rate that is needed to compensate investors for risk. This additional expected return is called the **risk premium.** As mentioned earlier, risk aversion suggests that as the cash flows become riskier, the risk premium increases. As we will see shortly, this intuition is correct, provided that risk is appropriately defined from the perspective of the investor.

As an example, assume that the rate of return on government bonds (the risk-free rate) is 7.0 percent. If the uncertainty associated with the cash flows of

Schmit Enterprises causes investors to require a 6.5 percent expected return as compensation for risk, then the risk premium is 6.5 percent. Adding the risk-free rate and the risk premium yields a 13.5 percent opportunity cost of capital for Schmit Enterprises. This is the discount rate that should be used when finding the present value of Schmit Enterprises's expected cash flows. If another firm, Browne Brothers Inc., had riskier cash flows than Schmit Enterprises, the risk premium for Browne Brothers would be higher than 6.5 percent, and the discount rate used to find the value of Browne Brothers would be higher. The important point is that the opportunity cost of capital for a particular expected cash flow should reflect the uncertainty about the expected cash flow. Thus, the valuation formula (equation 9.1) incorporates the expected value of cash flows (in the numerator) and the risk of cash flows (in the denominator).

Compensation for Risk

The risk premium for Schmit Enterprises in the previous example was assumed to be 6.5 percent. We now discuss determinants of the risk premium. Intuitively, as the risk of the cash flows increases, one would expect the risk premium to increase because investors require compensation for bearing more risk. We must recognize, however, that some risk can be eliminated by investors at virtually zero cost by holding well-diversified portfolios. If investors can diversify away some risk at zero cost, then they will not need to be compensated for this risk. Obviously, any security that provides compensation for risk that can be eliminated at zero cost will be highly desirable to well-diversified investors. However, competition among these investors will bid up the price of such securities until the investors receive compensation only for that risk that they cannot eliminate through diversification.[1]

To make these ideas more concrete, suppose that the stock of Schmit Enterprises is priced so that investors receive compensation for *all* risk, including risk that investors can eliminate through diversification. In particular, assume that 6.5 percent is the appropriate risk premium for risk that cannot be diversified away by investors, but that the stock is currently priced using 8.0 percent as the risk premium. Assuming a risk-free rate of 7.0 percent, the stock is therefore priced using a discount rate equal to 15.0 percent (when it should be using 13.5 percent) so that:

$$\text{Price} = \frac{\$97}{1 + 0.15} = \$84.35 \tag{9.3}$$

An investor buying a share of stock at $84.35 would expect a return of 15.0 percent—the expected value of each share at the end of the year equals $97, which is 15.0 percent higher than the purchase price of $84.35. If the investor were well-diversified, this would be viewed as a good investment because the ex-

---

[1] Students who have studied finance will notice that this is the logic underlying the capital asset pricing model (CAPM).

pected return is greater than the amount needed, 13.5 percent, to compensate the investor for that risk that cannot be eliminated through diversification. Other well-diversified investors also would view the stock of Schmit Enterprises as an attractive investment—that is, they would expect a return greater than what is needed to compensate them for risk that they could not diversify away. Stated differently, the price of the stock is too low because it reflects risk that investors can diversify away on their own. Well-diversified investors would start buying the stock, which would increase the price. As the price increased, the expected return would decrease. Investors would continue to buy the stock and bid up its price until the stock price reached $85.46, which produces the appropriate expected return of 13.5 percent. Thus, in equilibrium Schmit Enterprises's stock would be priced to provide compensation only for risk that could not be eliminated by investors holding diversified portfolios.

This discussion highlights that there are two types of risk.[2] Risk that can be eliminated by investors by holding diversified portfolios is called **diversifiable risk.** Risk that cannot be eliminated by diversification is called **nondiversifiable risk.** Recall from Chapter 3 the intuition for why risk can be eliminated by diversification: When holding a diversified portfolio, the good outcomes (high returns) of some firms tend to offset the bad outcomes of other firms. This "offsetting" effect will work when the events that affect one firm are uncorrelated with the events that affect other firms. Thus, the type of risk which can be diversified away is the risk due to events that are "firm specific," such as an explosion at a plant, theft, a decision by the government to award a company a new contract, and so on. Because the risk that can be diversified away is the risk of events that are specific or idiosyncratic to a particular firm, diversifiable risk often is called *firm-specific risk, idiosyncratic risk,* or *nonsystematic risk.*

In contrast, the risk due to events that affect all firms cannot be diversified away. For example, changes in general economic activity, as reflected in interest rate changes or the growth in gross national product (GNP), affect most firms. Consequently, risk associated with general economic activity cannot be diversified away by investors. Intuitively, when all firms are affected by an event, there are no good outcomes to offset bad outcomes in a portfolio of many stocks. Since risk that cannot be diversified away arises from common, marketwide events, nondiversifiable risk often is called *market risk* or *systematic risk.*

Figure 9–1 summarizes this discussion. The total risk of a firm can be divided into two categories: diversifiable risk and nondiversifiable risk. The appropriate discount rate (the required return) is unaffected by diversifiable risk. The intuition again is that investors can eliminate diversifiable risk on their own at very little cost so that investors do not require compensation for this type of risk. Nondiversifiable risk, however, affects the opportunity cost of capital because investors require compensation for risk that they cannot diversify away on their own.

---

[2] Various models are used to calculate the opportunity cost of capital for firms in practice and controversy exists regarding the appropriate measure of risk. However, almost all models adopt the fundamental principle that some risk can be diversified away by investors and therefore only nondiversifiable risk affects the opportunity cost of capital.

FIGURE 9–1

The components of a firm's total risk and their influence on the opportunity cost of capital

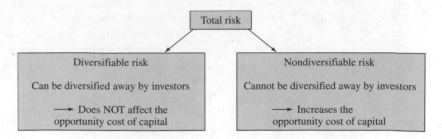

9.2 Risk Management and the Opportunity Cost of Capital

We now examine how risk management affects the discount rate (opportunity cost of capital) that should be used when valuing a firm. From the previous discussion we know that the discount rate equals the risk-free rate plus a risk premium. The risk-free rate is the rate of return on government bonds and cannot be influenced by firm decisions. Thus, if risk management is to affect the discount rate it must affect the risk premium. Recall that the risk premium depends only on the amount of nondiversifiable risk. As a result, if risk management decreases diversifiable risk only (the risk that investors can eliminate by holding diversified portfolios), the risk premium will be unaffected and so the opportunity cost of capital will be unaffected.

Risk management activities like insurance purchases and loss control expenditures typically only reduce a firm's diversifiable risk. The types of risk that insurance companies tend to insure also are risks that the insurance company can largely diversify by selling insurance to many different policyholders. If insurance companies can diversify the risk, then so can shareholders by holding well-diversified portfolios, and thus insurance purchases generally do not reduce a firm's opportunity cost of capital. The risk that is reduced through loss control also tends to be firm-specific risk. For example, the frequency and severity of workplace accidents and product failures are likely to be uncorrelated across firms. These firm-specific risks can be diversified by shareholders and so loss control activities usually will not decrease a firm's opportunity cost of capital.

Recall that nondiversifiable risk exists because there are unexpected events that affect the value of most firms. For example, an unexpected change in aggregate consumer demand is likely to change the value of all companies. Obviously, individual firm actions cannot influence the occurrence of these systematic events, but individual firm actions can reduce the sensitivity of the firm's cash flows to these events. For example, a firm could hedge against nondiversifiable risk, which would decrease the firm's opportunity cost of capital. Even when this occurs, however, one must be careful before concluding that firm's value has been increased. The reason is that, while a decrease in nondiversifiable risk will decrease the opportunity cost of capital, it also is likely to decrease the firm's expected cash flows. To see this, note that when a firm hedges nondiversifiable risk, it is shifting this risk to someone else who cannot eliminate it through diversification. The party who accepts nondiversifiable risk will require compensation for taking on this risk, and the cost of compensating the other party will decrease the firm's cash flows. As a consequence, reducing nondiversifiable risk has an ambiguous effect on value. The cost of shifting nondiversifiable risk to someone else (as reflected in lower expected cash flows) often will offset the benefit of reducing the discount rate. Provided everyone prices nondiversifiable risk in the same way, the two effects will offset each other perfectly. The amount that the firm must pay the other party for accepting the nondiversifiable risk would equal the amount by which the value of the firm would otherwise have increased from the lower discount rate.[3]

In summary, risk management is unlikely to decrease the opportunity cost of capital for firms with well diversified shareholders because risk management activities generally decrease the type of risk (diversifiable risk) that shareholders can eliminate on their own by holding diversified portfolios. If risk management does decrease nondiversifiable risk and therefore the opportunity cost of capital, the cost of doing so is likely to negate the benefits of reducing the discount rate.

Concept Check

3. Identify whether each of the following loss exposures is likely to involve nondiversifiable risk or diversifiable risk: (*a*) revenue losses for an automaker due to higher interest rates, and (*b*) property losses due to theft.

9.3 Risk Management and Expected Cash Flows

The previous section explained that corporate risk reduction is unlikely to affect the firm's opportunity cost of capital (the denominators in equation 9.2). Therefore, if corporate risk reduction is to increase shareholder wealth, risk reduction must increase expected cash flows to shareholders (the numerators in equation 9.2). We show how this can occur in this section. For concreteness, our discussion focuses on corporate insurance purchases. The main points, however, generally apply to other corporate activities, such as hedging and loss control, that reduce the variability of cash flows.

Table 9–2 provides an overview of the effects of corporate insurance purchases on a firm's expected cash flows to shareholders. The main disadvantage of purchasing insurance is that the firm must pay the loading on the insurance premium, which—holding all other factors constant—decreases expected cash flows. As introduced in Chapter 7, there are four main advantages of purchasing insurance:

1. By bundling insurance coverage with claim processing and loss control services, a firm may be able to lower the costs of obtaining these services.

---

[3] Similarly, insurers will demand compensation (in the form of a higher premium) for insuring nondiversifiable risk. Therefore, the effect of such insurance on a firm's opportunity cost of capital will be offset by lower expected cash flows because the firm must pay a higher premium loading.

TABLE 9–2   **Main Effects of Purchasing Insurance on Expected Cash Flows**

Description	Effect on Expected Cash Flows
Pay loading on insurance premiums	Decrease
Decrease cost of services from insurers • Claims processing services • Loss control services	Increase
Decrease likelihood of having to raise new funds • To pay for losses • To finance new projects	Increase
Decrease likelihood of financial distress • Decreases expected bankruptcy costs • Improves contractual terms with other claimants (i.e., lenders, suppliers, employees, customers)	Increase
Reduce expected tax payments • Tax benefits of insurance • Ability to increase debt-related tax shields	Increase

2. Insurance reduces the likelihood that the firm will have to raise new funds to finance losses or to finance new investment projects. Since raising new funds, either by borrowing from a bank or issuing new debt or equity securities, can be costly, insurance can be beneficial because it reduces the likelihood of having to incur these costs and of foregoing otherwise profitable investments because of these costs.

3. Insurance reduces the likelihood that a firm will experience financial distress, which lowers expected bankruptcy costs. Financial distress also can impose costs on other parties who contract with the firm, such as employees, suppliers, lenders, and customers. Firms with a higher likelihood of financial distress find that these other parties offer less attractive contractual terms—for example, employees may require additional compensation to work for a firm with a higher likelihood of financial distress. By reducing the likelihood of financial distress, insurance therefore increases the firm's expected cash flows.

4. Insurance can reduce a firm's expected tax payments. The direct tax effects of insurance are discussed in detail in Chapter 10. Risk reduction also can indirectly reduce expected tax payments by allowing a firm to increase its use of debt financing, which increases interest tax deductions.

Notice that many of the advantages of purchasing insurance result from decreasing the likelihood that either shareholders or other claimants will incur some additional cost, beyond the loss that is being insured. For example, insurance reduces both the probability that the firm will have to raise costly external capital and the probability that other claimants will incur costs due to financial distress. Thus, many of the benefits of insurance arise because insurance reduces the probability that some cost beyond the insured loss will be incurred. In this respect, insurance can be viewed as a loss control device: The purchase of insurance reduces the expected cost of indirect losses.

The remainder of this chapter illustrates the main cash flow effects of purchasing insurance with a series of examples. To present the ideas as simply as possible, we do not use an elaborate example that simultaneously incorporates all of the main effects; instead, each effect is examined in isolation. In practice, however, these effects are not mutually exclusive; they all are potentially relevant for a firm deciding how much insurance to purchase.

Insurance Premium Loadings

We begin by considering how the purchase of insurance would affect the share price of Schmit Enterprises if none of the benefits shown in Table 9–2 were present. Recall from section 9.1 that with no insurance Schmit's end-of-year per share cash flows will be $100 with probability 0.9 and $70 with probability 0.1 and that an opportunity cost of capital of 13.5 percent implies that the share price is $85.46. Note in this example that there are no taxes. And since Schmit Enterprises only exists for one year and its end-of-year cash flows are always positive, the firm will not have to raise new funds in the future, and it has no chance of financial distress. Finally, we will assume that if insurance is purchased, the insurer provides no services other than reimbursing the losses that the firm incurs. Under all these assumptions, none of the potential benefits of insurance listed in Table 9–2 exist.

Insurance with No Loading.   Suppose that Schmit Enterprises purchases a liability insurance policy with coverage equal to $30 per share of stock and a premium of $3 per share of stock. For simplicity we assume that the insurance premium is paid at the end of the year. Because the premium is equal to expected claim costs (0.1 is the probability of a claim and the size of a claim is $30 per share), the premium has no loading. In this case, the purchase of insurance will not change Schmit's expected cash flows and therefore will not change its share price.

To verify this, Table 9–3 summarizes how the insurance policy changes the

TABLE 9–3   **Probability Distribution for Schmit Enterprises's Cash Flow per Share with $30 of Insurance Coverage per Share and a Premium of $3 per Share**

Outcome	Probability	End-of-Year Cash Flow
No lawsuit	0.9	$100 – $3 = $97
Lawsuit	0.1	$100 – $30 + $30 – $3 = $97

Expected cash flow = (0.9 × $97) + (0.1 × $97) = $97

firm's cash flows. If a lawsuit does not occur, then the cash flow per share equals $100 minus the per share insurance premium of $3, which equals $97. If the firm loses the lawsuit, then the firm's cash flow per share equals $100 minus the loss of $30, plus the reimbursement from the insurance company of $30, minus the insurance premium of $3. Thus, insurance causes the cash flow to equal $97 regardless of whether a lawsuit occurs. Referring to Table 9–1, $97 also is the value of expected cash flows without the insurance policy.

In this case, the insurance policy does not change the firm's expected cash flows; it just makes cash flows more predictable. But from section 9.2 we know that the shareholders can diversify away the cash flow risk on their own so that insurance will not change the discount rate (13.5 percent). Consequently, the share price is unchanged by the insurance policy.

Insurance with a Loading.   Insurance premiums of course usually will exceed expected claim costs because of the insurer's administrative and capital costs. Suppose that the markup over claim costs is 40 percent, so that the insurance premium is $3(1.40) = $4.20 per share, which again for simplicity is paid at the end of the year. Under these conditions, the firm's cash flows are given by Table 9–4. If a lawsuit does not occur, then the firm's cash flow equals $95.80 ($100 per share minus the insurance premium of $4.20). If the firm loses the lawsuit, then the firm's cash flow also equals $95.80 ($100 minus the loss of $30, plus the $30 reimbursement from the insurance company, minus the insurance premium of $4.20). Comparing this scenario to Table 9–1 indicates that purchasing insurance at a premium of $4.20 causes Schmit's expected cash flow to be less than the expected cash flow without insurance ($95.80 versus $97). The difference is due to the loading of $1.20 on the insurance policy. The price per share with insurance equals $95.80/1.135 = $84.41, which is less than the share price if no insurance is purchased ($85.46). The lower price is due to the present value of the costs of the insurance policy's loading ($1.20/1.135). Intuitively, the firm can save the cost of the loading by not purchasing insurance.

These examples illustrate that by purchasing insurance a firm shifts its expected losses to an insurer. However, since the insurance premium exceeds the value of expected losses, purchasing the insurance policy reduces the firm's expected cash flows.

TABLE 9–4   **Probability Distribution for Schmit Enterprises's Cash Flow per Share with $30 of Insurance Coverage per Share and a Premium Equal to $4.20 per Share**

Outcome	Probability	End-of-Year Cash Flow
No lawsuit	0.9	$100 – $4.20 = $95.80
Lawsuit	0.1	$100 – $30 + $30 – $4.20 = $95.80

Expected cash flow = (0.9 × $95.80) + (0.1 × $95.80) = $95.80

Services Provided by Insurers

The previous example assumed that the insurer reimbursed losses but provided no other services. In practice, insurers frequently provide loss control services and almost always provide claims processing services; these services are bundled with the promise to pay claims. A firm, however, also can hire its own employees to provide these services or purchase them from noninsurance companies. In addition, many insurers sell these services without bundling them with insurance.

The key issue is whether bundling loss control and claims processing services with an insurer's promise to pay claims is the least-cost way of purchasing the services demanded by the firm. For a given level of quality, if the firm can obtain these services at the lowest cost through an insurance policy, then the firm would have an incentive to purchase insurance apart from any value obtained from the insurer's promise to pay claims.

To illustrate, assume that the cash flows in the Schmit Enterprises example are prior to the purchase of the loss control and claims processing services and that the cost for Schmit Enterprises to purchase these services in the absence of insurance is $1.50 per share. Then, without insurance, its cash flows will be either $98.50 ($100 − $1.50) or $68.50 ($100 − $30 − $1.50), and its expected cash flows will equal $95.50. As illustrated in Table 9–4, its expected cash flow with insurance is $95.80, which is $0.30 per share higher than without insurance. Assuming the insurer provides the same level and quality of services as Schmit Enterprises desires, the firm has higher expected cash flow by purchasing insurance. The reason is that the cost of purchasing these services when they are bundled with insurance is lower than the cost of purchasing these services elsewhere. Specifically, the implicit cost of the services bundled with insurance is the loading on the policy ($1.20 per share), whereas the cost of purchasing the services elsewhere is $1.50 per share.

Why would bundling services with the promise to pay claims result in lower costs? One reason is that with bundling the service provider has greater incentive to provide high quality service. For example, a firm that both provides loss control services and pays losses has an additional incentive to identify and undertake cost-effective loss control measures. A firm that both provides claims processing services and pays losses has an additional incentive to identify fraudulent claims. If the service and financial responsibility for claims are not bundled, additional resources must be expended in order to monitor the service provider and design contracts that provide proper incentives. When monitoring is too costly and contract design efforts ineffective, bundling the services with the financial responsibility for paying losses can be the least-cost method of obtaining services.

Insurance and the Likelihood of Having to Raise Costly External Funds

Raising New Funds to Pay for Losses.   In the Schmit Enterprises example, the firm had enough internal funds to pay the losses from a lawsuit. Sometimes, however, a firm will not have sufficient internal funds to pay all uninsured losses.

When this occurs, the firm must find a way to pay losses from future cash flows or else declare bankruptcy. Well-functioning financial markets provide a way of using future cash flows. For example, by borrowing money from a bank or issuing new debt or equity securities, a firm can raise the funds needed to pay losses and then use future cash flows to pay back the bank or the new investors. The use of bank borrowings or new security issues to pay losses does not imply that the loss is borne by the bank or the new investors. The loss is borne by the owners of the firm at the time of the loss because a portion of the firm's future cash flows will be used to repay the bank or the new investors.

An example will help illustrate these points. Consider Cather Inc., which, in contrast to Schmit Enterprises, is expected to operate over a two-year period. The first year's cash flows are uncertain because of the possibility of a lawsuit. Specifically, the firm will have cash flows equal to $15 per share with probability 0.9 and –$5 per share with probability 0.1. In essence, the firm has a 10 percent chance of suffering a $20 per share loss relative to its normal cash flow. If the loss occurs and the firm is uninsured, it must raise new funds or else go bankrupt. Fortunately for Cather, its second year cash flows are known to be $25 a share. If the uninsured loss occurs, Cather therefore can pay for the loss by borrowing money or issuing new stock and using the second year's cash flows to pay back the loan or the new investors. We will assume that Cather issues new stock, although borrowing the funds would yield the same conclusions.

We will initially assume that issuing new stock is costless in the sense that the firm only has to offer the new stockholders a rate of return equal to the opportunity cost of capital, which is assumed to equal 10 percent. In other words, there are no transaction costs, such as investment banker fees, and securities are properly priced so that investors do not receive more than the opportunity cost of capital. Under these conditions, if Cather raises $20 per share to pay for the loss (if it occurs), it must pay the new investors $22 ($20 × 1.1) at the end of the second year.

Table 9–5 compares the cash flows available for the original investors under two alternative methods of paying losses: (1) Cather purchases $20 of insurance coverage at the beginning of the first year and pays a premium of $2 per share (the expected claim cost) at the end of the first year, and (2) Cather issues $20 of new

---

TABLE 9–5   Cash Flow Comparison: Purchasing Insurance versus Issuing New Stock to Pay for Losses

Loss Financing Approach	Outcome	Cash Flows at End of Year 1	Cash Flows at End of Year 2 available for Original Shareholders
Purchase $20 of insurance coverage for a premium of $2 at the beginning of year 1	No loss	$13	$25
	Loss	$13	$25
Issue equity worth $20 at end of year 1 if loss occurs	No loss	$15	$25
	Loss	$15	$ 3

stock at the end of the first year if the loss occurs. If Cather purchases insurance, then its cash flows at the end of the first year are $13 ($15 minus the $2 premium) and $25 at the end of the second year, regardless of whether the loss occurs. If instead Cather issues new stock if the loss occurs, then cash flows depend on whether the loss occurs. If the loss does not occur, then shareholders receive $15 at the end of the first year and $25 at the end of the second year. If the loss occurs, then Cather raises $20 from new investors to pay for the loss; this leaves $15 for the original shareholders at the end of the first year. But at the end of the second year, the original shareholders only receive $3 because $22 must go to the new investors.

While issuing new stock to pay for the loss results in different cash flows for the firm compared to buying insurance, it does not result in a different stock price at the beginning of the first year. As illustrated in Table 9–6, the stock price if insurance is purchased equals the present value of the $13 first year cash flow plus the present value of the $25 second year cash flow, for a total $32.48. When the firm issues equity to pay for the loss, the stock price equals the present value of the $15 first year cash flow plus the present value of the expected second year cash flow (90 percent chance of $25 and 10 percent chance of $3), which again totals $32.48. Thus, in this example with no insurance premium loading and no transaction costs associated with issuing new securities, the shareholders would be indifferent between the two alternatives.

Although Table 9–6 illustrates that the stock price at the beginning of the first year is unaffected by whether the firm purchases insurance or issues equity if it is needed, the two loss financing strategies differ regarding stock price uncertainty in the future. If insurance is purchased, the stock price at the end of the first year will be certain since cash flows in this example are certain with full insurance. The end of the first year stock price with insurance will be $13 + $25/1.1 = $35.73, regardless of whether the loss occurs. If instead the firm issues equity if the loss occurs, then the end of year 1 stock price will depend on whether the loss occurs. Without a loss the stock price will be $15 + $25/1.1 = $37.73, and with a loss the stock price will be $15 + $3/1.1 = $17.73. Thus, the stock price drops by $20 (the size of the loss) if the loss occurs. This illustrates that by issuing equity to finance the loss payment, the original equityholders bear the cost of the loss.

TABLE 9–6   **Stock Price Comparison: Purchasing Insurance versus Issuing New Stock to Pay for Losses**

Loss Financing Approach	Stock Price at Beginning of Year 1
Purchase $20 of insurance coverage for a premium of $2 at the beginning of year 1	$\frac{\$13}{1.1} + \frac{\$25}{1.1^2} = \$32.48$
Issue equity worth $20 at end of year 1 if loss occurs	$\frac{\$15}{1.1} + \frac{(0.9)(\$25) + (0.1)(\$3)}{1.1^2} = \$32.48$

Issuing securities can be costly in practice because of investment banking fees and security registration costs. New securities also may be underpriced by the market, which implies that existing owners are selling securities for less than their true value. This underpricing is a cost imposed on existing owners—they are not fully paid for the part of the firm given to new investors. When choosing how to finance losses, a firm must compare the expected costs of issuing securities to the premium loading for insurance.

Suppose, for example, that the premium loading is 20 percent of expected claim costs or $0.40 per share ($0.20 \times 0.1 \times 20), while the total costs of issuing securities equals 25 percent of the funds raised or $5 per share ($0.25 \times 20). Since the probability that securities will be issued equals 0.1, the expected cost of issuing securities is $0.50 per share. Because the premium loading is less than the expected cost of issuing securities, the cost of financing losses is less with insurance.

In summary, this example illustrates three important points. First, if the firm has insufficient internal funds to pay uninsured losses, the firm must raise new funds by either borrowing or issuing new securities (assuming bankruptcy is not the best option). Second, when new funds are raised to pay for uninsured losses, the firm's owners at the time of the loss still bear the cost of the uninsured losses, because the value of their shares declines by the value of the loss. Third, when deciding how much insurance to purchase, the insurance premium loading must be compared to the expected cost of raising new funds following a loss.

Increased Likelihood of Raising New Funds for New Investment Projects. Even if a firm has sufficient internal funds to pay losses, the use of these funds can create an opportunity cost that was ignored in the previous example. The use of internal funds to pay uninsured losses implies that fewer internal funds will be available to finance new projects. Consequently, firms that use internal funds to pay uninsured losses are more likely to have to issue costly new securities to finance new projects. The costs of raising new funds reduce the value of new projects. In some cases, issuance and underpricing costs can be so high that a firm will forego what otherwise would have been value-increasing investment projects. In addition to savings on the costs of issuing securities, insurance can improve investment decisions in these cases.

To illustrate, assume Sommers Corp. will have a valuable investment opportunity available at the end of the year (e.g., building a new plant). In particular, if Sommers invests $25 million, the project will generate additional cash flows that have a present value of $27 million. Using the language of finance, this project is a positive net present value project, where **net present value (NPV)** is defined as the present value of the project's net cash flows. This particular project has NPV equal to $2 million ($27 – $25). Sommers Corp. has several alternative methods of financing the $25 million investment, including issuing new equity or new debt at the end of the year. Issuing securities, however, is costly because of security underwriting costs paid to investment bankers and because the new securities may be underpriced. The costs of issuing securities reduce the **adjusted net pres-**

ent value of the project; that is, the net present value minus the costs associated with financing the project.[4] For example, if the costs of issuing securities were equal to $1 million, then the adjusted net present value would be only $1 million ($2 – $1). If the costs of issuing securities were equal to $2.5 million, then the adjusted net present value would be negative ($2 – $2.5) and Sommers would not adopt the project.

As noted earlier, security issuance costs can be avoided if the new project is financed with internal funds. Consistent with this idea, most projects are financed with internal funds in practice. The problem is that Sommers may not have sufficient internal funds available. Assume, for example, that there is a 5 percent chance that Sommers will lose a lawsuit and be forced to pay damages of $30 million. If this occurs, Sommers will have insufficient internal funds to finance the new project and, without insurance, it will either have to issue new securities or forego the project. Alternatively, Sommers can ensure that sufficient funds will be available to finance the new project by purchasing liability insurance.

Suppose that a liability insurance policy with a $25 million limit has a premium equal to $1.34 million. Since the expected claim costs equal $1.25 million ($25 million × 0.05), the loading on the policy is $90,000 ($1.34 million minus $1.25 million).[5] Sommers must compare the premium loading to the expected cost of not having sufficient internal funds to finance the project. As described above, without insurance, Sommers will pass up the investment project if it loses the lawsuit and the cost of issuing securities equals $2.5 million. Since the probability of losing a lawsuit is 0.05, the expected cost of not having sufficient internal funds to finance the investment project is the net present value of the project ($2 million) times 0.05, which equals $100,000. Because the premium loading of $90,000 is less than the expected cost of foregoing the project ($100,000), Sommers should purchase the insurance.

In summary, because of the costs of issuing new securities, the lower cost method of financing new investment often is to use internal funds. The amount of internal funds available, however, is uncertain due to events such as liability suits. An uninsured firm sometimes will find that it has insufficient internal funds to adopt positive net present value projects. When this occurs, the firm will either have to forego the project or incur the costs associated with issuing new securities. Insurance can ensure that the firm will have sufficient internal funds to adopt positive net present value projects without having to incur the costs of issuing new securities.

---

[4] The costs of financing the project could be negative due to the interest tax shields on debt, in which case the adjusted net present value would exceed the net present value.

[5] The loading in this example is less than 10 percent, which is small compared to what would be observed in practice for liability insurance. The example nevertheless illustrates that risk reduction helps to preserve internal funds for investment purposes, which can increase value if raising external funds is costly. The premium loading on actual policies also reflects the expected cost of loss control and claim processing services, which are not considered in this example. Sommers presumably would need to purchase these services separately if the insurance policy were not purchased.

Concept Checks

4. If Sommers were uninsured, would it adopt the new project following a $25 million liability loss if the security issuance costs were $1.5 million instead of $2.5 million?

5. Would Sommers purchase the insurance policy described in the text if the premium were $1.5 million (instead of $1.34 million) and security issuance costs were $2.5 million?

Insurance and Financial Distress

A firm is "bankrupt" when it does not have sufficient funds to pay what it owes other parties (creditors) and therefore either must be legally reorganized to restructure the terms of its obligations or liquidated with the proceeds paid to creditors. The process of reorganizing or liquidating is costly—attorneys and accountants must be hired. Thus, actions that reduce the probability of bankruptcy can be beneficial because they reduce the probability of incurring these direct bankruptcy costs.

In addition to bankruptcy, a firm also can experience **financial distress** when it has difficulty meeting its obligations and therefore has a relatively high probability of bankruptcy. Financially distressed firms sometimes become bankrupt, but not always. Since bankruptcy and financial distress short of bankruptcy can impose costs on parties who have contractual relationships with the firm (such as employees, lenders, suppliers, and customers), the terms at which these parties will contract with the firm reflect the firm's probability of financial distress. Insurance can decrease the likelihood that a firm will experience financial distress and thereby improve the terms at which these other claimants are willing to contract with the firm. This in turn increases the firm's expected cash flows. To illustrate these effects, we will first focus on how the probability of bankruptcy affects contractual terms and then expand on the problems created by financial distress short of bankruptcy.

Manager Compensation Example.   Consider a simple example in which insurance changes the terms at which a manager will work for a firm because insurance decreases the probability of bankruptcy. J. R., the manager of Garven Corp., knows that he will not receive the compensation that he was promised if the firm goes bankrupt and that he will be forced to incur the costs of finding a new job. Since insurance reduces the probability that the firm will go bankrupt, insurance reduces the expected amount of compensation demanded by J. R. Consequently, the firm's expected costs decrease and its expected cash flows increase.

Specifically, assume that Garven's end-of-year cash flows prior to paying J. R. equal $1 million if the firm is not sued and $0 if it is sued. The probability of a suit is 0.05. Also assume that J. R. would work for $100,000 if he were certain to receive his promised compensation. The problem is that if Garven Corp. loses a lawsuit, the firm will not have any money to pay J. R. Since J. R. views working for this firm as risky, he will do so only if the firm promises to pay him

TABLE 9–7   **Cash Flows of Garven Corp. without Insurance**
(manager is promised $125,000 but receives it only if a lawsuit does not occur)

Outcome	Probability	Cash Flow before Managerial Compensation	Managerial Compensation	Net Cash Flow to Stockholders
No lawsuit	0.95	$1,000,000	$125,000	$875,000
Lawsuit	0.05	$ 0	$ 0	$ 0
Expected cash flow = (0.95 × $875,000) + (0.05 × $0) = $831,250				

$125,000. The additional $25,000 is demanded as compensation for the risk of not being paid what was promised and the hassle of finding another job. Because of the possibility of a lawsuit, J. R. knows that he will receive $125,000 with probability 0.95 and $0 with probability 0.05. His expected compensation therefore is $118,750.

Table 9–7 summarizes the cash flows of Garven Corp. without insurance. With probability 0.95, equityholders will receive $875,000 ($1 million minus the $125,000 in managerial compensation), and with probability 0.05, the firm will be bankrupt and equityholders will receive $0, in which case J. R. also will receive $0.

Now suppose that Garven Corp. purchases $400,000 of liability insurance coverage at a premium of $25,000. Since the expected claim cost equals $20,000 ($400,000 × 0.05), the premium loading is $5,000. The purchase of insurance, however, will keep the firm from going bankrupt if a lawsuit occurs, which implies that the managerial compensation contract can be changed if the firm insures.

Let's work through the effects of insurance on the firm's cash flows. If the lawsuit does not occur, cash flow before managerial compensation equals $1 million minus the $25,000 insurance premium. If a lawsuit does occur, cash flow before managerial compensation equals $0, plus the $400,000 of insurance proceeds, minus the $25,000 premium for a total of $375,000. Thus, with insurance the firm always has enough money to pay the manager, so that J. R. can be promised $100,000 with certainty. Table 9–8 summarizes the cash flows if Garven Corp. purchases insurance and the manager's compensation equals $100,000.

TABLE 9–8   **Cash Flows for Garven Corp. with $400,000 of Liability Coverage**
(premium equals $25,000 and the manager is promised $100,000)

Outcome	Probability	Cash Flow before Managerial Compensation	Managerial Compensation	Net Cash Flow to Stockholders
No lawsuit	0.95	$1,000,000 – $25,000	$100,000	$875,000
Lawsuit	0.05	$0 + $400,000 – $25,000	$100,000	$275,000
Expected cash flow = (0.95 × $875,000) + (0.05 × $275,000) = $845,000				

A comparison of Tables 9–7 and 9–8 indicates that the cash flows with insurance are at least as high as the cash flows without insurance in this example. Thus, insurance increases Garven's expected cash flows and its stock price because it reduces Garven's expected cost of managerial compensation. Without insurance expected managerial compensation is $118,750 (0.95 × $125,000). With insurance expected managerial compensation is $100,000. The savings in expected managerial compensation amounts to $18,750, while the premium loading is only $5,000. The increase in expected cash flows therefore is $13,750. The reason that insurance decreases the cost of compensating the manager is that it reduces the expected cost to the manager from possibly having to find a new job. In addition, the manager is risk averse and cannot diversify away the risk associated with being employed in the firm. In effect, the firm purchases insurance for its risk-averse manager (i.e., it guarantees that he will be paid), who in turn pays for the insurance by accepting lower compensation.

Implications for Other Claimants.   Insurance can alter the terms at which claimants other than managers contract with the firm as well. Suppliers, for example, are likely to contract with the firm at lower prices if the firm decreases the probability that it will become bankrupt. The effect of insurance on supplier contracts is likely to be greater when the supplier has to make specific investments in order to supply the firm. For example, if Regan's Parts needed to make or acquire specialized machinery to supply Garven Corp., Regan's Parts would require compensation for the risk that the specific value of its investment would be lost. Similarly, customers will be willing to pay higher prices if they know the firm is likely to be around in the future and able to service its products. The effect on product prices is likely to be greater when the firm sells products that will be used over time and for which the manufacturer has expertise in servicing.[6] A firm's lenders also are concerned with a firm's probability of bankruptcy. The interest rate that lenders charge will increase as the probability of bankruptcy increases because of the costs associated with collecting promised payments. As a result, lenders (and debtholders) often require that a firm be insured.

Financial Distress Prior to Bankruptcy.   The Garven Corp. example assumed that the firm could experience a large loss that would bankrupt the firm. You might have the wrong impression that only those losses that cause bankruptcy need to be insured to increase firm value. As we now explain, the issues just discussed also are relevant to situations where losses cause a firm to experience financial distress without actually going bankrupt. This is because financial distress

---

[6] Another scenario in which customers are likely to be concerned with the possibility that a firm will go bankrupt is when the product or service imposes the possibility of personal injury on the consumer. For example, air travelers may not be willing to purchase tickets (or will only purchase tickets at a lower price) from an airline that is financially weak because of fear that the airline will invest less in safety.

can create incentives that cause the firm's managers to make decisions that increase the likelihood of bankruptcy. Consequently, insurance that reduces the likelihood that a firm will experience financial distress apart from bankruptcy can be beneficial because it enables the firm to improve contractual terms with other claimants.

A general characteristic of the claims of bondholders, employees, customers, and suppliers is that these parties must be paid before the shareholders of the firm receive any funds. This characteristic can distort the investment choices of shareholders following a major loss in two ways. First, shareholders sometimes will have an incentive to forego good investment projects (positive net present value projects) following a loss that causes a firm to experience financial distress. Second, shareholders may have an incentive to invest in some negative net present value projects with high risk.

Some positive net present value projects may not be undertaken following a major loss that causes financial distress because the returns from the new investment will mostly accrue to other claimants who must be paid before shareholders. For example, suppose that if Mayers Inc. experiences a major flood that destroys its plant, Mayers Inc. will be unable to pay its lenders what they were promised unless the firm replaces the plant. The shareholders of Mayers Inc., however, may be reluctant to pay for replacement after the flood even if the cost of replacement is less than the total returns from replacement. The reason is that the returns from replacement following the flood will mostly accrue to the lenders. That is, replacement bails out the lenders (pun intended).

Flood insurance would provide the funds necessary to replace the equipment and therefore commit Mayers Inc. to replacement following a flood. Since insurance commits the firm to replacement, it alleviates lenders' concerns about being paid following a loss. Lenders therefore are willing to lend money at lower rates when the firm is insured. Stated differently, if the firm does not have insurance, lenders will raise the interest rate that will be charged, because they know that the firm sometimes will pass up good investment projects that would have increased lenders' payoffs. Consequently, this cost of not being insured is borne by shareholders in the form of a higher interest rate paid on the firm's debt. The appendix to this chapter provides a more detailed example of how insurance can solve the *underinvestment problem* that can arise following a major loss.

As noted, investment decisions also can be distorted in that financial distress may cause shareholders to have an incentive to invest in negative net present value projects with high risk. Intuitively, if a firm is close to bankruptcy, shareholders have little to lose if a high-risk project turns out bad. However, if the high-risk project turns out well, shareholders can earn a high return. Investors will price a firm's debt securities taking into account the likelihood that the firm will go into financial distress and invest in negative net present value projects. Corporate actions that reduce the likelihood of financial distress—like purchasing insurance—will therefore induce investors to pay higher prices for the firm's debt, because the likelihood that the firm will adopt risky projects with negative net present value has been reduced.

9.4 Summary

- The value of an asset equals the present value of its expected cash flows using the opportunity cost of capital as the discount rate.

- The opportunity cost of capital equals the risk-free rate of return plus a risk premium. The risk premium depends upon the amount of nondiversifiable risk associated with the cash flows.

- Risk management activities, such as purchasing insurance and engaging in loss control, typically do not affect nondiversifiable risk and therefore do not decrease the opportunity cost of capital.

- Corporate insurance purchases can affect expected cash flows in five key ways:

  1. Insurance premium loadings decrease expected cash flows.

  2. Services provided by insurers increase expected cash flows if the necessary premium loading is less than the cost of obtaining these services elsewhere.

  3. The reduction in the likelihood of having to raise new funds to pay losses or to finance new investment projects increases expected cash flows.

  4. The reduction in the likelihood of financial distress, including costly bankruptcy, improves contractual terms with nonowner claimants and therefore increases expected cash flows.

  5. The reduction in expected tax payments increases expected cash flows (see Chapter 10).

Key Terms

opportunity cost of capital   191
risk-free rate   191
risk premium   191
diversifiable risk   193

nondiversifiable risk   193
net present value (NPV)   202
adjusted net present value   202
financial distress   204

Questions and Problems

1. An analyst knows with certainty that Skipper Inc. will exist for two years and have the following cash flows per share:

	Year 1	*Year 2*
Revenue	$100	$100
Costs	$ 80	$ 80
Net cash flow	$ 20	$ 20

What is the stock price of Skipper Inc. if the opportunity cost of capital is 10 percent?

2. The analyst in problem 1 realizes that Skipper Inc.'s costs may not be $80 per share with certainty. Instead, each year there is a 10 percent chance that a worker will be seriously injured and that Skipper will have to pay the employee's medical expenses and lost wages. If an injury does occur, medical expenses and lost wages equal $5 per share, so that Skipper's costs equal $85 per share. If an injury does not occur (which has a probability of 0.9), then Skipper's costs equal $79.44 per share.

   (*a*) What is Skipper's expected net cash flow in each year?

(b) If the opportunity cost of capital is 10 percent, what is the stock price?

(c) Provide an argument for why the opportunity cost of capital should not change because of the risk of worker injury.

3. Suppose that Skipper Inc. (from problem 2) purchases workers' compensation insurance to cover the costs of medical expenses and lost wages. The premium for full coverage is $0.50 per share. What is the stock price? Compare your answer to that obtained in 2(b) and intuitively explain the relationship.

4. Redo problem 3 using a premium of $0.75 per share. Compare your answer to that obtained in problem 3 and intuitively explain the relationship.

5. If the risk-free rate equals 7 percent and the risk premium for Thistle Corp. is 5 percent, what is the opportunity cost of capital for Thistle? Suppose Thistle purchases insurance to cover property damage. What is likely to happen to its opportunity cost of capital?

6. Ambrose Motor Corp. has expected earnings before interest payments for the next year equal to $100 million if it does not lose a product liability lawsuit. Interest and principal payments on its debt equal $60 million, leaving $40 million for shareholders if it does not lose a product liability suit. The probability of losing a product liability suit is 0.02, and the expected damage if a suit is lost equals $50 million. If the suit is lost, the firm will be unable to make its promised payments to debtholders and it will have to renegotiate its debt payments. The legal and administrative costs of renegotiations (including the cost of managers' time) equal $5 million. Should Ambrose Motor purchase a liability insurance policy with a $50 million limit for a premium of $1.2 million? Explain.

7. Because of its relatively high probability of going bankrupt, Snow Corp.'s consumers are concerned about its ability to fulfill warranties, employees are demanding greater compensation for the risk of losing their jobs, and suppliers are demanding higher prices for the risk of losing the value of their specific investments. Assume that Snow's high probability of bankruptcy can be reduced by purchasing additional insurance coverage. What factors should Snow's managers examine when deciding whether to purchase additional coverage? Explain.

References

Froot, Ken; David Scharfstein; and Jeremy Stein. "A Framework for Risk Management." *Harvard Business Review,* December 1994. (*Provides examples of how risk reduction can avoid financing costs and improve investment decisions.*)

Mayers, David; and Clifford Smith. "On the Corporate Demand for Insurance." *Journal of Business 22* (1982), pp. 281–96. (*Analyzes the demand for insurance by corporations using modern financial theory.*)

Answers to Concept Checks

1. (a) The possible rates of return are 11.1 percent [(100 – 90)/90] and –22.2 percent [(70 – 90)/90].

   (b) The expected rate of return equals 7.8 percent [(11.1 × 0.9) – (22.2 × 0.1)].

2. There is an inverse relationship between expected return on a stock and the stock price, holding the expected cash flows constant.

3. (a) Since the level of interest rates affects the

present value of most firms, the risk due to changes in interest rates is likely to be nondiversifiable risk.

(*b*) Since a firm's property loss due to theft is largely the result of firm-specific events, the risk due to theft is likely to be largely diversifiable risk.

4. If the costs of issuing securities were $1.5 million, Sommers would still adopt the project since its net present value is $2 million. In this case, the cost of being uninsured is the lost net present value due to the cost of issuing securities (i.e., the $1.5 million).

5. Sommers would not purchase insurance because the premium loading would be $250,000 ($1.5 million minus $1.25 million), which exceeds the expected cost of foregoing the project ($100,000).

APPENDIX 9A
HOW INSURANCE CAN MITIGATE THE UNDERINVESTMENT PROBLEM

Mr. Mayers is planning to build a new plant to produce airplane parts. He has great ideas regarding how to build a more efficient plant than his competitors. After building the plant and operating for one year, he will sell the operation and retire to Hilton Head. The project requires a $30 million investment. Although he is quite wealthy, Mr. Mayers does not have $30 million sitting around and he therefore decides to borrow some money. He asks a bank how much he can borrow if he promises to repay $28 million at the end of the year. For simplicity, assume that the time value of money is zero and that the risk premium is zero. As a result, when calculating present values, the discount rate is zero.

The bank investigates what Mr. Mayers is planning to do with the borrowed funds (it wants to know whether he will be able to repay the $28 million). The investigation uncovers the following information. At the end of the year, the assets of the plant will be worth $35 million with probability 0.95. However, with probability 0.05, an explosion will damage the plant and the assets will be worth $20 million. If the explosion does occur, Mr. Mayers could invest an additional $10 million and restore the assets to $35 million. Notice that the $10 million investment following an explosion is a positive net present value project: A $10 million investment increases the value of assets by $15 million ($35 – $20). Figure 9A–1 summarizes this information.

The amount that the bank will be repaid at the end of the year depends on whether an explosion occurs and, if so, whether Mr. Mayers will invest the additional $10 million. If Mr. Mayers will commit to reinvesting, the bank will be repaid what was promised, $28 million, regardless of whether the explosion occurs. However, if Mr. Mayers cannot commit to reinvesting, the bank may not receive the promised payment of $28 million. With probability 0.95, the bank will receive $28 million, but with probability 0.05 the bank will only receive what the assets are worth following an explosion—$20 million. Figure 9A–2 summarizes the payoffs to the bank.

As Figure 9A–2 indicates, the amount that the bank is

FIGURE 9A–1

Asset values for Mr. Mayers's project

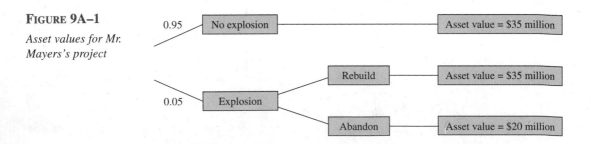

FIGURE 9A–2

Payoffs to the bank that lends Mr. Mayers money

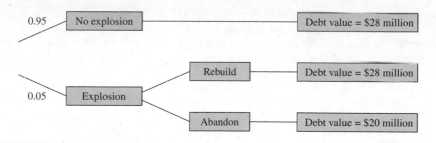

willing to lend Mr. Mayers depends on whether Mr. Mayers can commit to reinvesting. If he can commit, the bank will lend $28 million, because the bank is certain that it will be repaid (recall that the discount rate is zero). If Mr. Mayers cannot commit to reinvesting, the bank will lend less than $28 million because, with probability 0.05, the bank will receive only $20 million. Without a reinvestment commitment, the bank will be willing to lend the expected value of the amount repaid, which equals $27.6 million [(0.95 × $28) + (0.05 × $20)]. In summary, the amount that Mr. Mayers can borrow if he *can* commit to reinvesting is $28.0 million, and the amount that Mr. Mayers can borrow if he *cannot* commit to reinvesting is $27.6 million.

To see whether Mr. Mayers would like to commit to reinvesting following an explosion, we must compare the payoffs to Mr. Mayers if he commits to reinvesting to the payoffs if he does not commit to reinvesting following an explosion. This comparison will demonstrate whether Mr. Mayers would like to commit to reinvesting. (After doing this, we will consider whether Mr. Mayers can commit to reinvesting.)

If Mr. Mayers commits to reinvesting, he will receive $28 million from the bank, which implies that he will have to invest $2 million of his own money up front. With probability 0.95, the assets will be worth $35 million, of which $28 million will go to repay the loan, leaving $7 million for Mr. Mayers. Subtracting the initial investment of $2 million yields $5 million with probability 0.95. With probability 0.05, an explosion will occur and Mr. Mayers will have to invest an additional $10 million. By doing so, the assets again will be worth $35 million; the bank will receive $28 million, leaving $7 million for Mr. Mayers. However, once he takes into account the additional investment of $10 million and the initial investment of $2 million, he loses $5 million by reinvesting. The expected value of Mr. Mayers's cash flows if he can commit to reinvesting is {[0.95 × ($5)] + [0.05 × (–$5)]} = $4.5 million. That is, by building the plant and com-

mitting to reinvesting, Mr. Mayers expects to earn $4.5 million.

How much would Mr. Mayers earn if he builds the plant but does not commit to reinvesting? In this case, the bank will loan him $27.6 million, which implies that he has to invest $2.4 million of his own money. (This is a critical difference between committing and not committing.) With probability 0.95, the assets will be worth $35 million, the bank will receive $28 million, and Mr. Mayers will receive $7 million. After subtracting his initial investment, Mr. Mayers earns $4.6 million with probability 0.95. With probability 0.05, an explosion occurs, in which case Mr. Mayers gives the $20 million in assets to the bank and receives nothing. Thus, with probability 0.05, he loses his initial investment of $2.4 million. The expected value of his earnings equals [(0.95 × $4.6) + (0.05 × –$2.4)] = $4.25 million. Thus, by building the plant and not committing to reinvesting, Mr. Mayers expects to earn $4.25 million.

As a result, Mr. Mayers expects to earn more if he can commit to reinvesting ($4.5 million versus $4.25 million). The difference in value results because a positive net present value project is foregone if an explosion occurs and Mr. Mayers does not commit to reinvesting. Reinvestment of $10 million increases the asset value by $15 million, yielding a net present value of $5 million. An explosion occurs with probability 0.05; therefore the expected value that is lost by not committing is $0.25 million (0.05 × $5 million). This is the difference in expected payoffs to Mr. Mayers ($4.5 million minus $4.25 million).

Can Mr. Mayers simply tell the bank that he will reinvest if an explosion occurs? Mr. Mayers would like to commit to reinvesting, but the issue is whether the bank will believe him if he simply says, "Trust me—I will reinvest if an explosion occurs." The answer is no. The reason is that even though Mr. Mayers would like to commit to reinvesting, he will have no incentive to reinvest if an explosion actually occurs. In other words, his promise to reinvest is not credible. If an explosion occurs, Mr. Mayers realizes that he has to invest $10 million but will only get $7 million back. Therefore, he will not invest the additional money needed to restore the assets to their original value. The problem is that most of the returns from the investment will accrue to the bank.

Given the length of this example, it is worth recapping the analysis to this point. Mr. Mayers would like to commit to reinvesting, because by doing so he will receive more funds from the bank and consequently earn more money. But the promise to reinvest following an explosion is not credible. Once an explosion occurs, he has no incentive to invest because the returns from investment accrue to the bank. The bank therefore will assume that Mr. Mayers will not reinvest and will structure the loan accordingly.

Consider now how insurance can potentially solve Mr. Mayers's commitment problem. Suppose that Mr. Mayers buys property insurance coverage that will pay to repair the damage caused by an explosion for a premium of $600,000. Since the expected claim cost equals $500,000 ($0.05 \times 10 million), the premium loading is $100,000. With the insurance company paying the reinvestment costs, the assets of the firm always will be $35 million. The bank will be certain to receive what has been promised ($28 million), and Mr. Mayers will receive the remainder ($7 million). Since the bank's claims are risk free, it lends $28 million. Mr. Mayers then has to invest $2 million of his own money plus pay the

$600,000 insurance premium. He therefore earns $7 million minus $2 million minus $600,000, which equals $4.4 million. This amount is greater than what he earns if he does not purchase insurance ($4.25 million). By contracting with an insurer to provide the funds necessary for reinvestment following an explosion, Mr. Mayers commits to reinvestment. This increases the amount of money that the bank will lend him and therefore increases his return.

The important points are more general than this example may suggest. Whenever a firm borrows money, lenders will be concerned about the firm foregoing good investment projects when the firm is performing poorly. The reason is that most of the returns from these projects will accrue to lenders but will not benefit shareholders. Insurance helps ensure that the firm will reinvest following large losses.

An astute reader may notice that the underinvestment problem also can be solved by having the bank take over the firm and provide the funds for the reinvestment if an explosion occurs. Note, however, that the process of taking over the firm in financial distress also is costly. First, the bank has to monitor the firm's activities to see whether it is in financial distress and if the underinvestment problem has arisen. Second, attorney and accountant fees will have to be paid to take control of a financially distressed firm. The important point is that insurance may be the lower cost way of solving the underinvestment problem.

CHAPTER 10

Tax, Regulatory, and Accounting Factors Affecting Corporate Risk Management

Chapter Objectives

- Show how progressive tax rates induce firms to reduce risk.
- Explain how the different tax treatment of insurers and noninsurance companies provides a tax benefit to insurance.
- Illustrate that the tax treatment of depreciated property provides a tax benefit to property insurance.
- Show that risk reduction can increase a firm's use of debt financing and thereby create tax benefits.
- Describe insurance premium taxes and excise taxes that increase premium loadings.
- Describe government regulations that require businesses to buy insurance and influence the choice of an insurer.
- Identify and analyze how accounting rules affect risk management.

10.1 Tax Benefits Defined

A major portion of this chapter examines how tax issues affect corporate risk management. The chapter identifies the most important implications of the tax system; some of the more complicated details are omitted. Before describing specific tax effects, it is important to define the term "tax benefit." A transaction provides a **tax benefit** if it lowers the aggregate present value of expected tax payments for all parties involved in the transaction. For example, the purchase of property insurance by Cox Corp. provides a tax benefit if the present value of expected tax payments for Cox Corp. and the insurer are lower than the present value of Cox Corp.'s expected tax payments if it uses internal funds to finance property losses.

Several points about this definition of a tax benefit are important to emphasize. First, tax benefits are defined in terms of *expected* tax payments, not actual tax payments. Thus, the magnitude of tax benefits must be evaluated at the time loss financing decisions are made, not after losses have been realized. For example, tax benefits might exist if Cox Corp. purchases insurance, but unexpected events also might occur that would cause realized tax payments to be higher with insurance than with retention. Second, tax benefits are defined in present value terms, which highlights the fact that tax benefits may arise from shifting tax payments to later time periods.[1]

The third point is that the party that nominally receives a tax break may differ from the party that actually obtains the tax benefit. To illustrate, suppose that Bermuda insurers do not have to pay taxes on interest income that has been earned on funds set aside to pay future losses, but that US corporations are required to pay taxes on such interest income. Then the purchase of insurance by a US corporation from a Bermuda insurer could provide a tax benefit. The Bermuda insurer would nominally receive the tax break, but the actual benefit of the tax break could accrue to the US corporation. If Bermuda insurers compete with each other, then most or even all of the tax benefit would likely be passed through to US corporations in the form of lower insurance premiums. Because the party that receives the tax benefit can differ from the party that nominally receives the break, it is important to look at the tax effects on all the parties involved in a transaction.

Note finally that the definition of a tax benefit ignores any cost of obtaining the benefit. Thus, a transaction that provides a tax benefit does not necessarily increase shareholders' wealth. According to the definition, a tax benefit exists if a firm with a 34 percent tax rate makes a tax-deductible contribution of $1,000 to a charity. While the charitable contribution lowers the firm's taxes by $340 (34 percent of $1,000) and thus provides a tax benefit, the contribution will increase shareholders' wealth only if the contribution causes other cash flows to increase by more than $660 (the after-tax cost of the contribution). Thus, tax minimization is not the same as shareholder wealth maximization. (A firm could usually minimize tax payments by giving away all of its profits.)

In the next four sections of this chapter, we analyze the main tax benefits of insurance versus retention. These tax benefits arise because (1) effective corporate income tax rates sometimes are progressive; (2) the tax treatment of losses is different for insurers than for noninsurance companies; (3) the tax treatment of losses to depreciated property depends on whether the property is insured; and (4) the risk reduction provided by insurance may allow a corporation to increase its use of debt with tax-deductible interest payments. The first and fourth tax benefits apply to most risk-reducing activities (including hedging); the second and third are specific to insurance.

---

[1] The risk associated with tax payments would be reflected in the discount rate used to calculate the present value of expected tax payments.

10.2 Progressivity in Corporate Income Tax Rates

Overview

We introduced the idea in Chapter 7 of **tax rate progressivity;** that is, that progressive income tax rates (wherein tax rates increase as taxable income increases) allow a firm to lower its expected tax payments by reducing the variability of its before-tax income (e.g., by purchasing insurance). The intuition for this result is easily conveyed by considering how insurance affects a firm's tax payments when taxable income is volatile from year to year because of unexpected losses in some years. In years when losses are low and taxable income is high, the government takes a larger percentage of the firm's profits than in years when losses are high and taxable income is low. By purchasing insurance, a firm essentially lowers its taxable income in years when losses are low and increases taxable income in years when losses are high. This transfer of taxable income is beneficial because it lowers tax payments in years when losses are low by more than it increases tax payments in years when losses are high.

The curve in Figure 10–1 illustrates the relationship between taxable income and after-tax income when tax rates are progressive. When tax rates increase with taxable income, after-tax income increases at a decreasing rate. (Note that this is the same relationship between wealth and utility for a risk-averse person.) The figure also illustrates the effect of insurance on after-tax income in a simple example where a firm has a 50 percent chance of experiencing a $10 million loss each year. Without insurance, the firm has $12 million of taxable income in years without a loss and $2 million of taxable income in years when a loss occurs. By purchasing full insurance at a premium of $6 million, the firm's taxable income is always $6 million. As a result of progressive tax rates, the reduction in after-tax income in the years without a loss (distance between A and B) is less than the

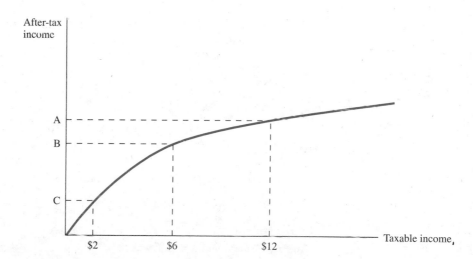

FIGURE 10–1

Effect of insurance on after-tax income when tax rates are progressive (in $ millions)

increase in after-tax income in the years with a loss (distance between B and C). Because the two outcomes are equally likely in this simple example, the firm would prefer to give up $(A–B) with probability 0.5 to receive $(B–C) with probability 0.5.

Numerical Example and Additional Insights

Suppose that DARCY Corp. has a tax rate of 34 percent if it has positive taxable earnings and a zero tax rate if it has negative taxable earnings, which is an extreme form of progressivity in tax rates. DARCY Corp. has a 0.02 probability that it will lose a lawsuit that will cost $30 million. Without a lawsuit, DARCY's taxable earnings equal $10 million. As illustrated in Table 10–1, DARCY's taxable earnings are either $10 million or –$20 million. Without insurance, DARCY's after-tax earnings equal either $6.6 million ($10 – $10 × 0.34) or –$20 million, implying that its expected after-tax earnings equal $6.068 million ($6.6 × 0.98 – $20 × 0.02).

Now suppose that DARCY purchases liability insurance with a $30 million limit for a premium of $600,000. This policy has a zero premium loading because expected claim costs equal $600,000 (0.02 × $30 million). Since the insurer pays the entire loss if it occurs, DARCY's taxable earnings will be $9.4 million with certainty ($10 million minus the insurance premium of $600,000). DARCY's expected after-tax earnings therefore equal $6.204 million ($9.4 – $9.4 × 0.34), which is $136,000 greater than without insurance.

Comparing DARCY's situation to another firm will help explain further how insurance lowers expected taxes for DARCY. Suppose that Barrese Inc. is faced with the same liability exposure as DARCY but that Barrese Inc. has taxable earnings of $50 million if it is not sued. The higher taxable earnings for Barrese ($50 million) than DARCY ($10 million) imply that Barrese Inc. will have posi-

---

TABLE 10–1   DARCY's Expected After-Tax Earnings (in $ millions) with Insurance versus Retention (tax rate when income is positive = 34%; tax rate when income is negative = 0%)

	No Lawsuit (probability = 0.98)	*Loses a Lawsuit (probability = 0.02)*
No Insurance		
Taxable earnings	$10.0	–$20
After-tax earnings	$ 6.6	–$20
Expected after-tax earnings = $6.6 × 0.98 – $20 × 0.02 = $6.068		
Full Insurance (with a $0.6 premium)		
Taxable earnings	$ 9.4	$ 9.4
After-tax earnings	$ 6.204	$ 6.204
Expected after-tax earnings = $9.4 – $9.4 × 0.34 = $6.204		

TABLE 10–2   Barrese's Expected After-Tax Earnings (in $ millions) with Insurance versus Retention (tax rate when income is positive = 34%; tax rate when income is negative = 0%)

	No Lawsuit (probability = 0.98)	Loses a Lawsuit (probability = 0.02)
No Insurance		
Taxable earnings	$50.0	$20.0
After-tax earnings	$33.0	$13.2
Expected after-tax earnings = $33 × 0.98 + $13.2 × 0.02 = $32.604		
Full Insurance (with a $0.6 premium)		
Taxable earnings	$49.400	$49.400
After-tax earnings	$32.604	$32.604
Expected after-tax earnings = $49.4 – $49.4 × 0.34 = $32.604		

tive earnings even if it loses the lawsuit ($50 million – $30 million). Thus, Barrese Inc. does not really face a progressive tax rate. As is illustrated in Table 10–2, this difference eliminates the tax benefit from insurance. Without insurance, Barrese's after-tax earnings equal $33 million ($50 – $50 × 0.34) with probability 0.98 and $13.2 million ($20 – $20 × 0.34) with probability of 0.02. Expected after-tax earnings without insurance therefore equal $32.604 million ($0.98 × $33 + 0.02 × $13.2). If Barrese purchases $30 million of liability insurance coverage for $600,000, its taxable earnings equal $49.4 million regardless of whether it loses a lawsuit. Its after-tax earnings with insurance therefore equal $32.604 million ($49.4 – $49.4 × 0.34), which is the same as without insurance.

The important difference between DARCY and Barrese is that without insurance Barrese is able to fully deduct the entire $30 million liability loss to lower its taxable earnings. DARCY, on the other hand, can only use $10 million of the $30 million loss to offset taxable earnings; the other $20 million in liability losses does not reduce its taxes. Of course, losses are not desirable, but if they occur a firm would like to fully utilize them to reduce taxable income. When uninsured, DARCY has a 0.02 probability that it will not be able to take a $20 million tax deduction that could be taken by a firm with higher taxable income (e.g., Barrese). The value of this deduction to such a firm equals the probability of the loss, 0.02, times the amount of tax that would be avoided by deducting the loss, $20 million, times the 34 percent tax rate. Multiplying these quantities yields $136,000, which is the amount by which insurance increases DARCY's after-tax income ($6.204 million – 6.068 million; see Table 10–1). Thus, by purchasing insurance, DARCY in effect is able to deduct the entire expected loss, thus reducing its expected tax payments and increasing expected after-tax earnings.[2]

---

[2] Premium loadings, which this example ignores, reduce the benefits of insurance.

Progressivity of US Corporate Income Tax Rates

The nominal tax rates on US corporations have limited progressivity. Taxable income between $0 and $50,000 is taxed at a 15 percent rate, between $50,000 and $75,000 at a 25 percent rate, and all taxable income above $100,000 is taxed at least at a 34 percent rate. In addition, firms can carry losses forward 15 years and backward 3 years to offset future or past profits. Thus, if a firm has negative taxable income in a given year, in effect it can obtain a refund based on taxes paid in the prior three years, or it can reduce the taxes it pays in future years.

The ability to carry losses forward and backward greatly reduces but does not eliminate the progressivity of the tax system for two reasons. First, when carrying losses backward or forward, a firm loses interest on the value of the tax deductions (i.e., the present value of the tax deductions declines). Second, when carrying losses forward, a firm is uncertain whether it will be able to fully deduct the losses in the future. The firm may go bankrupt prior to deducting all of the losses (or reach the 15-year limit before the full loss has been deducted).[3] The resulting effective progressivity in the tax code provides an incentive for firms to reduce the variability of taxable income.

10.3 Tax Treatment of Insurers versus Noninsurance Companies

Overview

When calculating its taxable income, a noninsurance company can only deduct losses that were paid during the year. In contrast, an insurer can deduct the discounted value of **incurred losses,** which equals losses paid during the year plus the change during the year in the discounted value of its liability for unpaid claims (the loss reserve). This distinction essentially allows insurers to deduct losses earlier than noninsurance companies, which all else equal increases the present value of expected tax deductions if a loss exposure is insured. Although the tax break is granted to insurers, competition among insurers for business will cause most or even the entire tax break to be given to policyholders through lower premiums.

Example and Additional Insights

To illustrate the distinction between paid losses and incurred losses, suppose that Crocker Snowblowers is subject to the risk that it will be sued as a result of its operations in year 1. The expected value and timing of loss payments are as follows:

---

[3] The tax code was changed in 1986 to reduce the ability of firms that acquire other firms to utilize the tax carryforwards of acquired firms. This change reduced the ability of firms to effectively "sell" loss carryforwards and thus increased effective progressivity. Alternative minimum tax provisions in the tax code also increase effective progressivity.

	Year 1	Year 2
Expected loss payments due to events occurring in year 1	$2 million	$2 million

Even though expected losses arise from events that occur in year 1, half of the losses are not expected to be paid until year 2 because of delays in the reporting of claims and delays in the liability system.

If Crocker Snowblowers retains the risk of liability suits (e.g., pays liability losses from its cash flow), it can deduct damage payments in the year they are paid. Thus, the decision to retain the liability risk would generate expected tax deductions of $2 million in both years 1 and 2.[4] With a 34 percent tax rate, each dollar of tax deductions reduces the firm's tax payments by 34 cents, or, stated differently, each dollar of tax deductions creates a tax shield of 34 cents. A **tax shield** is the amount by which tax payments are reduced as a result of the ability to deduct an expense when calculating taxable income. Therefore, $2 million of expected loss payments creates an expected tax shield equal to $0.68 million (0.34 × $2 million). Assuming that the appropriate opportunity cost of capital equals 8 percent, the present value (as of the beginning of year 1) of expected tax shields if Crocker retains the risk associated with its liability exposure is:

$$\frac{(\$2)(0.34)}{1.08} + \frac{(\$2)(0.34)}{1.08^2} = \frac{\$0.68}{1.08} + \frac{\$0.68}{1.08^2} = \$1.213 \text{ million}$$

Suppose instead that Crocker Snowblowers purchases full insurance from Tennyson Insurance, which has the same forecast of expected loss payments as Crocker Snowblowers (i.e., $2 million in year 1 and $2 million in year 2). Also assume that for tax purposes Tennyson anticipates recording losses in an unbiased manner (see below). As we will explain shortly, the different tax treatment implies that at the time the policy is written, Tennyson expects deductions for losses in year 1 and year 2 of $3.85 million and $0.15 million, respectively. The sum of expected loss deductions for Tennyson is the same as for Crocker Snowblowers, but the timing is different. Tennyson is able to deduct losses earlier. This timing difference increases the present value of expected tax shields.

With the aid of Table 10–3, we can explain how Tennyson calculates its expected loss deductions for its policy with Crocker Snowblowers. After one year, Tennyson expects to pay losses equal to $2 million and expects to have unpaid losses of $2 million. As a result, both the loss reserve (liability for unpaid losses) for the policy at the end of year 1 and the associated change in Tennyson's total loss reserve during year 1 from selling this policy equal $2 million. The undiscounted value of incurred losses equals paid losses ($2 million) plus the change in the loss reserve ($2 million), or $4 million. Using an 8 percent discount rate, the present value of unpaid losses (and the change in the present value of the loss

---

[4] As a follow-up to the discussion in section 10.2, note that in this example we are ignoring the possibility that Crocker faces a progressive tax system. In other words, Crocker is able to fully deduct any loss payments in the year they occur.

TABLE 10–3   Effect of Crocker Snowblowers Purchasing Insurance from Tennyson Insurance (in $ millions)

Expected values of:	*Beginning of Year 1*	*End of Year 1*	*End of Year 2*
1. Paid losses		$2.000	$2.000
2. Loss reserve	$0.00	$2.000	$0.000
3. Change in loss reserve		$2.000	–$2.000
4. Undiscounted incurred losses (1) + (3)		$4.000	$0.000
5. Present value of loss reserve (discounted value of 2)	$0.00	$1.852	$0.000
6. Change in present value of loss reserve		$1.852	–$1.852
7. Incurred losses for tax purposes (1) + (6)		$3.852	$0.148

reserve) at the end of year 1 is $2/1.08 = $1.852 million. The discounted value of incurred losses therefore equals paid losses ($2 million) plus $1.852 million, or $3.852 million.

At the end of year 2, the remaining $2 million in expected losses is expected to be paid. Since no additional losses are expected to be paid after year 2, the loss reserve and the present value of the loss reserve are expected to be zero. Consequently, the expected change in the present value of the loss reserve is –$1.852 = ($0 – $2)/1.08. The discounted value of incurred losses therefore equals $2 million in paid losses plus –$1.852 million in the change in the loss reserve, for a total of $0.148 million.

In summary, by selling the liability policy to Crocker Snowblowers, Tennyson expects to be able to reduce its taxable income by $3.852 million at the end of year 1 and by $0.148 million at the end of year 2. The expected tax shield equals 34 percent of incurred losses for tax purposes, which in year 1 equals $1.309 million (0.34 × $3.852 million) and in year 2 equals $0.050 million (0.34 × $0.148 million). The present value of the expected tax shields therefore equals

$$\frac{1.309}{1.08} + \frac{0.050}{1.08^2} = \$1.256 \text{ million}$$

The present value of the expected tax shield from insuring the loss exposure ($1.256 million) exceeds Crocker's present value of expected tax shields from retention ($1.213 million), which was calculated earlier. Thus, there is a tax advantage to insurance as a means of financing losses. The tax advantage in this case equals $43,184 ($1.256 million – $1.213 million).

The tax benefit arises because insurers are able to shield a greater amount of their income (in present value terms) from taxes than are noninsurance companies. This observation leads to a useful way of viewing this tax benefit. The additional income that an insurer can shield equals the income generated from investing the funds needed to pay expected future losses. In this example, $1.852 million ($2/1.08) is needed after year 1 to fund expected future loss payments, and the interest earned on these funds between years 1 and 2 equals $148,148

(0.08 × $1.85 million). This interest essentially escapes taxation under the insurer's tax treatment, but not under the noninsurance company's tax treatment. To confirm this, note that by avoiding tax on $148,148 of interest, an insurer would save $50,370 (0.34 × $148,148) in taxes at the end of year 2. The present value of these tax savings equals $43,184 ($50,370/1.08²), which is the tax advantage derived earlier. Thus, the different tax treatment of insurers and noninsurance companies implies that insurers can avoid tax on the interest earned on the funds needed to pay future losses; noninsurance companies cannot.[5]

The magnitude of this tax benefit can be very large, especially for lines of insurance such as liability insurance, where claims are paid many years after losses are incurred (i.e., there is a long claims tail). In many situations the tax advantage arising from the differential treatment of losses for insurers and noninsurance companies is the most important tax benefit of insurance.[6]

Tax Benefit with Overstated Loss Reserves

The tax benefit from the different tax treatment of insurers and noninsurance companies increases if insurers overstate loss reserves. While any overstatement of loss reserves eventually must be corrected in later years on a dollar-for-dollar basis, overstatement brings tax deductions earlier in time, thus increasing the present value of tax shields. We illustrate this effect in the appendix to this chapter.

You might conclude that the greater value of tax shields from overstating loss reserves leads some insurers to overstate loss reserves and thus charge a lower price to better compete for business. One factor that helps mitigate this incentive is that the overstatement of loss reserves decreases reported insurer capital. Insurers therefore must balance the tax benefits from overstating loss reserves against the costs that arise if any market participants infer that the insurer has higher insolvency risk as well as the regulatory costs from lower reported capital.

Concept Check

1. Suppose that Phillips Inc. has a products liability exposure where accidents this year are expected to cause loss payments equal to $3 million at the end of this year and $4 million at the end of next year. What is the present value of expected tax shields from this products

---

[5] To eliminate the tax advantage, the IRS would have to eliminate Tennyson's deduction of $0.15 million in the second year. This could be done by forcing the present value of the loss reserve to be increased each year to reflect the implicit interest earned over the year. To illustrate, when calculating the change in the present value of the loss reserve in year 2, if Tennyson had to use the present value of the loss reserve in year 1 plus implicit interest, then the prior year present value of the loss reserve would be $2 million ($1.85 × 1.08), which would imply that the discounted value of incurred losses in year 2 would be zero and the present value of expected tax shields with insurance would be the same as with retention.

[6] The tax benefit arising from the different tax treatment of insurers and noninsurance corporations was greater prior to 1986, because insurers did not have to discount incurred losses when calculating taxes.

liability exposure if Phillips retains its risk? Assume that the opportunity cost of capital is 10 percent and that the tax rate is 34 percent. What is the present value of expected tax shields that an insurer would have from deducting losses if it insured the same exposure?

10.4 Insuring Depreciated Property

Overview

Corporations also can obtain tax benefits from insuring depreciated property. The simplest way to explain this tax benefit is to assume that: (1) the value of existing property has been depreciated to zero (its book value is zero); (2) future depreciation expenses resulting from replacement of damaged property are the same whether the firm is insured or uninsured; and (3) the premium loading is zero (the premium equals the expected indemnity payment from the insurer). Under these assumptions, the purchase of property insurance has two tax effects. First, the firm is able to deduct the insurance premium when calculating taxable earnings, regardless of whether a loss occurs. Second, if a loss occurs, the firm will have to recognize a capital gain equal to the insurance indemnity payment. If the income tax rate exceeds the capital gains tax rate, the income tax savings from deducting the premium exceeds the expected capital gains tax payment.

As the following example illustrates, the actual tax treatment of depreciated property usually is more complex than this simple explanation might suggest. One reason is that property is not always depreciated to zero (assumption 1). Another reason is that when insurance proceeds are used to replace damaged property, firms have a choice of whether to recognize or defer the capital gain. If the gain is deferred, depreciation expenses following an uninsured loss differ from those following an insured loss. Although insurance still provides a tax benefit when the capital gain is deferred, it is more difficult to illustrate the result.

Example and Additional Insights

Suppose that Gaunt Corp. has a tax rate equal to 34 percent and the following property loss exposure:

$$\text{Property loss} = \begin{cases} \$0 & \text{with probability } 0.95 \\ \$4 \text{ million} & \text{with probability } 0.05 \end{cases}$$

Also assume that the property originally was purchased three years earlier, that the property's original cost was $4 million, and that the replacement cost of the property also is $4 million. Although the firm probably would use an accelerated depreciation method, assume for simplicity that Gaunt has used the straight-line method for tax purposes and that it is depreciating the asset over a four-year period. Since the property was purchased for $4 million three years ago, the property has been depreciated to $1 million; that is, its current tax basis equals $1 million. Finally, assume that if a loss occurs this year (year 1), the property will be immediately replaced, implying that the firm is able to begin taking a depreciation deduction for the new property this year.

To focus on the tax effects of insurance versus retention, assume that the insurance premium does not include a loading so that the premium for full replacement cost coverage equals $200,000 (expected claim costs equal 0.05 × $4 million). We also will ignore possible nontax reasons for purchasing insurance discussed in previous chapters (e.g., improvements in contracts with employees and customers, avoidance of the cost of issuing new securities, and so on) and any tax benefits not associated with depreciated property.

Retention. Table 10–4 summarizes the tax consequences if Gaunt retains the risk. If a loss does not occur, Gaunt will depreciate the asset from $1 million to $0, thus generating a depreciation tax shield of $0.34 million. If a loss occurs, Gaunt can deduct the lesser of the fair market value of the property or the tax basis. In this example, the tax basis ($1 million) is less than the fair market value. Thus, the loss generates a tax shield of $1 million times 0.34, which equals $0.34 million. Since Gaunt immediately replaces the property by purchasing another capital asset with a cost of $4 million, the new asset also generates a depreciation tax shield in year 1. Assuming that Gaunt uses a four-year straight-line depreciation schedule for the new property, the depreciation tax shield in year 1 is $0.34 million. The new property is further depreciated by $1 million in years 2 through 4, generating depreciation tax shields in each of those years equal to $0.34 million. The key points to notice are: (1) the loss eliminates the remaining depreciation tax shields on the book value of the lost property, but the firm receives a tax shield equal to the book value of the loss; and (2) the replacement of the property gives rise to additional depreciation tax shields on the new property.

TABLE 10–4   Tax Consequences of Retention for Gaunt Corp. (in $ millions; income tax rate = 34%)

Tax Shield	If No Loss Occurs (probability = 0.95)		If a Loss Occurs in Year 1 (probability = 0.05)	
	Year 1	*Year 2–Year 4*	*Year 1*	*Year 2–Year 4*
Uninsured loss	$0	$0	$0.34	$0
Depreciation	0.34	0	0.34	0.34
Insurance premium	0	0	0	0
Capital gains	0	0	0	0
Total tax shields	$0.34	0	$0.68	$0.34

Expected tax shields in year 1 = 0.95 × $34 + 0.05 × $68 = $0.357

Expected tax shields in years 2 through 4 = 0.95 × $0 + 0.05 × $0.34 = $0.17

Insurance and Recognition of a Capital Gain.   If insured, Gaunt can deduct the insurance premium, which gives it a tax shield equal to $0.34 \times \$200,000 = \$68,000$, regardless of whether a loss occurs. If a loss occurs, Gaunt can either (1) recognize a capital gain of $3 million, pay capital gains taxes, and then depreciate the new asset over time; or (2) defer the gain from the insurance proceeds, keep the tax basis on the new property at the old tax basis ($1 million), and limit its depreciation tax shields to the same level as if the property were not lost. We analyze the first option in Table 10–5.

By replacing the asset with the insurance proceeds and recognizing the capital gain, Gaunt obtains depreciated tax shields on the entire value of the new property ($4 million). In particular, $1 million of the new property is depreciated in the year of the loss and the remaining $3 million is depreciated in equal increments in years 2 through 4. Thus, Gaunt's depreciation tax shields if an insured loss occurs are the same as when it is uninsured (see Table 10–4).

The tax differences between insurance and retention in this case arise because Gaunt generates a tax shield on the insurance premium and it must pay a capital gains tax. The insurance premium tax shield equals 0.34 times $200,000, or $68,000, regardless of whether the loss occurs. The capital gains tax arises if a loss occurs. Following a loss, the firm must pay tax on the difference between the new tax basis ($4 million) and the old tax basis ($1 million). Assuming a 20 percent capital gains rate, the capital gains tax equals $0.6 million ($0.2 \times \$3$ million).

Table 10–5 summarizes the results. Notice that the expected tax shields in years 2 through 4 are the same with insurance as with retention (see Table 10–4). Insurance, however, raises the expected tax shields in year 1 from $0.357 million (without insurance) to $0.378 million. The difference equals $21,000. This benefit from insurance arises because the capital gains tax rate (20 percent) is lower than the income tax rate (34 percent). In this example, a capital gain of $3 million occurs with probability 0.05. Thus, insurance allows the firm to reduce its expected tax payments by $3 million (the capital gain) times 0.05 (the probability

TABLE 10–5   Tax Consequences of Full Insurance and Recognition of Capital Gain for Gaunt Corp. (in $ millions; income tax rate = 34%; capital gains tax rate = 20%)

Tax Shield	If No Loss Occurs (probability = 0.95)		If a Loss Occurs in Year 1 (probability = 0.05)	
	Year 1	*Year 2–Year 4*	*Year 1*	*Year 2–Year 4*
Uninsured loss	$0	$0	$0	$0
Depreciation	0.340	0	0.340	0.34
Insurance premium	0.068	0	0.068	0
Capital gains	0	0	−0.600	0
Total tax shield	$0.408	$0	−$0.192	$0.34

Expected tax shields in year 1 = $0.95 \times \$0.408 - 0.05 \times \$0.192 = \$0.378$

Expected tax shields in years 2 through 4 = $0.95 \times \$0 + 0.05 \times \$0.34 = \$0.017$

of the gain) times 0.14 (the difference in tax rates), which equals $21,000. In summary, insurance and recognition of the capital gain provide a tax benefit if the capital gains rate is less than the income tax rate.

Insurance and Deferral of the Capital Gain.   The second method of treating the insurance proceeds is to defer the capital gain; that is, keep the tax basis on the new property at the same level as the old property. In this example, the insurance proceeds would be used to purchase a new asset but the tax basis of the new property would be $1 million. The tax shields arising from this approach are presented in Table 10–6. Since a capital gain is not realized, there are no depreciation tax shields in years 2 through 4. Instead, the asset is replaced and then fully depreciated in year 1. Thus, regardless of whether a loss occurs, the firm receives a depreciation tax shield equal to $340,000 (0.34 times $1 million) plus the tax shield on the insurance premium, which equals $68,000. The total tax shield in year 1 therefore equals $408,000.

Comparing expected tax shields from insurance (see Table 10–6) to expected tax shields from retention (see Table 10–4) indicates that insurance increases the expected tax shield in year 1 by $51,000 ($408,000 – $357,000) and insurance reduces expected tax shields in years 2 through 4 by $17,000 per year. Notice, however, that $17,000 times three (the number of years) equals $51,000. Thus, the effect of insurance is to bring the tax shields forward in time, thereby increasing their present value.

In summary, regardless of whether the firm defers or recognizes the capital gain from using the insurance proceeds to purchase new assets, a tax benefit exists from insurance relative to retention. Comparing the deferral method to the recognition method, the tax benefit from deferral is more likely to dominate the tax benefit from recognition of the capital gain as (1) the difference between the income tax rate and the capital gains rate becomes smaller, and (2) the length of time required to depreciate the asset increases.

TABLE 10–6   **Tax Consequences of Full Insurance and Deferral of the Capital Gain (in $ millions)**

Tax Shield	If No Loss Occurs (probability = 0.95)		If a Loss Occurs in Year 1 (probability = 0.05)	
	Year 1	Year 2–Year 4	Year 1	Year 2–Year 4
Uninsured loss	$0	$0	$0	$0
Depreciation	0.34	0	0.34	0
Insurance premium	0.068	0	0.068	0
Capital gains	0	0	0	0
Total tax shield	$0.408	$0	$0.408	$0

Expected tax shields in year $1 = 0.95 \times \$408 + 0.05 \times \$0.408 = \$0.408$

Expected tax shields in years 2 through 4 = $0

10.5 Insurance and Interest Tax Shields on Debt

A firm's **capital structure** refers to the way that it has raised capital to finance its assets. At a general level, a firm's capital structure often is described by the value of its debt (i.e., the amount that it has borrowed) divided by the value of its equity (assets minus liabilities). For example, if a firm has $50 million in outstanding debt and the value of equity equals $50 million, then the debt-to-equity ratio is 1. Although the optimal capital structure for a particular firm is subject to debate, financial analysts generally agree that the principal advantage of using debt financing is that debt creates **interest tax shields;** that is, the interest payments on debt are deductible when calculating taxable income. In contrast, the firm cannot deduct dividend payments to equityholders. Thus, for a firm with a 34 percent tax rate, each dollar of interest paid to debtholders generates a tax shield of 34 cents, assuming the firm has sufficient earnings before interest and taxes to deduct the entire interest payment.

Debt financing, however, has some disadvantages, which generally stem from the possibility that the firm could experience financial distress. As discussed in Chapter 9, debtholders will be concerned about bankruptcy costs and whether the firm will adopt risky, negative net present value projects or fail to adopt positive net present value projects. Consequently, debtholders require additional compensation (higher promised interest payments) as the probability of financial distress increases. At some point, debtholders simply may refuse to lend any more money to the firm because the probability of financial distress is too high.

In Chapter 9 we discussed how risk reduction (e.g., purchasing insurance) lowers the probability of financial distress and therefore allows the firm to borrow funds at lower costs. Here, we make a related point. By reducing risk, firms might find it optimal to use more debt financing. The additional debt financing generates additional interest tax shields, which can increase firm value. Focusing purely on the effect of risk reduction on the amount of debt financing used, firms can be expected to decrease risk until the marginal cost of doing so equals the value of the additional interest tax shields generated by the additional debt.

Note that risk management affects a firm's capital structure and that a firm's capital structure affects its decision regarding how much risk to reduce. Thus, a firm's capital structure and risk management policy are interrelated so that these strategic decisions should not be made independently.

10.6 Insurance Premiums and Excise Taxes

Insurance premiums are subject to two other forms of taxation that can influence loss financing decisions. All states impose **premium taxes** on insurance transactions. Although there is some variation, premium taxes commonly equal about 2 percent of the premium. Premium taxes can differ depending on whether or not the insurer is domiciled (incorporated) in the state.[7] For example, some states impose higher premium taxes on insurers that are domiciled in other states. In response, other states have passed retaliatory taxes on insurers that are domiciled in states that impose higher premium taxes on nondomiciled insurers. The important point is that premium taxes increase the insurer's cost of providing insurance and thus can potentially influence the decision to purchase insurance or the choice of an insurer.

The federal government also imposes **excise taxes** if insurance is purchased from an insurer that is domiciled outside of the US (i.e., an alien insurer). The excise tax is 1 percent on reinsurance transactions and 4 percent on primary insurance transactions. Unlike premium taxes, the insurance buyer, not the insurer, nominally pays the excise tax on primary insurance. Similarly, the insurer, not the reinsurer, nominally pays the excise tax on reinsurance. The higher excise tax rate on primary insurance can influence the loss financing decisions of corporations, which we discuss in the next section.

10.7 Regulatory Effects on Loss Financing

Government regulation can influence loss financing decisions in two main ways.[8] First, the government may require companies to purchase insurance. Second, the government may restrict the pool of insurers from whom businesses may purchase insurance.

Compulsory Insurance

The main reason why the government sometimes makes business insurance compulsory is to reduce the likelihood that firms will be unable to fulfill their legal obligations to individuals or other firms. For example, as we will discuss in more detail in Chapter 16, firms are obligated to pay workers' compensation benefits to workers who become injured or ill as a result of their job. To ensure that firms are financially capable of paying workers' compensation benefits, firms must either purchase insurance or qualify as self-insurers (which usually is difficult for small firms). Similarly, automobile liability and truck liability insurance coverage often is compulsory if the firm that owns the cars and trucks does not qualify as a self-insurer. When insurance is mandatory, firms have no choice between retention and insurance.

---

[7] From the perspective of a particular state, a domestic insurer is an insurer that is domiciled in the state, a foreign insurer is an insurer that is domiciled in another state in the US, and an alien insurer is an insurer that is domiciled outside of the US.

[8] Price regulation also can affect loss financing decisions by affecting the premium loading (see Chapter 6). For example, if regulated premiums are less than competitive market levels, then a business will view insurance as having a low premium loading, which will increase the desirability of insurance, all else equal. Also see the discussion of this issue in Chapter 16.

Restriction on the Choice of Insurers

As we have mentioned in earlier chapters, insurance is regulated at the state level in the United States. Insurers can become licensed to sell insurance to cover risk exposures that are located in a particular state by meeting the state's licensing requirements. A licensed insurer in a particular state is called an **admitted insurer** for that particular state.[9]

An unlicensed or **nonadmitted insurer** also can sell insurance that covers a risk located in a state in which it is not licensed. However, the nonadmitted insurer must be licensed in at least one state and must sell nonadmitted insurance through an agent that has met the state's regulations for placing insurance with a nonadmitted insurer. Typically, agents placing insurance with a nonadmitted insurer face stricter regulations than agents placing insurance with an admitted insurer. Regulation of agents in principle substitutes for the lack of regulation of nonadmitted insurers.

While the specific regulatory provisions and their enforcement vary across states, a company (or individual) technically can buy insurance from a nonadmitted insurer only if it cannot obtain insurance from an admitted insurer. In some states, proof of being denied coverage from one or more admitted insurers is required. Thus, nonadmitted insurers typically provide coverage for exposures that are unusual or require very high limits. Because nonadmitted insurance coverage often is excess coverage (coverage in excess of some limit), the market for nonadmitted insurance also is called the **excess and surplus (E&S) lines market.** The market share of total commercial insurance premiums written by excess and surplus insurers has grown steadily over the past 25 years, but it is still a relatively small share (less than 10 percent of the total US market).

Due to the requirement that firms purchase insurance from an admitted insurer if it is available, admitted insurers sometimes serve as an intermediary between a firm that wishes to purchase insurance from a nonadmitted insurer. For example, Weiss Corp. may purchase insurance from ADM Insurance Company (an admitted insurer), who will then reinsure most or all of the exposure with NONADM Insurance Company (a nonadmitted insurer). This arrangement is called **fronting,** and the fronting insurer (ADM in this example) will charge a fee for providing the fronting service.[10]

Excise taxes provide another reason for using a fronting insurer. Recall that excise taxes on reinsurance transactions are 1 percent of the premium, while excise taxes on primary insurance transactions are 4 percent of the premium. As a result, paying insurance premiums to a primary carrier who then reinsures the bulk of the exposure with a non-US insurer may lower total tax payments. The

---

[9] In footnote 7, we described three types of insurers from the perspective of a particular state: domestic, foreign, and alien. All three types of insurers can be licensed by a state and thus all three can be admitted insurers.

[10] As discussed in Chapter 11, fronting often is used in offshore captive insurance transactions to satisfy state laws requiring that insurance be purchased from an admitted insurer or to satisfy third party requirements of a certificate of insurance from a rated insurer.

primary insurer would have to pay premium taxes on the primary insurance, but as long as the state's premium tax rate is less than 3 percent, the sum of the premium taxes on the primary insurance plus the excise taxes on the reinsurance will be less than the excise tax that otherwise would have been paid on primary insurance with a non-US insurer.

Another reason for a firm to purchase insurance through a fronting insurer is that a contractual party may require a certificate of insurance from a particular set of insurers (e.g., insurers with a high A. M. Best rating, as discussed in Chapter 5), although an alternative insurer is preferred by the insurance purchaser. For example, suppose that Thornton Corp. requires that its suppliers have liability insurance from an insurer that is A-rated from Best's, but that one of the suppliers prefers to have insurance from an unrated insurer (such as a captive insurer, which we discuss in Chapter 11). Then, the supplier can purchase insurance from an A-rated insurer, which in turn will reinsure the entire exposure with the supplier's preferred insurer.

Some of the reasons for using fronting insurers might suggest that a fronting arrangement is a sham transaction without economic substance. The fronting insurer, however, is liable for claims costs if the reinsurer becomes insolvent. Consequently, the fronting insurer has an incentive to monitor the solvency of the reinsurer prior to engaging in a fronting transaction, and the fee charged by the fronting insurer will reflect the insolvency risk of the reinsurer. The fact that a fronting insurer will cede the entire exposure for a relatively low fee indicates that the reinsurer has low insolvency risk. In essence, a fronting insurer acts as a guarantor that the reinsurer has low insolvency risk.

Fronting for nonadmitted insurers has come under regulatory scrutiny in recent years. Regulators' concern with fronting arrangements arises for two reasons. As mentioned, fronting insurers must assume the liabilities that were originally ceded to a nonadmitted reinsurer if the reinsurer becomes insolvent. Regulators' concern is that nonadmitted reinsurers may be poorly capitalized, which in turn jeopardizes the solvency of the ceding insurer. The second reason is that regulators may experience difficulty or high costs collecting payments from nonadmitted reinsurers if the fronting insurer becomes insolvent. As a result, either guarantee funds end up paying a greater share of the insolvent fronting insurer's liabilities or policyholders are uncompensated for some of their losses.

10.8 Financial Accounting Influences on Loss Financing

The decision to finance losses using internal funds as opposed to using insurance also influences financial accounting income statements and balance sheets. It is important at the outset to distinguish financial reporting from tax accounting. The Financial Accounting Standards Board (FASB) promulgates rules (called generally accepted accounting principles, or GAAP) that firms should follow in reporting information to investors. These rules can and often do differ from tax accounting rules. This section is concerned with financial reporting rather than taxes.

Generally, reported accounting numbers, in and of themselves, do not influence firm valuation (although exceptions will be noted below). Value depends on expected cash flows, the timing of these cash flows, and the risk of the cash flows. To the extent that reported accounting numbers provide information about cash flows, then they will appear to influence valuation. Thus, if Frickel Corp. announces unexpected positive accounting earnings and the announcement changes investors' expectations of cash flows, its stock price will likely increase. However, the valuation effect arises not from the accounting numbers per se but from the expectation of higher cash flows.

Consider another scenario. Suppose that Frickel Corp. alters its reported accounting earnings without changing its cash flows. In particular, assume that Frickel Corp. defers the recognition of some of its expenses to a later year, thus allowing it to report higher earnings this year. Will the stock price increase as a result of the higher reported earnings? The answer is probably not. Since value depends on cash flows, informed investors will likely "see through" the accounting manipulation and realize that cash flows have not been changed.

This discussion of accounting may suggest that, from a valuation perspective, the accounting effects of loss financing decisions are irrelevant. This conclusion, however, is too hasty, because there are potential indirect cash flow effects of accounting numbers. In the remainder of this section we describe the main accounting differences between insurance and retention and then describe the potential cash flow effects of financial accounting numbers.

Financial Accounting for Insurance Premiums and Uninsured Losses

Insurance premiums are reported as an expense in the year in which coverage is provided. Since insurance premiums reflect expected insured losses (not actual losses), an insured firm reduces its reported income by an amount that is directly related to the value of expected insured losses. With multiple year policies, the premium expense is allocated proportionately. If, for example, Frickel Corp. pays $20,000 for an insurance policy that provides coverage over a two-year period, a $10,000 expense will be recognized in each of the two years.

Uninsured losses are reported as an expense in the year in which they occur. For example, if Frickel Corp. experiences a $10 million uninsured loss in 1998, it would recognize the entire $10 million as an expense in 1998. Thus, an uninsured firm reduces its income by an amount that reflects actual losses (not expected losses). An uninsured firm cannot deduct contingency reserves that reflect the expected value of losses each year; instead, it must deduct actual losses when they occur.

Note that the financial reporting of uninsured losses differs from the tax reporting of uninsured losses. For financial reporting purposes, a firm should deduct losses in the year in which the losses occur, not when they are paid. In contrast, for tax purposes, a noninsurance firm can deduct losses only in the year the losses are paid. To illustrate this difference, suppose that Frickel Corp. knows that a liability suit has been filed alleging that an accident occurred because one of the firm's products was defective. Also assume that the suit is likely to take several years to be resolved. Once the company realizes that a loss from the liability suit is "probable" and can be reasonably estimated, then it should recognize an expense for the likely amount of the loss even if the loss may not be paid and deducted for tax purposes until some time in the future. Thus, reported income and shareholders' equity should be lowered in the year the loss becomes probable (Financial Accounting Standard SFAS 5).

Regardless of whether insurance premiums or uninsured losses occur, a firm's balance sheet will reflect the reported after-tax expense as a decrease in shareholders' equity. If the loss is paid in the same year that the expense is recognized, then the firm's reported assets will decrease by the same amount that shareholders' equity decreases. However, if the loss is not paid until some time in the future, then the firm's reported liabilities will increase by the amount of the after-tax expense. In the latter case, in the year the loss is finally paid, the liability for the unpaid loss will be removed and assets will decrease by the amount of the expense.

When comparing the effects of insurance versus retention on accounting earnings, the main difference is that insurance generally will result in smoother or less variable earnings. Stated differently, accounting earnings are less likely to experience large jumps when a firm is insured. To provide a simple illustration, suppose that Frickel Corp. is subject to the risk of a product liability suit. Assume that the probability of a suit is 0.05 and that damages equal $10 million. Ignoring administrative costs, capital costs, and the time value of money, the fair premium equals $500,000. The purchase of liability insurance for a $500,000 premium will decrease before-tax earnings by $500,000 regardless of whether a loss occurs. With retention (the payment of liability losses from internal funds), before-tax earnings depend on whether a loss occurs. If a loss occurs, then reported before-tax earnings will be reduced by $10 million. If a loss does not occur, before-tax earnings will be unaffected by the retention decision. Thus, retention results in greater variance in reported earnings. In this case, the greater variability in accounting earnings from retention mirrors the greater variability in cash flows from retention that was discussed in earlier chapters.

When considering the effects of insurance versus retention on a firm's accounting (as opposed to economic) balance sheet, insurance again will result in less volatile numbers. A simple example will illustrate the different effects. Suppose that if Frickel Corp. uses retention and a loss does not occur, it will have assets equal to $100 million, liabilities equal to $50 million, and shareholders' equity equal to $50 million. This scenario is summarized by the balance sheet on the top left of Table 10–7. If a $10 million loss occurs and is paid from the firm's internal funds, then Frickel's assets will fall by $10 million and its shareholders' equity also will fall by $10 million. The top right side of Table 10–7 gives Frickel's balance sheet if a loss occurs. The important point is that the firm's liability-to-equity ratio is subject to considerable variability depending on whether a loss occurs. In contrast, if Frickel Corp. purchases insurance for $0.5 million, then its assets and shareholders' equity will fall by $0.5 million regardless of

TABLE 10–7   Frickel Corp.'s Balance Sheet with Retention and with Insurance (in $ millions)

Balance Sheet with Retention and a $10 Million Loss	
Assets	*Liabilities + Shareholders' equity*
Assets = $100	Liabilities = $50
	Shareholders' equity = $50
Liability/Equity ratio = 100%	

Balance Sheet with Retention and No Loss	
Assets	*Liabilities + Shareholders' equity*
Assets = $90	Liability = $50
	Shareholders' equity = $40
Liability/Equity ratio = 125%	

**Frickel Corp.'s Balance Sheet with Full Insurance
(regardless of whether a loss occurs)**

Assets	*Liabilities + Shareholders' equity*
Assets = $99.5	Liabilities = $50
	Shareholders' equity = $49.5
Liability/Equity ratio = 101%	

whether a loss occurs. The bottom of Table 10–7 summarizes the firm's balance sheet with insurance.

Impact of Financial Accounting Numbers on Cash Flow

Suppose that Mr. Eastman, the risk manager of Seminole Corp., has analyzed the advantages and disadvantages of insurance versus retention discussed in this chapter and in Chapter 9 and has concluded that the present value of expected cash flows will be the same with insurance as with retention. After reporting his results at a meeting, Ms. Petroni, the company's accountant, tells Mr. Eastman that insurance is better than retention because it results in smoother (less variable) reported earnings. Mr. Eastman replies, "Financial accounting numbers are irrelevant to firm valuation; investors care about cash flows." Ms. Petroni goes back to her office and writes a brief report outlining how less volatile accounting numbers can influence the magnitude or variability of cash flows.

Her first argument is that less volatile earnings allow investors to predict earnings and thus cash flows more accurately, which means that investors will view the firm's cash flows as having lower risk and thus will pay a higher price for the firm's stock. (Mr. Eastman probably will not be very sympathetic to this argument because he believes that the only risk that matters for valuation is nondiversifiable risk and that the risk Ms. Petroni is talking about is firm-specific risk and therefore diversifiable.)

Ms. Petroni's second argument is that the firm's debt contracts state that the firm is technically in default if reported earnings fall below a certain level or the firm's liabilities-to-assets ratio increases above a certain level. The purchase of insurance implies that the firm is less likely to trigger default and therefore less likely to incur the costs of renegotiating its debt contracts. (Mr. Eastman is likely to find this argument persuasive.)

Ms. Petroni's third argument is that managers' bonuses (including Mr. Eastman's) are based on reported earnings. Less volatile earnings imply that earnings are more likely to be above the minimum level necessary for managers to receive a bonus. Thus, managers should purchase insurance. (Mr. Eastman probably will find this argument persuasive.)

Ms. Petroni's final argument is that insurance reduces earnings volatility, which in turn allows the firm's shareholders to monitor managers more effectively (at a lower cost). Her reasoning is that insurance reduces the extent to which factors that are outside of the control of managers influence earnings. Consequently, reported earnings are a more accurate representation of managers' performance. (Mr. Eastman, being a superior manager, will like this argument because it increases the likelihood that the board of directors will notice his efforts and skills.)

In summary, loss financing choices influence reported accounting numbers. While accounting numbers, in and of themselves, usually are not the most important consideration when making loss financing decisions, the accounting effects sometimes are relevant, especially when contracts (e.g., debt covenants and management compensation contracts) are written based on accounting numbers.

10.9 Summary

- A transaction provides a tax benefit if it lowers the aggregate present value of expected tax payments for the parties involved.

- When effective tax rates are progressive, reducing the variability of cash flows will lower expected tax payments.

- Insurers can deduct estimates of unpaid losses when calculating their taxable income, but noninsurance companies cannot. This difference provides a tax benefit to insurance. Essentially, insurers can earn the before-tax rate of return on funds set aside to pay future losses.

- The tax treatment of losses on depreciated property provides a tax benefit to property insurance.

- By lowering the variability in cash flows, firms might be able to borrow more funds than otherwise. The additional borrowing creates interest tax shields, which can increase firm value.

- Premium taxes and excise taxes increase the premium loading on insurance, thus reducing its attractiveness.

- Government regulation makes some insurance compulsory and restricts firms' choices of insurers.

- Fronting refers to the practice of purchasing primary insurance from one insurer that immediately reinsures most of the exposure with another insurer. Fronting is used to: (1)

comply with regulations that restrict the choice of insurers; (2) reduce excise taxes; and (3) satisfy third party demands that insurance be provided by a particular set of insurers.

• In contrast to the tax treatment of uninsured losses, the financial reporting of uninsured losses requires firms to recognize losses when they become probable and can be reasonably estimated.

• Insurance generally reduces the variability of reported income and balance sheet numbers. Since contracts often are based on accounting numbers, accounting effects can be important when considering loss financing alternatives.

Key Terms

tax benefit   213
tax rate progressivity   215
incurred losses   218
tax shield   219
capital structure   226
interest tax shields   226

premium taxes   226
excise taxes   227
admitted insurer   228
nonadmitted insurer   228
excess and surplus (E&S) lines market   228
fronting   228

Questions and Problems

1. True or false: "This transaction will reduce expected tax payments, therefore we should do it!" Briefly explain your answer.

2. True or false: "This insurance transaction does not provide a tax benefit, because the tax law gives the favorable tax treatment to the insurer." Briefly explain your answer.

3. Suppose that the Lai Jean Co. expects before-tax earnings of $5 million this coming year, assuming no liability losses. However, there is a 2 percent chance that Lai will lose a $10 million lawsuit during the year. Profits are taxed at a rate of 34 percent. Assume that Lai cannot carry losses forward or backward (e.g., it has had no profits in the past and it expects to close down next year). Would liability insurance with a $10 million limit for a premium of $225,000 increase expected after-tax earnings for this coming year?

4. Suppose that Neilson's Restaurants has a

liability exposure with expected loss payments equal to $3 million this year, $3 million next year, and $1 million in two years. Assume that Neilson's can fully deduct all losses when calculating its taxable income, that it has a 34 percent tax rate, and that the interest rate equals 10 percent.

(a) What is the present value of the expected tax shield arising from Neilson's liability exposure if retention is chosen?

(b) What is the present value of the expected tax shield arising from Neilson's liability exposure if its liability exposure is insured through the Tennyson Insurance Company? That is, what would Tennyson's expected tax shield equal?

5. Suppose that Gardner Manufacturing has assets that are worth $50 million. If these

assets are destroyed, Gardner plans to replace them at a cost of $50 million. Gardner uses the straight-line depreciation method and the nature of the assets requires that they be depreciated over a two-year period. For tax purposes, the assets already have been depreciated to zero. Assume that the probability that the assets will be destroyed during the coming year equals 0.05, the income tax rate is 34 percent, and the capital gains tax rate is 28 percent. Calculate the expected tax shield generated from the property in the coming year and in future years if:

(a) Gardner plans to use internal funds to finance replacement of the property if it is destroyed.

(b) Gardner purchases replacement cost insurance for a premium of $2.5 million and plans to recognize a capital gain if the insurance proceeds are used to replace the property.

(c) Gardner purchases replacement cost insurance for a premium of $2.5 million and plans to defer the capital gain if the insurance proceeds are used to replace the property.

6. Explain the practice of fronting. Does a fronting insurer provide a service other than allowing a business to circumvent unpleasant regulations? Explain.

7. Describe how tax accounting and financial reporting differ with regard to losses that occur in a given year.

8. Explain how (a) reported income, (b) reported balance sheet assets and liabilities, and (c) the variability of reported income each might affect a firm's cash flows.

References

Aird, Paul; Robert Witt; and Patrick Brockett. "Economic Overview of the Market for Excess & Surplus Lines Insurance." *Journal of Insurance Regulation* 9 (December 1990), pp. 234–58. (*Provides an overview of the excess and surplus lines market.*)

Mayers, David; and Clifford Smith. "On the Corporate Demand for Insurance." *Journal of Business* 55, (1982), pp. 281–96. (*Provides an overview of why corporations with diversified shareholders purchase insurance, including the tax reasons for purchasing insurance.*)

Answer to Concept Check

1. The tax shields generated by the exposure without insurance:

	End of Year 1	End of Year 2
Expected tax shields	$0.34 \times \$3 = \$1.02$	$0.34 \times \$4 = \$1.36$
Present value of tax shields = $2.05		

The tax shields generated by the exposure with insurance:

	End of Year 1	End of Year 2
Expected tax shields	$0.34 \times (\$3 + 4/1.1) = \$2.051$	$0.34 \times (\$4 - 4/1.1) = \$0.102$
Present value of tax shields = $2.153		

APPENDIX 10A
TAX BENEFITS WHEN INSURERS OVERSTATE LOSS RESERVES

Table 10A–1 illustrates the possible additional tax benefit from overstatement of loss reserves by insurers. Instead of reporting loss reserves in year 1 of $2 million, suppose that Tennyson plans to report loss reserves of $3 million (for comparison, see Table 10–3 in the chapter). The present value of the loss reserve is $3/1.08 = $2.778 million, which, when added to paid losses, gives a value of $4.778 million for the discounted value of incurred losses. In year 2, Tennyson plans to correct the overstatement in the prior year by reporting $0 for the loss reserve. The change in the present value of the loss reserve is therefore –$2.778 million, which, when added to paid losses, gives a value of –$0.778 million for incurred losses in year 2. The negative value for incurred losses implies that Tennyson reports higher taxable earnings in year 2.

The expected tax shield equals 34 percent of incurred losses for tax purposes, which for year 1 equals $1.624 million (0.34 × $4.778 million) and for year 2 equals –$0.265 million (0.34 × –$0.778 million). The present value of the expected tax shields therefore equals

$$\frac{1.624}{1.08} + \frac{-0.265}{1.08^2} = \$1.277 \text{ million}$$

This value exceeds the present value of expected tax shields that was calculated in section 10.3 with unbiased reporting ($1.256 million) by $21,600. The difference arises because Tennyson is able to bring some of its tax shields earlier in time by overstating loss reserves. In particular, by overstating loss reserves by $1 million, the discounted value of incurred losses is increased by $0.926 million in year 1. This overstatement generates an additional tax shield of $0.315 million (0.34 × $0.926) in year 1. The tax shield is reversed in year 2; that is, Tennyson has $0.315 million in higher taxes in year 2, but by pushing the tax shield forward, Tennyson essentially earns interest on the tax shield equal to $0.025 million (0.08 × $0.315 million). The present value of this interest is $0.025/1.08^2 = $21,600.

TABLE 10A–1   Effect of Crocker Snowblowers Purchasing Insurance from Tennyson Insurance When Tennyson Overstates Loss Reserves in Year 1 (in $ millions)

	Beginning of Year 1	End of Year 1	End of Year 2
1. Paid losses		$2.000	$2.000
2. Loss reserve	$0.000	$3.000	$0.000
3. Change in loss reserve		$3.000	–$3.000
4. Undiscounted incurred losses (1) + (3)		$5.000	–$1.000
5. Present value of loss reserve (discounted value of 2)	$0.000	$2.778	$0.000
6. Change in present value of loss reserve		$2.778	–$2.778
7. Incurred losses for tax purposes (1) + (6)		$4.778	–$0.778

Loss Financing Methods

Chapter Objectives

- Describe the major features of traditional commercial insurance contracts.
- Discuss the main types of loss sensitive insurance contracts.
- Describe the ownership and operational characteristics of captive insurers, why captives are formed, and their tax treatment.
- Explain the alternative methods of paying retained losses.
- Summarize trends in loss financing.

11.1 Traditional Insurance Contracts

Table 11–1 summarizes the most common insurance policies purchased by businesses. Traditional **commercial insurance contracts** require the insured to pay a fixed premium for coverage of a particular type of exposure (e.g., property, liability) over a relatively short time period, typically a one-year period. Although some contracts allow the policyholder to pay the premium in installments over the contract period, the premium payments are not sensitive to losses that occur during the contract period. In contrast, loss-sensitive contracts, which can be used to cover many of the same exposures, require the policyholder to pay premiums that depend on the losses that occur during the contract period (see section 11.2). Loss sensitive contracts often are multiyear contracts.

Basis of Coverage

Traditional commercial insurance contracts with fixed premiums usually shift a significant amount of the risk of unexpected losses during the policy period to the insurer. There are, however, different ways of defining losses that are covered un-

TABLE 11–1   **Brief Description of Commonly Purchased Commercial Insurance Policies**

Exposure	Policy	Brief Description
Property	Commercial property	Direct losses from fire, explosion, windstorm, and a variety of other perils.
	Loss of business income	Income losses from events that damage property and thereby interrupt operations.
	Auto physical damage	Damage to and theft of automobiles.
Liability	Commercial general liability	General liability coverage for premises, products, and many contractual liability exposures.
	Auto liability	Liability arising from automobile accidents.
	Workers' compensation and employers' liability	Benefits paid to injured and ill employees under state workers' compensation laws; coverage for employer liability for certain injuries not covered by workers' compensation.
Multiline property-liability	Commercial multiple peril	Package policies that could include property, liability, auto, and the like. Commercial package policy (CPP) and business owners package (BOP) are examples.
Marine	Ocean marine	Losses to vessels, cargoes, and freight charges in connection with water transportation plus liability to others.
	Inland marine	Property losses from transportation of goods on inland waterways and roadways, plus liability to others; includes floater policies that cover special items.
Benefits	Life	Group life insurance contracts to pay life insurance benefits provided to employees.
	Medical	Group medical expense insurance coverage to pay medical expense benefits provided to employees.
	Disability	Group disability insurance contracts to pay short-term and/or long-term disability benefits to employees.

der a policy, which in turn affects how much risk is shifted by a particular contract.

Most commercial property and liability insurance policies are **occurrence policies;** that is, the claim payments made by the insurer are based on losses that occur during the policy period, regardless of when a claim is filed. For property coverage, most claims are made within the policy period or soon after the end of the period. Occurrence-based liability coverage, however, often involves relatively long lags between the date of the occurrence (the date that the injury occurred) and the date that the claim is filed or made. This type of coverage provides broad protection to the buyer. For example, if Scordis Insurance Company sells liability coverage with the policy period equal to calendar year 1999, then all losses that occur in the year 1999 are covered, even if the policyholder does not get sued and therefore does not file the claim until the year 2005.

In response to policyholders filing product liability and environmental liability claims based on losses that occurred many years earlier (see Chapter 15), liability insurers have introduced claims-made coverage as an option in commercial general liability policies.[1] **Claims-made policies** cover losses for claims that are made during the policy period and that have occurred subsequent to a **retroactive date** stated in the contract. For example, if a claims-made policy provides coverage for the year 1999 and has a retroactive date of January 1, 1995, then claims that are made during 1999 for losses that occurred after 1994 will be covered, but claims for losses that occurred prior to 1995 will not be covered.

A useful way to compare the risk-shifting features of occurrence and claims-made liability policies is to compare the risk borne by a policyholder who purchases a series of one-year occurrence policies starting in 1995 and continuing to the present to the risk borne by the same policyholder if instead a series of one-year claims-made policies are purchased, each with a retroactive date of January 1, 1995. Under both types of policies, if a claim is filed this year, the insurer will pay the loss. However, the two policies do not shift the same amount of risk to the insurer. The reason is that if information is revealed about the likelihood of past losses (e.g., if a product sold in the past is found to be defective and causes damages), then the insurer can incorporate this information into the pricing of future claims-made policies that provide coverage for losses that have occurred in the past. In contrast, competition from other insurers generally will prevent the insurer from raising prices on future occurrence coverage (which provides coverage for future losses only) based on information about past losses, unless past losses increase expected claim costs for future occurrence coverage (see Chapter 6). Thus, claims-made policies generally impose greater risk on policyholders than do occurrence policies. With the exception of many medical malpractice liability policies and certain other types of "risky" coverage (e.g., environmental liability and directors and officers liability, which are discussed in Chapter 15), most liability policies provide coverage on an occurrence basis.

Deductibles and Self-insured Retentions

As discussed in Chapter 8, insurance contracts typically do not provide full coverage. Instead, policies almost always require the policyholder to bear some risk. Through the use of policy provisions like deductibles and limits, some element of retention exists even when a firm purchases a traditional fixed premium insurance policy. We will first address deductibles and related provisions and then turn to policy limits.

A useful method of describing the coverage provided by a particular policy is to use an **exposure diagram,** which visually displays how the contract apportions losses between the insurer and the insured. To illustrate, Figure 11–1 graphs the exposure of a firm that buys no insurance (i.e., the firm retains all the risk associated with a particular loss exposure). The horizontal axis identifies the possible losses from the exposure, and the vertical axis identifies the amount of loss

---

[1] Some commercial liability policies earlier in the 20th century were claims-made policies. Also, group medical expense policies are claims-made policies.

FIGURE 11–1

Losses paid by a firm that purchases no insurance

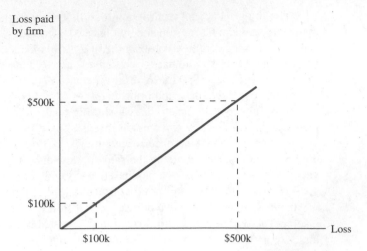

paid by the firm. When a firm retains all of its risk, it pays the entire loss. For example, if the loss is $10,000, then the firm pays $10,000; if the loss is $50,000, the firm pays $50,000. Consequently, if a firm buys no insurance, the 45-degree line from the graph's origin describes the firm's exposure to losses.

Whenever the line describing a firm's exposure to a loss has a positive slope, then the firm is retaining some of the risk. When interpreting exposure diagrams like Figure 11–1, it is important to keep in perspective that the losses measured on the horizontal axis are uncertain and that the graph identifies how much the insured will pay under any possible loss that may occur. Only one point on the graph will actually occur.

An insurance policy with a **deductible** of $2 million implies that the firm pays losses up to $2 million and that the insurer pays losses above $2 million. Deductibles can be per occurrence (claim) or aggregate. With a **per occurrence deductible,** the firm pays up to the deductible amount on each loss that is covered. For example, if Sharon Steel has a policy with a $2 million per occurrence deductible and it experiences five losses during the policy period with each loss equal to $1.5 million, then Sharon Steel would pay all losses. With an **aggregate deductible,** the firm pays all losses during the policy period until the aggregate amount paid equals the aggregate deductible. If Sharon Steel has a $2 million aggregate deductible in the example above, it would pay $2 million in total and the insurer would pay $5.5 million (assuming sufficient policy limits, see below).

While aggregate deductibles have the advantage of allowing the policyholder to place a cap on its loss payments for the policy period, they have the disadvantage of possibly promoting moral hazard, because once the aggregate deductible has been reached, the marginal cost of additional claims to the policyholder is zero (apart from any possible effect on future premiums). Thus, when the policyholder is likely to have considerable influence over the occurrence or severity of additional claims, per occurrence deductibles are more likely to be used, all else equal.

Firms with a per occurrence deductible policy sometimes purchase a **stop loss provision,** which caps the amount that the insured will pay during the policy period as a result of the accumulation of per occurrence deductibles. Thus, if Sharon Steel has a $2 million per occurrence deductible and a $4 million stop loss provision, then five losses of $1.5 million each would imply that Sharon Steel will pay $4 million and the stop loss insurer will pay $3.5 million.

The lower line in Figure 11–2 illustrates the amount of loss that the firm would pay with an aggregate deductible policy. The positive slope in the range of losses between $0 and $2 million indicates that the firm retains risk in this range. Notice that the lower line in Figure 11–2 does not take into account the premium paid for the insurance policy. The premium is easily incorporated by shifting the entire exposure line up by the amount of the premium. For example, if the premium for the aggregate deductible policy were $500,000, then the upper line in Figure 11–2 illustrates the sum of the premium and the amount of loss paid by Sharon Steel. Unless otherwise stated, we will not incorporate the premium in most of the diagrams.

Often the deductible amount ($2 million in the previous example) is called a **self-insured retention (SIR)** to indicate that losses below that point are self-insured or retained. A distinction sometimes is made between a deductible and a self-insured retention in the commercial insurance market. The term "deductible" (especially in reference to large deductible policies, see below) often indicates that the insurer will first pay all losses and then bill the insured for the amount of losses up to the deductible. In contrast, the term "self-insured retention" often indicates that the insurer will only pay losses once they exceed the self-insured retention level. When the insurer pays losses and then bills the insured for the deductible amount, the insurer usually will require that the insured provide a **letter of credit** from a bank that guarantees that the insured will pay losses as promised.

The choice between having the insurer pay losses up to the deductible

FIGURE 11–2

Losses paid by a firm that purchases a $2 million aggregate deductible policy

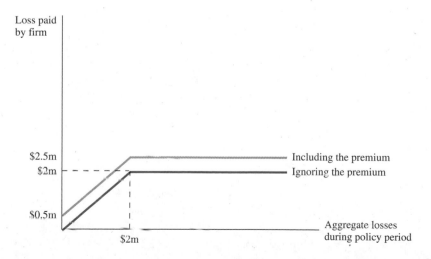

amount and then bill the insured or having the insured pay the self-insured retention depends in part on which party has a comparative advantage in processing
claims. If the insurer has an expertise in processing claims relative to the insured,
then having the insurer bill the policyholder can be advantageous. In addition, inefficiencies can occur in the processing of a high severity claim if a self-insured
retention is used, because both the insured and the insurer might have to be involved in processing and possibly litigating the claim. To avoid some duplication
of effort, it might be more efficient (lower cost) to simply have the insurer process
and litigate the claim and then bill the policyholder for the deductible. As we discuss further below, another reason to have the insurer pay the loss and then bill
the insured is to provide additional security to a third-party claimant (e.g., an injured worker under workers' compensation insurance).

Policy Limits and Excess Policies

The previous examples for deductibles and self-insured retentions (Figure 11–2)
ignored that insurance policies usually cap the amount that the insurer pays at
some **policy limit.** Both property and liability policies typically have per occurrence limits. (Claims-made liability policies have per claim limits.) Liability policies also usually have an annual aggregate limit.

The limit on a policy usually is stated as the maximum amount paid by the
insurer. For example, a policy that provides $3 million of coverage per occurrence
above a $1 million self-insured retention would require: (1) the insured firm to
pay the first $1 million of losses, (2) the insurer to pay the next $3 million of
losses, and (3) the insured to pay losses beyond $4 million on each occurrence.
Figure 11–3 shows the exposure diagram for this policy. Policies like this often
are called **excess policies,** because they provide coverage if losses are in excess

FIGURE 11–3

*Losses paid by a firm
that purchases a policy
that provides $3
million of coverage in
excess of a $1 million
per occurrence SIR*

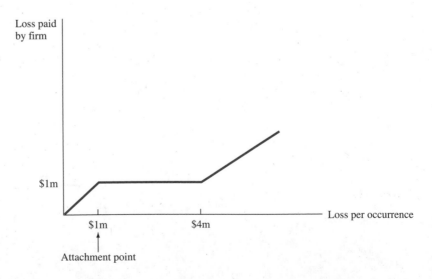

of some relatively large threshold, called the **attachment point.** Thus, the policy in our example provides $3 million of coverage with an attachment point of $1 million or, equivalently, $3 million of coverage in excess of $1 million. Excess policies can be structured to provide coverage above a self-insured retention or above the limit on another policy.

Layering Coverage.   Firms often purchase coverage in "layers" from different insurers, referred to as **layering coverage.** To illustrate, suppose that a firm purchases (1) a policy from insurer A that provides $3 million of coverage in excess of a $1 million self-insured retention (SIR), and (2) an excess policy from insurer B that provides $2 million of coverage in excess of $4 million. In combination, the two policies provide coverage over the range of losses from $1 million to $6 million. The firm's exposure to losses is shown in Figure 11–4. Large firms often have several layers of coverage and multiple insurers may participate in each layer, especially at the higher layers. An example of how the New York Transit Authority layered its coverage for the World Trade Center prior to its bombing in 1993 is provided in Box 11–1.

Layering helps to limit a particular insurer's exposure to a single loss and to distribute losses across insurers, thereby providing greater diversification. This explanation for layering is incomplete however, because the same diversification can be achieved if one insurer writes the entire coverage and then cedes the higher layer of coverage to a reinsurer. In the example above, instead of purchasing two policies from separate insurers, the firm could purchase one policy providing $5 million of coverage in excess of $1 million. The insurer selling that policy could then cede part of the coverage to a reinsurer. Greater diversification of risk occurs regardless of whether the insured or the primary insurer layers the coverage.

FIGURE 11–4

Losses paid by a firm that purchases two policies in layers (first policy provides $3 million of coverage in excess of $1 million per occurrence; the other policy provides $2 million of coverage in excess of $4 million on the same occurrence)

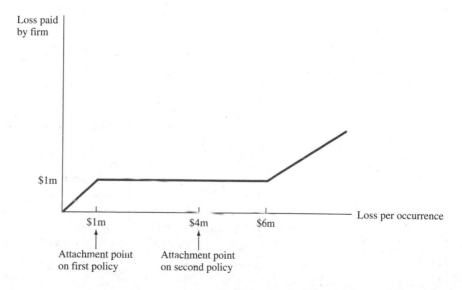

Box 11–1

Coverage for the World Trade Center Bombing

The World Trade Center in New York was bombed by a terrorist, causing property, liability, and business interruption losses of approximately $1 billion in February 1993. The New York Transit Authority had property and business interruption coverage of $600 million and liability coverage of $400 million. The multiple layers of property coverage and the multiple insurers that participated in the program are shown below:

Retention $100,000 per claim

1st layer $10 million from American Home Assurance and Home Indemnity

2nd layer $290 million from 11 companies

3rd layer $100 million from 5 companies

4th layer $100 million from 68 syndicates at Lloyd's of London

5th layer $100 million from 65 syndicates at Lloyd's of London

Source: "Blast Rips Businesses, Insurers," *Business Insurance,* March 8, 1993.

When would a firm find it more desirable to arrange the layering itself as opposed to having an insurer enter the reinsurance market to achieve the same layering? The answer depends on a number of factors, including the insured firm's costs of arranging the transactions versus the primary insurer's cost of transacting in the reinsurance market. In addition, because of the possibility of insurer insolvency and thus the failure to pay claims, the insured firm may find it desirable to be involved in the selection of those insurers that will ultimately provide the coverage. Finally, policies from multiple insurers can yield greater coverage protection from state guaranty funds should any of the insurers become insolvent because guaranty funds do not cover reinsurance.

Umbrella Liability Coverage.   Umbrella liability coverage is similar to excess coverage in that the policy provides excess coverage over other policies or self-insured retentions. The difference is that an umbrella policy covers liability losses from multiple exposures or perils. To illustrate, suppose that Lilly Inc. purchases the following set of policies: (1) an auto liability policy providing $1 million excess coverage above a $100,000 self-insured retention (SIR) per occurrence; (2) a products liability policy providing $10 million excess coverage above a $1 million SIR per occurrence; and (3) an umbrella policy providing $20 million of coverage per occurrence, excess of liability limits on the other two policies. Table 11–2 shows how these policies would apportion the losses between Lilly and the three insurers if Lilly incurs a $10.1 million auto liability loss and a $15 million products liability loss during the coverage period. In addition to providing coverage in excess of other policies' limits, umbrella policies often cover some losses not covered by another policy above a self-insured retention.

TABLE 11-2   Illustration of Coverage Provided by an Umbrella Insurer (umbrella coverage = $20 million per occurrence above limits on auto and products liability policies; auto policy coverage = $1 million above $100,000 SIR per occurrence; products liability coverage = $10 million above $1 million SIR per occurrence)

		Loss Paid by (in $ millions)			
	Amount of Loss	Insured Firm	Auto Liability Insurer	Products Liability Insurer	Umbrella Insurer
Auto liability loss	$10.1	$0.1	$1	$ 0	$ 9
Products liability loss	$15.0	$1.0	$0	$ 10	$ 4
Total loss	$25.1	$1.1	$1	$ 10	$ 13

11.2 Loss Sensitive Contracts

With **loss sensitive insurance contracts,** the premiums ultimately paid by the insured depend on the losses that occur (or are paid) *during the policy period.* Consequently, loss sensitive contracts typically shift less risk to the insurer compared with traditional fixed premium insurance contracts. Stated differently, loss sensitive contracts typically involve greater retention than traditional policies.

The ultimate amount paid by the policyholder under a loss sensitive contract is determined only after some time period has elapsed. To the extent that the insurer initially pays losses for the coverage period that eventually will be reimbursed by the policyholder, the insurer essentially provides a loan to the policyholder. Consequently, loss sensitive plans often will require that the policyholder provide a letter of credit from a major bank to guarantee that the policyholder will fulfill its obligation to make the agreed upon future payments.

Experience-rated Policies

As discussed in Chapter 6, experience-rated policies base the premium for the coming period on the individual insured's past loss experience. In contrast to the contracts described later in this section, experience-rated policies typically are not designed for the purpose of having the policyholder pay a large portion of unexpected losses during the coverage period. Instead, experience rating usually is used because (1) it reduces moral hazard, and (2) it formalizes how insurers will update their predictions of expected future losses based on the insured firm's past losses. Nevertheless, to the extent that past losses are given considerable weight in the determination of future premiums, experience-rated policies can be viewed as loss sensitive contracts.

Large Deductible Policies and Retrospectively Rated Policies

Recall that deductible policies often are structured so that the insurer pays all losses and then is reimbursed by the policyholder for the losses up to the deductible amount. When the deductible amount is set at such a high level that the policyholder expects to reimburse the insurer for substantial losses (e.g., $100,000 per injury in workers' compensation insurance), policies often are called **large deductible policies.** With these policies, the policyholder essentially retains a large amount of the risk, but the insurer temporarily finances the losses.

A related type of loss sensitive contract is called a **retrospectively rated policy,** or a retro. With these plans, an up-front premium usually is paid. However, the size of the total premium ultimately paid by the policyholder, known as the retro premium, depends on the magnitude of losses during the policy period. The policyholder must make an additional payment if the retro premium is greater than the up-front premium; the policyholder can receive a refund if the retro premium is lower than the up-front premium. Like large deductible policies, the insurer settles all the claims.

The retro premium is subject to both a minimum and a maximum amount, both of which are defined when the policy is initiated. For example, the following formula could be used: The retro premium (to be paid at a specified time after the policy period ends) will equal 90 percent of losses (including a loading for the insurer's loss adjustment expenses), with a minimum premium equal to $500,000 and a maximum premium equal to $3 million. As depicted in Figure 11–5, the minimum premium, the maximum premium, and the percentage of losses paid between the maximum and minimum determines the amount of retained losses under a retro policy. The greater the maximum premium and the greater the sensitivity of premiums to losses (90 percent in this example, although 100 percent is common), the more risk that is retained by the policyholder. One essential aspect of both retros and large deductible policies is that the insured retains a large portion of its risk; only the risk of very high losses is typically shifted to the insurer.

FIGURE 11–5

Exposure diagram for a firm that purchases a retrospectively rated policy (the minimum premium equals $0.5 million and the maximum premium equals $3 million)

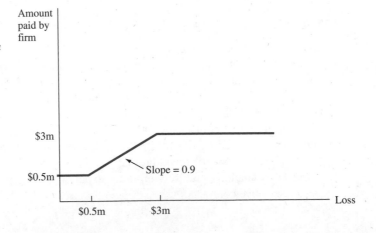

Retrospectively rated policies must specify the timing of retro premium payments. With a *paid loss retro,* the policyholder agrees to make payments that correspond to the insurer's payments for losses. Since losses that occur during the policy period may not be paid for several years, the paid loss retro policy often requires the insured to make periodic payments to the insurer over future years. The other possibility is to base the retrospective premium on incurred losses (the insurer's estimate of losses that eventually will be paid due to events that occur during the year). With an *incurred loss retro* policy, the retro premium payment at the end of the first year (or specified later date) will be based on losses paid as of this date plus the insurer's estimate of future loss payments for losses that occur during the coverage period. Thus, all else equal, the premium will be higher in the first year under an incurred loss retro policy than under a paid loss retro policy. Nevertheless, since insurers receive information over time concerning the value of loss payments for losses that occur during the policy period, incurred loss retros also can require periodic premium payments or reimbursements. For example, if subsequent to the policy period an insurer learns that its initial estimate of unpaid losses was too low, then it will recognize incurred losses, causing the insured to make a premium payment (provided the maximum premium has not been reached).

Why do businesses use large deductible and retro policies, instead of just purchasing an excess policy with a high attachment point? Tax reasons help explain why firms purchase policies based on incurred losses. As discussed in the previous chapter, when calculating its taxable income, a noninsurance business can deduct retained losses only when the losses are paid. Since insurance premiums are deductible, however, an incurred loss retro policy or a large deductible policy based on incurred losses may allow the business to deduct the value of losses incurred and thereby move its tax deductions for losses earlier.[2] Another reason for using a retro policy is that it might be an efficient way for the business to contract with the insurer to process claims, but at the same time, the business is able to retain risk. Finally, firms often purchase large deductible and retro policies to satisfy compulsory insurance requirements for workers' compensation and automobile liability insurance. In this way, the firm retains most of the risk of losses but satisfies regulatory requirements. The insurer serves the function of certifying that the business can pay its retained losses.

Related Loss Sensitive Plans

With large deductible and retro policies, the insured pays the insurer after the losses have occurred or have been paid. Consequently, the insured retains, at least temporarily, the use of the funds that eventually will be used to pay losses. As a result, these and other plans with this characteristic sometimes are called cash

---

[2] At one time paid loss retros were used to reduce taxes by having the insured pay a large advance premium, which would be tax deductible when paid, with the expectation of receiving a refund at the end of the retro period. Congress eliminated this potential advantage in 1986.

flow plans, because the buyer has greater initial cash flow than if insurance is purchased. While this can be advantageous if the funds are needed for other projects, it can have several disadvantages. If the business invests the funds that eventually will be needed to pay the insurer, then the business will have to pay a tax on the investment earnings of these funds. In addition, the insurer typically will require that the policyholder provide a letter of credit, which is costly to arrange and requires the policyholder to pay a fee to the bank.

Several innovative plans have been used in recent years to reduce the need for letters of credit but which continue to require the insured to pay most of the losses that occur. These plans require that the policyholder make up-front payments to the insurer (i.e., the policyholder essentially prefunds losses). However, the plans allow the insured to receive explicit investment income on the funds before losses are paid. If structured appropriately, these plans will be treated as insurance for tax purposes, which will allow the insured firm to deduct premium payments (prefunding payments) and allow the insurer to deduct incurred losses. Assuming the tax benefits are passed on to the insured firm via lower premium payments, these tax features essentially allow the insured firm to avoid tax on the investment income generated on funds used to pay losses that have been incurred but not yet paid.

With an **investment credit program,** the insured pays the insurer an amount to cover loss payments up to the desired deductible amount and the insurer, after subtracting some of the money for expenses, places the funds in a trust account. This account is used to pay losses and accrues interest at an agreed upon rate. Any funds that remain in the account after a certain length of time (depending on the length of the claims tail) are returned to the policyholder. If the account does not have sufficient resources to pay all the claims, then the insured will have to make additional premium payments. Provided maximum premium payments are set so that the insurer bears significant risk, these plans will qualify as insurance, thus providing tax benefits.

As discussed earlier, an insightful way of viewing the tax benefit arising from the different tax treatment of insurers and noninsurance companies is that the insurer is able to avoid paying tax on investment income that is generated from funds that are set aside to pay losses than have been incurred but not yet paid.[3] This way of viewing the tax benefit helps to explain why policyholders will sometimes combine an investment credit type plan with a **premium financing arrangement,** whereby it borrows the funds that are deposited with the insurer. In this way, the policyholder is able to deduct interest payments on the loan but avoid tax on the investment income that is generated to fund incurred losses that have not yet been paid. This arrangement can be viewed as a tax-arbitrage scheme—the policyholder's after-tax cost of paying off interest on the loan is less than the after-tax interest received on part of the borrowed funds, thus generating a certain profit.

---

[3] Note that insurers are taxed on investment income on capital, however.

Loss Portfolio Transfers

Insurance sometimes is purchased to cover losses that have already been incurred, but for which the timing and/or ultimate size of loss payments is uncertain. Thus, the premium depends on the losses incurred. Suppose, for example, that as a result of a manufacturing defect a firm expects that it will incur product liability claims of $200 million over the next five years. The exact dollar amount of losses is subject to some uncertainty, as is the timing of the payments. The firm can transfer the entire loss to an insurer, called a **loss portfolio transfer,** by paying the present value of expected (predicted) claim payments in one lump sum (or possibly in installments). In this situation, the insurer accepts some underwriting risk (the risk associated with the variability in the dollar amount of payments) and considerable timing risk (the risk due to the uncertainty of when payments will be paid). Provided that the insurer accepts considerable risk, the payment made by the insured firm is deductible and the insurer can deduct the present value of incurred losses, thus providing a tax benefit. In addition, for financial accounting reporting purposes, the insured firm can report the entire amounts paid to the insurer (the present value of expected losses) as an expense in the year they are paid. This can help smooth reported earnings.

Finite Risk Contracts

Insurers (and reinsurers) also offer multiple year loss sensitive plans that commonly are called **finite risk insurance** or **financial insurance.** The term "finite risk" is used to indicate that there is relatively little risk transferred to the insurer. In other words, the insured firm usually pays most of the losses. The contract period for finite risk contracts usually is three to five years. The insured firm pays premiums each year to the insurer who places the premiums in a fund (after taking out a fee). The fund accumulates interest at an agreed upon rate of return, and losses are paid from the fund. If the fund is insufficient to pay all the losses in a given year, then the insurer will pay losses up to a stated limit. However, the policyholder's future premium payments are used to reimburse the insurer. Any surplus remaining in the fund at the end of the policy period is returned to the insured firm. Together, these features imply that the policyholder pays most losses, but that the payments are smoothed over time. Thus, finite risk plans provide protection against the timing of loss payments but offer limited protection against unexpected loss payments over the course of the policy period.

An example will help illustrate the essential aspects of finite risk contracts. Suppose that a three-year contract is signed that (1) requires the insured firm to pay premiums of $4 million a year, (2) credits interest at 6.0 percent annually on the year's beginning balance, (3) provides the insurer with a fee equal to 10 percent of each premium, and (4) has an aggregate limit of $20 million for the three years. Table 11–3 illustrates the cash flows that would occur if paid losses in the three years equal $2 million, $4 million, and $5 million, respectively. We assume for simplicity that these loss amounts are paid at the end of each year. In the first

TABLE 11-3   Cash Flows (in $ thousands) from a Three-Year Finite Risk Contract (premium = $4 million; interest = 6% of beginning balance; $20 million aggregate limit)

	Year 1	Year 2	Year 3
At Beginning of Year:			
Balance from previous year	$ 0	$ 1,672	$ 1,377
Premium	4,000	4,000	4,000
Insurer's fee	−400	−400	−400
Beginning balance	3,600	5,272	4,977
At End of Year:			
Claim payments	−2,000	−4,000	−5,000
Interest on beginning balance	216	316	299
Ending balance	$ 1,816	$ 1,588	$ 276

year, the policyholder pays the premium of $4 million, the insurer takes its fee, and interest is earned on the balance. Since claim payments at the end of the first year equal $2 million, all claims are paid from the policyholder's fund. The ending balance in the fund after the first year equals $1,816,000. The premium payment in the second year increases the size of the fund, so that even though claim payments equal $4 million at the end of year 2, the policyholder's fund again is sufficient to pay all claims. The same scenario occurs in year 3; the policyholder's fund has enough money to pay all claims, leaving a surplus of $276,000. In this example, the $276,000 remaining in the fund at the end of the policy period would be returned to the policyholder. Alternatively, if another finite risk plan were established for the subsequent three-year period, the surplus at the end of the first three-year period could be used to reduce the premiums for the second three-year period.

Notice that in the example presented in Table 11-3 the insured firm has essentially paid all losses because claims were always below the amount in the fund. If losses were to exceed the amount in the fund, then the insurer would have to pay the losses up to the limit of $20 million. Thus, finite risk insurance is similar to a multiyear policy with a high deductible.

Table 11-4 illustrates the same policy as before, but with higher overall loss payments. In particular, claim payments equal $1 million, $12 million, and $1 million, respectively, at the end of years one through three. The large claim payment at the end of the second year depletes the policyholder's fund, so the insurer makes up the shortfall by paying $5,352,000. As a consequence, the policyholder's fund has a deficit after two years. In this example, the deficit is larger than the premium payment in the third and final year, which implies that the insurer will pay some of the insured's losses (up to the $20 million aggregate limit).

TABLE 11–4   **Cash Flows (in $ thousands) from a Three-Year Finite Risk Contract (premium = $4 million; interest = 6% of beginning balance; $20 million aggregate limit)**

	Year 1	*Year 2*	*Year 3*
At Beginning of Year:			
Balance from previous year	$ 0	$ 2,672	–$ 5,603
Premium	4,000	4,000	4,000
Insurer's fee	–400	–400	–400
Beginning balance	3,600	6,272	–2,003
At End of Year:			
Claim payments	–1,000	–12,000	–1,000
Interest on beginning balance	216	376	–120
Ending balance	$ 2,816	–$ 5,352	–$ 3,123

Finite risk contracts also can have provisions that make the policyholder pay a large percentage (e.g., 80 or 90 percent) of any deficit in the fund at the end of the policy period. The payment of the deficit usually can be paid in installments, thus allowing the policyholder to spread the cost over time. For example, in the previous example, a $3.123 million deficit existed at the end of the policy period. The contract could require that the policyholder pay 80 percent of this amount in equal installments over the subsequent three years. This $832,800 payment (0.80 × $3,123,000 ÷ 3) also could be added to the premium for another finite risk contract over the subsequent three-year time period.

This example illustrates that while the policyholder bears most of the risk of unexpected losses with finite risk plans, these plans allow firms to smooth their payments for losses over time. To highlight this feature, Figure 11–6 graphs the annual premium payments and loss payments under two successive three-year finite risk contracts. The premiums and losses for the first three-year period are the same as those used in Table 11–4. The premium payments for the second three-year period assume that the deficit in the first period is added to the premium payments for the second three-year period.

As discussed in the last chapter, the smoothing of loss payments can be beneficial from a tax standpoint. However, in order to obtain these tax benefits, the finite risk contract must be classified as insurance, which requires that a material amount of the risk associated with unexpected loss payments be shifted to the insurer. Having the insurer bear risk above a reasonable threshold (attachment point) usually can satisfy this requirement. The smoothing of loss payments over time also can have advantages because it reduces the variability of reported earnings. While financial analysis should in general focus on the present value of cash flows as opposed to accounting earnings, we discussed in the previous chapter how reported accounting numbers can influence expected cash flows and therefore be relevant when making financial decisions.

Figure 11–6

Illustration of how finite risk contracts smooth loss costs

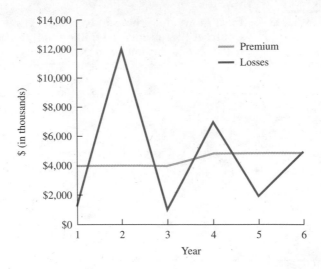

Concept Check

1. Briefly summarize the main reasons for purchasing a loss sensitive insurance policy.

11.3 Captive Insurers

An important method of financing losses for many large corporations is to make payments to a wholly owned subsidiary, called a **captive insurer,** which then pays losses. For reasons discussed below, captive insurers usually have insurance transactions with corporations other than the parent corporation, including the purchase of reinsurance to transfer risk of large losses. The typical relationships are illustrated in Figure 11–7, where solid lines indicate ownership relationships and dashed lines indicate possible insurance/reinsurance transactions with the captive insurer. If the captive only insures its single parent corporation and/or subsidiaries owned by the parent, it is called a **pure captive.** Often when captives insure other wholly owned subsidiaries of the parent, the transactions are called **brother-sister transactions** to indicate that the transactions are between corporations that have the same parent. Many captives have **unrelated business;** that is, the captive sells insurance to noninsurance corporations that are not owned by the captive's parent. In addition, many captives engage in reinsurance transactions with other insurers (including other captives). Finally, some captives have multiple parents (this relationship is not illustrated in Figure 11–7); these captives are called **group captives.**

Many US companies establish captive insurers "offshore" in places like Bermuda, Barbados, and the Cayman Islands. These locations impose few regulatory restrictions and offer favorable tax treatment relative to domestic captive insurance companies. However, several US states, such as Vermont and Colorado,

FIGURE 11–7

Ownership relationship (solid lines) and insurance transactions (dashed lines) involving captive insurers

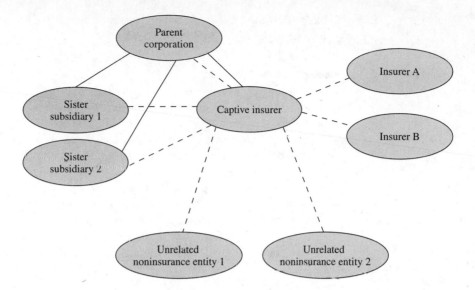

have offered favorable regulatory environments for captives in recent years. Regardless of where captives are established, few, if any, employees usually work where the captive is domiciled. Instead, management companies are hired or the parent's risk management department manages the captive's operations. Table 11–5 provides information on the number of captive insurers in various locations.

Many small- and medium-sized companies have insufficient exposures to justify the fixed costs of establishing and operating a captive. To provide some of the benefits of captives to these smaller businesses, existing captives and captive management companies have offered firms the ability to "rent-a-captive." In essence, an existing captive segregates the business of the renter from the other

TABLE 11–5   Locations of Captive Insurers in 1996

Location	Number of Captives
Bermuda	1,050
Cayman Islands	373
Guernsey	324
Barbados	167
Dublin	134
Isle of Man	134
Luxembourg	235
Vermont	293

Source: "Interest from Evolving Markets, New Uses Drive Captive Growth," *Business Insurance,* April 14, 1997.

business of the captive and returns the renter's underwriting profit and investment income to the renter, after subtracting a fee.

Motivations for Forming Captive Insurers

Tax and Regulatory Factors.   Loss financing through pure captives (single parent captives with no unrelated business) is, in essence, a form of retention (self-insurance). Several tax and regulatory factors help explain why a firm would go to the trouble and expense of forming a pure captive. Historically, an important motivation for creating a captive was to reduce expected tax payments. As discussed in Chapter 10, the different tax treatment of insurers versus noninsurance corporations gives rise to a tax advantage for insurance compared with retention. This tax advantage provides an incentive for firms to arrange loss financing transactions that will be treated as insurance for tax purposes. Thus, to the extent that captive transactions are treated as insurance transactions, firms can reduce expected tax payments relative to retention. We discuss the specific tax treatment of captives below.

Additional tax benefits can be obtained by locating captives offshore, in locations such as Bermuda and the Cayman Islands. These tax benefits arise if the captive's income does not have to be recognized by the parent as taxable income in the year it is earned. In this case, the taxes paid on the captive are subject to the tax treatment afforded insurers in the country in which the captive is domiciled. Since many offshore locations have lower tax rates on investment and underwriting income, the offshore location reduces expected tax payments relative to domestic captives. The issue of whether the parent must recognize the income of the captive as taxable income is complex. Prior to 1987, corporations could defer recognition of the underwriting income from an offshore captive indefinitely. If the country in which the captive was domiciled did not impose taxes on underwriting income, then corporations essentially could avoid taxation on the profits of their captive insurer. The Tax Reform Act of 1986, however, makes parents of most captives pay tax on their captive's profits in the year the profits are earned under Subpart F of the Internal Revenue Code.

Another potential motivation for establishing a captive is to allow the business to purchase excess insurance coverage directly from reinsurers. Since reinsurance transactions typically are subject to less stringent regulation, having a transaction classified as reinsurance (by first insuring through a captive, which then purchases reinsurance) can reduce regulatory constraints on the transaction. Excise taxes also create an incentive to have transactions with foreign insurers treated as reinsurance as opposed to insurance. Recall that excise taxes on foreign transactions equal 4 percent of insurance premiums, but only 1 percent of reinsurance premiums.[4]

---

[4] These savings also can be obtained by using a domestic insurer as a front. See Chapter 10.

A captive also allows a firm to retain a large portion of its risk and still satisfy compulsory insurance requirements, comply with restrictions on the selection of insurers, and meet third party demands for certificates of insurance from rated insurers, provided that the firm uses a fronting insurer. Specifically, a firm can purchase insurance through a fronting insurer that meets the necessary requirements (i.e., is an admitted insurer or satisfies the rating requirement of the party who demands a certificate of insurance). The fronting insurer then reinsures with the captive.

Risk Reduction.   Captives also can be used to reduce risk. When a captive sells insurance or reinsurance to unrelated entities, then the parent's exposures (and the parent's wholly owned subsidiaries' exposures) are pooled with the unrelated entities' exposures. Consequently, risk (the variance of average losses) is reduced as a result of the captive's transactions (see Chapter 3). Similarly, group captives reduce risk—the loss exposures of each owner are pooled together and each owner shares in the aggregate results of the group. Group captives often are formed to serve firms in a specific industry. Thus, provided that a captive has either multiple parents or unrelated business, captive transactions are not pure retention but instead are a form of insurance that reduces risk.

The Tax Treatment of Captive Transactions

General Legal Principles.   The tax courts have two sometimes conflicting principles that guide their decisions regarding the tax treatment of captive insurers. One principle is that risk reduction is important. That is, the courts will view with suspicion captive insurance transactions that do not reduce risk. The basis for this principle is a 1941 Supreme Court opinion (*Helvering v. LeGierse*) which states that insurance transactions entail "risk shifting" and "risk distribution."[5] Although experts differ in interpretation of the terms risk shifting and risk distribution, the courts have generally adopted a view that is consistent with the discussion in Chapter 3 on risk pooling. If a captive transaction results in a pooling of risk and therefore a reduction in the variance of average losses, then risk shifting and risk distribution exist, and the transaction is treated as insurance.

The courts also use the principle that the legal separateness of corporations should be respected (*Moline Properties v. Commissioner, 1943*). Using this principle, the tax courts will view transactions between a corporation and a separately incorporated captive as transactions between separate corporations that *could* constitute insurance. As discussed below, the use of this principle has led courts to view brother-sister captive transactions as insurance, even though these transactions result in little if any risk reduction.

---

[5] In addition, the courts often look to see if the transactions with the captive resemble insurance transactions in the "commonly accepted sense."

Captives That Only "Insure" a Single Parent.   Captives that only insure a single parent do not reduce risk for the parent corporation. This follows from the observation that the parent is the sole residual claimant to the captive's profits and only the captive transacts with the parent. Thus, any of the profits or losses of the captive are the direct result of the parent's payments to the captive and the parent's losses. From a risk-bearing perspective, pure captives are equivalent to self-insurance. Consistent with the risk-bearing effects, the tax law views these transactions as retention (*Carnation v. Commissioner, 1981*). The purchase of reinsurance, however, by the captive from an unrelated reinsurer is treated as insurance.

Captives with Unrelated Business.   When a captive insures or reinsures unrelated entities in addition to its parent corporation, the parent's loss exposures are pooled with the exposures of other entities. Consequently, captives that insure unrelated entities are essentially pooling arrangements that reduce the variance of the average losses of those parties transacting with the captive. Thus, the tax law treats transactions with captives that have unrelated business as insurance transactions.[6] Tax rulings on this issue have induced many captives to write unrelated business in an effort to achieve favorable tax status.

The question of how much unrelated business is needed for the transaction to be treated as insurance (for risk shifting and risk distribution to be material) is not settled. Of the cases addressing unrelated business (see footnote 6), the Harper case had the least proportion of unrelated business—approximately 30 percent. It is uncertain how the courts would rule if the percentage of unrelated business were less than 30 percent.

Captives That Only Insure a Single Parent and Sister Corporations.   As discussed earlier, in addition to insuring the parent corporation, some captives also insure other wholly owned subsidiaries of the parent corporation without providing insurance or reinsurance to any unrelated businesses. Before discussing the tax treatment of these brother-sister transactions, it is first useful to discuss two approaches that have not been adopted by the courts and taxing authorities.

One approach would be to treat the brother-sister transactions as unrelated business. Since the sister corporations are separate corporations from both the captive and the captive's parent, some experts have argued that the transactions between the captive and its sister corporations are just like unrelated business and, consequently, that both the parent's and the sister subsidiaries' transactions with the captive should be treated as insurance. Others, however, argue that since the parent wholly owns the sister corporations and the captive, the transactions between the sister corporations and the captive do not reduce the risk of the consolidated entity's cash flows. An owner of the parent, for example, would not view the transactions with the captive as reducing his or her risk because the owner bears the cost of unexpected losses whether or not the captive exists. The

---

[6] See *Harper v. Commissioner, 1991; AMERCO v. Commissioner, 1991; Ocean Drilling & Exploration Co. v. United States, 1991;* and *Sears, Roebuck and Co. v. Commissioner, 1991.*

captive simply changes the name of the legal entity that pays losses. This view leads to the recommendation that the brother-sister transactions should be treated as retention. That is, neither the parent's nor the brother-sister transactions should be treated as insurance.

In contrast to either of the views presented, the tax courts have adopted the following approach when the captive only insures its parent and its sister corporations: Transactions between the parent and the captive are not treated as insurance, but transactions between the sister subsidiaries and the captive (the brother-sister transactions) are treated as insurance (see *Humana Inc. v. Commissioner, 1989*) This approach was upheld in two 1997 cases, *Hospital Corporation of America v. Commissioner* and *Kidde Industries, Inc. v. The United States.* The logic given is that the parent's captive transactions do not reduce risk (and therefore are not insurance) because the parent owns all the corporations that the captive insures. The sister subsidiaries' transactions with the captive reduce risk because the sister corporation's exposures are being pooled with the exposures of entities that they do not own (i.e., sister corporations or the parent corporation).[7]

Risk Retention Groups

Although technically not captive insurers, risk retention groups have most of the characteristics of group captives. We therefore discuss them here. Prior to 1981, the formation of pooling arrangements among firms was hindered by the requirement that pooling arrangements generally had to satisfy state insurance regulations in order to legally provide primary insurance. Congress passed a law in 1981 that allows firms to bypass some state regulations and form groups to pool risk arising from products liability exposures. These groups, which are very similar to group captives, are called **risk retention groups.** In 1986, the law was expanded to allow risk retention groups for all liability exposures, except employers' liability and workers' compensation. In 1997, about 70 risk retention groups existed.

11.4 Methods of Paying Retained Losses

The methods that a firm can use to pay uninsured losses (retained losses) fall into three general categories: (1) using internal funds; (2) establishing lines of credit (precommitments from lenders to borrow funds needed to pay losses); and (3) raising external funds following a loss by borrowing money or issuing new equity

---

[7] One potential problem with the courts' rulings on this issue is that it creates an incentive for a parent simply to be a shell and place the vast majority of its loss exposures in wholly owned subsidiaries, which then insure through the captive. From the perspective of the primary risk bearer of corporate activities, the shareholders, these transactions do not reduce risk (i.e., the firm has essentially self-insured). However, brother-sister captive transactions might reduce risk for nonshareholder claimants of the subsidiaries.

securities. Regardless of whether losses are paid from internal funds, using lines of credit, or raising external funds, unexpected losses reduce the value of cash flows to the firm's shareholders at the time of the loss. Thus, when planning how to finance losses, any of these retention methods will increase the volatility of cash flows and thus the volatility of the firm's equity values compared with purchasing insurance.

Internal Funds

Cash Flows.   One source of internal funds to pay losses is the firm's cash flows from operations. The extent to which a firm can pay losses from its cash flows from operations depends on the level of potential losses and the probability distribution for cash flows. The greater the variability of cash flows, the less reliable they are as a loss financing method. For some firms, only relatively small losses can be paid from the firm's annual cash flows.

Dedicated Assets.   Since cash flows may not be sufficient to pay losses, firms sometimes try to set funds aside to pay losses when they occur. Generally, these funds are placed in liquid assets such as marketable securities. This is known as the **dedicated assets** approach to loss financing. While firms may attempt to build up assets gradually over time to pay losses, this approach suffers from the problem that large losses could occur before the firm has accumulated sufficient funds to pay the loss. As noted earlier, investment income on dedicated assets also generally will be taxable as income. The use of dedicated assets nevertheless can be a viable approach to financing losses in many cases. As suggested above, pure captives can be viewed as a mechanism for dedicating assets to finance retained losses.

Lines of Credit

Another way of financing retained losses is to use a **line of credit,** which involves arranging—prior to a loss—the terms at which the firm can borrow money. In essence, the firm negotiates with a bank for the option to borrow up to some predetermined amount of money at a specified interest rate during a specified time period. The firm then can draw down the line of credit to pay losses as needed. It is important to note that even though the funds needed to pay a particular loss are coming from a bank, the loan must be repaid and, consequently, the burden of paying the loss ultimately rests with the firm's shareholders at the time of the loss. Compared with paying the loss from cash flows or dedicated assets, a certain amount of time and effort is required to arrange lines of credit. In addition, the bank is likely to charge a higher interest rate (relative to the expected rate on a conventional loan) for the guarantee that it will provide the firm with funds when they are needed, especially if the amount of funds is large compared with the borrower's resources.

Issue New Securities

Instead of prearranging financing terms, a firm can attempt to arrange a bank loan following a loss. Alternatively, the firm can issue new debt securities or new equity securities to pay losses. As discussed in Chapter 9, raising new funds via the issuance of new securities often is costly due to transaction and underpricing costs. As with lines of credit, it is important to note that even though the funds needed to pay the loss nominally come from new investors if new securities are issued, the burden of the loss rests with the shareholders at the time of the loss.

11.5 Trends and Innovations in Loss Financing

During the past three decades, many large firms have increased (1) their retention levels and (2) their use of what is commonly called the *alternative market,* which includes captives, group captives, risk retention groups, and finite risk contracts. The trend toward greater retention and reliance on the alternative market has several explanations, including, at least in part, growth in understanding by managers and investors that risk reduction for diversified shareholders is beneficial only if it has positive effects on expected cash flows (see Chapter 9).

One economic factor that helps explain these trends is that, beginning in the late 1960s and continuing until the 1980s, larger fluctuations in the price of business insurance associated with the cycle of hard and soft markets (wherein periods of high insurance prices and low availability of coverage follow periods of low prices and readily available coverage) led businesses to look for alternative mechanisms for financing losses. This was especially true during the liability crisis in the mid-1980s, when premiums increased dramatically and coverage was restricted for some types of liability insurance. Increased volatility in insurance prices and availability generally discourages corporations from purchasing insurance. The increase in the number of insurer and reinsurer insolvencies in the late 1980s and early 1990s also may have reduced confidence in traditional commercial insurance by some risk managers.

The commercial insurance market has responded to the reduced corporate demand for traditional insurance by designing new products that offer corporations larger retentions, such as paid-loss retro plans, large deductible policies, and loss portfolio transfers. Commercial insurers also have increased their risk management services, including claims processing and loss control services. We will conclude this chapter by discussing two additional developments: (1) integrated, combined, or basket policies that may cover nontraditional as well as traditional insured exposures, and (2) structured debt instruments.

An emerging trend in loss financing is the use of insurance contracts based on losses across a variety of exposures. For example, instead of having separate coverage and limits for property, liability, and workers' compensation losses, some firms are purchasing contracts with indemnity payments and limits based on total losses from all three exposures (see Box 11–2). Policies also are being

Box 11–2

Examples of Combined Policies

Coca-Cola

In 1997, the Coca-Cola Company terminated its array of traditional insurance contracts and adopted an integrated risk program that combines most of its loss exposures in a single contract. The new policy provides an aggregate amount of coverage above a self-insured retention for each type of loss exposure covered.

Source: "All-in-One Insurance," *Financial Executive*, May/June 1997.

Honeywell Covers Pure Risk and Price Risk in One Policy

In July 1997, Honeywell Inc. initiated a program to finance losses from four different exposures: property, liability, directors and officers' liability, and currency fluctuations. By including coverage for currency risk exposures in the contracts, Honeywell was one of the first companies to combine pure and price risk into one policy. The loss financing program provides an aggregate limit and lasts two and one-half years.

Source: "Integrated Financing of Risk Gains Ground," *Business Insurance*, October 20, 1997.

written that combine exposures that traditionally have been insured by insurance companies with price exposures, such as currency risk, interest rate risk, and commodity price risk, which traditionally have been hedged using financial derivatives (see Chapter 13). An example of a contract covering both pure risk and price risk that also covers multiple years is provided in Box 11–2.

These contracts, which basically take the concept of umbrella liability policies one step further, are called various names by different insurers, such as **integrated, combined,** or **basket policies.** Their development is consistent with many of the explanations of why corporations purchase insurance in the first place. For corporations with diversified shareholders, insurance is most useful as a device to reduce exposure to large disruptive losses that either push a firm into financial distress or force it to raise costly external capital. From this perspective, the firm would like to avoid large aggregate losses regardless of whether they result from one type of exposure or from an accumulation of losses from multiple exposures. Combined policies provide exactly this type of coverage.

Another innovative method of financing losses is the use of **structured debt instruments** that bundle insurance in debt contracts. For example, a firm could raise $50 million by issuing debt securities but have the principal (or interest) on the debt be forgiven by lenders if a certain type of loss occurs, such as an earthquake. In essence, the debtholders provide the insurance by forgiving part of the debt if a major loss occurs. These types of structured debt instruments have been used to manage price risks for a number of years. For example, gold mining companies might issue debt with the payments linked to the price of gold. If gold prices decline, the firm's debt payments also decline. Box 11–3 provides an interesting example of the use of structured debt by an insurance company to reduce exposure to catastrophe losses.

Box 11–3

Insurers Issue Catastrophe-Linked Bonds

In July 1997, United Services Automobile Association (USAA), a large property and automobile insurer, raised capital by issuing bonds with the interest and principal payments on the bonds contingent on whether USAA experienced a hurricane catastrophe. More specifically, USAA established a wholly owned reinsurance subsidiary in the Cayman Islands, which then issued bonds worth $477 million. Using the proceeds from the bond issue as capital, the reinsurance subsidiary issued a one-year catastrophe reinsurance contract to USAA that covered 80 percent of insured losses between $1 billion and $1.5 billion from a single hurricane on the Gulf or the East coasts. Thus, the maximum loss paid by the reinsurer was $400 million (80 percent of $0.5 billion).

The bond issue had two tranches. The first tranch was worth $163.8 million and the other was worth $313.2 million. Investors who purchased the first tranch could only lose their promised interest payments. That is, if a catastrophe occurred, then the investors would receive less interest on their bonds than they were promised. Investors in the first tranch could not lose their promised principal payment, although if a catastrophe occurred the principal would not be

paid for 10 years. Investors who purchased the second tranch could lose both their interest and principal if a sufficiently large catastrophe occurred. To guarantee that the $163.8 principal payment for the first tranch would be paid after 10 years, $77 million of the $477 million was invested in 10-year government bonds that guaranteed a dollar return of $163.8 million in 10 years. The remaining $400 million from the bond issue backed the reinsurance contract issued to USAA. In return for taking the risk of losing their interest and/or principal, investors received a higher promised interest payment than most corporate bonds, with investors of the second tranch receiving a higher promised interest payment than investors in the first tranch.

Similar transactions also were undertaken by Swiss Reinsurance Co. and Tokio Marine & Fire Insurance Co. in 1997. Swiss Re issued bonds worth $137 million with interest and principal payments linked to the occurrence of an earthquake in California. Tokio Marine issued bonds worth $100 million with interest and principal payments linked to the occurrence of an earthquake in the Tokio area.

Source: Rodd Zolkos, "Catastrophe Bonds Take Risk Financing by Storm," *Business Insurance*, December 22, 1997.

11.6 Summary

- Traditional commercial insurance contracts are characterized by fixed premiums and usually one-year policy terms. These contracts require the insured to retain part of the risk exposure through the use of deductibles, self-insured retentions, and policy limits. High levels of coverage usually are obtained by layering excess coverage from multiple insurers.

- With loss sensitive insurance contracts,

premiums depend on losses that occur during the contract period. Retrospectively rated policies and large deductible policies are examples of loss sensitive contracts.

- A finite risk contract is a special type of multiyear loss sensitive contract that allows loss payments to be smoothed over time. Finite risk contracts may provide some of the tax advantages of traditional insurance if they involve material risk shifting.

- Large businesses often form captives (subsidiaries) to pay losses of the captive's parent and sister corporations. In part because of tax rulings, many captives also sell insurance to unrelated entities, including reinsurance to other insurers.

- Captives may provide tax advantages and allow corporations to purchase excess insurance in the reinsurance market. In combination with a fronting insurer, captives also allow corporations to self-insure but at the same time (1)

satisfy compulsory insurance laws, (2) comply with restrictions on the purchase of insurance from admitted insurers, and (3) meet third party requirements for certificates of insurance from rated insurers.

- Risk retention groups and group captives are pooling arrangements that reduce risk for their participants.

- Firms can finance retained losses by (1) using internal funds, (2) arranging lines of credit, and (3) raising new funds following a loss.

Key Terms

commercial insurance contracts   237
occurrence policies   238
claims-made policies   239
retroactive date   239
exposure diagram   239
deductible   240
per occurrence deductible   240
aggregate deductible   240
stop loss provision   241
self-insured retention (SIR)   241
letter of credit   241
policy limit   242
excess policy   242
attachment point   243
layering coverage   243
loss sensitive insurance contracts   245

large deductible policies   246
retrospectively rated policies   246
investment credit program   248
premium financing arrangement   248
loss portfolio transfer   249
finite risk insurance (financial insurance)   249
captive insurer   252
pure captive   252
brother-sister transactions   252
unrelated business   252
group captives   252
risk retention groups   257
dedicated assets   258
line of credit   258
integrated, combined, or basket policies   260
structured debt instruments   260

Questions and Problems

1. Draw an exposure diagram (i.e., illustrate the retained loss exposure) for a firm that has a building worth $2 million and purchases a property insurance policy with a $250,000 deductible.

2. Illustrate (with an exposure diagram) a firm's liability exposure if it purchases a liability policy providing $5 million of coverage in excess of $1 million.

3. Illustrate a firm's liability exposure if it layers the following set of policies on top of each other:
   (a) $3 million in excess of $2 million.
   (b) $5 million in excess of $5 million.

4. Distinguish between a per occurrence and an aggregate limit.

5. Using the finite risk contract described in the text, how much would the policyholder get

back at the end of three years if loss payments at year-end were

(*a*) $3 million in year 1; $3 million in year 2; and $3 million in year 3?

(*b*) $8 million in year 1; $1 million in year 2; and $1 million in year 3?

6. Suppose Porat Power Company establishes a captive insurer in Bermuda to "insure" its workers' compensation costs. Explain the various alternative ownership and operational characteristics that could describe the captive. What are the advantages of these alternatives?

References

Banham, Russ. "Shopping the Market for Finite Risk Products." *Risk Management,* September 1994, pp. 34–43. (*Practical overview of the variety of finite risk products, their uses, and tax and accounting issues.*)

Hein, Eric P.; and Michael J. O'Malley. "Two Birds with One Stone: How to Reduce Dependence on Letters of Credit and Accelerate Tax Deductibility." *Risk Management,* April 1996, pp. 59–71. (*Discusses retros, investment credit, and related loss sensitive plans.*)

Huebner, S. S.; Kenneth Black, Jr.; and Bernard C.

Webb. *Property and Liability Insurance.* 4th ed. Upper Saddle River, NJ: Prentice-Hall, 1996. (*Comprehensive treatment of traditional commercial property–liability insurance contracts for a wide variety of risk exposures.*)

Larkins, Ernest. "Taxation and the Future of Offshore Insurers." *Risk Management,* September 1, 1991, pp. 42–45. (*Provides detailed treatment of the taxation of captive insurers.*)

May, David. "All-in-One-Insurance." *Financial Executive,* May/June 1997. (*Provides a discussion and examples of integrated risk programs.*)

Answer to Concept Check

1. The main reasons for purchasing a loss sensitive insurance policy are (1) to obtain the tax benefits from insurance, (2) to purchase claims processing services from the insurer, and (3) to satisfy compulsory insurance laws.

Risk Management Decision Making

Chapter Objectives

- Describe methods used to identify risk exposures and to evaluate the potential frequency and severity of losses.
- Summarize practical, firm-specific influences on retention, insurance, and loss control decisions.
- Describe and illustrate the use of statistical analysis in risk management decision making.
- Describe and illustrate the use of discounted cash flow analysis in risk management decision making.

12.1 Risk Identification and Evaluation

As introduced in Chapter 1, the five major steps in the risk management decision making process are: (1) identify all significant risks that can cause loss and thus reduce firm value; (2) evaluate the potential frequency and severity of losses, including the expected value and variability of losses; (3) develop and select methods for managing risk in order to increase business value; (4) implement the risk management methods chosen; and (5) monitor the suitability and performance of the firm's risk management methods and strategies on an ongoing basis. This chapter focuses on the first three steps of this process.

Identifying Exposures

The first step in the risk management process is **risk identification:** the identification of loss exposures. Unidentified loss exposures most likely will result in an implicit retention decision, which may not be optimal. There are various methods of identifying exposures. For example, comprehensive checklists of common business exposures can be obtained from risk management consultants and other sources. Loss exposures also can be identified through analysis of the firm's financial statements, discussions with managers throughout the firm, surveys of employees, and discussions with insurance agents and risk management consultants. Regardless of the specific methods used, risk identification requires an overall understanding of the business and the specific economic, legal, and regulatory factors that affect the business.

Property Loss Exposures.   Some of the major practical questions asked when identifying property loss exposures are listed in Table 12–1. In addition to identifying what property is exposed to loss and the potential causes of loss, the firm must consider how property should be valued for the purpose of making risk management decisions. Several valuation methods are available. **Book value**—the purchase price minus accounting depreciation—is the method commonly

TABLE 12–1   Some Practical Questions in Identifying Property and Liability Loss Exposures

Type of Loss	Property Losses	Liability Losses
Direct Losses	1. What types of property are subject to damage or disappearance? 2. What factors (perils) can lead to loss? 3. What is the value of property exposed to loss? 4. Will the property be replaced if it is lost?	1. What parties might be harmed by the firm (customers, suppliers, and other parties)? 2. How might these parties be harmed? 3. What is the potential magnitude of damages? 4. What is the potential magnitude of defense costs?

Indirect Losses	1. Will the firm have to raise external funds to replace uninsured property?
	2. Assuming replacement, will the firm suspend or cut back operations following a direct loss?
	3. If the firm suspends or cuts back its operations:
	  (a) What is the potential duration and how much normal profit could be lost?
	  (b) What operating expenses would continue despite the suspension or slowdown?
	  (c) Will revenue losses continue after normal levels of production are resumed, and, if so, what actions might reduce these losses and at what cost?
	4. If the firm continues operating at preloss levels:
	  (a) What facilities or resources will be needed?
	  (b) What will be the additional cost from using alternative facilities or resources?
		1. Will revenues decline in response to possible damage to the firm's reputation?
		  (a) What is the potential magnitude of this loss?
		  (b) What actions might reduce the resulting indirect losses and at what cost?
		2. Will products and services likely be abandoned or products recalled in the event of large uninsured losses?
		3. Will the firm have to raise additional capital in the event that cash flows decline?
		4. Could large uninsured losses push the firm into financial distress?

used for financial reporting purposes. However, since book value does not necessarily correspond to economic value, it generally is not relevant for risk management purposes (except for the tax reasons discussed in Chapter 10). **Market value** is the value that the next-highest-valued user would pay for the property. **Firm-specific value** is the value of the property to the current owner. If the property does not provide firm-specific benefits, then firm-specific value will equal market value. Otherwise, firm-specific value will exceed market value. **Replacement cost new** is the cost of replacing the damaged property with new property. Due to economic depreciation and improvements in quality, replacement cost new often will exceed the market value of the property.

When making loss control decisions, it is important to measure the cost that will be imposed on the firm if the property is damaged. This cost equals the present value of the cash flows that would be lost plus the present value of the additional costs that are incurred (e.g., cleanup costs) if the property is damaged. In other words, the property should be valued as the firm-specific value plus the present value of these additional costs.

The firm also must consider whether the damaged property will be replaced. If it is to be replaced, then the cost of replacing the property becomes relevant. If it is to be replaced with new property, then the value that usually is relevant to insurance decisions is replacement cost new. If the replacement cost of the property exceeds the present value of future expected cash flows from replacement, then replacement will lower firm value.

To illustrate some of the factors involved in replacement decisions, suppose that Wells Corp. has property with a market value of $3 million, a replacement cost of $3.75 million, and that the property generates expected cash flows to Wells Corp. with a present value of $3.5 million. Since the value of the property in its current use exceeds its market value, the firm would not want to sell the property; instead, it would want to continue production. However, if the property were to be destroyed, Wells Corp. would not want to replace the property, because the replacement cost ($3.75 million) would exceed the present value of the net cash flows that would be generated ($3.5 million). This example assumes that replacement with new property does not increase the present value of the net cash flows generated. Note that if replacement with new property with a longer useful life were to increase the present value of net cash flows (e.g., to $4 million), Wells would increase its value by replacing the property following the loss.

If it is known prior to a loss that damaged property will not be replaced, the firm is likely to have less incentive to insure the replacement cost or perhaps even the market value of the property. For example, if Wells does not plan to replace the property and if a potential loss of $3.5 million will not cause indirect losses (e.g., worse contractual terms with bondholders or an increase in the cost of raising external funds), then insurance might not be purchased. On the other hand, damage to the property might cause indirect losses. For example, if the firm's net cash flows are reduced as a result of property loss, the firm might have to raise additional external funds to finance new investment. If so, the firm might increase its value by insuring the property for its market value (by purchasing actual cash value coverage), thereby reducing the need to raise costly external funds even though the property will not be replaced.[1]

Indirect losses also can arise from damage to property that will be repaired or replaced. For example, if a fire shuts down a plant for four months, the firm not only incurs the cost of replacing the damaged property, it also loses the profits from not being able to produce. In addition, some operating expenses might continue despite the shutdown (e.g., salaries for certain managers and employees and advertising expenses). These exposures are known as **business income exposures** (or, sometimes, business interruption exposures), and they frequently are insured with *business interruption insurance.* Note that business interruption losses also might result from property losses to a firm's major customers or suppliers that prevent them from transacting with the firm. This exposure can be insured with "contingent" business interruption insurance.

Firms also may suffer losses after they resume operations if previous customers that have switched to other sources of supply do not return. In the event that a long-term loss of customers would occur and/or a shutdown temporarily would impose large costs on customers or suppliers, it might be optimal for the firm to keep operating following a loss by arranging for the immediate use of alternative facilities at higher operating costs. The resulting exposure to higher costs is known as the **extra expense exposure.** Insurance purchased to reimburse the firm for these higher costs is known as *extra expense coverage.*

Liability Losses.   As we analyze in detail in Chapters 14 through 17, firms face potential legal liability losses as a result of relationships with many parties, including suppliers, customers, employees, shareholders, and members of the public. The settlements, judgments, and legal costs associated with liability suits can impose substantial losses on firms. Lawsuits also may harm firms by damaging their reputation, and they may require expenditures to minimize the costs of this damage. For example, in the case of liability to customers for injuries arising out of the firm's products, the firm might incur product recall expenses and higher marketing costs to rehabilitate a product.

Losses to Human Resources.   Losses in firm value due to worker injuries, disabilities, death, retirement, and turnover can be grouped into two categories. First, as a result of contractual commitments and compulsory benefits, firms often compensate employees (or their beneficiaries) for injuries, disabilities, death, and retirement. These types of losses are discussed in detail in Chapters 16, 18, and 19. Second, worker injuries, disabilities, death, retirement, and turnover can cause in-

---

[1] As noted in Chapter 8, property insurance policies can cover either the replacement cost or the *actual cash value* of the property. Actual cash value commonly is defined as replacement cost new less depreciation. A substantial number of court cases deal with disagreements over what this means. In many cases, actual cash value is treated as equivalent to market value. However, some court decisions might allow a corporation to argue that actual cash value equals firm-specific value if this is greater than the market value.

direct losses when production is interrupted and employees cannot be replaced at zero cost with other employees of the same quality. In some cases, firms purchase life insurance to compensate for the death or disability of important employees. Also, as the discussion of pension benefits in Chapter 19 will show, employment contracts can be designed to reduce employee turnover.

Losses from External Economic Forces.   The final category of losses arises from factors that are outside of the firm. Losses can arise because of changes in the prices of inputs and outputs. For example, increases in the price of oil can cause large losses to firms that use oil in the production process. Large changes in the exchange rate between currencies can increase a multinational firm's costs or decrease its revenues. As another example, an important supplier or purchaser can go bankrupt, thus increasing costs or decreasing revenues. We discuss how some of these types of losses can be managed using derivative securities in Chapter 13.

Evaluating the Frequency and Severity of Losses

After identifying the exposures, a risk manager ideally would obtain information about the entire probability distribution of losses and how different risk management methods affect this distribution. We illustrate how larger firms might estimate the relevant loss distributions in section 12.4. At this point, we simply will discuss how several summary measures of the probability distribution are often used. For example, risk managers summarize information about the probability distribution using frequency and severity measures, as well as expected losses and the standard deviation of losses during a given period. These measures help a risk manager assess the costs and benefits of loss control and retention versus insurance.

Frequency.   The frequency of loss measures the number of losses in a given period of time. If historical data exist on a large number of exposures, then the probability of a loss per exposure (or the expected frequency per exposure) can be estimated by the number of losses divided by the number of exposures. For example, if Sharon Steel Corp. had 10,000 employees in each of the past five years and over the five-year period there were 1,500 workers injured, then an estimate of the probability of a particular worker becoming injured would be 0.03 per year (1,500 injuries/50,000 employee-years). When historical data do not exist for a firm, frequency of losses can be difficult to quantify. In this case, industry data might be used, or an informed judgment would need to be made about the frequency of losses.

Severity.   The severity of loss measures the magnitude of loss per occurrence. One way to estimate expected severity is to use the average severity of loss per occurrence during an historical period. If the 1,500 worker injuries for Sharon Steel cost $3 million in total (adjusted for inflation), then the expected severity of worker injuries would be estimated at $2,000 ($3,000,000/1,500). That is, on average, each worker injury imposed a $2,000 loss on the firm. Again due to the lack of historical data and the infrequency of losses, adequate data may not be available to estimate precisely the expected severity per occurrence. With a little effort, however, risk managers can estimate the range of possible loss severity (minimum and maximum loss) for a given exposure.

Expected Loss and Standard Deviation.   The expected loss per exposure is the expected loss severity per occurrence times the probability of a loss per exposure (expected frequency per exposure). Expected loss obviously is an important element that affects business value (see Chapter 9) and insurance pricing (see Chapter 6). Thus, accurate estimates of expected losses can help a manager determine whether insurance will increase firm value. Continuing with the Sharon Steel example, the annual expected loss per employee from worker injury is 0.03 × $2,000 = $60. With 10,000 employees, the annual expected loss is $600,000. Ideally, many firms also will estimate the standard deviation of losses for the total loss distribution or for losses in different size ranges.

One way to summarize information about potential losses is to create a table for various types of exposures (property, liability, etc.) that provides characteristics of the probability distribution of losses for the particular type of exposure. An example for Sharon Steel's property exposures is provided in Table 12–2.

To create an accurate categorization of a firm's loss exposures (like Table 12–2), considerable information, time, and expertise are needed. For most companies, especially smaller ones and new ones, detailed data on loss exposures do not exist. Nevertheless, the framework of Table 12–2 still can be used. For example, each type of exposure can be classified as having low, medium, or high frequency and severity. Table 12–3 provides an example for Penn Steel Corp., a firm that is engaged in the same activities and is of the same size as Sharon Steel Corp.

Tables 12–2 and 12–3 both show that the standard deviation of losses for high frequency, low severity losses is low, while the standard deviation is high for low frequency losses with high potential severity. This relationship is fairly general: Infrequent but potentially large losses are less predictable and pose greater risk than more frequent, smaller losses. Using the type of information illustrated in these tables, firms pay particular attention to exposures that can produce potentially large, disruptive losses, either from a single event or from the accumu-

TABLE 12–2   Categorization of Sharon Steel's Property Losses

Property Exposures	Frequency of Losses per Year	Severity Range	Average Severity	Expected Loss	Standard Deviation
Damage to automobiles	100	$0–$20,000	$5,000	$500,000	$100,000
Stolen property	500	0–2,000	500	100,000	20,000
Small fires	1	100,000–500,000	125,000	125,000	400,000
Major fires	.05	500,000–10,000,000	2,000,000	100,000	800,000

TABLE 12–3   Categorization of Penn Steel Corp.'s Property Losses

Property Exposures	Frequency	Severity Range	Average Severity	Expected Loss	Standard Deviation
Damage to automobiles	Medium	$0–$20,000	Low	Medium	Medium
Stolen property	High	0–2,000	Low	Low	Low
Small fires	Low	100,000–500,000	Medium	Low	High
Major fires	Low	500,000–10,000,000	High	Low	High

lation of a number of smaller but still significant losses during a given period. We return to this issue in the next section, which discusses the benefits and costs of retention versus insurance.

12.2 Retention and Insurance Revisited

An integral aspect of the development and selection of alternative risk management methods is the measurement of benefits and costs in term of their effects on the firm's cash flows. Before getting into more detail on quantitative risk assessment and decision making, it first is useful to review some of the primary benefits and costs of retention versus insurance and to discuss a number of firm-specific factors and practical considerations that affect loss financing and loss control decisions.

As emphasized in Chapter 9, the retention decision involves a fundamental tradeoff between (1) the benefits to the firm from increased retention in the form of possible reductions in expected cash outflows for insurance, and (2) the expected costs to the firm that arise from greater risk (standard deviation of cash flows).

Benefits of Increased Retention

Building on the discussion in earlier chapters, potential savings to a firm from increasing retention include: (1) savings on premium loadings, (2) reducing exposure to insurance market volatility, (3) reducing moral hazard, (4) avoiding high premiums that may accompany asymmetric information, and (5) avoiding implicit taxes that arise from insurance price regulation. It also often is argued that increased retention is advantageous because it allows the firm to maintain the use of funds until losses are paid.

Savings on Premium Loadings.   A key factor motivating the retention of larger amounts of loss is the ability to save on some of the administrative expense and profit loadings in insurance premiums, thus reducing the expected cash out flows for these loadings. Specific sources of savings include lower commissions to insurance brokers, possible savings in underwriting expenses and administrative costs of claim settlement, and savings in state premium taxes (typically 2 percent of the premium) and implicit taxes for expected guaranty fund assessments. The savings also depend on the amount of profit loading that the firm can avoid paying by retaining more risk, which in turn depends on the insurer's capital costs and ability to reduce risk through diversification and reinsurance.

Potential savings in profit loadings also can depend on the degree of competition in insurance markets. While most insurance markets are competitively structured, the market for very large limits of business insurance often involves negotiation between the corporate buyer and a group of insurers that share the risk. In these instances, it has been suggested that insurers may achieve higher expected profits than is the case where many independent insurers are competing to sell coverage (see Box 12–1 later in this chapter).

Reducing Exposure to Insurance Market Volatility.   Another motivation for some corporations to increase risk retention has been the desire to reduce their vulnerability to annual swings in insurance prices due to the effects of shocks to insurer capital on the supply of insurance and/or the insurance underwriting cycle. Loss financing decisions often are part of a long-term business strategy or plan. Once a firm decides to insure a particular exposure, it may be costly to change its strategy in response to an insurance price increase. This is because an immediate large increase in the amount of risk retained can increase the probability of financial distress, increase the likelihood that the firm will not have sufficient internal funds to adopt positive net present value projects, and damage relationships with customers, suppliers, or lenders. Arranging alternative loss financing, such as accumulating internal funds or establishing a group captive, also can take time.

As a result of these influences, the demand for insurance by individual firms often is inelastic in the short run (i.e., comparatively unresponsive to a change in price in the short run). As a consequence, the purchase of insurance can lead to the perverse result: Even though a major purpose of purchasing insurance generally is to reduce uncertainty in cash flows, the volatility in insurance prices exposes the firm to uncertainty. When making long-term loss financing decisions, therefore, the volatility in insurance prices often is viewed by risk managers as a negative aspect of insurance, which leads them to increase retention.

Reducing Moral Hazard.   You learned in Chapter 8 that deductibles and other copayments reduce moral hazard. Without these contractual provisions, expected claim costs would be higher and therefore so would insurance premiums. Consequently, when moral hazard is more of a potential problem, firms have an incentive to retain more risk.

Avoiding High Premiums Caused by Asymmetric Information.   The inability of insurers to estimate claim costs precisely for all potential buyers causes some buyers to face prices that are relatively high compared to their true, unobservable expected claim costs. These buyers have an incentive to retain more risk (see the discussion of adverse selection in Chapter 8). Higher risk buyers would have the opposite incentive (i.e., they would retain less risk to the extent that they face a lower price for insurance because they are pooled with lower risk firms). Note, however, that the reasoning "We have lower expected claim costs than what the insurer thinks" might be seductive and somewhat dangerous. Recall that insurers have substantial incentives to forecast costs accurately. Firms also can provide insurers with any available evidence that their expected claim costs might be lower than predicted by the insurer.

Avoiding Implicit Taxes Due to Insurance Price Regulation.   In the case of workers' compensation insurance, some states periodically have had large residual markets characterized by significant cross-subsidies from the voluntary market to the residual market (see Chapter 16). To the extent that this occurs in workers' compensation or other lines of business insurance that have residual markets (e.g., commercial auto liability and some other types of liability coverage), any higher premiums needed to subsidize the residual market increase the incentives for firms that would be insured in the voluntary market to self-insure or otherwise increase their retention. Firms that can obtain subsidized coverage in the residual market will tend to purchase more coverage (retain less risk).

Maintaining Use of Funds.   It often is argued that another advantage of retention is that the firm gets to maintain use of the funds that otherwise would be paid in premiums until claim costs are paid. Given that competitive insurance premiums will reflect the present value of expected claim costs, it is not obvious that this argument is valid. The reason is that discounting expected claim costs to present value implicitly provides insurance buyers with a return on funds paid in premiums until claims are paid. As explained in Chapter 10, income tax rules for insurance versus self-insurance might even allow insurers to provide greater implicit after-tax returns to insurance buyers than could be obtained if buyers held the same amount of funds in similar assets to finance retained losses.

   It sometimes is argued that a firm should view its opportunity cost of paying premiums as equal to its opportunity cost of capital for general investment decisions, which will exceed the risk-free rate of interest due to the presence of nondiversifiable risk, whereas insurers will discount expected claim costs at the risk-free rate (or something close to the risk-free rate). However, this argument is problematic because theory generally suggests that the rate used to discount losses should depend on the risk of losses rather than whether the firm or the insurer pays the losses. As a result, the appropriate discount rate for losses is the same for the firm and the insurer (apart from any tax considerations). At a minimum, it is important for you to recognize that premiums in competitive insurance markets will provide some implicit return for the expected average time lag between the payment of premiums and claim costs.

Costs of Increased Retention

Increased retention obviously exposes the firm to greater risk. As you learned in Chapter 9, increased risk can be costly for a number of reasons. For example, the greater risk from increased retention increases the probability of costly financial distress with associated adverse effects on lenders, employees, suppliers, and customers, which causes them to contract with the firm at less favorable terms. Increased retention also may require the firm to raise costly external funds and forego some profitable investment opportunities. Moreover, increased retention may reduce expected tax shields and sacrifice possible advantages to insurance from bundling responsibility for claims payment with claims settlement. Other things being equal, the costs associated with increased retention will vary across firms depending on the nature of their ownership and operations.

Closely Held versus Publicly Traded Firms with Widely Held Stock.   The owners of closely held firms typically have a significant proportion of their wealth invested in the firm and thus are undiversified compared to shareholders of publicly traded firms with widely traded stock. Because the owners of closely held firms are not diversified, they have an incentive to retain less risk (purchase more insurance) than publicly traded firms with widely held stock.

Firm Size and Correlation among Losses.   If a firm has a large number of independent exposures, then the law of large numbers operates at the firm level, allowing the firm to predict its average loss per exposure more accurately. Consequently, one major benefit of insurance—the reduction in the variability of the average loss per exposure—is reduced. Larger firms with their generally larger cash flows also are better able to readily finance losses of any given size out of cash flow than are smaller firms, and they often are able to raise external funds at lower cost. Each of these influences reduces the demand for insurance by large firms. Positive correlation among losses across exposures increases the standard deviation of the average loss per exposure. Other things being equal, the increased risk from this positive correlation increases the demand for insurance (provided that insurers are able to achieve superior diversification).

Correlation of Losses with Other Cash Flows and with Investment Opportunities.   Firms whose losses are positively correlated with other cash inflows will have a lower standard deviation of total cash flows, other things being equal, and thus will tend to retain more risk. In these cases, firms have a natural hedge: When losses tend to be high, other cash flows also tend to be high, thus reducing the likelihood of financial distress and the need for external funds. For example, if a firm has more workplace injuries when demand for its products is unexpectedly high, the increased profits due to the increase in demand will at least partially offset the increase in worker injury costs.

A related result is that a positive (negative) correlation between losses and the rate of return on new investment will reduce (increase) the ability of the firm to pursue profitable investments without raising external funds, thus increasing (decreasing) the demand for insurance. The reason is that the demand for funds for new investment will tend to be high when losses are high and available internal funds are low. This case often is more applicable to hedging than insurance.

For example, reductions in oil prices are likely to reduce the rate of return on new investment in the exploration for oil. Firms in the oil industry will desire to invest less money in exploration following an oil price decline, and they will therefore have less incentive to hedge the risk of reductions in the value of their oil reserves due to lower oil prices (see Chapter 13).

Financial Leverage.   Firms with higher financial leverage (ratio of debt to equity) will have a higher likelihood of financial distress, holding the probability distribution of future asset values constant. Consequently, firms with higher leverage are likely to find risk reduction more advantageous (and vice versa; see Chapter 9).

Concept Check

1. Other factors held constant, which type of firm would be more likely to fully retain (self-insure) its workers' compensation losses?
   (*a*) A firm with an individual shareholder that owns 50 percent of the stock versus a firm in which no shareholder owns more than 1 percent of the stock.
   (*b*) A trucking firm with 5,000 drivers versus a manufacturing firm with 5,000 workers at a single plant.
   (*c*) A firm with revenues positively correlated with claim costs versus a firm with revenues uncorrelated with claim costs.
   (*d*) A firm with a large amount of debt in its capital structure versus a firm with no debt.

A Basic Guideline for Optimal Retention

The previous section highlights the basic tradeoff between the benefits of increased retention through savings on explicit and implicit loadings in insurance premiums and the costs of increased uncertainty. A basic guideline for optimal retention decisions in view of this tradeoff is: *Retain reasonably predictable losses and insure potentially large, disruptive losses.*

As noted above, potentially large, harmful losses that can cause financial distress and interrupt planned investment can arise from a single event, or they can arise from a series of smaller events during a given period. For example, a company that transports chemicals may face the possibility of very large liability claims from a single accident (e.g., several hundred million dollars). It also may face large aggregate claims in a given year if it has an unexpectedly large number of smaller claims (e.g., 50 claims averaging $3 million each). These two possibilities help explain the demand for per occurrence deductibles (or self-insured retentions) and stop loss provisions, which were discussed in Chapter 11. Later in this chapter we illustrate how per occurrence retentions and stop loss provisions alter the shape of the probability distribution of a firm's retained losses to reduce the risk of a large loss.

For individual firms, application of the guideline that firms should retain predictable losses but insure potentially large, unpredictable, and disruptive losses depends on the specific magnitude of the benefits and costs of increased retention, including managerial judgment about the magnitude of losses that can be tolerated without producing significant costs. For example, the point or points at which losses cease to be "reasonably predictable" and become "potentially disruptive" depends on many factors, including firm size, the cost of raising external funds, and the expected value and variability of cash flows apart from any losses. Due to special circumstances (e.g., compulsory insurance rules), retention strategies adopted by particular firms may vary substantially from this basic guideline. Box 12–1 provides an example of retention policy for a very large corporation, British Petroleum, which deviates to some extent from this guideline.

You also should recognize that while the underlying motives for buying insurance differ, this guideline also is applicable to risk management decisions by individuals and closely held businesses. For example, auto owners routinely choose per occurrence deductibles for automobile collision coverage by considering the tradeoff between increased risk and lower premiums for policies with larger deductibles. Moreover, risk management decisions by small, closely held businesses often reflect this tradeoff.

12.3 Benefits and Costs of Loss Control

Basic Cost-Benefit Tradeoff

As introduced in Chapter 1, loss control involves actions that change the probability distribution of losses. The two major types of loss control are increased precautions and reduced level of risky activity. While loss control affects the standard deviation of losses, its primary purpose generally is to reduce the expected value of losses. A basic tradeoff arises between the benefits of loss control from reducing the expected value of losses and the costs of increased precautions and reduced levels of risky activity.

In order to make loss control decisions to increase firm value, firms first must estimate the expected benefits and costs. Our focus in this section is on illustrating the major types of benefits and costs by discussing three specific examples of loss control. We also will point out some of the problems in measuring benefits and costs. Each example deals with voluntary decisions by firms. Government regulations that affect loss control are briefly addressed as appropriate in subsequent chapters.

Examples of Identifying Benefits and Costs

Installation of Automatic Sprinkler System.   Safety Supply stores large volumes of its products in a warehouse prior to shipment to distributors. Safety is considering the installation of heat- and smoke-activated sprinklers that will re-

Box 12–1

Retention Policy for a Giant Corporation: The Case of British Petroleum

The insurance purchasing strategy of British Petroleum (BP), a large oil company involved in the exploration, extraction, refinement, and distribution of oil and gas, provides an interesting example of risk management at a giant corporation. BP's strategy has been analyzed by Professor Neil Doherty of Wharton and Professor Clifford W. Smith, Jr., of the University of Rochester (see the references at the end of this chapter). During the five-year period preceding the Doherty-Smith analysis (1987–91), BP's accounting profits averaged about $2 billion per year with a standard deviation of approximately $1 billion. BP had over $50 billion of assets in 1991. In conjunction with a review of its insurance purchasing by Professors Doherty and Smith, BP revamped its strategy to purchase less coverage against large losses.

Local managers are allowed the discretion to purchase coverage for losses up to $10 million. In many cases, economies in having insurers administer claims, local rules governing the purchase of liability insurance, and local tax considerations favor insuring against losses of this magnitude. Losses in the $10 to $500 million range generally are not insured, in contrast to BP's previous policy. Doherty and Smith state that this strategy change was motivated by several factors: (1) BP had paid over $1.15 billion in premiums for coverage of these losses during the prior decade and had received only $250 million in claim payments; (2) coverage disputes with insurers were more likely for losses of this magnitude; (3) the impact of losses of this size on firm value was small, given BP's size; and (4) insurers have no advantage compared to BP in providing safety and loss control services.

Doherty and Smith attribute the first two factors to less competition in the market for very large limits of insurance coverage than for smaller limits and the fact that insurers have a greater incentive to dispute coverage for large complicated events. We note, however, that there is some uncertainty as to whether the low level of claim payments compared to premiums was due to chance as opposed to high prices at the time coverage was sold. Large shocks to liability insurer capital and subsequent price increases (see Chapter 6) also could have contributed to high prices.

For losses above $500 million, BP also does not purchase insurance. Doherty and Smith note that (1) insurance market capacity to provide coverage for losses this large is limited, (2) the ability to deduct losses from taxable income reduces demand for coverage, and (3) a loss of this size due, for example, to destruction of a major oil rig could increase the price of oil, thus mitigating the loss.

Is BP's strategy of allowing managers to insure small losses but generally retaining larger losses inconsistent with the basic guideline of retaining relatively predictable losses and insuring large, potentially disruptive losses? When considering this issue, you should recall the rationale for BP's strategy. First, small losses are insured only when it is advantageous to do so for reasons other than risk transfer (e.g., service, regulatory, and tax reasons). Second, a major reason that BP stopped insuring losses in the $10 to $500 million range was that losses of this size were not likely to seriously disrupt BP's operations and investment given the size of its profits and assets. For losses above $500 million, insurance capacity often is limited. Limited capacity can make retention desirable or the only feasible option for insuring very large losses, regardless of the basic guideline.

duce property damage in the event of a fire. The principal benefits from installing the sprinklers include reductions in expected cash outflows or increases in expected cash inflows that would arise from reducing expected fire damage. For simplicity we will assume that no risk of harm to employees or other people is involved and focus only on the benefits and costs associated with property damage.

The principal benefits from installing the sprinklers include: (1) reduced fire insurance premiums for direct damage to property and business interruption losses, and (2) reduced expected losses retained under per occurrence deductibles in Safety's fire insurance and for possible business interruption losses in excess of Safety's coverage limits. Safety probably can obtain reasonably accurate estimates of percentage savings in insurance premiums from insurance brokers, and it can assume a likely growth rate in premiums over time to estimate dollar premium savings. Safety might be able to estimate savings in uninsured losses from a historical analysis of its own or industry loss experience or by analyzing premium increases that would be needed if the firm were to buy more complete insurance coverage. Safety also might rely heavily on judgment to estimate reductions in uninsured losses.

The decision to install sprinklers involves two major costs. First, Safety will have to pay for the equipment and installation. Second, the sprinklers will involve routine maintenance and upkeep. The direct cost of purchase and installation will be known. The ongoing costs of maintenance and upkeep can be reasonably estimated based on discussions with sprinkler vendors, and they will be known for the duration of any maintenance agreement that Safety buys from the vendor.

As is true in many loss control decisions and, more generally, many other types of business investment decisions, the installation of sprinklers involves a comparatively large up-front investment in equipment and installation. The benefits in the form of lower insurance premiums and uninsured losses, as well as the costs of maintenance and upkeep, will be realized over the useful life of the sprinklers. Deciding whether to invest in sprinklers in order to increase firm value requires that Safety weigh the expected benefits and costs by discounting expected net cash flows to present value using an appropriate cost of capital. We illustrate this process in the context of a loss financing decision later in this chapter.

Installation of Safety Guards.   Presto Manufacturing uses drill presses in the manufacture of its products. Employees of Presto are exposed to serious injuries to their hands and arms from using the presses. Presto can retool its presses to include guards that will reduce the frequency and severity of injury to employees.

Like the sprinkler example, installation of the safety guards involves a comparatively large, up-front cost for Presto, as well as a minor increase in machine maintenance costs over time. Presto also believes, based on industry information and its own technical analysis, that the guards will reduce the normal output per employee by making it more difficult for employees to perform their tasks. As a result, holding wages fixed (see below), this effect will tend to increase Presto's labor costs per unit of output.

The benefits to Presto of installing the safety guards include lower workers' compensation insurance premiums in the form of possible up-front premium rate reductions for safer equipment and lower experience rating surcharges for poor experience (or greater rate reductions from experience rating due to better than average claims experience) if injuries are reduced. These benefits can be estimated with reasonable accuracy using insurance market data. Installation of the safety guards also will produce expected savings in Presto's retained workers' compensation costs (i.e., costs under its per occurrence deductible), which might be estimated with its own data, insurance market data, or managerial judgment. Another important benefit to Presto from installing the guards is that fewer accidents will mean fewer interruptions in production and lower costs of hiring/retraining either temporary or permanent replacement employees. These savings might be estimated using the firm's own data, industry data, and/or judgment.

A final potential benefit that Presto should consider when deciding whether to install the guards is the possible impact of greater safety on wages. Workers value safety, and safety is one dimension that affects job choice by workers. Numerous studies indicate that a tradeoff exists between wages and the risk of on-the-job injury: Higher risk jobs pay higher wages, other factors held constant. Thus, if Presto increases safety, then it should be able to attract and retain workers at lower wages over time. Presto may be able to estimate these savings from the evidence reported in these studies, or it may rely heavily on managerial judgment.

You should note that if workers are unable to assess safety accurately and underestimate the effect of the guards on safety, Presto's incentive to install the guards will be reduced. You will learn more about the tradeoff between wages and risk and its relation to workers' compensation laws and job safety legislation in Chapter 16.

Child-Resistant Packaging of Nonprescription Drugs.   No-More-Pain Drug Company markets a nonprescription pain medication that can provide relief for routine aches and pains in the head, neck, back, joints, and other body parts. No-More-Pain is considering modifying its packaging to make it more difficult for small children to open the bottle and swallow the contents. (The drug is toxic in large quantities.) Making this change requires large, up-front costs to retool No-More-Pain's packaging process. It also will require an ongoing increase in the cost of materials per unit sold.

A major benefit to No-More-Pain of increasing safety for children is that its premiums for product liability insurance will decline. The company can obtain an estimate of the potential savings by consulting with its insurance brokers. It can estimate savings in uninsured liability claims and defense costs using its own data, insurance market data, and judgment. Another potential benefit of changing the packaging is that it will reduce the likelihood of damage to No-More-Pain's reputation that could occur if one or more children were seriously hurt or killed from ingesting its product. The new packaging also makes it less likely that the company will have to undertake a costly product recall in the event of adverse loss experience. No-More-Pain can develop several scenarios for the probability and severity of these costs based on judgment and anecdotal evidence from prior injuries by its products and related products.

No-More-Pain also needs to consider the effect of the change in packaging on the price and demand for its product. To the extent that customers value the increased safety, No-More-Pain may be able to increase the price of its product without any loss of sales. Sales even may increase despite the price increase. On the other hand, based on some preliminary market research and trade publications, No-More-Pain is concerned that many of its customers will find it a hassle to open child-resistant caps on bottles. These customers might switch to cheaper "no-name" brands with easy-to-open bottles if No-More-Pain makes its bottles harder to open. The company also is concerned that some customers with small children might leave the bottle open in order to avoid taking off the cap. To the extent that this occurs, the benefits in the form of liability claims could be reduced if the courts continue to hold No-More-Pain liable for any injuries.

Qualitative versus Quantitative Decision Making.   In general, these examples make it clear that some of the important benefits and costs of loss control may be difficult to quantify. In many cases, the best that firms can do is to make educated guesses about the magnitude of benefits and costs. The next two sections of the chapter provide more detail on quantitative analysis in risk management decision making. While the tools that we cover are important in practice, you should keep in mind that many important decisions in risk management necessarily involve reasonable judgment based on limited information and data.

12.4 Statistical Analysis in Risk Management

You learned earlier that firms sometimes estimate the expected frequency, expected severity, expected loss, and standard deviation of loss for exposures in different size ranges as an input to making decisions about risk retention. In this section you will learn more about the use of statistical analysis in risk management decision making from the perspective of medium- to large-sized firms.

Small businesses are analogous to individuals in that they seldom experience large losses but must deal with a small probability that large, disruptive losses will occur. It generally will not be worthwhile for small businesses to spend resources trying to estimate the probability distribution of losses. The information would have little impact on the key decision as to how much risk they can reasonably retain. Instead, as is the case for individuals, decisions regarding deductibles and insurance policy limits depend largely on judgment, and they commonly are influenced by the advice of insurance agents and brokers. Loss control also depends largely on judgment and on insurance premium reductions that may be available if loss control is undertaken, as opposed to the statistical analysis of data.

For large firms, the value of information provided by statistical analysis is much more likely to exceed the cost of undertaking the analysis (the cost of data collection, analysis, and interpretation). The information provided is likely to be more meaningful and reliable, and large firms can spread the fixed costs of analysis over a larger number of exposures. Ideally, firms would like to have accurate estimates of the probability distribution of losses associated with each major alternative risk management strategy. In other words, for each risk management strategy, firms would like to know each possible loss amount during a year (measured on a present value basis, a complication that we ignore for simplicity until later in the chapter) and the associated probability that this amount of loss will occur.

While this ideal is seldom achieved in practice, a variety of approaches can be used as a means to improve decision making. These approaches usually involve approximating the total loss distribution, or at least estimating the expected value and standard deviation of total annual losses or costs. In addition, several approaches can be used to estimate the **maximum probable loss** (or cost) for the year, which is defined as the amount of loss (or cost) that is expected not to be exceeded in some large percentage of years, such as 90, 95, or 99 percent. For example, if the maximum probable loss at the 95 percent level for a firm is $5 million, this means that there is a 95 percent probability that annual losses will be less than $5 million (and a 5 percent probability that losses will exceed $5 million).[2]

The remainder of this section focuses on two common approaches to estimating loss distributions or key summary measures of these distributions: (1) relying on "large sample" probability distribution theory (i.e., assuming that the loss distribution can be approximated by the normal distribution), and (2) using computer simulation. It might be helpful for you to review Chapter 3, including the appendix, while studying this section.

Approximating Loss Distributions with the Normal Distribution

You learned in Chapter 3 that if losses are independent across exposures, then the probability distribution of the average loss per exposure approaches the normal probability distribution, with its familiar bell shape, as the number of exposures increases. This result is known as the *central limit theorem*. Thus, if a firm has a large number of exposures with zero or very low correlation in losses across exposures, the distribution of its average loss will be approximately normal. The distribution of the total loss for all exposures also will be approximately normal. For the normal distribution, knowledge of the expected value and standard deviation is sufficient to obtain the entire probability distribution. The expected value of the total loss distribution will equal the number of exposures times the expected loss per exposure. The standard deviation of total losses will equal the square root of the number of exposures times the standard deviation of loss for each exposure (see the appendix to Chapter 3).

---

[2] In financial risk management, the term *value at risk* is commonly used to indicate the same concept as maximum probable loss. That is, the value at risk is the maximum amount of value that can be lost from a given type of financial risk (or risks) at a specified probability level.

Illustration.   To illustrate how the firm might rely on the assumption that losses have the normal distribution, consider the case of Stallone Steel (a competitor of Sharon Steel). Stallone has obtained data on workers' compensation losses for each of its workers for the last five years and has adjusted the historical data to current values based on inflation (and possible changes in workers' compensation benefits). The sample mean loss per worker (total losses during the sample period/number of workers) is $300 and the sample standard deviation (see Chapter 3) is $20,000. Because Stallone has 10,000 workers, it is willing to assume that the total losses for the upcoming year will be normally distributed with expected total loss of $3,000,000 (10,000 × $300) and a standard deviation of total losses of $2,000,000 (100 [the square root of 10,000] × $20,000).

Using the properties of the normal distribution, Stallone can estimate both the probability that losses are less than any given amount during the year and the maximum probable loss at any desired level of confidence. For example, there is a 0.95 probability that any normally distributed random variable is less than its expected value plus 1.645 standard deviations. Thus, Stallone's maximum probable loss at the 95 percent level is approximately $6,300,000 ($3,000,000 + 1.645 × $2,000,000). Similarly, there is a 0.99 probability that any normally distributed random variable is less than its expected value plus 2.33 standard deviations, and Stallone's maximum probable loss at the 99 percent level is $7,660,000 ($3,000,000 + 2.33 × $2,000,000).

While the formulas are too complicated for us to cover here, the expected value and standard deviation of a normally distributed random variable that is "truncated" at particular points also can be readily calculated (using the right formula!). This means, for example, that if Stallone decided to purchase excess insurance with a $5 million annual aggregate retention, it could calculate the expected value and standard deviation of retained losses (losses less than the $5 million retention limit).

Problems and Limitations.   The principal limitation of assuming that losses are normally distributed is that the assumption often will be inappropriate in practice. First, the assumption is based on the central limit theorem, which simply describes a tendency as the number of exposures becomes infinitely large. Unless firms have very large numbers of exposures, the true distribution of total losses will likely exhibit positive skewness, and the difference from the normal distribution could be substantial. Compared to the true, positively skewed distribution, the normal distribution will tend to understate the probability of large losses. (We illustrate this result in the next section.) As a consequence, the firm will underestimate the likelihood of large, potentially disruptive losses.[3] This is not the type of mistake that firms wish to make.

Second, in many cases losses will not be independent across exposures. In

---

[3] Actuaries and statisticians have developed several approximation methods to allow estimation of the maximum probable loss at specified confidence levels that incorporate information about skewness in the distribution of losses.

the case of worker injuries, for example, many workers might be hurt in a single accident. Positive correlation in losses across exposures increases the standard deviation of total losses. Again, the result is that the procedure illustrated above will tend to underestimate the probability of large losses. In addition, the central limit theorem assumes independence so that assuming the normal distribution may produce significant errors even if a firm is very large.

A third limitation of the procedure illustrated above is that it does not facilitate analysis of per occurrence deductibles and policy limits. The reason is that the procedure provides estimates of the aggregate loss distribution only; it does not provide evidence about the loss distribution for individual losses (occurrences). As a consequence, while the method might help some firms make decisions about aggregate annual retention limits without per occurrence deductibles, it is not useful in the many cases where firms wish to consider limiting their exposure to losses from a single occurrence.

Computer Simulation of Loss Distributions

In many cases, realistic probability distributions for loss frequency and severity cannot be combined mathematically to derive the distribution of total losses. If, however, a firm is willing to estimate or make assumptions concerning the shape of the loss frequency and severity distributions, **computer simulation of loss distributions** using one of several software packages can be employed to estimate the probability distribution of total losses, as well as the effects of per occurrence deductibles and policy limits. Computer simulation also can be used to obtain the type of information illustrated in Table 12–2. In general, computer simulation of loss distributions often provides a versatile and valuable method of providing insight into the distribution of losses and the effects of alternative risk management strategies. It does not rely on the assumption that total losses are normally distributed. While more difficult to do accurately, it also is possible to incorporate in the simulation assumptions concerning possible correlation in losses across exposures.

Illustration.   We illustrate the method of computer simulation for the product liability exposure of Get-Well Pharmaceutical Company. Based on an analysis of its own data as well as industry data on product liability claims, Get-Well assumes that the frequency of lawsuits by consumers claiming damages for adverse reactions to drugs that it has manufactured can be reasonably approximated by a **Poisson distribution,** a probability distribution that often is used to describe accident probabilities. The Poisson distribution assumes that the probability that an event will occur (such as an accident) is constant in any small time period. However, you do not need to worry about the technical details of this distribution. All that you need to recognize is that this distribution often provides a reasonable description of reality and that it gives the probability that there will be zero claims, one claim, two claims, and so on during a given year (or other specified time period).

Get-Well believes that the expected number of lawsuits during the year is 30, but it also wishes to allow for parameter uncertainty (see Chapter 8) that arises

TABLE 12–4   Get-Well's Assumptions about Expected Claim Frequency

Legal Environment	Probability of Environment	Expected Annual Claim Frequency
Current standards applied	⅓	30
Stricter standards applied	⅓	20
More lenient standards applied	⅓	40

due, among other factors, to uncertainty associated with legal standards that will be applied to product-related injuries. Get-Well decides to allow for this uncertainty by making the assumptions shown in Table 12–4. In this way, Get-Well builds assumptions about uncertainty in the legal system into its analysis. In effect, it allows for increased risk due to dependence in claim frequency across exposures that can arise from changes in legal standards.

Based on analysis of historical data and published research on distributions for the severity of the costs of liability claims, Get-Well assumes that the loss severity will have the **lognormal distribution,** a distribution that is commonly used to describe the severity of property and liability losses.[4] For a random variable with a lognormal distribution, the natural logarithm of the variable's value has the normal distribution—thus the name *lognormal.* The lognormal distribution is characterized by positive skewness, as is true for most severity distributions. Get-Well estimates that the expected value of the severity distribution is $100,000 and that the standard deviation is $300,000. If desirable, Get-Well also could allow for uncertainty in these parameters, but we assume that you will get the main idea without us going to any more trouble.

The loss frequency and severity distributions for Get-Well are illustrated in Figure 12–1. The first panel shows the claim frequency distribution assuming a Poisson distribution with an expected value of 30. Note that the distribution is bell shaped for an expected number of losses this large. For lower expected numbers of claims per period, such as 0.1, which might describe the frequency of your having an auto accident, the distribution would be highly skewed (large probability of no loss, increasingly small probabilities for one, two, three losses, etc.). The second panel shows the sample frequency distribution obtained by randomly drawing 1,000 outcomes (i.e., from 1,000 "trials" of a simulation) from a Poisson distribution where the expected value varies according to the assumptions shown in Table 12–4. As can be seen, allowing for uncertainty in the expected value increases the variability of claim frequency compared to the first panel. The third panel shows the sample distribution of 1,000 trials from a lognormal distribution with expected value equal to $100,000 and standard deviation equal to $300,000. Note that most claims are less than $600,000, but some are much larger.

---

[4] For simplicity we assume that claim costs include defense costs and that all costs are discounted to present value.

FIGURE 12–1

Loss frequency and severity distributions for Get-Well

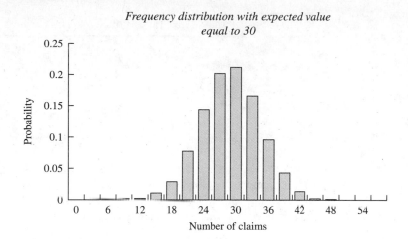

Frequency distribution with expected value equal to 30

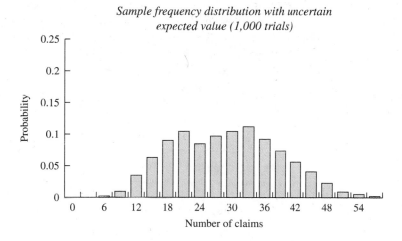

Sample frequency distribution with uncertain expected value (1,000 trials)

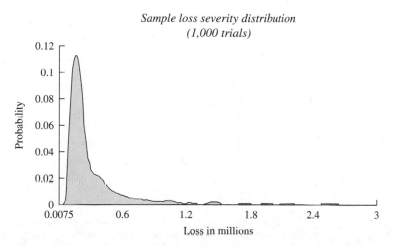

Sample loss severity distribution (1,000 trials)

TABLE 12–5 Alternative Insurance Policies for Get-Well

Policy	Per Occurrence Deductible	Per Occurrence Policy Limit	Aggregate Deductible	Aggregate Policy Limit	Premium
1	$ 500,000	$5,000,000	None	None	$780,000
2	$1,000,000	$5,000,000	None	None	$415,000
3	None	None	$6,000,000	$10,000,000	$165,000

Given these assumed distributions, Get-Well can use computer simulation to generate many years of hypothetical losses in order to estimate its probability distribution of losses and the effects of different insurance arrangements. The simulation proceeds as follows for each trial (year):

1. In the first step, an expected claim frequency is randomly sampled from the distribution shown in Table 12–4. The outcome of this step is either 20, 30, or 40.

2. In the second step, the number of claims is randomly sampled from a Poisson distribution with expected value determined by the first step. That is, if the first step produces an expected value of 20, then the sampled frequency distribution has an expected value of 20, and so on. The specific value drawn might be 4, 9, 19, 32, and so on.

3. In the third step, a claim severity amount for each claim is randomly sampled from a lognormal distribution with expected value of $100,000 and standard deviation of $300,000. For example, if the second step produces a claim frequency of 35, then 35 claim amounts are sampled in this step. The specific severities drawn might range from a very small loss to a loss in the millions of dollars.

4. Summing the claim severities sampled in step 3 yields the total loss for the given trial (year).

5. The effects of alternative insurance arrangements on the distribution of retained losses can be estimated using the output of the simulation by applying coverage limits and deductibles to the loss amounts generated in steps 3 and/or 4. For example, with a $500,000 per occurrence retention, Get-Well will retain the amount of each loss sampled in step 3 up to a maximum of $500,000.

6. Repeating steps 1 through 5 over many trials provides an estimate of the probability distribution of annual total losses and the probability distribution of annual retained losses for any arrangements considered in step 5.

We summarize the results of a 1,000 trial simulation of Get-Well's loss distribution and its retained losses for the three alternative insurance policies summarized in Table 12–5. The first policy provides $5 million of coverage per occurrence above a $500,000 per occurrence retention (deductible) for a premium of $780,000.[5] Get-Well pays the first $500,000 of any loss. The insurer pays any

---

[5] The premiums used in the example equal estimates of the expected value of insured claim costs obtained from the simulation, plus a loading charge equal to $25,000, plus 20 percent of expected claim costs, rounded to the nearest $5,000.

amount above $500,000 up to its limit of $5 million (a total loss of $5.5 million). There is no aggregate annual policy limit. The second policy provides $5 million of coverage per occurrence above a $1 million per occurrence retention for a premium of $415,000, again with no aggregate annual policy limit. The third policy provides an aggregate annual limit of $10 million in excess of a $6 million aggregate annual retention. There is no per occurrence limit or deductible. Get-Well pays the first $6 million of losses during the year; the insurer pays the next $10 million. Get-Well has to pay any losses above $16 million. The premium is $165,000.

Figure 12–2 shows the simulated distribution of total losses and retained losses for the alternative retention/insurance plans. Using the simulated distribution, Table 12–6 shows the mean, standard deviation, and maximum probable value of retained losses at the 95 percent level for each alternative. It also shows the maximum value of retained losses, the probability that total losses will exceed the insurance coverage limits, and the probability that retained losses will be less than or equal to $6 million. Since retained losses are only one component of the cost of risk, Table 12–6 also shows the mean total cost, defined as the mean value

FIGURE 12–2

Simulated distributions of retained losses for alternative retention arrangements (1,000 trials)

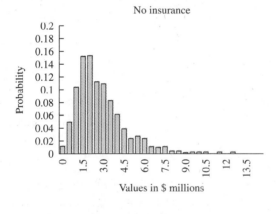

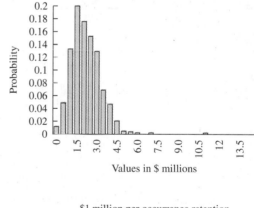

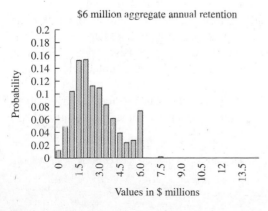

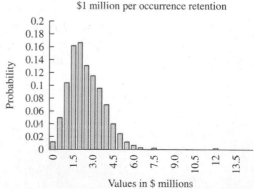

TABLE 12–6   **Simulation Results for Alternative Insurance/Retention Plans (1,000 trials in the simulation; all dollar values in $1,000s)**

Statistic	Policy 1 ($5 million excess $500,000 per occurrence retention)	Policy 2 ($5 million excess $1 million per occurrence retention)	Policy 3 ($10 million excess $6 million aggregate retention)	No Insurance
Mean value of retained losses	$2,414	$2,716	$2,925	$3,042
Standard deviation of retained losses	1,065	1,293	1,494	1,839
Maximum probable retained loss at 95% level	4,254	5,003	6,000	6,462
Maximum value of retained losses	11,325	12,125	7,899	18,898
Probability that losses exceed policy limits	1.1%	0.7%	0.1%	n.a.
Probability that retained losses ≤ $6 million	99.7%	98.7%	99.9%	92.7%
Premium	$780	$415	$165	$0
Mean total cost	3,194	3,131	3,090	3,042
Maximum probable total cost at 95% level	5,034	5,418	6,165	6,462

of retained losses plus the insurance premium, and the maximum probable total cost at the 95 percent level.

Based on the maximum probable total cost at the 95 percent level and the standard deviation of retained losses, the least risky strategy for Get-Well is the policy with the $500,000 per occurrence retention, followed in order of increasing risk by the $1 million per occurrence retention policy, the $6 million aggregate annual retention policy, and no insurance.[6] (Note, however, that this order does not hold for the maximum value of retained losses obtained in the 1,000 trials because more of a very large loss in one year was paid by the $10 million aggregate limit policy than by the $5 million per occurrence limit policies.) Due to savings on insurance premium loadings from increased retention, the ranking in terms of the mean total cost (premium plus mean retained loss) is reversed. The $500,000 per occurrence retention policy is the most expensive strategy, followed by the $1 million retention policy, the $6 million aggregate annual retention policy, and no insurance.

Based on this information, Get-Well can make an informed decision about which strategy to pursue. For example, it can decide whether the additional risk

---

[6] Because the premium is not random, the standard deviation of the total cost equals the standard deviation of retained losses.

reduction made possible by the $500,000 per occurrence retention policy compared to the $6 million aggregate retention policy is worth the additional expected cost of $104,000 ($3,194,000–$3,090,000).

Comparison of Results to Assuming the Normal Distribution.   We noted earlier that assuming that losses have the normal distribution can cause a firm to underestimate its maximum probable loss (at a given percentage level) if the true loss distribution is positively skewed. As can be seen in Figure 12–2, the simulated distribution of total losses for Get-Well is positively skewed. Consider what would happen if Get-Well assumed that total losses had the normal distribution with the expected value and standard deviation equal to the mean and standard deviation for the simulated distribution of total losses shown in the "no insurance" column of Table 12 6. The predicted maximum probable total loss at the 95 percent level assuming the normal distribution equals $6,067,000 (the mean value of $3,042,000 plus 1.645 times the standard deviation of $1,839,000). This amount is 6 percent lower than $6,462,000, the simulated value of the maximum probable loss at the 95 percent level. You also should recall that assuming the normal distribution for total losses would not allow Get Well to evaluate the effects of per occurrence retention and coverage limits.

Limitations of Computer Simulation.   Computer simulation can be a valuable tool in guiding decision making to the extent that reasonable assumptions or estimates of the shape and parameters (e.g., the expected value and standard deviation) of loss frequency and severity distributions can be obtained. The principal limitation of the method arises from parameter uncertainty: At best, the inputs to the simulation are only estimates of the true parameters and distributions. It might be especially difficult to incorporate accurate information about dependence in losses across exposures. Note, however, that parameter uncertainty can be incorporated in the analysis, as was illustrated for Get-Well in the case of claim frequency. In addition, different simulations can be run to examine the sensitivity of the results to different assumptions concerning the type and parameters of the assumed frequency and severity distributions. For example, Get-Well might examine the results assuming that claim frequency is described by one of the commonly used alternatives to the Poisson distribution.

12.5 Use of Discounted Cash Flow Analysis

The Net Present Value Criterion

In order to analyze the effects of risk management decisions that involve cash flows over multiple periods, it is necessary to discount the expected net cash flows to present value. Discounting cash flows was employed to determine the fair price of insurance in Chapter 6, to illustrate the effects of risk management on firm value in Chapter 9, and to illustrate the tax consequences of insurance versus retention in Chapter 10. In this section we review the key concept and illustrate its application in the context of loss financing. (Questions 9 and 10 at the end of the chapter contain additional examples.)

Assuming that cash flows occur initially (beginning of year 1) and then at the end of each year for n years, the discounted value of expected net cash flows equals:

$$\sum_{t=0}^{t=n} \frac{E(NCF_t)}{(1+r)^t} \tag{12.1}$$

where $E(NCF_t)$ is the expected value of the net cash flow in year t and r is the opportunity cost of capital. As noted in section 12.3, many risk management decisions involve a comparatively large up-front investment of funds that produces positive expected net cash flows in future years. For example, the decision regarding the installation of sprinklers was of this type. In these cases, the expression for the discounted value of expected net cash flows is known as the **net present value** of the investment. The net present value often is written in a slightly different way to emphasize the initial cash outflow for the investment (which we denote as I_0):

$$\sum_{t=1}^{t=n} \frac{E(NCF_t)}{(1+r)^t} - I_0 \tag{12.2}$$

Example: Forming a Captive Insurer

To illustrate the use of discounted cash flow analysis, consider the case of Long-Haul Trucking. Long-Haul currently has an annual self-insured retention of $500,000 per occurrence for both workers' compensation and auto liability insurance. The combined premium for its excess workers' compensation insurance, which pays losses without a per occurrence limit, and for excess auto liability coverage, with a $3 million per occurrence limit, is $2.15 million. Long-Haul is considering establishing a captive in Vermont to fund its retained losses. If it forms the captive, it will incur start-up costs in the amount of $140,000 for licensing the captive and one-time administrative costs. This expenditure can be regarded as the initial investment required to establish the captive.

If Long-Haul forms the captive, it will be able to obtain comparable excess coverage in the reinsurance market for an annual premium of $2 million, for a savings of $150,000. (Thus, in this example, other cash flows also occur at the time that the investment is made.) Long-Haul also plans to use a captive management firm to administer the captive on an ongoing basis. The fees paid to this firm will increase its total administrative costs by $30,000 per year. If it establishes the captive, Long-Haul also will use a fronting arrangement with an insurance company to meet state requirements concerning the purchase of coverage from an admitted insurer (see Chapter 10). The fronting insurer then will reinsure the coverage with the captive, which in turn will purchase the excess reinsurance coverage. The fee for this fronting arrangement is $80,000 per year.

TABLE 12–7   Change in Long-Haul's Expected Net Cash Flows from Establishing a Captive

	Time Period	
Type of Cash Flow	Beginning of First Year	End of Years 1, 2, 3, 4
Captive start-up costs	–$140,000	$ 0
Captive administration fee	–30,000	–30,000
Fronting fee	–80,000	–80,000
Reduction in excess		
Insurance premium	150,000	150,000
Total before-tax cash flow	–100,000	40,000
Income tax (34%)	34,000	–13,600
Total after-tax cash flow	–66,000	26,400

Long-Haul plans to pay the same amount to the captive to fund its retained losses as it maintains under its current program, and it will not change the way in which funds are invested. In addition, it does not plan to write outside business in the captive or to seek to have the transactions with the captive treated as insurance for federal income tax purposes. As a result, neither its investment income on assets dedicated to fund retained losses nor its income taxes will be affected by the establishment of the captive.

Table 12–7 shows the *change in expected cash flows* for Long-Haul from forming the captive assuming that premium payments and other expenses are paid at the beginning of each year and that all costs are tax deductible when paid.[7] For simplicity, the example assumes a five-year time horizon and that the fees and premium savings do not change during this period. Under these assumptions, Long-Haul will incur a net after-tax cash outflow of $66,000 upon establishing the captive (beginning of year 1) and a net cash inflow of $26,400 at the end of years 1 through 4.

Given these data and assuming an opportunity cost of capital equal to 10 percent, the net present value of establishing the captive is:

$$\text{NPV} = -66,000 + \frac{26,400}{1.1} + \frac{26,400}{1.1^2} + \frac{26,400}{1.1^3} + \frac{26,400}{1.1^4} = \$17,685 \quad (12.3)$$

---

[7] For most risk management decisions that involve capital expenditures, such as installation of sprinklers or safety equipment with a useful life of more than one year, tax rules do not permit the deduction of the full cost of investment when it is incurred. Instead, the firm is allowed to deduct the cost of the asset over a period of years in the form of depreciation. This yearly deduction for depreciation produces a tax savings (cash inflow) each year equal to the tax rate times the amount of depreciation for the year. Thus, on an after-tax basis, the investment produces an initial cash outflow equal to the cost of the assets and positive cash inflows in the form of reduced taxes over time as the initial cost is depreciated for tax purposes. Question 9 at the end of the chapter involves the deduction of depreciation for tax purposes in order to evaluate an investment in loss control.

Because the net present value is positive, the managers of Long-Haul can increase the firm's value by establishing the captive. The reason is that the savings in premiums from direct access to the reinsurance market outweigh the start-up costs and increased administrative costs.

Other applications of discounted cash flow analysis in risk management include choosing from a larger number of loss financing alternatives and making decisions concerning investments in loss control. With multiple loss financing options, it is customary to estimate the discounted value of expected net cash outflows for retained losses, insurance premiums, and other costs and choose the method with the lowest discounted cost. Since only two options were considered in the captive example, it was simpler to calculate the discounted value of the change in expected net cash flows from forming the captive compared to the current self-insurance arrangement. Investments in loss control commonly apply the net present value criterion once the size and timing of expected net cash flows have been estimated.

The Appropriate Cost of Capital

Basic financial theory suggests that the cost of capital used in discounting the expected net cash flows for a particular investment (or cost) should reflect the nondiversifiable risk associated with that particular investment. The key idea is that the rate of return required to compensate shareholders for risk will depend on the riskiness of the cash flows of the particular project from the shareholders' perspective. Since shareholders generally are assumed to be diversified, the appropriate way to measure the riskiness of the cash flows is by the amount of nondiversifiable risk.

In practice, risk managers sometimes must choose between two alternative (mutually exclusive) methods of financing losses that have different patterns of expenditures but do not materially affect the variability of *any of the firm's cash flows* (e.g., insurance premiums, losses, or other cash flows). In these cases, the appropriate cost of capital for discounting these expenditures is the risk-free rate of interest. For example, Long-Haul's decision to form a captive versus paying losses from internal funds does not change the expected value or the risk associated with retained losses. Consequently, the decision to form a captive depends critically on the present value of the costs of forming a captive (the fronting fees, administrative costs, etc.). Since these cash flows generally are certain or their risk is diversifiable, the cash flows associated with captive formation (or other retention methods that do not affect the level of retained losses) should be discounted at the risk-free rate of interest.

12.6 Summary

- Risk identification involves identifying the firm's significant exposures to loss using checklists, reviewing the firm's financial statements, and holding discussions with managers, employees, and insurance agents/outside consultants. Major loss exposures include: (1) property-related losses, including direct damage to property and indirect losses from a loss of profits and continuing or extra expenses; (2) liability losses; (3) losses to human resources; and (4) losses from external economic forces.

- Evaluating the frequency and severity of losses involves estimation or judgment of the likely frequency of loss, the potential severity of loss, and total losses during a period, including estimation of expected loss and the standard deviation of loss.

- A key loss financing decision for many firms is the determination of how much risk to retain and how much risk to insure in view of the major benefits and costs of increased retention (reduced insurance). Optimal retention for many firms involves the retention of comparatively predictable losses and purchasing insurance against large, potentially disruptive losses.

- Making loss control decisions to increase business value requires the identification and evaluation of the benefits and costs of specific loss control alternatives. These decisions often reflect reasonable judgment based on limited

information as opposed to statistical and financial analysis, especially for small firms.

- Larger firms often conduct a detailed statistical analysis to estimate the probability distribution of retained losses/costs for different types of losses and loss financing arrangements, or to estimate key features of these loss distributions, such as the expected value, standard deviation, and maximum probable loss.

- While loss distributions sometimes can be approximated with the normal distribution, problems and limitations of assuming the normal distribution often favor more elaborate and accurate estimation methods. In particular, computer simulation can be used in many cases to obtain more accurate estimates of losses and costs for different loss financing arrangements.

- Discounted cash flow analysis often is used by firms to compare the net present value of various loss control and loss financing decisions. This procedure requires an estimation of the expected value and timing of cash flows for each alternative and the choice of an appropriate discount rate in view of the risk of the cash flows.

Key Terms

risk identification   265
book value   266
market value   267
firm-specific value   267
replacement cost new   267
business income exposures   268

extra expense exposure   268
maximum probable loss   281
computer simulation of loss distributions   283
Poisson distribution   283
lognormal distribution   284
net present value   290

Questions and Problems

1. Rustbelt Inc. has a plant with market value equal to $25 million, firm-specific value of $30 million, and replacement cost new of $35 million. Assuming that replacement with a new plant will not increase

firm-specific value, should Rustbelt replace the plant if it is destroyed by an explosion? Why might Rustbelt buy fire insurance even if it would not replace the plant following a major loss?

2. Assume the same information in question 1 except that the firm-specific value with a new plant will increase to $40 million, given an increase in the plant's useful life following replacement. Will Rustbelt replace the plant if it is destroyed? How might its demand for insurance change compared to the situation presented in question 1?

3. Some observers argue that property-liability insurance prices and coverage are no longer cyclical and thus will be more stable in the future than in the past. If this argument is true, what effects would you predict for (a) business demand for insurance and (b) the formation of new group captives (see Chapter 11)?

4. The risk manager for a firm argues that retention limits should be increased in order to allow the firm to maintain the use of funds that otherwise would go for premiums until claims are paid. What questions would you ask the risk manager if you were his or her supervisor or if you were on the firm's board of directors?

5. The risk manager of Myopia, Inc., reasons that since most fire losses at Myopia's major plant are likely to be small, a good insurance strategy is to buy fire insurance with a limit equal to 50 percent of the plant's value and with a $500 per occurrence deductible and a 50 percent coinsurance clause (so that losses above $500 will be paid up to the coverage limit). The risk manager argues that this strategy makes sense because a significant portion of most losses will be covered since it is unlikely that any loss will exceed the coverage limit. What advice would you give to the risk manager or to Myopia's board of directors?

6. Lawn-Girl, Inc., sells self-propelled lawnmowers. Lawn-Girl's mowers currently include a device that shuts down the mower when both hands are removed from the handle. It is contemplating installing a device that will shut down the mower if the operator

removes either hand from the handle. Identify the principal benefits and costs to Lawn-Girl of installing the new device.

7. Bell Curve, Inc., estimates the expected value and standard deviation of its total liability losses for the forthcoming year as $10 million and $3 million, respectively. If Bell Curve assumes that total losses have the normal distribution, what is the predicted maximum probable loss at the 95 percent level? At the 99 percent level?

8. Describe the major steps involved in a computer simulation of loss distributions. Also describe the advantages of computer simulation (compared to assuming that losses have the normal distribution) and the limitations of computer simulation.

9. Wood Warehousing has property insurance on a replacement cost basis with a $5,000 per occurrence deductible. It can install automatic sprinklers in its warehouse for an initial cost of $10,000. The sprinklers will last five years (they would last much longer in real life). Annual upkeep of the sprinklers will be $1,000, payable at the end of each of the first four years from the time of installation. If Wood installs the sprinklers, it will deduct one-fifth of the installation price at the end of each year for five years as depreciation (a noncash expense) for tax purposes. Without the sprinklers, the firm believes that its expected cash outflow for losses less than the deductible will be $1,000 per year and that its insurance premium will be $10,000 per year. With the sprinklers, it believes that its expected cash outflow for losses less than the deductible will be $500 per year and that its insurance premium will be $7,000 per year. Wood's opportunity cost of capital for this decision is 10 percent. Retained losses are paid and deductible for tax purposes at the end of each year. Insurance premiums are paid at the beginning of the year and are deductible for tax purposes when paid. The tax rate is 34

percent. Should Wood install the sprinklers? Support your answer by calculating the net present value of installing the sprinklers.

10. Seward Go-Carts has annual sales of $150 million with an expected profit of $5 million. It currently has a retention limit for annual liability losses equal to $5 million. The premium for excess insurance coverage above the $5 million retention is $50,000. With the $5 million retention, its expected retained losses (including claims settlement costs) for accidents during the year equal $1 million. Half of all retained losses for accidents during the year will be paid at the end of the year; the remaining half will be paid at the end of the next year. If Seward changes its retention level to $2 million, the premium for excess coverage will be $170,000. Its expected retained losses for accidents during the year will drop to $900,000. Again, half of retained losses for accidents during the year will be paid at the end of the year; the remaining half will be paid at the end of the

second year. Premiums are paid at the beginning of the year. Seward's opportunity cost of capital for this decision is 10 percent. The tax rate is 34 percent. The decision horizon is one year of coverage because the firm can change its retention level again the following year. (Note, however, that cash flows associated with the decision occur over two years.)

(a) Calculate the present value of the after-tax *change in expected net cash flows* from reducing Seward's retention level from $5 million to $2 million.

(b) Calculate the present value of the after-tax change in net cash flows from reducing Seward's retention level *assuming that actual retained losses equal the retention limits* rather than the expected values.

(c) Which approach do you think that the firm should take? Why? What factors (other than the present values that you calculated) would be likely to influence its decision?

References

Doherty, Neil A.; and Clifford W. Smith, Jr. "Corporate Insurance Strategy: The Case of British Petroleum." *Continental Bank—Journal of Applied Corporate Finance* 6 (1993), pp. 4–15. (*Case study of retention and insurance strategy for a giant corporation.*)

Holler, Keith D. "The Confidence Game: Using Confidence Levels to Estimate Losses." *Risk Management,* August 1995, pp. 53–57. (*Practitioner-oriented introduction to estimation of losses, including the use of computer simulation.*)

Answer to Concept Check

1. (a) The firm with no shareholder who owns more than 1 percent of its stock would be more likely to self-insure. The 50 percent owner would have more incentive to purchase insurance because the owner would not be well-diversified and thus would face significant risk of loss if workers' compensation losses were much higher than expected.

(b) The trucking firm would be more likely to self-insure because the lower correlation in losses among workers reduces the variability of losses compared to the manufacturing firm, where many workers might be hurt in a single accident.

(c) The firm with revenues positively correlated with claim costs would be more likely to self-insure because the firm is naturally hedged (i.e., as losses go up so do its revenues). As a result, the variability of its profits would be lower without insurance compared to the firm whose revenues are uncorrelated with claim costs.

(*d*) The firm with no debt in its capital structure would be more likely to self-insure because it would have a lower probability of financial distress without insurance compared to the firm with debt.

13

Reducing Risk through Hedging and Diversification

Chapter Objectives

- Explain the basic derivative contracts (options, forwards, futures, and swaps) commonly used for hedging.
- Discuss similarities and differences between insurance contracts and derivative contracts.
- Explain differences between exchange-traded and over-the-counter derivative markets.
- Describe the major types of risk that are typically hedged using derivatives.
- Discuss the advantages and disadvantages of internal diversification of a firm's operations as a method to reduce its risk.

13.1 Introduction to Derivatives and Hedging

The traditional use of the term "risk management" suggests activities such as purchasing insurance and loss control that are used to manage pure risk. However, the term risk management increasingly is being used to indicate financial risk management: the hedging of financial price risk using derivative contracts like futures, swaps, and options. Perhaps because of the need for specialization, the two types of risk management often are performed by different people within the same corporation without consideration of the possible interrelationships. Ideally, both types of activities should be analyzed using the firm value maximization framework (see Chapters 2 and 9), taking into consideration that the optimal management of one type of risk (e.g., pure risk) depends on how other types of risk (e.g., price risk) are being managed. Indeed, there is some indication that such an integrated or holistic approach to risk management is being adopted by major corporations (see Box 11–2 for an example).

FIGURE 13–1

*The relation between
oil prices and
NeedOil's profits*

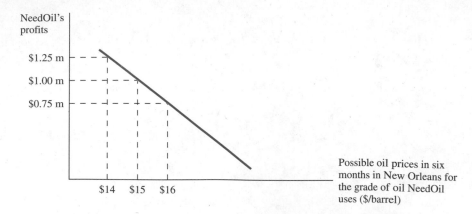

This chapter introduces some of the basic tools, terminology, and concepts used in financial risk management. Armed with this background, a major objective is then to identify and discuss similarities and differences between financial risk management and traditional risk management. We also briefly discuss the benefits and costs of internal diversification as another method that reduces business risk and that can in principle reduce the demand for both insurance and hedging.

Exposure Diagrams Revisited

To introduce some of the basic ideas of hedging with derivatives, we use a simple example of a firm called NeedOil that uses oil in its production process. If the price of oil increases, then the firm's costs will increase. On the other hand, if the price of oil decreases, the firm's costs will decrease. The important point is that the firm's costs are uncertain due to the price of oil being uncertain. We assume that NeedOil cannot pass on all incremental costs to customers and therefore that cost increases produce lower profits.

NeedOil's risk from uncertain oil prices can be illustrated using exposure diagrams similar to those introduced in Chapter 11. Figure 13–1 indicates that, holding other factors constant, NeedOil's profits are negatively related to the price of oil over the coming year. In particular, the horizontal axis gives the possible prices for the particular grade of oil that NeedOil will purchase in New Orleans in six months. If the price equals $15 a barrel, then NeedOil's profits will equal $1 million. However, if the price of oil is $16 a barrel, then NeedOil's profits will be only $750,000. The negatively sloped line in Figure 13–1 gives NeedOil's profits for each possible oil price.

Recall that the horizontal axis in an exposure diagram gives the possible outcomes for some random variable.[1] Only one of these outcomes will actually be

---

[1] The exposure diagrams presented in this chapter differ from those in Chapter 11 in that profits are graphed on the vertical axis here and costs were graphed on the vertical axis in Chapter 11.

realized. In this example, NeedOil does not know the price that it must pay for oil in six months. The horizontal axis gives possible oil prices and the vertical axis gives NeedOil's profits under these alternative outcomes. Only one point on the graph will occur. As with the exposure diagrams in Chapter 11, if the exposure diagram is not flat (horizontal), then the firm is exposed to risk.

Before showing how NeedOil can reduce its risk (flatten the line in Figure 13–1), two points are worth noting about the relation between NeedOil's profits and oil prices depicted in Figure 13–1. First, the relationship between oil prices and profits would not be known with certainty. Instead the relationship depicted in Figure 13–1 would be viewed as the relationship between oil prices and the expected value of profits, but generally there would be random variation in profits around the expected value. Second, considerable analysis (which is beyond the scope of this chapter) would be needed to determine the relationship between expected profits and possible oil prices. For example, the downward sloping line in Figure 13–1 could have been estimated using historical data on how NeedOil's profits varied with oil prices.

Concept Checks

1. Golddigger Inc. is a gold mining company. Draw a graph that identifies the likely relationship between gold prices and the value of Golddigger.
2. Zeiser Inc. is a construction company. Draw a graph that identifies the likely relationship between interest rates and the value of Zeiser Inc. Also draw a graph that identifies the likely relationship between government bond prices and the value of Zeiser Inc. (Hint: Higher interest rates reduce bond prices and the demand for new construction.)

Hedging with Call Option Contracts

The negatively sloped line in Figure 13–1 indicates that NeedOil is exposed to oil price risk. To reduce this risk, NeedOil must do something to flatten the line depicting the relationship between its profits and oil prices. If it could make the line horizontal over some range of oil prices, then it would eliminate its oil price risk over that range of prices (profits would be the same under different oil prices).

Suppose that NeedOil decides that it does not want to bear the risk that it will have to pay more than $15 a barrel for oil. That is, NeedOil wants to engage in some transaction that changes its profit line in Figure 13–1 from being negatively sloped when oil prices are above $15 to one that is flat when oil prices are above $15. NeedOil can do this by contracting with another party who will give NeedOil money when the price of oil rises above $15. For example, suppose that NeedOil signs a contract with OPTCO that requires OPTCO to pay NeedOil 250,000 times the difference between the actual price of oil in six months and $15, provided that the actual price exceeds $15. Under this contract, if the price of oil in six months turns out to be $16, then OPTCO will pay NeedOil $250,000; if the price of oil turns out to be $17, then OPTCO will pay NeedOil $500,000, and so on. On the other hand, if the price of oil ends up being less than $15, OPTCO will pay NeedOil $0.

So far, the description of the contract between NeedOil and OPTCO indicates that OPTCO will pay NeedOil money in six months if oil prices are higher than $15. Obviously, OPTCO will require compensation for agreeing to do this. In a sense, OPTCO can be viewed as insuring NeedOil against high costs due to high oil prices. OPTCO will demand compensation for selling this insurance. Let's assume that OPTCO requires a premium equal to $100,000. Taking into account this premium, but ignoring the time value of money, the payoff from NeedOil's contract with OPTCO is illustrated in Figure 13–2.

To identify NeedOil's exposure to oil prices after arranging this contract, we must add NeedOil's exposure diagram from its operations (Figure 13–1) to the exposure diagram from its contract with OPTCO (Figure 13–2). That is, for each possible oil price, we add the profits from operations to the payoffs from the contract with OPTCO. The following calculations indicate how this is done for three prices.

If oil price = $14 → Profits from operations (Figure 13–1)   = $1,250,000
                      Profits from OPTCO contract (Figure 13–2) = –$100,000
                      Total profits   = $1,150,000

If oil price = $15 → Profits from operations (Figure 13–1)   = $1,000,000
                      Profits from OPTCO contract (Figure 13–2) = –$100,000
                      Total profits   = $900,000

If oil price = $16 → Profits from operations (Figure 13–1)   = $750,000
                      Profits from OPTCO contract (Figure 13–2) = $150,000
                      Total profits   = $900,000

Figure 13–3 illustrates the total profits to NeedOil after engaging in the contract with OPTCO. No matter what happens to the price of oil, expected profits never fall below $900,000, which is the level of profits NeedOil would have if the price of oil were $15 minus the premium paid to OPTCO.

FIGURE 13–2

The relation between oil prices and NeedOil's payoff from its contract with OPTCO

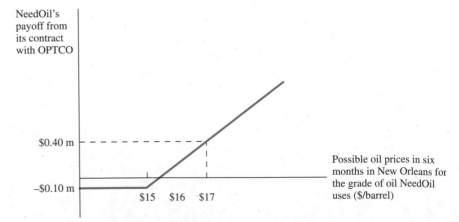

NeedOil's payoff from its contract with OPTCO

$0.40 m

–$0.10 m

$15 $16 $17

Possible oil prices in six months in New Orleans for the grade of oil NeedOil uses ($/barrel)

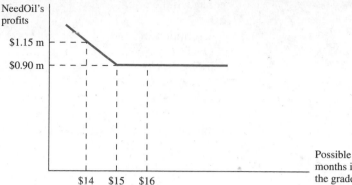

FIGURE 13–3

The relation between oil prices and NeedOil's profits from operations plus profits from contract with OPTCO

The transaction between NeedOil and OPTCO is an example of a derivative contract. A **derivative contract** is a contract whose payoff or value is derived from the value of something else, most commonly some other asset, but sometimes an index or other item. The asset on which a derivative contract is based is called the **underlying asset** of the derivative contract. In the example with Need-Oil, the underlying asset is the market value (price) of a particular grade of oil six months hence in New Orleans. Derivative contracts exist with underlying assets ranging from financial assets like bonds and stocks to commodities like orange juice, pork bellies, and lumber. The underlying asset of a derivative contract also could be an index that measures the level or rate of change in some economic variable. For example, derivatives could be based on a consumer price index or an index measuring the magnitude of insured losses from hurricanes in Florida.

The derivative contract purchased by NeedOil from OPTCO was an example of a call option contract. The buyer of a **call option contract** receives a positive payoff only if the value of the underlying asset exceeds some threshold, called the **exercise price** (or *strike price*). NeedOil's call option contract had an exercise price of $15. The price paid for a call option (the premium) is called the **option price;** NeedOil paid $100,000 for its call option, so the option price was $100,000.

An important feature of a call option is that the payoff is asymmetric: A buyer of a call option receives a payoff that increases linearly with the value of the underlying asset when the value of the underlying asset is above the exercise price, but the payoff is flat when the value of the underlying asset is below the exercise price. The asymmetric payoff to a buyer of a call option is illustrated in Figure 13–2.

We have discussed call options from the perspective of the buyer of the call option, NeedOil. Now consider the payoff to the seller of the call option – OPTCO. Graphically, OPTCO's payoff can be found by reflecting the mirror image of NeedOil's payoff on the other side of the horizontal axis. This payoff is illustrated in Figure 13–4. If the price of oil is high, OPTCO loses money on the contract, but if the price of oil is less than $15, OPTCO makes a profit on the contract. The possible gain from selling the option is limited to the price of the option, but the possible loss can be very large (a large increase in the price of oil will

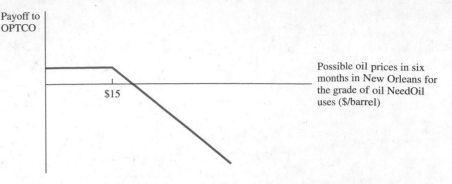

cause the seller to make a large payment). Notice that the payoffs to the option buyer (NeedOil) are opposite of the payoffs to the option seller (OPTCO) and therefore that the sum of the payments is always zero.

Hedging with Put Options

The other basic type of option contract is a put option contract. The buyer of a **put option contract** receives a positive payoff only if the value of the underlying asset falls below the exercise price. The payoff from a put option on oil with an exercise price of $15 is given by the kinked line labeled "put buyer" in Figure 13–5. Since the put buyer's payoff increases as oil prices fall, an oil producer could use a put option contract to hedge the risk of low oil prices.

For every put buyer, there is also a put seller. The payoff to the seller of a put option is the mirror image of the buyer's payoff reflected across the horizontal axis. This is illustrated in Figure 13–5 by the kinked line labeled "put seller." Notice that the seller's payoff is just the opposite of the buyer's payoff.

In summary, both call and put option contracts are derivative contracts that can be used to protect firm value from price changes that otherwise would decrease firm value. For firms whose value decreases when the value of the underlying asset increases, call options can protect firm value. For firms whose value decreases when the value of the underlying asset decreases, put options can protect firm value. Thus, option contracts have features like insurance contracts: Both option and insurance contracts can be used to generate cash when events occur that otherwise would have caused a loss in value. Just as a firm pays a premium for insurance, a firm pays a premium for an option contract.

Concept Checks

3. Golddigger Inc.'s value increases as gold prices increase. If Golddigger wanted to protect firm value against a possible decrease in the price of gold, would it use a call option or a put option? What would be the underlying asset?

4. Suppose that Zeiser Construction Co.'s value decreases as interest rates

FIGURE 13–5

Payoff from put options on oil with an exercise price of $15

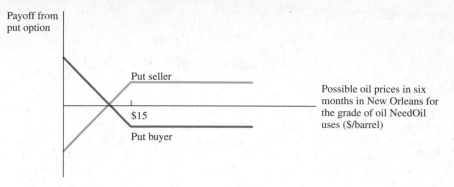

increase. If Zeiser wanted to protect firm value against an increase in interest rates, would it use a call option or a put option? What would be the underlying asset?

Cash Settlement versus Physical Delivery

Our presentation of call and put options has emphasized their similarity to insurance contracts. Specifically, the call option purchased by NeedOil provides cash to NeedOil if oil prices turn out to be high. This cash can then be used to offset the high cost of oil that NeedOil needs to purchase for its operations. Consequently, the call option "insures" NeedOil from losses resulting from high oil prices. Many derivative contracts are structured similar to NeedOil's call option; that is, they are settled in cash at the expiration of the contract. **Cash settled contracts** are purely financial transactions with cash payments based on (derived from) the value of some other commodity, security, or index; the underlying asset of the derivative contract (oil in our example) is not physically delivered.

Many derivative contracts, however, are based on the **physical delivery** of the underlying asset.[2] Indeed, the description of physical delivery contracts helps to explain some of the terminology used to describe options. With physical delivery, a call option on oil with an exercise price of $15/barrel gives the call option buyer the right (not the obligation) to buy oil at $15/barrel. For example, if the price of oil were $17/barrel, then the option buyer could force the option seller to deliver oil at $15/barrel. Thus, the term "call option" comes from the ability of the call option buyer to "call" the underlying asset away from the option seller for less than it is worth at the time of delivery.

---

[2] Even with physical delivery contracts, most traders do not actually take physical delivery. Instead, they "unwind" their positions by taking the opposite position prior to the contract's expiration. For example, NeedOil could purchase a call option on oil today and prior to the option's expiration sell the call option to someone else. If the price of oil increased during the intervening period, then the call option price would increase (see the next subsection) and NeedOil could use the gain to offset the higher price of oil that it must purchase for its operations.

Box 13–1

Some Option Terminology

European options can be exercised only at the expiration of the contract. If a call option contract is for six months, then the call buyer can only exercise the option at the end of six months. Thus, the ultimate payoff on European options is determined by the difference between the exercise price and the price of the underlying asset at expiration.

American options can be exercised any time prior to expiration. Thus, the ultimate payoff on American options can depend on the difference between the ex-

ercise price and the price of the underlying asset at any time prior to expiration.

The payoff on *Asian options* depends on the difference between the exercise price and the average of the prices of the underlying asset prior to exercise. Some Asian options can only be exercised at the contract expiration (like European options) and some Asian options can be exercised prior to the contract's expiration (like American options).

A put option gives the put buyer the right (not the obligation) to make the put seller purchase the underlying asset at the exercise price. If the value of the underlying asset is less than the exercise price, then the put buyer will exercise the option and make the put seller purchase the underlying asset for more than the asset is worth. Thus, the term "put option" comes from the ability of the put buyer to "put" the underlying asset to the put seller for more than it is worth at the time of delivery. (Box 13–1 summarizes some other terminology used to describe option contracts.)

The distinction between physical delivery and cash settled derivative contracts is inconsequential for our purposes. The essential point is that call options can be used to generate cash if the price of some commodity, index, or security turns out to be high. And put options can be used to generate cash if the price of some commodity, index, or security turns out to be low.

Basis Risk

The above examples illustrating how NeedOil might use options (and in later examples, forward contracts and other derivatives) to hedge its oil price risk are simplified by the assumption that the underlying asset of the derivative contracts also is the type of oil that NeedOil purchases for its operations. As a result, a perfect hedge can be constructed. In the option example, if oil prices increase beyond $15, then the lost operating profits can be exactly offset by increased profits from the option contract.

In reality, "the only perfect hedge is in a Japanese garden" (source unknown). The risk from an imperfect hedge is called **basis risk.** The *basis* for a hedge is the difference between the value of what's being hedged and the value of the hedging instrument. Thus, the basis for NeedOil is the difference between its oil costs and the payoff from the call option. If an increase in its oil costs is always offset by an equal increase in the payoff from the call option, then the hedge is perfect and there is no basis risk. However, if changes in NeedOil's oil costs are not always offset perfectly by the option's payoff, then there is basis risk. With basis risk, there is uncertainty in how good the hedge will actually work.

There are a number of sources of basis risk. For example, NeedOil may purchase a certain grade (sulfur content) of oil, but the derivative contract may be based on a different grade. NeedOil may purchase oil the last day of every month, but the derivative contract may mature during the middle of every three months. NeedOil may take delivery of its oil in New Orleans, but the derivative contract may be based on the price of oil delivered in New York. As a result of the differences in the factors affecting the value of its oil costs (and thus profits) and the factors affecting the value of a derivative contract, NeedOil is unlikely to find a perfect hedge for its oil costs.

13.2 Option Pricing

The Role of Supply and Demand

In the NeedOil example, we simply assumed that the price of the option equaled $100,000. We now examine the factors that affect the price of an option contract. Ultimately, the forces of supply and demand determine option prices. For example, suppose that the price of a particular option equals $100. If the number of option contracts that people want to purchase at a price of $100 exceeds the number of option contracts that people are willing to sell, then the option's price will increase.

Financial economists have developed a method, which is widely used by practitioners, for determining the price where supply and demand for options generally will coincide.[3] The key result of option pricing theory is that, for traders who can trade both the option contract and the underlying asset at relatively low costs, there is a critical price (called the no-arbitrage price) above which traders can profit from selling call options and below which traders can profit from buying call options. Using finance terminology, traders can make arbitrage profits (riskless profits without investing any money) if the price is above or below the no-arbitrage price and there are no transaction costs. As a consequence, traders always supply option contracts if the price is above the no-arbitrage price (which in turn depresses the price) and traders always demand call option contracts if the price is below the no-arbitrage price (which in turn increases the price). Option prices therefore should always be close to the no-arbitrage price.

---

[3] Financial economists Fischer Black, Robert Merton, and Myron Scholes developed the fundamental option pricing models during the early 1970s. Merton and Scholes were awarded the 1997 Nobel Prize in economics in large part for their work on option pricing. Black's death prevented him from receiving the award; Nobel Prizes are not awarded posthumously.

Influence of Underlying Asset, Contract, and Market Characteristics

Although option pricing theory is based on mathematical models that are beyond the scope of this book, some of the most important implications of these models can be explained intuitively. The basic option pricing model implies that the price of a call option at time t depends on five factors:

1. The price of the underlying asset at time t.
2. The volatility (standard deviation) of the return on the underlying asset per unit of time.
3. The exercise price.
4. The option's time to maturity (time to expiration).
5. The interest rate on government bonds.

The first two factors are characteristics of the underlying asset. The third and fourth factors are contract characteristics, and the final factor is a characteristic of the economic environment.

Price of the Underlying Asset. If the price of the underlying asset increases and the other four factors remain constant, then the call option price will increase. The intuition is that an increase in the current price of the underlying asset implies a higher expected value for the price of the underlying asset when the call option contract expires, which increases the expected payoff from buying the call option. Since the expected payoff increases as the price of the underlying asset increases, so does the option's price.

Volatility.   Greater *volatility* in the price of the underlying asset increases the price of the call option. At first, this result may seem strange—greater risk increases the price of the option. The reason for this result is that the payoff from an option is asymmetric. Increases in the price of the underlying asset beyond the exercise price continue to increase the payoff from a call option, but decreases in the price of the underlying asset below the exercise price do not cause additional losses. This asymmetry implies that more variability in the price of the underlying asset increases the expected payoff from the option.

A simple example, which is summarized in Table 13–1, illustrates the effect of increased volatility in the underlying asset on the payoffs from a call option with an exercise price of $100. Compare two scenarios for the price of the underlying asset at the option's maturity. In the low volatility scenario, the underlying asset has a 50 percent chance of being $110 and a 50 percent chance of being $90. Consequently, the payoff from the call option is either $10 or $0, yielding an expected payoff of $5. In the high volatility scenario, the underlying asset has a 50 percent chance of being $130 and a 50 percent chance of being $70. Note that the expected value of the underlying asset is $100 in both scenarios, but that the variance of the underlying asset's price is greater in the second scenario. The greater variance causes the expected payoff from the call option in the second scenario to be greater than the first scenario. In particular, the call option has a

TABLE 13–1   Illustration of How Greater Volatility in the Underlying Asset Increases the Price of a Call Option (exercise price = $100; each outcome is equally likely)

	Possible Outcomes for the Value of the Underlying Asset at Expiration	Possible Outcomes for the Payoff from the Call Option
Low volatility	$ 90	$ 0
	110	10
High volatility	$ 70	$ 0
	130	30

payoff of either $30 or $0, yielding an expected payoff of $15. Thus, even though the expected price under each scenario is the same, the greater volatility in the return on the underlying asset in the second scenario implies that the expected payoff from the call option is greater. Thus, greater volatility implies higher option prices, holding all other factors constant.

Exercise Price.   Compared to a call option contract with an exercise price of $20, an otherwise identical contract with a lower exercise price will have a higher price. The intuition is similar to that given above for why the call option price increases as the price of the underlying asset increases. A call option with a lower exercise price has a higher expected payoff to the purchaser of the call option. Consequently, a call option's price will be higher for option contracts with lower exercise prices, holding the other factors constant.

Time to Expiration.   Holding the other factors constant, an option's price is higher the longer the time to expiration. An option that expires in one year will have a higher price than an otherwise equivalent option that matures in six months. There are two reasons for this result. To see the first reason, assume that the price of the underlying asset at expiration will exceed the exercise price with certainty so that the call option will have a positive payoff with certainty. Then, as summarized in the first row of Table 13–2, the expected payoff at expiration will equal the expected value of the underlying asset at expiration minus the exercise price. Today's option price will depend on the present value of these cash flows, which equals the present value of the underlying asset minus the present value of the exercise price (see the second row of Table 13–2). We already have discussed how the option price depends on the current value of the underlying as-

TABLE 13–2   Payoff at Expiration and Call Option Price Assuming a Positive Payoff

Call option payoff at expiration	=	Expected value of the underlying asset at expiration	−	Exercise price
Call option price today	=	Value of the underlying asset today	−	Present value of exercise price

set and the exercise price. However, as the second row of Table 13–2 indicates, the option's price depends not just on the exercise price, but on the present value of the exercise price. Thus, the longer the time until the option expires, the lower will be the present value of the exercise price and thus the greater will be the option's price today given the current value of the underlying asset.

The second reason that the price of a call option increases with the time to expiration follows directly from the discussion of volatility. Holding the volatility per unit of time constant, the greater the time to maturity, the greater the total volatility and, consequently, the greater the price of the option. Intuitively, the longer the maturity, the greater the chance that the price of the underlying asset will increase by a large amount. Of course, there also is a greater chance that the price of the underlying asset will decrease by a large amount. Because of the asymmetric payoff from the call option, however, the greater total volatility arising from the greater time to maturity increases the price of the option, holding the other factors fixed.

Interest Rate.   The higher the level of interest rates, the higher is the price of the option, all else being equal. The intuition is similar to that given for the time to maturity. A higher interest rate lowers the present value of the exercise price, and thus the greater is the price of the option, holding the other factors constant.

This discussion has focused on the determinants of call options. These same factors affect the price of a put option. However, since the payoffs from a put option differ from the payoffs from a call option, some of the determinants of the price have the opposite effect for put options. Table 13–3 summarizes how each factor influences call and put option prices.

13.3 Hedging with Forward/Futures Contracts

Illustration

Let's return to our example of NeedOil. Recall that NeedOil's profits from operations are negatively related to the price of oil as indicated by Figure 13–1. Assume that NeedOil has decided to protect itself against increases in the price

TABLE 13–3   Determinants of the Price of European Call and Put Options

Determinants (holding other factors fixed)	Call Option Price	Put Option Price
As the price of the underlying asset increases	Increases	Decreases
As the exercise price increases	Decreases	Increases
As the volatility in the return of the underlying asset increases	Increases	Increases
As the time to maturity increases	Increases	Increases
As interest rates increase	Increases	Decreases

of oil. In the previous example, it purchased a call option contract to provide this protection, paying an option premium of $100,000. We now consider another way for NeedOil to obtain protection against increases in the price of oil above $15.

Suppose that a company called F-CO will provide protection against increases in oil prices, but that F-CO differs from OPTCO in that it does not make NeedOil pay a fixed premium. NeedOil, instead, only pays F-CO if the price of oil at the expiration of the contract falls below $15, and the more the price falls below $15, the more NeedOil must pay F-CO. Figure 13–6 illustrates the payoffs to NeedOil under its contract with F-CO for alternative oil prices at contract expiration. Just like NeedOil's option contract with OPTCO, if the price of oil exceeds $15, then F-CO pays NeedOil some money: If the price of oil equals $16, then F-CO will pay NeedOil $250,000; if the price of oil equals $17, F-CO will pay NeedOil $500,000. However, if the price of oil falls below $15, then NeedOil pays F-CO some money: If the price of oil falls to $14, then NeedOil must pay F-CO $250,000; if the price of oil equals $13, NeedOil must pay F-CO $500,000. Thus, the payoffs on this contact are symmetric around the $15 price.

Since the payoffs from the contract between F-CO and NeedOil are derived from the price of oil, the contract is another example of a derivative contract. There are two types of derivative contracts that have payoff structures like this contract: forward contracts and futures contracts. We will describe the differences between forward and futures contracts later. The important point for now is that a **forward contract** or a **futures contract** gives the buyer (NeedOil) a symmetric payoff that is equal to the difference between the actual price of the underlying asset and some predetermined price called the **forward price** or the **futures price.** In our example, the forward price is $15. Again, the important feature of forward and futures contracts is that the payoff is symmetric: If the price rises above the forward price, the buyer of the contract receives a positive payoff and if the price falls below the forward price, then the buyer receives a negative payoff.

Notice that the payoff to the buyer, NeedOil, from a forward contract is positively related to the price of oil. The payoff to the seller, F-CO, is just the opposite: The greater the price of oil, the more that F-CO has to pay. The lower the

Figure 13–6

NeedOil's payoff from its contract with F-CO

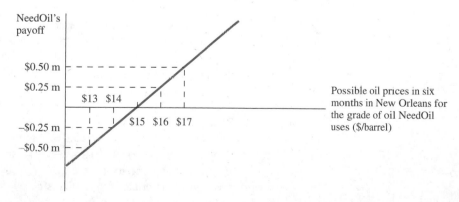

FIGURE 13–7

Payoff to F-CO, the seller of a forward contract

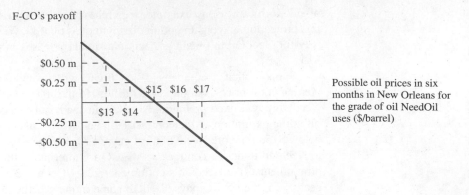

price of oil, the more that F-CO receives. Figure 13–7 illustrates the payoff to the seller of a forward contract.

We have described forward (futures) contracts assuming that the contracts are settled in cash. Some of the terminology, however, is derived from forward (futures) contracts based on physical delivery of the underlying asset. For example, by buying (taking a long position) in a forward contract, NeedOil essentially is agreeing to buy oil in six months (the expiration of the contract) at $15 a barrel (the forward price). Conversely, by selling (taking a short position) in a forward contract, F-CO is agreeing to sell oil in six months at $15 a barrel. Thus, the terms "forward" and "futures" are derived from the parties agreeing to transact at a fixed price (the forward or futures price) in the future. If the actual price of oil at contract expiration differs from the forward price, then one party gains and the other party loses. For example, if the actual price of oil in six months exceeds $15, then NeedOil is able to buy and F-CO must sell oil for less than it is worth.

Forward Prices

When a firm buys an option contract, it pays the seller a premium up front. In contrast, when a firm buys a forward contract, no cash exchanges hands. Instead, the payoffs all occur when the contract expires. Demand and supply in forward contracts are not adjusted by changes in an up-front price. Instead, demand and supply are adjusted by changes in the forward price. For example, if the forward price equals $15 and at that price the demand for forward contracts exceeds the supply of forward contracts, then the forward price will increase. Thus, you cannot choose a forward contract with a particular forward price; the forward price is determined by the marketplace.

The theory of forward (futures) prices has similarities to the theory of option pricing. As we discussed with options, if people can trade both the forward (futures) contracts and the underlying asset at relatively low costs, there is a critical price (called the no-arbitrage price). If the forward (futures) price is above the critical price, traders will be willing to sell forward (futures) contracts, thus putting downward pressure on the price. If the price is below the critical price, then traders will be willing to buy forward (futures) contracts, thus putting upward pressure on the price. The no-arbitrage forward (futures) price at time t for a contract that expires at time $t + T$ (T is the amount of time until the futures contract expires) satisfies what is called the **cost of carry relationship:**

Forward (futures) price = Spot price at time t + Cost of carry

where the cost of carry equals the sum of (1) the interest paid from t to $t + T$ on a loan that could finance the purchase of the underlying asset, (2) the cost of storing the underlying asset from t to $t + T$, and (3) the cost of insuring the underlying asset from t to $t + T$. Intuitively, the price paid in the future for the underlying asset (the forward or futures price) must be equal to the price paid today plus the cost of carrying the asset to the future.

As an example, suppose that the current spot price of oil is $16 a barrel, the interest rate equals 9 percent, and the cost of storing and insuring oil for one year is 1 percent of the value of the oil. Then the forward (futures) price on a contract that expires in one year would be expected to equal $16 + $16 × (0.09 + 0.01) per barrel, or $17.60.

Suppose that instead of being $17.60, the one-year forward price was equal to $18 a barrel. Then, a trader could sell (take a short position in) the forward contract at the $18 price, which is equivalent to agreeing to sell oil in one year at $18. Simultaneously, the trader could buy oil today and store and insure the oil for one year for a total cost of $17.60 a barrel. At the end of the year, the trader could use the oil it has stored to deliver on its promise to sell oil for $18. The trader would make $0.40 a barrel. If 1 million barrels were purchased initially and if the forward contract was for 1 million barrels, then the trader would make $400,000. If traders faced a situation like this, they would continue to sell forward contracts, which would eventually depress the forward price until it reached the $17.60 a barrel price implied by the cost of carry relationship.

13.4 Other Derivative Contracts

Constructing Other Derivatives

We have introduced call options, put options, and forward contracts. Futures contracts are essentially the same as forward contracts at this introductory level of analysis. Call and put options give asymmetric payoffs and forward and futures contracts give symmetric payoffs. While there are many other types of derivative contracts, they generally can be constructed from the basic contracts we have already described. For this reason, many practitioners and academics find it useful to view options and forwards as building blocks that can be used to construct other derivative contracts. The building block approach starts with the basic payoffs summarized in Figure 13–8.[4]

---

[4] Notice that even the blocks in the figure are redundant in that a forward contract can be constructed with options. In particular, the same payoff can be obtained by buying a forward contract or by buying a call option and simultaneously selling a put option.

FIGURE 13–8

Derivative "building blocks"

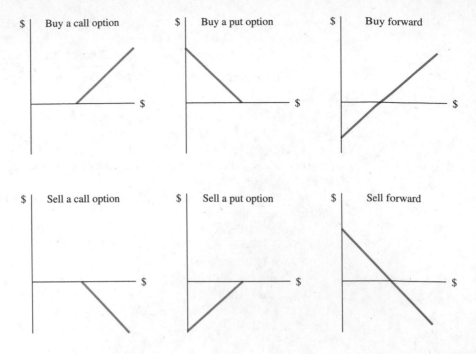

To illustrate the usefulness of the building block approach, suppose that NeedOil decides that it wants protection from high oil prices, but that it does not believe oil prices will rise above $18 a barrel. If NeedOil hedged by buying a call option with an exercise price of $15 (as was described earlier), it would be buying protection against any increase in oil prices above $15, including protection against oil prices above $18. Since it does not believe oil prices will rise above $18, it is buying protection that it deems as having little or no value. NeedOil therefore would like to have a derivative contract with a payoff that increases with prices between $15 and $18, but that does not increase when oil prices are above $18. The solid line in Figure 13–9 illustrates the payoff NeedOil wants (ignoring the cost of obtaining protection).

NeedOil can obtain its desired payoff by buying a call option with an exercise price of $15 and selling a call option with an exercise price of $18. To see this, you simply need to graph the payoff on each option separately and then vertically add the payoffs. Figure 13–9 illustrates the payoffs from the two options with dashed lines.

Swap Contracts

The final type of derivative contract that we will highlight is called a swap contract. **Swap contracts** have payoffs like a series of forward contracts. That is, instead of having just one payoff at the contract's expiration (or when the option is exercised), a swap contract has a series of payoffs over time. Each payoff depends

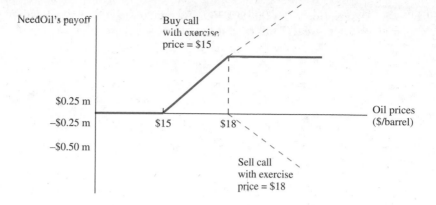

FIGURE 13–9

NeedOil's desired payoff from a derivative contract given its belief that oil prices will not rise above $18

on the difference between the market price of the underlying asset and a predetermined price.

To illustrate a swap contract, we will again use the example of NeedOil. In this example, NeedOil plans to purchase oil every six months for the next two years and it wants protection against high oil prices at each date. It therefore purchases a swap contract from SWAPCO with the payoffs described in Table 13–4. Notice that at each date, the payoff to NeedOil is just like the payoff from buying a forward contract. Thus, swap contracts can be viewed as a series of forward contracts.

The term "swap" is used because these transactions allow parties to reduce risk by swapping payments. Without hedging, NeedOil's payments for oil every six months would be uncertain; the payment would equal 250,000 times the price of oil at that time (P_t). By transacting with SWAPCO, NeedOil swaps its uncertain payment for oil for a certain oil payment. Specifically, SWAPCO gives NeedOil the funds needed to make its uncertain oil payment (250,000 times P_t) and NeedOil gives SWAPCO $15 times 250,000. By swapping its uncertain payments with certain payments, NeedOil reduces its risk.

In this example, the difference between the price of oil at a given date and $15 is always multiplied by 250,000. This is a common feature of swap contracts (and many other derivative contracts)—the difference between two prices is mul-

TABLE 13–4   Description of an Oil Swap Contract between NeedOil and SWAPCO
(P_t = Price of oil at time t)

	6 Months	*12 Months*	*18 Months*	*24 Months*
Payoff to NeedOil	$(P_{6\ months} - \$15) \times$ 250,000	$(P_{1\ year} - \$15) \times$ 250,000	$(P_{18\ months} - \$15) \times$ 250,000	$(P_{2\ years} - \$15) \times$ 250,000
Payoff to SWAPCO	$(\$15 - P_{6\ months}) \times$ 250,000	$(\$15 - P_{1\ year}) \times$ 250,000	$(\$15 - P_{18\ months}) \times$ 250,000	$(\$15 - P_{2\ years}) \times$ 250,000

TABLE 13–5   Description of an Interest Rate Swap Contract between NeedOil and SWAPCO
(r_t = **One-year T-bill rate at time** t)

	6 Months	12 Months	18 Months	24 Months
Payoff to NeedOil	$(r_{6\ months} - 5\%) \times$ $1 million	$(r_{1\ year} - 5\%) \times$ $1 million	$(r_{18\ months} - 5\%) \times$ $1 million	$(r_{2\ years} - 5\%) \times$ $1 million
Payoff to SWAPCO	$(5\% - r_{6\ months}) \times$ $1 million	$(5\% - r_{1\ year}) \times$ $1 million	$(5\% - r_{18\ months}) \times$ $1 million	$(5\% - r_{2\ years}) \times$ $1 million

tiplied by some number, called the *notional principal* (in this case 250,000), to determine the dollar payoff. While notional principal often is used to measure the value of outstanding swap contracts, notional principal usually is a flawed measure of how much money the parties could potentially gain or lose because potential swap payments depend on the units used for quoting prices and the volatility of prices, as well as the notional principal.

For example, if oil prices could vary between $13 and $17 during the time period covered by NeedOil's swap contract, then the payments made by NeedOil could vary between –$500,000 and $500,000. In this particular case, the notional principal understates the potential gain or loss in any given six-month period. For other types of swaps, like interest rate swaps, the notional principal greatly overstates the amount of money at risk. Table 13–5 gives an example of an interest rate swap. Here, the notional principal is $1 million and SWAPCO pays NeedOil the prevailing one-year T-bill rate minus 5 percent. For example, if the one-year T-bill rate in 12 months equals 6 percent, then SWAPCO pays NeedOil 1 percent times $1 million, or $10,000. If the one-year T-bill rate in two years equals 4.5 percent, then NeedOil pays SWAPCO 0.5 percent times $1 million, or $5,000. Even though the notional principal is $1 million, the likely payments are only a fraction of the notional principal. Thus, for interest rate swaps, the notional principal greatly overstates the amount of money at risk.

13.5 Comparison of Derivative and Insurance Contracts

We hope that you noticed that the payoff diagrams illustrated in the previous section have similarities to the diagrams in Chapter 11 describing features of insurance contracts.[5] Indeed, an insurance contract can be viewed as a derivative contract where the underlying asset is the value of losses experienced by the insured.

---

[5] As noted earlier, the exposure diagrams in this chapter have profits on the vertical axis, but the exposure diagrams describing insurance contracts in Chapter 11 have costs on the vertical axis.

While there are similarities between derivatives and insurance contracts, there are also important differences. In particular, the types of risk that tend to be hedged using derivative contracts have different characteristics from the risks that tend to be hedged using insurance contracts. As a consequence, insurance and derivative contracts generally differ with regard to transaction costs, basis risk, and liquidity.

Market Prices versus Specific Losses

Derivative contracts usually are used to hedge risk arising from unexpected changes in market prices; on the other hand, insurance contracts tend to hedge risk arising from losses specific to the insured. Contracts based on market prices are likely to be useful to many firms. For example, an option on oil prices or a forward contract on oil prices could be of interest to hundreds of companies that use or produce oil. In contrast, a contract derived from the liability or property losses of NeedOil often will be of interest to only one firm—NeedOil.

Basis Risk and Extent of Risk Reduction

An advantage of contracts based on firm-specific factors as opposed to market prices is less basis risk. Recall that basis risk can be viewed as uncertainty about the effectiveness of a hedge. When an insurance contract is based on a firm's liability losses, there is little uncertainty about the quality of the hedge—that is, if the firm experiences $10 million in insured losses, then it will be reimbursed for $10 million from the insurer (ignoring insurer insolvency). In contrast, with a derivative contract, a firm may experience a drop in profits of $3 million due to higher oil prices and the derivative contract used to hedge this risk may have a payoff of only $2 million because of basis risk. In short, since derivative contracts are not based on firm-specific outcomes, there is greater basis risk than with insurance contracts.[6]

Contracting Costs

The contracting costs for insurance tend to be higher than those for derivatives. This difference arises in part because of greater moral hazard and adverse selection problems with insurance and because of greater capital costs.

Moral Hazard and Adverse Selection.   When the underlying asset is a market price or an aggregate index (as is true with most derivative contracts), individual firms generally cannot influence the payoffs on the derivative contracts. For most

---

[6] Note, however, that more complete coverage and thus lower risk with insurance increase moral hazard. For this reason and others (administrative costs and adverse selection) insurance contracts almost always provide less-than-complete coverage (see Chapter 8), reducing the effectiveness of risk reduction.

insurance contracts, however, the value of the underlying asset is the loss experienced by the insured firm, which often is influenced indirectly, if not directly, by the actions of the insured party. Consequently, moral hazard problems tend to be more severe with insurance contracts. In addition, firms often have private information about expected losses, which creates adverse selection problems from the insurer's perspective. The moral hazard and adverse selection problems associated with contracts based on individual firm losses imply that considerable investigation and monitoring costs must be incurred when selling such contracts. In contrast, when contracts are based on market prices, which are outside of the influence of individual firms, fewer investigative and monitoring costs need to be incurred.

Capital Costs.   When market prices change, there tend to be winners and losers: Some firms increase in value and other firms decrease in value. Stated differently, situations often arise where firm values are negatively correlated. In this case, two firms can construct a derivative contract that will neutralize the effect of a price change on each firm's value. For example, an oil user can hedge by buying an oil forward contract and an oil producer can hedge by selling the same oil forward contract. Derivative markets therefore can bring the oil user and the oil producer together and create a contract that reduces price risk for both, without the two parties having to physically trade oil.

In contrast, the property and liability losses experienced by one firm typically do not trigger a simultaneous gain by another firm. That is, these types of losses tend to be independent (or even positively correlated) across firms. Consequently, substantial reduction in property and liability risks is achieved through diversification (i.e., by selling policies to many different policyholders). The marketing and underwriting costs associated with achieving diversification tend to be higher than the costs of matching two parties with negatively correlated exposures.

Moreover, because insurers hold capital to ensure that they will be able to perform their contractual promises (pay claims) to policyholders, the cost of holding this capital is an additional cost of insurance contracts. In contrast, once two parties with negatively correlated exposures have been identified, a comparatively small amount of capital is needed to ensure contractual performance on a derivative contract that hedges the risk of both parties. The reason is that the derivative contract will require a payment only when the firm's cash flows otherwise would be high. For example, an oil user who has purchased an oil forward contract will have to pay the seller of the forward contract (the oil producer) when oil prices are low, which is when the oil user has relatively high cash flows from operations. Conversely, the oil producer will have to pay the oil user when oil prices are high, which is when the oil producer has relatively high cash flows. Provided derivative contracts are used to hedge, the contractual parties should need comparatively little capital to bond their performance under the derivative contract. Insurers, on the other hand, typically hold considerable capital to bond their performance to policyholders.

Liquidity

Because of the greater number of parties who are potentially affected by market prices and because of lower transaction costs, derivative contracts tend to have greater liquidity than insurance contracts. In a **liquid market,** someone can sell or buy an asset quickly with little price concession. In contrast, in an illiquid market, someone trying to sell an asset may either have to wait to find a buyer who will pay the asking price or accept a much lower price in order to sell the asset quickly. The greater liquidity of derivative contracts implies that a firm can quickly establish a hedge using derivatives and also quickly remove a hedge at relatively lower cost. In contrast, modifying insurance contracts to provide more or less coverage can take a considerable amount of time and expense.

Summary

Table 13–6 summarizes the generalizations made in this section concerning the differences between derivative and insurance contracts. Of course, there are exceptions to each of the generalizations listed in the table. Also, in recent years, there have been attempts to introduce derivative contracts on risks that traditionally have been handled through insurance and reinsurance contracts. For example, in 1994, the Chicago Board of Trade introduced option contracts based on insured losses from catastrophes.

13.6 Markets for Derivatives

Over-the-counter versus Exchange-traded Derivatives

Earlier we mentioned that the payoffs from forward and futures contracts are similar. One difference in the two contracts is that forward contracts are traded in the over-the-counter (OTC) market and futures contracts are traded at exchanges

TABLE 13–6   Differences between Insurance and Derivative Contracts

Characteristics	*Derivative Contracts*	*Insurance Contracts*
Type of risk hedged	Market-price risk	Firm-specific risk
Number of firms potentially interested in a specific contract	Many	One (or few)
Basis risk	High	Low
Contracting costs (due to moral hazard, adverse selection, and bonding contractual performance)	Low	High
Liquidity (due to greater number of firms potentially interested in a particular contract and contracting costs)	High	Low

———

Box 13–2

Exchanges Try to Win More of Options Pie

As investor interest in trading stock options soars and the stock market itself surges to new heights, options exchanges are battling for a bigger share of the boom.

Their competitor: the privately negotiated, or over-the-counter derivative market.

Last month, the Chicago Board Options Exchange and the American Stock Exchange began offering custom-tailored options on a number of widely held and heavily traded stocks. Yesterday, the Philadelphia Stock Exchange announced it is awaiting Securities and Exchange Commission approval for a similar move. These "flex" options are like other options in that they give the investor, in return for a small premium payment, the right to buy or sell the underlying stock at a specified price at or before a certain date in the future.

But unlike other, standardized, exchange-traded stock options, the new flex products give the holders the freedom to pick a specific expiration date as well as offering them some leeway in setting the strike price. Until now, the pension funds and mutual funds that are the natural customers for these products would have had to turn to dealers to structure customized, over-the-counter derivatives to obtain a similar degree of flexibility.

"They're declaring war on the structured derivatives market," says Michael Schwartz, chief options strategist at Oppenheimer & Co. in New York. "There's a big effort under way to bring back to the exchange floor the kind of products that are now being done by the over-the-counter equity derivatives dealers."

Source: Suzanne McGee, "Exchanges Try to Win More of Options Pie," *The Wall Street Journal,* November 20, 1996.

like the Chicago Board of Trade. Call and put option contracts trade on exchanges as well as in the over-the-counter market. Swap contracts are traded over-the-counter.

An **over-the-counter (OTC) derivative** contract resembles a privately negotiated contract between two firms. For example, if NeedOil wanted to purchase an option contract to hedge its oil price risk, NeedOil could contact a financial institution in the OTC market, which could then tailor a contract to NeedOil's hedging needs. **Exchange-traded derivatives** are standardized contracts with the terms established by the exchanges. Since specific details are not subject to negotiation, contracting costs tend to be lower with exchange-traded derivatives than with OTC derivatives. While exchanges try to create standardized contracts that appeal to many participants, the standardization often implies that exchange-traded derivatives have greater basis risk than OTC derivatives.[7] As Box 13–2 illustrates, OTC derivatives and exchange-traded derivatives actively compete with each other. This competition has led exchanges to introduce more flexible derivative terms.

———

[7] The ability to tailor contracts to individual hedging needs makes OTC derivatives similar to insurance and reinsurance contracts.

Initially, financial institutions operating in the OTC market acted as *brokers* who would identify another firm that would transact with a party such as Need-Oil. Today, financial institutions operate more like *dealers,* taking positions directly with each firm. Thus, NeedOil could buy the option directly from the financial institution. Having sold a call option, the dealer would be exposed to oil price risk and thus the dealer probably would try to hedge this risk either by engaging in an offsetting transaction with someone else in the OTC market or by using exchange-traded options and futures contracts.

In addition to the ability to tailor contracts, there are other differences between the OTC and exchange markets. One difference is liquidity, the ability to buy or sell without making a large price concession. When the OTC market creates a contract that is tailored to one participant's needs, this contract tends to be illiquid. In contrast, if the contract were a standardized exchange-traded futures contract, there would likely be more liquidity. The greater liquidity arises in part because the standardized exchange contracts attract many traders.

The greater liquidity also is due in part to the method of ensuring that the parties who trade derivatives uphold their agreements. OTC contracts are bilateral contracts. That is, a buyer and seller are specified on the contract and if one party cannot fulfill its part of the contract, the other party becomes a creditor. As a result, when trading OTC contracts, firms assess the default risk (or credit risk) of the parties with whom they transact. In addition, if a firm wishes to reverse its position, the firm must negotiate with the specific counterparty to the contract. These features make OTC contracts less liquid.

Default risk is handled differently with exchange-traded contracts. When taking a futures position, a trader must post a performance bond, called a **margin.** The bond equals some percentage of the value of the contracts and must be posted either in the form of cash, letters of credit, or government bonds. The purpose of the bond is to ensure the solvency of the trader over the coming day of trading. Thus, at the end of each day, the margin account is monitored to see if there are sufficient funds to ensure solvency over the subsequent day.

As an example, suppose that the required margin is always 20 percent of the value of the contract and that Ms. Weiss takes a long position in (buys) one contract when the futures price equals $1,000. Then, Ms. Weiss must post margin equal to $200. Now suppose that over the course of the following day, the futures price falls to $900. Ms. Weiss has lost $100 ($1,000 – $900), which is subtracted from her margin account, leaving only $100. Since Ms. Weiss's position now is worth $900, she needs to have margin equal to $180 (20% of $900). Consequently, Ms. Weiss must add $80 to the margin account. If she does not add this amount, then her position will be closed; that is, she will have to take an offsetting short position in (sell) one contract.

The other important difference between OTC markets and exchange markets is that exchanges have a clearinghouse that acts as an intermediary in every transaction. As stated above, with an OTC contract, the buyer knows the identity of the seller. With exchange-traded contracts, a buyer is not matched with a particular seller. Instead, each transaction is with the clearinghouse. The number of contracts purchased by the clearinghouse must always equal the number that it has sold, but buyers and sellers are not explicitly matched. Thus, if a trader wants to reverse a position (sell the derivative the trader had previously purchased or buy the derivative contract the trader had previously sold), a specific counterparty does not have to be notified. Any counterparty willing to take the other side of the transaction may be used. The clearinghouse, along with the daily settlement and margin system for ensuring performance, helps create a liquid market.

Common Risks That Are Hedged with Derivatives

Although OTC contracts can be tailored to meet the specific hedging needs of individual firms, the types of risk that are most often hedged with derivatives are: (1) foreign exchange rates, (2) interest rates, (3) commodity prices, and (4) equity prices.

Foreign Exchange Derivatives.   With the increasing amount of trade among foreign countries and the increased volatility in exchange rates due to the breakdown in 1973 of the previous system of fixed foreign exchange rates, firms have become more interested in hedging against changes in foreign exchange rates. Most multinational companies utilize derivatives to manage their foreign exchange exposures. The most commonly used currency derivatives are swap contracts, which had notional principal of over $2.5 trillion in 1996.

Interest Rate Derivatives.   Several factors have contributed to the use of interest rate derivatives to hedge against changes in value due to interest rate changes. One factor is the high level and volatility of interest rates in the 1970s and 1980s, which resulted from high levels of expected inflation as well as changes in expected inflation. Also, in 1979 the Federal Reserve changed its policy of trying to stabilize interest rates directly and instead started targeting monetary aggregates. The consequence of this change in policy was to increase interest rate volatility substantially. Interest rate futures, options, and swaps are frequently used to hedge interest rate risk. The notional principal in 1996 of interest rate derivatives was close to $25 trillion.

Commodity Derivatives.   Derivative contracts on agricultural commodities have existed for a long time. For example, the Chicago Board of Trade has traded futures contracts since 1865, and forwards and options on agricultural products date back several centuries. Users and producers of commodities such as metals and oil also frequently trade both OTC and exchange-traded derivatives. The use of electricity derivatives also has grown significantly in recent years due in part to deregulation of the industry.

Equity Derivatives.   Equity derivatives are contracts derived from stock market indexes like the Standard and Poor's 500. Futures contracts exist that are based on US stock market indexes and on foreign stock market indexes, such as the Nikkei index for the Japanese stock market. In addition, options have traded on individual stocks for some time. The notional principal on futures and options in 1996 equaled about $480 million.

13.7 Reducing Risk through Internal Diversification

We conclude this chapter by briefly discussing another method that commonly reduces risk for many businesses: diversification of operations or internal diversification. The extent to which firms diversify their operations can reduce their demand for insurance and for hedging using derivatives. Firms diversify their operations by acquiring or investing in other firms or by adopting new projects whose cash flows are not perfectly correlated with the firm's other cash flows.

While modern acquisitions usually are not undertaken solely for the purpose of diversification, the benefits of risk reduction that were identified in Chapter 9 would apply in most cases. More generally, diversification often allows firms to reduce the variability of cash flows apart from insurance and hedging arrangements. A key issue is whether internal diversification increases firm value or is redundant or even harmful given (1) the ability of shareholders to diversify their individual portfolios and (2) the costs of diversification at the firm level.

To illustrate the benefits and costs of internal diversification, consider Sicherman Enterprises, a firm that makes golf clubs and has total value equal to $10 million. Sicherman is considering the acquisition of a sports clothing firm valued at $5 million. Sicherman's managers reason that some synergy will take place as a result of the ability to market both golf clubs and sportswear. **Synergy** exists when the combination of the parts has greater value than the sum of the individual values. In this case, Sicherman's managers believe that the marketing synergies will create $1 million in value. That is, by purchasing the sportswear firm, Sicherman's total firm value will increase to $16 million—$5 million from the existing value of the sportswear firm plus $1 million in value created by marketing synergies.

Another potential source of synergy is the benefit from reducing firm risk. Since the cash flows from producing and selling golf clubs are not perfectly correlated with the cash flows from producing and selling sports clothing, the acquisition will reduce the variability of Sicherman's cash flows. Intuitively, in situations where golf clubs sell poorly, there is a chance that clothing sales will be better than expected. This risk reduction could lower expected financial distress costs and/or expected tax payments (see Chapter 9).

Diversification at the firm level is not costless. First, considerable transaction costs are incurred in acquiring other companies (or in starting new operations). Perhaps more importantly, there are potential ongoing costs when a firm becomes involved in multiple activities. As a firm branches into other activities, managers may become less efficient, important information may not be as readily communicated internally, and agency costs may increase. These costs of internal diversification, known as *diseconomies of scope,* often will dominate the benefits from any risk reduction, especially in the case where firms branch into unrelated activities. For example, Sicherman might be able to achieve superior diversification if it acquires a firm that specializes in the sale of women's lingerie. But it is quite possible that the increased costs associated with managing both golf club production and underwear production would outweigh any benefit of reduced variability in its cash flows.

During the 1960s, firms tended to diversify and many conglomerates were formed. In recent years, however, the trend appears to be in the opposite direction. Managers and management consultants tend to believe that the managerial inefficiencies associated with large conglomerates dominate the synergies that can be created. As a consequence, there is greater emphasis on specializing in a firm's core competencies (i.e., firms are identifying what they do best and focusing their efforts on that activity). One other potential cost of attempting to diversify internally is that in some cases expanding into multiple activities can actually increase the risk of large losses. We will discuss this possibility, and how it can be mitigated through the use of subsidiary corporations, in Chapter 17.

13.8 Summary

- Derivative contracts are contracts with payoffs derived from the value of some other asset or index, called the underlying asset. The basic types of derivative contracts are: call options, put options, and forward (futures) contracts. Option contracts have asymmetric payoffs and forward (futures) contracts have symmetric payoffs as a function of the underlying asset. Swap contracts are equivalent to a series of forward contracts.

- By purchasing a call option on an underlying asset that is positively correlated with a firm's costs (and thus negatively correlated with profits, such as oil in the NeedOil example), a firm can hedge against losses from higher-than-expected costs. That is, the call option provides cash when the costs otherwise would be high (profits would be low). The purchase of the call option requires the firm to pay an up-front premium to the seller of the call option (similar to an insurance premium). Alternatively, a firm can "purchase" a forward (futures) contract on the underlying asset, in which case no up-front premium is required. Instead, the firm agrees to pay the seller of the forward contract if the underlying asset's price is low.

- By purchasing a put option on an underlying asset that is positively correlated with a firm's revenue (and thus positively correlated with profits), a firm can hedge against losses from lower-than-expected revenue. That is, the put option provides cash when the firm's revenue and profits otherwise would be low. Alternatively, a firm can "sell" a forward (futures) contract on the underlying asset, in which case the firm agrees to pay the buyer of the forward contract if the underlying asset's price is high.

- The determinants of call and put option prices are: (1) the current price of the underlying asset, (2) the exercise price of the option, (3) the time to expiration, (4) the volatility of the rate of return of the underlying asset, and (5) the risk-free rate of interest.

- The determinants of forward (futures) prices include: (1) the current price of the underlying asset, (2) the time to expiration, (3) the risk-free rate of interest, and (4) the cost of storing and insuring the underlying asset.

- Basis risk refers to the uncertainty associated with whether a particular derivative contract will be an effective hedge. In practice, most derivative contracts expose hedgers to some basis risk (i.e., the hedge does not work perfectly).

- The payoffs of derivative contracts are based on (derived from) the market prices of assets and indexes. Consequently, derivative contracts tend to be more liquid and subject to less moral hazard and adverse selection problems compared to insurance contracts. Capital costs associated with ensuring contractual performance tend to be lower with derivative contracts because the contracting parties' cash flows often are negatively correlated.

- The types of risk most commonly hedged with derivatives are: (1) foreign exchange risk, (2) interest rate risk, (3) commodity price risk, and (4) equity value risk.

- Internal diversification occurs when a firm engages in multiple activities. One of the benefits of internal diversification is the reduction in the variance of the firm's cash flows. The costs of internal diversification include greater agency costs and less efficient allocation of resources within the firm.

Key Terms

derivative contract   301
underlying asset   301
call option contract   301
exercise price   301
option price   301
put option contract   302
cash settled contracts   303
physical delivery   303
basis risk   304
forward contract   309

futures contract   309
forward price   309
futures price   309
cost of carry relationship   311
swap contracts   312
liquid market   317
over-the-counter (OTC) derivative   318
exchange-traded derivatives   311
margin   319
synergy   321

Questions and Problems

1. Draw an exposure diagram to illustrate a firm's exposure to interest rate risk if the firm is going to borrow $10 million six months from today. Assume the loan will be a one-year loan with all interest paid at the end of the year. Graph the relation between the firm's interest costs and interest rates. Also graph the relation between the firm's profit and interest rates assuming that higher interest costs cannot be passed on to consumers.

2. Draw an exposure diagram to illustrate the relationship between a firm's costs and the exchange rate between US dollars and British pounds if the firm plans to purchase goods from a British firm one year from today. Assume that the transaction is denominated in pounds, but that the firm is concerned about its costs in dollars. Also draw an exposure diagram to illustrate the relationship between a firm's profit and the exchange rate between US dollars and British pounds.

3. Draw an exposure diagram to illustrate the relationship between a gold mining firm's profit and the price of gold in three months.

4. Would a call option or a put option hedge the exposure of the firms described in problems 1, 2, and 3?

5. Would a long (buy) or a short (sell) forward position hedge the exposure of the firms described in problems 1, 2, and 3?

6. What is the difference between a forward contract and a swap contract?

7. Fill in the table below describing the payoffs on an interest rate swap contract under each of the scenarios for interest rates. Assume that under the terms of the swap, Strickler Inc. agrees to pay the swap dealer the six-month T-bill rate minus 4 percent at the end of each of the next three six-month periods and that the notional principal equals $2 million.

	6 Months	12 Months	18 Months
Six-month T-bill rate	3%	4%	4.5%
Payoff to Strickler			

8. What combination of derivatives would yield the following payoff (ignore the premiums paid for the options)?

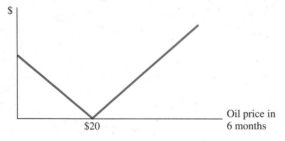

9. What combination of derivatives would yield the following payoff (ignore the premiums paid for the options)?

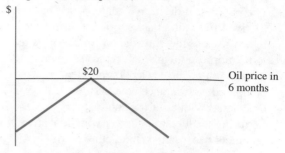

10. What combination of derivatives would yield the following payoff (ignore the premiums paid for the options)?

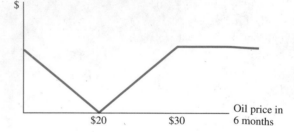

References

Smith, Clifford W., Jr.; and Charles Smithson. *Managing Financial Price Risk: A Guide to Derivative Products, Financial Engineering, and Value Maximization.* Burr Ridge, IL: Irwin Professional Publishing, 1995. (*Describes and analyzes how derivatives are used for hedging and also provides details on pricing models for options, forwards, futures, and swap contracts.*)

Stoll, Hans; and Robert Whaley. *Futures and Options: Theory and Applications.* Cincinnati, OH: South-Western College Publishing, 1993. (*Describes and analyzes how derivatives are used for hedging and also provides details on derivative pricing models.*)

Answers to Concept Checks

1.

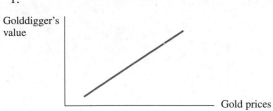

2.

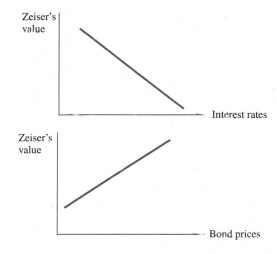

3. Golddigger would purchase a put option with the underlying asset being gold.

4. Zeiser would purchase a call option with the underlying asset being interest rates. Alternatively, because bond prices and interest rates are inversely related, Zeiser could purchase a put option with the underlying asset being bonds (e.g., US Treasury bonds).

PART IV

Legal Liability and Worker Injury Risk

Legal Liability for Injuries

Chapter Objectives

- Provide background on the general structure of US law.
- Describe basic legal liability rules and procedures, including negligence law.
- Describe the economic functions of the legal liability system.
- Explain the circumstances in which the assignment of legal liability affects safety incentives.
- Discuss the relationship between liability law and safety regulation.
- Briefly introduce various proposals for tort reform.

14.1 Some Background on the Law

The variety and potential magnitude of business liability exposures have increased tremendously in the past 30 years. Firms now are subject to liability risk in almost every aspect of their operations. For example, liability can arise from (1) employment practices (in addition to employer responsibility for paying workers' compensation benefits to injured workers), (2) products sold to consumers, (3) the disposal of waste or use of toxic chemicals, and (4) the actions of corporate boards of directors. The evolution of the US liability system has been subject to substantial controversy and debate. This chapter provides an introduction to the legal liability system that is necessary to understand issues related to legal liability risk. The subsequent three chapters examine specific types of liability (or responsibility for harm), including available insurance coverage and key management and public policy issues.

Table 14–1 summarizes the two main types of law: (1) common law, and (2) statutory law. **Common law** refers to the law that has evolved over time as a result of previous court decisions; it has not been enacted by a legislative body. The

TABLE 14–1   Sources and Branches of Law

Source of Law

Common law	Evolved over time through court decisions.
Statutory law	Enacted by government bodies.

Branches of Law

Criminal law	Applies to acts against the state.
Civil law	Applies to acts against other individuals or entities.
Contract law	Applies when a contract governs the relationship between the parties in the dispute.
Tort law	Applies when a contract does not govern the relationship between the parties in the dispute.

rule of precedent, which states that a court generally should follow the logic and rulings of prior court decisions, is the source of common law. In contrast, **statutory law** refers to laws that have been passed by a legislative body, such as a state legislature or the US Congress, and then signed into law by the executive branch (a governor or president). Although there are important exceptions, much legal liability is based on common law.

As shown in Table 14–1, law also can be categorized as either criminal or civil. **Criminal law,** which is usually the result of statutes, covers acts against the state (an individual state or local government, or the federal government). For example, since murder is contrary to the public interest, it is considered to be an act against the state and is therefore a violation of criminal law. In contrast, **civil law** deals with acts that cause losses to another individual, but for which the state (the public at large) has a less direct interest. There are in turn two branches of civil law: contract law and tort law. **Contract law** interprets contractual provisions and resolves disputes between contractual parties, such as when one party is harmed as a result of another party's failure to fulfill its contractual obligations. Parties found liable for breach of contract must pay monetary damages and, in some instances, perform their obligations under the contract. **Tort law** deals with wrongs done to someone where a contract does not govern the interaction that caused the harm. Parties held liable for injuries under tort law must pay the injured party monetary damages. For example, if an automobile hits and harms a pedestrian, the driver and the pedestrian do not have a contract to help them determine how the interaction will be handled; therefore, tort law handles the issue of who is responsible for the damages. In contrast, if an automobile dealer fails to deliver a car to a buyer at an agreed upon date and as a result the buyer suffers monetary losses, the issue of who is responsible for the damages is handled under contract law. The focus of this chapter is tort law. Unless otherwise noted, the term *liability* refers to tort liability.

14.2 Overview of Tort Liability Rules and Procedures

There are various ways of assigning liability for losses that arise from the interaction among parties who do not have contractual relations. As an example, consider the losses (medical costs) suffered by a pedestrian who has been hit by an automobile. The law could make the pedestrian responsible for his or her own losses regardless of the circumstances of an accident. Alternatively, the law could make the driver responsible for the pedestrian's losses regardless of the circumstances of the accident. Or an intermediate approach could be taken where the law examines the circumstances of the accident and decides who should be responsible for the pedestrian's medical expenses. The law also must allocate responsibility for the other potential losses suffered by the pedestrian, such as lost wages, mental anguish, and the like, as well as decide who is responsible for the driver's losses (if any were suffered).

When the law assigns liability for a general type of loss, the law is essentially allocating risk. For example, a rule that always makes the driver liable for all losses suffered in pedestrian accidents places the risk of such accidents on drivers and removes this risk from pedestrians. Drivers, in essence, are forced to insure all pedestrians. (The driver could in turn transfer this risk to an insurance company.) Thus, many of the tools and concepts that have been discussed earlier in this book are relevant for understanding the effects of alternative liability rules.

Basic Tort Liability Rules

Liability for harm to another person varies depending on the context. For example, liability arising from automobile accidents generally differs from liability arising from product injuries. This section provides an overview of the alternative methods of assigning liability. Section 14.3 elaborates on liability arising from negligence. Chapter 15 then elaborates on tort liability in specific situations (products, environmental, and corporate directors and officers' liability). As summarized in Table 14–2, liability of the party who "caused" the accident, who is known as the *tortfeasor,* can range from immunity from liability to always being held liable.[1]

No Liability.   While its incidence has decreased substantially over time, some institutions and some professions are immune from liability for certain types of actions. For example, charitable institutions and government entities sometimes are at least partially immune from being liable for losses suffered by peo-

---

[1] This description of tort liability omits intentional torts, such as libel and slander, invasion of privacy, copyright or trademark infringement, assault, and false imprisonment, where the action by the tortfeasor is intentional. The legal rules generally are different for each type of intentional tort. Liability for intentional torts that do not involve intentional harm or damage often is insurable.

TABLE 14–2   Brief Description of the Range of Alternative Tort Liability Rules

	Description	*Example*
No liability	Defendant cannot be held liable.	Charitable institutions in some cases.
Negligence	Defendant is liable if found negligent, but might be able to avoid liability using certain defenses.	Liability for damages caused by automobile accidents.
Strict liability	Defendant is liable even if not negligent, but might be able to avoid liability using certain defenses.	Liability of firms for damages resulting from defective products.
Absolute liability	Defendant is always liable; no defenses are available if the defendant caused the injury.	Liability for damages caused by the use of dynamite.

ple who use the institution's services. Another example would be the immunity from liability of foreign diplomats who harm US citizens while in the United States. When one party is immune from liability, the law implicitly makes other parties who interact with the immune party liable for their own losses. Perhaps more important for our purposes, the concept of no liability for harm is useful in explaining the rationale for alternative liability rules and the safety effects of these rules (see section 14.4).

Liability for Negligence.   A common way of assigning liability is to make one party liable for someone else's losses if the former party is negligent. The burden of proof under a **negligence rule** usually is on the plaintiff; that is, the plaintiff must prove that the defendant was negligent. (The conditions to prove negligence are discussed in the next section of this chapter.) An exception is the *res ipsa loquitor* rule ("the thing speaks for itself"), which switches the burden of proof to the defendant when the nature of the injury makes it highly improbable that the injury could have occurred without the defendant's negligence (e.g., a surgeon leaves a scalpel in the patient). A negligence standard is used to some degree in all states for determining liability for losses suffered from automobile accidents, and it is the standard used for medical malpractice. A negligence standard also is used in many business liability cases, including many product injury cases. As you will learn in more detail in the next chapter, persons injured by products commonly bring suits under the doctrine of strict liability as well, which we briefly explain in this chapter, and they sometimes can sue for breach of contract.

Strict Liability.   Under a **strict liability** standard, the defendant does not have to be negligent to be liable for the plaintiff's losses. As noted, strict liability often is applied in products liability cases. In these cases, the plaintiff generally has to show that the design, production, or warnings associated with the product were defective and unreasonably dangerous and that the defect caused the injury (see Chapter 15). But the plaintiff does not need to show that the product's defect was due to the manufacturer's negligence.

Absolute Liability.   According to the doctrine of **absolute liability,** the defendant is liable for the plaintiff's losses as long as the plaintiff can establish that the defendant's action caused the loss. The defendant does not have to be negligent, and the defendant has no defenses. Absolute liability traditionally has been limited to tort cases involving ultradangerous activities. For example, the common law applies absolute liability for injuries arising out of blasting operations and the use of explosives. Thus, if your parents' favorite and very expensive glass figurine topples from a shelf and crumbles when a road construction company blasts through rock three miles away, your parents can recover damages under the doctrine of absolute liability. They need only prove that the blast caused the loss, as opposed to mischievous behavior by the family cat. Similarly, if your neighbor's pet cheetah (there also are statutory laws against this sort of thing in most towns) jumps the fence and runs you down despite your being the fastest member of the track team, you or your family would be able to recover damages from your neighbor without having to prove negligence. Of considerably greater importance and seriousness, the concept of absolute liability (with restrictions on the types of damages that must be paid) provides the basis for workers' compensation laws governing workplace injuries, which we discuss in Chapter 16.

Damages

Tort liability law allows injured parties to recover damages for losses caused by tortfeasors. Courts can award two broad types of damages: compensatory damages and punitive damages.

Compensatory Damages.   As the name implies, **compensatory damages** are designed to compensate injured parties for loss. There are in turn two main types of compensatory damages: (1) special damages, and (2) general damages. **Special damages** refer to compensation to the plaintiff for monetary losses, such as medical expenses, lost wages, and the value of lost services from bodily injury, and repair/replacement costs and loss of use for property damage. Estimation of special damages can be complex; for example, it often is necessary to estimate the present value of future wage losses and medical expenses over many years.

General damages refer to compensation for nonmonetary losses, such as pain and suffering and loss of consortium with an injured or deceased spouse, and emotional distress from the death of a spouse or family member. These types of losses are very difficult to measure accurately. The courts and out-of-court settlements often rely on rules of thumb that relate general damages to special damages for certain types of injuries. For example, a rule of thumb for auto accidents might be to set general damages equal to two times special damages. These informal benchmarks can then be modified in view of the particular or unique circumstances in a case. Depending on the type of case, empirical studies of damages suggest that general damages commonly represent between one-half and three-fourths of total compensatory damages. The ultimate authority for determining general damages rests with the judge or with the jury in a jury trial. The amount of general damages that juries can be expected to award if a case goes to trial has a major effect on out-of-court settlements.

Punitive Damages.   Damages paid to the plaintiff that are not designed to compensate for the plaintiff's losses but which instead are meant to punish the defendant for the actions that led to the injury and to deter future actions are known as **punitive damages.** Punitive damages in principle are reserved for situations where the defendant recklessly or willfully disregarded the risk of harm to the plaintiff. While punitive damages are awarded in a small fraction of cases, punitive damage awards can be very large and sometimes vastly exceed the plaintiff's losses and compensatory damages.

In principle, the amount of punitive damages awarded reflects the goal of punishing the defendant and thus depends on the nature of the defendant's conduct and the severity of the risk of harm to the plaintiff. As we discuss in section 14.8, punitive damages have been highly controversial in recent years. Some observers argue that decisions to award punitive damages and the amounts awarded often reflect arbitrary and capricious behavior by juries. A number of cases brought before the US Supreme Court have invited the court to impose meaningful guidelines for punitive damages. To date these efforts have not been successful.

Joint and Several Liability

Often situations arise in which the actions of multiple parties combine to cause loss. For example, the family of a teenager who purchased computer cleaner at a store, sniffed it and got high, and then drove his car into a lake and drowned could name the producer of the computer cleaner, the store that sold the cleaner, and the contractor who designed the road as defendants (a situation similar to this actually happened in 1996—also see Box 14–1 later in this chapter). Under the doctrine of **joint and several liability,** each defendant can be held responsible for the entire damage.

You should note, however, that the plaintiff nevertheless can only recover damages once. If multiple parties are held liable under the doctrine of joint and several liability, the court might instruct one party to pay the plaintiff the entire amount of damages. The division of damages among the liable parties is then determined in subsequent negotiations or litigation between the liable parties. Similarly, if the plaintiff only sues and recovers from one defendant, this defendant may be able to seek recovery from other parties that were involved in causing the loss. The legal rules used in proceedings for determining the ultimate division of the cost of damages among multiple parties that cause a loss are extremely complex.

An important feature of joint and several liability is that if some parties are unable to pay, the full burden of paying damages will fall on other parties. As we discuss in Chapter 15, an important example is joint and several liability for environmental damages, which sometimes can make firms that contributed little to environmental damage responsible for the entire cleanup costs. Joint and several liability also provides incentives for plaintiffs to seek defendants with "deep pockets" (i.e., to name as defendants parties that have substantial assets or insurance to pay damages even if the party's role in causing the injury was minor compared to other parties with less ability to pay).

14.3 Liability from Negligence

Elements of Negligence

In most circumstances, four conditions must be satisfied to prove negligence: (1) legal duty by the defendant, (2) breach of duty, (3) proximate cause, and (4) injury to plaintiff.

Legal Duty.   In order to be held liable for negligence, the defendant must have had a duty to behave so as to protect other parties from harm. For example, a driver has a duty to stop at a stop sign and otherwise drive in a reasonably safe manner. In general, people and businesses have a duty to protect from injury those parties with whom they reasonably can be expected to come into contact. The law, however, usually does not impose a positive duty to come to the assistance of people who may be harmed by others or who may already be hurt.

Breach of Duty.   Assuming a legal duty, the defendant must have breached this duty by failing to exercise the required standard of care for the protection of the other party. In many nonbusiness liability cases, such as automobile accidents, the required standard of care to avoid a **breach of duty** usually is what a "reasonably prudent person" would have done in similar circumstances. In the case of professional liability, such as liability of a physician for alleged malpractice, the standard often is what a reasonable, adequately trained professional with the same area of expertise would have done in the same circumstances.

In many business liability cases (beginning with a US Supreme Court decision, *US v. Carroll Towing, 1944*), the courts often apply a specific economic standard for negligence in which the defendant is held to have exercised inadequate care if the business has failed to take **cost-justified precautions** to prevent harm. A precaution is cost-justified if the cost of taking the precaution is less than the expected reduction in harm that occurs if the precaution is taken.

To illustrate this economic standard, assume that a trucking company could reduce the expected harm to other people and property from truck accidents by $1 million if it limits the number of hours that each trucker can drive in a week, but that this action would increase the firm's costs by $800,000 because it has to hire more drivers. Then, under the economic standard for negligence, the trucking firm would be liable for the injuries caused by its failure to limit driving time because the expected benefit of the precaution ($1 million reduction in expected injury costs) exceeds the cost of the precautions ($800,000). If, on the other hand, limiting driving hours would cost $2 million, the business would not be found negligent for failing to spend $2 million to reduce expected injury costs by $1 million.

Application of the economic criterion for negligence requires the legal system to estimate the expected benefits and costs of additional precautions that could have been undertaken by the defendant. This process can be quite complicated in practice. We will discuss the safety incentives of liability law in detail in section 14.4. (Also see the appendix to this chapter.) For now it is sufficient to note that the economic criterion for negligence provides incentives for firms to take cost-justified precautions in cases where other incentives for doing so might be insufficient.

Proximate Cause. The third requirement for showing negligence is that the defendant's behavior is the **proximate cause** of the plaintiff's injury. In most cases, proximate cause is readily established. For example, if failure to stop at a stop sign results in a collision with another car or pedestrian and the injury would not have occurred but for the driver's failure to stop, this failure would be the proximate cause of the injury. Conversely, a defendant's action will not be considered the proximate cause of injury if the injury would have occurred regardless of whether the defendant failed to satisfy the standard of care required for protection of the other party. These results reflect what is known as the *sine qua non* or "but for" rule: If the injury would not have occurred but for the defendant's action, then the defendant's action is the proximate cause of the injury. An example that clearly illustrates this rule was provided many years ago by the Supreme Court of Minnesota when it refused to hold a railroad company liable for injuries to a driver who collided with a train after the train had failed to sound the legally required warning bell while approaching an intersection (*Sullivan v. Boone*). The court reasoned astutely that since the driver collided with the 68th car of the train, the accident would have occurred even if the bell had been sounded.

Complications sometimes arise in determining proximate cause when there are intervening events between the defendant's action and the ultimate injury. For example, assume that Fred leaves his keys in the car on the way to the door to pick up his date and that his car is stolen and crashes into a neighbor's car in the thief's haste to depart from the crime scene. The question arises as to whether Fred's failure to remove the keys could be considered the proximate cause of the damage to the neighbor's car so that the neighbor could successfully sue Fred. (Such a suit is likely since the thief is unlikely to have much money or liability insurance.) Or should the theft of the car instead constitute a superseding cause that prevents Fred from being liable? When dealing with these issues, many courts apply a *foreseeability test.* If a defendant should have reasonably foreseen that his or her action could create a significant risk of injury, then the defendant's action will be deemed the proximate cause of the injury even if there are unusual intervening events. A more elaborate and interesting case involving a complicated series of intervening events is described in Box 14–1.

Box 14–1

Negligence and Foreseeability

While the name of the driver has been changed, the following scenario is true. It happened in the Northeast during the early 1970s. Cases with similar results and implications have occurred elsewhere.

Jones noticed that the brakes on his old car were not working properly. He took the car to a service station about 5:30 PM. One of the rear brakes was defective. The mechanic did not have the part needed to make an immediate and permanent repair. He made a temporary repair and cautioned Jones to take the car home (Jones lived nearby) and bring the car back first thing in the morning. Jones drove 15 miles to a cookout where he apparently drank one or more beers. After leaving the cookout, Jones was spotted making an illegal pass by a state trooper. A high-speed chase ensued. Evidence later suggested that one of the brakes on Jones's car was not working properly, but it also appeared that Jones had no interest in stopping. Jones eventually approached a railroad crossing at the bottom of a long grade on a curve in the road. A train was entering the crossing at a speed of two miles per hour. Jones's car collided with the train and caromed into a phone booth lo-

cated nearby, severely injuring a person making a call (who lost both legs). Jones, who was uninsured, was not seriously hurt. The phone booth, which had been there for many years, was nine feet from the road and six feet from the railroad tracks.

The injured party sued Jones, the mechanic, the railroad, and the phone company. The jury, which visited the scene of the accident, held Jones and the phone company jointly and severally liable for negligence. The decision was upheld on appeal. The phone company argued that Jones's conduct and the other events should constitute a superseding cause and prevent the company from being held liable for negligence as a result of its placement of the phone booth. The court disagreed, holding that the phone company should have reasonably foreseen that its placement of the phone booth created a significant risk of injury to occupants (a question of fact for the jury to decide) and that the specific circumstances of the accident should not prevent liability. The phone company, which was self-insured, paid several hundred thousand dollars to the injured party, an amount that might seem low by today's standards.

Injury to Plaintiff.   The fourth condition for negligence is that the plaintiff has suffered loss, which essentially prevents people from bringing suits unless someone has been harmed. You learned earlier about the types of losses that are eligible for compensatory damages.

Defenses to Negligence

If all four conditions are established and the defendant is therefore negligent, the defendant may nonetheless be able to escape liability for the plaintiff's losses if the defendant can successfully use one of the defenses described below. A key aspect of a negligence rule is that the defendant's negligence is a necessary condition for the defendant to be liable, but not a sufficient condition. In many jurisdictions, defendants can avoid or at least reduce liability under a negligence rule (and sometimes under a strict liability rule) in two main ways: (1) prove that the plaintiff assumed the risk of injury, or (2) prove that the plaintiff also was negligent.

Assumption of Risk.   In some cases the defendant can avoid liability for damages using the **assumption of risk defense.** This requires the defendant to prove that the plaintiff voluntarily assumed a known risk. The logic underlying the assumption of risk defense is that if the plaintiff understood the risk involved in the activity and chose to participate in the activity anyway (e.g., downhill skiing or driving a vehicle that is known to have defective tires at a high rate of speed), then the plaintiff presumably was compensated for the risk in the form of a price concession or in any case valued the activity enough to undertake it despite the risk. Establishing the assumption of risk defense requires that the defendant prove that the plaintiff had knowledge of the particular risk and voluntarily assumed the risk. In modern times the courts have applied strict standards for proving that the plaintiff was aware of the risk, thus limiting the use of this defense.

Contributory and Comparative Negligence.   The second major type of defense that often may be available to the defendant is to establish that the plaintiff also was negligent. Under a **contributory negligence** standard, if the plaintiff also is shown to be negligent, then the defendant is not liable for any of the plaintiff's losses. For example, if a contributory negligence standard is applied to auto accidents with pedestrians and a pedestrian crosses the intersection against the light, then the driver might escape liability. Note that under a strict interpretation of the contributory negligence rule, any degree of negligence by the plaintiff prevents recovery.

Under a **comparative negligence** standard, the defendant can be found partially liable for the plaintiff's losses if the court finds that both the defendant's and the plaintiff's negligence contributed to the losses. Virtually all states have replaced the contributory negligence rule for auto accidents with a comparative negligence rule. While several types of comparative negligence rules exist, a typical rule would allow a person who is less than (or in some states less than or equal to) 50 percent responsible for the loss to recover damages from the other party. The damages, however, are reduced in proportion to the person's responsibility. For example, if a court finds that the defendant was 60 percent responsible, then the defendant will pay 60 percent of the plaintiff's losses. Compared to contributory negligence, comparative negligence rules tend to increase the number of losses that are compensated through the tort system.

14.4 Economic Objectives of the Tort Liability System

From an economic perspective, the tort system has two fundamental objectives: (1) to provide the right incentives for safety, and (2) to provide the right amount of compensation for accident victims. When trying to achieve these objectives, one must consider the transaction costs of operating the tort system and the costs of alternative methods of achieving these objectives. The following subsections explain each of the objectives in more detail. Before doing so, however, it is important to realize that the objectives often cannot be achieved simultaneously. The right amount of compensation for victims may yield the wrong incentives for safety and vice versa. Similarly, the transaction costs that would have to be incurred to achieve these objectives may imply that society should accept less than optimal safety incentives and less than optimal compensation for victims compared to a hypothetical world without transaction costs.

The objectives of the tort system should be familiar to you. The first goal—optimal safety incentives—means that we want the tort system to provide incentives for individuals and firms to optimally invest in loss control. The second goal—optimal compensation for victims—means that we want the tort system to provide the optimal amount of protection (insurance coverage) to people. The pursuit of these goals, however, must take into consideration the costs of loss control and the costs of insuring victims through the court system. Thus, the objective of the tort system can be succinctly stated as follows: The tort system should attempt to minimize the cost of risk to society, where the cost of risk includes expected accident losses, the cost of loss control, the cost of compensating victims (loss financing), and the cost of residual uncertainty (see Chapter 2).

By focusing on how the tort system affects loss control and victim compensation, our analysis ignores what some legal scholars view as important issues. For example, the distribution of wealth sometimes is affected by liability rules, and some people may view the reallocation of wealth as an objective of the tort system.[2] While the influence of liability rules on the distribution of wealth will be identified, we do not treat the redistribution of wealth as a fundamental objective. Also, some legal scholars focus on philosophical issues like social justice. We ignore these issues, apart from noting that some of the basic principles of tort law, such as the principle that persons who cause harm to others through negligence should compensate for injuries, have strong historical roots in both ancient secular and religious philosophy.

Optimal Safety (Optimal Loss Control)

As we have emphasized earlier in the book, it is rarely optimal to minimize the probability of loss or expected losses suffered by injured parties. Rather than attempting to achieve a "zero-risk" society, the tort system should provide incentives for people to invest in additional safety only if the additional benefits (marginal benefits) exceed the additional costs (marginal costs). The following example helps illustrate this point.

Suppose that Nielson Inc. produces riding lawnmowers that have the poten-

---

[2] From an ex post perspective, the tort system obviously redistributes wealth from persons that cause loss (or their liability insurance companies) to persons that are harmed. The discussion here refers to long-run effects of the tort system and the distribution of wealth and income in society.

tial of causing an injury to the consumer and that the loss suffered is $10,000. Thus, the expected loss to a consumer is simply the probability of an accident times $10,000. To simplify the analysis, assume that consumers are either risk neutral or that they can purchase full insurance at premiums equal to expected claim costs (zero premium loading). Under either of these assumptions, consumers only care about the expected loss from an accident and do not care about the uncertainty associated with losses.

If Nielson Inc. spends nothing on safety features, then the probability of an accident is 0.07. Nielson, however, can reduce the probability of an accident below 0.07 by incurring some costs. Table 14–3 lists the costs and the associated accident probabilities. To reduce the probability of an accident to 0.06, Nielson must spend $45 per mower; to reduce the probability of an accident to 0.05, Nielson must spend $130 per mower, and so on. Our objective is to identify the amount of money that Nielson should spend on making its mowers safer. We answer this question from society's perspective, not from the profit maximizing perspective of Nielson. Thus, we answer the hypothetical question: How much would fully informed consumers be willing to pay for safer mowers?

To answer this hypothetical question, we will start at the point where safety expenditures equal zero and the probability of an accident equals 0.07 and ask: Would a consumer who has to pay the cost of increased safety be willing to pay $45 to reduce the accident probability to 0.06? The answer is yes, because the benefit of the reduction in the accident probability is the reduction in expected loss, which equals $100 ($700 – $600). Stated differently, the marginal social cost to reduce the accident probability to 0.06 equals $45 and the marginal social benefit equals $100. Next, consider whether a consumer would be willing to spend an additional $85 on safety (for a total of $130) and thereby reduce the accident probability to 0.05. Again the answer is yes, because the additional $85 expenditure lowers expected losses by $100 (from $600 to $500). Thus, from society's perspective, Nielson should spend at least $130 on safety. Continuing, a consumer also would be willing to spend an additional $95 ($225 – $130) to reduce

TABLE 14–3   Analysis of Nielson's Safety Expenditures When the Severity of a Loss is $10,000

Safety Expenditure	Probability of Loss	Expected Loss to Consumer	Marginal Benefit to Consumer	Marginal Cost to Consumer
$ 0	0.07	$700	$ 0	$ 0
45	0.06	600	100	45
130	0.05	500	100	85
225	0.04	400	100	95
400	0.03	300	100	175
590	0.02	200	100	190
900	0.01	100	100	310

the accident probability to 0.04, because the additional benefit is $100 (expected losses are reduced from $500 to $400). A consumer, however, would not want to reduce the accident probability below 0.04, because the cost of lowering the probability to 0.03 equals $175 and the benefit of doing so is only $100.

Thus, the optimal amount of money that Nielson should spend on making each mower safer is $225, which would reduce the accident probability to 0.04. This amount minimizes the cost of risk. Spending less than $225 yields too little safety and spending more than $225 yields too much safety from the perspective of the consumer. The notion that a firm can spend too much on safety sometimes bothers students. It should be clear, however, that in a world of scarcity the costs of additional resources to make one activity safer implies that these resources cannot be spent on other activities (including other safety activities). Thus, at some point, the costs of additional safety expenditures exceed the benefits.

The point of this example is to clarify one of the objectives of tort law. In the context of this example, we would want the tort system to provide incentives for Nielson Inc. to spend $225 on safety. If the tort system provides incentives to spend less than $225 or more than $225, then the system has not achieved one of its objectives.

The main point of this section also can be illustrated graphically. In Figure 14–1, the level of safety as measured by the probability of *no* accident is listed on the horizontal axis and the marginal costs and marginal benefits of safety are measured by dollars on the vertical axis. Instead of discrete increments in safety, the graph assumes a continuum of possible safety levels (i.e., the probability of a loss can assume any value). As was true in the numerical example above, the marginal benefit of safety is assumed to be constant at $100 and the marginal cost of additional safety is assumed to increase with additional safety. The optimal level of safety is where the marginal cost and marginal benefit curves intersect.

FIGURE 14–1

Optimal level of safety is where the marginal benefit and marginal cost of safety are equal

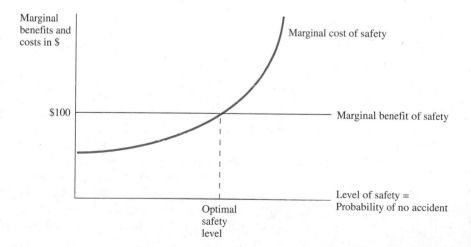

Optimal Compensation to Victims

The other objective of the tort system is to optimally compensate victims of accidents. Note that compensation awarded by the tort liability system is in many ways analogous to an insurance mechanism. Just as an insurance company compensates policyholders under certain conditions following a loss, the tort system compensates accident victims under certain conditions following a loss. Just as policyholders pay for insurance in the form of premiums, people pay higher prices for goods and services for the implicit insurance they obtain from the tort system. If the tort liability system systematically awards accident victims higher compensation for product-related injuries, then the prices of products will increase. In situations such as automobile accidents where a person can both cause harm to others and be harmed, the cost of liability insurance reflects the expected compensation awarded to victims of automobile accidents. If the tort liability system systematically awards greater compensation to automobile accident victims, then liability insurance premiums will increase. Thus, individuals implicitly pay for the insurance that is provided by the tort system.

Recognizing that the compensation aspect of the tort system is essentially an insurance mechanism has an important implication. When viewed solely from a compensation perspective (i.e., ignoring safety effects), the tort system should award compensation to a victim by answering the following hypothetical question: How much insurance coverage would the victim have wanted to purchase prior to knowing whether he or she would be involved in an accident if (1) the victim were fully informed about the risk of an accident, and (2) the terms of the insurance reflected the transaction costs, moral hazard, and adverse selection problems associated with offering insurance through the tort system?

Several aspects of this hypothetical question need elaboration. First, it is important to evaluate the amount of compensation from a *potential* victim's perspective, prior to knowing whether the person will be involved in an accident. Once losses have been incurred, the victim generally will want as much compensation as possible. The critical question, however, is how much compensation (insurance coverage) the victim would have been willing to pay for prior to knowing whether he or she would be involved in an accident. If compensation from the tort liability system exceeds the amount of insurance coverage that people are willing to pay for, then the legal system in effect forces people to buy too much insurance; people would prefer to spend their money in other ways. Similarly, if the compensation awarded by the tort system were less than the amount of coverage people are willing to pay for, then additional compensation would make people better off.

Second, the hypothetical question asks how much compensation from the tort system would people want if the terms of the insurance reflected the transactions costs, moral hazard, and adverse selection problems inherent in providing insurance through the tort system. The transaction costs include attorney fees and court costs. Moral hazard problems arise, in part, because some types of losses such as pain and suffering are difficult to measure. Adverse selection problems arise because the price paid for compensation provided by the tort system (e.g., which is embedded in product prices) typically is not differentiated across consumers, even though the expected losses of potential victims vary. As discussed in Chapter 8, transaction costs, moral hazard, and adverse selection lead people to want less than full insurance in most cases. A similar result holds for the insurance provided by the tort system: The transaction costs, moral hazard, and adverse selection problems associated with providing insurance through the tort system imply that most people will not be willing to pay for full insurance coverage (full compensation).

The US tort system generally attempts to compensate victims fully for their losses. In addition, there is widespread use of the **collateral source rule,** which precludes courts from reducing damages awarded by the amount of coverage provided by a plaintiff's first-party life, health, or property insurance. The use of the collateral source rule can imply that victims receive aggregate compensation from first-party insurance and damage payments in excess of losses, which is inconsistent with the result that people typically would not want to purchase full insurance. Thus, it appears that the US tort system forces many people to pay for more insurance than they probably desire.

One possible justification for this emphasis is that less than full compensation for damages (or reducing damages by the amount of the plaintiff's own insurance protection) could yield insufficient safety incentives (e.g., lowering victim compensation will reduce a manufacturer's incentive to make safe products or reduce a driver's incentive to take proper precautions) and that the US tort system places greater weight on optimal safety than optimal compensation. As an important example, we will explain in Chapter 15 that from a compensation perspective it might be better *not* to have pain and suffering compensation for product-related injuries. From a safety perspective, however, it might be better to have pain and suffering compensation.

In summary, the economic goal of the tort system is to minimize the cost of risk to society. That is, the tort system should provide optimal safety incentives (loss control) and optimal compensation to victims (insurance coverage), taking into account the costs of achieving these objectives. Unfortunately, these objectives probably conflict so that public policy must reflect a choice as to which objective to emphasize. The safety and compensation objectives will be central to the discussion of a number of liability issues in subsequent chapters.

14.5 Why Have a Tort System?—A Closer Look

The preceding section tacitly implied that a tort liability system might be needed to improve safety and compensation. This section examines when the tort system can improve safety incentives and victim compensation compared to an economy without a tort system (which is equivalent to what would occur with a no liability rule). In other words, we ask: When will the private marketplace fail to yield the optimal incentives for safety and the optimal amount of compensation to victims? We focus on two factors that can cause the private marketplace to yield nonoptimal safety: (1) imperfect information about the risk of harm, and (2) transaction costs that prevent people from achieving efficient outcomes without well-defined tort liability rules. We then note that similar results hold for the issue of whether the private marketplace will provide optimal compensation without a tort system.[3]

The Role of Information

Consider the Nielson Inc. example discussed earlier, where the optimal amount of safety expenditures from society's perspective equals $225. Instead of considering what is best for society, we now consider how much Nielson will spend on safety in various situations. The specific issue is whether the tort system is needed to induce Nielson Inc. to spend $225 on safety. We will show that the tort system is not needed if consumers are fully informed about the product's risk, because fully informed consumers are willing to pay more for safer products, which in turn gives manufacturers incentives to spend the optimal amount on product safety. However, if consumers underestimate product risk, then the tort system may be needed to induce Nielson to spend the right amount on safety.

Case 1: Full Information Implies Optimal Safety.   Consider first the case where consumers are fully informed and manufacturers are not liable for losses suffered by consumers who are injured using the manufacturer's products. If Nielson spent nothing on safety, then expected losses to consumers would be $700. Fully informed risk-neutral consumers (or fully insured consumers with no premium loading) would know that if they purchased a mower from Nielson they could expect losses (or have to pay a premium) equal to $700. Consequently, consumers would be willing to pay $700 less for a Nielson mower than for an otherwise equivalent mower that had no risk. If Nielson spent $45 on safety and thereby reduced the accident probability from 0.07 to 0.06, then consumers would increase the price that they would pay for the mower by $100. Nielson obviously would find the $45 safety expenditure a profitable move.

Now consider the next increment in safety. Consumers will pay an additional $100 per mower if Nielson lowers the accident probability to 0.05. Since the cost of doing this is an additional $85 (a total expenditure on safety equal to $130), it is in Nielson's own interest to lower the probability of an accident to 0.05. Continuing, since the cost of lowering the probability to 0.04 is $95 and since consumers will pay an additional $100 per mower for this change in the accident probability, Nielson will spend the additional $95 and lower the probability to 0.04. However, Nielson will not increase safety beyond this point, because the next increment in safety (lowering the probability to 0.03) will cost an additional $175 but will yield only an additional $100 in the mower's price. Thus, Nielson will spend $225 on safety, exactly what is optimal from society's perspective.

---

[3] Some people might argue that less than full information is due to transaction costs; it is more straightforward to analyze the information and transaction costs separately.

This example illustrates that *if consumers are fully informed about product risk, then the tort system is not needed to induce optimal safety.* The private marketplace provides manufacturers with the right incentives for safety. Informed consumers induce Nielson to consider appropriately the potential accident costs associated with risky products.

Case 2: Uninformed People and No Liability Implies Too Little Safety.   Now suppose that consumers are completely uninformed about product safety. How much would Nielson spend on safety if it is trying to maximize profits and if it is not liable for consumers' losses? The answer is zero. Nielson has no incentive to invest in safety, because consumers will not pay a higher price for a safer product. The private marketplace does not provide the right incentives to invest in safety. Although risky products impose accident costs on consumers, Nielson is not motivated to consider these costs because (1) consumers are unaware of them at the time they purchase products, and (2) Nielson is not liable for subsequent losses.

Case 3: Uninformed People and Full Liability Implies Optimal Safety.   To see how the tort system can improve safety incentives when consumers are completely uninformed, assume that Nielson is held liable for losses suffered by consumers who are injured using Nielson's mowers. In particular, suppose that every accident victim sues Nielson and each victim is fully compensated. Nielson therefore will view each additional safety expenditure as reducing the probability of losing a lawsuit. Since the tort system forces Nielson to pay all accident losses, Nielson will spend $225 per mower on safety, which is the optimal amount.[4]

Combining the results of cases 2 and 3, it is clear that one justification for making producers liable for all consumer losses is that consumers are uninformed. With no liability, Nielson has too little incentive to produce safe products when consumers are uninformed (case 2). By making Nielson liable for all consumer accident losses, Nielson has incentives to invest the optimal amount in safety (case 3). The next two cases expand this analysis by considering two other situations where Nielson is liable, but not to the optimal extent.

Case 4: Uninformed People and Less than Full Liability Implies Too Little Safety.   Suppose that the legal liability system only compensates accident victims for their monetary losses, instead of all losses. In our example, expected accident severity is $10,000. Suppose that one-half of this loss is nonmonetary (pain and suffering losses) and one-half is monetary (medical expenses and lost wages). If courts only award compensation for monetary losses, then victims will receive

---

[4] Note that if the economic criterion for negligence, discussed in section 14.3, is used to determine whether Nielson is liable, then Nielson also would have incentives to spend $225. That is, holding Nielson liable for failure to undertake cost-justified precautions would induce Nielson to spend the $225. If Nielson spent less than $225, its expected liability for damages would exceed the savings in safety expenditures.

only $5,000 from Nielson. In this case, Nielson will spend less than the optimal amount on safety. From Nielson's perspective, the benefit of making mowers safer is one-half of the societal benefit. That is, there is a divergence between the societal benefits of making products safer and the private benefits to Nielson. Consequently, when deciding how much to spend on safety, Nielson will spend too little on safety.

Using Table 14–3 we can calculate specifically how much Nielson will choose to spend. Starting from zero expenditure and an accident probability equal to 0.07, Nielson can reduce the probability of an accident to 0.06 by spending $45; thus, the marginal cost is $45. The marginal benefit to Nielson of reducing the probability to 0.06 is the reduction in expected liability costs, which equals the reduction in the probability of being sued, 0.01 (0.07 minus 0.06) times the amount of damages, which equals $5,000. Thus, the expected benefit is $50. Thus, Nielson will spend $45 to improve mower safety because doing so reduces its expected liability cost by $50. However, Nielson will not spend any additional amount on safety because the marginal cost will exceed the marginal benefit. This example illustrates that if the tort system undercompensates victims, then there will be too little incentive to invest in safety (provided people are completely uninformed).

This example also highlights a point made earlier about the possible trade-offs between optimal safety and optimal compensation. As discussed in Chapter 7, many people will not want to purchase insurance for nonmonetary losses such as pain and suffering. In addition, moral hazard problems associated with insuring nonmonetary losses imply that insurance typically will not be provided for such losses. This example illustrates that the tort system faces a potential conflict: If the tort system does not provide compensation for pain and suffering, which is likely to be optimal from a compensation perspective, then it may provide too little incentive for safety. As mentioned earlier, US courts typically attempt to compensate victims for nonmonetary losses. One explanation for this approach is that the US tort system places greater weight on optimal safety than optimal compensation in situations where a conflict between the safety and compensation objectives exists. Another interpretation is that the procedural process of personal injury cases, particularly the use of jury trials, causes awards to be influenced by sympathy for victims and not just optimal safety and compensation goals.

Case 5: Uninformed People and More than Full Liability Implies Too Much Safety.   As a final example, suppose that the tort system overcompensates each accident victim. For example, suppose that each accident victim receives twice the losses that are actually suffered. In this case, Nielson will spend more than what is socially optimal on safety. From Nielson's perspective, the benefit of making products safer is the reduction in expected liability costs, which exceed the true expected cost of unsafe products.

From Table 14–3, the benefit to Nielson of each increment in safety is a reduction in the probability of being sued (0.01) times the amount of damages ($20,000). Thus, the expected benefit to Nielson from each safety increment is

$200, which is twice the social marginal benefit. Thus, there is a divergence between private and social benefits: Nielson's private marginal benefit of additional safety exceeds the social marginal benefit. Consequently, Nielson will spend too much on safety. Nielson will decrease the accident probability until its private marginal cost exceeds its private marginal benefit, which occurs when the probability of an accident equals 0.02. Thus, Nielson will spend $590 per mower on safety. This example illustrates that if the tort system overcompensates victims, then firms will be given an incentive to invest in safety to the point where the cost of additional safety exceeds the benefit. In this case, buyers get very safe lawnmowers, but the mowers are too safe in that the additional safety is not worth the increase in price to the buyers. The buyers would prefer to have cheaper (less safe) mowers.

Concept Check

1. Suppose that consumers underestimate the probability of an accident by a factor of one-half. That is, when the true accident probability is p, consumers believe the probability is $p/2$. How much would Nielson spend on safety if it could not be held liable for consumers' losses? Would tort liability improve safety incentives in this case?

Transaction Costs and Assignment of Legal Rights

In some respects, the Nielson example is simpler than other scenarios where tort liability applies because the potential accident occurs in the context of a transaction between consumers and Nielson. The price at which the parties transact reflects the perceived risk involved in the exchange. If the parties are well informed, the private marketplace effectively deals with the risky situation. Other scenarios involving tort liability are complicated by the lack of a transaction prior to the potential accident. For example, pedestrians do not transact with all the drivers that could potentially hit them. In these scenarios, the private marketplace would require additional transactions to deal effectively with the risk. Due to the costs of arranging these additional transactions, the tort system may be a better mechanism for achieving the goals of optimal safety incentives and optimal compensation than the private marketplace.

To illustrate these concepts, consider the harm that can potentially arise from a factory that disposes waste in a river that people use for fishing. Assume that the waste has a 50 percent chance of damaging the fish in the river. Also assume that everyone knows that the cost of damaged fish equals $400 (in present value terms). Thus, the following probability distribution summarizes the loss from the waste that the factory places in the river.

$$\text{Cost to anglers} = \begin{array}{l} \$400 \text{ with probability } 0.5 \\ \$0 \quad \text{ with probability } 0.5 \end{array}$$

Assume that everyone is risk neutral or that full insurance can be purchased at a premium equal to expected claim costs. This assumption implies that we can ignore residual uncertainty and the cost of loss financing, so that the cost of risk associated with water pollution is simply the expected loss plus the cost of loss control (if any is undertaken).

Suppose that the factory can treat the waste prior to disposing of it in the river, which would eliminate the risk of loss to the anglers. We consider two scenarios for the magnitude of the waste treatment cost: (1) the treatment of waste costs $150, or (2) the treatment of waste costs $250. We first examine whether it is optimal from society's perspective to treat the waste before dumping it in the river. Then we examine whether the liability rule (whether the factory or the anglers are liable) affects whether the factory will treat the waste.

Optimal Level of Loss Control.   If the treatment cost is $150, it is optimal to treat the waste because the $200 benefit from treatment (anglers are spared a cost of $400 with probability 0.5) exceeds the cost. If the treatment cost is $250, however, it is optimal not to treat the waste because the benefit ($200) is less than the cost ($250). Stated differently, the cost of risk is minimized by treating the waste if the cost of treatment is $150, but the cost of risk is minimized by allowing pollution if the cost of treatment is $250. Panel A of Table 14–4 summarizes these results.

An important implication of this analysis is that it is not always optimal to eliminate pollution or other risks of harm. The costs of eliminating the pollution must be compared to the benefits. Because reasonable people can disagree about the magnitudes of the costs and benefits (unreasonable people are sure to disagree), arguments concerning the optimal amount of pollution are common. These issues are ignored in this example by assuming that everyone agrees on the costs and benefits.

TABLE 14–4   **Analysis of Factory Polluting River (benefit of waste treatment equals $200)**

		Cost of Treatment	
		$150	*$250*
Panel A	Socially optimal outcome	No pollution	Pollution
Panel B	Outcomes with zero transaction costs		
	Outcome if factory is liable	No pollution	Pollution
	Outcome if factory is not liable	No pollution	Pollution
Panel C	Outcomes if transaction costs equal $55		
	Outcome if factory is liable	No pollution	Pollution
	Outcome if factory is not liable	Pollution	Pollution

Does the Liability Rule Matter?   We now will demonstrate that in the absence of transaction costs, it does not matter whether the factory is liable: The factory will treat the waste if the treatment cost is $150; it will not treat the waste if the treatment cost is $250. Stated differently, with zero transaction costs, the factory will invest the optimal amount in preventing pollution regardless of whether it is liable for the losses imposed on anglers.[5]

Consider first the case where the cost of treating the waste is $150, so that it is optimal from society's perspective to treat the waste. Will the factory do what is optimal from society's perspective? If the factory is liable for the losses suffered by the anglers, then the factory obviously will consider the costs imposed on the anglers. Since the cost of treating the waste ($150) is less than the expected cost of compensating anglers for their losses ($200), the factory will treat the waste. Thus, if the factory is liable, we get the optimal outcome: The waste is treated.

Now suppose that the factory cannot be held liable, so that the anglers must bear the costs of pollution. In this case, it may at first appear that the factory will not consider the costs imposed on the anglers and therefore will not treat the waste. However, this conclusion is incorrect. If the cost of treating the waste is $150, then without transaction costs the anglers will join together and pay the factory to treat the waste. The cost to the anglers of paying the factory ($150) is less than the expected cost of pollution ($200); consequently, there will be no pollution even though the factory is not liable. Thus, when the cost of treating the waste is $150 and anglers can costlessly agree to pay the factory to treat the waste, the waste will be treated regardless of whether the factory is liable. Like the earlier discussion of product injuries when consumers are fully informed about the risk of harm, the key to this finding is that a contractual solution to the pollution issue exists. The tort system is not needed to solve the problem; the private marketplace handles it optimally.

Now suppose instead that the cost of treating the waste is $250 so that the waste should not be treated because the cost of doing so exceeds the benefits. If the factory is not liable, the anglers will not pay the factory to treat the waste, because the cost of treating the waste ($250) exceeds the expected cost to the anglers with no treatment ($200). If the factory is liable, then the factory is better off paying the losses to the anglers if they occur than treating the waste, because the expected cost of compensating the anglers ($200) is less than the cost of treating the waste ($250). Thus, regardless of whether the factory is liable, the waste is not treated.

As summarized in Panel B of Table 14–4, when the factory and the anglers can costlessly negotiate a solution to the pollution issue, it does not matter who is liable for the losses that occur. When it is optimal to avoid pollution (when the cost of treatment is less than the harm prevented), no pollution will occur. When

---

[5] This analysis originated in the work of Ronald Coase, who was awarded the Nobel Prize in economics in part for his work on these types of problems.

it is optimal to have pollution (when the cost of treatment exceeds the harm prevented), pollution will occur.

Assignment of Liability and the Distribution of Wealth.   You may object to the conclusion that the assignment of liability does not matter, because when the factory is not liable, the anglers have to pay the costs of preventing the pollution, but when the factory is liable the anglers do not have to pay. This point is valid: The assignment of liability can affect the distribution of wealth; anglers are better off if the factory is liable (factory owners are worse off). Nonetheless, in order to achieve the optimal level of safety, it does not matter whether the factory is liable or not—optimal safety takes place regardless of the liability rule.

The focus on safety may bother you. You might think that it is only fair that the factory should be liable for the losses imposed on the anglers. You should keep in perspective, however, that this notion of fairness is not universal. One could just as easily view the interaction between the factory and the anglers as one in which the anglers' decision to fish on that river created the risk and thus that the anglers should pay the cost of treating the waste. The key point is that fairness is a subjective notion. While fairness issues should not affect whether the waste should be treated, people's notions of fairness will affect who they think should pay for the treatment (if the waste should be treated). As a result, notions of fairness may well affect the assignment of liability in the real world.

The Zero Transaction Costs Assumption.   Zero transaction costs is a critical assumption underlying the conclusion that the assignment of liability does not affect whether the waste will be treated. To highlight the importance of this assumption, we now redo the analysis assuming that the anglers must incur $55 to organize themselves and negotiate a contract with the factory. Let's begin by assuming that the cost of treating the waste is $150, so that the optimal outcome is to treat the waste. If the factory is liable, then the factory will treat the waste, because the cost of treatment ($150) is less than the expected cost of compensating the anglers ($200). If, however, the factory is not liable, then the factory will not treat the waste, contrary to what the previous analysis showed and contrary to what is optimal. When transaction costs were zero, the anglers organized themselves and paid the factory the money needed to treat the waste. Now, however, the cost of organizing the anglers ($55) plus the cost of treatment ($150) exceeds the expected cost of pollution to the anglers ($200). Consequently, pollution will result even though it is optimal not to have pollution. This conclusion is illustrated in Panel C of Table 14–4.

This example illustrates that the liability rule can affect optimal safety incentives if there are positive transaction costs. In this case, transaction costs prevented a contractual solution to the pollution problem when the factory was not liable. Consequently, the liability rule should make the factory liable, because the factory invests optimally in pollution prevention only when it is made liable. (Thus, transaction costs in this example favor the same outcome that many people believe to be fair: The factory should be held liable.)

The key point is that liability rules can improve safety incentives when transaction costs prevent private contracting from providing the right safety incentives. For example, it would be too costly for every driver to privately contract with each other driver to determine how automobile accidents will be handled. Instead of private contracts, society is better off having the tort system govern these interactions. This reasoning suggests that, in addition to the case of underestimation of the risk of harm considered earlier, society should use tort liability when (1) interactions between people can cause harm, and (2) transaction costs prevent these people from entering into optimal contracts to deal with the potential harm.

Summary

This analysis illustrates that uninformed people and transaction costs provide a justification for assigning liability to certain parties. That is, uninformed people and transaction costs sometimes cause the private marketplace to handle the problems associated with accident risks suboptimally. You should not conclude, however, that tort liability is always the best solution to the problems that arise in the private marketplace. As we discuss below, other methods exist for dealing with safety and compensation issues. For example, government regulation with fines for noncompliance or taxes can help provide proper safety incentives, and social insurance programs can provide compensation to those who have been harmed. All of these methods of dealing with safety and compensation issues, however, are costly, which implies that the inefficiencies of the private marketplace must be compared to the inefficiencies (costs) of the methods used to deal with the shortcomings of the private marketplace.

While our discussion in this section has focused on safety incentives, similar points apply to the compensation (implicit insurance coverage) objectives of the tort system. If people are fully informed, private contracting generally will provide the implicit insurance coverage that people desire. However, if people underestimate some risks or if transaction costs prevent optimal contracts, then people may obtain too little insurance. In principle, the tort system can improve compensation in these situations.

14.6 Limited Wealth and Limited Liability

The safety and compensation objectives of the tort system may be undermined if the party who is liable for losses can escape liability for damages. People can avoid paying damages either because they do not have sufficient wealth or because their wealth is protected by limited liability (bankruptcy) rules. If the victim does not receive the optimal amount of compensation because of the defendant's limited wealth or limited liability, then the compensation objective is undermined. Similarly, if limited wealth or limited liability allow some people to avoid paying damages, then these people may invest too little in safety. Intuitively, if a person knows that he or she will not be forced to pay all the costs imposed on others, then the person might have insufficient safety incentives. After describing situations in which people do not have to pay full damages, we discuss how compulsory insurance in some cases may help solve the problems caused by limited wealth and limited liability.

Situations in Which People Can Escape Liability

Suppose that Mrs. Cagle, a retiree who has $10,000 in assets, is physically and mentally unable to work (i.e., she has no human capital). If the courts rule that Mrs. Cagle must pay $500,000 in damages to a pedestrian she hit with her car, then Mrs. Cagle will be unable to pay the entire damage. The court may force Mrs. Cagle to pay $10,000, but that is the limit of her liability. Since she has insufficient wealth to pay the entire judgment, Mrs. Cagle is **judgment proof** for damages in excess of her wealth (or in excess of the assets she would be allowed to keep if she filed bankruptcy).[6]

Suppose that the same situation occurs for Mrs. Cagle's son, Jules, a capable employee who has many years left to work. Jules has liquid assets of only $10,000, but he has human capital that is worth $2 million; that is, the present value of his future earnings equals $2 million. While Jules has sufficient resources to pay the entire $500,000 judgment over time, he does not have the liquid assets to pay the judgment immediately. The courts could force Jules to pay the entire judgment by making him pay a portion of his future earnings to the victim over time (i.e., the court could *garnish* future wages). However, because of the costs of collecting future earnings and the adverse effect such an action could have on Jules's incentives to produce in the future, the law usually does not garnish future wages (an exception sometimes occurs if a defendant engages in willful and reckless conduct). Thus, like his mother, Jules would likely be judgment proof for liability in excess of his liquid assets.

Owners of corporations also can escape liability (are judgment proof) for judgments made against the corporation that exceed the amount that the owners have contributed to the corporation. For example, if Mrs. Cagle pays $5,000 for shares of common stock of a corporation, then the most that Mrs. Cagle can lose from her investment is $5,000. If a judgment is made against the corporation which the corporation cannot pay, the individual owners (like Mrs. Cagle) will not have to pay the shortfall from their personal assets. Chapter 17 explores in more detail situations involving the use of corporate boundaries to limit liability.

Compulsory Liability Insurance and the Judgment Proof Problem

As discussed in Chapter 21, all states have laws that either encourage or require the purchase of auto liability insurance. In most states, auto liability insurance is compulsory. States also either mandate the purchase of workers' compensation insurance by businesses or require firms to meet detailed financial responsibility

---

[6] Complex federal and state laws determine how much wealth a person can retain after filing bankruptcy.

rules to qualify as a self-insurer (see Chapter 16), and some states make medical malpractice insurance coverage compulsory for physicians. Both the compensation and safety objectives of the tort system may be better achieved in some cases when parties with limited wealth and limited liability are required to purchase liability insurance.

In the example above, if Mrs. Cagle had liability insurance with a limit of $500,000, then the victim would have been fully compensated. And, to the extent that liability insurance premiums reflect the safety precautions taken by Mrs. Cagle with perfect accuracy, she will have the right safety incentives. For example, the premium reduction from taking a driver's training course may induce Mrs. Cagle to take a course that she would not have taken without insurance. Thus, accurately priced liability insurance can help restore the compensation and safety objectives of the tort system in situations in which limited wealth and limited liability undermine these objectives.

Compulsory liability insurance also might discourage people and businesses from engaging in risky activities that are valued less than the full cost of the activity. For example, compulsory auto liability insurance might cause some persons to give up driving who do not value driving enough to pay the premium for compulsory coverage. (Of course, other persons might instead decide to break the law and drive without coverage.) We discuss these issues further in Chapters 16 and 21.

In practice, liability insurance prices cannot reflect the expected loss with perfect accuracy, and the purchase of liability insurance can create a moral hazard problem that counteracts the positive safety effects of the insurance. For example, some drivers might drive less safely once they have purchased compulsory liability insurance because there is less likelihood that they will lose part of their limited wealth from a lawsuit. Intuitively, a poor uninsured person may act more cautiously in an effort to protect his or her limited wealth than would the same person with significant liability insurance. This possibility makes the effects of compulsory liability insurance on safety precautions theoretically ambiguous in some cases.

14.7 Tort Liability and Safety Regulation

The tort system is not the only mechanism available to solve the problems that arise from people being uninformed about risk and transaction costs. Government regulation and the use of taxes and subsidies to encourage and discourage certain activities also can be used to deal with these issues. For example, if the government knew that lawnmower manufacturers should spend $225 per mower on safety, the government could simply mandate that manufacturers spend $225. In this section, we discuss the tradeoffs between using the liability system and government regulation as a means of correcting the problems that the private marketplace does not optimally solve.

Determining the optimal level of safety expenditures requires (1) information about the causes of accidents, (2) an understanding of the methods and technology that can be used to reduce the frequency and severity of accidents, (3) an understanding of the costs of implementing safety measures, and (4) the willingness of people to pay for additional safety. All of this information is costly to obtain. Effective safety regulation requires that regulators obtain this information, whereas providing effective safety incentives through the tort system requires that private entities (firms and individuals) have this information. Thus, in some cases, economies of scale in obtaining and using safety information may exist and thus provide a justification for a greater emphasis on safety regulation versus tort liability. A related argument in favor of centralized safety regulation (over safety incentives via tort liability) is that regulation can reduce costly duplication of investments in safety research. On the other hand, when it would be too costly for the government to obtain the information available to private parties, or when it is important to keep information about the sources of risk and optimal loss control methods private (perhaps because this information is inseparable from valuable proprietary information about product design), tort liability is more likely to be an efficient method of obtaining optimal safety incentives (also see Box 14–2).

Additional tradeoffs between liability and safety regulation become more apparent by recognizing that safety regulation is essentially an ex ante approach and liability is an ex post approach. That is, safety regulation imposes restrictions or guidelines before an accident occurs to prevent accidents. The liability system waits until after an accident occurs and then makes one party pay for the victim's losses. (Of course, ex post liability affects ex ante safety decisions.) In some cases, the occurrence of a loss is so devastating that safety regulation has an advantage over the liability system, other factors being held constant. For example, it may make sense to rely more on safety regulation to deal with potential nuclear accidents than to use the liability system.

Box 14–2

Does Meeting Safety Regulations Imply No Liability?

For many types of risk, both regulation and liability coexist. An interesting question often arises in these circumstances: If a firm satisfies the safety regulations can it nevertheless be held liable for damages? The answer is yes. Critics of the tort system often contend that this is an unfair aspect of the tort system.

One justification for holding a firm liable even though it has met all safety regulations is that government standards must focus on typical or average risks of loss associated with many activities. While there may be economies of scale in risk assessment by the government in these cases, legal rules should provide firms with an incentive to use any additional or specific information that they may have concerning a particular risk. In some cases, the benefits (reduction in expected harm) of additional precautions beyond those implied in government standards may exceed the costs. Allowing injured parties to recover damages in these cases, despite the fact the firm has met the regulatory standard, provides the firm with the incentive to undertake cost-justified precautions.

A potential disadvantage of the liability system is that the party who is responsible for the loss might be judgment proof. As we discussed above, if the party who causes the loss does not have to pay the full amount of the loss, then there may be too little safety. Thus, in situations where the judgment proof problem undermines safety incentives, safety regulation has an advantage over tort liability, all else being equal. Given the different strengths and weaknesses of tort law and safety regulation, it is not surprising that both tools often are used to promote safety. When these tools are used jointly, compliance with a government safety standard generally does not necessarily prevent a defendant from being held liable for injuries (see Box 14–2). Another controversial issue, which is discussed in the appendix to this chapter, is whether government safety standards often involve costs in excess of the expected benefit from reduced injury costs.

14.8 Proposals for Tort Reform

During the mid-1980s, liability costs for many businesses and professions increased substantially. In response, many business and professional organizations lobbied state legislatures and the US Congress to pass tort reform legislation to reduce the magnitude of liability costs, and most states have passed some type of tort reform during the past 15 years. This section provides an overview of the major types of tort reform proposals and the problems they are meant to address.[7]

Modifying Incentives to Bring Suits

Most plaintiffs in the US hire their attorneys on a contingency fee basis; that is, the attorney receives a percentage of the damages awarded by the court or in a settlement, but if the plaintiff loses, then the attorney receives nothing. The use of contingency fees is much more frequent in the US than in other countries. One advantage of contingency fees is that they allow people access to the courts who otherwise could not afford to pay an attorney. In essence, the attorney finances the lawsuit for the plaintiff. Also, contingency fees can provide incentives for plaintiff attorneys to screen out cases that are not likely to succeed. However, critics of contingency fees argue that they lead plaintiff attorneys to take cases with a low probability of winning, but with potentially high damages. These speculative lawsuits, the critics contend, impose substantial costs on defendants. As a result, proposals often are made to place **limits on contingency fees.**[8]

---

[7] Considerable research exists on the effects of each of these proposals. Some references are provided at the end of the chapter.

[8] The United Kingdom has experimented with one approach to limiting contingency fees. It allows a conditional fee where the plaintiff attorney receives up to twice the compensation he/she would normally receive on an hourly basis if the plaintiff wins, but zero otherwise. Theoretically, this conditional fee induces plaintiff attorneys to turn down any case in which the probability of winning is less than 50 percent.

Unlike the systems in most countries, the US tort system generally does not require that losing plaintiffs pay any of the legal costs of a winning defendant. A common proposal for reforming the US system is the adoption of a **loser pays rule,** where the loser pays at least part of the winning side's legal costs. Proponents of a loser pays rule argue that it would reduce litigation in cases where the plaintiff has little chance of winning. A potential concern is that the adoption of a loser pays rule will reduce access to the justice system because plaintiffs will be averse to incurring the risk of paying the potentially large legal costs of the defendant. However, to the extent that plaintiff law firms can diversify this risk across many cases and have expertise in judging the merits of a case, plaintiff law firms would likely bear the risk of paying the defendant's legal costs under a loser pay system. Whether a loser pays rule nevertheless would have an excessively chilling effect on litigation and safety is hotly contested.

Reducing Damages

The United States also differs from most other countries in that tort cases are heard more frequently by juries, as opposed to judges. The reason for the frequent use of jury trials is that the US constitution and most state constitutions generally require a jury trial if either side requests one. Nevertheless, jury trials for personal injury cases have received considerable criticism from legal scholars for several reasons. Unlike judges, juries do not have to explain the reasoning for their decisions and juries are not bound by decisions in similar cases. Consequently, a jury adds uncertainty about the outcome, which in turn induces plaintiff attorneys to pursue speculative lawsuits. An additional criticism of juries is that they often are not capable of evaluating the expert testimony presented. Although it would be difficult to eliminate jury trials given the constitutional barriers, jury discretion in setting damages can be limited by legislation. For example, judges could be granted authority to set damages.

A number of state legislatures have enacted laws that limit or place **caps on pain and suffering awards.** Proponents of these reforms argue that because pain and suffering is difficult to measure, awards for pain and suffering have high variance, bear little relation to the loss actually suffered, and are not the type of compensation for which most consumers would be willing to pay. Proponents of reform further contend that the difficulty in predicting pain and suffering awards provides incentives for plaintiff attorneys to pursue speculative litigation with the threat of having an emotional and sympathetic jury ultimately determine the outcome. On the other hand, critics of caps on pain and suffering awards argue that caps reduce safety incentives.

Some critics of the tort system argue that juries often award excessive punitive damages and therefore advocate **limits on punitive damages.** One argument for punitive damages from a safety perspective is that because all victims of harm do not bring legal actions against the wrongdoer, damages in the cases that are brought need to exceed the losses that the specific victim suffered. Otherwise, the wrongdoer's expected total liability will be less than the expected total losses imposed on victims, and the wrongdoer will have too little incentive for safety (see case 4 earlier in the chapter). Punitive damages also could reflect society's desire to seek retribution against parties that inflict egregious harm on others.

Attempts to restrict punitive damages have met with limited success thus far. In 1991, the US Supreme Court refused to consider a case on punitive damages, *Pacific Mutual Life v. Haslip,* in which a life insurer was found to have defrauded a woman (Haslip) for $4,000. An Alabama court awarded the plaintiff the $4,000 and also assessed $1 million in punitive damages. Many observers interpret the Supreme Court's decision as implying that existing methods of limiting jury discretion on punitive damages are sufficient. The Supreme Court, however, did highlight that judges should instruct juries on the purposes of punitive damages and review jury awards. The court later overturned several punitive damage awards as excessive, but it has yet to impose clear guidelines for setting the appropriate amount of punitive damages.

A third proposal that would reduce damages is to alter the collateral source rule. Often accident victims receive compensation from sources other than the tort system. For example, private insurance, social insurance benefits, and charity help pay the losses suffered by accident victims and are therefore called collateral benefits. The basic issue is whether courts should take these other benefits into account when setting damages. From a safety perspective, the answer is no. If the sole purpose is to provide incentives for safety, then subtracting collateral benefits from total losses when setting damages would cause damages to be less than losses. As the example earlier in the chapter demonstrated (see case 4), if the damages that the defendant must pay are less than the losses imposed on the victims, then there will be too little incentive for safety. However, from a compensation perspective, the subtraction of collateral benefits makes sense; otherwise, victims would be overcompensated for their losses. During the latter part of the 1980s, several states enacted laws that restricted the application of the collateral source rule under certain conditions.

Limiting the Application of Joint and Several Liability

Recall that when defendants are jointly and severally liable, each individual defendant can be held responsible for the entire damages. While the doctrine of joint and several liability can be defended on the grounds that it provides compensation to victims, its justification from a safety perspective is more suspect. The reason is that joint and several liability can cause a party to pay more than the costs its actions have imposed on other parties. As explained earlier in the chapter (see case 5), imposing liability in excess of the losses actually imposed can provide too much incentive for safety.

During the latter part of the 1980s, the majority of the states enacted legislation on the use of joint and several liability. A few states completely eliminated the use of joint and several liability, but most states restricted its use, for example, by disallowing its use for noneconomic damages (pain and suffering). Other states disallowed its use when the plaintiff was more than 50 percent responsible for the damages.

14.9 Summary

- Liability rules allocate accident risk to various members of society and thereby affect incentives to engage in loss control (incentives to undertake risky activities and to take precautions). Also, by forcing some parties to compensate other parties (accident victims) for their losses, the tort liability system essentially forces the former party to provide insurance to victims.

- Liability rules range from (1) immunity from liability (e.g., charitable organizations in some circumstances), to (2) a negligence rule which holds people liable if they fail to exercise the required standard of care to prevent injury to another party, to (3) strict liability which holds manufacturers of defective products liable even if the manufacturer was not negligent, to (4) absolute liability.

- Compensatory damages in tort liability cases compensate victims for monetary losses (e.g., medical expenses, lost wages) and nonmonetary losses (e.g., pain and suffering). Punitive damages are damages in excess of the losses suffered by the victim.

- To recover damages under a negligence rule, a plaintiff generally must establish (1) the existence of a legal duty by the defendant to prevent harm to the plaintiff, (2) a breach of this legal duty by failing to exercise the required standard of care, (3) that the breach was the proximate cause of the plaintiff's harm, and (4) that an injury was suffered. Under a negligence rule (and sometimes under strict liability), a defendant in some cases may be able to avoid or reduce liability by showing that the plaintiff assumed the risk or that the plaintiff's negligence or actions contributed to the accident.

- The main objectives of the tort liability system from an economic perspective are to provide incentives for parties to engage in the optimal level of loss control and to provide optimal compensation (insurance coverage) to accident victims.

- When an accident risk exists in the context of a transaction between two parties, the two parties will engage in the optimal level of loss control and provide the optimal level of insurance to accident victims provided the parties are fully informed; a tort liability system is not needed in this case. If the parties are not fully informed, then one party may have insufficient incentives to engage in loss control and to provide the optimal level of insurance coverage in the absence of tort liability. In this situation, the tort system can improve upon free market outcomes.

- When contracting costs prevent potential accident victims from transacting with the parties who can cause damages, then the tort liability system may improve incentives to engage in loss control and to provide optimal insurance coverage to victims.

- Limited wealth and limited liability can cause some people to be judgment proof for damages imposed on others. In this case, victims may not receive optimal compensation and incentives for loss control may be insufficient. Compulsory liability insurance— forcing judgment proof people to purchase liability insurance—in some cases can improve victim compensation and loss control incentives.

- Government safety regulation and taxes also can be used to address the loss control and victim compensation problems that arise when people are uninformed or when transaction costs prevent these problems from being solved privately.

- A number of tort reform measures were proposed and enacted following the increase in liability insurance costs during the 1980s.

Key Terms

Questions and Problems

1. Ms. Schmit, a famous marathon runner and legal scholar, was out for a long run one day. While thinking about the arguments for and against joint and several liability, she crossed a street between intersections without looking for oncoming traffic. A speeding car hit her; luckily only her leg was injured. Medical expenses came to $750, but she was unable to run in the Boston marathon that year, something for which she had been training for the previous 10 years. Assume that the noneconomic loss (e.g., emotional distress and disappointment) of not being able to run in Boston is worth $100,000. Under each of the following liability standards, identify who is responsible for paying Ms. Schmit's medical expenses and her noneconomic losses.
   (a) Negligence rule with no defenses.
   (b) Negligence rule with a contributory negligence defense.
   (c) Negligence rule with a comparative negligence defense.
   (d) Absolute liability for drivers of vehicles involved in pedestrian accidents.

2. The liability standard for medical malpractice generally is a negligence rule. Compare the negligence rule to a liability standard where physicians are always liable for losses suffered as a result of a medical procedure on each of the following dimensions:
   (a) Physicians' incentives to provide care.
   (b) Victim compensation.
   (c) Legal costs.

3. Find the optimal level of safety (probability of an accident) from a societal perspective using the data on the costs of safety given in the table below. Assume that an accident imposes costs on a victim equal to $500,000.

Probability of Loss	Safety Expenditures
0.030	$ 0
0.020	1,000
0.015	2,000
0.012	3,000
0.0095	4,000
0.009	5,000

4. Graphically illustrate the solution to the problem in question 3.

5. Using the data in question 3, how much

would a profit-maximizing producer spend on safety if the tort liability system would award each victim $150,000?

6. Using the data in question 3, how much would a profit-maximizing producer spend on safety if the tort liability system would award $500,000 to each victim?

7. Using the data in question 3, how much would a profit-maximizing producer spend on safety if the tort liability system would award $500,000 to one-half of the accident victims?

8. Using the data in question 3, how much would a profit-maximizing producer spend on safety if the tort liability system would award $500,000 to each victim, but the producer only had $250,000 to pay liability awards and therefore the producer's liability was limited to $250,000?

9. Consider the same scenario as described in problem 8, but suppose that the producer is required to purchase liability insurance with a $500,000 limit. Assume that the insurance premium equals expected liability costs and that the insurer can costlessly observe the producer's safety expenditures. How much will the producer spend on safety?

10. One of the results of this chapter is that in an unregulated market without tort liability, producers would be induced to spend the optimal amount on product safety when consumers are fully informed. In an unregulated market without tort liability, if consumers overestimate the accident risk associated with products, what would happen to the amount that producers would spend on safety relative to the optimal amount?

References

Bernstein, David E. "Procedural Tort Reform: Lessons from Other Nations." *Regulation—Cato Review of Business and Government* 19 (1996). (*Discusses various tort reforms and their likely effects on litigation outcomes.*)

Demsetz, Harold. "When Does the Rule of Liability Matter?" *Journal of Legal Studies.* (*Classic article on how transaction costs cause the liability rule to affect resource allocation.*)

Lee, Han-Duck; Mark Browne; and Joan Schmit. "How Does Joint and Several Tort Reform Affect the Rate of Tort Filing? Evidence from State Courts." *Journal of Risk and Insurance* 61 (1994), pp. 295–316. (*Empirically examines the effect of tort joint and several tort reform on litigation.*)

Shavell, Steven. *Economic Analysis of Accident Law.* Cambridge, MA: Harvard University Press, 1987. (*Comprehensive economic analysis of tort law.*)

Viscusi, W. Kip. *Pricing Environmental Risks.* Center for the Study of American Business, Policy No. 112, June 1992. (*Analyzes the government's record of regulating environmental risk.*)

Answer to Concept Check

1. Nielson would spend $45 per mower on safety, which would reduce the probability of an accident from 0.07 to 0.06, because a consumer would be willing to pay an additional $50 for this increment in safety. (A consumer would view the accident probability being reduced by 0.005 [from 0.035 to 0.03], which when multiplied by the

loss of $10,000 would result in a savings in expected accident costs of $50.) Nielson, however, would not reduce the accident probability to 0.05 because the cost of this additional safety is $85, which exceeds the amount that a consumer would be willing to pay for the additional safety ($50). Thus, tort liability would improve safety incentives by inducing Nielson to spend the optimal amount on safety.

APPENDIX 14A
VALUING LOSS OF LIFE AND COST-BENEFIT ANALYSIS OF SAFETY REGULATION

Many situations involving accidents require that compensation be paid for the loss of a person's life. Similarly, when assessing the benefits of safety regulation, regulators must value life because many safety regulations affect the probability of death. While a discussion of how to value life can be troubling for some, it is necessary in many situations. Indeed, individuals implicitly make decisions on a daily basis that affect the probability of dying and thus they implicitly make tradeoffs about the value of their own life. For example, deciding to drive a small car versus a large car usually increases the probability of dying in a car accident. Thus, the choice of what car to buy often involves a choice between a lower car price and a lower probability of dying. The necessity of valuing life is highlighted by Box 14A–1.

While the courts and regulators use a variety of methods to value life, we present an approach that attempts to measure the value that people implicitly place on their own life. The idea is to infer the value of people's lives based on the compensation that they are willing to accept for an increased probability of dying. The typical setting in which this analysis is conducted is the labor market.

Suppose, for example, that a construction firm has two job openings. Assume that both jobs require the same skill and have the same working conditions, except that one job has a higher probability that the worker will be killed on the job. For simplicity, assume that one job has a zero chance of death and that the other job has a 0.0005 chance of death per year. Finally, assume that the firm must pay additional annual wages of $2,000 to attract an employee to accept the riskier job. The wage pre-

mium ($2,000) for the riskier job reflects the value that employees place on the increased probability of losing their lives. Implicitly, employees are acting as if $2,000 is equivalent to a 0.0005 chance of dying. Accordingly, the value employees place on their life is found by solving the following equation:

$$\$2,000 = 0.0005 \times (\text{Value of life})$$

Solving this equation yields a value for life equal to $4 million ($2,000/0.0005). Implicitly, an employee is valuing his or her life at $4 million when he or she is willing to accept this riskier job for a $2,000 wage premium.

This example was simplified to illustrate the approach to valuing life. Actual studies that use labor market data are more complex than the example suggests. For example, these studies attempt to control for the many factors that affect wages and apply the analysis to situations where the differential risks of dying generally are known. While it is important to recognize that valuing life in this manner depends on a number of assumptions and that the analysis does not yield a magical number on the value of a person's life, the approach yields a range of values that are useful for many purposes. For example, from a safety regulation perspective, regulators must decide whether to impose costly regulations that reduce the probability of death for a portion of the population. The costs of the regulation need to be compared to the benefits. The benefits can be measured by taking an estimate of the value of a life multiplied by an estimate of the number of lives saved due to the regulation. The value of life implicit in wage differentials between

Box 14A–1

Your Money or Your Life

Human life is precious, of course. But is it priceless?

That weighty question ought to be reserved for advanced philosophy seminars. Instead it is being debated in a setting—John Grisham-land—where the answers are practically guaranteed to be simple-minded.

Here's the setting: In 1991, an errant trailer broke off a pickup truck and careened straight into an Oldsmobile Cutlass station wagon parked at a Virginia tollbooth. The trailer punctured the car's gas tank, located behind the rear axle, and the car caught fire, killing a 13-year-old-boy. His parents sued General Motors, contending the station wagon's design was defective.

At the trial, now going on in Hollywood, Florida, the plaintiffs' lawyers introduced a "smoking gun" document found in GM's own files. Written in 1973 by a GM engineer named Edward Ivey, the memo calculates that there are a "maximum of 500 fatalities per year in accidents with fuel-fed fires where the bodies were burnt. Each fatality has a value of $200,000." Based on those assumptions, the memo calculates that each fatality costs GM "$2.40 per automobile in current operation."

A plaintiffs' witness who used to work for GM testified that an executive told him that, since it would cost $4.50 per vehicle to remedy this defect, GM had decided not to make the change. Naderite Clarence Ditlow gleefully went on television to conclude: "Hundreds of Americans have burned to death because of GM's callous disregard for human life."

GM's reaction has been predictable. The company angrily denies that it relied on the Ivey memo and indignantly declares, "General Motors believes that a dollar value *cannot* be placed on human life." If the company genuinely believes that, its shareholders should sue for mismanagement. More likely, the company simply believes that it cannot share some hard truths with an American jury.

In this case, the hard truth is that it's almost impossible *not* to put a value on human life when conducting any cost-benefit analysis, whether of a consumer product or a government regulation. Say the EPA is considering a new clean air rule. It figures the regulation will cost industry $100 million and save 200 lives. To figure out whether the regulation makes sense the EPA must calculate how much saving those lives is worth. Saying that we'll spend an infinite amount to save even one life isn't an option, since studies reveal that anything that reduces national wealth causes deaths in its own right.

For this reason, all federal regulatory agencies are required to conduct cost-benefit studies, many of which involve putting a price tag on human life. Courts do the same thing. In an airplane crash lawsuit, the relatives of Victim A—a 30-year-old investment banker with plenty of high-income years ahead of him—stand to win more than the family of Victim B—a 70-year-old retired factory worker. That is not to say that the banker's life is worth more in the kingdom of heaven, only that these kinds of distasteful calculations are inescapable in our material realm.

jobs of different risks is particularly appropriate for evaluating safety regulation, because safety regulation usually involves changes in probabilities of dying of similar magnitude to the differences in probabilities of dying in a labor market setting.

Congress now requires that most regulatory agencies

undertake a cost-benefit analysis of proposed regulations. Earlier safety regulations, however, were not subject to such a requirement. One study that has looked at the costs and benefits of earlier regulations has found that the government's record on safety regulations is varied. Using estimates of regulatory costs and the reduced

Courts do it. Governments do it. And it's perfectly OK. But when corporations engage in cost-benefit analysis, it's a scandal. Why? How can auto engineers avoid using cost-benefit analysis?

Imagine if car designers sat down and decided to make safety their only criterion in designing a car. The product they designed would probably resemble a Bradley Fighting Vehicle and have a price tag to match. In every car certain tradeoffs have to be made. Typically, the heavier a vehicle, the safer. Thus, it's hardly surprising that a recent study found that sport utility vehicles are more crashworthy than passenger cars.

Does that mean we should get rid of less-safe vehicles? Only if you don't want poor people (or daring people) to drive. The better alternative would be simply to publicize the risks of cars like the Ford Pinto, so buyers could make their own decisions about how much safety is worth to them.

But can you imagine what would happen if a manufacturer announced: "Our car is a great buy! It's cheaper than the standard midsize sedan and gets better gas mileage. Oh, and by the way: You're much more likely to be burned to a crisp while driving it."

Human psychology being what it is, nobody would buy the car—even though the ad is only making explicit a tradeoff that everyone makes anyway. And, of course, every tort lawyer in America would rush to the local courthouse to sue the automaker. This kind of honesty is *verboten* in public discussions. So GM is forced to go to great lengths to explain away an innocent document like the Ivey memo.

The courts, in theory, are supposed to be better equipped to balance these types of issues. Judge Learned Hand's famous formula holds that a defendant should be held liable for negligence only if the probability of an accident multiplied by the gravity of the resulting injury is greater than the burden of adequate preparations.

In GM's Florida case, the gravity of the injury is great, but its probability is pretty remote. To be exact, fatal rear-impact collisions with fire damage occur at a rate of one for every 23 billion miles traveled by owners of the station wagon in question. (That's almost a million trips around the Earth—if you could find a route!) So perhaps it's not so callous to avoid spending an extra $4.50 per vehicle for a redesigned fuel tank.

After all, even if GM were to move the fuel tank from the rear, it would just be opening up a new area of potential injury—and liability. Lots of lawyers have filed suits over GM trucks with side mounted fuel tanks; in those cases, the lawyers no doubt argue the fuel tanks should be located in the rear.

The reality is that certain activities are inherently dangerous. Driving is one of them. We simply have to accept the risks and not blame some big company every time fate is cruel to us. But try telling that to a jury.

Source: Max Boot, "Your Money or Your Life? That Depends," *The Wall Street Journal,* March 4, 1998, p. A18.

---

probability of dying as a result of the regulation, Table 14A–1 summarizes the estimated costs per life saved of various regulations. The estimates suggest that some regulations clearly were beneficial from a cost per life saved perspective. For example, the cost per life saved due to the regulation of unvented space heaters was estimated to be $100,000. On the other hand, a number of regulations appear to be unjustified from a cost per life saved perspective. For example, the estimated cost per life saved due to EPA asbestos regulations is estimated to be $104 million; the cost per life saved from arsenic regulation is estimated to be $764 million.

TABLE 14A–1   Costs per Estimated Life Saved of Various Safety Regulations

Regulation	Year Passed	Agency	Cost per Life Saved (in millions of $1984)
Unvented space heaters	1980	Consumer Product Safety Commission	$ 0.10
Passive restraints/belts	1984	National Highway and Traffic Safety Administration	0.30
Crane suspended personnel platform	1988	Occupational Safety and Health Administration	1.20
Grain dust	1987	Occupational Safety and Health Administration	5.30
Uranium mill tailings (inactive)	1983	Environmental Protection Agency	27.60
Asbestos	1989	Environmental Protection Agency	104.20
Arsenic/low-arsenic copper	1986	Environmental Protection Agency	764.00
Formaldehyde	1987	Occupational Safety and Health Administration	72,000.00

Source: W. Kip Viscusi, *Pricing Environmental Risks,* Center for the Study of American Business, Policy No. 112, June 1992.

CHAPTER 15

Liability to Customers, Third Parties, and Shareholders

Chapter Objectives

- Describe legal liability rules, insurance coverage, and public policy issues relating to products liability, environmental liability, and directors and officers' liability.

This chapter provides an introduction to three important types of legal liability for businesses: (1) liability for product injuries, (2) liability for environmental damage, and (3) liability for actions of corporate officers and directors. We emphasize at the outset that the law concerning these subjects is complex and varies across states. Our purpose is to provide an introduction to key aspects of the relevant law, explain and analyze the insurance market's response to changes in liability rules, and discuss key public policy issues that arise from these liability rules.

15.1 Products Liability

Legal Background

Evolution of Tort Liability. Products liability law has an interesting history that provides important insights about the evolving tort liability system. Prior to 1916, most injuries and illnesses resulting from products were covered under contract law, not tort law. A manufacturer could not be held liable unless the victim and the manufacturer had a direct contractual relationship. For example, if a manufacturer sold a product to a retailer who in turn sold the product to a consumer, then the manufacturer generally could not be held liable for the consumer's losses. Because of the contractual requirement (known as the *privity limitation*), manufacturers seldom were held liable for damages to injured consumers.

An important 1916 case, *MacPherson v. Buick,* established that consumers injured by defective products can recover damages under tort law. MacPherson was thrown out of his Buick and injured when one of the wooden spokes on a wheel collapsed. Even though Buick subcontracted the production of the wheel to another firm and Buick sold the car to a retailer, who in turn sold it to MacPherson, the court found that Buick was liable for damages. Importantly, the *MacPherson v. Buick* case determined that a contractual relationship is not needed for the injured party to recover damages from the manufacturer. As a result, manufacturers could be held liable for losses suffered by the ultimate consumers of their products. However, the case also made clear that a consumer could not recover damages unless the manufacturer had been negligent. While the negligence rule was generally used in products liability tort cases during the first half of the 1900s, courts eventually started to hold manufacturers liable even when they were not negligent; that is, the courts moved toward a strict liability standard.

An important case that helped establish the strict liability standard for certain kinds of product-related injuries was *Escola v. Coca-Cola Bottling Company* in 1944. Escola was loading coke bottles into a refrigerator when one of the bottles exploded, injuring her hand. The California Supreme Court ruled that Coca-Cola was liable for the losses even though it was not found to be negligent. Judge Traynor's opinion in the case clearly states that the negligence rule should be replaced by a standard that makes manufacturers liable whenever their products are defective.

> I believe the manufacturer's negligence should no longer be singled out as the basis of a plaintiff's right to recover in cases like the present one. In my opinion it should now be recognized that a manufacturer incurs an absolute liability when an article that he has placed on the market, knowing that it is to be used without inspection, proves to have a defect that causes injury to human beings.

Judge Traynor's opinion also clearly states that the reason for moving from negligence to strict liability is that manufacturers are best suited to provide consumers with insurance against losses from product injuries:

> Those who suffer injury from defective products are unprepared to meet its consequences. The cost of an injury and the loss of time or health may be an overwhelming misfortune to the person injured and a needless one, for the risk of injury can be insured by the manufacturer and distributed among the public as a cost of doing business . . . Against such a risk there should be general and constant protection and the manufacturer is best suited to afford such protection.

The *Escola v. Coca-Cola* case helped establish victim compensation (insurance) as an important objective of products liability law.

The *Second Restatement of Torts,* published in 1965, outlined legal doctrines that should be applied in tort law. Regarding products liability, it stated that manufacturers are liable if consumers are harmed as a result of using a product that is "unreasonably dangerous" and "defective" (see section 402A). The important point is that, under this doctrine, courts do not focus on the manufacturer's actions (as they would under a negligence rule) to determine whether the manufacturer is liable; instead, courts focus on whether the product is unreasonably dangerous and defective. However, determining in some cases when a product is unreasonably dangerous or defective may involve an analysis very similar to that used in assessing negligence, as we explain below. The *Second Restatement* also stated that contributory negligence is not an allowable defense by manufacturers. The doctrines in the *Second Restatement* were adopted by almost all states in the subsequent decade.[1]

There are three general types of product defects: (1) manufacturing defects, (2) design defects, and (3) warning defects. Depending upon the alleged defect (and the jurisdiction), manufacturers can defend themselves by arguing that the consumers (1) assumed the risk, or (2) engaged in the unforeseeable misuse of the product, in which case the defendant's liability may be reduced in a manner similar to a comparative negligence standard.[2]

A **manufacturing defect** exists if a particular product deviates from what the manufacturer intended. In most jurisdictions, if a product differs from the normal production run and a consumer is harmed as a result of the defect, then the manufacturer is liable; the manufacturer has no defense and the courts give no consideration to the costs and benefits of eliminating the manufacturing defect. The example of the exploding Coke bottle in the *Escola v. Coca-Cola* case illustrates a manufacturing defect. The manufacturer did not intend for the bottle to explode under normal conditions; thus, the explosion of one bottle suggests that that particular bottle was different from the normal production run and thus defective.

A **design defect** exists if foreseeable risks of harm presented by the product could have been reduced by the adoption of a reasonably safer design (or discovered and corrected through more exhaustive testing of the product). To determine whether a product is unreasonably dangerous, most jurisdictions use some form of a cost-benefit analysis. A manufacturer's liability depends on the court's answers to questions such as: Could the defect have been corrected at a reasonable cost? To answer this question, both the plaintiffs and the defendant usually employ engineering experts to testify on issues related to the feasibility and costs of alternative safer designs. Thus, when deciding whether a design defect exists, courts consider issues similar to those considered under a negligence standard. Since a finding that a product has a design defect implies that all the products of that particular design are defective, the costs associated with losing a design defect case usually are greater than the damages in that particular case. Box 15–1 provides a few examples of design defects that have led to large liability awards.

A **warning defect** exists if the product has not been properly labeled or the risks associated with using the product have not been properly explained. In most jurisdictions, courts will hold manufacturers liable if the danger was foreseeable

---

[1] The *Second Restatement* is soon to be replaced by the *Third Restatement*.

[2] Recall from Chapter 14 that contributory negligence, which prevailed until the 1970s, precludes recovery altogether if the plaintiff is at all negligent. Comparative negligence, which has replaced the previous rule in most jurisdictions, reduces the amount of the plaintiff's recovery to reflect his or her relative negligence.

Box 15–1

Examples of Design Defects

Examples of design defects that have led to large liability awards include:

- Liability of a manufacturer of three-wheel, all-terrain vehicles for injuries to children harmed when the vehicles overturn.

- Liability of an auto manufacturer for failing to install a rollbar to minimize injury if the vehicle overturns.
- Liability of a pick-up truck manufacturer for injuries caused by the explosion of a side-mounted fuel tank.

and the manufacturer failed to provide a warning that could have reduced the risks of harm. The foreseeability requirement essentially implies that courts consider issues similar to those under a negligence standard. Some jurisdictions, however, do not require that the danger was foreseeable and instead hold manufacturers liable if a warning would have prevented the harm that was caused by the product (under the assumption that if the warning had existed, then the consumer would have heeded the warning and prevented the harm). Manufacturers' liability based on warning defects explains, in large part, the proliferation of warning labels and pamphlets that are attached to many products. Box 15–2 provides examples of warning defects that have led to large liability awards.

In summary, since producers are strictly liable for product defects, the important issue is whether a product is defective. Deviation from the normal production run is taken as evidence of a manufacturing defect and thus manufacturers effectively are strictly liable for injuries resulting from such a defect. When determining whether a product has a defective design or warning, courts generally examine the manufacturer's knowledge and behavior. In this sense, the liability rule is somewhat analogous to negligence for design and warning defects.

Contractual Liability.   In addition to tort liability, firms also are subject to liability under contract law as a result of warranties that are made when products and services are sold to consumers. An **express warranty** is an explicit statement (promise) that a product or service will perform according to some standard. An **implied warranty** is an implicit performance guarantee that usually accompanies the sale of any product or service (e.g., that the product will be reasonably fit for its intended use). Consumers who are injured as a result of products not performing according to implied or express warranties can sue the seller for damages.

As an example of a breach of an express warranty, suppose that Mr. Madden buys a step-ladder that has a sticker stating that it will safely support a person weighing up to 300 pounds. If Mr. Madden is injured when the ladder breaks under his weight (which is less than 300 pounds), he can sue the manufacturer on the grounds that the ladder did not perform as the company expressly said it

Box 15–2

Examples of Warning Defects

Examples of warning defects that have led to large liability awards include:

- Liability of a crane manufacturer for an inadequate warning that the operator could be harmed if the crane contacted electrical wires.

- Liability of a refinishing fluid manufacturer for injuries caused by combustion of the fluid when used too close to an open flame.
- Liability of a manufacturer of a nonstick cooking spray for deaths to teenagers who deliberately inhaled the substance.

would. As an example of an implied warranty, suppose that Mr. Jordan purchases a basketball. While playing a game at the local YMCA, he goes up for a rebound. While his head is above the rim, the ball bursts when it hits the rim and inflicts damage to Mr. Jordan's face. In this scenario, the ball was not fit for ordinary use, and Mr. Jordan therefore can sue the ball manufacturer for the damages suffered.

Insurance Coverage

Insurance coverage for products liability generally is provided by a firm's Commercial General Liability (CGL) insurance policy.[3] As the name suggests, the CGL policy provides liability insurance coverage for property damage and bodily injuries for a wide range of liability exposures. The CGL policy, however, excludes some specific types of exposures that are insured by separate policies, such as auto liability and workers' compensation, or that are uninsurable for other reasons, such as war (see Chapter 8). As we will discuss later in this chapter, there are important exclusions for environmental hazards. The CGL policy also provides that the insurer has a duty to defend the firm in the case of a lawsuit and that the insurer pays the defense costs.

In 1986, the CGL policy was changed to allow liability coverage to be written on either an occurrence basis or a claims-made basis, as opposed to an occurrence basis only. Recall from Chapter 11 that under an occurrence policy the insurer pays claims if the loss occurred during the policy period, regardless of when the claim is filed. Under a claims-made policy, the insurer pays claims if the claim is filed during the policy period, provided that the loss occurred after the retroactive date of the policy. Claims-made coverage usually is only purchased for hazards that involve a large risk of unexpected increases in claim costs for the insurer, such as environmental liability, directors and officers' liability, and some product and professional liability exposures.

---

[3] Prior to 1986, the policy was called Comprehensive General Liability, also referred to as the CGL.

Issues

Critics of the products liability system contend that the scope and scale of products liability has expanded to the point that both the safety and compensation objectives of the liability system have been undermined. In response to these criticisms, a number of state legislatures have passed product liability reforms, and federal legislation has been proposed. After discussing whether the current system meets its safety and compensation objectives, we discuss some product liability reform measures.

Product Safety.   As discussed several times earlier in the book, safety can be increased by (1) taking more precautions (e.g., greater product safety features or warnings), and (2) decreasing the level of the risky activity (e.g., selling fewer products that might cause harm). From a public policy perspective, there are two main safety issues: (1) Do producers and consumers have incentives to take proper precautions to prevent accidents? and (2) Do consumers purchase the right amount of risky products? Arguments can be made that strict products liability is justified because it provides incentives for manufacturers to take the right amount of safety precautions when designing, manufacturing, and selling their products and because it induces consumers to purchase the right amount of risky products. As we will see shortly, however, counterarguments also can be made.

Regarding the issue of manufacturers' safety incentives, strict liability for all consumer losses provides strong incentives for manufacturers to make safe products. As analyzed in detail in the previous chapter, if consumers are uninformed about product risk, then manufacturers will have too little incentive to produce safe products in the absence of liability. Thus, strict liability for all accident losses provides incentives for manufacturers to invest in more safety.

Another potential problem remedied by making manufacturers strictly liable is that consumers who are uninformed about product risk might otherwise consume too many risky products. To illustrate, suppose that consumers are uninformed and producers are not liable for damages. Then, the product's price will reflect only the manufacturing and distribution costs; the price will not reflect the expected losses that consumers could suffer. Consequently, the product's price is less than the true cost of consuming the product. Uninformed consumers therefore may buy too much of the risky product relative to what they would consume if they were informed about the product's risk. Making the manufacturer liable for damages can help correct this problem, because the product's price will reflect the producer's expected liability costs and thus consumers' expected losses. Since the price reflects consumers' expected losses, even uninformed consumers will make consumption choices based on the true cost of consuming the product. Making producers strictly liable for all consumer losses therefore helps correct the problem of overconsumption of risky products by uninformed consumers.

The weight given to these arguments for strict liability depends, in part, on your view of how well the marketplace works to give manufacturers incentives to make safe products in the absence of liability (or under a negligence standard) and whether consumers would make the right consumption choices regarding risky products in the absence of liability (or under a negligence standard). As discussed in the previous chapter, if consumers properly evaluate product risks, then manufacturers will have the right safety incentives without liability. Similarly, if consumers properly evaluate product risks, then consumers will not consume an excessive amount of risky products. Thus, the safety justification for the existing products liability system is premised on consumers underestimating product risk. While some would argue that consumers do not understand product risks, it is worth noting two points. First, the extent to which people become informed about product risks depends in part on whether manufacturers are liable for damages. To the extent that consumers view themselves as being insured by the products liability system, their incentive to gather information about product risks declines. Second, consumers' lack of information could cause them to overestimate product risk, which undermines the argument that manufacturers need to be held liable for safety reasons.

Regarding manufacturers' safety incentives, strict liability and a negligence rule are likely to have similar effects. In particular, a negligence standard that examines the costs and benefits of additional safety measures is likely to give manufacturers the right incentives to make safe products. If a manufacturer fails to undertake cost-effective safety measures, the courts will find it liable. Thus, from the perspective of manufacturers' safety incentives, there is little advantage of a strict liability standard over a negligence standard, if the negligence standard is appropriately used. On the other hand, because product prices will not reflect the expected costs of non-negligent injuries under a negligence rule, too many risky products might be purchased compared to strict liability if consumers underestimate the risk of injury.

Problems with strict liability from a safety perspective may arise when other firms in the chain of supply (for example, retailers) and consumers can influence the frequency and severity of accidents. For example, strict liability for defective products may give consumers too little incentive to use defective products safely. This problem is an example of the moral hazard problem discussed several times earlier in the book; if consumers are fully insured, then their incentives to take precautions are reduced. The effect of strict liability on consumer safety is uncertain. Some people argue that consumers are unlikely to increase their risk of injury because of the potential for a large damage award if injured. On the other hand, the observation that people increase their level of precautions in response to an increase in the probability of incurring small fines (e.g., driving slower when more police are patrolling) suggests that people also might decrease their level of precautions in response to an increase in the probability of receiving large damage awards. Indeed, some people have staged accidents in order to possibly receive a large award or settlement.

Whether the current products liability system provides the right safety incentives depends on a number of factors, including the damages awarded by courts, their assessment of the costs and benefits of additional safety efforts by manufacturers and consumers, and the implementation of procedures and standards of proof. These factors are likely to vary across jurisdictions as well as across individual cases within a jurisdiction. Some commentators argue that courts make systematic errors by holding manufacturers liable when the manufacturer could not have foreseen the danger or when the danger was created by the consumer's misuse of the product, and by awarding excessive damages, especially for pain and suffering. To the extent that these charges are true, then manufacturers are likely to have excessive incentives to make products safe. This point was illustrated in the example in the previous chapter where Nielson overinvested in safety when the courts awarded damages that were greater than consumer losses. While it is unlikely that courts award excessive damages in all cases, at a minimum there is little doubt that the courts have introduced considerable uncertainty into products liability.

In response to the high expected value and variance of product liability costs, many manufacturers claim that they have withdrawn products from the marketplace. In some cases, withdrawing dangerous products is beneficial. In other cases, however, the products withdrawn actually may have reduced risk relative to other products. For example, some analysts have argued that certain pharmaceuticals have been withdrawn as a result of products liability even though the evidence is that the vast majority of people would experience a reduction in risk through their use. Small airplanes provide another example. Products liability has increased the cost of new airplanes, so pilots are induced to fly older planes which are often more risky.

Compensation for Injury.   Even though one of the main justifications of the current products liability system is as an insurance system (see the quote of Justice Traynor earlier in the chapter), the current system nonetheless can be criticized on the grounds that it provides excessive compensation (insurance coverage) to victims. Under the existing system, courts generally try to compensate victims fully for medical expenses, lost wages, and pain and suffering. As discussed in Chapters 8 and 14, full insurance coverage rarely is desired by consumers because of transaction costs and moral hazard. The legal fees and court costs associated with providing insurance through the tort system are akin to the transaction costs associated with private insurance contracts. Also, to the extent that consumers' behavior affects the likelihood and severity of product injuries, the insurance provided by the tort system is subject to moral hazard. Moral hazard problems are especially severe for noneconomic losses. The transaction costs and moral hazard problems suggest that consumers would demand less than full coverage (compensation) for product-related injuries.

Moreover, as discussed in Chapters 8 and 14, many consumers are unlikely to demand insurance coverage for noneconomic losses, such as pain and suffering, even if the insurance had no loading and was not subject to moral hazard. To the extent that compensation for noneconomic losses is awarded, the courts force consumers to purchase insurance coverage that many of them do not want. That is, most consumers would prefer to have lower pain and suffering compensation if injured (lower insurance coverage) and lower product prices.

As discussed in Chapter 14, one interpretation of why the courts award full compensation to accident victims is that the courts are concerned with giving manufacturers the right incentives to produce safe products, which may require full compensation to victims. Other explanations for the courts' attempts to provide full compensation are that (1) courts do not understand or they reject the insurance theory underlying the argument for less than full compensation, and (2) other factors, such as jury sympathy, play a role in determining victim compensation.

Regressivity of Current System.   The wealth redistribution effects of the products liability system are interesting because they violate many people's notions of fairness. In particular, lower income people, on average, tend to be hurt by having insurance bundled with products.

To illustrate this point, note first that product prices reflect producers' expected liability costs, which in turn reflect the average level of damages awarded in products liability suits. Second, all consumers typically pay the same price for the same type of product (poor people pay the same price for a stepladder as do rich people). The problem is that the expected liability awards vary across people in predictable ways so that poor people typically receive lower awards. This occurs because courts typically award damages for lost wages, which vary with income. Also, evidence indicates that pain and suffering awards are greater for people with higher incomes (perhaps because pain and suffering awards are linked to monetary losses). Thus, the insurance coverage that is bundled with products is greater for higher income consumers. To the extent that higher income people buy the same risky products and pay the same prices as lower income people, the products liability system is therefore like a regressive tax: Lower income people pay the same price but receive less insurance coverage for the insurance implicitly bundled with products.

Products Liability Reform Proposals.   A number of products liability reform measures have been adopted by individual states and proposed (but not passed) at the federal level. These reforms include measures that would (1) reduce the potential liability of producers (e.g., by curtailing joint and several liability, capping pain and suffering awards, imposing limitations on punitive damages, and altering the collateral source rule so that plaintiffs cannot be compensated twice for the same losses); and (2) reduce the incentive of plaintiffs' attorneys to file marginal cases (e.g., by adopting a loser pays rule and reducing contingency fees for plaintiffs' attorneys).

A reform proposal that is unique to products is the adoption of a **statute of repose,** which states that products liability suits must be brought within a certain number of years (e.g., 20 years) after the product has been purchased. One justification for a statute of repose is that product safety deteriorates over time with or without proper consumer care. Given a strict liability standard, a statute of repose is a way of limiting manufacturer liability for product deterioration that would be excessively costly to prevent or when consumers are likely to have a significant influence on the product's safety.

Concept Check

1. Which liability standard would generally make it most difficult for a person injured by a product to recover from the manufacturer: negligence, strict liability, or absolute liability?

15.2 Environmental Liability

Legal Background

With increasing frequency, individuals exposed to toxic chemicals in the water, air, or soil are suing the firms that have contributed to the contaminants. The recent history of both common and statutory environmental law helps indicate how the scope of a firm's liability for environmental hazards has expanded dramatically during the past 30 years.[4]

Common Law. For many years, diffuse environmental hazards, such as loud noise and gradual pollution, were handled under nuisance law, which requires that the plaintiff demonstrate that the hazard is "serious, continuing, and unreasonable," and that the plaintiff is not hypersensitive to the hazard. Strict liability was reserved for situations where the environmental damage was caused by sudden events that occurred because someone brought something unnatural to the area and when losses were easily linked to a particular event (i.e., cause and effect were easily identified). The application of strict liability usually was based on an 1868 English case, *Rylands v. Fletcher,* in which the defendant's dam broke and flooded the plaintiff's mine. Although the defendant was not negligent, the court ruled that he was liable for the plaintiff's losses, because the losses clearly were the result of the defendant bringing something unnatural to the area (water), which had subsequently escaped.

Scientific advances have altered common law in two ways. First, we have improved our ability to measure small amounts of contaminants in the air, water, and soil over the past 50 years. Second, scientists have demonstrated that some illnesses may be linked to our exposure to certain contaminants. These advances have led some courts to interpret gradual leaks of potentially toxic substances into the environment as being equivalent to sudden events that directly lead to illness or death. To illustrate how gradual releases of potentially toxic substances might be equated to a sudden event that directly causes damage, consider the case of an underground storage tank that develops a hole and then gradually releases into the groundwater a substance that, when given in high doses to laboratory animals, causes cancer. The emergence of the hole in the tank is the sudden event, analogous to the dam breaking in the *Rylands v. Fletcher* case. The evidence from laboratory animals provides a way of arguing that the cancer that some residents of the area have developed is a direct effect of the hole. Using this line of reasoning, courts have begun to use a strict liability standard in cases involving low-level, gradual releases of potentially toxic substances.

---

[4] This section is largely based on an article written by Peter Huber, titled "Environmental Hazards and Liability Law" (see the end-of-chapter references).

Box 15–3

Notable Cases of Environmental Contamination

Love Canal

Between 1942 and 1953, the Hooker Chemical Company dumped 21,000 tons of hazardous waste into a landfill in the Love Canal area of Niagara Falls, New York. The dumpsite was selected because of the sparse population and because the clay soil would contain the potentially toxic substances. Despite Hooker's warnings to local officials of the potential danger, local officials pressured Hooker into selling the land to the city so that it could be developed. The city subsequently sold some of the land for further development. The development damaged the safety measures undertaken by Hooker (linings and layers of clay) and the potentially toxic substances eventually leaked. In 1980, the level of contaminants in the groundwater and soil were deemed to be so high that 700 residents of the area were forced to move. Despite an explicit provision in the original sales contract absolving Hooker of any liability, 1,300 current and former residents of Love Canal sued Hooker Chemical and the city of Niagara Falls. The suit was settled in 1984 for $20 million. According to numerous studies, Love Canal residents have not experienced a higher rate of disease than the general population.

Three-Mile Island

Following the nuclear accident at Three-Mile Island, Pennsylvania, in 1979, 280 residents of the area sued the operator of the nuclear power plant, General Public Utilities Corporation. The plaintiffs sought damages for economic losses associated with relocating and medical expenses, as well as damages for emotional distress. The suit was settled in 1982 for $20 million in economic damages and $5 million for creation of a public health fund.

Times Beach

Waste oil, containing the potentially toxic substance dioxin, was sprayed near the town of Times Beach, Missouri, during the 1970s. In 1983, the EPA, under the authority of the Superfund law, bought the land in the town and began to clean up the site. A few former residents of the area successfully sued the parties responsible for spraying the waste oil, alleging they had an increased risk of cancer. More recent evidence has questioned the toxicity of dioxin.

Agent Orange

As a result of exposure to agent orange in Vietnam, 2.4 million veterans and relatives of veterans sued Dow Chemical Company as well as other firms. The plaintiffs received $180 million in 1985.

Statutory Liability.   An important source of statutory liability is the Comprehensive Environmental Response, Compensation, and Liability Act of 1980 **(CERCLA),** usually known as the **Superfund law.**[5] The Superfund law was passed, in part, because of the Love Canal incident described in Box 15–3. The stated purpose of Superfund is to provide the funds needed to clean up waste dumps and accidental spills of toxic substances. The funds are obtained from taxes on petroleum and chemical companies and from recoveries from those who

---

[5] In addition to the federal Superfund law, many states have environmental laws governing cleanup and victim compensation.

have dumped waste in the cleanup sites. Most courts interpret the Superfund law as imposing strict, retroactive, and joint and several liability on owners, former owners, and anyone who has dumped waste at the site, including transporters of that waste.

An example will illustrate the scope of liability. Suppose that the EPA determines that a waste site needs to be cleaned up. The EPA then identifies the parties who have dumped waste at the site. The retroactive part of the liability standard implies that the EPA can hold someone liable who dumped at the site many years earlier. The strict liability standard implies that a party can be held liable even though it took all the cost-effective safety precautions known at the time that the waste was dumped. The joint and several liability standard implies that each party who dumped at the site could be held liable for the entire cleanup costs regardless of how little they contributed to the contamination. The liability of firms linked to the waste site does not end with the strict, retroactive, and joint and several liability associated with EPA cleanup suits. Often, common law cases, seeking damages for bodily injury and property damages, follow EPA lawsuits.

Initially, CERCLA was expected to last five years and clean up about 400 sites (at least one from each state). Each time the program's life has ended, however, Congress has voted to continue its activities. Over 30,000 potential cleanup sites have been identified, with about 1,500 classified as priority sites. From 1980 through 1995, the EPA spent about $20 billion to clean up about 300 sites and to partially clean up about 500 sites. A large percentage of these costs are used to pay attorneys, consultants, and overhead expenditures. In 1994, litigation costs accounted for over 20 percent of the Superfund budget.

Insurance Coverage

The history of private market insurance coverage for environmental hazards reflects an opposite trend to the scope of liability: As the common law and statutory liability for environmental hazards have expanded, insurers have curtailed coverage, especially in basic liability policies. Large environmental liability claims, in many cases for policies written many years earlier, have contributed to significant financial problems at numerous insurance companies.

Prior to 1970, most comprehensive general liability (CGL) policies did not specifically address the issue of environmental hazards, but being *general* liability insurance policies, they covered environmental damages that were neither expected nor intended by the insured business. As environmental liability increased during the 1960s, insurers began to alter policies to exclude coverage arising from pollution, except if the event causing the pollution was "sudden and accidental." By 1973, almost all CGL policies included the **sudden and accidental clause.** Some insurers offered a separate policy, called an environmental impairment liability (EIL) policy, to cover gradual pollution.

As discussed earlier, courts increasingly found firms liable for low-level, gradual releases of potentially toxic substances during the 1970s and 1980s under the logic of the *Rylands* case (that such releases were equivalent to sudden releases with a clear cause and effect). In addition, the introduction of the Superfund law in 1980 increased firms' liability for environmental hazards. Naturally, when firms experience environmental liability losses, they look to their liability insurers to pay the losses. Since pollution usually occurs over many years, multiple policies can potentially provide coverage. Complicating matters further, many of the policies have an exclusion for all but sudden and accidental pollution. The result has been enormous litigation between insurers and policyholders over whether policies cover environmental losses—with no end in sight.

Coverage of Cleanup Costs.   One of the issues that frequently arose in insurance policy disputes during the 1980s was whether the policy would cover the costs arising from Superfund actions. The standard CGL policy provides coverage for liability payable "as damages." Thus, the issue is whether Superfund costs should be viewed as damages. Insurers have made two arguments to deny coverage for Superfund costs. First, some of Superfund's actions can be classified as preventative and thus insurers argue that the costs of these actions are not damages, but instead are loss-control expenditures. Second, in some instances, the EPA requires that a firm clean up a site, as opposed to the EPA undertaking the clean up and then holding the firm liable for the cleanup costs. Insurers argue that when the policyholder cleans up a site, the cleanup costs are not damages and therefore are not covered. Most state courts have settled these disputes in favor of the policyholder.

Coverage Trigger.   One of the main sources of dispute over environmental claims relates to what has come to be called the **trigger of coverage.** That is, disputes arise over what policies are triggered by a claim and, if more than one policy is triggered, how claim costs are to be divided among the various policies. The answer seems straightforward: Occurrence policies cover damage for injury that occurs during the policy period and claims-made policies cover damage for injury that has occurred since the retroactive date and for which a claim is filed during the policy period. However, a number of situations arise where it is difficult to identify when the injury occurred. To illustrate, consider the case of a plaintiff who is awarded damages as a result of a chemical leak that started in 1971. The plaintiff was exposed between 1971 and 1975, he first learned of the disease in 1980, and he filed a claim in 1982.

Depending on the case and jurisdiction, the courts have adopted several alternative triggers of coverage. A *continuous trigger* rule states that all policies that provided coverage between the date of first exposure (1971 in our example) to the date the damage was first manifested (1980) provide coverage, usually in proportion to the number of exposure years. An alternative continuous trigger rule would trigger all policies between the first exposure and the time a claim was filed (1982). An *exposure trigger* rule would trigger all polices that were in place while the plaintiff was exposed to the substance (1971 through 1975). A *manifestation trigger* rule states that the policy that provided coverage when the injury was first manifested (1980) provides coverage, which often implies that only one policy is triggered. More recently, some courts have adopted an *injury-in-fact trigger,* which bases the trigger on specific facts (evidence) concerning when the substance actually harmed the plaintiff. In some cases this has produced results similar to the continuous trigger rule.

Gradual Pollution and the Absolute Pollution Exclusion.   Another important issue relating to insurance coverage disputes is whether claims related to gradual pollution are covered under the policies that contain an exclusion for all but sudden and accidental losses. Many courts have found that these policies provided coverage even when the pollution was gradual and occurred over many years. The courts' decisions in these cases have been based on one of several arguments. For example, policyholders sometimes argue that the exclusion is ambiguous. As discussed in Chapter 8, contract ambiguities often are settled in favor of the policyholder. Policyholders also have argued that, even though the pollution has occurred over several years, they were unaware that it was occurring. The revelation that the pollution occurred was sudden and the consequences of the pollution were unintended. Thus, they argue, the exclusion for all but sudden and accidental pollution does not apply. In 1986, insurers responded to the courts' tendency to provide coverage by changing the exclusion for all but sudden and accidental pollution to an **absolute pollution exclusion** that excludes coverage for virtually all pollution. Thus, as courts expanded liability and broadened their interpretation of insurance coverage (arguably beyond what insurers originally intended), insurers responded by explicitly restricting coverage.

     The law and insurance coverage for environmental hazards continues to evolve. The absolute exclusion for environmental liability in the CGL policy has increased demand for EIL coverage, and this market experienced dramatic growth during the 1990s. On the legal front, some courts have found, despite its name, that the absolute pollution exclusion is not absolute. For example, a Louisiana Supreme Court in 1994 found that the absolute pollution exclusion is ambiguous and does not bar coverage for some types of environmental claims. Two other states also have ruled that the absolute pollution exclusion does not necessarily bar coverage (see Box 15–4).

Issues

Safety.   There is little doubt the increased liability from common and statutory law (e.g., Superfund) has increased incentives for firms to take more precautions when handling or disposing of potentially hazardous substances. Some analysts, however, argue that the law has provided excessive safety incentives in some instances. For example, joint and several liability and the tendency of some courts to find liability when only a tenuous link exists between a firm's actions and losses suffered by victims might lead a firm with substantial net worth to take excessive precautions with respect to environmental issues.

     Critics of the Superfund law also argue that the EPA spends excessive resources (obtained from businesses and insurers) on cleaning up sites that have little chance of posing harm to area residents. Many studies indicate that the inci-

Box 15–4

The Pollution Exclusion Debate

After studying the genesis of pollution exclusions in general liability insurance policies, two state supreme courts late last year ruled in favor of policyholders by narrowing the scope of the absolute pollution exclusion.

The Illinois and Massachusetts high courts ruled the exclusion does not bar coverage for carbon monoxide-related bodily injury claims that do not involve "traditional environmental pollution." After all, the courts found, cleanup costs resulting from gradually and abruptly occurring pollution were the only insurable, contaminant-related risks that insurers sought to exclude when the industry introduced the 1970 and 1985 pollution exclusions.

As the decisions demonstrate, the nearly 30-year battle over the scope of the pollution exclusion is far from over. Policyholders and insurers remain sharply divided—even when interpreting the same evidence—over the intentions of the insurance industry.

Insurers, not surprisingly, protest that the Illinois and Massachusetts courts awarded policyholders coverage that insurers had specifically barred in the absolute pollution exclusions.

Source: Dave Lenckus, "Drafting History Debated: Policyholders, Insurers Spar over Intentions behind Pollution Exclusion," *Business Insurance*, January 5, 1998.

dence of disease for people living near cleanup sites is not significantly higher than elsewhere. So why does the EPA spend resources cleaning up sites? Critics contend that the EPA overstates health risks because the EPA's risk assessment is based on worst case scenarios for each of multiple contributing factors. The probability that one of the factors will take on its worst value is remote and the probability that all the factors will take on their worst values is next to impossible. Even in situations where sites are potentially hazardous, the EPA is criticized for its selection of remedies. The EPA usually attempts to remedy the situation by cleaning up the site for any potential future use. Thus, even if a site is unoccupied, the EPA attempts to make it safe for a residential community. Alternatives, like limiting future use of the site and paying the relocation costs of existing residents, could be more cost-effective and preferred by many residents. In a few specific cases, the EPA has been criticized for increasing risk of exposure to toxic substances because its cleanup efforts have freed some of these substance into the environment when they were previously encased.

Compensation.   It is reasonable to assume that people would want to have insurance coverage against diseases and property damage caused by environmental hazards. To a large extent, private insurance for medical expenses, disability, and life insurance provides the types of coverage people are most likely to desire Thus, the compensation for medical expenses, disability, and loss of life provided by the tort system for environmental hazards is likely to be redundant, at least in part, for many people. Private insurance coverage is not available, however, for the loss in property value or the pain and suffering and emotional distress associated with environmental hazards.

Legal Costs.   A large amount of legal costs has been incurred as a result of environmental liability (estimated at up to one-half of total costs). Considerable litigation has occurred determining whether a firm is liable for cleanup costs and for personal losses suffered by individuals. In addition, as noted earlier, insurers and policyholders have litigated extensively over policy coverage. Part of the reason for the high litigation costs is that state courts vary in their interpretation of the liability rules and insurance coverage. The question is whether an alternative method exists that would compensate victims and pay cleanup costs and yet involve lower legal costs. For example, instead of using the liability system, additional taxes could be assessed on manufacturers and insurers to pay cleanup costs and compensate victims.

Incentives to Develop Former Industrial Sites.   Critics of Superfund also argue that it has deterred the development of former industrial sites because of the possibility that new owners may be held liable for cleanup costs in the future. This problem is likely to be especially severe in older cities, where manufacturing was once the major industry. An advantage of locating in suburban areas is the avoidance of potential environmental liability. This problem likely has contributed to the urban decline in many cities and has had a disproportionate effect on lower income people.

15.3 Directors and Officers' Liability

Legal Background

As with other types of legal liability, directors and officers' liability has expanded during the last two decades. Directors and officers of corporations have a legal duty to act in the interest of shareholders. If they breach this duty, they can be held personally liable for the losses suffered by shareholders.[6] Directors and officers' liability is one method of providing incentives for managers to act in shareholders' interests. As discussed in Chapter 2, the managerial labor market, the market for corporate control, compensation contracts, and monitoring by shareholders also help to ensure that managers act in shareholders' interests.

State incorporation law holds that directors and officers have a duty of care and a duty of loyalty to shareholders. The **duty of care** generally is interpreted as requiring directors and officers to make informed decisions. That is, directors and officers must seek information and consider the pros and cons of a decision. Generally, the burden of proof is on the plaintiff when a duty of care violation is alleged. Also, the courts use the principle, called the **business judgment rule,** that they will not question informed decisions. Thus, even if a business decision turns

---

[6] Directors and officers also can be sued by nonshareholder claimants.

out to have produced poor results (e.g., it decreased shareholder wealth), the courts will not hold directors and officers liable, provided that the decision was an informed decision. If the courts did not follow the business judgment rule, then the courts would be overseers of all major corporate decisions and in essence become corporate managers.

The **duty of loyalty** applies when a corporate decision involves a potentially material conflict of interest between shareholders and officers and directors. Consider, for example, a decision by the directors to accept a management buyout offer when some of the directors are part of the management team that is proposing the buyout. As part of the buyout team, the directors want as low a price as possible, but as agents for shareholders, the directors want as high a price as possible. When faced with such situations, directors and officers are required to act in the interests of shareholders, and courts hold them to a much higher standard than in duty of care cases. Not only must directors and officers become informed (as the duty of care requires), they also must take whatever steps are necessary to ensure that decisions are in shareholders' best interests.

In addition, officers and directors can be held liable for violating federal securities laws. The Securities Act of 1993 and the Securities Exchange Act of 1934 impose a number of requirements on a firm and its officers and directors. For example, firms are required to disclose information that is relevant to investors in a timely manner. If the firm fails to do so, then officers and directors, as well as the firm, can be sued by shareholders.

Shareholder suits can be classified as either derivative or direct. **Derivative suits** are brought by shareholders on behalf of the corporation. Any court-awarded damages or settlements are received by the corporation. In contrast, in **direct actions suits,** plaintiffs bringing the suit (and their attorneys) receive the damages and settlements. Direct actions against officers and directors can be either individual actions or class actions. *Class actions* are suits brought on behalf of a group of plaintiffs that are alleged to have been harmed.

Shareholder suits alleging that officers and directors violated their duty of care or duty of loyalty often are related to corporate activities like acquisitions and bankruptcies. It is not surprising, therefore, that the number of shareholder suits increased during the 1980s with the increased takeover activity and bankruptcies of financial institutions during that period. Shareholder suits alleging violation of securities laws often are associated with the process of going public through the initial public offering of equity securities and with seasoned equity offerings. In these cases, the purchasers of the new securities claim that officers and directors failed to disclose material information. Also, as we discuss in more detail below, a large number of shareholder class actions have been filed in recent years against the officers and directors of publicly traded companies alleging that managers failed to disclose information in a timely manner.

Indemnification and Insurance Coverage

Before describing directors and officers' insurance policies, we first must describe corporate **indemnification** of officers and directors, which refers to the reimbursement by the corporation for officers and directors' legal costs and losses

TABLE 15–1   Summary of the Types of Officers and Directors' Losses That Can Be Indemnified by Corporations in Many States

Type of Action	Corporation Can Indemnify
Derivative actions	Litigation expenses
Direct actions	Litigation expenses and judgments, fines, and settlement amounts

from settlements, judgments, and fines. As summarized in Table 15–1, many states limit the extent to which officers and directors can be indemnified based on the type of suit that is filed. For derivative actions, indemnification can cover only litigation expenses. However, for direct actions, indemnification can cover judgments, settlements, and fines, as well as litigation expenses. The logic for limiting indemnification for derivative suits lies in the observation that if indemnification also covered judgments and settlements, then the corporation would be paying damages to itself.

Prior to the mid-1980s, almost all states had indemnification laws as described in Table 15–1. Around that time, courts began to hold officers and directors liable in circumstances where they previously had not. As a result, insurance premiums increased, which caused firms to look for new ways of compensating officers and directors for damages awarded in derivative suits. In response to corporate lobbying efforts, a number of state legislatures passed laws expanding the ability of firms to indemnify officers and directors for judgments and settlement amounts in derivative actions.

Directors and officers' (D&O) insurance generally has two parts. One part provides coverage for officers and directors for losses that are not indemnified by the corporation. The other part provides coverage to the corporation for indemnification costs. Many policies include per director deductibles as well as aggregate deductibles. In addition, many policies have a coinsurance provision that requires officers and directors to pay some percentage of losses above a limit. D&O insurance policies generally are claims-made policies. Unlike CGL policies, D&O insurance policies do not permit the insurer to take over the defense of the claim. An explanation for this difference is that the reputation of the officers and directors often is at stake in a shareholder suit and therefore that officers and directors often would want to be involved in their defense and in settlement decisions.

D&O insurance policies typically have a number of exclusions, which are important for understanding the incentives of officers and directors to settle cases (see below). A common provision excludes coverage for claims that arise as a result of an officer or director gaining illegal personal profit. Thus, insurers may deny coverage for damages resulting from a director's violation of his or her duty of loyalty (i.e., where a conflict of interest with shareholders exists). Another important provision excludes coverage for damages that are "uninsurable under the law." A fundamental legal principle states that as a matter of public policy, people should not be insured for liability damages that arise from their willful misconduct. This exclusion can be used to deny coverage for known violations of security laws.

Issues

Incentives to Settle Securities Class Actions.   A controversial issue related to directors and officers' liability in the 1990s was the number of class actions alleging that public firms failed to disclose material information in a timely manner. The following circumstances are typical of these suits. Suppose that Posey Inc. announces that its annual earnings are substantially less than expected and that its stock price immediately falls 20 percent. A day or two later, an attorney files a class action alleging that directors and officers had the negative information long before it was released and therefore that the managers committed fraud and misrepresentation by failing to release the information for a period of time, called the *class period.* Because the firm's stock price did not reflect the negative information during the class period, investors who purchased shares during the class period and held their shares through the end of the class period suffered losses and are eligible for compensation.

Many analysts believe that a large proportion of securities class actions are **strike suits** (i.e., they have little or no merit but they are filed to coerce management into a settlement). Managers often have strong reason to settle, in part because of their directors and officers' insurance contracts. As noted above, defendant managers who are found guilty of fraud and misrepresentation can be held personally liable for alleged plaintiff shareholders' losses. In most instances, the magnitude of alleged damages easily exceeds managers' wealth. D&O insurance and corporate indemnification typically will pay settlement amounts, but exclusions in the D&O insurance policies allow the insurer to deny coverage if managers are found by the court to have committed fraud and misrepresentation. Thus, managers face a decision of fighting the class action in court (which carries a small probability of incurring very large personal losses) or settling out of court (which ensures that their immediate personal financial losses will be relatively small).[7]

The Merit of Securities Class Actions.   As noted, considerable controversy exists regarding the merit of a large proportion of class actions alleging violations

---

[7] A natural question is why D&O insurers go along with a settlement if a case has no merit. The insurer would appear to be better off fighting the case in court, because, even though insurers may lose a few cases at trial, the fact that there are large numbers of cases suggests that most of the risk of large average losses is diversified away. One answer is that the settlement costs are lower than the expected legal fees from fighting the case. A second possibility is that insurers typically are not given control of the officers and directors' defense. Finally, insurers may be fearful of bad-faith suits (see Chapter 8). If the insurer convinces directors and officers to fight the case in court and they lose, then the officers and directors might sue the insurer for bad faith. Thus, insurers usually acquiesce to the desire of officers and directors to settle cases.

of securities laws. Critics of these suits claim that (1) the suits typically have little merit; (2) they are brought solely to coerce a settlement, which mainly benefits attorneys; (3) large costs are imposed on corporations defending these suits; and (4) the effect of these suits on corporate disclosure is the opposite of what the securities laws were originally intended to accomplish. With respect to the last criticism, it is argued that instead of promoting information disclosure, firms are reluctant to provide forward-looking information that may not be realized due to chance. For example, statements that the managers expect sales to increase significantly over the next year could be used in a shareholder suit alleging the statement was misleading if the forecast turns out to be inaccurate ex post, no matter how accurate the prediction ex ante (i.e., given information available at the time the prediction was made).

Plaintiffs' attorneys counter that class actions compensate victims of corporate fraud and misrepresentation. In addition, plaintiffs' attorneys argue that by imposing personal costs on fraudulent managers, these suits encourage the timely release of accurate information, which reduces information asymmetries in the stock market and thus lowers the cost of capital in the United States. They also point out that since plaintiff attorneys have incentives to identify disclosure violations, taxpayers are not burdened with enforcement costs.

In December 1995, Congress passed the Securities Litigation Reform Act of 1995. One aspect of the law is intended to deter plaintiffs' attorneys from filing suits with little or no evidence that fraud has occurred except for the fact that the firm's stock price has dropped by a large percentage. The law also gives firms a safe-harbor provision intended to reduce the likelihood that firms will have to pay damages for forward-looking statements.

15.4 Summary

- Products liability law has evolved from contract law to negligence to strict liability for product defects. Product manufacturers can be held liable under strict liability for design, manufacturing, or warning defects.

- Making manufacturers strictly liable for all consumer losses can improve safety incentives when consumers are uninformed about product risk, because strict liability gives manufacturers proper incentives to make safe products and induces consumers to purchase the right amount of risky products. However, it also is argued that the application of strict liability in practice may lead to excessive safety and higher prices, discourage innovation, and encourage continued use of older, less safe products. Strict liability for all consumer losses is likely to force consumers to purchase more implicit insurance coverage than they desire.

- Liability for environmental damage under common law expanded greatly during the last half of the 20th century, and Superfund legislation expanded liability for the cleanup of waste sites. As liability expanded, insurers first attempted to restrict coverage in CGL policies to only sudden and accidental pollution; subsequently, they introduced an absolute pollution exclusion in these policies. Pollution coverage now is available through customized environmental impairment liability (EIL) policies, which usually are sold on a claims-made basis.

- Directors and officers of corporations have a duty of care and a duty of loyalty to shareholders. If they breach these duties, they can be sued by shareholders. Directors and officers also can be sued by shareholders for violations of securities laws that require firms to disclose material information in a timely manner. Depending on the state and corporate charter, directors and officers are indemnified by their corporations for legal defense costs and/or settlements and awards. D&O insurance coverage often is purchased to cover (1) some nonindemnified losses to directors and officers, and (2) some corporate costs of indemnification.

Key Terms

manufacturing defect   367
design defect   367
warning defect   367
express warranty   368
implied warranty   368
statute of repose   373
CERCLA or Superfund law   375
sudden and accidental clause   376
trigger of coverage   377

absolute pollution exclusion   378
duty of care   380
business judgment rule   380
duty of loyalty   381
derivative suits   381
direct action suits   381
indemnification   381
strike suits   383

Questions and Problems

1. Compare the incentives of manufacturers to design safe products under the following scenarios for products liability:
   (a) Consumers cannot sue manufacturers for injuries.
   (b) Manufacturers have strict liability for defective products.

2. Critically evaluate the following statement: "Strict liability for products is socially beneficial because it provides correct safety incentives for manufacturers and consumers."

3. Provide an argument that the US products liability system results in excessive compensation to victims.

4. Provide an argument that strict liability lowers legal costs compared to a negligence rule.

5. Chapter 14 summarized the advantages and disadvantages of government regulation versus legal liability. Apply those arguments to critically evaluate the following statement:

"As a society, we should place more reliance on government regulation than on personal injury suits to influence firms' disposal of potentially toxic substances into the air, water, and soil."

6. Outline a procedure for assessing whether the benefits of Superfund cleanup operations are worth the costs.

7. Explain how increased uncertainty concerning products liability risk and possibly large punitive damages will affect the fair premium for products liability insurance.

8. Using the factors that influence the willingness of insurers to supply insurance coverage and consumers' willingness to pay for coverage (i.e., the insurability of risk, see Chapter 8), provide an explanation for why insurers have restricted coverage as the courts have expanded liability for environmental damage.

9. Suppose that an officer of a corporation has been sued for $2.5 million, where the suit alleges that the officer knowingly failed to disclose relevant information to investors. The officer believes the case has no merit, but because of the uncertainties of court cases, the officer estimates that the probability of losing the suit at a trial is 0.01. The expected legal fees from going to trial equal $100,000.

The plaintiff attorney has made a settlement offer of $0.5 million.

(a) Assuming that the officer is uninsured, what is the officer's expected cost of going to trial?

(b) Assuming that the officer is uninsured, explain why the officer may accept the settlement offer.

References

Abraham, Kenneth. "Cleaning Up the Environmental Liability Insurance Mess." *Valparaiso Law Review* 27 (1993), pp. 601–36. (*Analyzes insurance policy disputes related to environmental claims.*)

Epstein, Richard. *Modern Products Liability Law.* Westport, CT: Quorum Books, 1980. (*Provides a detailed discussion of the history and effects of products liability law.*)

Huber, Peter. "Environmental Hazards and Liability Law." In *Liability: Perspectives and Policy,* eds. R. Litan and C. Winston. Washington, DC: The Brookings Institution, 1988. (*Provides background and discussion of the problems in environmental liability.*)

Priest, George. "The Insurance Crisis and Modern Tort Law." *Yale Law Journal* 96 (1987), pp. 1521–90. (*General discussion of the effects of expanding liability and uncertain legal costs on liability insurance markets and the insurability of liability risk.*)

Romano, Roberta. "Corporate Governance in the Aftermath of the Insurance Crisis." In *Tort Law and the Public Interest: Competition, Innovation, and Consumer Welfare,* ed. Peter Schuck. New York: W. W. Norton, 1991. (*Analyzes shareholder suits and their effect on insurance prices and coverage during the 1980s.*)

Answer to Concept Check

1. Negligence, because the injured party has to prove that the manufacturer did not use reasonable care (cost-justified precautions). Strict liability requires proof that the product was defective and unreasonably dangerous, although this sometimes involves standards similar to negligence. With absolute liability, the injured party would only need to prove that the product caused the injury.

CHAPTER 16

Responsibility/Liability for Employee Injuries

Chapter Objectives

- Describe the history and basic features of workers' compensation laws.
- Explain the economic rationale for workers' compensation laws.
- Explain the major features of workers' compensation and employers' liability insurance.
- Review problems in workers' compensation related to cost growth and insurance price regulation and briefly discuss related reform legislation.
- Briefly discuss workplace safety regulation and other sources of employer liability for harm to employees, including violations of the Americans with Disabilities Act.

16.1 Overview of Workers' Compensation Laws

All states have workers' compensation laws that govern employer responsibility for workplace injuries to employees. Certain types of federal employees (e.g., railroad and maritime workers) are governed by comparable federal legislation, while other federal employees are governed by state laws. Many countries besides the United States have similar laws. As we describe in more detail below, **workers' compensation laws** have two important features: (1) employers are required to pay specified benefits for economic loss to injured employees without regard to employer fault or negligence, and (2) employees are not allowed to sue employers for injuries under tort law.

Prior to the enactment of state workers' compensation laws beginning in the second decade of the 1900s, employer responsibility for workplace injuries to employees was governed by tort liability law. Employers were legally responsible for employee injuries only if the employee could prove that the injury was caused by the employer's negligence. Prior to the 1880s three main defenses were available to employers even if the employee could prove negligence.

First, employers sometimes could avoid liability using an assumption of risk defense, arguing that for obviously hazardous jobs the employee assumed the risk of injury in return for a higher wage. Second, employers were not held liable if they could prove contributory negligence by the employee. Third, according to the fellow servant rule, employers were not held liable if they could establish that the employee's injury was caused by the negligence of a fellow employee. While some employers voluntarily provided compensation to injured employees, these defenses, along with the requirement of proving employer negligence, resulted in many employees not receiving any compensation from the employer for workplace injuries. In addition, very few employees had individual insurance to provide compensation for such injuries.

Starting in the 1880s, many states enacted **employer liability laws.** These laws generally prohibited employers from using one or more and commonly all three of their traditional common law defenses. Employer liability laws still apply today in cases where a workplace injury is not governed by workers' compensation legislation. In these cases, the worker must prove employer negligence in order to recover damages in a lawsuit, but the employer's defenses are limited by the state's employer liability law.

As noted, workers' compensation laws in the United States began to be adopted by the states during the early twentieth century. All states had enacted workers' compensation laws by 1948. These laws require most employers to pay specified economic losses of injured employees. Thus, they essentially mandate that employers insure workers against specified losses caused by work-related injuries and diseases. We provide an overview of workers' compensation benefits in the next section of this chapter.

Injured employees subject to workers' compensation laws do not have the right to sue their employers for injury under tort liability. Employer immunity from tort liability claims by injured employees is known as the **exclusive remedy** rule; that is, the employee's only remedy against the employer is to obtain benefits under the workers' compensation law. While employers are required to pay specified benefits for economic loss, the laws do not require the employer to compensate employees for pain and suffering. Note, however, that if some party besides the employer contributed to the injury, the worker may be able to sue that party for pain and suffering and any monetary losses not covered by workers' compensation (see Box 16–1).

Although the enactment of workers' compensation laws prevented injured employees from suing to recover economic losses not covered by workers' compensation and damages for pain and suffering, the laws were supported by employees and unions because they ensured that employees would receive specified compensation for economic loss without having to prove negligence by the employer. Employers generally favored the laws because they eliminated the employer's exposure to tort liability claims for employee injuries, which could involve significant defense costs and potentially large awards for pain and suffer-

Box 16–1

Worker Injury Suits against Nonemployers

The exclusive remedy rule only applies to the employer. Thousands of tort liability suits for workplace injuries are filed each year against other parties that contributed to the injury. A major example is when a worker is injured by a machine that was manufactured by another business. In these cases employees often recover damages in a product liability suit against the machine manufacturer for pain and suffering and any monetary losses not covered by workers' compensation. The employer's workers' compensation insurer (or the employer if it is self-insured) is subrogated (see Chapter 8) to the employee's tort rights to the extent of any workers' compensation benefits paid and generally will seek to recover these costs from the product manufacturer. Another common situation where a worker could sue under tort liability is when the worker is hurt from an on-the-job automobile accident caused by another driver. Again, the workers' compensation insurer or the self-insured employer is subrogated to the employee's tort rights against any at-fault driver to the extent of any workers' compensation benefits paid.

Because of these tort liability cases, for a given type of injury and amount of loss, an employee will receive more money if some other party is at fault than if the injury only involves the employer. Some people suggest that this is inequitable, proposing either that workers be allowed to sue their employers or that employee/employer suits against other parties be restricted. We discuss the disadvantages of extending tort liability rights (and allowable employee suits against employers under the so-called *dual capacity doctrine,* see Box 16–3) later in this chapter. A disadvantage of restricting suits against nonemployers that contribute to workplace injuries is that safety incentives could be reduced for these firms or parties.

ing. Employer support for workers' compensation strengthened following an increase in the frequency of tort liability suits by injured employees that accompanied the enactment of employer liability laws. In addition, many employers already had begun to provide limited benefits for economic loss to injured employees without regard to negligence. We discuss the economic rationale for workers' compensation laws in detail in section 16.3.

Coverage under workers' compensation is compulsory for specified types of employment in all but one state—Texas. Some states do not apply workers' compensation laws to employers with fewer than two or sometimes three or four employees. Some states exclude certain categories of employment, such as domestic services, from their workers' compensation laws. In these cases, employers can and typically do voluntarily choose to be governed by the workers' compensation law; a few of these states require the employee's consent. In order to be governed by a workers' compensation law, an employee's injury must be work-related in that it must arise out of and during the course of employment. Whether an injury satisfies this test is sometimes difficult to determine (see Box 16–2).

Workers' compensation laws require employers to either purchase workers' compensation insurance or meet specified eligibility standards in order to qualify to self-insure workers' compensation benefits. Workers' compensation insurance

---

Box 16–2

When Is Injury Work-Related?

Workers' compensation benefits are payable for injuries and occupational disease that *arise out of and during the course of employment*. In some cases it is not clear whether this requirement is met. If a dispute arises between the employer/workers' compensation insurer and the employee about whether an injury is covered, in most states the issue is settled by the state's workers' compensation commission. (A few states rely on the court system.) Examples of injuries and illnesses that may involve uncertainty about whether they are compensable by workers' compensation and how they are typically treated are shown below:

- On-the-job heart attack: May be compensable if conditions of employment gave rise to unusual risk of heart attack.

- Stress-related illness: Often compensable only if the employment involved stressful conditions above and beyond the ordinary conditions for that particular type of employment.

- Injuries while traveling to and from work: Generally not compensable, even if the employee has regular use of a company car; injuries incurred while using a vehicle for work (e.g., sales calls) are compensable, but not while using a vehicle for personal errands.

- Out-of-town travel within the United States: Injuries en route generally are compensable; injuries while off duty (e.g., in the hotel) may be compensable if the employer selects the accommodations.

- Foreign travel: Off-duty injuries are likely to be compensable if the location involves unusual risk compared to the United States.

---

prices traditionally have been subject to comprehensive regulation. In addition, six states (Ohio, Nevada, North Dakota, Washington, West Virginia, and Wyoming) require workers' compensation insurance to be purchased from a state government insurer. These government monopolies are known as **monopolistic state funds.** About one-third of the states have state insurers, known as **competitive state funds,** that compete with private insurers and/or serve as the residual market.

Concept Check

1. How does a workers' compensation law differ from an employers' liability law?

16.2 Workers' Compensation Benefits

Workers' compensation benefits are paid for work-related bodily injuries and occupational disease. The specific types and amounts of benefits vary widely across states, and the details are complicated. Our purpose here is to acquaint you with the major types of benefits (and hint at some of the complexity). Understanding the basic structure of benefits is important for understanding the operation of the system, the economic rationale for workers' compensation, and the problems that have arisen with workers' compensation in many states.

There are three main types of workers' compensation benefits: (1) payment of medical expenses; (2) payments for lost income associated with total or partial disability, whether temporary or permanent (i.e., the disability is expected to continue until normal retirement age or death, whichever comes first); and (3) death benefits in the form of payments to survivors of workers that are killed on the job.[1] Medical expenses represent 40–50 percent of total workers' compensation benefit payments in the typical state. A large majority of benefits for loss of income are for permanent partial disabilities. Benefit payments for permanent total disability and death represent a very small fraction of total payments.

Medical Benefits

Most jurisdictions provide for payment of all medical expenses associated with covered injuries and diseases without limitation during the lifetime of the employee. Medical benefits usually are paid without any deductible or co-insurance for the employee. Consistent with full insurance coverage for losses aggravating moral hazard (see Chapter 8), there is evidence that utilization of medical care for injuries covered by workers' compensation is greater than for nonoccupational injuries where medical expense insurance coverage often is subject to deductibles and co-insurance.

About half the states allow employers to (1) specify the physicians who shall initially treat the employee and (2) approve treatment by other physicians. This can reduce moral hazard because physicians then have an incentive to control costs in order to maintain their relationships with employers and workers' compensation insurers. In addition, increases in workers' compensation medical expenses during the 1980s led many states to adopt fee schedules for workplace injuries. These schedules specify the level of fees that physicians can receive for treating injured workers. In an effort to control costs, some states also have allowed employers to implement various types of managed care that provide employers and workers' compensation insurers with a greater ability to control costs. You will learn more about how moral hazard affects utilization of medical care and how managed care can reduce utilization in Chapter 18.

Disability Benefits

Total Disability Benefits.   Injured workers who are unable to work commonly receive benefits equal to two-thirds of their pre-injury wage. The maximum weekly benefit usually is capped at an amount equal to 100 percent of the state's average weekly wage. Many states also specify a minimum weekly benefit. To illustrate typical benefits, suppose that the state's average weekly wage is $400. Then an employee with a pre-injury wage of $300 would receive a weekly bene-

---

[1] A majority of states also pay specified benefits for vocational rehabilitation (e.g., compensation during a period of retraining, transportation expenses, prostheses, etc.). Comparable benefits usually are provided in other states even if they are not specifically enumerated in the workers' compensation law.

fit of $200 while disabled (two-thirds of $300). If instead the employee's pre-injury wage was $700, the employee would be paid the maximum benefit of $400 (since two-thirds of $700 exceeds the maximum benefit amount of $400). These benefit maximums, along with benefit minimums in many states, produce a higher wage replacement rate for lower paid workers than for higher paid workers. Workers' compensation benefits are not subject to federal and state income taxes, which increase the wage replacement rate compared to pre-injury wages on an after-tax basis. Some—but not all—states index benefits payable following an injury to increases in the state's average weekly wage.

Many states have a three-to-seven-day waiting period following the onset of the disability before benefits are paid. These waiting periods help to control costs and reduce the moral hazard (see below) associated with less serious injuries. If the duration of the disability exceeds a specified number of days (e.g., 21), then benefits usually are paid retroactively for the waiting period.

A **temporary total disability** ends when the worker can return to work. Total disability that is expected to continue until death or retirement age is known as **permanent total disability.** Almost all states pay permanent total disability benefits based on the amount of time from the onset of injury until a specified retirement age (e.g., age 65). Some states specify a maximum limit on the total amount of benefits paid (e.g., $200,000) or cap the duration of benefits at a lower amount (e.g., 500 weeks). In many permanent total disability cases, the injured worker and the workers' compensation insurer (or self-insured employer) agree to a lump sum settlement equal to the present value of future benefits instead of having benefits paid over time.

Like most insurance benefits, workers' compensation disability benefits (and other types of disability insurance benefits) are subject to a moral hazard problem. This problem has two dimensions. First, some injured workers may fake or exaggerate injuries in order to avoid working and become eligible for benefits. Second, some injured workers may delay returning to work following an injury because the marginal benefit of working may be small compared to not working and collecting workers' compensation benefits.

To illustrate the moral hazard problem, consider a worker with pre-injury wages of $500 per week before taxes and after-tax wages of $380. If the worker becomes eligible for temporary total disability payments, assume that he or she will receive $333 per week, which equals two-thirds of $500 (and is less than the maximum weekly benefit in the state). Compared to collecting workers' compensation benefits of $333 per week, the worker would gain only $47 per week after taxes ($380 − $333) by working. Thus, in this example, a worker that returns to work following an injury and temporary disability would make roughly $1 per hour from working ($47 per week more for a 40-hour work week) compared to receiving workers' compensation benefits.

Because the proportion of after-tax wages that is replaced by workers' compensation benefits is higher for lower paid workers than for higher paid workers (and perhaps because lower paid jobs are less attractive/stimulating than higher paid jobs), the moral hazard problem is more severe for lower paid jobs. For example, for the worker who makes a much higher wage, such as $1,500 per week, the moral hazard problem is lower because the worker only receives the maximum weekly benefit of $400 while disabled. Employers and workers' compensation insurers often attempt to mitigate moral hazard by monitoring and investigating claims and by using physician reports that certify whether the worker is able to work.

Permanent Partial Disability Benefits.   Payments for **permanent partial disability** are made to workers who experience permanent injuries that partially reduce the worker's earnings capacity. For example, if a person whose job routinely involves lifting heavy objects herniates a disk in his or her back, the injury may permanently prevent the worker from working in this capacity. If the worker can work only in jobs that pay less following the injury (for example, in lower paying service jobs), he or she has suffered a loss of earnings capacity that is compensable under workers' compensation laws. Payments for permanent partial disability usually follow a period of temporary total disability. As noted above, permanent partial disability payments generally represent a large proportion of total disability payments.

Most states combine two methods of determining permanent partial disability payments: (1) scheduled payments, and (2) payments based on an estimated reduction in earnings capacity. With the first approach, scheduled injuries will be compensated at amounts listed on a benefit schedule. Fixed benefit amounts will be scheduled for well-defined injuries, such as the loss of one or both limbs, fingers, eyes, hearing, and so on. For example, a state might have a benefit amount of $50,000 for loss of a thumb and $75,000 for loss of an eye. Scheduled amounts vary widely across the states.

A large proportion of permanent partial injuries are not amenable to using the simple schedule method. Examples include most injuries to shoulders, necks, backs, and other joints; these injuries reduce earnings capacity but do not prevent gainful employment. Although the rules and procedures for determining amounts of compensation in these cases are complex, the typical approach is to base compensation on the estimated percentage reduction in earnings capacity.[2] For example, assume that the worker with the herniated disk is estimated to have experienced a permanent reduction of earnings capacity of 50 percent (compared to 100 percent for total disability) and that the worker's predisability weekly wage was $600. Then the worker's weekly earnings loss would be estimated at $300 (0.5 × $600) and the weekly permanent partial disability benefits would be estimated at $200 (2/3 × $300). (This amount would be capped if it were greater than the statewide average weekly wage.) The $200 then would be multiplied by the number of weeks that benefits would be payable, which might be a fixed number of weeks (e.g., 300), or, if shorter, until retirement age. Assuming a 300-week period, the total benefit in this example would be $60,000 ($200 × 300). This benefit often would be discounted to present value (subject to state rules on the discount rate) and paid as a lump sum to the worker.

---

[2] The fact that several states refer to some of these injuries as scheduled injuries even though flat payment amounts cannot be specified adds to possible confusion.

Because an injured employee's true reduction in earnings capacity must be estimated for permanent partial disability cases, disputes between the employee and the employer and/or workers' compensation insurer are common. Injured employees often retain an attorney to negotiate settlements with the employer and/or the workers' compensation insurer. Many states provide that the employee's attorney fees are paid by the employer/insurer. If the employee and the employer/insurer cannot agree on a settlement, most states have a workers' compensation commission that will resolve the dispute (parties may be able to appeal the commission's decision to the courts). A few states allow direct access to the court system.

As an alternative to negotiated settlements for permanent partial disability based on the estimated reduction in earnings capacity, a few states have experimented with paying employees an amount equal to their actual wage loss over time. These experiments have met with little success due to two main problems. First, it is administratively costly to keep track of employees and their current wages. Second, actual wage-loss systems are subject to the moral hazard problem described above for total disability payments. They reduce the incentive for the employee to return to work and to obtain a higher paying job. This effect increases the costs of a wage-loss system.

Survivor Benefits

In addition to payment of a flat amount toward burial costs (e.g., $1,000–$5,000), all states pay workers' compensation benefits to surviving spouses and eligible children of workers that are killed on the job. The total weekly benefit usually is similar in magnitude to payments for total disability (two-thirds of the pre-injury wage). Some states pay a lower percentage of the pre-injury wage, such as 50 percent, if there are no children or if there is only one child and no surviving spouse. Depending on the jurisdiction, the duration of benefits often is limited by a number of factors, such as the remarriage of a spouse or a child's 18th birthday.

Concept Check

2. A state requires workers' compensation weekly disability benefits equal to 60 percent of pre-injury weekly wages but no more than the statewide average weekly wage of $540. How large must a worker's weekly wage be before his or her benefit will be less than 60 percent of the pre-injury wage?

16.3 Why Have Workers' Compensation?

You might wonder why we ask this question. Many students find the rationale for workers' compensation to be self-evident. The reasoning is: If workers are hurt on the job, then the employer should pay—end of story! However, life is seldom so simple. The economic rationale for workers' compensation rests on whether it can minimize the cost of risk by maximizing the welfare of workers compared to alternative systems that might be used.

Recall that workers' compensation laws combine mandatory provision of insurance coverage by employers with employer immunity from tort liability (exclusive remedy). Possible alternatives to the current system of workers' compensation include: (1) no mandatory workers' compensation benefits and no tort liability for employers; (2) no mandatory benefits but employees can recover from employers under tort law if the employer is negligent (no exclusive remedy); and (3) mandatory benefits but employees also can sue negligent employers for damages under tort law, thus allowing workers to receive workers' compensation benefits and seek compensation for the types of losses that are not covered under workers' compensation (e.g., pain and suffering and any lost wages in excess of allowed benefit maximums).

Note that there are many possible variations. For example, employers might be held strictly liable under a system that allows employees to sue, as opposed to requiring the employee to prove negligence on the part of the employer. Our discussion assumes that employees would have to prove negligence to keep things simple and because employees must currently prove employer negligence to recover for injuries that are not governed by workers' compensation.

As was true of our discussion of the rationale for tort liability in Chapter 14, the economic rationale for workers' compensation rests on its effects on safety, compensation for injury (including the extent to which persons uninsured for injuries might impose costs on other parties), and administrative/dispute resolution costs. Given the background provided in Chapter 14, our discussion in this section is comparatively brief.

Who Pays for Injury Costs?

To understand the rationale for workers' compensation compared to alternative methods, as well as issues associated with the design of workers' compensation benefits, you first need to recognize that laws or contracts that require employers to pay part or all of the cost of employee injuries will tend to reduce wages over time by the amount necessary for employers to recover these costs. Indeed, economic theory and evidence both suggest that this is the case. The intuition is that the demand for labor by employers depends on the marginal value added by workers (worker productivity) and the *full marginal cost* of labor to the employer, which includes the cost of worker injuries that the employer must pay, as well as the cost of employee benefits (see Chapters 18 and 19) and wage-based taxes paid by employers, such as social security taxes. In the context of workers' compensation, this means that employers primarily care about the total cost of employing a given worker, not how it is divided between wages and workers' compensation costs.[3]

Because employees as a group ultimately bear injury costs, there is no free lunch. Other things being equal, worker injury compensation systems that in-

---

[3] In Chapters 18 and 19 we discuss how the division of total compensation between employee benefits and cash compensation is relevant to employers to the extent that it affects factors such as employee productivity and turnover, as well as income taxes paid by employees.

TABLE 16–1   Theoretical Comparison of Alternative Systems for Dealing with Workplace Injuries

Mandatory Benefits	Tort Liability	Safety Incentives	Compensation	Administrative/Dispute Resolution Costs
No	No	Inadequate if employees underestimate risk	Inadequate	Low
No	Yes	Adequate	Excessive if employer is negligent; otherwise inadequate	High
Yes	No	Adequate with labor market incentives and safety regulation	About right	Moderate
Yes	Yes	Adequate or possibly excessive	Excessive if employer is negligent	Highest

crease what employers have to pay eventually will reduce wages, and if wages cannot be reduced, fewer workers will be employed.[4] Note that we are referring to a long-run, aggregate tendency. In the short run, employers are affected by changes in injury costs and those better at controlling costs can profit compared to other firms. Nonetheless, as a result of this long-run, aggregate tendency, the relevant question for employees to ask before they know whether they will be injured is: *What is the best method of providing compensation for workplace injuries given that we have to bear the costs?*

Some groups dispute this view. Leaders of organized labor groups, for example, often argue that the cost of greater payments by employers for injuries (and benefits) simply will reduce employer profits. However, if profits are at competitive levels, any increase in the cost of employer obligations for workplace injuries that cannot be offset by savings in wage payments will cause employers to hire fewer workers. Alternatively, it may lead to some increase in the prices of products, which also will tend to reduce employment due to reduced demand for goods and services following the price increase.

Benefits and Costs of Different Arrangements

Given the preceding background, you now are ready for an overview of the benefits and costs of traditional workers' compensation (mandatory benefits without tort liability) compared with three alternatives: (1) no mandatory benefits and no tort liability, (2) no mandatory benefits with tort liability, and (3) mandatory benefits with tort liability. Table 16–1 highlights the main differences in the systems.

---

[4] Some increase in the prices of goods and services also is possible (see below), but employees as a group then will have to pay higher prices and thus have lower real wages.

No Mandatory Benefits and No Tort Liability.   Consider first the case where employers are not required to provide compensation for workplace injuries and cannot be sued by employees. This "no remedy" case is analogous to the case of no liability for harm discussed in Chapter 14. In essence, we are analyzing safety and compensation in an unregulated market with no employer liability.

With neither mandatory workers' compensation benefits nor tort liability, employer safety decisions will reflect the benefits and costs to employers. It may at first appear that employers will invest virtually nothing on workplace safety. However, if employees are well informed about the risk of injury, increases in safety will allow employers to pay lower wages to the extent that the increased safety is valued by employees. With well-informed employees, this system will produce the right amount of safety: Employees will get the level of safety that they desire given that they have to pay for greater safety through lower wages.

Evidence indicates that higher risk jobs require higher wages, which is consistent with employee demand for safety providing significant incentives for employers to increase safety. Potential adverse publicity following major workplace accidents provides additional safety incentives for employers. Thus, even in an unregulated market with no tort liability, employers have substantial incentives to reduce workplace injuries. Given the complexity of many workplace environments and possible causes of injuries, however, many employees may not be sufficiently informed for safety to be adequate under a "no remedy" system.

Specifically, if employees underestimate the risk of injury, they will demand too little safety, and the no remedy system will produce too little safety. The employers' savings in wages from increasing safety will be insufficient to induce the employer to provide the level of safety that would be demanded by workers if they were better informed (and other influences, such as potential adverse publicity, may not fully offset this problem). As a result, one rationale for either workers' compensation or tort liability is to prevent suboptimal safety.

A second problem with no workers' compensation and no tort liability for workplace injuries is that many workers probably would fail to buy insurance coverage for workplace injuries or to negotiate employee benefit packages that would pay medical expenses and loss of income for their injuries. Many workers, especially lower paid workers, currently are uninsured for medical expenses for injuries and illnesses that are not work-related (see Chapter 18). In addition to possible hardship to uninsured people, a significant proportion of medical costs for the uninsured ends up being borne by other parties (insured persons and taxpayers). Thus, uninsured workers commonly impose costs on other parties. Workers' compensation reduces this problem for on-the-job injuries. Tort liability for employers would provide implicit insurance for injuries caused by employer negligence.

No Mandatory Benefits with Tort Liability.   We now examine workplace safety, compensation for injury, and administrative costs if employers can be held liable for workplace injury under a negligence standard. In this case, tort liability for employers would have the potential to provide proper safety incentives to employers without mandatory workers' compensation benefits, provided that employers have liability insurance or sufficient assets to pay damages. Compulsory liability insurance or requiring proof of adequate assets might be necessary to prevent some employers from being judgment proof (avoiding liability) and therefore having excessively risky workplaces and inadequate compensation for injured employees. However, even ignoring the problem of judgment-proof employers, a number of problems arise with the tort liability/no workers' compensation benefits approach.

First, as was discussed in Chapter 14, in order to provide parties with proper incentives to consider the full cost of harm they might cause to other parties, tort liability violates the principle of optimal compensation by requiring damages for pain and suffering and by providing payments that duplicate other sources of recovery to the injured party. Second, the tort liability system produces large costs for dispute resolution, as well as substantial uncertainty associated with the possibility of punitive damages. Both of these factors would increase injury costs and thereby reduce wages and/or employment. Third, unlike a workers' compensation system that compensates monetary accident losses regardless of whether the employer is negligent, a tort liability system would leave some employees uninsured for these losses.

Workers' Compensation: Mandatory Benefits without Tort Liability.   Consider next the effect of the traditional workers' compensation system on safety, compensation, and administrative costs. To the extent that workers underestimate the risk of workplace injury, mandatory workers' compensation benefits provide greater incentives for safety than would exist with neither mandatory workers' compensation benefits nor tort liability for injuries. Because employers must pay for injury costs as defined by law, increased safety has the potential to lower employer costs by reducing self-insured claim costs or workers' compensation insurance premiums (see below). While in the long run such savings will tend to benefit employees through increased wages and employment, in the short run, employers that can lower these costs can expand output, compete more effectively for labor, and increase profits compared to other employers.

The failure of mandatory workers' compensation benefits to encompass all economic losses and nonmonetary losses (pain and suffering) in principle could lead to suboptimal safety compared to tort liability. However, the design of workers' compensation benefits is more consistent with principles of optimal compensation and generally involves significantly lower dispute resolution costs than tort liability. In addition, government regulation of workplace safety can be and is used to supplement private incentives for safety, which in principle further reduces the potential advantage of tort liability as a means to promote safety.

You need to be aware, however, of at least one caveat to this favorable view of workers' compensation. If a workers' compensation system provides benefits greater than what employees are willing to pay for, has few cost controls, and is plagued by fraud and comparatively high dispute resolution costs in determining whether the injury is work-related and the magnitude of disability, a point might be reached where employees can be made better off by providing them with a nonworkers' compensation benefit package and allowing employees to sue employers for negligence. In fact, many employers in Texas that have opted out of workers' compensation, and insurers that sell specialized benefit packages and liability insurance to these employers, argue that this solution is preferable to workers' compensation for many employers and workers.

Mandatory Benefits with Tort Liability.   Now consider the possibility of adding tort liability to mandatory workers' compensation benefits (i.e., eliminating employer immunity from tort liability and thus ending exclusive remedy). Some people advocate this change, including a number of lawyers and law professors. Under this system, workers would receive workers' compensation benefits and also be allowed to sue employers for uncovered economic losses and pain and suffering if the injury is alleged to be caused by employer negligence. Punitive damages also could be sought in some cases (in principle if the employer engaged in willful disregard of worker safety). Advocates argue that this change is necessary to increase workplace safety and hold employers accountable for the full costs of their actions.

Until the costs are considered, combining tort liability with workers' compensation might first seem like the best of both worlds. It would combine the advantages of workers' compensation with improved safety incentives from the tort system. However, the additional compensation would violate principles of optimal compensation and result in large dispute resolution costs and substantial uncertainty for employers. The likely result would be lower wages and less employment. The current consensus is that the additional safety that might arise from such a system would not be worth the costs, which would largely be borne by employees over time.

Not knowing whether you will be injured and assuming that you would have to accept lower wages to cover the increased costs (thus preventing any subsidy), ask yourself whether you would like to be covered by workers' compensation *and* have the right to sue your employer for uncovered economic losses, pain and suffering, and punitive damages. If you understand the material in this section and in Chapter 14, we suspect that your answer will be no.

Concept Check

3. If a worker knew for certain that he or she was going to be hurt on the job (and the employer did not know this), which of the four systems described in this section would the employee most likely prefer? Explain how this employee's preference might be different if he or she did not have this prior knowledge.

16.4 Workers' Compensation Insurance and Self-insurance

The private workers' compensation insurance market, with 1996 premium volume of $25.1 billion, is the largest business property-liability insurance market in the United States and the third largest market overall behind personal auto insurance and homeowners insurance.[5] The four largest private workers' compensation insurers in the United States in 1996 were: (1) American International Group, with 6.9 percent of countrywide premiums; (2) CNA Insurance Group (6.8 percent); (3) Liberty Mutual Group (6.4 percent); and Travelers Property/Casualty Group (4.9 percent). While comprehensive data on self-insurance are not readily available, rough estimates suggest that approximately 35–40 percent of workers' compensation claim costs are self-insured. Workers' compensation insurance prices traditionally have been subject to comprehensive price regulation, and this remains true today in a majority of states.

Description of Insurance Coverage

In most states insurers are required to issue a policy developed by the National Council on Compensation Insurance (NCCI), the leading insurance industry advisory organization that specializes in workers' compensation insurance, or a policy that is substantially similar to this contract. The policy has two main coverage parts: (1) workers' compensation insurance and (2) employers' liability insurance.

The **workers' compensation insurance coverage** part of the workers' compensation and employers' liability insurance policy simply requires the insurer to pay all benefits required by the state's workers' compensation law for work-related bodily injury or disease without limitation. There are no exclusions, but insurers are allowed to seek reimbursement from the employer in some circumstances (e.g., if the injury results from willful misconduct by the employer). For accidental bodily injury, the insurer whose policy is in effect on the date of the accident pays the claim. For occupational disease, the claim is paid by the insurer whose policy is in effect on the last day of exposure to the hazard that caused the disease. The latter provision has helped reduce disputes over which insurer should pay compared to the case of occurrence-based liability coverage discussed in the last chapter.

The second part of the workers' compensation and employers' liability insurance policy is the **employers' liability insurance coverage** part. This coverage provides employers with specified limits of coverage for tort liability suits by employees (or family members) for bodily injuries or disease that are not governed by workers' compensation. Examples of suits for which the insurer agrees to defend the employer and pay damages include, where permitted by common law or statute: (1) suits by a spouse of an injured employee for the value of lost services due to the injury; (2) suits by a family member that is injured in conjunction with injury to the employee; and (3) **dual capacity suits,** which allege that the injury resulted from the employer acting in a dual capacity, such as a suit

---

[5] Premium data obtained from *Best's Aggregates & Averages, Property-Casualty, United States,* 1997 edition (Oldwick, NJ: A. M. Best Co.). These data do not reflect workers' compensation premiums paid to state-run insurers.

Box 16–3

Dual Capacity Suits

Some tort liability suits have allowed injured employees to recover damages for pain and suffering and any monetary losses not covered by workers' compensation based on the argument that the injury occurred while the employer was acting in a second, distinct capacity from its primary capacity as employer. As mentioned in the text, this has occurred when the employer has provided negligent medical care to an employee. Another example would be if an employer-owned and -operated cafeteria served contaminated food that harmed employees. The basic idea behind the dual capacity doctrine is that when employers assume functions that are not integral to the employment relationship, exclusive remedy should not apply. Thus far the courts have refused to extend the dual capacity doctrine broadly. For example, employers that manufacture their own equipment that in turn injures a worker have not been successfully sued for products liability based on the argument that the employer acted in a dual capacity as product manufacturer.

for medical malpractice if the employer negligently provides emergency medical care (see Box 16–3). Exclusions include but are not limited to losses covered by workers' compensation benefits (they are paid by the workers' compensation coverage), injuries to employees that are knowingly employed in violation of the law (e.g., minors), and injuries that are intentionally caused by the employer (such as an employer striking an employee).

Insurance Pricing, Residual Markets, and State Funds

Pricing.   Insured employers generally pay premiums equal to a **class rate** per $100 of payroll times the amount of the firm's payroll (in $100s) in different occupational (industry) classifications. The NCCI (or other rating advisory organization) begins by projecting the loss cost per $100 of payroll for each of approximately 500 occupational classifications in each state. This projection, which is known as the **prospective loss cost,** thus varies across states and occupational classifications. A total rate then is determined by adding a loading for expenses and profit (which reflects anticipated investment income) to the prospective loss cost. In recent years many states have required each insurer to determine this loading, as opposed to the prior practice (still followed in some states) of having the loading determined by the rating advisory organization and added to the prospective loss cost to produce an **advisory rate.** A significant majority of states require prior regulatory approval of prospective loss costs and expense/profit loadings.

   To illustrate these concepts, consider three employment classes used in most states: (1) wholesale beer or ale dealers, (2) tree pruning/spraying, and (3) attorneys and other law firm employees. The prospective loss costs for these three classes per $100 of payroll for a given state and year might be, for example, $4, $15, and $0.50, respectively. Consistent with historical loss experience, these numbers indicate large differences in expected claim costs for these classes.[6]

If the advisory organization or individual insurer loading for expenses and profit (including an offset for expected investment income) equaled 20 percent of the class rate, then the class rates per $100 of payroll would be $5, $18.75, and $0.63, respectively, for the three classes. (These class rates equal the prospective loss costs divided by 0.8, which produces the 20 percent loading for expenses and profits.) Thus, the total premium for tree pruning employees with a total payroll of $100,000 using this class rate would be $18,750 ($18.75 × 1,000). Similarly, the total premium for a law firm with payroll of $1 million using the class rate would be $6,300.

Depending on the state and the characteristics of the employer, the class rate for each job classification then is modified by one or more of the following factors to produce the final rate that a particular employer is charged for each class:

• Many states permit individual insurers to file (subject to regulatory approval) a percentage deviation from prospective loss costs (or advisory rates) developed by the advisory organization to reflect better or worse than average expected experience in the insurer's target markets. The percentage deviation usually must be the same for all classes. For example, an insurer might file for a 10 percent reduction compared to advisory organization prospective loss costs and file its own expense and profit loading. (A few states permit independent rate filings that do not use advisory organization prospective loss costs.)

• All states mandate that an **experience rating** system be used except for small employers. These systems generally modify the employer's rate for the coming year either up or down depending on whether the employer's loss costs have been greater or lower than the expected average experience for the class during the preceding three years. This system produces a rate that reflects a weighted average of the expected average experience for all employers in the class and the particular employer's own loss experience during the experience period. The weight given to the employer's own experience increases with its payroll to reflect greater credibility of loss experience (less random variation) for larger employers.

• Additional charges and discounts may be added because loss costs and expenses (e.g., commissions to agents) per $100 of payroll decline with firm size. The effect of these modifications is to produce rates per $100 of payroll that decline commensurately with expected costs.

• Many states permit **schedule rating,** whereby insurers can modify the rate for a particular employer within allowable percentage ranges (e.g., up to plus or minus 25 percent) to reflect the underwriter's evaluation of the employer's expected claim costs based on analysis of factors such as safety programs.

---

[6] These numbers are consistent with historical loss data in one state.

• Large employers may have the final rate paid for a given year adjusted over time based on loss experience during the same year under retrospective experience rating systems (see Chapter 11).

• Many insurers pay dividends to employers whose historical loss experience has been better than expected.

If regulators approve class rates that are high enough to cover the expected costs of most employers in each class, then rate deviations, schedule rating, and dividend plans can be used by insurers to lower prices for those employers in each class that are predicted to have better loss experience than implied by the class rate. The outcome from using these procedures in many states is a refined pricing system in which rates are closely related to expected claim costs for different employers. As we discuss further below, however, significant distortions in supply can occur if regulators refuse to approve class rates that are large enough to cover the expected costs of insuring most employers.

Residual Markets and State Funds.   You learned earlier that six states mandate the purchase of workers' compensation insurance from a monopolistic government insurer known as a monopolistic state fund. These government monopolies offer coverage to all employers at rates determined by the state. States that allow private insurance do not require each insurer to offer coverage to each employer that applies for coverage. If an employer is unable to readily find an insurer that is willing to provide coverage voluntarily because, for example, price regulation prevents insurers from charging a high enough price, the employer is able to obtain coverage in the **residual market.**

About one-fourth of the states use a competitive state fund as the residual market. As the name implies, competitive state funds sometimes also compete with private insurers in the voluntary market. The remaining states with private insurance generally provide that employers that cannot readily obtain voluntary coverage will be charged a regulated price and randomly assigned to insurers in proportion to each insurer's premiums for workers' compensation insurance written voluntarily.[7] In most of these states, workers' compensation insurers have developed reinsurance pools in lieu of these assignments. Most of the pools are administered by rating advisory organizations (most often the NCCI).

Under the pooling system, insurers contract with a number of servicing insurance carriers who issue residual market policies, collect premiums, and settle claims in exchange for a fee paid by the pool. The net financial results of the residual market pool then are split among all insurers that participate in the pooling arrangement in proportion to the amount of premiums that an insurer received in a given year for policies that it wrote voluntarily. This system therefore involves insurer specialization in administering residual market policies and reduces the risk that individual insurers otherwise might face from highly uncertain

---

[7] Self-insurers are excluded from the system; they do not participate in the residual market.

cash flows if they were randomly assigned individual employers with varying degrees of price inadequacy due to regulation.[8]

As we will discuss further below, residual markets in many states became very large during the 1980s and produced large deficits and cross-subsidies from the voluntary market to the residual market due to inadequate residual market premium rates through the early 1990s. As a result, regulators in many of these states began to approve significantly higher rates for employers insured in the residual market compared to employers insured voluntarily.

Self-insurance and Large Deductible Policies

As noted at the beginning of the chapter, employers are required to purchase workers' compensation insurance unless they meet minimum financial requirements for qualifying as a self-insurer. These requirements generally prevent small- to medium-sized employers from self-insuring workers' compensation claims on an individual basis. However, since the early 1980s, many states have passed laws permitting **group self-insurance** for these employers, which enables a group of companies to combine together to jointly self-insure benefits. Group self-insurance has contributed to growth in self-insurance in recent years. It also is commonly believed that self-insurance has grown in many states as commercial insurance in the voluntary insurance market became less attractive to many employers because voluntary market rates in effect were increased to make up for inadequate residual market rates (see above).

Self-insurers often use outside firms known as **third-party administrators** to settle workers' compensation claims, and this practice is customary for group self-insurance. Otherwise, the employer must settle its own claims. Workers' compensation self-insurers and self-insurance groups often purchase excess insurance to protect against large losses from a single claim and/or in total for a given year.

Until the 1990s regulation generally only permitted comparatively small deductibles under workers' compensation insurance policies. Thus, employers basically had two choices: (1) self-insurance (if they could qualify) with excess insurance above a large retention, and (2) workers' compensation insurance with low deductibles. At this time some states began to permit the sale of **large deductible policies** in the voluntary market (generally defined as policies with per injury deductibles of $100,000 or more). Under these policies, the insurer has to settle and pay the full amount of the claim to the injured employee, but the insurer then seeks reimbursement from the employer for the amount of the claim below the deductible.

Like traditional workers' compensation policies with little or no deductible,

---

[8] During the past several years a number of insurers in some states have withdrawn from these pooling arrangements, opting instead to receive direct assignments and in many cases then entering into a separate contract with one or more insurers to service the business.

the payment of mandatory workers' compensation benefits under large deductible policies is guaranteed by the insurer, thus mitigating the potential judgment proof problem (see Chapter 14), but the employer does not have to pay for full (or nearly full) coverage. Thus, these policies offer employers an intermediate risk-sharing option compared to traditional policies and self-insurance.[9] The market for large deductible policies grew rapidly in many states beginning in the early 1990s, which contributed in part to a 16 percent reduction in countrywide workers' compensation insurance premium volume during 1992–1996.

Second Injury Funds

All states have a **second injury fund** that allows insurers and self-insured employers to be reimbursed for the estimated increase in benefit costs when a subsequent ("second") injury occurs to an employee that was previously injured. The cost of the combined reimbursements then is spread among insurers and self-insurers in proportion to their total claim costs. The original rationale for second injury funds was to increase employment opportunities for workers with an earlier injury. The concern was that employers would be reluctant to hire an employee that had previously lost the use of an arm because injury to another arm or leg might produce a total disability, which would require larger workers' compensation benefits than if the worker had not been hurt previously. With the second injury fund, this increased cost is spread among all employers, thus reducing the disincentive to hire the worker.

In modern times, second injury funds in some states have been plagued by high costs. Injuries in some states are eligible for reimbursement even if the employer did not know of the prior injury at the time of hire. This tends to increase second injury fund assessments and associated administrative costs. It is not clear that the ability to be reimbursed for these "undiscovered" injuries will have much if any effect on hiring. A disadvantage of second injury funds is that they might reduce the incentive of an insurer or self-insurer to dispute questionable claims. The reason is that any increase in investigation or dispute costs will be borne by the insurer or self-insurer but any reduction in the amount of payment also will reduce reimbursement from the second injury fund (and thus benefit other employers/insurers).

Another problem is that it is very difficult to estimate the incremental effects of second injuries to backs and other soft tissues. This measurement problem might induce insurers/employers go out of their way to argue that the injury was aggravated by a prior injury. Finally, some observers question the need for these funds in modern times, especially in view of federal legislation designed to increase employment opportunities for disabled persons (see below).

---

[9] Because they have much lower premiums than traditional policies, large deductible policies also reduce the implicit taxes that the employer might have to pay to subsidize the residual market (see below).

16.5 Problems and Reforms in Workers' Compensation

The workers' compensation system and insurance market experienced considerable turmoil in the 1980s and early 1990s. Workers' compensation claim costs grew rapidly in many states during the 1980s. For example, benefit costs per $100 of payroll increased approximately 5 percent per year during this time, and increases in the average indemnity and medical cost per injury involving lost wages averaged 10 percent per year or more in many states before leveling off in the 1990s. The causes of this cost growth include: (1) increases in medical care costs in excess of wage and general medical care cost inflation; (2) growth in benefit levels in many states; (3) compensation for new types of injuries, including cumulative injuries, due to repetitive motion and expansion (in some states) of the ability to receive benefits for job-related stress; (4) increased dispute resolution costs and greater settlements for difficult to measure, permanent partial disabilities; and (5) increased claims fraud (e.g., faked or exaggerated injuries, or seeking compensation for injuries that occurred away from work).

This growth in workers' compensation costs and insurance premiums during the 1980s was accompanied by deteriorating financial results for workers' compensation insurance. Insurers commonly argued that state regulators failed to al-

FIGURE 16–1

Workers' compensation insurance residual market premiums as a percent of total workers' compensation insurance premiums: 1977–1996 (countrywide aggregates for NCCI states; data reported in NCCI Management Summary, *annual editions)*

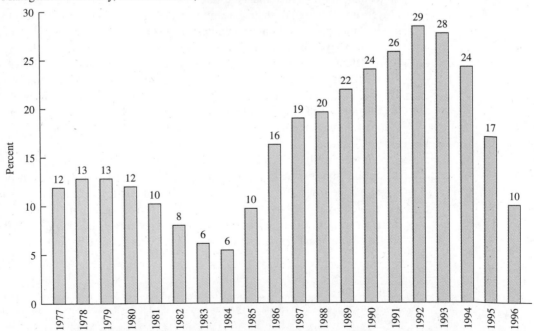

low rate increases commensurate with cost increases. These arguments are plausible. Regulators often approved rate increases much smaller than requested, and they were subject to substantial pressure from many employers to deny or at least delay rate increases that were necessary to keep pace with rapid growth in expected claim costs. Consistent with regulatory constraints on rate increases in the presence of rising costs, the nationwide workers' compensation insurance residual market increased sharply during the 1980s (see Figure 16–1). By 1992, the residual market share of premiums had grown to over 50 percent in a number of states (see Figure 16–2).

Recall that insurers generally are responsible for residual market deficits in proportion to their voluntary market premiums. As a result, if residual market rates are too low to cover expected costs, insurers know that they will have to contribute to the resulting deficit in proportion to their voluntary market premiums. When they write a policy voluntarily, their charge for the residual market deficit therefore will increase. This effectively increases the cost of selling a policy vol-

FIGURE 16–2

Workers' compensation insurance residual market premiums as a percent of total workers' compensation insurance premiums by state in 1992 (states with data reported by the NCCI; data reported in NCCI Management Summary, *1992)*

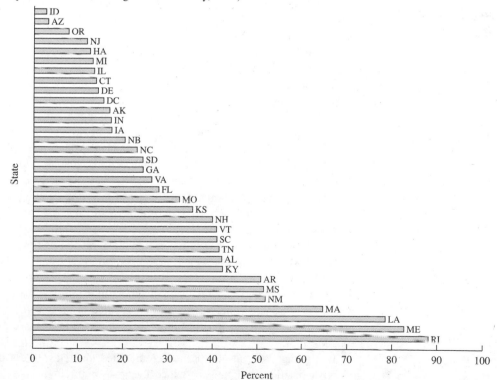

untarily. In order to cover the total expected costs of selling a policy voluntarily, the insurer needs to charge a high enough premium to cover the expected costs for the particular employer plus the cost of higher assessments for the residual market deficit.

For example, assume that an insurer estimates that it needs a premium of $20,000 to provide coverage to an employer without any residual market deficit, but if the insurer writes the policy, it estimates that the present value of its future assessments for the residual market deficit will increase by $2,000. Then the insurer will require a premium of at least $22,000 to write the policy. The required premium might be higher than $22,000 because of substantial uncertainty associated with the size of assessments, as well as uncertainty concerning whether regulators will approve future rate increases for the voluntary market that are sufficient to cover increases in expected costs.

In many cases, regulators approved higher voluntary market rates to help make up for residual market rate inadequacy, and insurers often had the flexibility to lower dividends and schedule rating discounts that previously had been provided to many employers insured voluntarily, thus increasing the net price charged to many employers insured in the voluntary market in order to offset expected deficits for the residual market. As a result, these actions produced a cross-subsidy from the voluntary to the residual market. Employers insured in the voluntary market were charged more than their expected costs in order to offset all or part of the cost of expected deficits for the residual market. In many states this enabled private insurers to cover more of their total costs and reduced pressure for them to exit the market.

As suggested earlier, higher rates in the voluntary market to finance residual market deficits might cause more businesses to self-insure, thus avoiding subsidies to other employers. To the extent that this occurs, the size of the voluntary market is further reduced. Escalating growth in the residual market and an inability to shift residual market deficits to a shrinking voluntary market led to insurance company exits and the virtual collapse of the voluntary workers' compensation insurance market in a few states (such as Maine, see Figure 16–2).

There also is evidence that inadequate residual market rates for higher risk employers aggravated claim cost growth. This result is predicted to the extent that regulatory caps reduce modifications in class rates from experience rating and/or allow higher risk employers to grow more rapidly by reducing their workers' compensation insurance costs.

The 1980s claims cost surge and regulatory responses threatened to undermine the historical basis of workers' compensation legislation. Many observers viewed legislation to control claim costs as essential to preserve the system and maintain substantial private sector involvement in the provision of workers' compensation insurance. Others disputed that regulation produced inadequate rates and argued that cost-benefit control measures deprived injured workers of needed compensation.

Beginning in the late 1980s, numerous states adopted workers' compensation reform legislation designed to reduce the growth in claim costs. Examples of changes include: (1) adoption of medical expense fee schedules and permission for employers to adopt managed care practices to help control workers' compensation medical costs; (2) changes in disability benefit administration designed to encourage employees to return to work after injury and to clarify calculation of permanent partial disability benefits; (3) restrictions on the compensability of stress-related claims; and (4) actions to increase detection of, prosecution of, and penalties for workers' compensation claims fraud.

Many states also made changes in their systems of voluntary and residual market price regulation to reduce residual market deficits and cross-subsidies from the voluntary market to the residual market, including (1) regulatory approval of significantly higher class rates for the residual market compared to the voluntary market; (2) elimination of premium discounts for larger employers insured in the residual market; and (3) increases in experience rating surcharges (discounts) for worse (better) than average loss experience for employers insured in the residual market. These changes in price regulation and in benefit design and administration were associated with slower claim cost growth, improved insurer financial results, and declining residual markets and residual market deficits during the mid-1990s.

16.6 Government Safety Regulation and Other Sources of Liability

The Occupational Safety and Health Act

The federal **Occupational Safety and Health Act** (OSHA) became effective in 1971. This act, which applies to all private sector businesses engaged in commerce with employees, provides for the promulgation and enforcement of comprehensive safety standards by the Occupation Safety and Health administration or, if approved by the US Department of Labor, by state administrators. About one-half of the states have received approval to administer and enforce their own standards and laws. Under OSHA, businesses are subject to unannounced safety inspections and can be cited and fined for safety violations. Severe violations also can result in criminal penalties for managers. The law also requires detailed record-keeping and reporting of occupational injuries by employers.

OSHA has been criticized by many businesses and academics for imposing costs on businesses without having a major, demonstrable effect on safety. Many of the voluminous standards are alleged to represent attempts at micromanagement of safety by government bureaucrats. It is argued that the additional incentives for safety provided by OSHA are small and that they are not necessary given the strong incentives provided by workers' compensation laws, employee demand for safety, and the adverse effects of occupational injuries on business productivity. In addition, the enforcement of the law has been criticized for failing to target higher risk employers.

Studies of the effects of OSHA have failed to demonstrate a consistent negative effect on serious injury rates, but this in part may reflect difficulty in disentangling the possible effects of OSHA from the downward trend in serious injuries and fatalities that began prior to the enactment of OSHA. In recent years, the Occupational Safety and Health administration and some of its state counter-parts have experimented with ways of simplifying standards and improving the cost-effectiveness of standards and inspections.

Americans with Disabilities Act

The federal **Americans with Disabilities Act** (ADA) was enacted in 1990 and became effective in 1992. The ADA applies to businesses engaged in interstate commerce with 15 or more employees. The law makes it illegal to discriminate against qualified workers with disabilities. In particular, the law makes it illegal to deny employment or a particular type of job to a disabled person unless the individual is unable to perform the job. The law also requires businesses to reasonably accommodate disabled workers by, for example, providing ready access to facilities (e.g., ramps for wheelchairs) or redesigning jobs and equipment. Employers are relieved from the accommodation requirements if they would create "undue hardship" (substantial difficulty or expense).

Disabled persons can sue employers under tort liability for violating the ADA. At the time of its adoption, many business groups predicted large compliance costs and an explosion in litigation due in part to the vague and somewhat open-ended nature of the requirements. Early experience suggests a significant increase in litigation, but defenders of the ADA argue that litigation is relatively infrequent and that it generally has focused on egregious cases of discrimination. As suggested earlier, some observers argue that the ADA has largely eliminated the need for second injury funds as a means of promoting employment of previously injured workers. However, it currently appears unlikely that a political consensus will emerge for doing away with second injury funds.

Other Sources of Liability

Apart from responsibility for worker injuries under workers' compensation laws and potential liability to disabled persons under the ADA, businesses in recent years have faced increased frequency of lawsuits from current, prospective, and former employees that allege harm from a number of causes. The most important sources of liability include: (1) suits by employees alleging that they were wrongfully terminated or discharged; (2) suits by employees claiming that they were negligently subjected to extreme stress (if the injury is not covered by workers' compensation) or verbal harassment; (3) suits against employers alleging that the employer engaged in or failed to take reasonable actions to prevent sexual harassment; (4) suits claiming age, sex, or racial discrimination in hiring, promotion, or firing; and (5) suits alleging damages due to unfavorable or inaccurate written or oral comments made by the employer to a prospective employer of a former employee.

These suits commonly seek damages for alleged harm due to lost income, damage to a person's reputation, or mental distress. Many of these exposures generally can be insured with **employment practices liability insurance,** subject to a variety of exclusions, including intentional harm (see Box 16–4). The provisions of this insurance vary significantly across insurers. Expected claim costs

Box 16–4

Economy: More Firms Insure against Worker Suits— Discrimination Complaints Boost Once-Obscure Coverage

A sharp rise in employee-discrimination suits—highlighted by the recent case against Texaco Inc.—is prompting more companies to turn to a once-obscure form of insurance to help cover the cost of such litigation.

Known as employment practices liability insurance, the policies protect companies facing huge legal bills or damage awards from workers alleging discrimination or wrongful discharge based on race, sex, age, or physical handicap. So far, the insurance has appealed mainly to small and medium-size companies, which can get coverage of up to $1 million for about $7,500 in annual premiums.

Major corporations such as Texaco, however, have felt less pressure to buy such policies, in part because their big balance sheets allow them to weather the litigation costs more easily. But insurance executives expect that to change. One factor, they say, is the widespread publicity given to the discrimination suits against Texaco and other companies such as the US unit of Japan's Mitsubishi Motors Corp. Insurers also are moving to improve the terms of their policies and to offer coverage of up to $100 million.

Some insurance experts believe sales of employee practices insurance, which currently total about $100 million a year, could hit $1 billion within three years and $2 billion within a decade. Insurance experts say employment practices coverage was available through Lloyd's of London as long as a decade ago, but it wasn't until earlier this decade that major US insurers began selling the policies. Today as many as 20 carriers sell some form of the specialized coverage, including units of American International Group Inc., Chubb Corp., and Reliance Group Holdings.

Although policies initially sold in the United States generally provided no more than $5 million in protection, a unit of insurance broker Marsh & McLennan Cos. teamed earlier this year with a unit of Exel Ltd., of Hamilton, Bermuda, to offer policies with limits of up to $100 million. Such higher policy limits are expected to appeal to some of the nation's biggest employers. Exel said it has sold eight policies so far, and among those now considering a purchase is Microsoft Corp.

Scott Lange, the computer software company's director of risk management, said lawsuits alleging discrimination pose a threat of "big exposure" to companies nationwide, despite their best efforts to do the right thing. He said he finds Exel's policies "interesting" and "if we find the pricing and terms to be reasonable, we're likely to participate in this market. I think in the eyes of most [large corporations], it's a viable product."

But brokers say it remains a tough sale to many big companies, partly because corporate attorneys worry that they will have to give up at least some control over how they handle a discrimination suit if an insurer is footing the defense bill.

Coverage under the policies can vary greatly. Some policies specifically exclude claims arising out of reorganizations, mass layoffs or plant closures. Some policies also exclude punitive damages, and most exclude coverage for intentional or willful acts although the definition of those terms varies. One reason for this exclusion: Certain state laws prohibit insurance for intentional wrongs. Policies also differ on the extent to which an employer would have to go along with an insurer's desire to settle a case out of court.

Source: Leslie Scism, "Economy: More Firms Insure against Worker Suits: Discrimination Complaints Boost Once-Obscure Coverage," *The Wall Street Journal*, November 15, 1996.

from these liability exposures often can be reduced substantially with risk identification and loss control. For example, many employers have reduced their exposure to suits alleging inaccurate or prejudicial remarks to prospective employers of former employees by indicating only whether and how long the person was employed.

16.7 Summary

- State workers' compensation laws have two main features: (1) employers are required to pay specified benefits for monetary loss to injured employees without regard to employer fault or negligence, and (2) employees are not allowed to sue employers for injuries under tort law (i.e., workers' compensation is the employee's exclusive remedy).

- Workers' compensation benefits include medical benefits, benefits for total disability, benefits for permanent partial disability, and survivor benefits. For permanent partial disability payments, which represent a large proportion of the total cost of disability benefits, the amount of benefits for some injuries generally is specified in a schedule. For nonscheduled injuries, benefit amounts generally are based on the worker's estimated loss of earnings capacity.

- Alternative approaches to workers' compensation include (1) no mandatory employer-provided benefits and no tort liability of employers; (2) no mandatory benefits with employer tort liability for injuries; and (3) mandatory benefits with tort liability for employers. Compared to these alternatives, workers' compensation systems provide reasonable safety incentives and compensation for monetary loss. They also produce lower dispute resolution costs than would be the case with tort liability. Many workers are likely to find the broad structure of workers' compensation laws attractive compared to alternative systems given that workers bear the cost of whatever system is chosen.

- Employers subject to workers' compensation laws are required to purchase workers' compensation insurance or to meet state rules to qualify as a self-insurer. Six states have government monopoly workers' compensation insurers known as monopolistic state funds. Some states have state insurers, known as competitive state funds, that either compete with private insurers or serve as the residual market.

- Workers' compensation insurance policies cover workers' compensation benefits and employer tort liability for certain work-related injuries not governed by workers' compensation. Workers' compensation rates vary across numerous occupational classes in each state. A variety of methods, including experience rating, are used to modify the rate to reflect differences in expected claim costs across employers within an occupational class.

- From the mid-1980s through the early 1990s, workers' compensation claim costs grew rapidly, insurance company financial results deteriorated, and state residual markets mushroomed. Large residual markets in some states produced large operating deficits and cross-subsidies from the voluntary to the residual market. Residual market shares and deficits have since declined in conjunction with residual and voluntary market rate increases and with slower growth in claims due in part to state legislation enacted to reduce cost growth.

- Extensive government regulation of safety exists at both the federal and state level. Whether safety regulation has a material effect and is cost-effective have been subject to considerable debate.

- Many businesses are exposed to tort liability claims for employment practices that cause injuries apart from bodily injury and disease governed by workers' compensation law. Major tort liability exposures include allegations of illegal discrimination based on factors such as age, sex, race, and disability, and allegations of wrongful termination. Many of these liability exposures can be insured in the developing market for employment practices liability insurance.

Key Terms

workers' compensation laws   387
employer liability laws   388
exclusive remedy   388
monopolistic state funds   390
competitive state funds   390
temporary total disability   392
permanent total disability   392
permanent partial disability   393
workers' compensation insurance coverage   400
employers' liability insurance coverage   400
dual capacity suits   400
class rate   401

prospective loss cost   401
advisory rate   401
experience rating   402
schedule rating   402
residual market   403
group self-insurance   404
third-party administrators   404
large deductible policies   404
second injury fund   405
Occupational Safety and Health Act   409
Americans with Disabilities Act   410
employment practices liability insurance   410

Questions and Problems

1. Assume a statewide average wage of $500 and a workers' compensation weekly disability benefit equal to two-thirds of the pre-injury wage but no more than 100 percent of the statewide average weekly wage. What percentage of pre-injury weekly wages would be replaced by workers' compensation benefits for (a) a worker with pre-injury weekly wages of $600? (b) a worker with pre-injury weekly wages of $2,000? Graph the relationship between the workers' compensation wage replacement rate and pre-injury wages. How would the graph change if the replacement rate were calculated after income taxes?

2. Compare and contrast permanent partial disability claims under workers' compensation with a tort liability claim for a comparable injury arising out of an off-the-job auto accident.

3. Assume that there is no workers' compensation law but that employers can be sued by employees for on-the-job injuries. Assuming that the government would not prohibit such a contract, describe a contract between an employer and its employees that

would have the same effect as a workers' compensation law. Would it be mutually beneficial for the employer and employees to negotiate this contract? Explain.

4. Imagine that you are on a spaceship and must decide between landing and living for five years on one of two planets. All you know about the two planets is that (a) one requires employers to pay workers' compensation benefits but also allows employees to sue their employer for negligence, and (b) the other has a traditional workers' compensation system (mandatory benefits are the employee's exclusive remedy). Which planet would you pick and why? Would your answer differ if you knew that you would suffer an on-the-job injury within two months of landing but that overall injury rates were the same for the two planets? Explain.

5. In which case will the argument for government regulation of safety be stronger? (a) Workers are well informed about injury risk versus workers underestimate injury risk. (b) There is workers' compensation with exclusive remedy versus there is a workers'

compensation system without exclusive remedy.

6. A business with a high risk of injury to employees that faces correspondingly high workers' compensation premiums argues that its workers' compensation insurance rate should be lowered by regulation to make coverage more affordable and reduce the adverse effects of high workers' compensation premiums on its ability to hire more workers and pay them higher wages. Explain why you agree or disagree with this firm's argument.

7. Self-insurers do not have to contribute toward workers' compensation insurance residual market deficits. Explain how this might affect the demand for workers' compensation insurance.

8. Which is likely to have a greater variance for the typical firm: (a) the average claim cost per $100 of payroll for workers' compensation claims, or (b) the average cost of damages, awards, and defense costs per $100 of payroll for tort liability suits alleging racial discrimination, sexual harassment, excessive stress, and so on?

References

Danzon, Patricia; and Scott Harrington. *Rate Regulation and Cost Growth in Workers' Compensation Insurance.* Washington, DC: American Enterprise Institute, 1998. (*Detailed discussion of price regulation, the resulting cross-subsidies, and the effects on growth in claim costs.*)

Hood, John. "OSHA's Trivial Pursuit." *Policy Review,* Summer 1995, pp. 59–64. (*Argues that federal safety regulations have achieved little compared to private incentives for workplace safety.*)

Meindersma, Sandra Jane. "Employers under Fire—

Managing Employment Practice Liability." *Risk Management,* January 1996, pp. 22–30. (*Reviews employment practice exposures and available insurance.*)

Rejda, George. *Social Insurance.* New York: Prentice-Hall, 1994. (*Provides detailed discussion of the history and features of workers' compensation.*)

United States Chamber of Commerce. *Analysis of Workers' Compensation Laws,* annual. (*Detailed statistics on workers' compensation benefit and coverage provisions across states.*)

Answers to Concept Checks

1. An employers' liability law restricts defenses available to employers in defending tort liability suits brought by injured employees. A workers' compensation law requires the employer to pay specified benefits to injured workers and eliminates tort liability claims against the employer.

2. If the worker's weekly wage exceeds $900 ($540/0.60), the worker's benefit will be less than 60 percent of wages because the benefit is capped at $540. If, for example, the worker's weekly wage was $1,000, the weekly benefit would equal 54 percent of the worker's pre-injury wage ($540/$1,000).

3. The worker who knew that he or she would be hurt probably would prefer to receive mandatory benefits without regard to negligence by the employer and also have the right to allege negligence and sue under tort liability for pain and suffering and any uncovered monetary losses. If the worker did not know that he or she would be hurt and realized that wages would have to be lowered to cover the cost of the system in place, the worker probably would prefer workers' compensation with its exclusive remedy rule.

CHAPTER 17

Issues in Liability Risk and Its Management

Chapter Objectives

- Explain how the doctrine of limited liability allows businesses to reduce tort liability risk and describe the rationale and limitations of this doctrine.
- Discuss how businesses are liable for the actions of agents, employees, and independent contractors and describe the effects of applicable legal doctrines on incentives for loss control and the cost of risk.
- Explain how businesses manage liability risk through hold harmless and indemnity agreements and the effects of these agreements on the cost of risk.
- Provide an overview of key strategic and operational issues in the management and administration of liability and workers' compensation claims.

17.1 Risk Shifting through Limited Liability

Chapter 14 briefly discussed the doctrine of limited liability, the resulting judgment proof problem, and the possible effects of this doctrine on safety. For corporations, the limited liability doctrine holds (except in unusual circumstances discussed below) that shareholders cannot be held liable for claims against the corporation that exceed the value of the corporation's assets. As a result, the liability of shareholders is limited to their ownership interest in the corporation: Claimants against the corporation generally cannot reach the personal assets of individual shareholders or other business assets of corporate shareholders (e.g., other assets of a parent corporation). In this section you will learn more about (1) limited liability for corporations and its relation to tort liability risk and its management, including how limited liability sometimes can lead to excessive risk of injury; (2) the rationale for limited liability despite this problem; and (3) exceptions to the doctrine.

Limited Liability as Insurance against Loss

We begin by explaining a fundamental point: Compared to a system of unlimited liability, limited liability essentially provides shareholders with insurance against losses that exceed corporate assets. Consider a corporation with assets of $10 million, and initially assume that the corporation has no debt. What happens if the business causes injuries that produce tort liability awards against the corporation equal to $12 million? The doctrine of limited liability holds that the claimants can obtain only the value of the corporation's assets. Therefore, only $10 million will be available to claimants; $2 million will be unpaid.

If, contrary to actual legal rules, unlimited liability existed, then the tort claimants could obtain the remaining $2 million from the personal wealth of individual shareholders or other business assets of corporate shareholders. Thus, compared to the doctrine of unlimited liability, in this example, limited liability reduces the loss to shareholders by $2 million. The effect of limited liability is directly analogous to insurance against losses in excess of $10 million. The limited liability rule is equivalent to giving shareholders an insurance contract that pays losses above an aggregate deductible equal to the value of the corporation's assets.

Figure 17–1 illustrates the payoff to shareholders with a limited liability rule when the corporation has no debt in its capital structure. Up to the value of assets, shareholders bear the full cost of tort claims (i.e., tort claims reduce shareholder wealth dollar for dollar). However, because of limited liability, the loss to shareholders is capped at an amount equal to the value of assets. This figure looks just like Figure 11–2, which showed the amount of loss borne by a business that buys an insurance policy for losses in excess of an aggregate deductible.

FIGURE 17–1

How limited liability limits losses with no debt claims

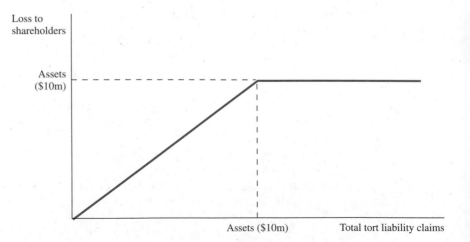

If the business has issued debt to finance investment, the situation becomes a little more complicated, but the same basic result holds. To illustrate, assume that the firm has $15 million in assets but that it owes $5 million to lenders (i.e., one-third of its assets are financed with debt and two-thirds with equity). Now what happens if $12 million in tort claims arise? In this case, the firm's assets are less than its total liabilities (debt plus tort claims). The value of the firm's stock is zero. Because tort claimants have legal priority over lenders (i.e., tort claims are satisfied before the claims of lenders), tort claimants will receive $12 million. Lenders will receive the remaining assets of $3 million, but lenders do not receive the other $2 million that they are owed.

Note that with debt the loss to shareholders from tort liability claims in this example is still limited to $10 million by the doctrine of limited liability. Share-holders can lose only the excess of assets over the amount owed to lenders ($15 million – $5 million). In this case, the lenders can be viewed as having provided the shareholders with $5 million of insurance coverage against losses above $10 million. If tort liability claims exceed the $10 million, lenders in effect pay the excess up to the total value of assets. If tort claims exceed the total value of assets ($15 million), tort claimants will be paid $15 million and lenders will receive nothing.

These simple examples should convince you that limited liability allows risk shifting that is analogous to insurance. Without borrowing by the firm, the risk of losses in excess of assets is shifted from shareholders to tort claimants. With bor-rowing, the risk of losses in excess of the firm's equity value is shifted first to lenders and, if claims exceed the value of assets, to tort claimants. An important implication is that the financing decisions of corporations (how much debt and equity are used) affect who bears risk in the economy.

The Case of Parents and Subsidiaries.   The organization of a corporation—whether subsidiary corporations or operating divisions are used—also affects who bears risk. To see this, consider a parent that has two subsidiaries (A and B), no debt, and no assets besides the stock of the subsidiaries. Each subsidiary has assets of $25 million, so the parent has consolidated assets of $50 million. Each subsidiary has a 0.01 probability of a $50 million tort liability claim and a 0.99 probability of no claim. Also assume for simplicity that the probability that both subsidiaries have a tort claim is zero. Finally, if a tort claim occurs, assume that the parent will use the subsidiary's assets of $25 million to pay the claimants and declare the subsidiary insolvent, thus limiting the reduction in the parent's assets to $25 million. (We discuss later why the parent sometimes might decide to use its remaining assets, in effect the assets of the other subsidiary, to pay all claims.)

How does limited liability affect the risk to the parent and thus its share-holders under these assumptions? Table 17–1 shows the probability distribution, expected value, and standard deviation of (1) losses to the parent (or corporate group) when the parent has limited liability for claims against its subsidiaries, and (2) losses to the parent if the parent does not have limited liability so that the par-ent will have to use assets from the other subsidiary to pay the full claim. In this

TABLE 17–1   **Illustration of Risk Reduction with Limited Liability of Parent for Claims against Subsidiaries**

	Parent Loss Distribution (values in $ millions)	
	Limited Liability for Parent	*Unlimited Liability for Parent*
Probability:		
0.98 (no claim)	$ 0.0	$ 0.0
0.01 (claim against A)	25.0	50.0
0.01 (claim against B)	25.0	50.0
Expected value	0.5	1.0
Standard deviation	3.5	7.0
Expected value of unpaid claims	0.5	0.0

example, the probability distribution with unlimited liability for the parent equals the probability distribution of total damage claims because tort claims cannot exceed the parent's assets. The table also shows the expected value of unpaid tort claims in each case. We also have assumed that the limited liability rule does not affect the probability of a tort claim. As you will learn below, this assumption is not as innocent as it might first appear. It is nonetheless useful at this point to highlight the risk reduction associated with limited liability.

As illustrated in Table 17–1, compared to unlimited liability for the parent, limited liability (1) reduces the expected loss to the parent by $0.5 million, (2) increases the expected value of unpaid claims by $0.5 million, and (3) reduces the standard deviation of losses to the parent by 50 percent (from $7 million to $3.5 million). The risk reduction indicated by the lower standard deviation is directly analogous to the risk reduction that would occur with a liability insurance policy that pays claims in excess of a per occurrence deductible (retention limit) equal to $25 million (see Chapter 11). In essence, the parent is insured for claims above a $25 million deductible (the value of assets) for each subsidiary.

This example suggests that the judicious use of subsidiary corporations can allow a parent corporation to limit its exposure to large tort liability claims that otherwise might seriously weaken or even threaten the viability of the parent and other subsidiaries. This does not mean, however, that parents automatically will declare subsidiaries bankrupt and walk away from tort claims or other obligations that exceed a subsidiary's assets.[1] In many cases parents will have an incentive to pay claims in excess of a subsidiary's assets in order to avoid adverse effects on the reputation of the parent and other subsidiaries. Limited liability nonetheless

---

[1] As an example, State Farm Mutual provided about $3 billion to its major subsidiary insurer to pay its claims from Hurricane Andrew in 1992.

provides a valuable risk-reducing option for the parent: It gives the parent the option to walk away and thereby preserve other assets, including valuable investment opportunities, if the cost of paying the claims exceeds the adverse reputation effects from not paying claims.

Who Pays for the Implicit Insurance?   You may be wondering whether firms have to pay for the implicit insurance protection provided by limited liability. The answer depends on the situation. For example, when firms borrow money, lenders routinely consider the likelihood that they will not be repaid in full because of limited liability, and they require the borrower to pay more for credit because of this risk. This increase in the promised interest rate on the loan can be viewed as a charge (premium) for the implicit insurance provided by the lender due to the limited liability of the borrower. Similarly, and related to the discussion in earlier chapters, consumers (including business customers) who might be harmed by a firm's products and not have their damages fully paid because of limited liability might therefore reduce the price that they are willing to pay for the firm's products. The price reduction could be viewed as a premium for the implicit insurance provided by product users as a result of limited liability for product manufacturers.

The Moral Hazard Problem

As discussed in Chapter 14, limited liability reduces the ability of the tort liability system to provide optimal safety incentives, which in some cases can lead to an excessive risk of harm. To elaborate, limited liability implies that firms may not bear all of the costs of tort liability claims. Thus, when making decisions about which activities to pursue, firms may not consider all of the costs that they impose on others. Consequently, some firms will engage in excessively risky activities. If the parties that may be harmed are able to charge a price (an implicit premium) to the firm that perfectly reflects the expected value of unpaid claims from the firm's activities, then the moral hazard problem disappears.[2] Of course, due to costly and imperfect information, perfect pricing of this sort is infeasible in the real world. In some cases the risk may not be priced at all. This outcome might occur, for example, for the risk of environmental damage to persons that have no relation to the firm.

Our earlier example assumed no moral hazard; that is, we assumed that the probability and severity of tort claims did not depend on the limited liability rule. However, because the parent would not have to pay the amount of the claim above $25 million with limited liability, its incentive to invest in precautions to reduce the probability of a claim or the amount of claim could be lower than if the par-

---

[2] This situation is conceptually identical to that described for moral hazard in general in Chapter 8. If insurance premiums reflect all of the effects of the insured on expected claim costs with perfect accuracy, there is no moral hazard.

ent did not have limited liability. As a result, the expected amount of damages could be higher with limited liability, and the social cost of risk would not be minimized. Similarly, because firms may not have to bear all of the costs of tort liability claims, their investments might be tilted toward projects that create greater risk of harm than would be the case with unlimited liability.

The moral hazard problem associated with limited liability is reduced by a number of factors in addition to the possible ability of potential claimants to charge some price for the implicit insurance protection. Just as deductibles reduce moral hazard with conventional insurance, the fact that valuable assets must be lost before liability for tort claims is capped by limited liability reduces the moral hazard problem. For this reason alone, the moral hazard problem is likely to be negligible for firms with substantial assets. In addition, all of the factors that encourage firms to reduce risk by hedging or insurance (e.g., the effect of risk on expected bankruptcy costs, possible loss of profitable investment opportunities, and so on) will mitigate the tendency to take on excessive risk. Finally, as we discuss below, the courts may not enforce limited liability in cases of severe moral hazard.

Why Have Limited Liability?

Why have limited liability for tort claims given the potential for moral hazard? Entire books have been written on the rationale for limited liability for debt, tort, and other claims. The simple answer is that it commonly is believed that limited liability increases productive investment compared to unlimited liability and that the value of this increased investment outweighs the costs of excessive risk taking.

Again, an insurance analogy may be helpful. Without insurance against property and liability losses, risk aversion might greatly reduce the amount of risky but productive investment. Insurance is socially valuable because it reduces risk and facilitates productive activity. But insurance is not perfect—it generally is characterized by moral hazard and a variety of other problems that reduce its value and increase the cost of risk. Imperfect and costly information make it infeasible for insurance pricing to eliminate moral hazard. As a result, it often is optimal to reduce insurance protection through the use of deductibles and other forms of partial insurance (see Chapter 8). Similarly, it can be argued that limited liability is socially valuable despite the moral hazard problem. As noted above, moral hazard from limited liability is mitigated by the partial nature of the insurance protection: The firm's equity must be lost before the insurance kicks in.

Individual Shareholders.   One specific advantage of limited liability for individual shareholders is that it facilitates separation of the management and risk-bearing functions in a firm. That is, without the protection of limited liability, individuals often would be much less willing to invest without engaging in more costly monitoring of managers or becoming managers themselves. Since the people who are more efficient at bearing risk (people with money) are not necessarily the people who are good managers, the absence of limited liability would yield an economy with less effective managers and, more important, less investment in risky yet productive activities. Another argument for limited liability is that without limited liability the risk of owning a firm's stock would depend on the total wealth of all of its shareholders, because the amount of damages that one shareholder might have to pay would depend on the wealth of all shareholders. At a minimum, this would complicate stock valuation and individual decisions about which stocks to own. In addition, each investor would likely incur costs monitoring every other investor's wealth, which would increase the total cost of investing in stocks and of holding a diversified portfolio.

Limited Liability for Parent Corporations.   The preceding arguments are less applicable to limited liability for parents of subsidiary corporations. Some people believe that the rationale for limited liability is much weaker in this case, especially for tort claims. A few lawyers and law professors even have suggested elimination of limited liability for parent corporations. While the issues are complicated, you should be aware of two related points. First, elimination of limited liability for parent corporations in many cases would not reduce and sometimes even might increase moral hazard and the expected value of unpaid liability claims. The reason is that if limited liability for parent corporations were eliminated, fewer firms would combine under common ownership and some existing corporate groups would split up to reduce the risk of having to use assets in one subsidiary to pay claims against another subsidiary.

To illustrate using our earlier example, without limited liability the parent simply could divest one of the subsidiaries. The relationship between subsidiaries A and B would end. The assets of either firm therefore would never be available to pay tort claims against the other. The expected value of unpaid liability claims would not decrease. For each firm there still would be a 0.01 probability of an unpaid tort claim in the amount of $25 million (the $50 million claim minus $25 million in assets). There also is little or no reason to expect that firms A and B would have more incentive to invest in loss control. In addition, if corporate groups were to split into unaffiliated entities, the possibility that a parent might pay tort claims in excess of the value of a subsidiary's assets in order to avoid damage to the group's reputation would disappear.

The second and related problem that would arise if limited liability for parent corporations were eliminated is that any resulting division of corporate groups into unaffiliated entities would sacrifice any valuable synergies that otherwise might occur from affiliation, such as possible cost savings in raising capital. While valuable synergies might provide incentives for continued affiliation (or new affiliations), if limited liability for parents were eliminated, the reduction in value from splitups that did occur and future affiliations that would not take place still would weaken any case for eliminating limited liability. Our own view is that eliminating limited liability for parent corporations might primarily encourage large numbers of costly lawsuits and possibly create a severe recession.

Exceptions to Limited Liability

In some cases courts have refused to uphold limited liability and instead have forced shareholders to pay claims in excess of corporate assets or equity. This outcome is colorfully known as **piercing the corporate veil** or simply veil piercing. The possibility of veil piercing reduces the ability of shareholders to rely on limited liability as a risk-shifting device, and it is another factor that reduces moral hazard associated with limited liability. We stress, however, that veil piercing is not common. Courts do not routinely hold shareholders liable for claims in excess of corporate assets or equity.

While the law is fairly complex in this area, veil piercing has occurred in two main types of tort liability situations. The first is where the corporation is closely held with the primary shareholders directly involved with the firm's decisions or actually responsible for operations (e.g., they are owner/managers) and the firm engages in obviously risky activity with limited assets and insurance. You should note that moral hazard would appear to be severe in this case. One advantage of limited liability, the separation of management and risk bearing, also is not present. Thus, the benefits of limited liability are comparatively small, and the moral hazard problem is comparatively large.

The second main situation in which veil piercing has occurred for tort liability claims is for parent-subsidiary relationships where the parent has strong control over or common management with the subsidiary and the subsidiary has engaged in obviously risk activity with relatively little capital. Again, it can be argued in this situation that the benefits of limited liability are low compared to the costs. Box 17–1 discusses an example of veil piercing in a parent-subsidiary relationship involving liability for environmental damages and cleanup.

Another situation in which a parent might be held liable for claims against a subsidiary is where the parent makes statements or behaves in a way that causes potential claimants to assume that the parent guarantees the obligations of the

---

Box 17–1

Liability of a Parent for Subsidiary Torts: The Case of Superfund

One of the most important areas of debate regarding limited liability of parents for subsidiaries has involved environmental liability under Superfund (see Chapter 15). In a key case decided in 1989 that has been followed in other cases, Kayser-Roth Corporation, an apparel manufacturer, was held liable for damages and cleanup costs associated with the activities of its wholly-owned subsidiary Stamina Mills, a textile mill that had been dissolved in 1979. The government brought action against Kayser-Roth, arguing that the corporate veil should be pierced. The court agreed because Kayser-Roth had exercised practical control of the subsidiary's decision making and had appointed its board of directors.

subsidiary. A variant would involve misrepresentation of material facts to potential claimants. These situations have been more common for debt or other financial obligations as opposed to tort liability claims for bodily injury or property damage.

Concept Check

1. Explain intuitively why limited liability might cause a firm to take on excessive risk of tort liability.

17.2 Liability for Actions of Employees and Other Parties

Vicarious Liability Doctrine

A fundamental legal doctrine in tort law is that in relationships between principals and agents, the principal is liable for the negligence and related torts (e.g., any strict liability) of the agent in performing his or her duties for the principal. This doctrine is known as **vicarious liability** and is sometimes called *imputed negligence.* In this context, "agent" is a general legal/economic term to indicate any party that is acting on behalf of another party known as the principal. The most important principal-agent relationship governed by the vicarious liability doctrine is the relationship between an employer (the principal) and an employee (the agent). But the doctrine is much broader than this. If, for example, you agree to run an errand for a friend using your car and negligently run down a pedestrian, your friend (the principal) conceivably could be sued and held liable because you would be acting as your friend's agent.[3]

The injured party in these situations can sue both the agent and the principal but can only recover the amount of the loss. In some cases, the principal might subsequently sue the agent to recover money that the principal had to pay because of the agent's negligence. However, suits by employers against employees in this context are rare for several reasons. First, because employees are risk averse, it usually is advantageous for employers to guaranty employees either implicitly or explicitly with liability insurance that they will not suffer loss of personal assets for ordinary negligence. General business liability insurance policies, for example, usually explicitly include employees as insureds under the policy. Second, without either explicitly insuring the employee or an implicit guaranty that the employer will not sue the employee, suits by the employer would in many cases recover little money because many employees have comparatively little wealth and will not have liability insurance coverage for business torts.

The rationale for vicarious liability is that it provides the principal, the party that is directing and managing the activity, with incentives to train, supervise, and monitor agents in order to reduce the risk of harm to other parties. The doctrine also prevents principals from using financially weak, uninsured, and thus judgment proof agents as a method of avoiding responsibility for harm. As a result,

---

[3] Your friend would be protected by your auto liability insurance, however (see Chapter 21).

holding principals liable for the torts of agents increases safety and reduces the judgment proof problem that arises because agents have limited liability (due to their limited personal wealth).

Liability of Businesses for Actions of Independent Contractors

Does vicarious liability apply to the actions of independent contractors who are hired by businesses to perform some task (e.g., to construct a building)? Before turning to this question, you need to learn a little about the difference between an independent contractor and an employee (agent). The common law distinguishes independent contractors from employees on a variety of dimensions, including (1) whether the business actively supervises and directs the other party (i.e., dictates how the work should be done as opposed to what result is expected), and (2) whether the business establishes hours of work, provides tools and equipment, and so on.[4] If a business does either or both of these things, the other party will be considered an employee (or agent). If not, the party is an independent contractor. (You should be aware that the terminology can be a little confusing here. For example, some insurance "agents" are legally considered to be independent contractors.)

The original common law rule was that businesses (or individuals) that hired independent contractors could not be held vicariously liable for the torts of the contractor. While this rule still is applied in some narrow instances, there are so many exceptions that for most intents and purposes a business faces substantial risk of liability if the contractor injures some other party. There are three main situations where the firm can be held liable.

First, we hinted above that sometimes there is ambiguity or disagreement over whether a party is an employee or an independent contractor. If the court determines that the party is acting as an employee, which has occurred in many cases, the business that hired the party can be held vicariously liable. Second, many states have held that protecting the public safety constitutes a **nondelegable duty.** This means that the business cannot delegate the duty to keep the public safe to an independent contractor. As a result, if the contractor injures a member of the public, the business that hired the contractor can be held vicariously liable. The third situation does not involve vicarious liability, but it has substantially the same effect: The business must pay damages. Many cases have held businesses liable for negligence in failing to take reasonable precautions to select a safe contractor. In these instances, the business is sued for damages directly by the injured party.

As a result of these exceptions, businesses have limited ability to shift legal responsibility for harm by using independent contractors. Some people suggest a "deep pockets" rationale for these exceptions: The primary purpose is to allow the injured party access to the business's assets or insurance coverage, which often

---

[4] Whether a party is an employee or independent contractor also has important tax implications which are beyond the scope of this book.

might be larger than for the independent contractor. In a sense this may be true, but the pejorative context of the term "deep pockets" would appear to be inappropriate for describing the general legal rules. (How they are applied in some cases may be another matter.)

The economic rationale for significant limitations on shifting legal liability risk through the use of independent contractors is that these limitations help reduce the cost of risk. Limited liability might cause contractors with few assets and little or no liability insurance to have too little incentive for safety if the parties that might be harmed by the contractor (such as members of the public) cannot force the contractor to bear the expected costs of its actions. If contractors with few assets and little or no liability insurance do not have to bear the full cost of their actions, they also might be able to charge a lower price than firms with substantial assets at risk and/or liability insurance. Note that the issue here is not one of desirable variation in price and quality. The key point is that limited liability may allow some firms to have levels of safety and prices that are too low to minimize the cost of risk, and these low prices might tempt firms to hire such contractors if the firms cannot be held liable for the contractors' actions.

In short, if firms could routinely avoid the risk of legal liability for injury by using independent contractors, they would have less incentive to seek and pay the higher price required to cover the costs of contractors that bear more of the expected cost of harm to other parties. As a result, an unlimited ability of businesses to shift legal liability risk to independent contractors would result in lower than optimal safety in society.

One drawback to legal rules that hold firms liable for the actions of independent contractors is that they might reduce the incentives of contractors to be safe if the contractor has more of an effect on safety than the principal but the rules allow the costs of injuries to be shared with the principal. However, as we elaborate in the next section, these situations can be handled by agreements between the firm and the contractor that reallocate the ultimate financial responsibility for harm.

Concept Check

2. Other things being equal, compare the expected cost of liability claims from a lawsuit for a small construction business with no liability insurance or assets at risk to a comparable business that buys substantial liability insurance.

17.3 Hold Harmless and Indemnity Agreements

Businesses routinely use two closely related types of contracts to manage their liability risk in view of the legal rules described in the preceding section. A **hold harmless agreement** is a contract between (in the simplest case) two parties in which one party agrees to hold the other party harmless for losses that arise out of some activity. This means that if the party that is to be held harmless (party B) is ordered to pay or agrees to settle damages under circumstances covered by the agreement, then the other party (party A) will pay the injured party on behalf of party B. An **indemnity agreement** is similar except that party B (known as the indemnitee) pays the injured party and is then reimbursed by party A (known as the indemnitor).

In some principal-agent relationships, agents agree to hold harmless or indemnify principals for injuries caused by the negligence of the agent. For example, independent contractors routinely agree to hold harmless or indemnify businesses that hire their services for liability due to negligence of the contractor. Manufacturers often agree to hold harmless or indemnify product retailers for possible liability of the retailer for injuries caused by manufacturing defects. Similarly, retailers that modify products prior to sale may agree to hold harmless or indemnify the manufacturer if the modifications contribute to consumer injury. These contracts often are also used in lessor-lessee relationships. For example, the lessee may agree to hold harmless or indemnify the lessor for injuries on the premises that result from the lessee's negligence.

Effect on the Cost of Risk

Hold harmless/indemnity agreements help minimize the cost of risk by allowing the contracting parties to reallocate financial responsibility for harm away from what might occur from application of the underlying legal doctrines governing liability.[5] To understand the key idea, first recall that limitations on the ability of businesses to shift legal liability for harm to independent contractors are desirable because they encourage businesses to deal with safe and financially responsible contractors. However, given these legal limitations, it often will be advantageous for the parties to use a hold harmless or indemnity agreement to ensure that financial responsibility for injuries caused by the independent contractor will be borne fully by the contractor.

Making the contractor bear full responsibility for the contractor's negligence gives the contractor proper incentives to invest in loss control. Without the hold harmless or indemnity agreement, part of the cost of injuries might be borne by the business that hired the contractor, which would reduce the contractor's incentives to take precautions. While this point is closely related to what you learned about the incentives provided by the tort liability system in Chapter 14, it is useful to provide a simple numerical example to make sure that you understand it.

Table 17–2 shows expected injury costs for different levels of precautions under two scenarios. Under the first scenario, the contractor bears the full cost of injuries and will minimize costs by spending $9,000 on precautions, producing expected injury costs of $6,000 and total expected costs of $15,000. The second scenario assumes that the contractor only bears 50 percent of injury costs, with

_____

[5] To some extent this reallocation is similar to the reallocation of liability in the example of the factory polluting the river in Chapter 14.

TABLE 17–2   Investment in Loss Control by a Contractor (all costs in $1,000's)

Cost of Precautions	Contractor Bears Full Injury Cost		Contractor Bears 50% of Injury Cost	
	Expected Injury Cost	*Expected Total Cost*	*Expected Injury Cost*	*Expected Total Cost*
2	20	22	10	12
5	12	17	6	11
9	6	15	3	12
14	4	18	2	16

the remainder borne by the firm that hires the contractor. In this case, the contractor will spend only $5,000 on precautions to minimize the contractor's costs. For the contractor this produces expected injury costs of $6,000 and expected total costs of $11,000. Expected total injury costs and expected total costs for both parties, however, will be $12,000 and $17,000, respectively. Thus, sharing responsibility between the contractor and the business that hires the contractor increases expected total costs by $2,000 ($17,000 – $15,000).

The business and the contractor can reduce expected total costs by $2,000 if the contractor spends $9,000 on precautions instead of $5,000. If the contractor agrees to hold harmless or indemnify the business, it will bear 100 percent of injury costs and spend the $9,000, thus minimizing total expected costs for the activity and allowing the business and the contractor to share the increased expected profit. The division of gains between the two parties will be affected by their negotiating skills and/or competitive conditions in the market for independent contractor services. However, the key point is that the parties have an incentive to enter into a hold harmless or indemnity agreement to provide incentives for cost minimization. This generally will be achieved by allocating responsibility to the party that is best able to control the risk.[6]

A second motive for entering into hold harmless and indemnity agreements is to reduce dispute resolution costs in the event that an injury occurs. Absent this type of agreement, both parties may be held liable by the court, with one party ordered to pay. This party then will seek to recover all or part of the damages from the other party, thus producing significant dispute resolution costs (attorney fees and so forth). By helping to clarify who is responsible in advance, hold harmless and indemnity agreements make post-injury disputes between the parties less

---

[6] It sometimes is argued that one of the parties might be better able to bear risk (e.g., by having access to insurance at more favorable terms), and that this might influence who holds whom harmless. While this possibly might have some effect in some cases, it still generally will be preferable to have the party best able to control the risk hold harmless or indemnify the other party. If the other party can buy insurance with a lower loading, then it could buy the insurance and charge the contractor for the protection.

common. The process is not perfect; disputes sometimes arise despite the agreement. In addition, some types of hold harmless and indemnity agreements may not be enforceable in court (see Box 17–2).

The Role of Insurance

The party that agrees to hold harmless or indemnify the other party commonly is required to bond (back up) its promise to pay by purchasing liability insurance and providing evidence of insurance to the other party. The required purchase of liability insurance (or in some cases some other form of security, such as a bank letter of credit) further reduces the judgment proof problem. Moreover, the fact that liability insurance premiums are based on factors related to the contractor's expected claim costs, including information on prior claims experience, further enhances incentives for safety.

An important practical issue for risk managers is the type of evidence to require. Two main methods are used. First, the insurer may issue a **certificate of insurance** to the party that is to be held harmless or indemnified that indicates that the other party has insurance and the amount of coverage purchased. Second, the insurance policy may be endorsed to list the business that is to be held harmless or indemnified as an "additional named insured," thus making the business an insured party under the contract. Being named as an additional insured provides greater legal rights, and the business is more likely to be notified of

---

Box 17–2

Enforceability of Hold Harmless and Indemnity Agreements

Hold harmless and indemnity agreements typically require party A to hold harmless or indemnify party B only in the case that the injury is due to the *sole negligence of party A*. Enforcement of these contracts sometimes is challenged by party A. For example, party A may argue that it was coerced into signing the agreement, or that it did not agree to bear a particular type of risk. Some courts have held in these situations that the contract is enforceable only if there is a "clear and unequivocal evidence of the parties' intent" to shift risk. These types of disputes, which should be less common when valid liability insurance is in force to back the agreement, make it important for risk managers to draw up the agreements as clearly as

possible, to be knowledgeable about applicable case law in different states, and to consider the likelihood that the other party might renege on its promise.

Many states will not enforce a contract where party A agrees to hold harmless or indemnify party B for injuries caused by the *sole negligence of party B* as against public policy, and there is little economic rationale for such agreements. Some hold harmless or indemnity agreements require party A to hold harmless or indemnify party B for injuries caused by the *joint negligence of A and B*. Some states will not enforce these agreements, which again indicates that many risk managers need to be familiar with differences in state practices.

changes in limits or cancellation of coverage on a timely basis than with a certificate of insurance.

In addition to liability insurance, independent contractors also are routinely required to provide evidence of workers' compensation insurance or qualified self-insurance for their employees. If the firm uses a contractor with employees that are not covered by workers' compensation (if, for example, the contractor has only one or two employees and is not required to be covered by workers' compensation in a given state), or if the contractor has violated the rules requiring insurance or qualified self-insurance, exclusive remedy may not apply in some jurisdictions. The business that hires the contractor then may be sued in tort for injuries to the contractor's employees. In other jurisdictions exclusive remedy may apply, but the firm that hires the contractor may be required to pay workers' compensation benefits to injured employees of the contractor.

Summary of Incentive Effects

Assuming that insurance is purchased in the business/independent contractor example, the role of legal rules and hold harmless and indemnity agreements backed by insurance in helping to minimize the cost of risk can be summarized briefly as follows. First, limits on the ability of businesses to shift legal liability risk to independent contractors encourage businesses to hire safe and financially sound contractors. Second, hold harmless and indemnity agreements are used to reallocate or clarify responsibility for damages in order to provide proper incentives for safety and reduce costly disputes between the parties. Third, the required purchase of insurance by the contractor helps guaranty that the contractor will honor the commitment, reduces the judgment proof problem, and further enhances incentives for safety by giving an advantage to safe contractors with good safety records.

Concept Check

3. Using the information in Table 17–2, how much would the contractor spend on safety without a hold harmless or indemnity agreement if it only had to pay 25 percent of injury costs? How much would the expected total cost of precautions and injuries increase compared to the case where the contractor has to hold harmless or indemnify the firm that hired it?

17.4 Claims Management and Administration

Liability and workers' compensation claims management and administration have a significant effect on the firm's cost of risk. In this section, we briefly address three issues: (1) general strategy, (2) monitoring the performance of insurers and third-party administrators, and (3) claim cost allocation to operating divisions or subsidiaries. Box 17–3 contains a number of practical tips for investigating and dealing with product liability claims.

Box 17–3

Dealing with Product Liability Claims

What should a firm do when it gets the news that its product has injured someone? According to the *Journal of American Insurance,* there are a number of dos and don'ts, including:

- Act promptly, create a case file, and gather relevant information about the injury, who was involved, when the accident occurred, whether the product was used properly, and so on.
- Obtain and keep the product involved because it might be valuable as evidence.
- Do not make negative statements about the product, including comments about any prior complaints or problems with the product; instead, make positive statements about the product and the firm's concern with the customer.
- Try to be helpful and cooperative with the injured party, telling the person that the firm wants to be of assistance in dealing with the problem.
- Contact the firm's product liability insurer as soon as it becomes apparent that a material incident has occurred and definitely after the firm receives a summons or complaint.

Source: "A Product Liability Guide for Manufacturers," *Journal of American Insurance,* Third Quarter, 1988.

General Claims Strategy

The overall strategic objective of liability and workers' compensation claims management is to minimize the expected sum of (1) claim costs, (2) claim settlement and dispute resolution costs, and (3) indirect costs such as adverse effects on the firm's reputation that could increase its cost of contracting with various parties. When insurance is purchased, the insurer bears defense costs and takes primary responsibility for negotiating and settling claims. As we discuss further below, it is therefore important for the firm to pick an insurer that has a claims settlement strategy that is compatible with the firm's overall objective. Workers' compensation self-insurers that use a third-party administrator also need to choose an administrator with compatible objectives.

While many strategic issues are similar for liability and workers' compensation claims, the fact that employers are required to pay valid claims without regard to fault or negligence and the closer, ongoing relationship between employers and employees than between employers and tort liability claimants, such as customers, can give rise to differences in strategy. Employers usually have strong economic incentives to pay legitimate workers' compensation claims promptly without having the employee retain legal counsel with associated increases in dispute resolution costs. In addition, in the long run, both employers and employees have an interest in controlling the cost of claims. Nonetheless, problems can arise for injuries that are difficult to verify and measure with the result that settlement of these claims often is more similar to liability claims. We comment further on these and other differences between liability and workers' compensation claims where appropriate.

Incentives to Settle.   Over 90 percent of tort liability cases settle without trial, and a similarly large proportion of workers' compensation claims are settled without a hearing before either a workers' compensation insurance commissioner or judge. Defendants and plaintiffs in liability cases both have strong incentives to settle before trial, because avoiding trial reduces legal costs for both parties. In addition, the parties usually are risk averse (or, in the case of businesses, have incentives to behave as though they were risk averse). Settling before trial avoids the uncertainty associated with the outcome of a trial. Cases that go to trial usually involve either mutual optimism by the parties (i.e., they both expect a good result from a trial) or have much larger stakes due to reputation effects or effects on the settlement of other suits (see below).

Workers' compensation claims commonly settle before formal dispute resolution because the injury is clearly work-related and there are no factual disputes about the required benefit payment. For cases where it is not clear that the injury is work-related or where the extent of disability is unclear, settlement before formal dispute resolution again reduces legal costs and avoids the uncertainty associated with a hearing.

Reputation Effects.   In some cases, defendants have an additional incentive to resist claims and avoid settlement when admitting liability may damage their reputation for safety with an adverse effect on their future ability to sell goods and services. For example, before medical malpractice suits became commonplace beginning in the 1970s, physicians were reluctant to settle claims because it would be construed as an admission of malpractice that might lead to significant damage to the physician's ability to practice, including the ability to obtain referrals from other physicians. For this reason, older malpractice policies did not give malpractice insurers the right to settle. This aversion to settlement declined as malpractice suits became more widespread (and thus less scandalous and less indicative of poor practice). Malpractice insurance now often gives insurers the right to settle just as is the case for most other types of liability insurance.

In other cases, refusing to settle or perceived excessive toughness in negotiations might damage a business's reputation. For example, if these actions receive extensive negative publicity that makes the business look stingy (e.g., they are the subject of a "60 Minutes" episode), there may be significant damage to the firm's general reputation that adversely affects sales. With respect to injured employees, an aggressive posture in trying to settle permanent partial disability claims for the lowest possible amount and/or to get workers back to work early might damage the firm's relations with other workers and make it more costly for the firm to attract and retain employees.

Effects of Multiple Suits.   If a defendant in a liability case or an employer in certain types of difficult-to-value workers' compensation cases will likely face many similar claims over time, the incentive to spend more resources to achieve a favorable outcome increases if this outcome will establish a precedent for other cases. For example, the defendant business or employer may attempt to establish a reputation for toughness in negotiation that will lower costs for other claims. Some observers suggest that this incentive stacks the deck in favor of corporate defendants or employers against individual plaintiffs or employees. The counter-argument is that liability plaintiffs' attorneys and attorneys that represent injured workers will in many cases also have greater incentives to achieve a favorable outcome that could influence other cases.

A related issue is when one or both parties desire to keep the details of a settlement private in order to not have the settlement influence other litigation. In these cases, the party that desires privacy (usually the defendant in a liability case who does not want the details to increase demands by plaintiffs in other cases) may be willing to offer a more generous settlement in order to keep the details private in what is known as a "sealed settlement."

Nuisance Suits and Fraud.   A nuisance suit is a suit where the plaintiff's case is known to be very weak by both parties. In these cases, the defendant often will nonetheless minimize the sum of defense and claim costs by offering to settle the case for an amount that essentially buys off the plaintiff to save on defense costs. A limitation of this strategy is that it may increase the frequency of similar suits. As a result, a key strategic decision is whether to invest significant amounts of money fighting these low-value suits in an attempt to establish a reputation for toughness and thereby deter these types of suits.

Fraudulent or exaggerated workers' compensation claims raise similar issues. The employer has to decide whether to incur greater costs fighting these claims in the short run with the hope of reducing the present value of total costs over time. This decision must consider the possible adverse effects on legitimate claimants. While fraud might be suspected, in some cases the claim may be legitimate. Fighting the claim will harm the employee with possible adverse effects on relations with other employees.

Releases and Advance Payments.   Payments are not made to most plaintiffs in liability cases unless the plaintiff signs a contract, known as a **release,** that releases the defendant from any obligation to make additional payments. **Advance payments** are payments made by the defendant (or insurer) to the plaintiff prior to receiving a release. Possible advantages to advance payments are: (1) they might sometimes reduce harm to the plaintiff and thus damages in some instances (e.g., paying the plaintiff's expenses to get necessary medical treatment), and (2) they might ultimately encourage a more favorable settlement if the plaintiff has a cooperative attitude and/or is uncomfortable with litigation.

Advance payments generally will be disadvantageous in cases where it is not clear that the defendant is liable as they may be construed as an admission of liability. A serious drawback to advance payments in many other instances is that they can significantly reduce the incentive for a noncooperative plaintiff to settle the case. A major factor that creates pressure for plaintiffs to settle is that they do not want to wait for the money.

Lump Sum versus Structured Settlements.   The vast majority of liability suits are settled with a lump sum payment. Large settlements sometimes are paid over time, however, in what is called a **structured settlement.** The typical practice is for the defendant or the defendant's insurer to purchase an annuity contract to make periodic payments to the plaintiff instead of a lump sum settlement. In some cases these deals have been arranged to provide the annuity payment at a lower after-tax cost than would be the case if the plaintiff were paid a lump sum and then to purchase an annuity on their own from the proceeds. This cost savings has allowed the structured settlement to be advantageous to both the plaintiff and the defendant.

As noted in Chapter 16, most workers' compensation claims for permanent disability are settled in a lump sum rather than paid over time. Workers (and any legal counsel) usually prefer lump sum payments. Lump sum awards also avoid the disincentive for work that can arise with periodic benefit payments given that these benefits normally cease if the recipient returns to work.

Monitoring Performance of Insurers and Outside Contractors

As briefly discussed in Chapter 9, bundling responsibility for settling and paying claims in liability insurance contracts generally provides strong incentives for the insurer to minimize the sum of claim payments and claim settlement costs. This result also generally holds for insured workers' compensation claims. There are a number of issues that firms need to consider when selecting an insurer and evaluating insurer performance.

Recall that insurers usually are legally responsible for defending and settling claims and that they have the legal authority to settle claims. In the case of potentially large liability claims that could have significant adverse reputation effects or could affect other claims in the future that might not be insured by the same insurer, risk managers will need to select insurers that will be willing to work closely with the firm to meet its objectives in view of these issues. However, advance agreement on strategy and an appropriate price may be difficult when there is substantial uncertainty about the types of losses that could occur and the possible effects of different settlement strategies. In some cases it may be possible for insurers and their policyholders to agree on a strategy for dealing with such claims after they occur, perhaps including price concessions or adjustments to achieve a mutually beneficial result. In other cases, disagreements over settlement strategy may arise that result in a termination of the relationship or litigation between the firm and its insurer.

A related issue is the possible incentive conflict that can arise between a liability insurer and a policyholder in cases where it may be fairly obvious that the claim will ultimately settle for an amount equal to or greater than the policy limit. The insurer might then be tempted to delay paying the claim as long as possible to maintain use of the funds. If this behavior occurs, it may expose the policyholder to risk that the amount ultimately needed to settle the claim will increase (i.e., forcing the plaintiff to wait can increase the amount demanded to settle the case). Because the increase in the settlement amount is in excess of the policy limit, the policyholder will be responsible for the increased cost.

Insurer incentives to engage in this type of behavior are mitigated by: (1) an interest in having a long-term relationship with the policyholder, (2) possible adverse effects on the insurer's reputation and thus the insurer's ability to sell or renew coverage to other parties, and (3) the possibility that the policyholder or injured party might successfully sue the insurer for failing to negotiate in good faith. In addition, risk managers can reduce this risk by carefully selecting an insurer and monitoring the insurer's settlement efforts after the claim.

When liability claims are not insured, firms sometimes will have to employ outside attorneys. For self-insured workers' compensation claims, firms often find it desirable to use outside administrators (third-party administrators or TPAs; which we discuss in Chapter 16) given the specialized expertise of these firms and the possible advantage of having a third party intervene in potentially adversarial situations between the employer and the employee.[7] In these situations, the outside attorneys and claims administrators are paid by fees. In contrast to insurers, they are not responsible for paying the cost of claims. As a result, they may have less incentive to pursue strategies that reduce claim costs and thus total costs for firms that use their services. Risk managers need to select these parties carefully, based on their reputations for quality, and monitor their performance over time.

A problem that often arises in practice is how to determine whether a TPA has done a good job in controlling costs. In some cases, data may be available to compare the average claim costs (or other variables such as the average time needed to settle a claim) for a particular TPA to other TPAs or to workers' compensation insurers. Risk managers also can review and compare factors such as the TPA's pursuit of subrogation rights and second injury fund recoveries to gather additional information about performance.

Claim Cost Allocation

An important practical issue associated with administering liability and workers' compensation claims is how to best allocate costs to operating divisions (or subsidiaries). The method used to allocate costs can have a material impact on (1) managers' incentives to control costs, (2) performance measures for the divisions, and thus (3) managerial compensation, to the extent that it is linked to these performance measures. A general principle is that if division managers have information and authority to make decisions to control certain types of costs, then it is desirable to allocate these costs to the division to increase incentives for cost control.

When claims are insured, cost allocations often can be made by allocating relevant premiums for liability or workers' compensation coverage. For uninsured

---

[7] TPAs also are often used for self-insured medical insurance claims.

claims, the firm needs to decide how to allocate claim costs in view of the fact that realized costs in a given period may be highly variable due to random fluctuations. If claim costs turn out to be very high in a given period due to chance (bad luck), allocating the entire cost will give a distorted picture of performance, and it may expose managers to excessive risk if their compensation is directly linked to a performance measure that reflects the entire cost of claims.

For this reason it often will be desirable to smooth cost allocations over time. For example, the division might be charged an amount based on a moving average of costs in the current and prior years. Sometimes this process is taken one step further by attempting to estimate and charge for expected costs using methods similar to those that would be used by insurers, including the use of experience-rating charges. Although use of a captive is not essential, these approaches often are formalized when the firm has a captive insurer. Premiums paid by divisions to the captive allocate the cost of claims across divisions.

Concept Check

4. Reinterpret the example in Table 17–2 to explain how allocating all relevant expected injury costs to a division manager can provide the manager with incentives to invest in loss control to minimize the cost of risk.

17.5 Summary

- The doctrine of limited liability limits the liability of corporate shareholders to the value of corporate assets. The protection provided by limited liability is analogous to insurance protection against large tort liability claims for both individual shareholders of a corporation and a parent corporation with multiple subsidiaries.

- Like insurance in general, limited liability can lead to moral hazard and excessive risk of injury because corporations might not have to pay for all of the harm they might cause from risky activities.

- Courts sometimes allow tort claimants to recover from corporate parents for torts of subsidiary corporations if the subsidiary's assets are insufficient to pay damages. Known as piercing the corporate veil, allowing recovery from parent corporations is most likely when moral hazard is severe and the social benefits of limited liability are negligible.

- Principals generally are liable for the torts of their agents, which includes liability of employers for torts of employees in the course of their employment. Firms that use independent contractors often can be held liable for torts of the contractor in order to mitigate the judgment proof problem and encourage safety.

- Hold harmless/indemnity agreements backed by liability insurance help reduce the cost of risk by allocating the ultimate responsibility for harm to the party best able to reduce injury costs and by reducing costly disputes between the parties.

- Risk aversion and savings on dispute resolution costs motivate plaintiffs and defendants to settle most cases before trial. The general overall goal of defense and claims settlement for businesses that face tort liability claims is to minimize the expected total costs of damages and defense. Factors that influence strategy in specific instances include potential adverse effects of fighting claims on a firm's reputation and the effects of settlement on the frequency and severity of other suits.

- Appropriate procedures for allocating injury costs to divisions or subsidiaries can improve incentives to control costs and thus reduce the cost of risk.

Key Terms

piercing the corporate veil   422
vicarious liability   423
nondelegable duty   424
hold harmless agreement   425
indemnity agreement   426

certificate of insurance   428
release   432
advance payments   432
structured settlement   433

Questions and Problems

1. A corporation has assets of $100 million and owes $30 million to a bank. Given limited liability, what is the maximum amount of loss to the corporation's shareholders from tort claims? What is the maximum loss to the bank from tort claims against the corporation? Explain how the bank is providing implicit liability insurance to the corporation's shareholders. Also explain how the bank can charge a premium for this insurance.

2. Rework the example in Table 17–1 assuming that each subsidiary has assets of $40 million. Then rework the example assuming that each subsidiary has assets of $50 million and that the probability of a tort liability suit increases to 0.02 for each subsidiary. Does limited liability of the parent for torts of the subsidiaries reduce risk for the parent in the latter case? Why or why not?

3. Other things being equal, is the moral hazard problem associated with limited liability likely to be worse for the risk of product-related injuries to consumers or for the risk of environmental damage to the public? Explain.

4. Other things being equal, is the moral hazard problem associated with limited liability likely to be worse for firms with substantial profitable future investment opportunities or firms that have few if any such opportunities? Explain.

5. You have just inherited $10 million. Rather than kicking back and avoiding all work, you are contemplating starting and operating a landscaping business with a friend that would require each of you to invest $5,000 for equipment. Your friend suggests that the business be formed as a corporation so that you won't have to buy a lot of expensive liability insurance to protect your inheritance from tort claims from people that you conceivably might injure. Given your knowledge of veil piercing, what do you tell your friend?

6. Argue the case for eliminating the limited liability of parent corporations for tort liability claims from parties that do not have a contractual relationship with the firm. Then argue the case for keeping limited liability in these situations.

7. Firms A and B form a joint venture to produce and service machines used by tire manufacturers. Firm A will build the machines; firm B will set up the machines and perform maintenance. What type of hold harmless or indemnity contracts should the

firms enter into in order to minimize the cost of risk associated with possible tort liability claims from workers who are injured by the machines?

8. A business faces a nuisance suit that demands $3,000 in damages. The business and the plaintiff both know that no damages will be awarded if the case goes to court. It will cost the business $2,000 to fight the case and win in court. Ignoring the timing of payments, the time value of money, and the possible effect of settlement on other cases, what is the maximum settlement offer that the firm will make?

9. Consider the same scenario in question 8 and assume that the firm can settle the case for $1,500. Also assume that if the firm settles the case, it will face nine identical cases in the future. If the firm refuses to settle, it will discourage some of these suits. Again ignoring the time value of money, how many suits would have to be deterred in order for the firm to minimize its costs by refusing to settle any suits versus settling each suit for $1,500?

10. Liability insurance contracts generally require the insurer to defend policyholders (and incur the cost of defense) and give the insurer the right to settle suits. Explain why these provisions in the contract are normally desirable from the standpoint of policyholders who must pay for the cost of coverage. Also describe circumstances where conflicts over defense/settlement strategy might arise between the liability insurer and the policyholder.

References

Cooter, Robert D.; and Daniel L. Rubinfield. "Economic Analysis of Legal Disputes and Their Resolution." *Journal of Economic Literature* 27 (1989), pp. 1067–97. (*Detailed discussion of the economics of negotiating and settling liability claims.*)

Easterbrook, Frank; and Daniel Fischel. "Limited Liability and the Corporation." *University of Chicago Law Review* 52 (1989), pp. 89–117. (*Detailed discussion of the rationale for limited liability and its incentive effects.*)

Answers to Concept Checks

1. Because of limited liability, a firm may not have to pay the entire cost of harm that it causes to other parties. Unless these parties can induce the firm to consider the full cost of potential harm by somehow charging the firm an appropriate price, the firm has less incentive to avoid activities that may give rise to large injury costs, especially since any profits from the risky activities will accrue to the firm.

2. Because of limited liability, the expected cost of liability claims for a small construction firm with no liability insurance or assets at risk will be smaller than the expected cost of injuries to other parties because the firm will be judgment proof, at least for sizable losses. In contrast, a comparable business that buys liability insurance will bear the expected cost of liability claims up to the limit of the policy because the insurance premium will reflect these expected costs. (Liability insurance will not eliminate moral hazard, however, because of imperfect experience rating and the fact that the magnitude of harm to other parties could exceed the limit of insurance.)

3. A revised version of Table 17–2 is shown below for the case where the contractor has to pay only 25 percent of injury costs:

Investment in Loss Control by Contractor ($1,000s)

	Contractor Bears Full Injury Cost		Contractor Bears 25% of Injury Cost	
Cost of Precautions	*Expected Injury Cost*	*Expected Total Cost*	*Expected Injury Cost*	*Expected Total Cost*
2	20	22	5	7
5	12	17	3	8
9	6	15	1.5	10.5
14	4	18	1	15

The contractor would minimize its expected total cost by spending $2,000, which would produce expected total costs of $7,000 to the contractor. The expected injury cost if $2,000 is spent on precautions is $20,000, producing total expected costs of $22,000. If the contractor has to indemnify or hold harmless the firm that hired it, it would spend $9,000 on precautions, producing total expected costs of $15,000. Thus, the total expected cost increases by $7,000 (from $15,000 to $22,000) if the contractor has to pay only 25 percent of injury costs.

4. Apart from other influences (e.g., monitoring by senior managers), a division manager that is only charged with a portion of expected injury costs might have incentives comparable to a contractor that has to bear only part of injury costs. Thus, the division manager might spend too little on precautions (e.g., less than $9,000) in order to increase the expected income of the division. Allocating all relevant expected injury costs to the manager would increase his or her incentives to spend the optimal amount on precautions ($9,000).

Benefit Plans and Social Security

Employee Benefits: Overview and Group Medical Coverage

Chapter Objectives

- Explain the major types of employee benefits and why firms provide employee benefits.
- Describe and analyze group medical expense coverage, including traditional fee-for-service arrangements, health maintenance organizations, and other forms of managed care.
- Summarize key group medical expense plan coverage provisions and pricing issues.
- Discuss causes of high health care costs and why many people are not insured for medical expenses.
- Briefly describe alternative proposals for reforming the US health care system to control costs and increase the number of insured people.

18.1 Major Types of Employee Benefits

Employers usually voluntarily offer a variety of benefits to employees in addition to cash wages. The most common types of benefits are insurance programs (medical insurance, life insurance, disability insurance, and dental insurance) and retirement plans. Other examples of employee benefits are paid vacations and maternity/paternity leave. This chapter and Chapter 19 discuss benefit plans that are voluntarily offered by employers. The compulsory federal social security program, which pays benefits to retired and disabled workers and survivors of deceased workers and medical expenses for the elderly population, is discussed in Chapter 20.

Employee benefits represent a substantial proportion of total employee compensation costs for many employers. Table 18–1 provides the percentages of US employees who receive various types of benefits by type and size of employer.

TABLE 18-1   Percentage of US Employees Receiving Various Types of Benefits in 1994

Type of Benefit	Description	Medium and Large Private Businesses	Small Private Businesses	State and Local Government
Medical insurance	Covers eligible medical expenses for employee and covered dependents through fee-for-service arrangement or health maintenance organization	77%	66%	87%
Retirement plan	Defined contribution or defined benefit pensions and related retirement savings plans	80	42	96
Life insurance	Typically term life insurance with death benefit equal to a multiple of salary (e.g., 1-2 times salary)	87	61	87
Short-term disability insurance	Replaces a percentage of lost wages for short-term disability (e.g., up to six months)	53	n.a.	n.a.
Long-term disability insurance	Replaces a percentage of lost wages for long-term disability (e.g., up to age 65) with offset for any disability benefits paid by social security	42	20	30
Dental insurance	Covers eligible dental expenses for employee and covered dependents	57	28	62

Source: Data obtained from Bureau of Labor Statistics *Report on Employee Benefits.*

These data indicate that larger employers are more likely to provide benefits than smaller employers and that government employees are more likely to receive benefits than employees of private enterprises. For private employers, estimates indicate that aggregate employee benefit plan costs represent between 20 and 25 percent of total compensation costs. For some firms, employee benefit costs represent over one-half of total compensation.

Who Pays the Cost of Benefits?

Employee benefit plans that do not require workers to contribute directly toward the cost of benefits through payroll deductions are know as *noncontributory plans.* Plans that require workers to contribute part of their wages or salary are known as *contributory plans.* In both contributory and noncontributory plans, an implicit tradeoff between employer contributions and wages is likely to exist, at least in the long run. That is, higher employer contributions will result in lower wages, all else equal. Similarly, in order to attract equally qualified employees, an employer that does not pay for any benefits will have to pay higher wages than an employer that pays part or all of the cost of benefits.

While in the long run employees are likely to pay the full cost of their benefits via higher payroll deductions and lower wages, short-run increases in employee benefit costs are likely to reduce employer profits. For example, employers are likely to experience lower short-run profits if the cost of medical expense insurance or self-insured medical expense benefits suddenly increases. The fact that employers bear the risk of employee benefit costs in the short run helps explain why employee benefit plans often fall under the topic of risk management. The other reason employee benefit plans fall under risk management is that many employee benefits provide insurance protection for employees. Consequently, the tools and institutional knowledge needed for corporate risk management also are needed to manage employee benefits plans.

Flexibility in Choice of Benefits

In some cases employees have no choice regarding their benefits; the employer offers a particular benefit package for all employees. Usually, however, employees have some choice as to the benefits they receive, especially in contributory plans. Employee choice is maximized with **cafeteria benefit plans** (often known as "flexible benefit plans"), in which employees typically receive a core (minimum) package of required benefits and credits to select from a menu of optional benefits. If employees are offered the option of receiving cash instead of benefits, the entire value of the credits is taxable as income (and the tradeoff between wages and benefit costs becomes explicit). The primary advantage of cafeteria plans is that employees are able to choose benefits that better meet their needs. Disadvantages include increased adverse selection (discussed later in the chapter) and administrative costs for record keeping, providing employees with information about options, and so on.

A related method of providing employees with some choice regarding benefits and of utilizing the tax advantages of benefits is through a **flexible spending account.** With a flexible spending account, the employee chooses to reduce salary by some amount, such as $1,000. This amount can be used to pay for a variety of benefits, including uninsured medical and dental expenses and dependent child care. The advantage of a flexible spending account is that the employee is not taxed on the amount of salary that is used for this purpose (e.g., the $1,000).[1] However, to qualify for favorable tax treatment (see below), the employee must incur the expenses and request reimbursement within a specified period. The fact that unused amounts of the salary reduction are forfeited is known as "use it or lose it."

18.2 Why Firms Provide Employee Benefits

If employees pay for their benefits in the long run, a natural question is: Why are benefits provided through an employer as opposed to workers purchasing them individually? Instead of providing employee benefits, businesses could pay

---

[1] For contributory plans, a similar mechanism commonly is used for employee contributions toward the cost of medical expense coverage in order to exclude the amount contributed from the employee's taxable income.

higher cash wages and allow employees to contract for benefits on their own. The explanations for why employers provide employee benefits fall into three main categories. One important reason for employer provided benefits is that taxes paid by the employer and employee generally are lower if the employer provides the benefits as opposed to paying higher cash wages and having the employee purchase the benefits individually. A second reason for employer provided benefits is that percentage loadings for administrative expenses in group insurance premiums are lower than for individual insurance. Finally, employers sometimes find that employer provided benefits promote employee productivity. We now examine each of these explanations in more detail.

Income Tax Advantages of Employee Benefits

Employee benefit plans that receive preferential income tax treatment are called **qualified plans.** As discussed in Chapter 10, the tax benefits of a particular transaction can be assessed only by examining the tax payments of all parties involved. In the case of employee benefits, it is necessary to examine the tax treatment from both the employer's and the employee's perspective.

The federal income tax treatment of employee benefits generally is the same as the tax treatment of cash wages from the employer's perspective. Both benefits and wages are deductible expenses. Consequently, the income tax effects to an employer of paying an additional $100 in cash wages are the same as paying an additional $100 in employee benefits. The major tax advantage of employee benefits therefore arises from the personal income tax treatment of employee benefits versus cash wages.[2] Specifically, the tax advantage exists because: (1) the cost of qualified employee benefit plans either is not taxed or is tax deferred at the personal level, whereas salary and wages are taxed in the year earned, and (2) employees generally are not able to obtain the same tax treatment if benefits are purchased individually.

To illustrate the main tax benefit, suppose that the annual cost of medical insurance for Helen is $4,000 regardless of whether it is purchased through the employer or individually by Helen. Consider two potential compensation packages for Helen:

Package 1:   Salary = $40,000 and no medical insurance

Package 2:   Salary = $36,000 plus medical insurance

---

[2] State income tax rules generally are similar. For most workers, the social security system provides additional tax incentives to substitute employee benefits for cash wages. The social security system is financed mainly through payroll taxes equal to specified percentages of payroll paid by both the employer and the employee (see Chapter 20). Since the value of many employee benefits is not subject to payroll taxes, employees can save on payroll taxes by taking a greater portion of their total compensation in the form of employee benefits as opposed to cash wages. However, since social security benefits are tied to the taxes paid by a particular employee, the substitution of employee benefits for cash wages might reduce social security benefits as well. Thus, the net effect of social security on employee benefits is complex.

The after-tax cost to the employer is the same for both packages; however, the tax treatment of the two packages differs for Helen. Assume, for example, that Helen has a 20 percent income tax rate and that she cannot deduct any of the cost of individual medical insurance from her taxable income.[3] With package 1, Helen then has after-tax income of $32,000 [$40,000 × (1 − 0.20)], from which she purchases health insurance at a cost of $4,000, leaving $28,000 to spend on other goods and services. With package 2, she has after-tax income of $28,800 [$36,000 × (1 − 0.20)] to spend on other goods and services. The difference of $800 is the tax savings on the cost of medical insurance (0.20 × $4,000).

While the initial cost of qualified employee benefits is not taxable, the benefits from some plans, such as retirement plans and disability insurance, may be taxed if and when they are received. For example, retirement income is taxed when it is received. Thus, there is a deferral of taxes on the contributions to retirement plans. Qualified retirement plans also have the feature that taxes on investment income are deferred until funds are withdrawn. Tax deferral is beneficial because it reduces the present value of tax payments. Tax deferral also can be beneficial if the tax rate applied in the future is expected to be lower than the current tax rate. Chapter 19 examines the tax benefits of qualified retirement plans in more detail.

Cost Savings with Group Insurance

Group insurance purchased by an employer (implicitly purchased by employees in the form of lower wages) can be less costly than having each employee individually purchase the same amount of insurance. One reason for the lower cost is that the insurer's administrative costs of marketing, underwriting, billing, and premium collection are lower with group insurance than with selling separate policies to each individual employee. Thus, group insurance through an employer has a lower percentage expense loading than individual insurance. Another cost savings associated with employer provided benefits is that the total costs of designing benefits and selecting an appropriate insurer are lower than if each individual were to arrange for their own benefits.

Group insurance also can reduce adverse selection problems relative to providing insurance on an individual basis. Because of the heterogeneity in individuals applying for medical insurance and life insurance, insurers typically find it cost effective to gather information which will help them predict expected claim costs and thus classify applicants. Without classification (charging all applicants the same price), insurers could experience severe adverse selection problems (see Chapter 6). That is, individuals with higher (lower) expected claim costs could purchase higher (lower) amounts of coverage than with classification. Classifica-

---

[3] Individual medical insurance premiums are deductible if the premiums and other deductible medical costs exceed 7.5 percent of the person's (adjusted) gross income. Self-employed persons can deduct only part of the cost of coverage.

tion is never perfect, however; therefore, some adverse selection is likely to occur despite insurers' efforts to classify individuals.

With group insurance, individual members of the group typically have limited opportunities to choose their level of coverage. Consequently, group insurers need to worry less about adverse selection even though they generally do not classify individual members. Group insurance therefore can reduce classification costs and adverse selection if individual members of the group have limited choices.[4] The mitigation of adverse selection helps to explain why group insurance often is mandatory or why coverage options are limited for a particular firm.

Productivity and Employee Benefits

Another reason for including benefits in an employee compensation package is that suitably defined benefit plans can increase productivity. As discussed in more detail in Chapter 19, deferred compensation (such as retirement benefits) can be structured to induce employees to work harder and to reduce employee turnover. Other types of benefits also can enhance labor productivity by improving morale and the retention of key employees. In addition, productivity can be enhanced by employee benefits such as medical insurance if the benefits improve the health of employees, reduce time away from work, and reduce turnover.

Regulatory Restrictions on Employee Benefits

The regulatory restrictions on employee benefits are numerous and complex. We have no intention of trying to learn or memorize them fully ourselves, much less pretend that you should do so. (Of course, if your career plans are in the employee benefit area, then you will have to learn many of the regulations and keep track of how they change every year.) Nevertheless, you should be aware that employee benefits can be subject to restrictions from a number of sources, including federal laws dealing with labor contracts and labor relations, antidiscrimination laws, the tax code, and state laws dealing with insurance contracts. We discuss some of the regulations dealing with group medical insurance later in the chapter and with retirement plans in Chapter 19.

Concept Check

1. Explain why the income tax treatment of qualified employee benefits will likely cause higher paid employees to demand a greater proportion of their total compensation in the form of benefits than lower paid employees.

18.3 Overview of Group Medical Expense Coverage

One of the most common and important types of employee benefits is **group medical expense coverage,** whereby the employer provides employees with insurance coverage to pay eligible medical expenses. Almost 90 percent of people

---

[4] Insurers still are likely to classify groups to prevent adverse selection at the group level.

with private (i.e., nongovernmental) medical expense insurance in the United States are enrolled in employer-based group plans.

Traditional Fee-for-Service Insurance Arrangements

From the 1940s through the 1980s, the predominant form of employer-based group medical expense insurance was a fee-for-service arrangement. These arrangements have become much less common since that time, especially in their pure form. Knowledge of these arrangements is nonetheless important for understanding the development of health maintenance organizations and other managed care alternatives to traditional fee-for-service plans.

Traditional fee-for-service arrangements have several main features:

- Employers provide coverage for specified medical expenses, either self-insuring or purchasing insurance to cover all or part of the costs.
- Employees and covered dependents have substantial discretion (choice) over what doctor or hospital to use when care is needed.
- When an employee or covered dependent receives medical care, the health care provider charges a fee to the employee and/or insurer for the services provided (thus the name "fee-for-service"). Depending on the plan, the provider either bills the employee, who is then reimbursed by the insurer, subject to deductibles and coinsurance, or the provider bills the insurer directly. In the latter case, the employee either pays the provider for any charge not covered by the plan or reimburses the insurer.

Large employers generally self-insure most or all of the benefits under these plans, in many cases using an insurer or third-party administrator to administer the insurance benefits. Small- to medium-sized employers commonly purchase group medical insurance to pay benefits from either a commercial insurance company or Blue Cross–Blue Shield organization (see Box 18–1). In noncontributory plans, employers provide medical expense coverage without an explicit premium contribution from employees. Contributory plans require employees to pay a part of the cost as an explicit payroll deduction. Most plans that provide coverage for an employee's dependents are contributory.

There are two main methods of arranging insurance protection for employees under fee-for-service plans: (1) provide basic coverage with "supplementary" major medical insurance, and (2) provide "comprehensive" major medical insurance without separate benefits under basic coverage.

Under the first approach, employees generally receive **basic benefits** in the form of coverage for hospitalization, surgery, physician services apart from surgery (for example, while hospitalized or following a period of hospitalization), and specified diagnostic tests. These benefits often are subject to small deductibles and the benefit is limited (e.g., 60 days of hospitalization per illness, or a specified maximum number of physician visits). The costs of routine care, such as periodic physical examinations or physician visits for "minor" illnesses (e.g., visits for colds and infections) usually are limited or in many cases excluded from the basic benefits package. Coverage generally is provided for "usual, customary,

Box 18–1

Blue Cross–Blue Shield Organizations

Blue Cross–Blue Shield (BC–BS) organizations originally were formed during the 1930s and 1940s as nonprofit (and therefore income tax-exempt) associations of health care providers who offered services to covered workers and other consumers for annual premiums. Although there was little material difference, these plans differed from indemnity insurance policies in that groups of hospitals and doctors agreed to provide specified health care services in exchange for premiums, as opposed to having an unrelated insurer pay hospitals and physicians for services rendered. Blue Cross plans provided hospital services; Blue Shield plans provided physician services. Most separate Blue Cross and Blue Shield plans later merged to provide both hospital and physician services.

Modern BC–BS organizations operate as separate entities in almost all states; a few states have more than one BC–BS organization. Most of these organizations operate in the same general manner as other medical expense insurers. BC–BS organizations have a large share (e.g., up to 50 percent or more) of the group medical expense coverage market in many states. The Congress repealed the federal income tax exemption for BC–BS plans in 1986. Some states exempt the plans from state premium taxes. In part due to loss of their income tax-exempt status, some BC–BS entities converted to mutual insurance companies during the mid-1980s. Beginning in the mid-1990s, a number of BC–BS organizations converted to stock insurance companies, a trend that could continue. Many BC–BS organizations have diversified their operations by creating HMOs, by expanding into lines of insurance beyond medical insurance, and by providing claims processing services for self-insured employer medical plans.

and reasonable" charges and/or based on a fee schedule. If the hospital or physician charges more than what is defined as reasonable or specified in the schedule, then the employee has to pay the excess.

In addition to basic benefits, the employee typically receives additional protection in the form of supplementary **major medical coverage.** The major medical coverage pays eligible expenses not covered by the basic benefits package, subject to an annual deductible (for each family member or less often for the family as a whole) and a co-insurance clause that requires the employee to pay a specified percentage (e.g., 15–25 percent) of expenses in excess of the deductible. Major medical coverage usually provides a large lifetime limit on total benefits, such as $500,000 to $1 million; some plans have no upper limit. Common exclusions include elective cosmetic surgery, vision and dental care, and medical expenses payable under workers' compensation.

Many major medical plans cap the employee's maximum out-of-pocket cost for eligible expenses during the year using a **stop loss clause** or "out-of-pocket maximum," which specifies that the major medical coverage will pay 100 percent of eligible expenses (usually including some services not covered by the basic plan) once the employee has paid a specified amount under the co-insurance clause (or under both the deductible and co-insurance clause). For example, the stop loss clause might limit the employee's maximum out-of-pocket cost from the application of co-insurance to $1,500 in a year. This limit could apply to all costs for the employee and covered dependents, or it could only apply to the employee's expenses with a higher stop loss amount, such as $3,000, to cap total co-insurance costs (or in some plans total deductible and co-insurance costs) for the family. Note that major medical coverage and the stop loss clause apply only to eligible expenses. Medical expenses that are not eligible are paid in full by the employee. In many plans, ineligible expenses include amounts charged by physicians in excess of the amount that the plan is willing to pay for specified services. Thus, in some cases employees may have material out-of-pocket costs in addition to the maximum amounts specified by the stop loss clause.

The splitting of coverage into basic benefits and major medical benefits reflects to some extent the historical development of employer provided group medical coverage and associated insurance products. When group medical coverage first became common, employers often started with hospitalization coverage and later added coverage for surgery and other physicians' services. Major medical coverage eventually was developed to protect against large losses not covered by the basic benefits package.

The second approach to providing benefits under a fee-for-service arrangement is simply to use stand-alone major medical insurance, sometimes known as "comprehensive major medical coverage." There is no separate package of basic benefits. Eligible expenses simply are covered subject to a lifetime limit on costs, if any, and subject to a deductible, co-insurance, and, if included, a stop loss provision.

Fee-for-Service and Utilization of Health Care Services

The health care system has three major players: (1) health care providers, such as physicians, nurses, and hospitals; (2) employees/individuals who seek and consume health care; and (3) employers/insurers who provide insurance to pay the unexpected health care costs of individuals. The main point of this section is to show how the incentives of these parties under traditional fee-for-service arrangements can increase overall medical expenses.

An important characteristic of health care is that providers typically know more about the services needed than do consumers. For example, if a physician recommends a particular test or procedure, most consumers are not qualified to question the physician and many consumers are reluctant (or find it costly) to obtain second opinions except for major treatments. As a consequence, providers in many cases have considerable influence over the demand for the product that they provide. In the extreme, providers can create demand for their services. The influence of providers on the demand for their services is strengthened to the extent that someone other than the consumer, such as an insurer, pays most of the costs of services recommended by the provider.

Moral Hazard with Fee-for-Service.   Group medical coverage in general and fee-for-service coverage in particular leads to moral hazard, which increases the cost of medical care. There are two aspects of the moral hazard problem associated with group medical coverage. First, the group nature of coverage implies that any premium contributions of employees and foregone wages to pay for the employer's contribution generally are not closely related to the individual employee's expected claim costs. As a result, before they are hurt or become ill, employees (and covered dependents) might behave in ways that are riskier than would be true if the employee's cost of insurance was more closely related to the employee's risk. For example, employees might be more likely to smoke or maintain lifestyles that are more conducive to illness or injury. This type of "ex ante" (before injury or illness) moral hazard is not unique to fee-for-service coverage; it also occurs with alternatives to fee-for-service, such as health maintenance organizations.

Second, moral hazard associated with group medical coverage can lead to excessive utilization of health care once a person develops an ailment. This "ex post" (after injury or illness) moral hazard is especially pronounced for fee-for-service coverage that allows ready access to medical specialists and that includes comparatively small deductibles and co-insurance percentages. Under a fee-for-service arrangement, the provision of health care services is separate and distinct from the provision of insurance. This separation of the provision of insurance from the provision of care aggravates moral hazard because insureds and providers have limited incentives to economize on costly medical care when most of the costs are paid or reimbursed by insurers and employers.

Understanding Excessive Utilization.   To elaborate, medical insurance benefits under fee-for-service arrangements imply that patients typically bear only a small part of the cost of care. Consequently, patients tend to demand too much care, or they are at least willing to accept care that is recommended by providers without paying significant attention to costs. Since providers' revenues increase as more services are provided, providers have an incentive to provide care that provides any real prospect of benefiting the patient, given that much of the provider's costs are paid by insurance rather than the patient. Providers also might have an incentive to provide extra care to reduce the likelihood of a malpractice suit. In some cases, providers might even have an incentive to provide unnecessary care.

It is important for you to get a firm handle on what we mean by the term *excessive utilization*. While most people have an intuitive understanding of this idea, it can be a little hard to pin down precisely. We define **excessive utilization** as occurring when a patient receives care for which the cost of providing the care exceeds the expected benefit to the patient, where the expected benefit to the patient depends on the value that a typical person would place on the expected improvement in health status (including any lessening of risk that the condition will worsen). We define the idea in terms of the value to a typical person to avoid subtle issues dealing with how a person's income might affect their valuation of care (e.g., a high income person might be willing or able to pay more for health care and thus place a higher monetary value on the care than a low income person).

To illustrate how excessive utilization can arise with fee-for-service arrangements, assume that the cost of providing a particular service to a patient is $100 but that the expected benefit to the patient of receiving the care is only $50. Thus, the cost exceeds the benefit, and the total cost of risk will be lower if the care is not provided. If the patient had to pay the full cost of the care and knew the expected benefit, he or she would choose not to receive the care, thus reducing the cost of risk.

Now consider what happens if the patient has to pay only $20 (20 percent) of the cost with the person's medical insurance paying the other $80. Then the patient will demand the care (and/or the physician or other health care provider will encourage the care) because the marginal cost to the patient is $20 and the marginal benefit is $50. The provider will provide the care because it benefits the patient and because the full $100 cost is covered by the patient and the insurer. However, because the care is provided even though the cost exceeds the benefit, the cost of risk goes up by $50.

The moral hazard problem associated with providing care to a given patient is illustrated further in Figure 18–1 under the plausible assumption that as additional care is provided, the marginal benefit to the patient declines and the marginal cost of providing care increases. The optimal amount of care is Q*, the point at which the marginal cost equals the marginal benefit. Up to Q*, the marginal benefit from an additional unit of care exceeds the marginal cost; beyond this point the marginal cost exceeds the marginal benefit. Because the patient has to pay only part of the cost of additional care (e.g., a co-insurance percentage), the marginal cost to the patient is less than the full marginal cost of providing the additional care. As a result, care will be provided until the marginal benefit to the patient equals the marginal cost to the patient, so that with insurance Q^I units of care are provided. The difference between Q^I and Q* represents excessive utilization of care.

FIGURE 18–1

Excessive utilization due to moral hazard

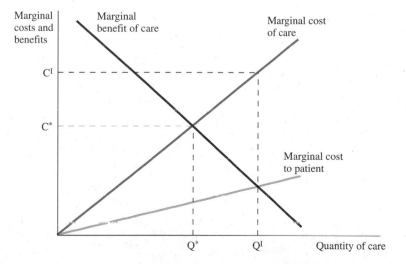

Note that employees as a group will have to pay for excessive utilization over time in the form of lower wages and/or higher explicit contributions toward the cost of coverage. Also note that excessive utilization implies that employees receive excessive quality of health care (i.e., more care than a fully informed employee would choose to have if covered under an optimal insurance arrangement that only provided care for which the expected benefits exceeded the costs; see below). While in some cases care may be provided that has no expected benefit to the patient, the more fundamental problem concerns the provision of care with positive expected benefits that do not exceed the costs. Thus, the incentives provided by fee-for-service coverage lead to higher quality of health care than employees in general are willing to pay for. In practice, this problem is manifested in many ways, including excessive visits to the doctor and specialists, excessive days in the hospital, excessive investment in diagnostic testing devices and other medical technology, and so on. The good news is that people will be healthier; the bad news is that they would prefer a little less health and a little more money for other things.

If employees have to pay the full cost of insurance in the form of either lower wages or higher contributions toward the cost of coverage, they have an incentive to demand insurance coverage that helps reduce the moral hazard problem. In an ideal world where the expected benefits of care and the costs of care could be measured without cost by the insurer, insurance contracts could be written that would exclude coverage of any care with a cost higher than the expected benefit. However, the optimal amount of care (i.e., where the marginal expected benefit equals the marginal cost) is not observable. It generally cannot be determined or verified by the insurer without incurring a cost. As a result, the moral hazard problem cannot be eliminated by simply excluding payment for excessively costly care.

To highlight how uncertainty concerning the optimal amount of care is the underlying cause of excessive utilization in traditional fee-for-service arrangements, compare the medical insurance example to auto physical damage insurance. When a person wrecks his or her car, there are a variety of reasonably accurate and low cost sources of information to determine how much it will cost to repair the car so that it is in roughly the same condition as it was before the wreck (i.e., to "make the car well"). Thus, physical damage insurance is written on a repair cost basis (see Chapter 21) without producing inordinately large verification costs for insurers or pervasive excessive utilization of the services of body shops. The insured might like to get some scratches repaired that are unrelated to the wreck or get an expensive, custom paint job, but the insurer simply can refuse to pay for this type of excessive quality. In contrast, because of uncertainty about the optimal amount of medical care, it is much more difficult/costly for insurers to intervene in physician-patient relationships.[5]

---

[5] We do not mean to imply that the problem of excessive quality does not arise in automobile physical damage insurance, but simply that the problem is much worse for medical expense coverage.

Reducing Moral Hazard under Fee-for-Service Arrangements

Rapid growth in health care costs during the 1980s and early 1990s led many employers to modify traditional fee-for-service arrangements to help control costs. This section briefly describes some of these changes before turning to the subject of health maintenance organizations and how they address the moral hazard problem. Recall first that in Chapter 8 you learned about several means of reducing moral hazard in insurance contracts, including having the policyholder pay part of the loss, experience rating, and claims investigation and monitoring by insurers. Apart from the growth of health maintenance organizations, many employers have modified traditional fee-for-service arrangements in several ways in order to limit moral hazard.

Numerous employers have changed benefits and employee contribution rules to encourage cost control. For example, deductibles and other forms of copayments by patients have been increased.[6] You should note that increased cost-sharing by patients can reduce excessive utilization even though patients are not knowledgeable about medical care. The reason is that with increased cost-sharing, consumers will demand more information from physicians about the expected benefits of costly treatments. In addition, consumers will choose physicians based, in part, on their reputations for providing cost-effective care (at least in theory). Consequently, in an effort to develop a reputation for providing high-quality, cost-effective care, physicians will be less likely to suggest treatments with small expected benefits relative to the costs.

In addition to increased cost-sharing, many employers now offer employees a choice of cost-sharing arrangements and require them to contribute more toward the cost if a more expensive plan is chosen. This approach, which often is used in conjunction with the employer providing a choice between fee-for-service coverage and coverage under a health maintenance organization, provides employees with a financial incentive to take less complete insurance coverage that is less subject to moral hazard.

Another major and very important approach to cost control under fee-for-service type arrangements has been the adoption of a variety of methods that incorporate some form of **managed care,** where the insurer becomes more active in monitoring/managing the provision of health care services, often in conjunction with less flexibility for employees to choose providers. For example, most fee-for-service plans now have requirements for review by the insurer before certain types of procedures, tests, or hospital admissions are approved for coverage. In effect, traditional fee-for-service arrangements—where decisions on care were made almost exclusively by the physician and patient—have largely disappeared. The growth of managed care has required insurers and other plan administrators to develop additional expertise in evaluating care.

---

[6] This includes reducing maximum fees that the plan will pay for services. Note also that moral hazard is mitigated by nonmonetary costs borne by patients, such as the time and hassle involved in seeing physicians, receiving medical tests, and so on.

In an attempt to reduce costs further, some employers/insurers also have contracted with providers to provide treatment at discounted prices. Under these **preferred provider organizations,** employees that go to a provider that is not included in the agreement have to pay more of the cost of care. This saves the plan money and encourages the employee to go to a preferred provider. Providers are willing to enter into these arrangements with large employers or insurers in order to obtain a large volume of business from covered workers.

Health Maintenance Organizations

Another form of managed care that addresses the moral hazard problem is the health maintenance organization. **Health maintenance organizations** (HMOs) either merge the provision of care and insurance functions into one entity or involve contracts between the HMO and physicians that reduce the moral hazard problem. The proportion of employees covered by HMOs grew very rapidly in the 1990s. Many of the earliest and largest HMOs have been corporations that are unrelated to traditional health insurers. In recent years most of the largest health insurers and Blue Cross–Blue Shield organizations have established HMOs to supplement their fee-for-service insurance operations.

The distinction between HMOs and fee-for-service arrangements has become blurred as fee-for-service arrangements have adopted the various forms of managed care described earlier. A key difference, however, is that workers covered by an HMO generally must receive care from physicians that are associated with the HMO (see below), whereas fee-for-service plans generally allow greater choice of physicians, including access to specialists. In addition, HMOs usually have more influence on the types of care that will be provided compared to fee-for-service plans with some form of managed care.

HMOs generally charge employers a fixed annual fee, called a capitation fee, in exchange for providing a wide range of medical care services to employees. The benefits provided are usually comprehensive, including some coverage for routine care. HMO coverage may involve small copayments for some services, but it usually does not involve annual deductibles and co-insurance.

There are several types of HMOs. Under an *individual practice association,* the HMO contracts with physicians to provide covered services on a fee-for-service basis. However, the compensation contract with physicians provides incentives for cost control (e.g., a reduction in fees or possible termination of the agreement if utilization of care exceeds certain levels or a bonus if utilization is below certain levels) and/or provisions that allow close monitoring of the physician by the HMO. Under a second type of HMO, sometimes known as a *group practice plan,* groups of physicians contract with the HMO, agreeing to provide covered services for a per capita fee. Under both of these approaches, the physicians often treat non-HMO patients as well as HMO patients. Under a third type of HMO, services are provided by a group of physicians that are employed by the HMO, which may also own one or more hospitals.

Incentives for Cost Control.   An HMO has a strong incentive to control costs in order to increase profits and allow it to compete more effectively with other HMOs and fee-for-service plans. Compared with fee-for-service plans with some form of managed care and especially compared with traditional fee-for-service plans, the HMO is able to exert more control over physicians and/or provide physicians with greater incentives to control costs, thus reducing moral hazard. Note that linking physicians' compensation to their success at controlling costs can provide greater incentives for cost control in the same way that experience rating can provide greater incentives for cost control in other insurance arrangements.

Under an HMO, employees usually choose a primary care physician from the group of physicians that have contracts with (or are employed by) the HMO. Employees (and covered dependents) generally must see this physician when they are ill, and the primary care physician largely determines whether the patient will have access to care by a specialist. (Special provisions govern payment of emergency care by non-HMO physicians or hospitals.) As a result, primary care physicians commonly serve a **gatekeeper function:** They control access to specialists and other forms of costly care. A number of HMOs have recently modified this approach by using what are known as *point of service plans.* With these plans, an HMO primary care physician manages the employee's care. However, employees can seek care from non-HMO physicians if they are willing to pay a higher proportion of the cost of treatment.

Evidence suggests that HMOs experience higher utilization of certain types of "walk-in care" than fee-for-service arrangements, which probably is attributable to lower copayments for these types of care. However, HMOs experience lower utilization of more costly types of care. For example, HMOs on average have fewer days of hospitalization per covered employee, fewer surgeries, and fewer consultations with specialists. In view of the fact that some employers give employees a choice between fee-for-service coverage and one or more HMOs, this result in part reflects the tendency for less healthy employees to choose fee-for-service coverage even though they usually have to pay a higher contribution toward the cost of coverage than if they were to choose an HMO. The reason is that people with health problems or that are concerned that problems might be imminent want more freedom of access to specialist care. However, evidence suggests that HMOs have fewer hospitalizations, surgeries, and specialist visits even after controlling for the tendency for HMO enrollees to be healthier than people covered by fee-for-service plans.

HMOs and the Quality of Care.   HMOs reduce incentives for excessive care and thereby control costs relative to traditional fee-for-service plans. However, HMOs often are criticized for providing too little care or poor quality care. While other forms of managed care have been similarly criticized, much of the attention has focused on HMOs. Indeed, the growth in HMO enrollment has been associated with an "HMO backlash." Many enrollees have complained about limited access to specialists and other forms of care. Some states have passed laws that have limited the discretion of HMOs to control costs (see Box 18–2).

While HMOs have strong incentives to control costs, a number of factors in principle reduce the risk that HMOs on average will tend to provide inadequate quality (i.e., that they will have *too little* utilization of care). First, if an HMO provides too little initial care for a problem, it may have to pay for more expensive care if the problem worsens. Second, although federal law prevents many HMOs from being sued and held vicariously liable under tort law for malpractice by HMO physicians and hospitals, individual physicians and hospitals that are part of HMO networks nonetheless can be sued for malpractice by HMO patients.

Third, HMOs compete with other HMOs and fee-for-service plans for enrollees based on a combination of price and quality. The resulting market discipline should help control any tendency for HMOs to provide inadequate quality over time. To be sure, if workers are uninformed about differences in coverage and quality among HMOs and fee-for-service plans, the possibility exists that many workers might mistakenly prefer coverage with too many restrictions in order to reduce their contributions toward a plan's cost or increase cash wages. If so, market discipline will provide less incentive for HMOs to provide good quality, and many workers might be disappointed by the types and quality of care that ultimately are provided. However, many workers might be expected to learn more over time, especially given publicity associated with the HMO backlash, so that fewer mistakes will be made.

When considering the question of whether HMOs are likely to provide (or have provided) inadequate quality and possible government restrictions on HMOs, you also should be aware of how the incentives and desires of patients

---

Box 18–2

The HMO Backlash

As HMOs and other forms of managed care expanded rapidly in the 1990s, limitations on choice of physician and types of care provided by HMOs were subject to increased criticism. Some states have enacted legislation restricting HMOs and, in some instances, other forms of managed care; other state legislatures are considering such legislation. In some states, legislation has been proposed that basically would ban HMOs by requiring group medical plans to allow workers to choose a physician and have access to specialists. Other proposals that are being debated and have been adopted in some states include:

- Requiring HMOs to provide broader coverage of emergency care by non-HMO physicians.

- Requiring HMOs to allow treatment by non-HMO physicians for an additional charge to the patient (i.e., requiring point of service plans).

- Requiring larger insured employers to offer workers a fee-for-service plan as an alternative to an HMO (subject to a higher contribution from the worker).

- Establishing specified procedures for patients to appeal denials of certain types of care by HMOs.

- Prohibiting "gag rules" in which HMOs may attempt to keep physicians from discussing certain types of care with patients.

may change once they become ill or hurt. Prior to illness or injury, employees may be willing to accept limitations on the quality of care that they will receive if they need medical treatment in order to save money on the cost of coverage. However, once a person is hurt or becomes ill, he or she has a strong incentive to seek the highest quality care possible when the costs are spread among the insured pool. Even if employees are fully informed about how HMOs work and the quality of care compared with fee-for-service plans, they might rationally choose an HMO but then turn around and complain about the quality of care and seek to expand their options for receiving care once they need treatment. This behavior could produce substantial political pressure for restrictions that might be too severe from the perspective of fully informed workers who do not know what their future medical needs will be but who have to pay the cost of care through lower wages or contributions. In any case, to the extent that any such efforts by HMO patients are successful, the treatment and cost differences between HMOs and fee-for-service plans will narrow.

Concept Checks

2. Assume that an employee has a choice between (*a*) comprehensive major medical coverage with a $250 annual deductible, 20 percent co-insurance, and a $1,750 stop loss limit on co-insurance charges, and (*b*) HMO coverage with no deductibles and co-insurance. The required employee contribution for employee coverage is $20 per month lower for HMO coverage. Other things being equal, which plan would most likely be chosen by a 22-year-old person just entering the labor force? By a 45-year-old with a chronic back problem?

3. Suppose that the comprehensive major medical coverage described above is chosen. If the employee incurs $750 of eligible medical expenses during a year, how much of this expense will be paid by the employee and how much will be paid by the insurer?

18.4 Group Medical Plan Provisions and Pricing Issues

In this section you will learn about a number of coverage provisions and pricing issues for group medical coverage including: (1) coverage for dependents, (2) cross-subsidies among employees that are inherent in group coverage, (3) government mandated benefits that must be included in group plans, (4) portability of coverage when employees change jobs, and (5) renewability of group health insurance.

Dependent Coverage

Most group health care plans offer coverage for the employee and the employee's eligible dependents. Plans usually require a small employee contribution or sometimes no contribution for employee coverage and a significantly higher contribution for dependent coverage. The contribution for dependents may be a flat charge per pay period regardless of how many dependents are covered or there may be a higher charge for coverage of children than for spouse-only coverage.

When both a husband and wife without children work for employers with group health plans, they often will minimize their contributions to the cost of coverage by each receiving coverage from their own employer. An exception would be when one plan does not require an additional contribution for spouse coverage and the spouse's coverage requires a contribution. In this case, the spouse working for the employer that requires a contribution may decide to be covered under the other spouse's plan. A possible limitation of this strategy is that if this spouse later wants to be covered under his or her own employer's plan, he or she may have to provide evidence of insurability. When parents with children both work for firms with medical plans, the choice of dependent coverage commonly will be made based on a comparison of the coverage terms and required contributions for the two plans.

In the event that a person is covered by more than one plan, the plans will coordinate payments for covered expenses. While this sometimes can be complicated, a standard coordination of benefits provision holds that the employee's plan is primary for the employee and excess for a covered spouse with children covered by the plan of the parent whose birthday falls earliest in the year.

Cross-Subsidies in Group Medical Coverage

Apart from differences in required employee contributions for different types of plans (e.g., HMO versus fee-for-service) or depending on whether dependents are covered, employee contributions for group medical coverage usually do not vary across workers for a given firm. That is, employees choosing the same plan typically make the same contribution even though their expected claim costs may vary. Since it is unlikely that wages typically vary to reflect these differences in risk, some employees are subsidized by others. For example, an employee who smokes and has five dependent children is likely to be subsidized by a nonsmoking employee without dependents. However, as suggested by our earlier discussion of why firms provide benefits, lower risk employees still might prefer the group medical plan over individual coverage because of the tax and administrative cost advantages of group insurance. Recall that the administrative cost savings for group plans are in substantial part due to the absence of risk classification for individual workers.

Mandated Benefits

We explained earlier that employees have limited flexibility to choose types of benefits under group medical coverage. Limitations on choice are necessary to help control adverse selection, especially since the cost of coverage to individual employees is not closely related to differences in expected claim costs among employees. The coverage provisions of group medical plans agreed upon by employers and employees generally will provide benefits that the typical employee desires given the cost of providing benefits. Because employees are heterogeneous, some employees might prefer alternative benefits.

In recent years, many states have mandated that employer group medical plans (and sometimes individual plans) provide certain types of benefits, such as minimum benefits for alcohol/drug use treatment and mental health services, and payment for a specified minimum period of hospitalization for childbearing. Similarly, in 1996 the US Congress enacted legislation requiring that medical plans for firms with 50 or more employees provide minimum coverage of 48 hours hospitalization for normal childbirth and 96 hours for cesarean births. This law also included some restrictions on the ability of group medical plans to limit coverage for mental health services.

An argument often used to justify certain types of government **mandated benefits** is that private decision making by employers and employees might fail to provide desirable coverage to employees with special needs, thus creating hardship for these employees and perhaps having part of the costs of uninsured treatment fall on other parties. Opponents argue that mandated benefits increase the cost of coverage without benefiting many employees and increase cross-subsidies among employees. They also argue that much of the political pressure for mandates comes from those health care providers who gain business if certain types of coverage are required or expanded.

Portability of Coverage

An important issue that has received substantial attention in recent years is the portability (or lack of portability) of group medical coverage when employees are terminated or change jobs. One reason employees may lose coverage when they change jobs is that fee-for-service group medical plans usually contain a **pre-existing conditions clause,** which excludes coverage for new employees for any ailment for which the person received medical treatment in the prior 12 months. Therefore, employees that have pre-existing conditions (or dependents with pre-existing conditions) will not be covered under a new plan for the cost of treating these conditions for 12 months. Pre-existing condition clauses are relatively uncommon for HMOs. HMOs that were established under federal legislation enacted in the early 1970s to spur the growth of HMOs cannot exclude coverage for pre-existing conditions, and competition has led many other HMOs to forego using these clauses.

The rationale for a pre-existing conditions clause is that it controls costs by reducing the adverse selection that otherwise could occur. For example, some persons might seek employment to obtain coverage for known medical problems. A problem with the pre-existing conditions clause is that it can discourage some employees from making desirable job changes, if, for example, the new job does not provide HMO coverage without a pre-existing conditions clause. Under the provisions of some insured group health plans, employees are allowed to convert their group coverage to individual coverage with the insurer without proving insurability. However, the individual coverage sometimes is less comprehensive and commonly requires a higher premium.

In 1985, the US Congress enacted the Consolidated Omnibus Reconciliation Act of 1985 (COBRA), which required group health plans for firms with 20 or more employees to offer continued coverage to employees (and covered dependents) for a period of up to 18 months following the date that the employee is terminated or quits. (Coverage must be offered for three years if the employee dies and to dependents in the event of a divorce.) Persons who wish to continue coverage must notify their employer within 60 days of leaving the job, and they must pay a premium for coverage that cannot exceed 102 percent of the employer's cost of providing coverage.

In 1996 the US Congress enacted a law to further enhance the portability of group medical coverage for many employees. The law still permits plans to exclude coverage for pre-existing conditions for 12 months, but previous coverage under another employer's plan can be used to satisfy the 12-month period as long as the employee has not gone without coverage for 63 days or longer between jobs. Thus, a person who has been covered for a year under a prior plan who obtains a new job within approximately two months will not have a gap in coverage due to the pre-existing conditions clause in the new employer's plan.

Renewability of Small Group Health Insurance

Insurers commonly offer individual (as opposed to group) health insurance policies that provide **guaranteed renewable coverage**. At the end of the policy period, the insurer must renew coverage regardless of the health of the insured. While the premium can increase to reflect the expected experience for the individual's rating class, the premium cannot be increased on an individual basis to reflect possible deterioration in the individual's (or covered dependents') health. In effect, the contract does not allow individual experience rating and thus provides insurance against a rate increase due to deterioration in a person's health. To emphasize, the individual is exposed to the risk of rate increases based on changes in the average expected claim cost for his or her rating class, but there can be no surcharge based on the individual's own health.

You learned above that small employers commonly insure their obligations to pay medical expenses under their group medical plan. An interesting feature of small group medical insurance contracts is that (without a legislative mandate, see below) these contracts generally are not offered on a guaranteed renewable basis. As a result, if the health of one or more employees deteriorates, the employer may face a large rate increase at renewal or, in some cases, be denied renewal. The inability of small employers to be protected against rate increases when one or a few employees become seriously ill reduces the incentive for small employers to offer group medical coverage.

Why are small group policies not guaranteed renewable (unless required by law) when individual policies with this feature are routinely available? If an insurer offers a guaranteed renewable contract, it has to charge a higher price at renewal to employers with good experience in order to cover the insurer's total expected costs because it cannot selectively increase the price for employers with poor experience to reflect their higher expected claim costs. The underlying problem in the small group market appears to be the ability of small employers with good health experience to readily qualify for a lower rate with a new insurer. Thus, if an insurer offered guaranteed renewable coverage, it would lose many of the employers with good experience to other insurers who could charge them a lower premium based on their good experience. As a result, the insurer would have to increase the rate substantially for the employers that it renewed, which primarily would have poor experience, thus defeating the purpose of the guaranteed renewal feature.

Why does the ability of individual insureds that remain healthy to qualify for new, low rate coverage not prevent guaranteed renewable individual health insurance? The answer to this question appears to be that the direct costs, inconvenience, and hassle of qualifying for new coverage are proportionally larger for individuals than for small employer groups. These higher costs deter the "best risks" from leaving the insurance pool if the insurer charges the same rate to them and to people that have experienced a deterioration in health compared to the average person in the rating class.

Over 30 states have enacted legislation to address the lack of guaranteed renewability in the small group health insurance market. While the details vary and the laws are complex, they generally require each insurer to offer coverage at a rate that does not consider the health of individual employees, and the laws restrict the magnitude of rate increases at renewal. They also prevent new insurers from excluding coverage for pre-existing conditions. As a result, these laws make it much more difficult for a new insurer to price its products or design coverage in a way that would allow small employers with good health experience to obtain significantly lower rates than employers with poor experience.

Concept Check

4. (*a*) Explain why a majority of employees might prefer group medical insurance that provides very limited benefits for mental illness/ psychological problems. How will these employees be affected if the state mandates large benefits of this type? (*b*) Answer the same question with respect to hospitalization coverage for childbirth.

18.5 Health Care Cost Inflation and the Uninsured Problem

Two issues were subject to intense debate in the United States during the late 1980s and early 1990s. First, as illustrated in Figure 18–2, the rate of increase in the cost of medical care exceeded the general inflation rate by a sizable margin. Cost growth slowed substantially in the mid-1990s due in large part to greater use of HMOs, other forms of managed care, and increased cost-sharing under fee-for-service plans. Nonetheless, the medical care consumer price index (CPI) in-

FIGURE 18–2

Annual percentage changes in medical care CPI and overall CPI: 1981–1997

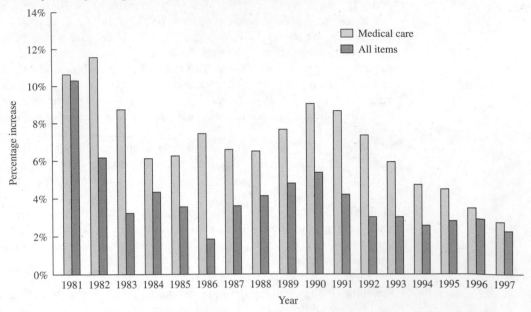

Source: Data obtained from Bureau of Labor Statistics.

creased 213 percent during the period 1981–1997, an average (geometric) annual increase of 6.9 percent. The overall CPI increased by 95 percent during this period, a 4 percent average annual increase. Health care expenditures per capita increased at an average annual rate of approximately 9 percent. The total cost of health care represented approximately 14 percent of the US gross domestic product (GDP) in 1997, compared with 9 percent of GDP in 1980.

The second issue relates to the number of people without medical expense insurance. In the mid-1990s, approximately 41 million people in the United States (approximately 15 percent of the population) did not have private or government medical insurance at any point in time. Many of these uninsured persons were employed or were dependents of employees. Thus, although most people obtain their medical expense insurance from employer-based group plans, a large number of employees do not have such coverage. It is estimated that between 4 and 5 million employees that are uninsured have rejected employer coverage, presumably to avoid paying a contribution toward the cost.

In this section, we discuss some of the factors that have led to high medical costs and inflation in medical costs, characteristics of uninsured people, and the reasons that large numbers of people are uninsured. Our purpose is to provide you with perspective to help you understand the nature and scope of these problems. Broad proposals for dealing with these issues are discussed in the following section.

Why Does Health Care Cost So Much?

A number of factors contributed to rapid growth in health care costs through the early 1990s, including: (1) moral hazard and resultant excessive utilization, (2) increased demand for high quality care and technological advances, and (3) aging of the population. Increased costs associated with uninsured persons and medical malpractice litigation also led to higher costs.

Moral Hazard/Excessive Utilization.   One factor that contributed to rapid growth in health care costs up to the mid-1980s was growth in the amount of insurance coverage for medical expenses under fee-for-service plans that required relatively little cost-sharing by employees. In particular, many insurance plans up through the mid-1980s basically offered first dollar coverage (i.e., there were little or no deductibles or co-insurance). As discussed above, this type of coverage provides little incentive for consumers and providers to keep health care costs low. In an effort to control costs, many of these plans increased deductibles and co-insurance provisions in the 1980s and early 1990s.

Demand for Increased Quality of Care and Technological Advances.   The demand for high quality health care increases with income. Thus, substantial income growth for many persons in the United States over time would be expected to increase the quality of care and the cost of health care as a proportion of GDP apart from any moral hazard. Higher quality of care often has been achieved through expensive technological advances. For example, technological advances have been especially prominent in keeping premature babies alive and in extending the life of the elderly. It is often very difficult to determine the extent to which these improvements in quality are excessive due to moral hazard or efficient due to changes in income and technological capability.

Increased Elderly Population.   An important factor leading to higher aggregate health care costs is simply that the proportion of the US population that is elderly has increased substantially during the past several decades (see Chapter 20). Other things being equal, increased age of the population will lead to a higher proportion of GDP going toward the cost of health care. The increased proportion of elderly individuals in part reflects declining birth rates over time and in part reflects greater quality of health care, which can keep people alive longer.

Other Factors.   While we have pointed out that too much insurance causes higher health care costs, too little insurance also can increase costs. Even though uninsured poor people may not be able to pay for their health care, they typically are not denied health care. The costs tend to be shifted to other parties or entities, including group medical expense plans, thus increasing the costs of these plans. Another problem is that the uninsured often receive health care in inefficient (high cost) ways. For example, instead of seeing a physician who can treat an illness in its early stages at relatively low costs, poor uninsured people may wait to obtain medical care in the hope that the illness will subside. If the illness continues and/or gets worse, they may finally seek care in an emergency room, which is a high cost method of providing care. In addition, the amount of treatment needed may be greater than otherwise would have been needed if the illness had been treated earlier or if diagnostic tests had been performed.

Another factor that many people argue has led to higher health care costs is the increased frequency and severity of medical malpractice suits. During the mid-1970s and again in the mid-1980s, malpractice liability insurance premiums increased dramatically, at least in part because of a higher frequency of suits and increases in damages awarded by the courts. In addition to producing higher malpractice insurance premiums, increased frequency and severity of medical malpractice liability suits is likely to increase health care costs because providers will be more likely to practice defensive medicine—that is, providers are more likely to require extensive tests and treatment to reduce the likelihood of a malpractice suit. (As suggested above, the growth of HMO coverage and other forms of managed care in the 1990s has shifted the debate toward whether too little care might sometimes be provided under these plans.)

The Uninsured: Who, Why, and Effects on Others

As noted above, approximately 15 percent of the population is not covered by any public or private medical expense insurance. In most cases, uninsured persons with acute illnesses or injuries receive emergency and follow-up care at hospitals and/or clinics. Much of the cost of unpaid bills for these persons is shifted to other parties in the form of higher charges for physicians and hospital services. Some uninsured persons with severe medical problems who cannot work will be eligible for public medical insurance under the Medicaid program, which is financed by state and federal income taxes. As a result, much of the cost of medical treatment for the uninsured is shifted to insured people and taxpayers.

When thinking about the scope of the uninsured problem, you should be aware that a large majority of uninsured people is uninsured for a relatively short period of time. For example, it is estimated that about one-half of the uninsured persons remain uninsured for less than four months and that almost three-quarters are uninsured for nine months or less. Many of these people are young, comparatively healthy, and/or between jobs. Some have not taken advantage of the ability to extend coverage under COBRA; others have rejected employer provided coverage (see above). It is estimated that 15 to 20 percent of the uninsured are uninsured for a period of two years or longer. Many of these long-term uninsured people are employed without group medical coverage or have turned down coverage. Many are younger and healthier than the general population.

There are a variety of factors that contribute to large numbers of persons being uninsured for medical expenses.[7] High medical costs naturally will lead to uninsured individuals, because as medical costs increase, medical insurance cov-

---

[7] About 1 percent of the population is chronically uninsurable due to adverse health conditions, but many of these persons are insured in high risk health insurance pools that many states have created to make coverage available at subsidized rates.

erage becomes less affordable. Another factor that affects the demand for insurance is whether the person has other sources of indemnity for medical expenses (see Chapter 7). To the extent that poor people can shift the cost of their health care to other people in ways described above, the incentive to purchase insurance is reduced further as its price increases.

Many people have the misperception that the employer pays the cost of medical expense insurance and thus employers are to blame for the large numbers of working people without insurance. This view, however, fails to recognize that, at least in the long run, employees pay for their employee benefits. The fact that large numbers of working people are uninsured therefore implies that many employees are unwilling (or cannot afford) to give up enough wages to receive medical expense coverage through employer-provided group medical plans, especially given that large numbers of uninsured workers have declined coverage.

18.6 Health Care Reform

Tradeoffs Involving Cost, Quality, and the Scope of Insurance

The twin problems of the high cost of health care and significant numbers of uninsured people create a serious dilemma for policymakers because of two unavoidable tradeoffs. First, increasing access to health insurance (reducing the number of uninsured people) tends to increase health care costs. The reason is that, other things being equal, extending health insurance to more people will lead to more health care being provided and higher total costs (even if some care is then provided more efficiently). Second, attempts to reduce costs for the insured population generally will lead to some reduction in the overall quality of care. The goal in principle is to reduce excessive utilization, that is, to cut back on quality for which people are unwilling to pay. In practice, however, it will likely be difficult to reform the US system in ways that achieve this goal accurately. In addition, it is important for you to realize that there will be little or no "free lunch" (lower cost without lower quality) under any reform proposal.

These policy tradeoffs are highlighted in Figure 18–3, which illustrates the relationship between the best achievable average health per person and expenditures on health care per person. Thus, the figure illustrates the level of health that could be achieved at each level of expenditure if the health care system were fully efficient. As more money is spent, the best achievable level of average health increases, but plausibly at a decreasing rate.

Different groups of people would be located at different points on the graph. For example, suppose that the point I_1 represents the (hypothetical, of course!) position of persons that currently have medical expense insurance. The fact that this point is below the best achievable health-expenditure curve indicates that there is some waste in the system. In principle, either greater health could be achieved with the same expenditure or the same level of health could be achieved by a lower expenditure. For example, the point I_2 would give the same level of health as I_1 but at a lower cost.

FIGURE 18–3

Maximum achievable health versus expenditures per person

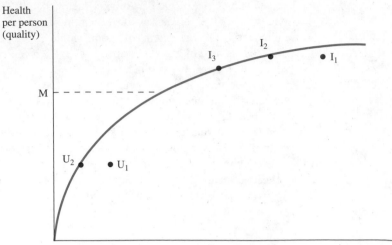

With the exception of health care providers or other parties that might benefit when useless care (care which has no effect on health) is provided, people generally agree that we should make changes that cut costs without reducing health. However, although some might disagree, most people appear to believe that large sums are not spent on useless care. This means that most proposals that would cut expenditures on health care would lead to some reduction in quality. For example, a proposal might primarily involve a movement down the curve for the insured group (e.g., from point I_1 to point I_3). Such a reduction in expenditures and a reduction in quality would be desirable to this group if it eliminated excessive quality (i.e., if these people preferred to spend those resources on other goods and services).

Now consider the point U_1, which represents the hypothetical position of people that are currently working but uninsured. The point could plausibly fall below the best achievable health level for the given expenditure for reasons mentioned earlier (e.g., some uninsured people might receive expensive care in emergency rooms or fail to obtain routine care, which might lead to more costly problems later). In general, most people can agree that it would be better to be at point U_2 than U_1: It provides the same level of health at a lower cost. Alternatively, people agree that it would be better to have the same level of expenditure as U_1 but attain the best achievable level of health (i.e., get more health for the buck).

Now suppose that society feels that the minimum health status for any group of people should be no less than M. This minimum might be achieved in part by actions that provide all people with health insurance. Of course, the expansion of insurance coverage might increase excessive utilization due to moral hazard. More important, it is clear from Figure 18–3 that this minimum level of health can be achieved for the uninsured only if their expenditures increase. The question then arises: Who should pay the increase in cost?

Compelling currently uninsured people to pay might be problematic, given that they generally have lower than average income. However, the alternative of requiring currently insured people to pay more to help pay for expanded coverage for currently uninsured people is inconsistent with the goal of reducing their costs. A third alternative is to force currently insured people to sacrifice some quality but keep their expenditures (payments) constant. The resulting excess of expenditures over costs for the currently insured group could then be used to increase the quality of the uninsured group. None of these alternatives appear to be very attractive to a majority of people.

In summary, health care reform proposals to control costs will lead to some reduction in health (quality), and they entail the risk of an excessive reduction in quality. Proposals to increase the number of insured people generally will increase total health care expenditures, and someone will have to pay for this increase.

Possible Approaches to Reform

Given this background, we now turn to major approaches that have been suggested for reforming the US health care system in order to deal with the problem of high costs and to increase the number of insured people. We emphasize that there are numerous complicated proposals. Our purpose is simply to acquaint you with several broad approaches to reform.

Nationalization or Quasi-nationalization of Medical Care and Insurance. One approach to reforming the health care system would be for the government to nationalize the provision of medical care and medical expense insurance, as has essentially been done in Canada and the United Kingdom. The government basically could specify what insurance would be provided to all people and how the insurance would be paid for. In order to control the total cost of care, the government could assume ownership of hospitals and health care facilities, employ all physicians, and set expenditure limits in ways that restrict (ration) the amount of care provided. A less intrusive but still comprehensive version of this approach would be for the government to allow private entities to provide specified insurance and medical care, with prices for insurance and medical care and expenditure limits set by the government.

Under this approach, the government in effect would attempt to specify one or more points on the health-expenditure curve for different groups of people and achieve the desired points by central planning or extensive regulation. The key point is that the government would determine how much is spent on what types of services and thus the quality of care. A large majority of American voters presently have little appetite for this sort of radical change (which some pundits call the "US Postal Service approach" to health care reform), perhaps because of the potential for lower quality care and waiting lists (rationing) for costly treatments.

Universal Private Sector Insurance.   Another set of proposals would require most people (except the very poor and the elderly) to be insured by private insurance that provides a minimum level of benefits. This expansion of coverage typically would be achieved by: (1) requiring employers either to provide coverage to employees or to pay an earmarked tax that would be used to subsidize the cost of coverage for people not covered at work (known as the "play-or-pay" approach), and (2) requiring the self-employed and any workers who do not obtain coverage at work to buy a minimum level of individual medical insurance, perhaps at subsidized rates for lower wage workers.

Because this approach would expand coverage, it would tend to aggravate the moral hazard problem, depending on the extent to which newly insured persons were covered by HMOs or other forms of managed care. For this reason, proposals for universal coverage sometimes also include proposals for government regulation of the prices of health care services or government-established limits on expenditures. The more comprehensive the proposals for government regulation of prices and services, the more this approach resembles quasi-nationalization of the medical care system and medical insurance.

Play-or-pay proposals that would mandate all employers to provide minimum levels of group medical coverage or pay additional taxes have received extensive debate. Proponents of this approach argue that it would: (1) alleviate hardship for uninsured workers and their dependents, (2) reduce the extent to which the cost of care for these persons is shifted to other employers and other parties, and (3) reduce the use of inefficient and expensive care by uninsured persons. As we suggested above, a possible problem is an increase in excessive utilization of health care services, especially if the additional insurance coverage is not accompanied by managed care and employee cost-sharing. In addition, this proposal would reduce wages and reduce employment of lower paid workers. Subsidizing the cost of coverage to alleviate these effects would require that other employees and other taxpayers pay the subsidies.

Selective and Limited Intervention.   A more cautious approach to reform focuses on specific problems related to the cost and availability of health care and addresses these problems with targeted, limited intervention. To a great extent this approach has been followed in many states, such as through the enactment of legislation addressing the lack of guaranteed renewability in small employer group insurance, or legislation creating state-mandated insurance pools for individuals with chronic and expensive-to-insure health problems. This approach also is reflected in some federal legislation, such as COBRA and the previously described 1996 law allowing prior coverage to count toward meeting the requirements of a pre-existing conditions clause when a person changes jobs. The selective and limited intervention approach often is criticized for not doing enough to control costs and to reduce the number of uninsured persons.

Providing Incentives through Changes in Tax Law.   The last broad approach to reform that we will introduce would modify the income tax treatment of medical expense insurance to provide increased incentives for cost control. One major proposal that has been extensively debated would eliminate (or significantly limit) the current tax subsidy to group medical coverage by requiring employees to pay tax on employer contributions toward the cost of coverage and eliminating the tax deductibility of employee contributions.

The key idea underlying this proposal is that the current tax treatment leads employees to demand and employers to provide too much insurance coverage (relatively low deductibles and co-insurance) for small losses, which exacerbates the moral hazard problem. If the "tax subsidy" to medical expense insurance is eliminated, it is predicted that employees will demand less costly insurance arrangements that are less prone to moral hazard. The predicted result is less utilization of care for which the expected benefits do not exceed the costs and substantial savings in costs over time (and perhaps more complaints about quality, an increased HMO backlash, and so on).

The proposal to eliminate the tax subsidy to group medical coverage has been criticized on a number of dimensions. Some people question whether employees will be wise or informed enough to make intelligent decisions about what coverage to demand and what care to receive if they have to pay a greater share of the cost. Another criticism is that this change would further discourage some employees from receiving any group medical coverage and would therefore exacerbate the uninsured problem. Finally, some people are concerned that this change would substantially increase income taxes and are therefore opposed. Although a reduction in other income taxes could accompany the change, some people are understandably skeptical that there would be a dollar-for-dollar reduction.

Another type of proposal that has received extensive attention would in effect expand tax breaks associated with medical care by allowing employees (and the self-employed) to establish tax sheltered **medical savings accounts (MSAs).** The US Congress enacted legislation in 1996 that permitted MSAs on an experimental basis for a four-year period for self-employed workers and employers with fewer than 50 employees. Under an MSA, the person buys or receives insurance protection that provides protection against "catastrophic" losses but which contains a substantial deductible (e.g., $3,000 per year). An amount equal to 75 percent of the deductible can then be contributed to the MSA on a tax-sheltered basis. Money can be withdrawn from the account to reimburse the person for annual medical expenses less than the deductible. Money that is not withdrawn accumulates toward retirement on a tax-deferred basis (i.e., no current income taxes are paid on the money deposited or on investment income on these funds). Funds may be withdrawn for any purpose prior to retirement subject to normal income tax and a 15 percent penalty tax.

Like proposals to eliminate the tax subsidy to medical expense coverage, MSAs encourage participants to economize on the cost of care because receiving additional care reduces their MSA balance. The MSA concept has been highly controversial, however. Opponents of MSAs have expressed fear that severe adverse selection will result if employees are allowed to choose between MSAs and more traditional coverage. It is argued that many younger, healthier employees will opt for MSAs, thus increasing the cost of more comprehensive coverage arrangements for older employees or employees with health problems and undermining traditional notions of risk-sharing in employer-provided group medical plans.

18.7 Summary

• Many employees receive a material amount of their total compensation in the form of employer-related retirement plans and group life and health insurance. Obtaining benefits through work often is advantageous compared to employees purchasing individual coverage because: (1) qualified employment-related benefits reduce income taxes for employees, and (2) administrative expense loadings in group insurance premiums are lower than for individual insurance. Employer provided benefits also can promote greater productivity among employees.

• Traditional fee-for-service arrangements for medical expense coverage pay specified medical expenses through basic and/or major medical coverage that include deductibles and co-insurance requirements. Employees receive treatment from the physicians and hospitals that they choose; physicians and hospitals are compensated by fees for services rendered. These arrangements can lead to excessive utilization of health care due to moral hazard.

• In order to control costs and reduce excessive utilization, many fee-for-service plans have been modified to incorporate some form of managed care in which the types and amounts of medical care are subject to considerable monitoring by the insurer or employer. Health maintenance organizations, which merge the provision of health care and insurance and therefore provide the HMO with substantial incentives to control costs, have grown rapidly in the 1990s. Whether HMOs sometimes provide inadequate care has been hotly debated. Some states have adopted regulations that limit the ability of HMOs to control costs.

• The federal government and many states have mandated that employer-provided group medical plans provide certain types of benefits. Federal law also has been changed to enhance portability of coverage by lessening the extent to which coverage can be denied for pre-existing conditions. Many states have adopted laws to encourage or mandate guaranteed renewability of group medical expense coverage for small employers.

• The problems of rapid increases in health care costs during the 1980s and early 1990s and increases in the number of uninsured persons generated numerous proposals for health care reform. The main approaches include nationalization of medical care and medical insurance, universal private sector insurance, and better incentives for appropriate utilization of care through changes in the tax law. Key unresolved dilemmas include how to reduce the number of uninsured persons without increasing total costs and how to weed out excessive utilization without producing inadequate quality.

Key Terms

cafeteria benefit plans   443
flexible spending account   443
qualified plans   444
group medical expense coverage   446

traditional fee-for-service arrangements   447
basic benefits   447
major medical coverage   448
stop loss clause   448

Questions and Problems

1. Suppose that Helen's marginal income tax rate is 28 percent. Compare her after-tax income and her group medical costs under three scenarios: (*a*) She receives $38,000 in salary and pays $2,000 for individual medical coverage, (*b*) she receives $36,000 in salary and group medical coverage on a noncontributory basis with the employer's contribution to the cost of coverage equal to $2,000, and (*c*) she receives $37,000 in salary and group medical coverage on a contributory basis with the employer's contribution equal to $1,000 and her required (tax deductible) contribution equal to $1,000. What would the difference be between (*a*) and the other two scenarios if individual insurance costs Helen $2,200 due to a higher expense loading?

2. Given the rationale for why firms provide benefits, why do you think firms seldom provide personal auto insurance to employees as an employee benefit?

3. Rick has basic coverage and supplementary major medical with a $300 deductible, 15 percent co-insurance, and a $1,500 stop loss on co-insurance payments. How much will the major medical coverage pay if Rick incurs $1,000 in expenses during the year that are not covered by basic coverage but that are eligible for major medical? If he incurs $5,000 in eligible expenses? At what level of eligible expenses will major medical coverage begin to pay 100 percent of additional expenses?

4. A patient pays $100 for a test that costs $400 to provide. How large must the expected benefit to the patient be to avoid excessive utilization?

5. Explain how each of the following would affect the degree of excessive utilization of medical care in a fee-for-service plan: (*a*) the time, hassle, and inconvenience of seeing a doctor and receiving tests and treatment, and (*b*) the number of primary care physicians and specialists in a community.

6. Compare incentives for reducing excessive utilization under: (*a*) a group practice HMO where the group receives a capitation fee per enrollee, and (*b*) an individual practice association HMO where physicians' fees do not depend on utilization.

7. How does a preferred provider organization differ from a health maintenance organization?

8. Explain how requiring employees to contribute toward the cost of dependent coverage for medical care will reduce cross-subsidies among employees. What disadvantages might exist in varying employee contributions for employee coverage in relation to each employee's expected claim costs in order to further reduce cross-subsidies?

9. Individual life insurance policies are guaranteed renewable with the additional feature that the maximum premium rate that can be charged in any year is specified in the contract. Individual medical expense insurance policies often are guaranteed renewable, but there is no limit on the maximum premium rate that can be charged

for the class at renewal. Given what you learned about the determinants of insurance prices in Chapter 6, what do you think might account for this difference? (Hint: Consider possible differences in risk to insurers between life insurance and medical expense insurance.)

10. Explain how the federal income tax subsidy to employer provided medical expense coverage might contribute to excessive utilization of medical care and how limiting or eliminating the subsidy could reduce excessive care.

11. Explain why limiting or eliminating the tax subsidy for group medical coverage may increase the number of people that are uninsured for medical expenses. If the tax subsidy were eliminated, would the fact that most uninsured workers are paid relatively low wages affect the size of any increase?

References

Pauly, Mark. "Taxation, Health Insurance, and Market Failure in the Medical Economy." *Journal of Economic Literature* 14 (1986), pp. 629–75. (*Comprehensive survey of the economics of medical care and medical care coverage.*)

Rottenberg, Simon. "Unintended Consequences: The Probable Effects of Mandated Medical Insurance." *Regulation: Cato Review of Business & Government,* Summer 1990, pp. 21–28. (*Discusses possible adverse effects of requiring employers to provide health insurance.*)

Weisbrod, Burton. "The Health Care Quadrilemma: An Essay on Technological Change, Insurance, Quality of Care, and Cost Containment." *Journal of Economic Literature* 29 (1991), pp. 523–52. (*Detailed discussion of problems and incentives in the provision of medical care.*)

Answers to Concept Checks

1. Higher paid employees will have a higher income tax rate while working and therefore will prefer to receive a greater proportion of their compensation in benefits that either are not taxed or are tax deferred. The deferral of tax decreases the present value of tax payments, plus the employee's tax rate might be lower during retirement, which would lower the nominal amount of tax paid. Note that the demand for insurance protection and retirement plans also is likely to increase with income apart from tax considerations.

2. A 22-year-old person just entering the labor force is more likely to choose the HMO option. The HMO has lower monthly costs, and it has no deductibles or co-insurance. The main disadvantage of the HMO is that the employee will have limited flexibility in the choice of physicians. Since this person is likely to be healthy and therefore not require major medical attention from specialists, he or she will not find this disadvantage to be very costly. In contrast, the 45-year-old person with a chronic back problem will be more willing to pay the higher costs (both in premiums and expected deductible and co-insurance payments) associated with the comprehensive major medical coverage so that he or she can retain the option of seeing specialists in the case that extensive care or surgery becomes desirable.

3. Total expenditure = $750

   Amount paid by employee =
   $$\$250 + 0.20\,(\$750 - \$250) = \$350$$

   Amount paid by insurer =
   $$0.80\,(\$750 - \$250) = \$400$$

4. (*a*) Because most employees perceive that they have little (if any) chance of becoming mentally ill (Los Angeles residents excluded), they often will be unwilling to pay for extensive insurance coverage for the costs associated with such treatment, especially given the possibility of excessive utilization.

Given that employees pay for their benefits, at least in the long run, by foregoing other forms of compensation (e.g., cash wages), if the state mandates more extensive benefits for mental illness, then many employees will be forced to purchase insurance that they prefer not to have. (*b*) The same points apply for mandated hospitalization coverage for childbirth, except that a much larger proportion of the working population is likely to view these benefits as being valuable.

Retirement Plans

Chapter Objectives

- Describe the major types and features of employment-related retirement plans, including defined benefit and defined contribution plans.
- Explain the tax and incentive effects of retirement plans.
- Explain the growing use of defined contribution plans.
- Introduce self-employed plans and individual retirement accounts (IRAs), including Roth IRAs.
- Discuss government regulations and government insurance affecting defined benefit plans.

19.1 Overview of Retirement Plans

One risk faced by every individual is that their human capital (ability to earn a living) will decline. Productivity, especially physical productivity, generally declines after some age, which in part explains why people choose to stop working at some point and retire. There are three ways that people provide for retirement income. In this chapter, we focus on private employment-related retirement plans. Another important source of retirement income comes from the mandatory federal government program, commonly called social security, which we will discuss in Chapter 20. In addition, many people save additional money for retirement outside of private pension plans.

Saving through employment-related retirement plans differs from private saving in several important respects, which are emphasized throughout the chapter. First, employment-related retirement plans receive special tax treatment that generally makes them a preferred method of saving for retirement. A second advantage of employer-sponsored retirement plans is that they can affect employee incentives; in particular, these plans can improve employee productivity and reduce employee turnover. Offsetting some of the tax and incentive benefits is the disadvantage that retirement plans are subject to numerous government regulations. Some of the regulations limit the extent to which people can save through retirement plans. Other regulations, such as those that restrict one's ability to use savings in retirement plans prior to retirement, reduce the desirability of saving through such plans.

Employer-sponsored retirement plans can be divided into two general categories: defined benefit plans and defined contribution plans. A majority of employees in the United States are covered by defined benefit plans, but a majority of plans are defined contribution plans. In the past two decades, there has been a gradual shift away from defined benefit plans and toward defined contribution coverage. After describing the two types of plans, we will discuss some of the reasons for the shift toward defined contribution plans.

Defined Benefit Plans

In a **defined benefit plan,** an employer promises employees a monthly retirement benefit that is defined by a benefit formula. Hourly workers often have a benefit formula that equals a flat amount times the employee's number of years of service. For example, employees might be promised $50 a month times years of service. A worker with 20 years of service would receive $1,000 a month during retirement. This type of benefit formula is not indexed to inflation during the employees' preretirement years; consequently, the benefit formula typically is adjusted periodically to correct for the effects of inflation.

The benefit formula for salaried employees typically is based on the number of years of service and the employee's salary during the final years of service. For example, a salaried employee's monthly benefit might equal 2 percent times the number of years of service times the employee's average monthly salary during the last five years of service. As an illustration, suppose an employee worked 20 years and during the last five years of employment earned $3,000 a month. Then, the monthly retirement benefit would be $1,200 ($0.02 \times 20 \times \$3,000$). An important feature of a benefit formula that is based on the employee's final salary (or average of salaries during the final years of service) is that retirement benefits are automatically indexed to preretirement inflation, assuming that wages increase with inflation.

The retirement benefit as a percentage of the employee's final salary is called the **replacement rate.** For the previous example, the monthly retirement benefit was $1,200 and the final salary was $3,000; thus the replacement rate was 40 percent ($1,200/$3,000). An employee who worked 30 years with the same salary history would have a monthly benefit of $1,800 or a 60 percent replacement rate ($1,800/$3,000). Few defined benefit plans have explicit indexing of benefits to postretirement inflation. Thus, the replacement rate can overstate the actual purchasing power of retirees if inflation occurs following retirement. During the high inflation period of the 1970s, some employers increased retirees' pension benefits to make up, at least in part, for the effects of inflation even though the employer had no contractual requirement to do so.

When benefit formulas depend on the employee's final salary, the retirement benefit can be greatly reduced if the employee switches employers. To illustrate, suppose that Mr. Sherris works for two employers over the course of his career and that both employers sponsored a defined benefit plan that provided a monthly retirement benefit equal to 2 percent times final salary times years of service. If Mr. Sherris's service with the first employer was 15 years and his final monthly salary was $4,000 and his service with the second employer was 10 years and his final monthly salary was $6,000, then his retirement benefit would equal

$$(0.02 \times 15 \times \$4,000 + 0.02 \times 10 \times \$6,000) = (\$1,200 + \$1,200) = \$2,400$$

which gives a replacement rate of 40 percent ($2,400/$6,000). In contrast, if Mr. Sherris had worked for just one employer for all 25 years, then his retirement benefit would be $3,000 (0.02 × 25 × $6,000) for a replacement rate of 50 percent. Thus, changing employers will result in a lower retirement benefit, assuming that salaries and benefit formulas remain the same.

Since sponsors of defined benefit plans promise to pay employees a retirement benefit in the future, a potential issue is whether the employer will fulfill its promise. For example, the employer may not exist when some employees retire or the employer may not have sufficient funds to pay the promised benefits. The concern about employers defaulting on pension promises is reduced by requiring that employers make contributions to a fund, called a pension fund, based on the present value of the new benefits that have been accrued by employees during the year. Some defined benefit plans also require employees to contribute to the pension fund. We will return to the potential problem of the employer not fulfilling its promises later in the chapter when regulation and government insurance for defined benefit plans are discussed.

For now, we will assume that employer default on pension promises is not a problem. Also, although it ignores some practical complications (which will be discussed later), assume that if the pension fund has excess assets, then the employer can remove the excess funds and use them for purposes other than compensating employees. Under these assumptions, the employer bears all the investment risk associated with the pension fund; that is, higher than expected investment earnings on the pension assets benefit the employer and lower than expected investment earnings hurt the employer by requiring additional contributions to the pension fund.

In summary, the essential aspects of a defined benefit plan are that (1) the employer promises employees a retirement benefit defined by a formula, (2) the employer, and sometimes employees, contribute to a pension fund each year so that sufficient funds accumulate to pay the promised benefits, and (3) the employer bears most of the risk associated with investment performance.

Defined Contribution Plans

With a **defined contribution plan,** the employer—and often the employee—makes a specific (defined) contribution to a fund. The contributions are invested on behalf of the employee, and the employee's retirement benefit depends on the investment returns. The greater the investment returns, the greater the employee's retirement benefit. Thus, the employee bears the investment risk in a defined contribution plan.

To illustrate, suppose that Vickie's salary is $50,000 and that her employer will contribute 10 percent of her salary if she contributes 5 percent to a defined contribution plan. Then, the annual contribution equals $7,500 (Vickie contributes $2,500 and the employer contributes $5,000). The contributions are invested on behalf of Vickie until she retires. Employees usually have a choice as to how the funds are invested; for example, Vickie might be able to choose among stock funds, bond funds, real estate funds, and money market funds. Each year of service, Vickie and her employer would make additional contributions, which also would be invested. At retirement, Vickie would receive the accumulated value of the contributions and the earnings on the contributions. These funds could be taken as a lump sum or they could be used to purchase an annuity that would provide Vickie with a fixed monthly income until death. Employees, however, cannot obtain the use of defined contribution funds prior to retirement unless a particular hardship, such as a permanent disability, death, or high family medical expenses, strikes the employee.

While defined benefit plans fix the benefit employees receive during retirement, defined contribution plans fix the employer's contribution to the plan. The benefit that the employee receives and thus the employee's replacement rate depends on the return earned on the contributed funds until retirement. As a result, an important distinction between defined benefit and defined contribution plans is that the employee bears the risk associated with investment earnings under a defined contribution plan. The uncertainty about the return in a defined contribution plan can make retirement planning with these plans more difficult for the employee than with defined benefit plans.

Concept Check

1. A treasurer of a major corporation states: "The pension fund assets had a negative return this year. Therefore, we will have to contribute more money to the fund over future years than was expected." Does this corporation sponsor a defined contribution or a defined benefit plan?

19.2 Tax Advantages of Retirement Plans

An important factor leading to the widespread use of employment-related retirement plans is the preferential tax treatment granted these plans. To explain these tax advantages, we will compare the after-tax amounts that can be accumulated via saving through a **qualified retirement plan** (one that qualifies for favorable tax treatment) versus saving outside of a qualified retirement plan. Two important aspects of the US tax code influence the tax advantage of retirement plan savings. First, contributions to qualified defined benefit and defined contribution plans are not subject to personal income taxes until retirement benefits are received. Second, earnings on assets in qualified retirement plans are not taxed until they are received. As we will show, the deferral of tax on both contributions and invest-ment earnings implies that saving through a qualified retirement plan allows an employee to earn the before-tax rate of return, whereas saving outside of a qual ified plan gives an employee the after-tax rate of return. This difference can be substantial.

Saving Outside of a Qualified Retirement Plan

Suppose that Vickie's employer is considering whether to make a $1,000 contri-bution to a defined contribution plan on her behalf. The alternative is for the em-ployer to pay the $1,000 to Vickie in the form of cash wages, which Vickie would then invest for retirement. (For simplicity, we ignore social security taxes that are payable on wages.) Assume that, in either case, the savings will earn a 10 percent annual before-tax rate of return over two years, which is when Vickie will retire. Also assume that Vickie has a constant 28 percent income tax rate.

If the $1,000 is paid to Vickie in the form of cash wages, then she would have to pay income tax on the $1,000, which implies that she could invest $720 [$100 $\times$ (1 − 0.28)]. This amount would earn a before-tax rate of return of 10 percent per year. However, the investment earnings would be taxed each year, which im-plies that Vickie's after-tax return is 7.2 percent [10% $\times$ (1 − 0.28)] per year.[1] Thus, if Vickie were to save the $1,000 in before-tax wages (or $720 in after-tax wages), she would accumulate $827.41($720 $\times$ 1.072^2) for retirement.

In general, each dollar of before-tax wages that is invested for T years out-side of a retirement plan would yield

$$(1 - \tau)[1 + r(1 - \tau)]^T \qquad\qquad (19.1)$$

where τ is the individual's tax rate (assumed constant over time) and r is the annual before-tax rate of return. This amount will be compared in the next two sections to the amount that would be available if the individual could either defer tax on investment earnings or defer tax on both investment earnings and contri-butions to a retirement plan.

Effect of Deferral of Tax on Investment Earnings

Now suppose that Vickie can invest in an account in which tax on investment earnings is deferred until retirement. We examine this tax feature in isolation be-cause, while qualified retirement plans have this tax advantage as well as the ad-vantage of deferring tax on contributions to retirement plans, other financial prod-ucts, such as some forms of life insurance and annuities, allow for tax deferment of only investment earnings. In addition, income taxes on contributions to some individual retirement accounts (IRAs) and 401(k) plans (discussed later) are not deferred but investment earnings are tax deferred.

---

[1] We briefly discuss the effects of investing in stocks and tax-exempt securities below.

If Vickie receives $1,000 in before-tax wages, then after paying income tax she will have $720 to save for retirement. These savings would earn 10 percent a year and, since the investment earnings are not taxed as they are earned, she would accumulate $871.20 ($720 × 1.1²) prior to paying tax on the investment earnings. The difference between the accumulated savings and the initial investment equals the investment earnings. Therefore, she must pay tax on $151.20 ($871.20 − $720). Given her 28 percent tax rate, she would have to pay tax of $42.34, leaving $828.86 after taxes. Note that this amount exceeds what she would have if she were unable to defer tax on the investment earnings, which from the previous section we know equals $827.41. While this difference is small, in examples using longer time periods the tax advantage of deferring tax on investment earnings can be substantial.

In general, each dollar in before-tax wages would allow an individual to invest $(1 − τ) in an account that defers tax on investment earnings. Assuming an annual before-tax rate of return of r, this $(1 − τ) would grow to the following amount after paying taxes at the end of T years:

$$\$(1 - \tau) \; \{ \underbrace{(1 + r)^T}_{\substack{\text{Accumulated saving} \\ \text{from \$1 prior to paying} \\ \text{tax on investment earnings}}} - \; \tau \underbrace{[(1 + r)^T - 1]}_{\substack{\text{Investment} \\ \text{earnings on \$1}}} \} \qquad (19.2)$$

The second term in the bracketed expression is the tax rate, τ, times the investment earnings, where the investment earnings is the difference between the ending value of the fund and the initial amount contributed.

Effect of Deferring Tax on Both Investment Earnings and Contributions

We now consider the tax treatment of qualified retirement plans, which in addition to the deferral of investment earnings allows an investor to defer tax on contributions to the retirement plan. Continuing with our example, if $1,000 is contributed to a qualified plan on behalf of Vickie, then she will not have to pay tax on the $1,000 until she retires in two years. Moreover, since taxes on the earnings in the retirement plan also are deferred, Vickie will accumulate $1,210 ($1,000 × 1.1²) prior to paying taxes when she retires in two years. She will have to pay tax on the entire amount, which means that after taxes, she will have $871.20 [$1,210 × (1 − 0.28)]. This amount exceeds the amount she would have if she saved outside of the retirement plan ($827.41) and the amount she would have if she saved in an account where only the investment earnings are tax deferred ($828.86).

In general, tax deferral of contributions and earnings implies that each dollar of before-tax wages that is invested in a qualified retirement account for T years will grow to

$$(1 + r)^T (1 - \tau) \qquad (19.3)$$

Comparing this expression to the amount that $1 will earn after taxes outside of a pension plan (equation 19.1), $[1 + r (1 - \tau)]^T (1 - \tau)$, indicates that the essential difference between saving in a qualified retirement plan and saving outside of a qualified retirement plan is the difference between earning the before-tax rate of return and the after-tax rate of return. That is, saving $1,000 through a qualified plan is the same as receiving $1,000, paying tax on this amount, and then earning the before-tax rate of return, r, until retirement. Saving outside of a qualified plan is the same as receiving $1,000, paying tax on this amount, and then earning the after-tax rate of return, $r(1 - \tau)$, until retirement.

Figure 19–1 illustrates the difference between the accumulated amounts under the three different tax scenarios analyzed here assuming a 10 percent annual before-tax rate of return and a 28 percent tax rate for various times until retirement. As you can see, there is a substantial difference between the accumulated value of savings available in a nonqualified account versus an account in which investment earnings are tax deferred and versus a qualified retirement account (investment earnings and contributions are tax deferred).

Since the essential tax advantage of a qualified retirement plan is that savings accumulate at the before-tax rate of return (i.e., you avoid paying tax on investment earnings), it is important to compare returns from investing in retirement plans to other tax-advantaged ways of investing, such as the returns from investing in municipal bonds or low dividend paying stocks. Municipal bonds are tax advantaged because the investor does not have to pay federal income tax on the interest received. Low dividend paying stocks are tax advantaged because capital gains, which would be expected to be higher if dividends were lower, are taxed at a lower rate than dividend income if they are realized. In addition, unrealized capital gains can be deferred until death and then passed on to heirs without having to pay tax on the capital gains in some cases.

Securities that are tax advantaged generally offer lower before-tax expected returns than other securities with the same risk. To illustrate this conceptual point,

FIGURE 19–1

Comparison of accumulated value of $2,000 in before-tax wages under different tax treatments (Assumptions: 10 percent rate of return, 30 percent tax rate)

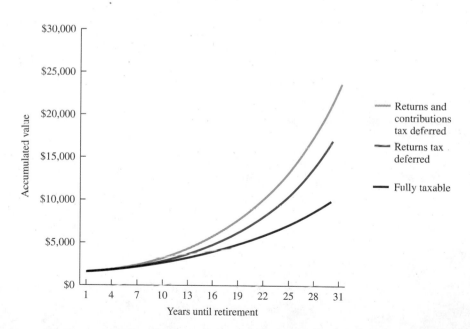

suppose that a US government bond and a municipal bond have the same risk and that the US government bond is paying a 10 percent rate of return. The interest on the US government bond is taxed, but the interest on the municipal bond is not. If the municipal bond also provided a 10 percent return, then investors with a positive tax rate would never buy US government bonds. Consequently, the municipal bond would be expected to provide a return less than 10 percent. If all investors had a 28 percent tax rate, then the municipal bond would be expected to pay 7.2 percent. If the municipal bond paid more than 7.2 percent, then all investors would prefer municipal bonds because they would offer a higher after-tax return than US government bonds. Similarly, if the municipal bond pays less than 7.2 percent, then all investors would prefer US government bonds.

Since the returns on tax-advantaged securities (e.g., municipal bonds) are reduced relative to the returns on tax-disadvantaged securities of the same risk (e.g., US government bonds), a higher return can be earned by investing in tax-disadvantaged securities in a qualified retirement plan than can be earned by investing in tax-advantaged securities (either within or outside of a qualified account). To illustrate using the previous example, investing in US government bonds through a qualified plan will yield a 10 percent annual return, but investing in municipal bonds (either within a qualified account or a nonqualified account) will yield a return of only 7.2 percent. Thus, all else equal, the most tax-disadvantaged securities are the best investments within a qualified plan.

Lower Tax Rates during Retirement

The previous examples assume that people's tax rates are constant over time. To the extent that people are expected to have a lower tax rate during retirement, then the tax advantages of retirement plans increase. For example, suppose that an employee has a 36 percent tax rate while working and expects a 28 percent tax rate during retirement. Then, deferring tax on contributions and investment earnings provides a greater tax benefit than previously described because, in addition to deferring taxes (and thus decreasing the present value of tax payments), the absolute amount of taxes paid is lower due to the lower tax rate during retirement.

Tax Advantages of Defined Benefit Plans

The previous example illustrated the tax advantage of saving through a qualified retirement account versus saving through a nonqualified account by comparing a defined contribution plan to a nonqualified private investment account. In both cases, a sum of money was invested in an account until retirement; the only difference in the two methods of savings was in the tax treatment. Since defined benefit plans operate differently than defined contribution plans, the tax benefits of defined benefit plans may not be apparent. However, the tax benefits from a defined benefit plan are the same as a defined contribution plan that provides equivalent retirement benefits.

Perhaps the easiest way to see that the tax benefits from a defined contribution and defined benefit plan are the same from an individual's perspective is to recognize that with defined benefit plans employers and sometimes employees must make contributions to a pension fund so that promised benefits can be paid from the fund. These contributions are then invested until employees retire. Thus, the retirement benefits that employees receive from a defined benefit plan are equivalent to a series of employer and employee contributions to a pension fund and the accumulation of the earnings on those contributions. In this sense, defined benefit plans are similar to defined contribution plans—employees receive retirement benefits as a result of employer and employee contributions and the earnings on those contributions. These contributions are not taxable to the employee when the contributions are made, and the earnings on the pension assets are not taxed as they are earned. However, since the retirement benefits are taxable, the contributions and investment earnings that are used to pay the defined benefit are tax deferred. Thus, a defined benefit plan provides the same tax benefits as a defined contribution plan with equivalent benefits.

Concept Check

2. Consider the following three investment options:
    (*a*) A $1,000 investment in Treasury bonds in a qualified retirement plan.
    (*b*) A $1,000 investment in municipal bonds in a qualified retirement plan.
    (*c*) A $1,000 investment in municipal bonds outside of a qualified retirement plan.
    Assume that the Treasury bonds and the municipal bonds have the same risk. Compare the after-tax retirement income that would be available from (*a*) versus (*b*), (*a*) versus (*c*), and (*b*) versus (*c*).

19.3 Incentive Effects of Employer-sponsored Pension Plans

The first employer-sponsored retirement plan in the United States was created by American Express in 1875, and a number of large firms introduced retirement plans prior to the introduction of federal income taxes in 1913. Although taxes are a major factor in explaining the growth of employer-sponsored retirement plans, the fact that employers established plans prior to the existence of tax benefits strongly suggests that there are important incentive effects of retirement plans. In this section, we explain how retirement plans can be used (1) to increase employee productivity by inducing greater employee effort and by reducing turnover, and (2) to promote retirement at an age when employee productivity often declines.

Increasing Productivity

One way to induce employees to put forth greater effort is to defer part of their compensation and make the receipt of their deferred compensation contingent upon their performance. Retirement plans, of course, provide deferred compensation. These plans therefore can induce employees to work harder—provided that workers lose part of their retirement benefits if they are fired. As we discuss below, participation and vesting schedules and the backend loading of retirement benefits can induce employees to put forth greater effort early in their careers because these features cause them to lose part of their benefits if they leave the firm.

Employers often provide training to workers that increases the employees' human capital and therefore their productivity. If this training is transferable to other employers, then the employer providing the training is confronted with the potential problem that the worker will quit, in which case, the original employer will have paid the training cost but will not have received the anticipated benefit of the training. Employers who provide training therefore need some method of compensating employees so that the employees forfeit some of their compensation if they leave. Again, retirement plans with participation and vesting schedules and with backend loading of benefits can provide the answer. Without these mechanisms, employers would be less likely to provide the training that increases employee productivity.

Participation and Vesting Requirements.   Many retirement plans do not allow employees to participate until they have worked at the firm for some period of time, for example, two years. Prior to satisfying the participation requirements, an employee is not entitled to retirement benefits. Therefore, once the employee satisfies the participation requirement, his or her total compensation is bumped up. As a result, participation requirements provide incentives for employees to not quit and to work harder so as not to be fired.

In addition to participation requirements, plans typically have **vesting requirements,** which cause participants to forfeit part or all of their retirement benefits due to employer contributions if they leave prior to being fully vested. (Employees always are entitled to benefits based on their own contributions to the plan.) An employee's retirement benefits are vested if he or she receives the irrevocable right to those benefits. In other words, the benefits cannot be taken away. A commonly used vesting schedule is **cliff vesting** after three years, whereby an employee receives full retirement benefits after three years of service. Another commonly used vesting schedule is **graded vesting,** whereby an employee's retirement benefits are vested gradually over time (e.g., 20 percent vested after two years, 40 percent vested after three years, 60 percent vested after four years, 80 percent vested after five years, and 100 percent vested after six years). We will discuss the regulations on vesting schedules later in the chapter. The important point for this discussion is that plans that do not provide immediate vesting provide employees with some incentive to work hard and to stay with the firm. Both defined benefit and defined contribution plans have vesting schedules.

Backend Loading of Benefits.   Defined benefit plans offer another way of structuring benefits so that employees will lose part of their benefits if they leave the firm. With most defined benefit formulas, benefits are backend-loaded, which means that relatively larger retirement benefits are accrued late in a person's service with the company. To see how benefits are backend-loaded, consider the following defined benefit formula:

Annual retirement benefit

= 2.0% × Years of service × Annual salary during last year of service

Now examine the benefits that Jack would accrue each year if he started working for VanDerhei Inc. at the age of 30. Assume that his initial salary is $25,000 and that his salary grows 4.0 percent each year. For simplicity, we will assume that there are no participation requirements and that he is immediately vested.

After working one year, Jack's accrued benefits would equal 0.02 × 1 × $25,000 = $500/year. That is, if Jack left Vanderhei Inc. after one year, his annual retirement benefit from Vanderhei Inc. would be $500. In his second year, Jack receives a 4.0 percent raise so his salary increases to $26,000 and his accrued annual benefit equals 0.02 × 2 × $26,000 = $1,040. If Jack leaves after two years, he will receive $1,040 annually during retirement. Thus, his additional accrued retirement benefit as a result of his second year of service is $540 ($1,040 − $500). An important point to notice is that the higher salary in the second year is, in essence, applied to the first year of service under this type of benefit formula since the accrued benefit is determined by multiplying the final salary by the number of years of service. Indeed, each year that Jack's salary increases, his accrued benefit increases for previous years of service because that higher salary is applied to all previous years of service. If we continued to calculate Jack's additional accrued benefit for each additional year of service, we would find that, as-

FIGURE 19–2

Jack's additional accrued annual retirement benefit under a defined benefit plan with initial salary = $25,000 and salary growth = 4.0%

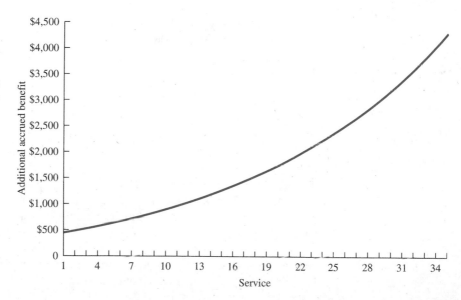

suming that his salary grows at a 4 percent rate over time, the additional accrued benefit increases at an increasing rate over time, as depicted in Figure 19–2 on page 485.

To highlight the difference in the additional accrued benefit at different service levels, we will calculate the accrued benefit in Jack's final year of service. Jack's annual salary in his 34th year will equal $91,210 [$25,000 × (1.04)^{34}], and his salary in his 35th (and last) year will equal $94,858 [$25,000 × (1.04)^{35}]. If Jack left the firm after 34 years of service, his annual retirement benefit would equal $62,023 (0.02 × 34 × $91,210). If instead he worked an additional year, his retirement benefit would increase to $66,401 (0.02 × 35 × $94,858). Thus, by working his 35th year with the firm, Jack would accrue an additional annual benefit of $4,378 ($66,401 – $62,023). In comparison, Jack accrued an additional retirement benefit of only $500 in his first year of service. Thus, the majority of Jack's retirement benefits were accrued late in his career.

Since accrued benefits are heavily backend-loaded with most defined benefit plans, these plans provide employees with incentives not to be fired and thus to work harder. In addition, these plans encourage workers not to quit. To illustrate the magnitude of the losses an employee can suffer from leaving a firm with a defined benefit plan, suppose that Dick has been working for Ippolito Inc. for the past 15 years and that he expects to work an additional 15 years. The issue is whether he will work the last 15 years with Ippolito Inc. or with another firm, Bulow Corp. Both firms have the same defined benefit formula: 2 percent times years of service times final salary. Dick's current salary is $50,000 and he expects it to grow at a 5 percent rate until he retires—regardless of his employer. Thus, Dick's final salary is expected to be $103,947 [$50,000 (1.05)^{15}]. If he stays with Ippolito Inc. then he expects that his annual retirement benefit will be 2 percent times 30 years of service times $103,947, which equals $62,368 for a 60 percent replacement rate. If instead he switches employers, then he will receive a retirement benefit from Ippolito Inc. equal to 2 percent times 15 years of service times $50,000, which equals $15,000, plus a retirement benefit from Bulow Corp. equal to 2 percent times 15 years of service times $103,947, which equals $31,184. Thus, Dick's total retirement benefit is $46,184 for a replacement rate of 44.4 percent. Switching employers in this case reduces annual retirement income by $16,184 ($46,184 – $31,184). This example illustrates that defined benefit plans can provide powerful incentives to stay with one firm.

Inducing Retirement

The backend loading of retirement benefits can create a problem for employers—since additional service results in higher benefits, employees may delay retirement well beyond the point where their productivity warrants their continued employment. Simply stated, some people will work too long. Under current law, most employers cannot force employees to retire at a certain age. Most defined benefit plans therefore deal with this problem by structuring benefits to provide incentives for employees to retire at certain ages.

A plan's **normal retirement age** determines the age at which a retiree receives full retirement benefits. The normal retirement age can be defined using the employee's age and/or the employee's years of service with the company. Retirement plans typically do not give additional retirement benefits to employees who continue working beyond the normal retirement age. Thus, the lack of additional benefits beyond the normal retirement age is an important method by which employers can induce employees to retire. Also, benefits often are structured to induce early retirement. Under many defined benefit plans, employees can retire earlier than the normal retirement age. When an employee retires early, benefits usually are reduced relative to normal retirement benefits, but they may not be reduced as much as would be projected given the fewer years of service and a greater number of years for which benefits would be expected to be received. In essence, plans can be structured so that employees receive a "retirement bonus" if they retire early.

19.4 Types of Defined Contribution Plans

Money Purchase and Profit Sharing Plans

One of the most common types of defined contribution plans is a **money purchase plan,** in which the employer makes an annual contribution on behalf of the employee regardless of the firm's profits. The contribution usually is stated as a percentage of the employee's salary but can be a flat amount. In some instances employers require that employees also make contributions to the plan. A profit sharing plan is another common type of defined contribution plan. As the name suggests, the employer's contribution to a **profit sharing plan** depends on the firm's profits. With some profit sharing plans, contributions are based on an explicit formula (e.g., 5 percent of pretax profit) and in other plans the contributions are at the discretion of the corporation's board of directors. Profit sharing contributions usually are allocated across employees based on the proportion of the employee's salary as a percentage of total payroll costs.

401(k) Plans

Section 401(k) of The Revenue Act of 1978 allowed a new form of defined contribution plan that has become known as a 401(k) plan. The distinguishing feature of a **401(k) plan** compared to other defined contribution plans is that employees can elect (subject to limitations) to make tax-deferred contributions, in addition to the employer's tax-deferred contributions. Recall that a tax-deferred contribution implies that the employee does not pay tax on the contribution until the money is withdrawn from the plan (usually at retirement). The use of 401(k) plans has grown tremendously in the past two decades.

Many firms have adopted 401(k) plans in addition to their other defined benefit or defined contribution plans. Employee participation in 401(k) plans typically is voluntary and the level of employee contributions if they do participate is voluntary. Employees also typically have more discretion in how the funds of their 401(k) plan are invested compared to other defined contribution plans.

An interesting feature of many 401(k) plans is that employers often match employee contributions. For example, an employer may match employee contributions dollar-for-dollar. Whereas employee contributions are immediately vested, employer contributions can be subject to vesting requirements. Box 19–1 provides four potential explanations for employer matching of 401(k) contribu-

---

Box 19–1

Employer Matching of Employee 401(k) Contributions

Nondiscrimination Rules

One explanation for employer matching is that regulation requires that employer-sponsored plans follow nondiscrimination rules, which do not allow highly compensated employees to make contributions that far exceed the contributions of lower paid employees. The details are of nondiscrimination rules are not important for our purposes (but are extremely important to benefit plan managers). The important point is that nondiscrimination rules induce employers to provide an incentive for lower paid employees to contribute to 401(k) plans, which in turn allows highly compensated employees to make larger contributions. Employer matching of contributions is a method of inducing lower paid employees to make contributions.

Incentives

A second explanation for employer matching relates to incentives. Since the matching contribution can be subject to vesting rules, employees have incentives to remain with the firm to get its matching contributions. Thus, employer matching can increase productivity and reduce turnover, just like other retirement plans.

Aligning Compensation and Productivity

A third reason an employer may match employee contributions is that it more closely aligns compensation with employee productivity when employees have different skills and/or willingness to work. For example, suppose that there are two types of workers; one type is more productive than the other is, but the employer cannot identify the more productive workers until they have worked a long time period (or alternatively that for legal considerations the firm finds it costly to fire workers once they have been found to be of the low productivity type). Also assume that the more productive workers tend to be people that are more concerned about the future than less productive workers and therefore that the more productive workers will tend to save more than the less productive workers do, all else being equal. Under these conditions, the more productive workers would be the people who would make larger contributions to their 401(k) plan. If the employer matches employee contributions, then the employer pays the more productive workers more than the less productive workers, which helps reduce turnover of the more productive workers.

Taxes

A final explanation for employer matching has to do with taxes. Payroll taxes (e.g., social security taxes) apply to employee contributions, but they do not apply to employer contributions. Thus, from a tax management perspective, total tax payments are reduced if employees accept lower wages in exchange for an employer match of the employees' 401(k) contributions.

tions. The matching feature increases the administrative costs of 401(k) plans compared to money purchase or profit sharing plans.

Employees can withdraw (or borrow funds) funds from their 401(k) plans prior to retirement under certain hardship conditions. For example, funds possibly could be withdrawn to pay family medical expenses, to pay for college tuition, or to purchase a principal residence. The funds withdrawn are subject to tax in the year they are withdrawn.

Employee Stock Ownership Plans

With all defined contribution plans, contributions are allocated to individual employee accounts and the money is invested in various assets on behalf of employees. In all of the defined contribution plans discussed so far, the proportion of the funds in an employee's account that can be invested in the sponsoring firm's stock is limited by regulation to 10 percent. The purpose of this regulation is to force employees to hold somewhat diversified portfolios. One type of retirement plan, however, is not subject to this regulation. An **employee stock ownership plan (ESOP)** is a defined contribution plan that is required to hold at least 50 percent of its assets in the sponsoring firm's stock. ESOPs have another distinguishing feature relative to other retirement plans—they can be leveraged. That is, an ESOP plan can borrow money to purchase stock for employees. ESOP loans are repaid using the sponsoring firm's contributions.

The unique features of ESOPs have made them an important financing tool for some corporations and a means of placing stock in friendly hands to prevent takeovers. ESOPs also have been promoted as a means of (1) improving employee productivity by tying employee compensation to the firm's stock price, and (2) improving labor relations, although there is limited evidence consistent with these effects. ESOPs also have received tax advantages beyond other retirement plans. An important disadvantage of ESOPs as retirement plans is that they force employees to hold poorly diversified portfolios. Employees enrolled in an ESOP have both their employment income and their retirement income tied to the fortunes of the firm. For this reason, ESOPs are required by regulation to allow employees reaching the age of 55 to diversify the funds in their ESOP accounts.

Simplified Employee Pensions

Employers without other qualified retirement plans can with minimal paperwork establish retirement plans called **simplified employee pension (SEP) accounts** for each of their employees. The employer then can make tax-deductible contributions up to 15 percent of employee compensation, or $30,000 (in 1998). These SEP accounts must be established for each employee over the age of 21 who has worked for three of the last five years. From the employee's perspective, the contributions and investment earnings are tax deferred as in other qualified retirement plans.

Growth in Defined Contribution Plans

While the majority of employees who participate in employer-sponsored retirement plans are enrolled in defined benefit plans, enrollment in defined contribution plans has grown dramatically in the past 15 years. The growth in defined contribution plans primarily reflects the growth in 401(k) plans. One reason for the recent growth in 401(k) plans is that the IRS did not clarify the tax treatment of these plans until the early 1980s. The growth in defined contribution plans in general also can be attributed in part to the effects of increased regulation of defined benefit plans. First, the regulatory burden and administrative costs of operating defined benefit plans have increased. Second, there are economies of scale in the administration of defined benefit plans, which makes smaller firms more likely to choose defined contribution plans. A shift in the US economy toward smaller firms therefore also helps explain the increased use of defined contribution plans. Third, the increased regulations on vesting and early retirement provisions in defined benefit plans make their use as an incentive mechanism less effective. A fourth potential explanation is that the economy has changed in a way that has increased the benefits and decreased the costs of greater labor mobility; as a result, firms are less likely to adopt defined benefit plans, which reduce labor mobility. Finally, regulatory restrictions on a firm's ability to remove excess pension assets from defined benefit plans (see below) reduce some of the advantages of these plans from a corporate financing perspective, as well as from a labor contracting perspective.

19.5 Self-employed (Keogh) and Individual Retirement Accounts (IRAs)

Keogh Plans

Self-employed individuals can establish retirement plans called **Keogh plans** for themselves and all full-time employees. These plans can be either defined benefit or defined contribution plans. From a regulatory and tax perspective, they are treated very similarly to corporate-sponsored retirement plans.

Individual Retirement Plans (IRAs)

An important source of retirement income for many people, especially those who are not participants in employer-sponsored plans, is an **individual retirement account (IRA).** In addition, participants in employer-sponsored plans can in some circumstances augment their retirement savings through IRAs. There are two basic types of IRAs: traditional IRAs and Roth IRAs. The latter type was introduced in 1998. Regardless of the type of IRA, contributions are limited to $2,000 a year and withdrawals made prior to age 59½ can trigger an excise tax of 10 percent, unless death or permanent disability occurs.

Traditional IRAs.   People who are not participating in an employer-sponsored retirement plan can make tax-deductible contributions to a traditional IRA up to $2,000 per year. The earnings on these funds are tax deferred. All withdrawals from a traditional IRA are taxed as income. The combination of tax-deductible contributions and tax-deferred investment earnings make traditional IRAs similar to corporate sponsored retirement plans from an individual tax perspective. To illustrate, a $2,000 IRA contribution that earns a before-tax rate of return of r for T years will grow to $2,000 $(1 + r)^T$. If the individual's tax rate at retirement is 30 percent, the amount accumulated after-tax will be $0.7 \times \$2,000 \ (1 + r)^T = \$1,400 \ (1 + r)^T$. In effect, the IRA allows the individual to earn the before-tax rate of return on $1,400. As we will see, an advantage of a Roth IRA is that the individual can in effect earn the before-tax rate of return on a larger amount (the entire $2,000).

Individuals who are participants in employer-sponsored plans also can make tax-deductible contributions to an IRA if they earn less than a certain amount ($40,000 for individuals and $60,000 for couples filing jointly in 1998). After these cutoffs, the ability to make contributions is phased out as income increases. Starting in 1998, individuals who cannot make tax-deductible contributions to an IRA still can contribute to an IRA up to $2,000 a year. While the contributions are not tax deductible, the investment earnings on the IRA funds are tax deferred until the funds are withdrawn during retirement.

Roth IRAs.   Roth IRAs differ from traditional IRAs in that (1) contributions to a Roth IRA are not tax deductible, and (2) withdrawals during retirement from a Roth IRA are not taxed. (Traditional IRAs have the opposite treatment—contributions are tax deductible and withdrawals are taxed.) Thus, once money is placed in a Roth IRA, it is no longer taxed (assuming it is not withdrawn early), which implies that investment earnings on the entire contribution to a Roth IRA escape taxation. A maximum contribution of $2,000 to a Roth IRA that earns a before-tax rate of return of r for T years will yield $2,000$(1 + r)^T$ in retirement income.

An important difference between a Roth IRA and a traditional IRA is that the Roth IRA effectively relaxes the constraint on the amount of money on which an individual can earn the before-tax rate of return. With a traditional IRA, a maximum contribution of $2,000 by an individual with a 30 percent tax rate effectively allows the individual to avoid tax on the investment earnings generated from $1,400 [$2,000$(1 - 0.3)$]. With a Roth IRA, a maximum contribution of $2,000 by an individual with a 30 percent tax rate effectively allows the individual to avoid tax on the investment earnings generated from $2,000. For individuals who do not find the traditional IRA constraint binding (those who wish to contribute less than $1,400 of after-tax earnings in our example), the Roth IRA would not dominate a traditional IRA.

A potential disadvantage of the Roth IRA compared to the traditional IRA arises when investors expect to have a lower tax rate during retirement. Since the traditional IRA gives a tax deduction when the contribution is made and then taxes withdrawals during retirement, investors with lower tax rates during retirement under some circumstances can achieve higher retirement income with a traditional IRA.

19.6 Retirement Plan Provisions and Regulations

There are numerous contractual provisions in any retirement plan, and many of the provisions are influenced by detailed and complex regulations. In this section we provide a broad overview of some of the more important provisions and regulations. The regulatory restrictions on retirement plans greatly expanded with the passage of the **Employee Retirement Income Security Act (ERISA)** of 1974 by the US Congress. ERISA has been changed numerous times since 1974.

Nondiscrimination and Vesting Rules

To qualify for preferential tax treatment, employer-sponsored retirement plans must satisfy certain rules. As noted in Box 19–1, qualified plans must meet complex **nondiscrimination rules** that allow a broad range of employees to participate and that ensure that benefits do not disproportionately favor highly compensated employees. Qualified plans also must be operated solely for the benefit of the plan's beneficiaries, and funds contributed to retirement plans cannot be diverted for other corporate purposes.

As mentioned earlier, an important provision in retirement plans is the vesting schedule, which determines when employees receive the right to the benefits resulting from the employer's contributions. Recall that cliff vesting means that benefits are not vested at all until a certain number of years of service have been completed and then benefits are fully vested. ERISA sets the maximum length of service for cliff vesting at five years. Graded vesting means that benefits are vested gradually over time. If graded vesting is chosen, regulation requires that benefits be vested at least 20 percent after three years, 40 percent after four years, 60 percent after five years, 80 percent after six years, and 100 percent after seven years.

Funding Requirements

The risk that the employer might not fulfill its promises to pay benefits to employees under a defined benefit plan is handled in a number of ways, including required funding rules and mandatory pension insurance. With respect to funding, sponsors must make periodic contributions to a pension fund from which the promised benefit will be paid. Although sponsors have some discretion over their contributions, ERISA imposes minimum funding requirements on sponsors of defined benefit plans. For example, new benefit accruals must be funded immediately and shortfalls in funding must be amortized over time.

To assess funding adequacy for defined benefit pension plans, it is useful to examine the firm's pension plan balance sheet. A comparison of the value of the pension assets and the value of the pension liabilities provides a snapshot of the plan's funding status. The value of **pension assets** is the market value of the assets held in the pension fund; the value of **pension liabilities** is the present value of the promised benefits to employees. As discussed in Box 19–2, there are various ways of calculating the value of a plan's pension liabilities. When pension assets exceed pension liabilities, the plan is *overfunded.* When pension assets are less than pension liabilities, the plan is *underfunded.* For example, General Motors had some pension plans in 1996 that were underfunded and some plans that were overfunded. The underfunded plans had assets equal to $40.2 billion and liabilities equal to $44.2 billion; the overfunded plans had assets equal to $31.1 billion and liabilities equal to $26.0 billion.

Box 19–2

ABO and PBO Measures of Pension Liabilities

Measuring pension liabilities can be complex. To calculate pension liabilities, one must make assumptions about numerous factors, such as employee turnover rates, death rates, and discount rates. In addition, the calculation of pension liabilities requires an assumption about the nature of the firm's pension contract with employees. To illustrate the latter point, consider the plan described earlier in which Jack's salary is initially $25,000, his salary grows 4.0 percent each year, he retires in 35 years, and he is immediately vested. The benefit formula is 2.0 percent times years of service times final salary. After one year of service, Jack's accrued benefit is $500 (0.02 × 1 × $25,000). What is the firm's pension liability after one year? One approach is to calculate the pension liability assuming that Jack's participation in the plan ends after one year. Under this assumption, the firm would have to pay Jack an annual benefit of $500 when he retires. Thus, the pension liability would equal the present value (discounted over 34 years) of the value of a $500 annual retirement annuity. This method of calculating the pension liability is called the *accumulated benefit obligation (ABO)* and is based on the view that the labor contract is a one-year contract.

An alternative approach is to calculate the pension liability assuming that Jack's participation in the plan will continue until his retirement. According to this approach, this first year of service is expected to create a benefit equal to 2 percent of his projected final salary. Assuming Jack works for 35 years, his projected final salary is $94,858 [25,000 × (1.04)³⁵]. Thus, the pension liability is the present value of the value of a $1,897 (0.02 × 1 × $94,858) retirement annuity, nearly four times the value of the ABO in this case. This method of calculating the pension liability is called the *projected benefit obligation (PBO).*

The difference between the accumulated benefit obligation and the projected benefit obligation depends on a number of factors, including the age of the participants, the benefit formula, and the expected salary growth. In general, the pension liability will grow at a faster rate over time if ABO is used. Stated differently, if a firm funded its plans so that pension assets always equaled ABO, then pension contributions initially would be low but would increase rapidly over time. Funding so that the value of pension assets always equaled PBO would result in a more uniform pattern of contributions. Most pension economists would view the PBO measure as the better way of measuring an ongoing firm's pension liability because its more uniform growth pattern more accurately reflects how employees pay for their pension benefits through foregone wages.

Pension Insurance

Despite most firms' attempts to adequately fund their pension plans and despite regulations on funding, pension plans can become underfunded for a variety of reasons. For example, the return on the plan's assets could be less than expected, or interest rates could decline, thus increasing the present value of pension liabilities, or any one of a number of assumptions needed to calculate promised pension benefits (e.g., employee turnover, employee wage growth, death rates) could differ from expectations.

ERISA created the **Pension Benefit Guaranty Corporation (PBGC)** to insure employees' promised benefits in defined benefit pension plans against the contingency that a firm terminates an underfunded plan. Under the PBGC insurance program, the PBGC will pay promised benefits (valued at the time of termination, see below) up to a maximum amount if a pension plan is terminated with insufficient funds to pay promised benefits. Employers sponsoring defined benefit plans are charged an annual premium for the compulsory insurance. The history of the PBGC insurance program illustrates some of the problems associated with insurance programs that are not structured to take into account moral hazard problems.

When the PBGC was first created, each firm sponsoring a defined benefit plan was charged an annual premium equal to $1 per participant. Because the premium was independent of the funding of a firm's plans, some employers probably paid more than their expected claim costs and other employers certainly paid less than their expected claim costs. Insurance arrangements that charge all insureds the same premium despite differences in expected claim costs normally would suffer from adverse selection—the high-risk (high-expected claim cost) sponsors would buy the insurance and the low risk would not. The compulsory nature of the program mitigated such adverse selection, although in the long run some firms might have selected out of the insurance program by switching to defined contribution plans.

The more important problem with the premium schedule was that it reduced the incentive of some firms to contribute sufficient funds to pay all their promised benefits (i.e., it created a moral hazard problem). Essentially, a firm could shift part of the expected cost of compensating its employees to the PBGC by promising employees pension benefits and then not fully funding those benefits. Although the source of this moral hazard problem was the fixed premium schedule, the insurance program incorporated several factors that, at least in principle, could have helped reduce the moral hazard problem. For example, funding requirements could have prevented firms from not fully funding the promised benefits. However, the rules gave firms sufficient discretion over funding so that some plans still became significantly underfunded. In recent years, though, the funding requirements have been tightened.

One factor that helped reduce the moral hazard problem associated with the PBGC insurance was that, when an underfunded plan was terminated, the PBGC could claim up to 30 percent of the sponsoring employer's net worth. That is, if a firm wanted to make the PBGC pay the unfunded pension liabilities, then the firm had to give the PBGC 30 percent of the firm's equity value. This restriction effectively prevented financially strong firms from making the PBGC pay unfunded pension liabilities. It did not, however, eliminate the moral hazard problem for financially distressed firms whose net worth was close to zero. It also provided incentives for firms to spin off divisions that had underfunded pension plans in an effort to protect the rest of the corporation's assets from being claimed by the PBGC (see Chapter 17).

Another factor that mitigated moral hazard is that the PBGC does not guarantee all promised pension benefits. In addition to the limit on the level of benefits guaranteed, the PBGC's guarantee applies only to benefits based on employees' salaries at the time the underfunded plan is terminated, not benefits based on projected salaries. As a result, an underfunded plan termination is likely to impose losses on employees whose benefits are backend loaded. Since employees are not fully insured, they have an incentive to stop firms from terminating underfunded plans. Stated differently, the PBGC insurance has an important co-insurance provision (employees are not fully insured) that helps to reduce moral hazard.

Employers, however, have a way of circumventing the co-insurance aspect of the insurance. After terminating an underfunded plan, employers can compensate employees for their losses by establishing a follow-on plan that gives employees the difference between their promised benefits and the PBGC guaranteed benefits. With such a follow-on plan, employees will not try to block the termination of an underfunded plan. Since follow-on plans eliminate the co-insurance associated with the PBGC insurance, the PBGC has actively sought to prevent follow-on plans. One of the more important cases involving follow-on plans was the LTV case, in which the PBGC was successful in stopping LTV from establishing a follow-on plan (see Box 19–3).

Two laws enacted in the 1980s gave the PBGC the means to reduce "abuses" of the insurance program. Both the Single Employer Pension Protection Act of 1986 (SEPPA) and the Pension Protection Act of 1987 (PPA) restrict the ability of a firm to use the PBGC insurance to walk away from its pension promises. In particular, firms seeking to make the PBGC pay unfunded pension liabilities must demonstrate that the pension plan termination is necessary for the continued existence of the firm. In addition, these laws have expanded the PBGC's claims against a firm's assets when an underfunded plan is terminated beyond the 30 percent net worth claim.

In part because of the moral hazard and in part because the initial premium level ($1 per employee) was too low given the PBGC's exposure even in the absence of moral hazard, the PBGC was forced to increase the premium several times. In 1987, a variable premium schedule was adopted. All employers now pay a base annual premium of $19 per employee, but employers with underfunded plans pay an additional premium that increases with the amount of underfunding (0.9 percent of unfunded vested liabilities).

Box 19–3

The PBGC Battles with LTV over the Termination of Underfunded Pension Plans

Following a downturn in the steel industry in the 1980s, LTV Corporation, a large steel company, filed for bankruptcy. In 1987, the PBGC forced LTV to terminate three pension plans that were underfunded by about $2.5 billion. LTV had completely stopped funding these plans. By terminating the plans, the PBGC took over the responsibility of paying the $2.5 billion in underfunding.

LTV then established new follow-on plans that essentially restored employees' benefits to the level promised prior to termination. From LTV's and its employees' perspective, the forced termination together with the follow-on plans were a blessing—employees lost little if any promised benefits, but the PBGC was going to pay $2.5 billion of the cost.

The PBGC tried to stop LTV from establishing the follow-on plans. The PBGC's main point was that if LTV could pay the benefits promised in the follow-on plans, then LTV should have to pay the $2.5 billion in underfunding. LTV initially won in lower court rulings, but the PBGC appealed the case to the US Supreme Court. In 1990, the Supreme Court ruled in favor of the PBGC.

Excess Assets in Defined Benefit Plans

Just as plans can become underfunded, plans can accumulate pension assets in excess of pension liabilities (i.e., they can become overfunded). An important issue for the financial management of defined benefit plans and for participants in these plans is who owns the excess assets. The answer to this question depends on the ability of firms to remove excess assets from the plan. A firm can remove excess assets either gradually, by reducing future contributions, or all at once, by terminating the plan and taking the excess through a **pension asset reversion.**

During the 1980s, a large number of firms removed excess assets through reversions. These reversions were criticized because reversions require that the plan be terminated, which potentially can impose losses on employees because, as discussed earlier, retirement benefits for a terminated plan are based on employees' salaries at the time of the termination. Even if a new plan with the same benefit formula were established, employees could suffer losses, because the service under the new plan would not include the service under the old plan. Just as the earlier example showed how Dick would lose pension benefits if he changed employers, employees of a firm that terminates a plan could experience losses.

In an effort to discourage pension asset reversions, Congress imposed an excise tax (in addition to the normal income tax) on the value of excess pension assets claimed in reversions. Currently, the excise tax is 20 percent, provided that 25 percent of pension surplus is used as a cushion for a replacement plan or that employee benefits are increased by 25 percent; otherwise, the excise tax is 50 percent. These rules reduce firms' incentives to fund their defined benefit plans because, once the money has been placed in the fund, only a small portion can be recovered all at once through a reversion.[2]

19.7 Summary

- The primary reasons that employers offer retirement plans are to reduce taxes for employees and to improve labor productivity.

- With a defined contribution plan, the employer and usually the employee contribute to a fund, according to a defined schedule (e.g., 5 percent of salary). These contributions are invested on behalf of the employee, and the employee receives retirement benefits equal to the accumulated value of all contributions and the associated investment earnings. Thus, employees bear most of the investment risk in defined contribution plans.

- With a defined benefit plan, an employer promises employees a benefit during retirement that is defined by a formula. The employer (and sometimes the employees) contributes to a fund, and the defined benefits are paid from the assets in the fund. If the assets have a lower than expected return, then the employer has to make additional contributions to pay the promised benefits. Consequently, the employer bears most of the investment risk associated with pension assets.

- Qualified retirement plans satisfy the regulations necessary to receive preferential tax treatment. In a qualified plan, contributions and earnings on the pension assets are tax deferred to the employee. The combination of tax deferral of contributions and tax deferral of investment earnings implies that employees essentially earn the before-tax rate of return on money contributed to a qualified plan. The returns that can be earned by saving for

retirement through a qualified plan can materially exceed those that can be earned outside of a qualified plan.

- Often the benefit formula in a defined benefit plan is structured so that benefits are strongly backend loaded. The backend loading of benefits implies that employees can suffer large losses in the value of their retirement benefits if they leave the firm or if the firm terminates the plan prior to retirement. Consequently, the backend loading discourages turnover, which provides greater incentives for employers to make investments in training employees and provides employees with incentives to put forth greater effort.

- Section 401(k) plans have grown dramatically in the past two decades. These plans are defined contribution plans that allow employees to make discretionary tax-deferred contributions subject to some limitations. Employers often match employee contributions.

- Individual retirement accounts (IRAs) allow people who are not participants in employer-sponsored plans to save for retirement and receive the same tax benefits as qualified plans. Participants in employer-sponsored plans also can contribute to IRAs under some circumstances. Annual contributions to IRAs, however, are limited to $2,000. Roth IRAs were introduced in 1998. The tax treatment of Roth IRAs and traditional IRAs differs.

- ERISA, which was introduced in 1974, regulates private pension plans. It imposes participation, vesting, and nondiscrimination

---

[2] In 1987, Congress denied firms the ability to make tax-deductible contributions to plans that have pension assets equal to 150 percent of the accumulated benefit obligation (ABO). Critics of the excise tax and the funding limitations argue that these initiatives could lead to underfunded plans and more claims against the PBGC.

rules that plans must satisfy. It also mandates minimum funding of defined benefit plans.

- Defined benefit plans can be overfunded or underfunded (i.e., the value of pension assets can exceed or fall short of the present value of promised benefits). ERISA established the PBGC to insure the promised benefits of employees who participate in underfunded plans that terminate.

Key Terms

Questions and Problems

1. If saving through a retirement plan allows an individual to reduce tax payments relative to saving outside of a retirement plan, then why would anyone save outside of a retirement plan?

2. Determine the replacement rate in the following scenarios if an employee is enrolled in a defined benefit plan with the following benefit formula: 2.5% × Years of service × Final salary
   (a) Service = 10 years; final salary = $50,000
   (b) Service = 10 years; final salary = $75,000
   (c) Service = 20 years; final salary = $75,000

3. Determine the replacement rate (as a percentage of final salary) for an employee who is enrolled in a defined contribution plan in which the employer annually contributes 10 percent of salary and the before-tax rate of return each year equals 8 percent under each of the scenarios listed below. Assume that the cost of a $100 life annuity at retirement equals $900. That is, by giving an insurance company $900 at retirement, the insurer will give the retiree $100 every year until he or she dies.
   (a) Five years of service; constant salary = $50,000
   (b) Five years of service; salary in years 1–3 equals $50,000; salary in years 4–5 equals $75,000

4. Suppose that Ken is enrolled in a defined contribution plan in which the employer contributes 10 percent of his salary each year. Ken is earning $60,000 this year and his tax rate is 30 percent (which is not expected to change). Assume that the before-tax rate of return is 8 percent.
   (a) What is the additional amount of funds that Ken will have when he reaches

retirement in 10 years as a result of this year's service?

(b) Suppose that Ken's employer is planning to stop contributing to the defined contribution plan. Assume that Ken would like to keep his retirement funds the same as they would have been with the defined contribution plan. If Ken's only opportunity to save for retirement is in a nonqualified savings plan (no tax benefits), how much would Ken need to receive in additional salary (which he would then save) to achieve his objective?

5. What is the accumulated value of a $1,000 contribution to a qualified defined contribution plan under each of the circumstances described in the table below?

Tax Rate	Before-tax Rate of Return	Investment Period
10%	10%	5 years
30	10	5 years
30	5	5 years
30	5	10 years

Suppose instead that the $1,000 is paid to an employee who then invests the funds in a nonqualified account. What is the accumulated value under each of the circumstances in the table? Compare the results.

6. A complicating feature of the tax code is that interest and dividends are taxed at a higher rate than capital gains for individuals. A lower capital gains tax rate reduces the desirability of investing in assets with high expected capital gains within a tax-deferred account. The reason is that in a tax-deferred account investment earnings are taxed at the ordinary income tax rate even if some of the earnings are from capital gains. Thus, when deciding to save through an account with tax-deferred earnings, one must compare the advantage of deferring tax versus the disadvantage of potentially paying a higher tax rate on some of the earnings. To illustrate, suppose that Travis is going to retire in 10 years, the annual before-tax rate of return is 10 percent, one-half of this return is from capital gains, his income tax rate is 30 percent, and his capital gains tax rate is 20 percent. Will Travis have more money at retirement by saving $1,000 of before-tax wages in a qualified account or will he have more money by saving in an account with no tax benefits?

7. Would an employee want to invest his or her defined contribution plan funds in municipal bonds? Explain.

8. Describe how the tax advantages of qualified employer-sponsored retirement plans would change under each of the following conditions:
(a) The employee is expected to have a lower tax rate during retirement than while working.
(b) The employer is expected to have a higher tax rate in the future than currently.

9. Predict some of the likely consequences from Congress passing a law requiring that all defined benefit plans be fully portable (i.e., when an employee switches employers, the new employer will have to provide a pension based on service with prior employers).

References

Allen, Everett; Joseph Melone; Jerry Rosenbloom; and Jack VanDerhei. *Pension Planning.* 8th ed. Burr Ridge, IL: McGraw-Hill Professional Book Group, 1997. (*Comprehensive discussion of the institutional characteristics of retirement plans.*)

Ippolito, Richard. *Pensions, Economics, and Public*

Policy. Homewood, IL: Pension Research Council, 1986. (*Analyzes public policy issues related to pensions.*)

Ippolito, Richard. *The Economics of Pension Insurance.* Homewood, IL: Pension Research Council, 1989. (*Examines the economic reasons for having government insurance of private pensions and the economic effects of PBGC insurance.*)

Ippolito, Richard. *An Economic Appraisal of Pension Tax Policy in the United States.* Homewood, IL: Pension Research Council, 1990. (*Examines US tax policy toward pensions.*)

Ippolito, Richard. *Pension Plans and Employee Performance.* Chicago: The University of Chicago Press, 1997. (*Focuses on the incentive effects of pensions—especially defined contribution plans.*)

Answers to Concept Checks

1. The corporation sponsors a defined benefit plan.

2. (*a*) would provide a higher retirement income than (*b*).
   (*a*) would provide a higher retirement income than (*c*).
   (*b*) would provide the same retirement income as (*c*).

Social Security

Chapter Objectives

- Describe social security retirement, survivor, and disability benefits and the financing of these benefits.
- Explain the major factors that determine the implicit rate of return on contributions to pay-as-you-go retirement programs, such as social security.
- Discuss possible rationales for the social security retirement program versus alternatives to social security and proposed modifications to the social security retirement program.
- Describe the social security Medicare program and its financing.

20.1 Overview of Social Security

The US social security program, which was first enacted in 1935, is known more formally as the **Old-Age, Survivors, Disability, and Health Insurance (OASDHI)** program. This giant federal program has two broad components: (1) the **Old-Age, Survivors, and Disability Insurance (OASDI)** program, which provides monthly retirement benefits, benefits to dependents of deceased workers, and disability benefits; and (2) the federal **Medicare** program, which provides medical insurance to retirees and nonretirees aged 65 and over and to certain disabled persons under age 65. Coverage under OASDI is work-related: People become eligible for coverage by working and paying social security payroll tax. Coverage is compulsory for most workers. Primary exceptions include federal government employees hired before 1984 and some state and local government employees covered by alternative programs. Medicare coverage also is compulsory for almost all workers.

The social security program is a social insurance program that provides a floor of protection that many workers supplement with private pensions, savings, and insurance coverage. As you will learn in this chapter, social security has some features that are similar to private pensions and insurance arrangements and some features that are not. Similar to private pensions and insurance, the program is (1) largely self-supporting, in that OASDI benefits are largely financed through OASDI payroll taxes; (2) the amount of OASDI benefits payable to a worker increases with the amount of payroll taxes paid by the worker and by the employer on the worker's behalf; and (3) the payment of benefits is based on specified events (e.g., retirement, death, and disability) and is not conditional on meeting a means test (i.e., demonstrating financial need).

The absence of a means test distinguishes the OASDI program from pure welfare programs. Unlike private pensions and insurance, however, OASDI benefit formulas provide comparatively higher benefits in relation to taxes paid for lower paid workers than for higher paid workers. In addition, earned (accrued) benefits are not funded in advance. Instead, current benefits for retirees and other beneficiaries are paid largely from payroll taxes on current workers on a "pay-as-you-go" basis.

In 1997, nearly 44 million Americans were receiving monthly OASDI benefit payments totaling $362 billion, with an average monthly benefit of approximately $690. The Medicare program had total expenditures of $214 billion.[1] OASDHI expenditures represented approximately 20 percent of total expenditures by the federal government, exceeding any other program, including national defense. OASDHI payroll taxes represented about 25 percent of total tax revenues.

20.2 Old-Age, Survivors, and Disability Insurance (OASDI) Benefits

Eligibility

Workers and specified dependents become eligible to receive OASDI benefits by paying compulsory OASDI payroll taxes (which are described in detail in section 20.3). The types of coverage for which a worker is eligible depend on the amount of wages that have been earned and the length of time that the worker has been in the work force. The unit of measurement for determining coverage is known as a *quarter of coverage*. In 1998, for example, a worker would be credited with one quarter of coverage for each $700 in annual earnings (up to a maximum of four per year). The amount of earnings required for a quarter of coverage is increased each year to reflect growth in national average wages. Eligibility for specific benefits depends on the number of quarters of coverage.

---

[1] Information on expenditures and most other statistics reported in this chapter were obtained from the *1998 Annual Report of the Board of Trustees of the Federal Old-Age and Survivors Insurance and Disability Trust Funds* and *Status of the Social Security and Medicare Programs—A Summary of the 1998 Annual Reports,* Social Security and Medicare Boards of Trustees, Washington, DC, April 1998.

TABLE 20–1   **Summary of Old-Age, Survivor, and Disability Insurance (OASDI) Benefits**

Type of Benefit	Benefit Payable	Cessation of Benefits	Required Insured Status	Amount of Benefit
Retirement	Retired worker aged 62 or older	Death	Fully insured	100% of PIA at age 65
	Spouse aged 62 or older (or divorced spouse if married at least 10 years)	Death (or divorce if married less than 10 years)	Fully insured	50% of worker's PIA at age 65 (or 100% of working spouse's own PIA, if greater)
	Spouse under age 62 with dependent child under age 16 or disabled child	Nondisabled dependent child reaches age 16	Fully insured	50% of worker's PIA
	Unmarried dependent children	Age 18 (19 if full-time elementary or high school student; no age limit if disabled before age 22)	Fully insured	50% of worker's PIA
Survivors	Spouse under age 60 with dependent child under age 16 or disabled child	Age 60 or nondisabled child reaches age 16	Fully or currently insured	75% of worker's PIA
	Spouse aged 60 or older (or divorced spouse if married at least 10 years)	Death	Fully insured	100% of PIA at age 65
	Disabled spouse aged 50–59	Age 60 or cessation of disability	Fully insured	71.5% of worker's PIA
	Unmarried dependent children	Age 18 (19 if full-time elementary or high school student; no age limit if disabled before age 22)	Fully or currently insured	75% of worker's PIA
	Deceased worker with dependent parents aged 62 and older	Death; remarriage subject to certain limitations	Fully insured	82.5% of worker's PIA at age 62 (150% total for two parents)
Disability	Disabled worker	Death, cessation of disability, or age 65 (when retirement benefits begin)	Disability insured	100% of worker's PIA
	Dependents (similar categories to retirement benefits)	Limits generally similar to retirement benefits	Disability insured	Similar to retirement benefits

Note: PIA equals primary insurance amount. Maximum benefits payable to a family generally range from 150–180 percent of the eligible worker's PIA. Normal retirement age is scheduled to gradually increase from age 65 to age 67 for people that reach age 62 during the period 2000 to 2022. Retirement benefits are adjusted downward for retirement prior to normal retirement age and adjusted upward for retirement after normal retirement age.

Types of OASDI Benefits

Retirement Benefits.   Table 20–1 summarizes the major types of OASDI benefits. Workers with either 40 quarters of coverage or an average of at least 1 quarter of coverage per year from age 21 until age 62 or the age of death or disability (whichever comes first) are said to be *fully insured* and qualify for monthly

retirement benefits (which sometimes are called old-age benefits, after the program's name). Retirement benefits represented two-thirds of total OASDI benefits paid in 1997.

Covered workers become eligible to receive retirement benefits at age 62. The *normal retirement age* for workers that reach age 62 before the year 2000 is 65. The normal retirement age then will gradually increase until it reaches a maximum of 67 for workers that reach age 62 in the year 2022 or later. Workers that retire and request benefits prior to the normal retirement age receive reduced benefits; workers that delay retirement receive higher benefits. Retirement benefits also are payable to eligible dependents, such as spouses and dependent children (see Table 20–1).

Survivor Benefits.   Eligible beneficiaries of fully insured workers who die prior to retirement age receive monthly **survivor benefits.** These survivor benefits represented 20 percent of total OASDI benefits paid in 1997. For workers who are fully insured at the time of death, monthly benefits are payable to spouses with dependent children, dependent children, and spouses age 60 and above (or age 50 and above if the spouse is disabled) without dependent children. A deceased worker's spouse and dependent children also qualify for survivor benefits if the worker is *currently insured,* which requires the worker to have had at least 6 quarters of coverage during the 13 quarters ending in death (or, if earlier, the quarter of any disability or when the person reached age 62). A single, lump sum death benefit of $255 also is paid when a fully or currently insured worker dies.

An important limitation on survivor benefits is that a spouse's benefit will cease when the youngest child reaches age 16 unless the spouse has reached age 60 (age 50 if disabled). Thus, if a covered male worker dies and has a 30-year-old wife and a 4-year-old child at the time of death, the spouse's benefit would cease when the wife reaches age 42 (the child reaches age 16). The child's benefit would continue until age 18 (age 19 if the child is still in high school). The wife again would qualify for benefits at age 60 (age 50 if disabled at the time of the worker's death or within seven years of the worker's death). The resulting gap in survivor benefits for many spouses is known as the social security blackout period.

Disability Benefits.   Workers who are fully insured with at least 20 quarters of coverage during the 40 quarters ending with the onset of disability are said to be *disability insured* and qualify for monthly **disability benefits;** less restrictive eligibility rules apply to younger workers. Disability benefits represented 13 percent of total OASDI benefits paid in 1997. Benefits are paid to disabled workers and dependents, including dependent children and the worker's spouse if there are dependent children.

In addition to meeting the quarters of coverage requirement to qualify for disability benefits, workers must meet the definition of disability. The worker must have "a mental or physical impairment that prevents the worker from engaging in any substantial gainful employment," and the disability must be expected to last for at least 12 months or result in death. This definition of disability is more stringent than the definition found in many individual and group disability plans. A five-month waiting period is required following the onset of disability before benefits are paid.

OASDI Benefit Amounts

Primary Insurance Amount.   The social security retirement program is a special form of a defined benefit retirement plan (see Chapter 19). The basic monthly benefit payable to a worker who retires at normal retirement age is known as the **primary insurance amount (PIA),** which depends on the worker's earnings history. As shown in Table 20–1, survivor and disability benefits also depend on the worker's PIA, and benefits payable to eligible dependents are expressed as a percent of the worker's PIA.[2] In addition, the total of all benefits payable to a worker and eligible dependents is subject to a family maximum that generally varies from 150 to 180 percent of an eligible worker's PIA.

A retired worker's PIA is calculated in two steps. (An analogous procedure is used for survivor and disability benefits.) In the first step, the worker's **average indexed monthly earnings (AIME)** is calculated. While the precise procedure is complicated, the basic idea is to first adjust or index the retired worker's annual earnings that were subject to OASDI tax (see below) up through the second year prior to age 62 (the index year) for growth in national average wages since the time the wages were earned. (The second year prior to death or disability is used for survivor and disability benefits.) For example, if the worker became 62 in 1994, his or her annual wages earned in 1980 would be multiplied by the ratio of average annual wages in 1992 to average annual wages in 1980. The highest 35 years of indexed wages and any wages earned following the index year are then summed and divided by the number of months during this period to produce the AIME.[3]

In the second step, the worker's PIA is obtained by applying a formula to the worker's AIME. In 1998, the PIA would equal: (1) 0.9 times the first $477 of AIME; (2) 0.32 times the amount of AIME, if any, between $477 and $2,875; and (3) 0.15 times the amount of AIME, if any, in excess of $2,875. For example, the PIA for a worker with an AIME of $3,000 would be

$$[0.9 \times \$477 + 0.32 \times (\$2,875 - \$477) + 0.15 \times (\$3,000 - \$2,875)] = \$1,215.41$$

The values $477 and $2,875, which are known as "bend points," increase each year in conjunction with growth in national average wages.

Figure 20–1 illustrates how the PIA varies as a function of a worker's AIME. As earnings increase, so does the PIA. The maximum PIA ($1,344 in 1998) is

---

[2] Note that while the benefit payable to a 65-year-old spouse on behalf of a retired worker equals 50 percent of the worker's PIA, a spouse who also worked and is fully insured is entitled to 100 percent of his or her own PIA at age 65 if it exceeds 50 percent of the spouse's PIA.

[3] Alternative rules for choosing the number of years are used for workers that became 62 prior to 1991.

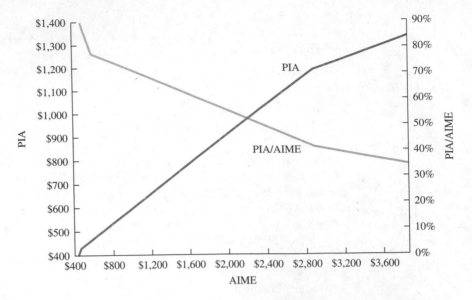

achieved by workers who earned at least the maximum amount of earnings subject to OASDI taxes each year during the earnings measurement period. However, given the bend points in the formula, the increase in the PIA as the AIME increases is not linear up to this maximum. Instead, the PIA formula gives greater weight to lower earnings than higher earnings.

Figure 20–1 also shows the ratio of the PIA to a worker's AIME. This ratio provides one measure of the OASDI earnings replacement rate (i.e., the extent to which OASDI benefits replace a worker's prior earnings). Note that the greater weighting of lower wages produces a replacement rate that declines as wages increase. Another method of calculating the replacement rate is to divide a worker's PIA by the worker's average monthly earnings in the year immediately before retirement (or the date at which other benefits begin). Table 20–2 shows replacement rates relative to earnings in the year before retirement for workers with several different levels of preretirement wages (assuming that each worker's wages grew by the national growth rate in average taxable wages each year prior to retirement).

Cost-of-living Adjustment.   Monthly OASDI benefits are subject to a yearly **automatic cost-of-living adjustment (COLA)** based on the percentage change in the consumer price index (CPI). Thus, these benefits are protected against reductions in purchasing power due to general price inflation.

During the mid-1990s it often was argued that indexing social security benefits to the CPI produced an increase in real benefit levels for the typical retiree and that correcting the price index used to adjust benefits would reduce future expenditures substantially. The reason that the CPI adjustment might overstate inflation for many beneficiaries is that retirees on average purchase a "basket of goods" characterized by lower inflation than reflected in the overall CPI. A num-

TABLE 20–2   Old-Age Benefits and Replacement Rates Compared to
Earnings in Prior Year for Workers Retiring at Age 65 in 1998

Preretirement Earnings Level	1997 Annual Earnings	1998 Annual Benefits	1998 Benefits/ 1997 Earnings
Low earnings (45% of national average)	$12,161	$ 6,824	56.1%
Average earnings	27,026	11,270	41.7
High earnings (160% of national average)	43,268	14,538	33.6
Maximum earnings (earned maximum taxable wage base or more each year)	65,400	16,124	24.7

Source: Benefits and replacement rates obtained from *1998 Annual Report of the Board of Trustees of the Federal OASDI Trust Fund,* Table III.B5. Preretirement earnings are assumed to grow by the annual growth rate in national average taxable earnings. We calculated 1997 earnings for low, average, and high earnings categories by dividing the reported annual benefit by the replacement rate.

ber of technical corrections to the CPI formula appear to have reduced concern with this issue, at least for the time being.

Earnings Test.   As noted earlier, social security benefits are not subject to a **means test;** that is, people do not have to show that they have little or no income/ wealth from any source to qualify for benefits. Instead, benefits are payable for specified contingencies (retirement, disability, or death of a covered worker). Social security retirement benefits, however, are subject to an **earnings test:** "Retirees" under age 70 who elect to receive benefits have their benefits reduced if they receive wages above specified maximums (which are adjusted annually based on growth in national average earnings). In 1998, for example, persons aged 65 through 69 would have their retirement benefits reduced by $1 for each $3 in annual earnings above $14,500 (producing a 33 percent implicit tax rate on wages above this amount). Beneficiaries under age 65 would have benefits reduced by $1 for each $2 in annual earnings above $9,120 in 1998 (producing a 50 percent implicit tax rate).[4] The earnings test does not apply to retirees aged 70 and above. The distinction between a means test and the social security earnings test is not a distinction without a difference. In contrast to a means test, the earnings test does not apply to nonwage/salary income, such as investment income and payments from private pension plans.

The earnings test produces a nontrivial reduction in total benefits paid to beneficiaries under age 70, thus reducing the cost of the retirement program. On the other hand, the earnings test creates a significant disincentive to work for beneficiaries less than age 70. As noted above, for example, a 65–69-year-old person

---

[4] Special rules apply in both cases for the first year of retirement. Excess earnings of the retired worker can offset other family members' benefits, but any excess earnings of these other family members only affect their own benefits.

who is receiving benefits would in effect face a 33 percent tax rate in the form of lost retirement benefits for excess earnings above the exempt amount—in addition to applicable federal, state, and local income taxes, as well as social security payroll taxes.

Income Taxation of Benefits.   OASDI benefits for higher income recipients became subject to federal income tax in 1984. While the details are complicated, 50 percent of social security benefits is taxable as income once the sum of adjusted gross income, tax-exempt interest, and one-half of annual social security benefits exceeds specified thresholds ($25,000 for individual returns or $32,000 for joint returns; these thresholds are not indexed to wage growth or inflation). Up to 85 percent of benefits is taxable for persons with total income that exceeds higher thresholds ($34,000 for individual returns or $44,000 for joint returns). The income taxes on benefits to higher income beneficiaries, which are used to help finance benefit payments, tilt after-tax benefits even more toward social adequacy versus individual equity.[5]

20.3 OASDI Financing

OASDI and HI Payroll Tax

With the exception of the use of income taxes on OASDI benefits paid by higher income beneficiaries and interest income on assets in the OASDI trust funds, OASDI benefits are financed almost exclusively from **payroll taxes.** (These taxes are known more formally as "Federal Insurance Contribution Act" taxes and usually are shown as "FICA" on your pay stub.) Both the employer and the employee pay an OASDI tax rate of 6.2 percent on the employee's annual wages up to a specified **maximum taxable wage base.** The maximum taxable wage base, which equaled $68,400 in 1998, increases each year according to growth in national average wages.

In addition to the OASDI tax, both the employee and the employer pay a tax for Medicare Part A Hospital Insurance (see section 20.7) equal to 1.45 percent of all wages; there is no maximum wage base. Thus, the combined OASDHI tax rate payable by both the employee and employer on wages up to the maximum taxable wage base is 7.65 percent (6.2 percent for OASDI plus 1.45 percent for HI). This tax rate has increased substantially since the inception of social security (see Figure 20–2).[6]

---

[5] Although taxing benefits annoys many higher income beneficiaries, the receipt of benefits substantially in excess of contributions by many higher income retirees that retired prior to the early 1990s (see below) annoys many "baby boomers" who pay higher social security taxes to support these benefits.

[6] Self-employed persons pay OASDI taxes equal to 12.4 percent of wages up to the maximum taxable wage base. This rate equals the combined employer-employee rate (2×0.062). Similarly, they pay 2.9 percent (2×0.145) of all wages to finance Medicare Part A. Self-employed persons are allowed to deduct one-half of their OASDHI taxes from their income subject to federal income tax, which places the income tax treatment on a par with employees who cannot deduct their share of payroll taxes but are not taxed on the employer's share (see below).

FIGURE 20–2

History of social security payroll tax rates

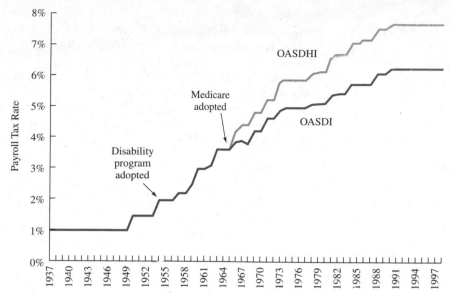

Source: Data obtained from *1998 Annual Report of the Board of Trustees of the Federal OASDI Trust Funds,* Table II.B1.

To illustrate the amount of OASDHI taxes paid, an employee making $30,000 in 1998 would pay $2,295 [$30,000 × (0.062 + 0.0145)]. The employer also would pay this amount, producing a total tax of $4,590. An employee with wages of $100,000 in 1998 would pay $5,690.80, which equals 0.0765 (the combined OASDHI rate, 0.062 + 0.0145) times the maximum taxable wage base of $68,400, plus 0.0145 (the Medicare Part A rate) times $31,600 (the excess of wages over $68,400). The employer would match this amount, producing a total tax of $11,381.60. The employee earning $30,000 effectively pays a 15.3 payroll tax, and the employee earning $100,000 effectively pays an 11.4 percent payroll tax. Thus, total social security taxes effectively increase at a decreasing rate, just as social security benefits increase at a decreasing rate as wages increase. Whether social security is on average a progressive system (i.e., a system that transfers wealth from higher income persons to lower income persons) is not immediately obvious, but studies examining this issue generally conclude that the system is progressive (at least looking toward the future; see below).

Payroll taxes for social security significantly decrease the after-tax income of workers. Indeed, almost half of all employees pay more in social security taxes (combining employer and employee payments) than in income taxes. At least part of the employer's share of social security taxes generally is believed to be borne largely by workers in the form of lower wages. That is, long-run wages are lower by an amount that reflects a significant proportion of the employer tax. Moreover, at least part of any payroll tax paid by employers that is not offset by lower wages might be expected over time to produce higher prices for goods and services, as opposed to lower business profits (returns to capital).

When viewed as an employee benefit, the income tax treatment of social security payroll taxes is less favorable than the treatment of contributions to qualified retirement plans (discussed in the last chapter). Like employer contributions to a qualified retirement plan, the amount of OASDHI tax paid by the employer is not taxable as income to the employee. However, the worker's share of total OASDHI taxes is not deductible from his or her income subject to federal and state income taxes. Thus, workers' OASDHI taxes come out of after-tax wages, in contrast to tax-deductible employee contributions to a qualified retirement plan. On the other hand, only part of social security benefits is taxable as income to beneficiaries, and then only for higher income beneficiaries; whereas all benefits received from qualified plans are taxable as income.[7]

Concept Check

1. (a) How much OASDI tax and HI tax would be paid by an employee with wages of $20,000 in 1997? By an employee with wages of $80,000? (b) What would the employer pay in each case?

Pay-as-you-go Financing

As is true for social insurance programs in most western developed countries, social security benefits are financed using what is commonly called **pay-as-you-go financing.** In contrast to contributions to private pensions and individual deferred annuities, payroll taxes are not invested when collected to fund the payment of accrued benefits (i.e., benefits earned to date, see Chapter 19) for participants in the program. Instead, payroll taxes on current wages are largely used to pay benefits to current beneficiaries. Any short-term excess of current taxes over expenditures is credited to social security trust funds. (There are separate funds for old-age/survivor benefits, disability insurance, and the hospital insurance program.)

In 1983 Congress enacted scheduled increases in OASDI payroll tax rates to build a temporary surplus to help finance increased retirement benefit costs after the turn of the century. As a result of these tax rate increases and economic growth, the OASDI trust funds had assets of $656 billion at year-end 1997, which represented 171 percent of benefits projected for 1998. Despite the size of the trust funds, however, benefits accrued to date are largely unfunded. As we explain more fully below, combined OASDI trust funds are expected to grow for another 15 years or so and then be exhausted rapidly during the third decade of the next century.

Social security "surpluses" (excesses of current tax revenues over benefit payments) are used to purchase special issue, US government bonds. The interest earned is credited to the trust funds. The purchase of government securities with any positive cash flow from social security reduces the amount that the federal government otherwise would have to borrow to finance any nonsocial security expenditures in excess of general tax revenues (assuming that positive cash flow

---

[7] Note also that because the cost of providing employees with employee benefits as opposed to higher cash benefits is not subject to social security payroll tax, this increases the incentive for employees to take compensation in the form of employee benefits (see Chapter 18).

from social security does not encourage Congress to spend more or discourage cuts in spending for other programs). You should note that this process is largely equivalent to the US Treasury spending positive social security cash flow on other government programs and issuing an IOU with interest to the social security trust funds.

Projected OASDI Deficits

Each year the board of trustees of the Social Security administration prepares 75-year projections of program expenditures, tax revenues, and trust fund balances under a variety of assumptions. Based on the "intermediate" assumptions concerning wage and employment growth, the OASDI program faces a substantial long-term deficit (see Figure 20–3). Annual payroll taxes are projected to exceed expenditures until approximately 2015 but then projected expenditures increase above projected tax revenues. The OASDI trust funds will begin to decline once credited interest on securities held is insufficient to cover the shortfall. Under these assumptions, the OASDI trust funds are projected to be exhausted around the year 2032. The total projected funding deficit over 75 years represents 2.19 percent of projected taxable payroll. As we elaborate later on, a variety of changes to the system are being discussed for reducing or eliminating the projected deficit.

Long-range social security projections are subject to considerable error. However, assuming that these projections are reasonably accurate (in contrast to some earlier projections), the question arises as to how this state of affairs came about. The simple answer is that, during the 1960s and 1970s, Congress repeat-

FIGURE 20–3

OASDI projected taxes and benefits as percentages of taxable payroll and projected balance in OASDI trust funds as a percentage of projected annual benefits

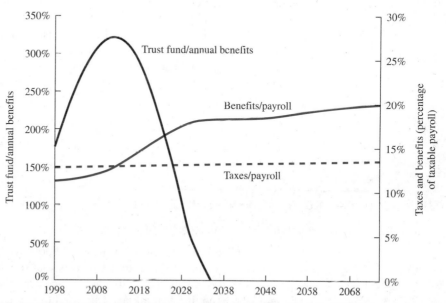

Source: Data obtained from *1998 Annual Report of the Board of Trustees of the Federal OASDI Trust Funds*, Tables II.F13 and II.F20.

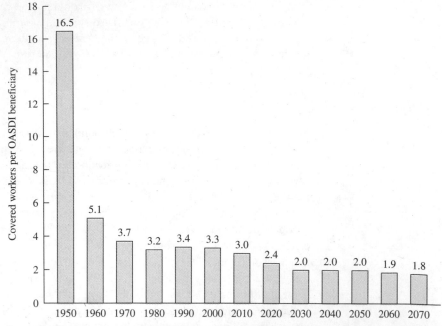

Source: Benefits and replacement rates obtained from *1998 Annual Report of the Board of Trustees of the Federal OASDI Trust Funds,* Table II.F19.

edly expanded the program and increased benefits based on favorable economic and demographic projections that were not realized. While payroll tax rates also increased substantially during this period, low real wage growth during parts of the 1970s and 1980s and unexpected (or at least unprojected) increases in the number of retirees compared to the size of the work force due to declining birth rates have led to the projected deficit. The ratio of workers paying taxes to OASDI beneficiaries is projected (based on the board of trustees' intermediate assumptions) to be 2.0 in the year 2030, compared to the current value of 3.4, and a value of 5.1 in 1960 (see Figure 20–4). Under a pay-as-you-go system, a significant decrease in the ratio of workers to beneficiaries over time means that the tax per worker has to be significantly higher to finance a given level of benefits.

20.4 Understanding Pay-as-you-go Systems

Economic and Demographic Factors Affecting Benefits and Taxes

To help you understand the effects of wage and population (employment) growth on social security financing and the value of social security to workers who pay for the system, it is useful to examine the average benefit per recipient that can be paid in a year assuming that all taxes are used to pay benefits. This assumption highlights the essence of pay-as-you-go systems. If all taxes are used to pay benefits in a given year, the average benefit equals total tax revenues divided by the number of beneficiaries. Total tax revenues equal the product of the (combined employee-employer) payroll tax rate, the average annual taxable wage per worker, and the number of workers. As a result, the average benefit can be expressed as:

Average benefit

= Tax rate × Average taxable wage × Ratio of workers to beneficiaries

This expression makes it clear that, for a given tax rate, the average benefit that can be paid under a pay-as-you-go system increases with the ratio of workers to beneficiaries, which in turn depends largely on population (employment) growth. The average benefit also increases with the level of wages, which depends on productivity growth. Conversely, the payroll tax rate that is needed to pay a given average benefit decreases as wage rates increase and as the ratio of workers to beneficiaries increases, as is seen by rearranging the terms in the above expression as follows:

Tax rate

= Ratio of workers to beneficiaries × Average benefit /Average taxable wage

For 1997, a combined employer-employee payroll tax rate of 11.2 percent was needed to pay OASDI benefits given that the ratio of covered workers to beneficiaries was 3.4. If this ratio had been 5.1 (the 1960 value; see Figure 20–4), a tax rate of only 7.4 percent would have been necessary to pay the same average benefit. If the ratio of covered workers to beneficiaries was 2.0 (as projected for the year 2030), a tax rate of 18.9 percent would be required to pay the same average benefit.

More generally, these expressions for the average benefit and tax rate make it clear that slow wage and population growth will produce either smaller benefits or higher tax rates if a pay-as-you go system is to be self-financing.[8] These expressions also illustrate how the long-range projected deficit for the OASDI program might be substantially reduced or eliminated without changes in benefits or taxes: Real wage growth could increase more rapidly than projected, or people, including you and your classmates, could surprise the social security forecasters by having more children. This increased birth rate would increase the number of workers compared to the number of retirees (and thus compared to the total number of beneficiaries).

Historical and Projected Implicit Rates of Return with Pay-as-you-go Financing

Has the social security program been a "good deal" for retirees to date? Will it provide a good deal to future retirees? While a worker's payroll taxes are not in-

---

[8] Increases in the maximum taxable wage base, which increase the average taxable wage, also permit higher benefits and/or a lower payroll tax rate for a given level of wages and ratio of workers to beneficiaries.

vested to fund his or her future benefits, an **implicit rate of return on payroll taxes** paid by a worker can nonetheless be calculated. While the details of the calculation generally are complicated, the basic idea is to solve for the rate of return that would be needed *if the tax payments had been (or were to be) invested* in order to accumulate a fund equal to the present value of the worker's expected monthly benefits at retirement. A similar approach is to compare the present value of expected benefits at retirement to the accumulated value of assets that could have been generated by investing payroll taxes in specified securities, such as government bonds. If the present value of expected benefits exceeds (is less than) the accumulated value of taxes, then the implicit rate of return from social security exceeds (is less than) the average return that could have been earned if the payroll taxes for the worker had been invested in the specified securities.

Historical Returns.   Analyses of implicit returns under the social security retirement program indicate that the program was attractive for most workers that retired up until the early 1990s. Implicit returns were especially high for persons that retired prior to the 1980s due to legislated benefit increases prior to that time and because earlier retirees were awarded significant benefits even though they had paid taxes during only a fraction of their working years.[9] Implicit rates of return were very high (and highest) for lower paid workers due to the weighted benefit formula, but they also were very good for higher paid workers. In addition, the absolute increase in wealth from participating in the program (which can be measured as the difference between the present value of a worker's expected social security benefits at retirement and the accumulated value of the worker's taxes at reasonable interest rate assumptions) was larger for higher paid workers than for lower paid workers.

Future Returns.   As suggested by our earlier discussion of the projected long-range OASDI deficit, the days of attractive implicit returns on payroll taxes are over for many if not most workers. Going forward, projections indicate comparatively low implicit returns on average and especially low and even negative implicit returns for higher paid workers, at least if both employee and employer taxes are considered. As a result, if social security were not compulsory for young and middle-aged workers, many of these workers would withdraw from the program. These withdrawals would greatly reduce the ability of the program to subsidize returns to lower paid workers.

We discussed earlier how wage growth and the ratio of workers to retirees, which depends on population growth, primarily determine the level of benefits that can be paid at a given payroll tax rate. The same framework can be used to analyze the implicit rate of return on payroll taxes for the average worker under a mature, pay-as-you-go system (i.e., a system with stable payroll tax rates and where all retirees have paid taxes over their entire work life). Under a mature,

---

[9] An analogous result occurs when new private defined pension benefit plans are created that give significant credits to workers for service prior to plan adoption.

pay-as-you-go system, the implicit rate of return depends primarily on wage and population (employment) growth. Intuitively, larger wage growth over time means that retired workers who paid taxes when wages were lower can be paid higher benefits from higher national wage levels during retirement, thus increasing their implicit returns. Higher population growth means that relatively more workers can be taxed to provide benefits to retired workers, again increasing the implicit rate of return.

With constant growth rates in wages and population and a number of other simplifying assumptions, it can be shown that *the long-run implicit rate of return on payroll taxes under a mature, pay-as-you-go retirement program equals the growth rate in wages plus the growth rate in population.* Thus, for example, if the (long-run) annual growth rate in wages is 4 percent and the population growth rate is 1 percent, the long-run implicit return would be 5 percent. If the population growth rate were 3 percent instead of 1 percent, the implicit return would be 7 percent. (The appendix to this chapter develops this relationship between implicit returns, wage growth, and population growth for a pay-as-you-go retirement program under simple assumptions.) Similarly, the long-run real (after-inflation) implicit rate of return, as opposed to the nominal return, on payroll taxes with a pay-as-you-go program depends on the real (after-inflation) growth rate in wages and the population growth rate. Under simplifying assumptions, *the long-run implicit real rate of return on payroll taxes equals the real growth rate in wages plus the population growth rate.*

If the population growth rate is small, a real rate of return equal to the growth rate in real wages plus the population growth rate might not be attractive to many workers. Real growth in wages on average equals the growth rate in worker productivity, which generally has been in the 1–2 percent per year range in recent decades. Small population growth rates are the norm in Western developed economies. The current birth rate in the United States, for example, will produce little population growth over the long run. With a productivity growth rate of 2 percent and zero population growth, the long-run implicit real rate of return on payroll taxes would be 2 percent, which is approximately equal to the average real rate of return on riskless government bonds in recent decades.

Whether the rate of return available under a mature pay-as-you-go system compares favorably with long-run returns that would be available on savings is complicated because it depends on factors such as the relationship between real wage growth and the long-run real rate of interest on riskless bonds, the expected return available on risky investments, risk associated with implicit rates of return on social security, and the risk tolerance of investors. However, it is safe to conclude that average implicit real rates of return in the 2–3 percent range are significantly lower than the average real returns that have historically been realized in the past and presumably can be expected in the future on a balanced portfolio of corporate stocks and bonds. As noted above, due to the social adequacy aspect of the benefit formula, higher paid workers can anticipate implicit returns that are lower than this average level and could easily be negative for the highest paid workers.

Illustration. Table 20–3 provides evidence consistent with the preceding discussion of historical and future implicit returns. It compares the present value of expected benefits to the accumulated value of payroll taxes for hypothetical male workers who retire at normal retirement age during various years based on calculations from a 1992 study by Robert Myers and Bruce Schobel. This study compares the present value of expected retirement benefits to the accumulated values of taxes based on numerous assumptions for workers at two different wage levels: (1) workers earning the national average wage each year prior to retirement, and (2) workers earning the maximum wage subject to OASDI tax each year. While the study's results are based on the employee's share of payroll taxes only, we converted these estimates to reflect combined employer-employee taxes.[10]

The results shown in Table 20–3 indicate that prior to 1991 the present value of expected benefits at retirement age exceeded the accumulated value of taxes for both average and maximum earners. The ratio of the present value of expected benefits to accumulated taxes is larger for the average earner than for the maximum earner, which reflects the social adequacy feature of the weighted-benefit formula. The absolute difference between the present value of expected benefits and accumulated taxes prior to 1991, however, is greater for the maximum earner than for the average earner. In other words, the total gain compared to the accumulated value of taxes was higher for higher paid workers. This makes it very difficult to argue that higher paid workers subsidized lower paid workers during the first 50 years of the program.

The results for later years present a different picture. For maximum earners retiring in 1991 and later years, accumulated taxes exceed the present value of expected benefits. The ratio of the present value of expected benefits to accumulated taxes for maximum earners retiring in 2027 is 49 percent. In effect these workers receive no benefit from employer taxes paid on their behalf (recall that employers pay half of the combined tax). For average earners, the accumulated taxes exceed the present value of expected benefits for workers that retire in 2002 and

---

[10] Myers and Schobel note that "conversion from one to the other is a trivial calculation." The specific assumptions used by these authors that provide the basis for Table 20–3 include: (1) workers survive until normal retirement age and then receive benefits; (2) investment returns used to accumulate taxes for years prior to 1991 equal 2.25 percent for 1937–1950, the returns paid on the special-purpose US government bonds acquired by the social security trust funds for 1951–1990, and the projected interest rates (intermediate assumptions) for 1991and later years reported in the *1991 OASDI Trustees Report;* (3) expected retirement benefits are discounted using a 2 percent real interest rate and for mortality using historical and projected postretirement mortality rates for different age cohorts from the *1991 OASDI Trustees Report.* Thus, the present value of expected benefits at retirement reflects the probabilities of survival after reaching age 65, but the accumulated tax estimates assume that the worker survives until retirement. The accumulated tax calculations reflect taxes used to pay survivor benefits, as well as taxes for retirement benefits. While this overstates the accumulated value of taxes needed to pay retirement benefits only, assuming that workers survive until retirement overstates the present value of expected benefits for the typical worker who participates in the program.

**TABLE 20–3   Estimated Present Value of Expected Retirement Benefits
Compared to Accumulated Value of Taxes for Male Workers
That Retire at Normal Retirement Age**

Year of Retirement	Earnings Level	Accumulated Taxes (3)	Present Value of Expected Benefits (4)	Absolute Gain or Loss (4) – (3)	Relative Gain or Loss (4) / (3)
1960	Average	$ 1,974	$ 13,986	$ 12,012	709%
	Maximum	2,756	15,731	12,975	571
1970	Average	7,020	23,376	16,356	333
	Maximum	9,040	26,347	17,307	291
1980	Average	24,502	66,531	42,029	272
	Maximum	34,258	84,400	50,142	246
1991	Average	101,084	117,409	16,325	116
	Maximum	166,722	159,896	–6,826	96
2002	Average	237,232	202,760	–34,472	85
	Maximum	439,554	298,295	–141,259	68
2009	Average	369,762	280,228	–89,534	76
	Maximum	735,118	431,644	–303,474	59
2020	Average	653,034	496,001	–157,033	76
	Maximum	1,481,788	787,309	–694,479	53
2027	Average	889,310	683,981	–205,329	77
	Maximum	2,197,030	1,084,443	–1,112,587	49

Source: Data obtained from Robert Myers and Bruce Schobel, "An Updated Money's-Worth Analysis of Social Security Retirement Benefits," *Transactions* (Society of Actuaries) 44 (1992), pp. 247–70. We adjusted the reported figures to reflect combined employer-employee taxes. Average earner earned the national average wages each year from age 21 until the year prior to retirement; maximum earner earned wages equal to the maximum earnings subject to OASDI taxes.

later years. Although Myers and Schobel do not analyze lower paid workers, the present value of expected benefits presumably would still exceed the accumulated taxes for many workers with less than average earnings.

Based on the findings of this and other studies, there is little doubt that workers who retired up until the late 1980s generally received favorable implicit returns and that average returns will be low in the future and negative for many higher paid workers. Specific calculations, however, must be based on numerous assumptions, and realized results over time for different groups of workers will reflect changes in economic and demographic factors compared to the values projected at any point in time. For example, stronger real growth in wages and higher than projected birth rates will increase implicit returns to all workers.

In addition, specific workers may receive returns much different from the average worker. For example, females generally have higher implicit returns than males due to their longer life expectancy at retirement. (The results of the Myers and Schobel study indicate that the present value of expected retirement benefits for average earner females who retired in 1991 was 141 percent of the accumulated value of combined employer-employee taxes, compared to the

116 percent value for males shown in Table 20–3.) Moreover, all else being equal, married couples with one spouse who does not work outside the home for pay and thus who is not a covered worker are entitled to a retirement benefit equal to 150 percent of the worker's PIA (see Table 20–1). The 50 percent spouse's benefit significantly increases the implicit return on payroll taxes paid for these workers.

Concept Checks

2. Other things being equal and assuming that total taxes equal total benefits, how would each of the following affect the average benefit that can be paid over time to retirees under a pay-as-you-go plan?
   (*a*) An increase in the payroll tax rate.
   (*b*) A decrease in population growth.
   (*c*) A long-run increase in the unemployment rate.
3. Other things being equal, how would each of the following affect the long-run implicit rate of return available with a pay-as-you-go retirement program?
   (*a*) An increase in the birth rate.
   (*b*) A decrease in real productivity growth.
   (*c*) A cure for cancer (assuming no increase in the retirement age).

20.5 Why Have Social Security?

Why have the social security retirement program or, alternatively, should there be some other type of compulsory retirement income program or no program at all? Arguments for government insurance in general often suggest that problems associated with private insurance, such as moral hazard, adverse selection, and correlated losses, limit the amount of private insurance that is sold and sometimes provide a rationale for government insurance. For example, it sometimes is argued that mandatory government insurance can mitigate adverse selection by forcing lower risk persons or businesses to buy coverage or that government insurance possibly might produce economies of scale in administrative costs. A counterargument is that governments generally will not be able to design insurance arrangements that are better able to mitigate these problems than private insurance arrangements. In addition, it often is suggested that government insurance arrangements in practice may have fewer incentives for controlling moral hazard, thus driving up costs, and that political pressure may cause prices for government insurance to be substantially inadequate, at least for some buyers.

With respect to the social security retirement program, the discussion in the previous section suggests that it is difficult to make a compelling case for the program given the low implicit rates of return that are likely to be available in a mature, pay-as-you-go system. Opinions concerning the efficacy of the OASDI program vary widely, even among people that have carefully studied the program. At one end of the spectrum, some observers regard the OASDI program as an ingenious method of providing a floor of inflation-protected income with an appropriate emphasis on social adequacy. At the other extreme, some people regard the program's history as one in which several generations of workers essentially voted themselves large wealth transfers at the expense of future generations— with a significant reduction in both private savings and economic growth as byproducts. Going forward, they regard the program as a sneaky form of redistribution which leads subsidized beneficiaries to believe that they are not the recipients of government handouts financed by taxes on other people.

We obviously will not resolve this debate. We can, however, increase your understanding of the program and help you to develop an informed opinion by discussing three additional aspects of pay-as-you-go systems that affect their attractiveness (or lack thereof) over the long run: (1) the ability to finance automatic cost-of-living adjustments; (2) the possible advantages of a compulsory retirement program with a social adequacy component (i.e., with what basically amounts to cross-subsidies from higher to lower paid workers); and (3) the possible effects of social security on savings, capital formation, and economic growth. While the discussion focuses on retirement benefits, much of what we say also applies to the social security survivor and disability benefit programs.

Self-financing COLAs

One argument for a public, pay-as-you-go retirement plan is that it might provide an efficient, self-financing means of indexing retirement benefits to postretirement inflation. Moreover, private annuity contracts (see Chapter 23) that provide inflation-indexed benefits for a fixed, advance premium are not available. One explanation for the lack of privately provided inflation-indexed benefits is that changes in indexed benefits due to inflation will be very highly correlated across pension plan participants or annuitants. As a result, providing indexed benefits would expose pension plan sponsors and insurance companies to substantial risk that cannot be reduced by selling large numbers of contracts or other types of insurance. The resulting need to hold a large amount of capital to guarantee indexed benefits drives up the cost of providing these contracts and makes them unattractive. Retirees therefore face the risk that unexpected inflation during retirement could significantly erode the purchasing power of any fixed monthly benefits financed through preretirement savings.

A pay-as-you-go mandatory retirement system potentially can solve the correlated risk problem that impedes inflation-linked private benefits. To illustrate, recall that for a given payroll tax rate and ratio of workers to retirees, the average benefit that can be paid from current taxes depends on average wages. As a result, as long as increases in wages on average keep pace with inflation, tax revenues will tend to grow automatically with inflation. As a result, indexing benefits to inflation is essentially self-financing under a pay-as-you-go system. Inflation leads to higher wages and thus taxes, which in turn can be used to pay higher benefits. Thus, a pay-as-you-go program might be desirable given that correlated risk generally prevents inflation-indexed retirement benefits from being offered in the private marketplace.

To be sure, retirees can partially hedge reductions in retirement income purchasing power without a government program by investing retirement funds in assets with returns that are positively correlated with inflation (e.g., by investing in real estate). However, this strategy is imperfect and exposes retirees to significant risk. In 1997 the US Treasury began selling bonds with returns indexed to inflation. Investing retirement savings in these bonds could allow retirees to be protected against inflation, but the expected yields on these bonds are significantly lower than on traditional government bonds (risk reduction is not free). Thus, despite the introduction of inflation-indexed government bonds, one advantage of pay-as-you-go social security benefits is the ability to readily finance inflation-indexed benefits.

Compulsion and Social Adequacy

The decades of high or reasonably attractive average implicit returns under social security are over (absent much higher economic growth and birth rates than are currently projected). The difficult question therefore arises as to whether there is anything inherently desirable about forcing people to participate in a social security retirement program that provides higher implicit returns to workers with low wages and relatively low or negative returns to average and higher paid workers.

Subsidizing Low Wage Workers May Be Inevitable.   In a world without a social security retirement program or alternative government program, many lower paid workers might save little for retirement so that many elderly persons would have very low income without any government program. This outcome probably would not be politically viable for a variety of reasons. For one, workers who fail to save can vote for politicians that support transfer payments. In addition, due to compassion or altruism, many workers who would save for their own retirement may support policies that require them to finance payments to workers who save little or nothing. Some form of income transfer program also might be supported because it would reduce the need for younger people to provide direct support to elderly parents, and because it would reduce possible spillover effects from large numbers of poor, elderly people (e.g., higher crime rates if grandma becomes a burglar).

The adoption of some program that provides some subsidy to people that save little for retirement therefore appears inevitable. Workers who view the social security program as a "bad deal" and who would like to pull out need to recognize that taxes on middle and higher wage workers will likely be used to transfer income to retirees with low preretirement wages with or without social security. One advantage of the compulsory social security retirement program in this regard is that it requires workers to pay something in order to receive subsidized benefits. While payroll taxes are not saved and invested, workers in essence are required to contribute something toward the cost of their benefits.

"Earned" rather than Means-tested Benefits.   There also are several potential advantages of paying "socially adequate" benefits without regard to need (i.e., to not having a means test). The costs of administering a means test are avoided, and any means test will likely involve some evasion (e.g., hiding wealth). Making benefits contingent on a means test also can significantly reduce the incentive for some people to save. Moreover, it sometimes is argued that the absence of a means test and the (admittedly erroneous) belief by many lower paid workers that they have paid the full cost of their benefits enhance self-esteem. Holding income constant, many elderly parents and their working children might be happier if the parents receive social security benefits instead of means-tested benefits or increased support from their children.

Effect on Savings, Capital Formation, and Economic Growth

The effects of social security on savings, capital formation, and economic growth also should be considered when deciding whether it is desirable to have such a system. The effect of social security on aggregate savings has been debated for many years. Recall that pay-as-you-go financing does not produce any significant amount of savings. If the promise of future social security benefits reduces incentives for many workers to save for retirement and aggregate savings therefore decline, less capital will be available for investment, thus raising the cost of capital and reducing investment and economic growth. Downward pressure on savings also may arise because social security payroll taxes reduce disposable income. And, to the extent that payroll taxes increase the cost of labor, social security taxes will reduce employment and aggregate output. Less savings will tend to occur if fewer people work and if people on average work fewer hours.

The extent to which social security reduces savings is uncertain in theory and practice. Some economists argue that because favorable implicit rates of return on taxes throughout most of the program's history have increased the total wealth of covered workers, at least part of this additional wealth probably has been saved. It also has been argued (we are not making this up!) that social security might encourage workers to save money to help their children pay higher payroll taxes in the future. A more important practical issue is how much additional savings would be generated if social security were substantially modified to promote savings. This issue plays an important role in a number of social security reform proposals that we describe briefly in the next section.

20.6 Proposed Changes and Alternatives to Social Security

Policymakers currently are debating a variety of changes or alternatives to the social security retirement program, in large part because projected future deficits very likely will necessitate some action. A number of proposals attempt to eliminate projected deficits without fundamentally altering the system; other proposals would fundamentally alter the system. In general, unless the government re neges on the promise to pay benefits that have been accrued to date by covered workers, the projected OASDI deficits imply that substantially higher taxes of some kind will be needed.[11]

Changes That Would Maintain the Basic Structure of OASDI

Changes in Benefits and Payroll Taxes.   One approach to eliminating the projected OASDI deficit without fundamentally altering the system is to enact benefit reductions and/or payroll tax increases. Proposals for reducing benefits include reducing the cost-of-living adjustment or omitting the adjustment in one or more years, increasing the normal retirement age above currently scheduled amounts, and reducing after-tax benefits by making more benefits taxable as income. Proposals for raising payroll taxes include raising the payroll tax rate and raising or eliminating the limit on the amount of wages subject to OASDI tax. Benefit reductions will cause current and future retirees who have already paid substantial taxes to bear a significant part of the cost of eliminating the deficit. Payroll tax increases will shift more of the cost of the deficits to younger and future workers.

Investing Trust Fund Assets in Common Stocks.   Another proposal would maintain the basic program but require that all or part of the projected excess of tax revenues over expenditures for the next 15 years or so be invested in common stocks. The main rationale would be to achieve higher returns for the OASDI trust fund. Positive social security cash flow probably would be invested in stock index funds to help resolve the thorny issue of which stocks to pick (but an index would have to be specified). Unanswered questions concerning this proposal include its effect on stock prices and on any overall federal deficit if these funds are no longer used to buy government bonds, as well as the possible adverse ramifications if stock returns are significantly lower than expected.

Crediting the Trust Funds with Any Operating Budget Surplus.   It has recently been proposed that any surpluses for the federal operating budget (i.e., from programs other than social security) be credited to the social security trust funds to reduce the social security deficit, as opposed to reducing income taxes or reducing the national debt. It is currently uncertain whether material operating surpluses will arise and, if so, whether they will be credited to social security. However, the use of any surplus of general revenues over general operating costs to shore up the OASDI program would move the system away from its historical self-supporting basis.

---

[11] While estimates vary considerably, the unfunded liability for OASDI benefits accrued by workers to date (including persons currently receiving benefits and current workers that are eligible for future benefits based on payment of taxes to date) has been estimated to exceed $5 trillion.

Changes That Would Modify the Basic Structure of OASDI

Privatization Proposals. Other proposals for dealing with the long-range OASDI deficit would modify the basic structure of the program. Perhaps most important, a number of **privatization proposals** would require workers to invest either part of the current OASDI tax or an additional percentage of wages in tax-deferred accounts similar to individual retirement accounts (see Chapter 19). One approach would offset part of the retirement income from these accounts against promised benefits. An alternative approach would gradually replace the social security retirement program with compulsory individual retirement savings accounts, perhaps with a subsidy for lower income workers. One potential advantage of these approaches is that they might yield higher overall returns to workers than with a purely pay-as-you-go system. A second potential advantage is that they could increase savings and economic growth.

Note that privatization proposals for replacing the pay-as-you-go retirement plan with individual accounts (with or without any subsidy to low wage workers) most likely would not eliminate the need for benefit reductions for current or future retirees or higher taxes on workers unless the government reneges on its promise to pay accrued benefits. In other words, unless the government reneges, partial or full privatization of social security still would likely require many workers to pay significant taxes to pay unfunded benefits in addition to contributing to their individual accounts.

Converting Social Security to Welfare. Another alternative to social security would be a means-tested retirement benefit financed perhaps all or in part with general revenues as opposed to payroll taxes. Retirees with income or wealth lower than specified minimums would eventually receive payments analogous to welfare. Other workers eventually would rely exclusively on private pension plans and other private savings; they would not qualify for benefits. Higher overall taxes on workers still would be needed to pay social security benefits accrued prior to adoption of a means test unless the government reneges on its promise to pay these benefits without a means test.

Rapid adoption and implementation of a means test would produce large negative implicit returns for workers in their 40s, 50s, and 60s who have already paid large amounts in OASDI taxes (although this in part might be offset by their possibly paying lower taxes in the future compared to alternative approaches). As noted previously, means tests also are imperfect, costly to administer, and possibly degrading to recipients.

The welfare approach also would have to address a difficult tradeoff between adequacy of means-tested benefits and incentives for saving. Any level of means-tested benefits deemed reasonably adequate might discourage large numbers of workers from saving anything for retirement, thus increasing the costs of the program, which would have to be borne by taxpayers. This incentive (moral hazard) problem helps explain why most proposals for fundamentally modifying social security involve some form of compulsory savings.

20.7 Medicare

Medicare Benefits

Medicare benefits for specified medical expenses are available to most persons aged 65 and above and to certain disabled people under age 65. There are two main parts of Medicare: (1) Medicare Part A Hospital Insurance and (2) Medicare Part B Supplementary Medical Insurance.

Medicare Part A Hospital Insurance (HI) provides coverage for up to 90 days of inpatient hospitalization for each "spell of illness," subject to a deductible for each spell and co-insurance for the 61st through the 90th days. There also is a lifetime reserve of an additional 60 days. Part A also provides up to 100 days of coverage in a skilled nursing facility, as well as coverage of certain home health care services and hospice care.

Hospitals have been reimbursed under Medicare since the late 1980s according to a schedule of payments for different *diagnostic related groups* (DRGs). Under this system, which is intended to control costs and reduce excessive utilization, hospitals are paid scheduled amounts (which vary by geographic location and whether the hospital is urban or rural) for different ailments (diagnoses), as opposed to being paid for charges on a fee-for-service basis.

Medicare Part B Supplementary Medical Insurance (SMI) pays 80 percent of expenses above a $100 annual deductible for physicians' services, outpatient hospital services, home health care visits not covered by HI coverage, and a wide variety of other medical services. Most prescription drugs are not covered (unless the person is hospitalized). As is discussed further below, a monthly premium is required for SMI coverage. All persons covered by the HI program are covered unless they reject coverage.

Physicians are reimbursed under the SMI program based on a fee scale (known as the *resource-based relative-value scale*), as opposed to charges. The fee scale is designed to reflect the time, skill, and intensity of the service provided, as well as geographical differences. Physicians that accept "assignment" of Medicare claims agree to accept these fees as payment in full. They bill Medicare directly for fees above the annual deductible and 20 percent co-insurance paid by the patient. Medicare pays 95 percent of the fee schedule for services provided by physicians who do not accept assignment of claims, and the maximum amounts that these physicians can charge their patients is limited. The patient pays the physician and then is reimbursed by Medicare subject to the annual deductible and co-insurance. In an effort to control rapidly rising Medicare costs (see below), the program has been modified in recent years to encourage Medicare beneficiaries to be covered by a health maintenance organization (HMO) instead of the traditional program.

Medicare Financing

Recall from Section 20.3 that the Medicare HI program is financed with a payroll tax equal to 1.45 percent of all wages. This amount is paid by both the employee and the employer (self-employed workers pay 2.9 percent). Like OASDI, the HI program faces significant projected deficits. Despite enactment of legislation in 1997 to control cost growth, the HI Trust Fund is projected to be depleted by the year 2008. At year-end 1997, the long-range (75-year) projected deficit was 2.1 percent of payroll based on the Medicare Board of Trustees' intermediate assumptions.

The SMI program is not financed by payroll taxes. Beneficiaries pay monthly premiums that are modified each year to cover approximately 25 percent of the total cost of the program. The monthly premium in 1998 was $43.80. The remaining 75 percent of costs for the SMI program is financed in large part with general Treasury revenues (i.e., individual and corporate income taxes and so on) and in small part by interest on assets in the SMI Trust Fund.

Like the HI program, the amount of general revenue financing needed for SMI coverage is projected to continue to grow rapidly in the future, thus putting upward pressure on any federal budget deficit. Proposals for addressing this problem include measures to help control medical expenditures, such as more managed care, and increasing premiums to pay a larger share of SMI costs, perhaps by raising premiums for higher income retirees.

Private Coverage to Supplement Medicare

Medicare covers about half of all medical expenses for covered persons due to deductibles, co-insurance, and other limitations on coverage. Many persons purchase private medical insurance to supplement Medicare, which commonly is known as "medigap" coverage. To reduce the likelihood that some financially unsophisticated, elderly people will be duped by unscrupulous insurers and agents (e.g., in extreme cases by selling them multiple high-priced, low-benefit policies), most states have legislation providing some standardization of medigap coverage and regulating the marketing of these policies. Federal legislation concerning the coverage and marketing of medigap policies applies absent state legislation.

20.8 Summary

- The federal Old-Age Survivors, Disability, and Health Insurance (OASDHI) program provides monthly benefits (known as OASDI benefits) to retired workers, eligible dependents of deceased workers, and disabled workers. The health insurance program (Medicare) provides limited coverage for hospitalization and other specified medical expenses for persons aged 65 and older and for certain disabled persons under age 65.

- OASDI benefit amounts are based on the worker's average earnings subject to OASDI payroll taxes prior to receiving benefits, with past earnings adjusted for subsequent wage

growth. Eligible beneficiaries do not have to satisfy a means test to receive benefits. The benefit formula provides relatively greater benefits compared to payroll taxes paid for lower paid workers, thus stressing social adequacy of benefits. Benefits are automatically adjusted each year to reflect changes in the consumer price index.

- Employees pay a payroll tax equal to 6.2 percent of wages up to the maximum taxable wage base in a year ($68,400 in 1998) to finance OASDI benefits. The employer matches this amount. In addition, the employee and employer each pay 1.45 percent of the employee's entire wage to finance Medicare Part A Hospital Insurance (HI). Medicare Part B Supplementary Medical Insurance (SMI) is financed with monthly premiums from covered persons and with general tax revenues.

- OASDHI benefits are financed on a pay-as-you-go basis. Current payroll taxes are largely used to pay current benefits without advance funding of the projected cost of accrued benefits. Although the OASDI trust funds are expected to grow substantially for another decade, significant long-run deficits are projected for both OASDI and the Medicare HI program.

- Until around 1990, the social security retirement program on average provided attractive implicit rates of return on payroll taxes paid by workers and employers prior to retirement. The average implicit rate of return for subsequent retirees is projected to be relatively low and negative for many higher paid workers. As is true concerning projected OASDI deficits, low implicit rates of return are due in large part to increases in the number of beneficiaries compared to the number of workers paying taxes.

- Important characteristics of the pay-as-you-go social security system include: (*a*) the ability of the pay-as-you-go approach to provide cost-of-living adjustments on a self-financing basis, since inflation generally increases wages and thus payroll tax revenues; (*b*) the requirement that workers who otherwise might save little for retirement pay something in exchange for future support by other persons; (*c*) the absence of a means test, thus avoiding the disadvantages of means testing; and (*d*) the potential adverse effects of the program on savings and economic growth.

- Proposals for reducing or eliminating projected OASDHI deficits and otherwise modifying social security include: (*a*) raise payroll taxes; (*b*) reduce future benefits; (*c*) replace all or part of the retirement program with compulsory individual savings; and (*d*) make workers satisfy a means test to receive benefits. Regardless of the approach or approaches used, current and future workers almost surely will have to pay higher taxes unless the government reneges on its promise to pay all benefits accrued as of the date of any change in the system.

Key Terms

Questions and Problems

1. Briefly describe the major categories of OASDI and Medicare benefits.

2. Using the payroll tax rates discussed in the text and the maximum taxable wage base for

1997 of $68,400, calculate the payroll tax (OASDI and HI combined) that would be paid by the employee and the employer for each of the following amounts of annual wages: (*a*) $10,000; (*b*) $25,000, (*c*) $50,000; (*d*) $75,000; and (*e*) $150,000.

3. Graph the ratio of the payroll tax paid by an employee to wages for the amounts of wages in question 2.

4. How do each of the following affect the social adequacy of social security benefits compared to individual equity?
   (*a*) The formula used to derive the primary insurance amount,
   (*b*) Limiting the maximum amount of wages subject to payroll tax.
   (*c*) Making higher income beneficiaries pay income tax on part of their social security benefits.

5. A regressive tax is a tax that represents a greater proportion of income or earnings for lower income people than for higher income people. Is the financing of social security with payroll taxes regressive? Does the way in which benefits are designed to promote social adequacy affect your answer?

6. Contrast pay-as-you-go financing with financing of private pension plan benefits.

7. Other factors held constant, explain how each of the following factors would affect the average amount of benefits that could be paid under a pay-as-you-go retirement plan:
   (*a*) A decrease in the payroll tax rate.

(*b*) Removal of the maximum limit on annual wages subject to OASDI tax without increasing the maximum benefit payable.

(*c*) A long-run increase in productivity growth.

(*d*) A long-run increase in the birth rate.

8. How does the social security earnings test differ from a means test?

9. The following changes would reduce social security expenditures for and/or increase tax revenues from higher paid workers and thus help eliminate the projected long-range OASDI deficits: (*a*) remove the maximum limit on wages subject to OASDI tax without increasing the maximum benefit amount; (*b*) subject all social security benefits for higher income beneficiaries to income tax; and (*c*) eliminate benefits for high income beneficiaries. Why might these changes undermine support for social security and ultimately lead to more radical changes?

10. Why is it likely to be very costly for private pension plan sponsors and insurance companies to provide guaranteed automatic cost-of-living adjustments to pension and annuity benefits? How does pay-as-you-go financing of retirement benefits facilitate the provision of automatic cost-of-living adjustments to benefits?

11. Briefly explain the possible effects of the social security retirement program on private savings and economic growth.

References

1998 Annual Report of the Board of Trustees of the Federal Old-Age and Survivors Insurance and Disability Insurance Trust Funds. Washington, DC: US Government Printing Office, 1998. (*Comprehensive discussion of OASDI financing, including projected benefits, taxes, and trust fund balances. Available at Social Security administration's website: http://www.ssa.gov.*)

Boadway, Robin W.; and David E. Wildasin. *Public Sector Economics.* 2nd ed. New York: Little, Brown, 1984. (*Chapter 14 contains an informative introduction to the economics of social security and welfare, including redistributive aspects and effects on savings.*)

Myers, Robert J.; and Bruce Schobel. "An Updated Money's-Worth Analysis of Social Security

Retirement Benefits." *Transactions* (Society of
Actuaries) 44 (1992), pp. 242–70. (*Detailed
comparisons of the present value of expected
social security retirement benefits to accumulated
payroll taxes.*)

Rejda, George E. *Social Insurance and Economic
Security.* 5th ed. Englewood Cliffs, NJ: Prentice
Hall, 1994. (*Comprehensive treatment of social
security and other social insurance programs.*)

Robertson, A. Haeworth. *Social Security: What Every*
Taxpayer Should Know. Washington, DC:
Retirement Policy Institute, 1992. (*A user-friendly
introduction to social security benefits and
financing issues.*)

*Status of the Social Security and Medicare Programs—
A Summary of the 1998 Annual Reports.*
Washington, DC: US Government Printing Office,
1998. (*Summary information on OASDI and
Medicare financing. Available at
http://www.ssa.gov.*)

Answers to Concept Checks

1. (*a*) The worker with $20,000 in wages
   would pay $1,240 (0.062 × $20,000) in
   OASDI taxes and $290 (0.0145 ×
   $20,000) in HI taxes. The worker with
   $80,000 in wages would pay $4,240.80
   (0.062 × $68,400, the 1998 OASDI
   maximum taxable wage base) in OASDI
   taxes and $1,160 (0.0145 × $80,000) in
   HI taxes (there is no maximum wage
   base).

   (*b*) The employer would match the amounts
   calculated above.

2. (*a*) An increase in the payroll tax increases
   the average benefit that can be paid
   because more tax revenues are available
   to pay benefits.

   (*b*) A decrease in population growth
   decreases the average benefit that can be
   paid because there will be relatively
   fewer workers compared to beneficiaries
   at any point in time.

(*c*) A long-run increase in the
unemployment rate decreases the average
benefit that can be paid because there
will be fewer workers paying taxes.

3. (*a*) An increase in the birth rate increases
   population growth and the number of
   future workers paying taxes compared to
   the number of retirees at any point in
   time, thus increasing the long-run
   implicit rate of return.

   (*b*) A decrease in real productivity growth
   reduces real wage growth, which in turn
   will reduce payroll tax revenues available
   to pay beneficiaries and thus reduce the
   implicit rate of return.

   (*c*) A cure for cancer would reduce the long-
   run implicit rate of return because it
   would increase the number of
   beneficiaries compared to the number of
   workers.

APPENDIX 20A

IMPLICIT RATE OF RETURN ON PAYROLL TAXES WITH PAY-AS-YOU-GO FINANCING

The effects of wage and population growth on implicit
returns under a pay-as-you-go retirement program can be
illustrated easily using the simple assumption that people
live for two periods. In the first period, they are born,
work, and pay taxes. In the second period, they retire, receive benefits, and then die. We also will assume that all

people have the same wages in a given period and that retirees in a given period all receive the same benefit. We emphasize that the key implications of this analysis also hold for more realistic assumptions.

Assuming that all taxes in a given year are used to pay benefits, it is first useful to write the expression for average benefits that was used in the text in a slightly different way:

$$\text{Benefit}_t = \tau \times \text{Wage}_t \times \text{Workers}_t/\text{Retirees}_t$$

where, for period t, Benefit_t is the average benefit, Wage_t equals wages earned by each worker, Workers_t is the number of workers, Retirees_t is the number of retirees, and τ is the payroll tax rate. If wages then are assumed to grow at a rate of g per period, wages during period t equal $1 + g$ times wages in period $t - 1$ [i.e., $\text{Wage}_t = (1 + g)\text{Wage}_{t-1}$]. Likewise, if the population grows at a rate of s per period, the number of workers that pay taxes in period t equals $1 + s$ times the number of retirees in period t [i.e., $\text{Workers}_t = (1 + s)\text{Retirees}_t$]. (Note that Retirees$_t$ = Workers$_{t-1}$; workers in period $t - 1$ become retirees in period t.) Substituting these relations into the above expression, the benefit paid to retirees in period t can be written:

$$\text{Benefit}_t = \tau \times (1 + g)\text{Wage}_{t-1} \times (1 + s)$$

Period t retirees had to pay taxes on their wages prior to retirement to receive this benefit. The amount of tax paid was $\tau \times \text{Wage}_{t-1}$ (the payroll tax rate times the wages while they worked).

Armed with these results, we now can get to the punchline. The implicit rate of return in this simple case can be calculated directly by comparing the retirement benefit to the tax paid by the retiree. The rate of return equals the excess of the benefit over the tax paid divided by the tax paid. Given that the tax paid is $\tau \times \text{Wage}_{t-1}$, the rate of return equals:

$$\text{Rate of return}_t = (\text{Benefit}_t - \tau \times \text{Wage}_{t-1})/(\tau \times \text{Wage}_{t-1})$$

Substituting the earlier expression for the benefit in period t, the expression for the rate of return for period t retirees reduces to:

$$\text{Rate of return}_t = (1 + g)(1 + s) - 1 \approx g + s$$

where $\approx$ indicates "is approximately equal to." In words, the implicit rate of return on taxes paid equals the growth rate in wages plus the population growth rate.

Thus far we have considered the nominal rate of return, as opposed to the real (after-inflation) rate of return. As noted in the text, it can be readily shown that *the real implicit rate of return on taxes paid equals the real growth rate in wages plus the population growth rate.* Because real wage growth will be approximately equal to productivity growth, this result implies that the real implicit rate of return will approximately equal the productivity growth rate plus the population growth rate. As we mentioned above, this result holds for more realistic assumptions. For example, the same simple result arises when workers work and are retired for multiple periods when the growth rate in wages and the population growth rate are constant over time.

PART VI

Personal Insurance

CHAPTER 21 Automobile Insurance

Chapter Objectives

- Describe personal exposures to loss arising out of automobile ownership and use and personal auto insurance coverage for these losses.
- Explain major features of personal auto insurance pricing and underwriting.
- Explain compulsory auto insurance laws and the rationale and effects of these laws.
- Explain no-fault auto insurance laws and the rationale and effects of these laws.

21.1 Overview of Auto Loss Exposures and Insurance

Thirty-five million auto accidents occurred in the United States in 1996, killing approximately 43,000 people and producing $120 billion in economic loss (*The Fact Book 1998,* Insurance Information Institute). Personal auto insurance, which protects against many losses associated with auto accidents, is the largest line of property-liability insurance in terms of premium volume, with 1996 written premiums of $108 billion. Commercial auto insurance premiums totaled another $18 billion. The largest four personal auto insurers, with national premium market shares shown in parentheses, were: State Farm Insurance (22.2 percent), Allstate Insurance (12.3 percent), Farmers Insurance (5.3 percent), and Nationwide (4.0 percent). All of these insurers are direct writers that primarily rely on exclusive agents to market coverage, and 69 percent of the personal auto insurance market is written by direct writers as opposed to insurers that primarily rely on independent agents and brokers.

The major loss exposures arising out of automobile accidents are: (1) legal liability for harm that you may cause others as a result of your negligence, (2) bodily injury to you and members of your family, and (3) property damage to and/or theft of your vehicle(s). Table 21–1 summarizes these exposures and indicates insurance coverage that is available to cover part or all of these losses. It shows auto insurance coverages that are available with the **personal auto policy.** This contract, along with very similar versions offered by many insurers, is the largest selling type of auto policy and is the focus of this section. Table 21–1 also shows other (i.e., nonauto) insurance that may be available to pay for losses from auto accidents. In a majority of states, these nonauto coverages, which include individual and group medical expense coverage, disability insurance, life insurance, and social security, represent major sources of payment for auto-related losses.

The personal auto policy includes four main types of coverage: (1) "third-party" liability coverage for liability to third parties harmed by negligence of an insured person; (2) "first-party" medical payments coverage for the insured, or in states with no-fault or related laws, personal injury protection coverage for the insured's medical expenses *and* loss of income; (3) uninsured and underinsured motorists coverage for losses caused to an insured by drivers without liability insurance and drivers with comparatively low liability insurance limits; and (4)

TABLE 21–1   Automobile Loss Exposures and Insurance for Losses

Type of Loss	Auto Insurance Coverage	Other Insurance That May Apply
Your legal liability for negligently causing (1) bodily injury to others, including economic losses and pain and suffering; (2) property damage to others, including loss of use; and (3) defense costs	• Your liability coverage	• Your personal "umbrella" liability insurance coverage (see Chapter 22)
Your economic losses from bodily injury	• An at-fault driver's liability coverage • Your "first-party" medical payments coverage or personal injury protection coverage • Your uninsured or underinsured motorists coverage if other driver is at fault (and uninsured or underinsured)	• Your group or individual medical/disability/life insurance • Workers' compensation insurance if work-related injury • Social Security disability, survivor benefits, or Medicare
Your pain and suffering	• An at-fault driver's liability insurance • Your uninsured or underinsured motorists coverage if other driver is at fault	• None
Collision damage to your vehicle	• An at-fault driver's liability coverage • Your collision coverage • Your uninsured or underinsured motorists coverage if other driver is at fault	• None
Other damage to and theft of your vehicle	• Your "other than collision" (comprehensive) coverage	• None

coverage for physical damage to or theft of insured autos. This section provides a brief overview of these coverages. We emphasize that while personal auto policies are written in language that most buyers can understand, these contracts nonetheless are reasonably complex with numerous clauses and definitions. Our purpose is to acquaint you with key provisions rather than provide a comprehensive restatement of coverage terms and conditions.

Liability Coverage

The **auto liability coverage** in the personal auto policy provides broad coverage for liability for bodily injury and property damage to other parties arising out of the use of an automobile by an insured person. As is customary with liability insurance, the insurer also agrees to defend the insured and bear the defense costs and is responsible for negotiating and settling claims.

Personal auto liability coverage may be sold with a "single limit" that specifies the maximum amount that the insurer will pay for all damages from a single accident. (The policy does not include an aggregate annual limit.) For example, a policy with a single limit of $300,000 will pay up to $300,000 for liability for bodily injury and property damage, regardless of how many persons or autos are damaged by the insured. Alternatively, the policy can include separate limits ("split limits") that specify the maximum that the insurer will pay per accident (1) to each injured person for bodily injury, (2) in total to all injured persons for bodily injury, and (3) for total property damage. For example, split limits equal to $100,000 per person for bodily injury, $300,000 per accident for bodily injury, and $50,000 per accident for property damage would pay: (1) up to $100,000 for bodily injury to each person injured by the driver in an accident, (2) no more than $300,000 in total if more than one person is hurt, and (3) up to $50,000 for total property damage regardless of how many vehicles are damaged by the insured.

As of 1998, 43 states and the District of Columbia have **compulsory liability insurance laws** that mandate the purchase of a minimum amount of auto liability coverage by auto owners. The minimum amounts generally are specified as split limits with the per person minimum for bodily injury generally ranging from $10,000 to $50,000 (see Table 21–2). All states also have **financial responsibility laws** that penalize drivers with fines and possible loss of driving privileges under certain conditions if they negligently cause accidents and are unable to pay specified minimum amounts of damages. Financial responsibility laws predate compulsory insurance laws. Purchasing liability insurance with limits equal to or greater than the minimums specified in a state's financial responsibility law satisfies both the financial responsibility law and any compulsory liability insurance law.

The minimum liability coverage available in a personal auto policy from most insurers equals the "basic limits" that are required under the state's financial responsibility law/compulsory liability insurance law. Most insurers also offer higher limits for higher premiums. When you travel out of state, the liability limits under the personal auto policy automatically adjust to provide the limits required by law if they are higher than in your home state.

TABLE 21–2   Compulsory Auto Insurance Coverages and Minimum Liability Limits in 1998

State	Compulsory Coverages	Minimum Liability Limits	State	Compulsory Coverages	Minimum Liability Limits
Alabama	FR only	20/40/10	Montana	Liability	25/50/10
Alaska	Liability	50/100/25	Nebraska	Liability	25/50/25
Arizona	Liability	15/30/10	Nevada	Liability	15/30/10
Arkansas	Liability	25/50/15	New Hampshire	FR only	25/50/25
California	Liability	15/30/5	New Jersey	Liability, PIP, UM	15/30/5
Colorado	Liability, PIP	25/50/15	New Mexico	Liability	25/50/10
Connecticut	Liability, UM, UIM	20/40/10	New York	Liability, PIP, UM	25/50/10
Delaware	Liability, PIP	15/30/10	North Carolina	Liability	25/50/15
DC	Liability, UM	25/50/10	North Dakota	Liability, PIP, UM	25/50/25
Florida	PDL, PIP	10/20/10	Ohio	FR only	12.5/25/7.5
Georgia	Liability	15/30/10	Oklahoma	Liability	10/20/10
Hawaii	Liability, PIP	35/15/10	Oregon	Liability, PIP, UM	25/50/10
Idaho	Liability	25/50/15	Pennsylvania	Liability, PIP	15/30/5
Illinois	Liability, UM	20/40/15	Rhode Island	BIL, UM	25/50/25
Indiana	Liability	25/50/10	South Carolina	Liability, UM	15/30/5
Iowa	Liability	20/40/15	South Dakota	Liability, UM	25/50/25
Kansas	Liability, PIP, UM	25/50/10	Tennessee	FR only	20/50/10
Kentucky	Liability, PIP	25/50/10	Texas	Liability	20/40/15
Louisiana	Liability	10/20/10	Utah	Liability, PIP	25/50/15
Maine	Liability, UM	20/40/10	Vermont	Liability, UM, UIM	20/40/10
Maryland	Liability, PIP, UM	20/40/10	Virginia	FR only	25/50/20
Massachusetts	Liability, PIP, UM	20/40/8	Washington	Liability	25/50/10
Michigan	Liability, PIP	20/40/10	West Virginia	Liability, UM	20/40/10
Minnesota	Liability, PIP, UM, UIM	30/60/10	Wisconsin	FR only	25/50/10
Mississippi	FR only	10/20/05	Wyoming	Liability	25/50/20
Missouri	Liability	25/50/10			

Note: Minimum liability limits are per person/per accident for all persons injured/property damage liability limits. Liability = property damage and bodily injury liability; PDL = property damage liability only; BIL = bodily injury liability only; PIP = personal injury protection; UM = uninsured motorists; UIM = underinsured motorists; and FR = financial responsibility law.

Sources: Compulsory Auto Insurance, *Insurance Issues Update,* March 1998; *The Fact Book 1998* (Insurance Information Institute); and Insurance News Service. Personal injury protection coverage and tort limitation information obtained from miscellaneous trade publications.

The policy covers the liability of the "named insured," which includes a resident spouse and other family members residing in the same household (including college students temporarily away from home while attending school). These persons are covered for liability arising out of use of a "covered auto" and any other auto with reasonable belief that they have the permission of the owner (subject to a number of exclusions, several of which we note below). The policy also covers liability of any person using the insured's covered auto(s), again with a reasonable belief that they have permission to do so. Covered autos are defined to include vehicles specifically listed in the policy, newly acquired vehicles, trailers owned by the insured, and temporary substitute autos, such as an auto used while a listed auto is being repaired.

Thus, you are insured under your personal auto policy for use of any auto with the permission of the owner, and people that you permit to use your covered auto(s) also are insured under your policy. In addition, if you borrow another person's car with permission, you will be covered under the car owner's personal auto policy, if any, and if you lend your car to someone else, the driver will be covered under his or her own policy, if any. If a person is covered under more than one policy, the general rule (there are exceptions) is that insurance on a covered auto is primary and other coverage is excess. For example, if you borrow your friend's car, your friend's insurance is primary and yours is excess.[1]

Liability coverage under the personal auto policy contains many exclusions. Several of the major ones include (but are not limited to): (1) intentional injury or damage; (2) losses to property owned by, transported by, rented to, or in the insured's care, which often are covered under homeowners insurance; (3) bodily injury to an employee covered by workers' compensation; (4) coverage for a vehicle that is being hired out to the general public, such as using your car as a taxi; (5) certain types of business vehicles, for example, those used in the automobile business and large trucks; (6) vehicles used without a reasonable belief that the owner has given permission; and (7) vehicles with less than four wheels, such as motorcycles, which generally can be covered by adding an endorsement to the policy. Note that business use of an auto by an insured person is covered unless subject to a specific exclusion.

Medical Payments Coverage

By purchasing optional first-party **auto medical payments coverage,** the auto owner can receive payment for medical expenses arising out of an accident. Coverage is for medical expenses for the named insured and family members hurt in any auto and other persons that are hurt while occupying a covered auto. Coverage limits generally are comparatively low, such as $1,000 to $10,000 per injured person, with many persons purchasing amounts in the $1,000 to $2,500 range. In part this reflects that many persons have individual or group medical insurance that pays much of the cost of medical expenses associated with auto accidents. Payments under auto medical payments coverage are not contingent on fault and generally are not coordinated with other medical insurance that the person may have. Thus, the insured usually can recover from both policies. Exclusions to auto medical payments coverage are largely similar to those for liability coverage.

In states with no-fault or related laws, the personal auto policy includes **personal injury protection coverage** for the named insured, family members, and parties hurt while occupying a covered auto instead of medical payments coverage. In contrast to medical payments coverage, personal injury protection coverage generally provides limited coverage for loss of income in addition to medical

---

[1] The policy also covers the liability of any other person or organization arising out of an insured person's use of a covered auto (or other auto not owned by this other person or organization) on behalf of the person or organization. For example, if you used your car for your employer, your employer would be protected under your policy (and have excess coverage under its own policy).

expenses. In some states, purchase of personal injury protection coverage is optional (see Table 21–2). Other states make purchase compulsory with benefit amounts specified by law, in contrast to optional medical payments coverage. States with no-fault laws also limit tort liability. You will learn more about personal injury protection coverage and no-fault laws in section 21.4.

Uninsured and Underinsured Motorists Coverage

If an insured person is legally entitled to recover damages from the owner or operator of a motor vehicle who has not purchased auto liability insurance, whose insurer is insolvent or denies coverage, or who is a hit-and-run driver, **uninsured motorists coverage** allows the insured to recover damages *from his or her own insurer* up to the policy limit. Coverage for bodily injury includes all amounts that the insured presumably would have been able to recover if the driver had collectible liability insurance, including medical expenses, loss of income, and pain and suffering. Insured persons include the named insured and resident family members, any other person occupying a covered auto, and any person legally entitled to recover damages, such as surviving dependents of an insured person that is killed.

While uninsured motorists coverage is first-party coverage between the insurer and the insured, roughly half of insured persons with uninsured motorists claims hire an attorney to negotiate settlements with their insurers. Disagreements are subject to arbitration, but the result is not binding; that is, the parties can continue to litigate if the award exceeds the minimum policy limits under the state's compulsory liability/financial responsibility laws. Some exclusions to uninsured motorists coverage are similar to those for liability coverage (for example, using a vehicle without a reasonable belief of permission), while others are unique.

A related type of coverage that is available as an option in the personal auto policy is **underinsured motorists coverage.** As is true for uninsured motorists coverage, underinsured motorists coverage allows an insured person to recover damages from his or her own insurer that in principle could have been obtained from an insured, at-fault driver, including damages for pain and suffering. The difference is that underinsured motorists coverage applies when the at-fault driver has liability insurance with limits that are less than the insured's underinsured motorists limits. The maximum amount payable under underinsured motorists coverage is the difference between the underinsured motorists coverage limit and the at-fault driver's liability insurance limit.

Assume, for example, that you purchased underinsured motorists coverage with split bodily injury limits of $50,000 per person/$100,000 per accident and were harmed by a negligent driver with liability limits of $25,000 per person/$50,000 per accident. If your total damages were $75,000, you would recover $25,000 from the driver's liability coverage and $25,000 ($50,000 − $25,000) from your underinsured motorists coverage. Thus, you would need an underinsured motorists coverage limit of $75,000 to have all of your damages covered. An exception arises for people with multiple cars in states that allow "stacking" of uninsured motorists coverage limits, in which case the courts may allow the limits to be multiplied by the number of cars insured under a policy or may add up the limits in separate policies. Because the limits are effectively higher in these situations, stacking increases the costs of uninsured motorists coverage.

Students often have two questions regarding these coverages. First, you might wonder why uninsured motorists coverage exists if all drivers are required to have liability insurance. The answer is simple: As we elaborate later in the chapter, many people break the law and drive without required liability insurance. The second question is: Why is there separate coverage for uninsured and underinsured motorists instead of having combined coverage that, along with the at-fault driver's liability coverage (if any), would provide the policyholder with a specified level of protection (such as $100,000 per person/$300,000 per accident)? Note that if the coverages were combined, then purchasing coverage equal to the state's basic liability limits would be equivalent to having uninsured motorists coverage equal to these limits and no underinsured motorists coverage.

The economic rationale for separating the two coverages is not obvious. As a practical matter, uninsured motorists coverage was developed first. Underinsured coverage then was added as an option later, which may have been simpler than doing away with the existing uninsured motorists coverage and substituting new, combined coverage. It also might be easier to explain separate coverages in a way that most people can understand.

In any case, many states mandate the purchase of a minimum amount of *uninsured motorists* coverage equal to the minimum amount of liability coverage specified by the state's compulsory liability/financial responsibility law. Coverage for property damage caused by uninsured motorists varies widely among the states. Some states mandate property damage coverage under uninsured motorists coverage; others make it optional, sometimes by automatically including property damage coverage with bodily injury coverage unless the insured rejects coverage in writing. The purchase of *underinsured motorists* coverage usually is not mandatory. However, some states encourage people to buy both uninsured and underinsured motorists coverage limits equal to their liability insurance limits by requiring insurers to provide equal limits automatically unless the insured signs a form rejecting higher limits.

One interesting feature of uninsured and underinsured motorists coverage is that they provide first-party compensation for pain and suffering. We are aware of no other first-party insurance that does this. This coverage of pain and suffering does not necessarily imply that many or most people who buy these coverages are revealing a desire to insure pain and suffering losses. You just learned that purchase of these coverages often is either required or encouraged by law, and state law requires that both uninsured and underinsured motorists coverage include coverage for pain and suffering. Thus, the purchase of pain and suffering compensation through uninsured and underinsured motorists coverage may in part reflect the interests of politically influential groups that might benefit from such coverage, such as attorneys who represent policyholders seeking recovery under these coverages.

Damage and Other Losses to Autos

The personal auto policy provides two optional coverages for damage and theft to vehicles: **collision coverage** and **other-than-collision coverage.** These coverages apply to autos listed in the policy and newly acquired autos if requested by the owner within 30 days. Nonowned autos, such as an auto that you have permission to use but do not own or use on a regular basis, including a temporary substitute auto, also are covered on an excess basis over the owner's insurance. Coverage of nonowned autos includes car rentals, at least for personal use as car rental firms generally do not automatically provide physical damage coverage (see Box 21–1). Many insurers exclude liability and physical damage coverage for autos rented for business use unless an endorsement to the policy is purchased.

Box 21–1

Coverage for Rented Cars and Foreign Travel

So you just landed for your dream vacation and are picking up your rental car. How is the insurance handled? In most states, car rental companies provide liability insurance limits equal to the minimum required by the state with the cost built into the daily rental fee. If your personal policy has higher limits, it generally will serve as excess coverage. Alternatively, you can shell out a daily fee to get higher limits from the car rental company. In a few states car rental firms provide excess coverage over your policy if you pay a daily fee. In at least one state (California), they provide no liability coverage without a fee. If you do not have an auto and personal auto liability coverage, you may then need to pay for the coverage from the rental company to comply with the state's compulsory insurance and financial responsibility laws.

With respect to physical damage and theft coverage, your personal auto coverages (if you have them) generally will cover a rental, but it's a good idea to check with your agent to make sure that you have coverage. Losses will be paid above any deductible. Some people nonetheless decide to shell out $10 to $20 a day to buy collision coverage available from the car rental company. While this coverage is comparatively expensive, there is no deductible, and it substantially eliminates the likelihood that a rental agent will discover a slight scratch or crack in the windshield when you return the car, thus requiring you to fill out papers and perhaps miss your flight home. Some credit cards provide cardholders with automatic collision coverage for car rentals up to a specified limit.

As noted in the text, some personal auto insurers no longer provide liability or collision coverage for rentals used for business purposes unless the insured purchases an endorsement to coverage. You also should be aware that the personal auto policy only provides coverage for the United States, its territories and possessions, Puerto Rico, and Canada. Thus, if you vacation in Mexico or England you will not be covered for any car rental (or if you take your own car). You will be offered and sometimes required to buy medical coverage, physical damage coverage, and theft coverage from the rental company (although again some credit card companies offer collision coverage for foreign travel that might be accepted by the rental company). If you cannot afford the coverage or cannot stand the thought of buying the required coverage, you probably should either take the train or vacation in areas where your personal auto policy provides coverage. Finally, if you take your own car to Mexico, some people suggest that it is a good idea to obtain liability coverage from a Mexican insurer in order to be protected against loss and to avoid potential hassle by the police if you are involved in an accident.

Collision coverage covers the upset (rollover) of a covered auto or impact with another object. Other-than-collision coverage covers theft of the vehicle and damage from "missiles" or falling objects, explosion, earthquake, windstorm, hail, water, flood, vandalism, riot, glass breakage, and contact with a bird or animal. Other-than-collision coverage in auto policies used to be called "comprehensive coverage," and this terminology is still commonly used on an informal basis. One might guess that the newer, awkward name reflects the desire of insurers to avoid litigation from policyholders that might argue that a "comprehensive" policy should pay for everything without exclusion! Exclusions under collision and other-than-collision coverage include but are not limited to damage from wear and tear, freezing, and mechanical breakdown; loss to custom furnishings and equipment; and loss to campers or trailers not listed in the policy unless newly acquired and the damage occurs within 30 days of acquisition; as well as several exclusions similar to those under liability coverage.

Losses under these coverages are covered above a deductible. The size of the deductible may differ between the coverages. Losses are paid on a repair cost basis up to the actual cash value of the vehicle for a total loss. There also is limited coverage of additional transportation expenses until a vehicle is repaired or a new auto is obtained. The insurer has the option to declare the auto a total loss and pay the actual cash value. In this case, the insurer has the right to take the vehicle; that is, it has the right of *salvage*. While this sometimes annoys people, it helps lower premiums, and the insurer usually has a comparative advantage in disposing of the auto, selling parts, and so on, compared to most policyholders. (We know this to be true in our case.)

Whether the loss is total or partial, if a dispute arises concerning the amount of settlement, the policy includes an appraisal provision, which allows either party to demand an appraisal. Each party then selects and pays an appraiser, and these two appraisers select and split the cost of an umpire. If the appraisers do not agree, the difference is submitted to the umpire, who decides which party to agree with or works out an agreeable compromise, thus determining the settlement. The appraisal provision reduces litigation but, in a few cases, policyholders still may sue the insurer, alleging bias or fraud by the umpire.

21.2 Auto Insurance Pricing and Underwriting

The pricing and the underwriting of automobile insurance have long been a source of controversy to many consumers, regulators, and insurers. During the 1980s and early 1990s the average price of auto insurance nationally grew much faster than the overall rate of inflation, as is illustrated using the auto insurance and overall consumer price indexes during 1981–1997 in Figure 21–1. The auto insurance CPI increased 206 percent during 1981–1997, an average annual (geometric) percentage increase of 6.8 percent. The overall CPI increased by 95 percent during this period, an average annual increase of 4 percent.

The average premium per car insured varies widely across states and drivers.

FIGURE 21–1

Auto insurance and all items consumer price indexes

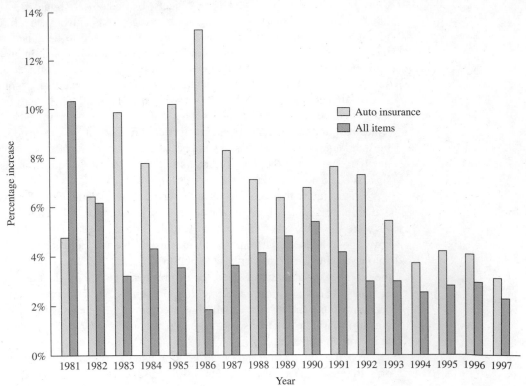

Source: Bureau of Labor Statistics.

Table 21–3 and Figure 21–2 illustrate the variation across states in combined expenditures for auto liability, medical payments/personal injury protection, collision, and comprehensive coverage per vehicle with liability insurance in 1996. As you know and as we discuss further below, many drivers, such as young drivers and those who live in higher cost urban areas, face premium rates that are substantially greater than average.

You learned about the basic economics of insurance pricing in Chapter 6. The key idea is that there are strong incentives for insurers to base prices on the discounted expected costs of providing coverage, where costs include expected claim costs, administrative costs, and the cost of holding capital to increase the likelihood that the insurer will have sufficient funds to pay claims. In this section you will learn about the major rating factors used in personal auto insurance pricing, about auto insurance underwriting, and about government regulation that affects auto insurance pricing and underwriting.

TABLE 21–3   Average Auto Insurance Expenditure per Vehicle with Liability Coverage and Average Auto Liability Insurance Residual Market Share

State	Average Expenditure per Auto and Rank 1996		Residual Market Share and Rank 1995		State	Average Expenditure per Auto and Rank 1996		Residual Market Share and Rank 1995	
Alabama	$578	33	0.02%	42	Montana	$ 479	44	0.09%	32
Alaska	751	16	1.67	16	Nebraska	475	45	0.01	45
Arizona	785	12	0.02	40	Nevada	803	9	0.05	34
Arkansas	558	34	0.04	35	New Hampshire	621	26	0.55	19
California	791	11	0.94	18	New Jersey	1,099	1	3.04	10
Colorado	751	15	0.01	46	New Mexico	660	22	0.19	25
Connecticut	899	5	1.98	15	New York	960	3	14.67	4
Delaware	806	8	2.99	11	North Carolina	518	41	23.92	2
DC	993	2	8.66	5	North Dakota	402	51	0.01	43
Florida	783	13	0.15	26	Ohio	553	36	0.00	51
Georgia	627	25	0.13	27	Oklahoma	545	39	0.09	31
Hawaii	959	4	3.57	9	Oregon	585	30	0.01	46
Idaho	465	47	0.03	39	Pennsylvania	687	19	2.68	12
Illinois	638	24	0.09	33	Rhode Island	870	6	4.55	8
Indiana	548	38	0.01	44	South Carolina	602	28	41.02	1
Iowa	445	50	0.02	41	South Dakota	448	49	0.03	37
Kansas	495	43	0.53	20	Tennessee	557	35	0.10	30
Kentucky	581	31	0.12	28	Texas	726	17	4.69	7
Louisiana	802	10	0.37	21	Utah	581	32	0.00	50
Maine	470	46	0.27	22	Vermont	514	42	2.55	13
Maryland	759	14	4.85	6	Virginia	550	37	1.63	17
Massachusetts	833	7	14.72	3	Washington	666	21	0.03	38
Michigan	697	18	2.22	14	West Virginia	671	20	0.27	23
Minnesota	654	23	0.03	36	Wisconsin	533	40	0.01	48
Mississippi	604	27	0.26	24	Wyoming	452	48	0.01	49
Missouri	599	29	0.11	29	Total US	685		3.60	

Note: Average expenditure includes premiums for liability, medical payments/personal injury protection, collision, and comprehensive coverage.
Sources: National Association of Insurance Commissioners, Automobile Insurance Plans Service Office, and Insurance News Network.

Rating Factors

Auto insurance rates charged to different consumers reflect differences in the discounted expected costs of providing coverage. In order to classify different persons into homogeneous groups with respect to expected claim costs, insurers generally use rate classification systems that include (1) driver classes that reflect the characteristics of individual insureds, and (2) **territorial rating** to reflect expected differences in claim costs for people that live in different geographical areas (holding individual characteristics constant). Of course, physical damage rates also depend on the value and type of vehicle. Liability insurance rates sometimes also depend on the type of vehicle, given evidence that certain vehicles, such as red cars (not really) and high performance cars, are more likely to be in-

FIGURE 21–2

Average auto insurance expenditures by state in 1996

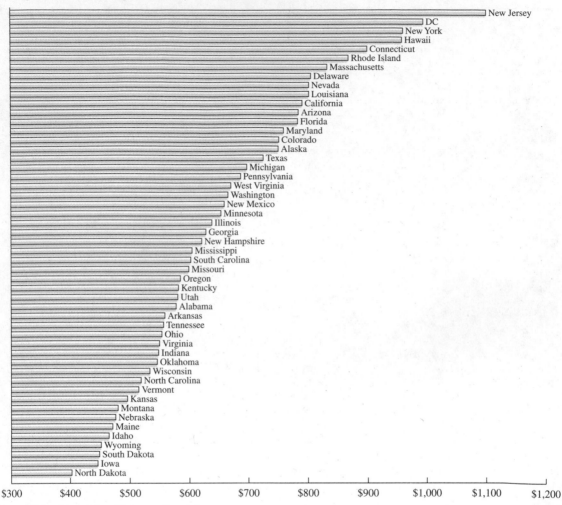

Source: National Association of Insurance Commissioners.

volved in at-fault accidents. We will briefly explain the major factors considered in establishing driver classes and the use of territorial rating factors.

Driver Classes.   Insurers generally assign an applicant to a driver class based on a number of primary characteristics, including the person's (or household's) driving record. Major factors that commonly are used besides driving record are summarized first before turning to the use of driving record.

• Age: Other factors held constant, claim costs generally are higher for persons up to approximately age 30 than for older drivers. There also is evidence that people aged about 55–65 have lower claim costs than people aged 30–55 but that average claim costs are higher at advanced ages. Thus, other things being equal, rates generally start out high for young drivers, decline with age until approximately age 30, and then level off. Many insurers then provide discounts for older drivers until they reach an advanced age, at which point some insurers charge a higher rate than for drivers aged 30–55.

• Gender: Young males (up to approximately age 30) have higher average claim costs than young females and thus generally pay higher rates than females at these ages.

• Marital status: Up to age 25–30, married males and females generally have lower average claim costs (per vehicle) than unmarried males and females. As a result, many insurers offer a discount to young married persons.

• Use of the automobile: Average claim costs vary according to whether vehicles are driven to work or are used for business or farm work. A typical rating plan will have higher rates for autos driven to work than for those that are not. It is common to have two classes for cars driven to work based on approximate commuting mileage. For example, an insurer might have one rate for autos driven to work less than 20 miles per day (e.g., 10 miles one way) and a higher rate for autos driven more than this amount. Autos customarily used for business will pay a higher rate due to higher expected claims costs; automobiles primarily used on farms typically have lower costs and thus are charged a lower rate.

• Number of automobiles and accompanying homeowners coverage: Many insurers provide a multiple car discount to reflect possibly lower expected claim costs per auto in multiple car households and, more importantly, savings in administration costs. Some insurers also provide a discount if the person buys both auto and homeowners coverage from the same insurer to reflect reduced administrative expense loadings that are possible in these cases.

• Miscellaneous factors: Many companies (sometimes due to state law requirements) include discounts for youthful drivers who have completed an approved driver education program and for good students. There is evidence that driver education helps reduce accident costs for young drivers, at least during the first year or two following completion of the course. The evidence that good students have lower claim costs is somewhat weaker (although "bookworms" may study more and drive less). Some factors of this sort might be used to help an insurer target and keep customers with high renewal rates and opportunities for selling multiple types of coverage (see below).

Driving Record.   Another very important factor that affects rates is the driving record of insured persons in the household. Students often want to know whether their rates will increase if they have had an accident or traffic violation. Because practices vary across insurers (and across states in large part due to differences in regulation) instructors often cannot give a precise answer. However, your agent/insurer will know and can provide you with the rules that apply to you. The theory is simple: In principle, rate increases for past accidents and traffic violations will reflect the predicted effect on expected costs during the next policy period.

That is, if past accident involvement or tickets affect predicted claim costs, rates will be adjusted to reflect the effect of this information.

In practice and unless constrained by regulation, accidents that produce a specified minimum amount of damage often will lead to a percentage rate increase due to the loss of a "safe driver" discount. Additional accidents and/or certain types of violations can produce additional charges as the person accumulates accident and violation "points" and associated surcharges. At-fault accidents generally will lead to some rate increase for a negligent driver. Accidents between two people where neither party is at fault often produce rate increases for both people given evidence that these accidents are associated with higher accident frequency in the future. Accidents between an at-fault party and a party that is not at fault sometimes will not produce a rate increase, or only a small increase, for the party that is not at fault. You might ask: Why should my rate go up if I'm not at fault? The answer is that evidence often suggests that persons involved in accidents that are not at fault nonetheless are more likely to have subsequent accidents. Insurers that ignore this information in order to be fair will face adverse selection. Many insurers will not increase rates if an insured's car is damaged while parked. Similarly, other-than-collision claims often do not produce rate increases.

Again, the key idea is that insurers have strong incentives to use information as long as it helps predict costs. Sometimes the results do not seem fair to people who have their rates go up. In these situations, they might shop around to see whether another insurer provides a better deal. Some states have detailed regulations governing surcharges for accidents and violations. In a few states, the government specifies what insurers must do. In these cases, when people get upset and blame their insurer, at least part of the blame may be misplaced.

Territorial Rating.   Other things being equal, claim costs vary significantly across states and areas within states. In general, large cities have the highest average claim costs, followed by suburban areas, smaller cities, and small towns or rural areas. Figure 21–3 illustrates these differences using data on liability claim frequency in a number of large cities compared to claim frequency in the remainder of the state in which each city is located.

Insurers develop rating territories to reflect these differences. Buyers pay a rate that is based on where they live (where the vehicle is garaged). An exception often is made for college students who take a car to school while temporarily residing at a different location. In this case, the car usually is rated based on the student's permanent residence (i.e., where mom and/or dad live). Unless constrained by regulation, different insurers often use different territorial boundaries and have different price differences across territories. This provides additional motivation for buyers to compare prices across insurers.

Government Restrictions on Rating Factors.   As we discussed briefly in Chapter 6, some state governments have prohibited the use of certain rating factors in automobile insurance. For example, several states have prohibited the use of gender and/or marital status. At least one state (Massachusetts) has prohibited

FIGURE 21–3

Claim costs and coverage territory: Bodily injury liability claim frequency in selected large cities as a percentage of claim frequency in remainder of state (five-year aggregates in the 1980s)

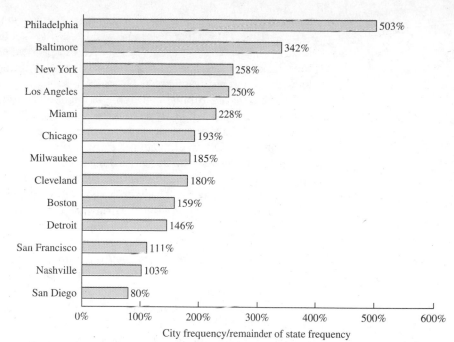

Source: *Factors Affecting Urban Auto Insurance Costs* (Insurance Services Office and National Association of Independent Insurers, 1988).

the use of age, substituting years of driving experience. A number of states have restricted territorial rating, either by mandating the use of certain territories or limiting rate differences that can be charged between adjacent territories. When these restrictions prevent insurers from charging rates commensurate with differences in predicted costs, insurers have a clear incentive to avoid sales to people for whom rates are less than predicted costs. As we discuss more below, this tends to increase the size of the state's auto insurance residual market. In some cases, insurers may at least in part be able to work around these restrictions by target marketing to particular types of drivers or territories. You learned about possible behavioral effects of restrictions that could increase the cost of risk and fairness issues associated with restrictions in Chapter 6.

Underwriting

An insurer's rating plan produces different rates for numerous driver classes and territories. These plans are complex and produce a large number of rating classes, each with a distinct rate. For example, ignoring differences associated with the type and value of an auto, an insurer in a large state might have 300–400 driver classes and 30–40 territories. Assuming 300 driver classes and 30 territories would produce 9,000 (300 × 30) driver class/territory combinations.

However, this complexity in rating classes is not the end of the story. Most states do not require insurers to offer coverage to all applicants. Insurers establish **underwriting criteria** that determine whether a given applicant will be sold coverage. An insurer's rates depend on these criteria. For example, the underwriting criteria might be designed to reflect information about the applicant that is not included in the insurer's rating plan, but which is related to expected claim costs and administrative costs. Similarly, the criteria might relate to the expected length of time that the person will be likely to renew coverage, which determines how long the insurer will have on average to recover up-front underwriting and policy issue costs that are not fully recovered in the first period's premium. Moreover, the criteria might be designed to attract customers that will be likely to buy multiple types of insurance from the insurer, thus allowing the company to spread certain types of fixed underwriting and distribution costs across a larger policy base.

In general, insurers with more "stringent" criteria for coverage sell policies to people who have lower expected claim costs and/or require a lower expense loading. Prospective buyers who do not meet the insurer's criteria generally will have higher expected claim costs and/or require a higher expense loading than contemplated in the insurer's rate structure. They therefore may not be eligible to obtain coverage from this particular insurer. However, they almost always will be able to find an auto insurer that does not employ the same criteria and therefore will be willing to insure them at a higher rate that reflects the higher expected costs, unless regulation prevents insurers from charging adequate rates to these buyers. In this way, variation across insurers with respect to underwriting criteria produces variation in rates across insurers for similar driver classes and territories. The result is that policyholders are sorted into more homogeneous groups with respect to expected claim costs and required expense loadings.

A few examples of underwriting criteria might help illustrate this process and its effects. A few auto insurers only offer coverage to people who totally abstain from alcohol. If these people on average have lower expected claim costs than other people, the insurer might be able to attract them with a lower premium and make a nice profit in the bargain (at least until other companies enter the nondrinker market). In addition, teetotalers won't have to subsidize social drinkers. Another insurer may have information that people in certain types of occupations have higher expected claim costs on average. It might then deny coverage to people in these occupations who apply for coverage, charge lower rates to people in other occupations, and again make a nice profit if the insurer's information is accurate and other companies do not quickly adopt similar strategies.

Similarly, recent evidence suggests that people with poor credit histories (e.g., a bad credit rating or bankruptcy in the past few years) have higher auto insurance claim costs on average than people with good credit histories. People with poor credit histories on average also might require a higher expense loading because of the greater likelihood of nonpayment of premiums and a lower expected renewal frequency. As a result, some insurers have begun to use credit history as an underwriting criterion. As a final example that was suggested earlier, many insurers, including many of the larger direct writers, have designed their marketing strategies and underwriting criteria to attract buyers who are likely to have good loss experience, renew coverage for a long period, and buy multiple policies.

Should the Government Restrict Underwriting?   Some people get annoyed by insurer underwriting practices and argue that the ability of insurers to underwrite should be heavily restricted by the government.[2] A handful of states have substantially constrained the ability of insurers to underwrite, in some cases by requiring each insurer to accept virtually all applicants. There generally is a close connection between regulatory prohibitions on rating factors and restrictions on underwriting. For example, if the government prohibits the use of a person's gender as a rating factor, then it may need to restrict insurer underwriting. Otherwise, some insurers may readily circumvent the prohibition by offering rates commensurate with the expected cost of insuring young females and then denying coverage to most young males.

When thinking about whether underwriting is socially beneficial, you should keep in mind that if restrictions prevent rates from being closely related to expected costs, they can distort behavior in ways that increase the cost of risk. In addition, we noted above that insurer underwriting practices do not prevent significant numbers of drivers from finding an insurer that is willing to accept them given their cost characteristics. Underwriting does not force large numbers of drivers into the residual market unless price regulation keeps the rate that can be charged below expected costs (see below). In most states that do not substantially restrict underwriting, an active specialty insurance market, known as the **nonstandard insurance market,** exists to serve drivers with characteristics that suggest significantly above-average expected claim and/or administrative costs.

Given the preceding discussion and the discussion in Chapter 6, you also should recognize that the use of underwriting criteria that do not separate buyers into more homogeneous groups would not be rewarded in the marketplace. Instead, the use of criteria that do not predict costs often will cause insurers to lose money due to adverse selection. It also is usually very difficult and costly to enforce constraints on underwriting given strong market incentives for insurers to charge prices commensurate with expected claim costs.

You might be wondering why insurers don't simply develop more rating classes with different prices that reflect their underwriting criteria and then accept all applicants at a price that reflects expected costs. (If you are, you are to be commended because this indicates that you are thinking about what you are reading.) One reason is that a single insurer seldom will have or find it cost-efficient to develop the expertise needed to prosper in all market segments. In other words, there are gains from specialization in different cost segments and underwriting helps achieve specialization. For example, it might not be efficient for an insurer to develop, market, and price to serve customers at all income levels due to income-related differences in the value of cars and homes, the amount of assets at risk from a lawsuit, the need for life insurance, the expected length of time that policies will be renewed, and so on.

In addition, to a certain extent, an insurer's underwriting criteria are proprietary. As a result, if an insurer obtains or develops information that helps it to

---

[2] Recall also from Chapter 6 that theory suggests the possibility that insurers may engage in excessive risk classification (and thus underwriting) in some instances.

more accurately classify drivers, it can use the information to establish underwriting criteria and thereby benefit its customers and make money without having its competitors immediately catch on. In contrast, rating plans almost always are filed with regulators and are therefore public information. Thus, rating plans can be quickly copied by competitors. If insurers had to announce all of their new ideas and analysis to the world, they would have less profit potential from investing resources to develop more accurate classifications. This would reduce their incentive to develop more accurate rating/underwriting systems that reduce cross-subsidies among buyers.

Cancellation and Nonrenewal.   Insurers usually give agents authority to issue policies (or "bind" coverage) before underwriting is completed. If additional investigation discovers new information indicating that the applicant does not meet the insurer's underwriting criteria, the insurer may be able to cancel the policy. This most commonly occurs when the applicant has failed to provide full and accurate information on the application for coverage. Similarly, events may occur during the coverage period, such as serious at-fault accidents or traffic violations, that cause the applicant to no longer meet the insurer's criteria. In these cases, the insurer may notify the customer that his or her coverage will not be renewed.

The personal auto policy allows the policyholder to cancel at any time, by giving the insurer advance written notice, and to receive a premium refund specified in the company's rate manual. If the policy has been in force for less than 60 days, the insurer can cancel by providing 10 days written notice for nonpayment of a premium and 20 days notice in other cases. Thus, this contractual provision allows the insurer to issue a policy before fully investigating whether a policyholder is acceptable and then cancel coverage if it is determined that the applicant does not meet its criteria. After 60 days (or after renewal), the policy only allows the insurer to cancel for nonpayment of a premium, suspension or revocation of a driver's license, or material misrepresentation. However, at the end of a policy period (generally six months or in some cases one year), the contract allows the insurer to deny renewal for any reason with 20 days written notice.

Many states have further limited the right of insurers to cancel coverage within a policy period. For example, cancellation within 60 days of issue also may be restricted to nonpayment of a premium, suspension or revocation of the owner's driver's license, or material misrepresentation or fraud. While much less common than restrictions on cancellation, some states only allow insurers to deny renewal for reasons specified by state law. In a few states, for example, insurers are required to renew coverage unless an owner or other insured is at fault in a serious accident or is convicted of a serious violation (e.g., driving under the influence).

Residual Markets

All states have automobile insurance residual markets that enable drivers who might otherwise find it difficult to obtain coverage to obtain coverage at a regulated price. As is illustrated in Table 21–3 (page 543) and Figure 21–4, the share of personal autos covered by liability insurance that is insured in the residual market varies widely across states. A large majority of states have very small residual markets. In 1995, for example, the residual market for auto liability coverage insured less than 1 percent of insured cars in 34 states. On the other hand, a handful of states have large residual markets.

The most important factor that explains differences in residual market share across states is regulation of prices and underwriting that prevents insurers from charging rates high enough to cover expected costs for some drivers. States with large residual markets restrict insurer rate classification (i.e., driver classes or territories) and/or in effect set a maximum permissible rate that is inadequate for insurers to cover their costs of insuring many drivers voluntarily. One method of limiting maximum rates is simply to establish residual market rates below expected costs for some drivers, which then in effect prevents insurers from charging higher rates to many of these drivers.

Another factor that can cause a state's residual market to become larger is prior approval regulation of rate changes. About half the states have prior ap-

FIGURE 21–4

States with auto liability insurance residual market shares of at least 0.5 percent in 1995

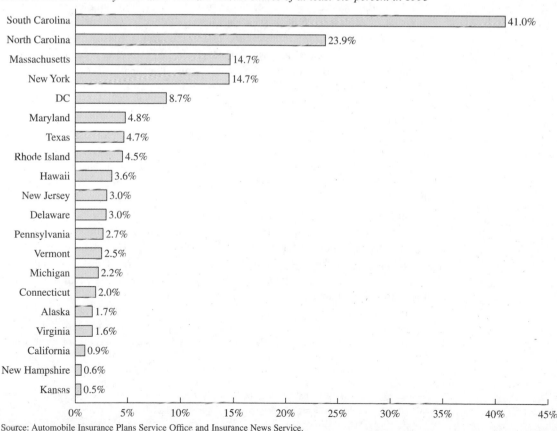

Source: Automobile Insurance Plans Service Office and Insurance News Service.

proval regulation for auto insurance. If regulators in these states do not approve rate increases commensurate with growth in expected claim costs, insurers will be less willing to take on new customers and more likely to deny renewal to some existing customers. Regulatory restrictions on rate increases are especially likely when costs are growing rapidly because of political pressure exerted by consumers against large rate increases. If cost growth slows and regulators are more willing to approve higher rates, the residual market will tend to decline in size, as insurers become more willing to write coverage voluntarily. Thus, to some extent, prior approval regulation will have temporary effects on residual market size. Restrictions on rate classification and maximum prices that can be charged to some consumers have a more permanent effect on residual market size.

There are four types of auto insurance residual markets. The common features are (1) guaranteed access to coverage at a regulated rate, and (2) any residual market deficit (excess of losses and expenses over premiums) is spread broadly across auto insurers and/or auto insurance policyholders.

Over 40 states use an **assigned risk plan.** (These plans are officially called "automobile insurance plans." We use the traditional name because it conveys useful information about how these plans work.) Applicants who have difficulty obtaining coverage can apply (using an agent) to the state's assigned risk plan, which is administered by insurers. The plan assigns applicants to individual insurers at rates that have been approved by regulators. Assignments are made in proportion to an insurer's total volume of auto insurance that it writes voluntarily in the state. For example, an insurer that writes 10 percent of the total voluntary business will get 10 percent of the assignments. The insurer issues the assigned policy, receives the premium, and is responsible for paying claims. Assigned risk plan rates in most states are significantly higher than rates charged by the leading voluntary insurers.

A few states with large residual markets use a **reinsurance facility** instead of an assigned risk plan. Under this approach, *each insurer is required to issue coverage to virtually anyone who applies to the insurer* using rates that have been approved by the government. Thus, underwriting is prohibited. Insurers are then allowed to reinsure policies for which they believe the rates are too low in a state reinsurance pool, known as the reinsurance facility. Because the rates are too low on business that is reinsured, the facility chronically loses money. Two different approaches have been used to deal with reinsurance facility deficits: (1) charge the deficit to all insurers in proportion to their total share of business that is not reinsured, and (2) charge the deficit directly to all insured drivers in the form of a recoupment fee set by the government.[3]

---

[3] Recoupment fees are used, for example, in South Carolina, the state with the largest residual market in 1995. While the fee for a given insured does not depend on whether his or her policy has been reinsured in the facility, it does depend on the person's driving record, with hefty charges for a poor record (e.g., about $1,000 over three years for one ticket for speeding more than 10 miles per hour over the limit). This system has substantially annoyed a majority of drivers and currently is being phased out, along with elimination of most of the restrictions on underwriting and rating that led to a large residual market.

Another type of residual market used in several states is a **joint underwriting association.** In this system, agents can submit applications to a number of insurers under contract with the state to issue residual market policies. These insurers receive fees with the net financial results (usually a deficit) for the residual market divided among all auto insurers in the state in proportion to their share of the voluntary auto insurance market. Maryland uses a **state insurer** as the residual market, with any deficits of its state insurer divided among auto insurers in proportion to their share of the voluntary auto insurance market.

Because large residual markets are caused by rate inadequacy, large residual markets produce large operating deficits. With a reinsurance facility and recoupment fees, other drivers directly subsidize the residual market deficit. In other cases, policyholders insured in the voluntary market also usually end up paying higher rates to subsidize the residual market. In fact, rates must eventually go up for the voluntary market if insurers are to cover their total expected costs of providing coverage. (We explained the effects of expected residual market deficits on voluntary market prices in some detail when we discussed workers' compensation insurance residual markets in Chapter 16.) Thus, large residual markets and deficits produce a system of cross-subsidies where some policyholders are in essence taxed through higher charges to offset, at least in part, inadequate residual market rates.

Concept Checks

1. Distinguish the use of underwriting criteria from the use of rating factors by insurers.
2. Can auto insurers underwrite in states that have assigned risk plans? In states with reinsurance facilities? In states with joint underwriting associations?

21.3 Should Auto Insurance Be Compulsory?

Many people fail to buy auto liability insurance voluntarily. Many other drivers are uninsured for medical expenses/loss of income that could result from an accident. To some extent, this lack of coverage might simply reflect that some people might not have the money to pay for insurance, or that they possibly might underestimate the risk of loss so that insurance looks like a bad deal (see Chapter 7). But a major reason why people fail to buy these coverages is that part or most of the costs of accidents will fall on other parties. For example, a driver with few assets is essentially judgment proof and thus has limited economic incentive to buy auto liability coverage. Similarly, if an uninsured person will receive medical care if injured in an automobile accident with the costs paid by other parties, the person will have much less incentive to buy insurance.

Economic arguments for compulsory insurance laws in these cases focus on the possibility that compulsory insurance can reduce the cost of risk by getting people to consider more of the costs of their actions when deciding whether to drive, what kind of car to buy, how safely to drive, and so on. However, many observers have criticized compulsory insurance laws in theory and in practice on a number of dimensions. We will first briefly review the economic rationale for compulsory insurance and then turn to some of these criticisms. We also will point out the effects of the laws on the revenues and costs of various parties and briefly introduce you to the issue of whether these laws are fair.

Economic Rationale

Effect on Decisions to Drive.   We will begin by ignoring the issue of how safely people might drive if they are not insured for liability or their own economic losses and instead focus exclusively on the effects of compulsory insurance on the decision to drive. The key idea is as follows: Without compulsory insurance, some people will drive even though the full costs that arise when they drive exceed their benefits from driving. Compulsory insurance will make some of these people give up driving, thus reducing the cost of risk.

Assume for example that the cost to Jack of having a car and driving compared to relying on alternative transportation is $150 per month. This amount includes the cost of the car, gas, and the expected costs of uninsured accidents that would be borne by Jack or any insurance that Jack has purchased against these losses. Also assume that the expected cost of harm to others when Jack drives without auto liability and medical coverage is $50 per month. This would include the expected damage to others from Jack's negligence and any expected medical expenses for Jack that would be borne by other parties. Thus, the total costs when Jack drives are $200 per month.

If Jack places a value on driving (compared to not driving) of at least $200, then the benefits of driving to Jack outweigh the total costs. However, if Jack only values driving at $175, then the total costs on all parties exceed the benefits to Jack by $25 ($200 – $175). But Jack will nonetheless drive (unless forced to buy insurance) because his benefits exceed the costs borne by him. In this case the cost of risk is not minimized when Jack drives, because the cost of driving ($200) exceeds the benefit of driving ($175).

Assume now for simplicity that Jack can buy auto liability and medical insurance coverage at a premium equal to the expected cost ($50). If a compulsory insurance law forces Jack to buy this coverage if he drives, then he will face a total cost of driving (including premiums) of $200. With the compulsory insurance law, Jack's benefits from driving ($175) are less than Jack's costs ($200). Therefore, in principle, he will give up driving. In this way, compulsory insurance reduces the cost of risk by getting people not to drive unless they value driving by an amount more than the costs associated with their driving.

We will call this argument for compulsory insurance the "pay or take the bus" rationale. You either pay for coverage and drive, or you give up driving and take the bus, walk, and so on. We think that this type of argument represents one reason that economists often puzzle people. Our guess is that if 10,000 randomly chosen adults were asked why auto liability insurance is compulsory, only a handful would say that it is important to have people give up driving who do not value driving more than the total costs. Many people might strongly support "getting uninsured drivers off the road," but this really is not the same point.

We conclude this brief discussion of the effect of compulsory insurance on the decision to drive with two observations. First, the fact that an argument seems obscure to many people does not mean it is a poor one. The "pay or take the bus" rationale is sound in principle. Second, if most people in America value driving a lot, then compulsory insurance will cause comparatively few people to give up driving: Most people will pay rather than take the bus.

Safety Effects.   A related rationale for compulsory insurance is that it might encourage people to drive more safely. This too can reduce the cost of risk. For example, a judgment proof driver without liability insurance will often have too little incentive to take precautions to reduce harm to other drivers. Forcing the person to buy auto liability insurance with premiums based on the person's driving record can encourage greater safety.

This argument also is relevant for compulsory auto medical coverage—even for people with group medical coverage. Making drivers buy auto medical coverage with premiums tied to their driving record will provide greater safety incentives than when group insurance is used because the cost of group coverage to the employee is unlikely to depend on the person's driving habits. On the other hand, the lower expense loading and other advantages of group insurance would have to be considered before concluding that the cost of risk could be reduced by making people buy auto medical coverage that would pay for losses up to the limit, with group medical serving as excess coverage. As we discuss in the next section, this issue also arises in the context of auto no-fault laws.

Criticisms and Limitations of Compulsory Insurance

Compulsory auto liability insurance laws have been criticized for a number of reasons and have several limitations in practice. Some of these criticisms and limitations also apply to compulsory auto medical or loss of income coverage.

Regressive Impact on the Distribution of Income/Pressure for Subsidies.   To the extent that compulsory insurance laws get people to buy coverage, they tend to shift income from low-income people with few assets to higher-income people with more assets. The reason is simple: Low-income people are the ones most likely to be affected by compulsory insurance laws, and they will be forced to pay more of the costs of losses that previously fell on other people who, on average, have higher incomes and assets. For example, with compulsory liability insurance, previously insured drivers should see some reduction in the cost of uninsured motorists insurance as more low-income drivers pay for liability coverage. Similarly, group medical coverage is more prevalent for middle-income and upper-income workers than for low-wage workers or the unemployed. The cost of group coverage might decline if compulsory medical coverage reduces the cost of hospital bad debts that might in part be shifted to group medical expense plans.

Some people are uneasy about whether compulsory coverage is fair given its regressive impact on the distribution of income (see Box 21–2). The regressive effects can be reduced if the cost of coverage is subsidized. This could be achieved, for example, by using price regulation to limit the price of auto coverage in low-income urban areas where the unregulated price would be high. As a practical matter, low-income people who are forced to buy expensive liability coverage also might exert substantial political pressure for subsidies that outweighs pressure against subsidies.

While any rate subsidies in response to compulsory insurance reduce the burden of compulsory insurance on low-income persons, they also reduce the

---

Box 21–2

Are Compulsory Liability Insurance Laws Fair?

Like Ishmael and Queequeg in Melville's *Moby Dick,* opponents of compulsory auto liability laws sometimes make for strange bedfellows. For example, some liberals oppose the laws because they harm many low-income people. The regressive impact of the laws is difficult to reconcile with accepted liberal philosophies of fairness/justice, such as the "maximin" criterion for justice enunciated by John Rawls in his book, *The Theory of Justice.* The maximin criterion holds that differences in wealth across people are fair only if they maximize the welfare of the least well-off people in society. Rawls argues that people would rationally support this criterion if they had to decide on how to organize society without knowing what their talents or circumstances would be—for example, if people had to decide on the rules of the game without knowing anything about whether they would be good at it compared to other people. Some people say that compulsory liability laws are at best very difficult to reconcile with this notion of justice.

On the opposite end of the spectrum, libertarians are not very excited about compulsory liability insurance, either. Robert Nozick's classic exposition of libertarian philosophy in his book, *Anarchy, State, and Utopia,* specifically rejects compulsory liability insurance as representing an unjust intrusion of the state on private decisions. The reason is that it forces people to incur large costs just because they *might* be-

have in a way that is harmful to others. (We suspect that Nozick might support tough financial responsibility laws that do not force people to pay for expensive coverage before they harm others.)

On the other hand, compulsory auto liability insurance laws might be consistent with what can be called the "Do the Right Thing" argument. (We don't know whether Spike Lee has ever thought about this.) The idea is that responsible people will buy liability insurance to make sure that they can pay for at least part of the harm that they may cause others and that it is ethical for people to behave responsibly. This idea has its roots in ancient Greek philosophy and the Old Testament. For example, while silent about insurance companies and trial lawyers, Aristotle's concept of "corrective justice" and the discussion of responsibility for harm in Chapters 20–21 in the book of Exodus both more or less support the idea that people should bear responsibility for the harm that they cause.

The extent to which a majority of people hold "Do the Right Thing" views and whether this materially influences their support for compulsory liability laws is not clear. It is possible that a majority of people support these laws just because they think that they will save money when other people are compelled to buy coverage, regardless of whether this savings actually is achieved to any significant extent in practice.

ability of these laws to reduce the cost of risk by making low-income persons bear
the costs of their actions. Previously insured drivers might now pay lower premiums for uninsured motorists coverage but have to pay higher premiums for other
coverage to finance subsidies to low-income persons. Under these conditions, the
effects on different people and the cost of risk can become quite murky. In addition, rate subsidies often lead to other distortions, such as large residual markets
and decreased incentives to take care.

Weak Enforcement.   While detailed data on uninsured drivers are not available,
it is estimated that 15–20 percent of drivers violate compulsory insurance laws
nationwide. Allowable penalties for a first-time violation usually include a fine,
such as $100–$250, and possible suspension or revocation of the driver's license
or vehicle registration, with harsher penalties for subsequent violations. However,
the penalty for first-time violators is not mandatory in many states and often is
not imposed. Some states have recently increased penalties and improved enforcement. (Several states also have adopted laws that prevent uninsured drivers
from suing other drivers for pain and suffering damages.) Nonetheless, some people suggest that relatively weak penalties and enforcement lead to a perverse result: low-income, honest people "pay through the nose" for liability insurance
that benefits other people, while low-income, dishonest people break the law.

While weak enforcement reduces the political pressure that arises when low-
income people with little wealth are told that they have to buy expensive insurance that benefits other parties in order to drive a car, this argument for weak enforcement comes close to saying that strictly enforced compulsory insurance is
not politically viable. This raises the question: Then why bother to have the laws?
An answer is that some people will comply with the law, thus helping to reduce
the cost of risk. In addition, people who break the law might drive more safely in
order to avoid getting caught and having to pay a fine and demonstrate that they
have purchased coverage in the future. In this regard, compulsory insurance laws
may be like speed limits. They are not very threatening, but they get people to
slow down, at least a little.

Alternatives to Compulsory Insurance

It might surprise you that most insurance company trade organizations have traditionally opposed compulsory auto liability insurance. At least in part, this reflects the belief that forcing people to buy products that do not benefit them much
will likely lead to other problems, such as efforts by regulators to regulate the
price of coverage to make it affordable. Insurers and other opponents of compulsory liability laws often recommend returning to financial responsibility laws
with tougher sanctions. People would not have to buy coverage, but if they cause
an accident and do not have coverage they will face significant fines and a possible loss of driving privileges.

Instead of compulsory liability insurance, at least one state (Virginia) requires drivers who do not want to buy coverage to pay an annual fee to the state
that is less than the cost of liability coverage for many buyers (e.g., $400). The

funds are used to reduce the cost of uninsured motorists insurance. While South Carolina adopted a similar law effective in 1999 and other states are considering this type of change, the future of compulsory liability coverage appears to be secure (at least for the time being!). A majority of voters appear to support compulsory liability insurance laws (see Box 21–2). Politically powerful trial lawyer groups also generally support the laws.

Concept Check

3. What effect will compulsory auto liability insurance laws have on the demand for personal injury lawyers? (This question is not as easy as it seems if you consider the impact of compulsory liability on the number of uninsured motorist claims.)

21.4 Should Tort Liability Be Limited with No-fault Laws?

No-fault Compared to Tort Liability

Under tort liability systems for auto accidents, drivers that cause accidents can be sued for damages by injured parties under a negligence standard. For the reasons discussed in the previous section, most drivers are required to pay at least part of the costs they impose on others. Under a **pure no-fault** approach to compensating auto accident victims, tort liability for auto accidents would be eliminated. Instead, drivers would bear their own losses. For the same types of reasons given for compulsory liability insurance under a tort system, a no-fault system usually requires drivers to purchase first-party personal injury protection (PIP) insurance that will pay their own losses (or be covered for these losses by other types of health insurance). Without some medical cost and loss-of-income insurance, some drivers could shift the cost of accidents to others in society. Thus, first-party health coverage for losses from auto accidents would be required under a pure no-fault approach, but liability insurance would not be needed because drivers could neither sue nor be sued for damages.

Table 21–4 lists the 24 states as of early 1998 with either compulsory or optional PIP coverage and whether these states limit tort liability. No state has adopted a pure no-fault system.[4] However, during the 1970s, 15 states (Colorado, Connecticut, Florida, Georgia, Hawaii, Kansas, Massachusetts, Michigan, Minnesota, Nevada, New Jersey, New York, North Dakota, Pennsylvania, and Utah) adopted **compulsory no-fault laws** for automobile insurance with two main features. First, the purchase of first-party PIP coverage with specified benefits for medical expenses and loss of income was made compulsory for auto owners. Second, tort liability for bodily injury arising from auto accidents was limited but not eliminated.[5] These laws often are called "modified" no-fault to contrast them with pure no-fault. We will resist this temptation because we feel that this naming con-

---

[4] Pure no-fault is used in New Zealand.

[5] Most no-fault statutes apply only to personal autos and exclude motorcycles. Only Michigan limits tort liability for property damage.

TABLE 21–4 Personal Injury Coverage and Limits on Tort Liability in 1998

State	PIP Coverage	Tort Limitation	Threshold
Arkansas	Optional		
Colorado	Compulsory	Yes	Dollar
Delaware	Compulsory		
DC	Optional		
Florida	Compulsory	Yes	Verbal
Hawaii	Compulsory	Yes	Dollar
Kansas	Compulsory	Yes	Dollar
Kentucky	Optional	Choice	Dollar
Maryland	Compulsory		
Massachusetts	Compulsory	Yes	Dollar
Michigan	Compulsory	Yes	Verbal
Minnesota	Compulsory	Yes	Dollar
New Hampshire	Optional		
New Jersey	Optional	Choice	Verbal
New York	Compulsory	Yes	Verbal
North Dakota	Compulsory	Yes	Dollar
Oregon	Compulsory		
Pennsylvania	Optional	Choice	Verbal
South Carolina	Optional		
South Dakota	Optional		
Texas	Optional		
Utah	Compulsory	Yes	Dollar
Virginia	Optional		
Wisconsin	Optional		

Sources: No-Fault Auto Insurance, *Insurance Issues Update* (March 1998), and *The Fact Book 1998* (Insurance Information Institute).

vention conveys little information (compared to "limited" or "partial" or even "half-a-loaf" no-fault) and therefore should itself be "modified."

Kentucky enacted what is appropriately known as a **choice no-fault law** during this period that allows auto owners to choose whether to buy PIP coverage and limit their tort liability. In addition, several states enacted so-called "add-on laws" that mandated purchase of PIP coverage without limiting tort liability, and several others made insurers offer optional PIP coverage without making people buy it, again without restricting tort liability. Three states (Connecticut, Georgia, and Nevada) subsequently repealed their compulsory no-fault laws, and two states (New Jersey and Pennsylvania) converted to choice no-fault, largely in response to rapid claim cost growth under their compulsory no-fault laws.

You should note that compulsory no-fault laws are similar to workers' compensation laws in that they specify mandatory insurance benefits for injuries and limit (although in the case of no-fault they do not eliminate) tort liability. No-fault laws thus might be viewed as state-mandated covenants among drivers to limit tort liability (the right to sue and be sued) coupled with mandatory first-party insurance. We will now (1) describe PIP coverage and tort limitations, (2) discuss the rationale for and against no-fault, including its possible effects on safety, and (3) explain the effects of no-fault on premiums for auto insurance and group medical insurance. This discussion focuses first on compulsory no-fault; we then discuss choice no-fault and alternative no-fault proposals.

PIP Benefits and Limitations on Tort Liability with Compulsory No-fault

PIP Benefits.   The magnitude of required PIP benefits for medical expenses and loss of income varies widely across states with compulsory no-fault laws. For example, the minimum amount of total benefits for medical expenses and loss of income is less than $10,000 in Massachusetts, approximately $50,000 in New York, over $100,000 in Colorado, and unlimited (due to unlimited medical coverage) in Michigan. Like first-party medical payments coverage in states without no-fault laws, drivers and occupants of the vehicle are paid these benefits for injuries without regard to fault, and the policyholder must pay a premium that reflects the cost of providing these benefits. PIP benefits generally are primary and group/individual medical expense coverage is excess.[6] As a result, mandatory PIP benefits produce a reduction in the costs of group/individual medical insurance. (Our later discussion for simplicity focuses on the possible effects on group medical costs.)

Limitations on Tort Liability.   Compulsory no-fault laws limit tort liability in two ways. First, an injured party who receives PIP benefits generally cannot sue another driver for losses covered by PIP coverage. Second, and very important, an injured party cannot sue for pain and suffering unless the magnitude of the injury satisfies a **threshold** specified in the no-fault law. Some states (see Table 21–4) specify a "dollar threshold" that requires economic losses (usually medical expenses) to exceed a specified dollar amount. In recent years the dollar thresholds used in different states generally have ranged from $2,000 to $4,000. Other states use a "verbal threshold" that generally eliminates suits for pain and suffering unless there is "significant permanent injury." The ultimate effect of a verbal threshold depends on how its specific wording is interpreted by the state's court system. Michigan's verbal threshold generally is regarded as having the strongest limitation on suits for pain and suffering compared to other states' verbal and dollar thresholds. It has eliminated suits for pain and suffering in a large majority of at-fault accidents.

We emphasize that no real world no-fault law eliminates tort liability. There is no "pure" no-fault, and most laws still allow large numbers of lawsuits. As a result, persons with assets to protect or who wish to comply with state compulsory liability/financial responsibility laws still need to buy auto liability insurance, and it often won't be cheap.

---

[6] Drivers in Michigan can make PIP coverage excess over group or individual medical insurance coverage and receive a premium reduction.

The Rationale for and against No-fault

Does no-fault have the potential to reduce the cost of risk? Academics, legislators, and other parties have debated the pros and cons of no-fault for 30 years. Most recently, debate has focused on choice no-fault, and a federal choice no-fault bill has been introduced in Congress. The advantages of no-fault primarily relate to its ability to improve compensation compared to the tort liability system. The disadvantages relate to its possible effects on safety. However, the key issue that many consumers focus on is how no-fault will affect the cost of insurance, especially the cost of auto insurance.

More Efficient Compensation with No-fault.   In Chapter 14 you learned about a number of disadvantages of the tort liability system when viewed solely as a compensation (insurance) system. Compared to traditional tort liability systems, all no-fault laws to some extent increase compensation for economic loss through first-party insurance and reduce compensation for economic loss and pain and suffering through third-party liability insurance. From the perspective of optimal compensation, this has several advantages:

• The reduction in coverage for pain and suffering is potentially beneficial from the perspective of optimal compensation if consumers generally would not be willing to purchase coverage for pain and suffering voluntarily.

• More economic losses are covered by insurance because, among other reasons, more people will have first-party coverage that pays even when no other driver is at fault.

• Payment for loss generally is faster with PIP coverage than with a tort liability suit.

• There is less duplication of coverage because PIP benefits and group medical benefits are coordinated. With tort liability the injured party's medical insurance does not reduce the person's tort claim for damages (see Chapter 14), and group medical insurers sometimes do not have or exercise the right of subrogation against negligent drivers.

• Dispute resolution costs are lower with no-fault because there are fewer tort liability suits. Bodily injury liability suits almost always involve attorney representation for the injured party, and they often produce significant defense costs for the liability insurer. While some policyholders hire an attorney to represent them when seeking recovery for losses covered by their PIP coverage, a majority of PIP claims are settled without attorney representation for the claimant and without significant dispute resolution costs for insurers.

Effect on Safety and the Decision to Drive.   A major argument that has been used against no-fault is that limitations on tort liability will lead to less safety and more accidents. This key idea follows directly from the main rationale for tort liability in the first place: Tort liability often is necessary to get people to consider the expected cost of harm to others when making decisions about risky activities and precautions. In principle, limits on tort liability will cause more costs of driver negligence to fall on other parties, thus reducing incentives not to be negligent. Limits on tort liability also will encourage some people to drive who value driving less than its full cost, including expected harm to others (recall "pay or take the bus").

These predictions hold when tort liability is restricted, other things being equal. But it also is important to consider that other things will not be equal if no-fault is adopted. In particular, under the traditional tort system, many drivers buy only small amounts of medical payments coverage, are covered by group medical insurance, or are basically uninsured for most medical expenses that would arise from an auto accident. Other things being equal, requiring these drivers to buy primary PIP coverage will increase incentives for safety and perhaps encourage some drivers who value driving less than the full cost to give up driving. This is because medical expense/loss-of-income insurance premiums are more closely tied to precautions and the decision to drive under no-fault.[7]

In principle, premiums for PIP coverage will depend on accident involvement, traffic safety violations, and whether the driver was "at-fault" as long as these factors help predict future accident involvement. Thus, reduced safety incentives under experience-rated liability insurance when tort liability is limited will at least in part be offset by improved safety incentives associated with experience-rated PIP coverage. In addition, persons will have to consider the cost of PIP coverage when they decide whether to drive. As a result, the overall effects of no-fault on safety and the decision to drive are uncertain in theory. If no-fault were to reduce safety and increase accidents in practice, the state might be able to increase penalties for traffic violations or even levy fines for at-fault accidents in a way that would limit any adverse effects on safety.

Have no-fault laws affected accident rates? Quite a few studies have examined this issue, mostly by comparing motor vehicle fatality rates between states with and without no-fault and, less commonly, before and after the adoption of no-fault. The results of these studies do not demonstrate any consistent effect of no-fault. This in part may reflect that tort limitations and PIP benefits under many no-fault laws are modest so that it is hard to estimate their effects on accident rates.

Retribution and Fairness.   A common argument against no-fault with strong limitations on tort liability is that it would be unfair to allow a drunk and/or grossly reckless driver not to be sued for causing a severe injury. There are at least two responses to this argument: (1) do not limit tort liability in these specific cases, and/or (2) increase fines and other legal penalties for these cases, which might achieve more punishment/retribution than simply having the person's liability insurance premium go up. However, the more that people like to sue or derive psychological or emotional satisfaction from recovering from another driver's liability insurer, the more advantageous is traditional tort liability compared to no-fault.

---

[7] Limitations on compensation for pain and suffering also might cause drivers to drive more safely to avoid being injured.

How Does No-fault Affect Premiums?

Now, for the issue that some of you have been waiting for: Will no-fault reduce my auto insurance premium? We first discuss the possible effects in principle and then discuss the evidence concerning existing laws. We also address the effects on group medical insurance costs. Our discussion of the "theory" will not consider possible effects on safety and the decision to drive. Compared to the main effects discussed, these effects generally would be expected to be small.

Effect on Auto Insurance Premiums.   The overall effect of a no-fault law on average auto insurance premiums depends on the effects on liability premiums and PIP premiums:

1. Liability insurance premiums will decline for three reasons: (*a*) injured parties who have losses paid by PIP coverage will not be able to sue the at-fault driver for these losses; (*b*) suits for pain and suffering will be reduced by the state's threshold for such suits; and (*c*) auto liability insurers' defense costs will decline accordingly. The greater the amount of PIP benefits and the stronger the state's threshold for pain and suffering suits, the greater will be the reduction in liability insurance premiums.

2. Premiums for PIP coverage increase directly with the magnitude of required benefits. PIP premiums will reflect the expected cost of benefits paid to persons injured by at-fault drivers that previously would have been paid by at-fault drivers' liability insurance. PIP premiums also will reflect the expected cost of losses to persons who are not injured by at-fault drivers with liability insurance and thus who would not be compensated by auto insurance without mandatory PIP coverage (apart from small amounts of auto medical payments coverage that might be purchased voluntarily).

In general, large mandatory PIP benefits with little restriction on lawsuits for pain and suffering will cause average premiums to go up. There is evidence that this occurred in some states that originally adopted no-fault laws with large PIP benefits and low dollar thresholds ($250–$1,000) for pain and suffering suits (e.g., Nevada, New Jersey, and Pennsylvania). In contrast, if the threshold for pain and suffering suits is strong enough, the reduction in liability insurance premiums can exceed the magnitude of required PIP premiums so that total auto premiums will decline.

It is difficult to measure these effects with existing laws. However, simulated analysis of hypothetical PIP benefit amounts and tort thresholds using data on injury losses suggests that material limitations on suits for pain and suffering coupled with moderate PIP benefits could produce total liability and PIP premiums 25–40 percent lower than liability insurance premiums without no-fault (see the Carroll et al. study listed at the end of the chapter). The reason is that reduced payments for pain and suffering and lower dispute resolution costs are more than sufficient to pay PIP benefit costs for persons that are not injured by at-fault drivers and thus who would have received on average little compensation through voluntary auto medical payments coverage.

FIGURE 21–5

Effect of no-fault on auto insurance premiums

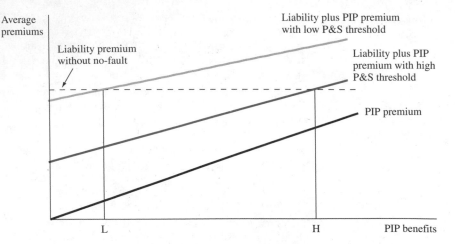

Figure 21–5 illustrates these effects graphically for laws with low and high thresholds for pain and suffering (P&S) suits. If PIP benefits are less than L, the restriction of pain and suffering suits by the low threshold cuts liability costs enough to produce an average premium for combined liability and PIP coverage that is lower than the average liability premium without no-fault. With the high tort threshold, PIP benefits will produce a lower average combined premium than the average liability premium without no-fault as long as PIP benefits do not exceed H. A stronger threshold might permit even higher PIP benefits before no-fault would increase average premiums.

Effect on Premiums for Group Medical Coverage.   The focus of many consumers and much of the political debate about how no-fault affects auto insurance premiums, while perhaps understandable, is a bit shortsighted. To the extent that PIP benefits are primary and group medical benefits are excess, group medical insurance costs will decline as mandatory PIP benefits are increased. Other things being equal, this will allow employers to pay higher wages or reduce employee contributions to group medical insurance costs without increasing the employer's total cost of labor (see Chapter 18). To be sure, this benefit to employees is likely to be much less visible than the effects of no-fault on auto insurance premiums.

As we noted earlier, a possible disadvantage of having PIP coverage primary compared to group medical insurance is that the expense loading for auto PIP coverage sold to individuals generally is higher than for group insurance (or administrative costs for group self-insurance). In addition, auto PIP premiums are not income-tax deductible, whereas the costs for group coverage usually are not taxed as income to the employee. These factors suggest that it might be advantageous (to people who prefer lower taxes) to make auto PIP coverage excess, as is done in a few states. However, making PIP coverage excess can create administrative problems associated with verifying other insurance and providing a suitable premium reduction for PIP coverage given that the amount of group medical coverage differs across drivers. Moreover, making auto coverage excess will reduce safety incentives by reducing the extent to which premiums for medical/loss-of-income coverage for auto accidents will depend on a person's driving record, and less of the expected costs of accidents will be considered by people when deciding whether to drive.

Choice No-fault

Auto insurance company trade associations historically have supported no-fault. Physician and hospital groups generally have supported mandatory PIP benefits because these laws make it more likely that people injured in auto accidents will have medical insurance. Trial lawyers have strongly resisted no-fault and have fought to prevent increases in thresholds in existing laws. In a few states the outcome of political battles over no-fault has been the adoption of choice no-fault.

As the name implies, choice no-fault allows drivers to decide whether to purchase PIP coverage and accept some modification in tort rights. Under current choice no-fault laws, drivers who opt for no-fault generally cannot sue other drivers for losses covered by PIP coverage and cannot sue for pain and suffering unless losses exceed a specified threshold. In exchange, drivers who choose no-fault receive a mandatory reduction in their liability insurance premiums. However, drivers who do not choose no-fault still can sue them.[8]

Two other types of choice no-fault laws have been proposed. One proposal would allow people who do not choose no-fault to sue each other without limitation. People who choose no-fault would have their exposure to tort liability and their rights to sue others limited. If person A did not choose no-fault and was harmed by person B who did, A could recover damages from his or her own insurer from coverage similar to uninsured motorists coverage. Thus, compared to people who chose no-fault, people who rejected no-fault would have to pay more for liability insurance and pay for the right to recover damages from their own insurer if they were hurt by an at-fault driver that had chosen no-fault. An alternative proposal would allow persons that rejected no-fault to sue everybody, but drivers who had chosen no-fault could sue them in turn.

We noted earlier that compulsory no-fault laws might be viewed as agreements among drivers to limit tort liability (the right to sue and be sued) coupled

---

[8] The premium reductions that must be given are designed to reflect the total savings in liability claim costs. The savings in liability claim costs for a given insurer need not equal the reduction in premiums. For example, while most of a given insurer's customers might accept no-fault, many of them may harm drivers who have not chosen no-fault, and the insurer will have to defend them and pay claims without any restriction on tort liability. Insurers and regulators have developed "risk exchanges" to deal with this problem by, in essence, requiring insurers that have cost savings greater than the reduction in premiums to compensate insurers whose costs savings are less than the reduction in liability insurance premiums.

with mandatory first-party insurance. Viewed within this framework, choice no-fault laws make participation in the agreement to limit tort liability voluntary. However, you can see that choice no-fault laws and proposals are not necessarily simple. This complexity reduces the attractiveness of some of these proposals. But if you like the idea of limiting your rights to sue in exchange for limits on your exposure to liability, choice no-fault may be better than no no-fault.

Other Proposals to Limit Tort Liability

Another type of no-fault proposal that has been suggested in some states would restrict recovery for pain and suffering in lawsuits without making the purchase of PIP coverage compulsory. People could still sue for economic loss and perhaps recover attorney fees. They also could choose to buy some PIP coverage or simply rely on individual/group health insurance to cover their losses.

A more radical proposal would restrict lawsuits for both economic loss and pain and suffering without mandating PIP coverage, as is done in a few states for uninsured drivers. How would people be compensated for economic losses if they could not sue? The same way that they are now compensated if they are hurt in an auto accident and no one else is at fault. They could rely on group or individual health insurance or buy auto medical coverage or optional PIP coverage. As is now the case, low-income uninsured persons generally would receive "free" medical care with the costs falling on other parties.

The possibility of restricting tort liability for economic loss and pain and suffering without requiring PIP coverage has received little discussion. Perhaps this is because it would exacerbate the uninsured problem and reduce incentives for safety. This lack of discussion also may reflect the notion (enunciated in early court decisions on the constitutionality of no-fault laws) that if people give up tort rights they have to be given some other "remedy" (such as the *obligation* to buy first-party coverage). But this linkage is not very tight. A person that "gives up some rights" when tort liability is restricted automatically receives something in return—reduced exposure to lawsuits from other people.

Concept Check

4. Assume that restrictions on recovery of damages for pain and suffering in lawsuits are adopted without mandating purchase of PIP coverage. Describe the possible effects on safety and the decision to drive compared to: (*a*) the traditional tort liability system, and (*b*) a compulsory no-fault law (restrictions on tort liability with compulsory PIP coverage).

21.5 Summary

- The personal auto policy includes four main coverages: (1) coverage for liability to third
parties harmed by the negligence of an insured person; (2) coverage for medical payments or,

in some states, personal injury protection coverage for medical expenses and loss of income; (3) coverage for losses caused by uninsured or underinsured motorists; and (4) coverage for physical damage to and theft of insured autos.

- Personal auto insurers generally use rate classification systems that reflect driver characteristics such as age, sex, marital status, whether the car is driven to work or for business, driving record, and the geographic territory in which the auto is located. Rates are lower for insurers with more stringent underwriting criteria.

- All states have auto insurance residual markets that allow drivers to obtain coverage who would not be insured voluntarily due to rate inadequacy. Most states use an assigned risk plan. The residual market is very small in a majority of states because insurers are allowed to charge rates commensurate with the expected costs of insuring different people. A few states require each insurer to accept almost all applicants but they then may reinsure applicants for which rates are perceived as inadequate in a state reinsurance facility.

- Almost all states make the purchase of auto liability insurance compulsory; a number of states mandate the purchase of personal injury protection coverage. Economic arguments for compulsory insurance focus on the possible benefits of getting people to reflect more upon the costs of their actions when deciding whether to drive, what kind of car to buy, and how safely to drive—as opposed to having these costs fall on others. Compulsory insurance laws are criticized for weak enforcement in many states and for having a regressive impact on the distribution of income, which increases pressure to subsidize rates for certain groups through price regulation.

- Some states have compulsory no-fault laws that require drivers to purchase specified personal injury protection coverage and restrict tort liability. A few states have choice no-fault laws that allow drivers to elect whether to buy personal injury protection coverage and have restricted tort liability rights. No-fault laws with moderate personal injury protection coverage limits and material restrictions on tort liability have the potential both to improve the efficiency of compensation and to reduce auto insurance premiums. One argument against no-fault is that restricting tort liability might lead to more accidents; another criticism is that some no-fault laws have not reduced premiums.

Key Terms

personal auto policy   534
auto liability coverage   535
compulsory liability insurance laws   535
financial responsibility laws   535
auto medical payments coverage   537
personal injury protection coverage   537
uninsured motorists coverage   538
underinsured motorists coverage   538
collision coverage   540
other-than-collision coverage   540
territorial rating   543

underwriting criteria   548
nonstandard insurance market   549
assigned risk plan   552
reinsurance facility   552
joint underwriting association   553
state insurer   553
pure no-fault   558
compulsory no-fault laws   558
choice no-fault law   559
threshold   560

Questions and Problems

1. Why might a person rationally buy liability insurance with limits greater than his or her limits on underinsured motorists coverage?

2. Develop an argument for how uninsured motorists and underinsured motorists insurance might be improved from the perspective of optimal compensation.

3. In view of moral hazard, explain why it might be optimal for a person to have a lower deductible for other-than-collision coverage than for collision coverage.

4. Describe the major rating factors used in automobile insurance.

5. Consider an auto insurance policy that for a period of five years would guarantee annual renewal to the policyholder at the same premium rate the insurer charges to drivers that have not had accidents or tickets. In other words, the contract would guarantee the policyholder against rate increases that otherwise would occur from a poor driving record. (Thus, to some extent it would be similar to guaranteed renewable health insurance discussed in Chapter 18.) Do you think that people would be willing to pay enough for this contract to allow the insurer to cover expected costs over the life of the contract? Explain.

6. Explain why insurers have the incentive to sell coverage voluntarily to a driver as long as the price that can be charged is greater than or equal to the expected costs of providing coverage (i.e., the fair premium). Why does this imply that residual markets usually will lose money?

7. Explain what might happen to accident rates if compulsory auto liability insurance laws were repealed and tort liability were restricted without mandating the purchase of PIP coverage. How could the government promote greater driving safety if these changes were made?

8. Explain how compulsory insurance laws might lead to fewer accidents for people who disobey the law and drive without coverage.

9. Argue (*a*) the case for compulsory auto liability insurance laws, and (*b*) the case against these laws. Do the same thing for compulsory PIP coverage assuming no restriction on tort liability.

10. What are the similarities between the key features of workers' compensation laws and auto no-fault laws?

11. Who would benefit most from restrictions on tort liability for auto accidents, a high-risk driver or a low-risk driver? Answer the same question if restrictions on tort liability are combined with mandatory PIP coverage in a no-fault system.

12. Many state legislators are personal injury lawyers. How might this affect the likelihood that no-fault is adopted and the main features of no-fault laws that are adopted? Do you think that voting on no-fault legislation represents a conflict of interest for these lawyer/legislators? Why or why not?

References

Carroll, Stephen, et al. *No-Fault Approaches to Compensating People Injured in Automobile Accidents.* Rand Institute for Civil Justice Report R-4019-ICJ. Santa Monica, CA: Rand, 1991.

(*Discussion and analysis of the effects of no-fault on compensation and premiums.*)

Cummins, J. David; and Sharon Tennyson. "Controlling Automobile Insurance Costs." *The Journal of*

Economic Perspectives 6 (1992), pp. 95–115. (*Discusses how claim cost increases are the major cause of premium increases and possible approaches to controlling costs, including no-fault.*)

Harrington, Scott. "Taxing Low Income Households in Search of the Public Interest: The Case of Compulsory Automobile Insurance." In *Insurance, Risk Management, and Public Policy: Essays in Honor of Robert I. Mehr,* eds. Scott Harrington and Sandra Gustavson. Boston: Kluwer Academic, 1994. (*Detailed discussion of the economics, fairness, and politics of compulsory auto insurance laws.*)

O'Connell, Jeffrey; and Robert H. Joost. "Giving Motorists a Choice between Fault and No-Fault." *Virginia Law Review* 72 (1986). (*Detailed analysis of choice no-fault.*)

Answers to Concept Checks

1. Rating factors are used to place drivers in a specific rate class. Insurers then employ underwriting criteria to determine whether to offer coverage to the applicant at the class rate.

2. Auto insurers can underwrite in states with assigned risk plans and joint underwriting associations. An insurer can deny coverage to an applicant, who then can apply for coverage through the assigned risk plan or through a servicing insurer for the joint underwriting association. In states with reinsurance facilities, each insurer is required to offer coverage to most applicants, but the insurer can use some underwriting criteria to determine whether to retain the risk or reinsure the coverage in the state reinsurance facility.

3. Because more people will have liability insurance to pay tort liability settlements, compulsory liability laws tend to increase the number of lawsuits and thus the demand for personal injury lawyers. However, because compulsory liability will reduce the number of uninsured motorists, the increase in demand will be offset in part by reductions in the number of uninsured motorist claimants who would have hired an attorney.

4. (*a*) Unless greater penalties for unsafe driving are adopted or enforcement of motor vehicle codes is increased, incentives for safety will likely decline, and more people will drive compared to the traditional tort system because liability insurance costs will decline and thus have less effect on safety and the decision to drive.

   (*b*) Incentives for safety will likely decline and more people will drive compared to a compulsory no-fault law because experience-rated compulsory PIP coverage raises the cost of driving and provides increased incentives for safety.

Homeowners Insurance

Chapter Objectives

- Describe homeowners insurance and personal umbrella liability insurance policies.
- Describe property insurance arrangements for catastrophic perils, including FAIR plans, the National Flood Insurance Program, and beach and windstorm plans.
- Analyze the impact of catastrophes on property insurance and the market's response to large catastrophes.

22.1 Homeowners Insurance

Homeowners insurance is the second largest line of personal insurance for property-liability insurers, behind auto insurance. In 1996, United States homeowners insurance premiums equaled $24.5 billion, making the homeowners market in the United States about 19 percent of the personal property-liability insurance market. (The remaining 81 percent is auto insurance.) Most insurers writing homeowners policies are multiline insurers who also sell personal auto and life insurance. Over 500 companies sell homeowners insurance across the United States, and the market shares of the leading insurers within each state generally are not large. The largest five writers of homeowners insurance in the United States (with 1996 national market shares in parentheses) were State Farm (24.2 percent), Allstate (12.2 percent), Farmers Insurance Group (5.5 percent), Nationwide (3.6 percent), and USAA (3.5 percent). All of the top five insurers are direct writers; all but USAA also ranked in the top five for personal auto insurance.

Types of Policies

Homeowners policies are multiple-line, multiple-peril policies. They provide first-party property, third-party liability, and third-party medical expense coverage. Property is covered from losses due to multiple perils (e.g., fire, windstorms, and theft). In some cases, the policy lists the perils that are covered (a **named peril policy**). In other cases, the policy covers all perils except those specifically excluded (known as an **open peril policy** or **all risk policy**).

Homeowners policies are standardized to a large extent. That is, the policy structure and language, as well as the types of coverages, the exclusions, and so on, generally are similar across insurers. Most insurers sell policies that are very similar if not identical to the standard policy forms that have been developed by the Insurance Services Office (ISO), a private organization that provides rating and policy form services to the insurance industry. There are six basic types of policy forms: HO1 (basic form), HO2 (broad form), HO3 (special form), HO4 (contents broad form), HO6 (condominium unit owners form), and HO8 (modified coverage form).[1] The different forms generally apply to different types of situations; forms HO1, HO2, HO3, and HO8 are for homeowners, HO4 is for renters, and HO6, as is obvious from its name, is for condominium owners. The most common homeowners policy by far is the **HO3 policy.**

Description of Major Coverages

Policies for homeowners typically provide six basic coverages. These coverages, which are listed in Table 22–1, are labeled A through F. The first three coverages provide reimbursement for property damage, and the other three provide reimbursement for loss of use, liability losses, and medical expenses, respectively. Next to the name of each type of coverage in Table 22–1 is a brief description of how the amount of coverage is determined under the HO3 form. Homeowners policies also provide a number of other coverages, such as coverage for debris removal and fire department service charges.

TABLE 22–1   Homeowners Insurance Coverages

Type of Coverage	*Amount of Coverage in HO3 Policy*
A. Dwelling	Chosen by policyholder
B. Other structures	10% of dwelling coverage
C. Unscheduled personal property	50% of dwelling coverage
D. Loss of use (e.g., additional living expenses if dwelling cannot be occupied)	20% of dwelling coverage
E. Personal liability	$100,000*
F. Medical payments to others	$1,000 per person*
	$25,000 aggregate limit*

*These limits can be increased.

---

[1] HO5 and HO7 policy forms once existed, but have since been discontinued.

The amount of dwelling coverage (A) chosen by the policyholder determines the amount of coverage for other structures (B), personal property (C), and additional living expenses (D). For example, if the policyholder chooses $100,000 of dwelling coverage, then the HO3 policy provides $10,000 for other structures, $50,000 for personal property, and $20,000 for additional living expenses. The limits for liability and medical coverage for others (i.e., persons injured other than the insured or family members) are not contingent on the amount of dwelling coverage chosen. The basic limit for personal liability coverage is $100,000 and the limit for medical coverage for others is $1,000 per person, although these limits can be increased.

Table 22–2 summarizes the differences between the main HO policy forms

TABLE 22–2   Overview of Property Coverage under Different Homeowners Policy Forms

| | Perils Covered | | | Percent of Homeowners Policies | |
| | A, B, & D | | | | |
Policy Form (user)	Dwelling Coverage, Other Structures, and Loss of Use	C Coverage for Personal Property	Additional Coverages	1977	1995
HO8 (Homeowner)	Basic list, except coverage for theft is subject to $1,000 limit and does not extend "off the residence premises"	Basic list, except coverage for theft is subject to $1,000 limit and does not extend "off the residence premises"	List below minus "collapse"	0%	< 1%
HO1 (Homeowner)	Basic list	Basic list	List below minus "collapse"	14%	< 1%
HO2 (Homeowner)	Expanded list	Expanded list	List below plus "ordinance and law"	41%	6%
HO3 (Homeowner)	Open peril	Expanded list, but can be changed to an open peril policy through an endorsement	List below plus "ordinance and law"	45%	93%
HO4 (Renter)	NA	Expanded list	List below plus "building additions and alterations"	NA	NA
HO6* (Condominium owner)	Expanded, but coverage for plumbing discharge and freezing differs; also can be changed to open peril policy through an endorsement	Expanded, but coverage for plumbing discharge and freezing differs; open peril coverage available through an endorsement	List below plus "ordinance and law"	NA	NA

Notes: NA means not applicable.

*Dwelling and other structures coverage are combined.

Basic list perils covered: Fire, lightning, windstorm, hail, explosion, riot, civil commotion, vehicles, aircraft, smoke, vandalism, malicious mischief, theft, and volcanic eruption.

Expanded list perils covered: Basic perils plus falling objects, weight of ice, snow, sleet, plumbing discharge, rupture of hot water and air conditioning systems, freezing of plumbing, and artificially generated electricity.

Additional coverages: Debris removal, reasonable repairs, plants and trees, fire department service charge, property removed, fund transfer and credit cards, loss assessment, glass or safety glazing material, and collapse.

Source: Percent of policies obtained from *Homeowners Insurance: Threats from Without, Weakness Within,* Insurance Services Office, 1996.

with respect to property coverage. The four policies for homeowners (excluding renters and condominium owners) are listed in order of the comprehensiveness of coverage provided by the form; that is, HO8 offers the least comprehensive coverage, followed by HO1, HO2, and HO3. Coverage differences are evident by comparing the entries in the columns titled "Perils Covered" and "Additional Coverages." A third dimension on which the coverage of the policy forms differs is the method of loss settlement, which is discussed below. Table 22–2 also provides estimates of the percentage of all policies purchased by homeowners (excluding renters and condominium owners) represented by the different policy forms in 1977 and 1995. Ignoring HO8, which did not exist in 1977, the sale of more comprehensive coverage has expanded as indicated by the shift of HO1 and HO2 policies to HO3 policies over time. In 1995, 93 percent of homeowners policies were HO3 policies.

Homeowners insurance **dwelling coverage** (coverage A) covers the policyholder's main residence and attached structures. The property insured by a homeowners policy must be primarily used as a place of residence and not for business purposes. While limited amounts of business activity can be conducted at a residence without jeopardizing coverage under a homeowners policy, if a person's main residence also is where a significant amount of business is transacted, a separate business property policy may be needed.

Other structures coverage (coverage B) covers structures not attached to the main residence, such as detached garages, garden sheds, swimming pools (above and in-ground), and fences. As stated above, the amount of coverage for other structures is limited to 10 percent of the dwelling coverage. This limit is an aggregate limit; that is, it applies across all other structures, not separately for each structure. Additional coverage can be purchased through an endorsement.

Unscheduled personal property coverage (coverage C) covers items that are owned or used by the insured regardless of whether they are lost or damaged at the insured's home or away from home. The limit for coverage C under HO3 equals 50 percent of the dwelling coverage, but the limit can be increased through an endorsement. The typical homeowners policy, however, excludes or limits coverage for specific items. For example, motor vehicles are excluded, as are animals and sound equipment in a car. Coverage sublimits apply to many items that could potentially be very valuable, such as silverware, jewelry, and guns. As explained in Chapter 8, coverage limits for these items help make the coverage more suitable for the typical buyer and thereby reduce classification costs. Additional coverage for items with sublimits can be purchased using an endorsement to the policy or with a separate contract, called a *personal articles floater.*

Loss of use coverage (coverage D) provides reimbursement for additional living expenses if the dwelling cannot be used because it is damaged or because civil authorities prevent its use. As an example of the latter situation, authorities could prevent people from living in a neighborhood because of potentially dangerous pollution. Loss of use coverage also provides coverage for lost rental income if a portion of the residence can no longer be rented.

Personal liability coverage pays for judgments, settlements, and defense costs for bodily injury and property damage liability that arise from accidents at the residence or may result from certain actions of the insured away from the residence. **Coverage for medical payments to others** pays the medical expenses of nonresidents who are injured while on the premises. This coverage is provided without regard to fault or negligence of the insured. For example, if a visiting child falls off of a swing and breaks an arm, the homeowners policy will cover medical expenses up to $1,000.

Excluded Perils.   Homeowners policies exclude coverage for a number of perils. One way this is done is through a named-peril policy, which excludes coverage for all perils not named. In addition, named-peril policies have specific exclusions to reduce ambiguity about what is not covered under the policy. Open peril policies, like the HO3 form, specifically name perils that will not be insured.

Examples of exclusions include property losses caused by intentional acts, normal wear and tear, smog, and animals owned or kept by the insured.[2] These exclusions can be explained using the principles presented in earlier chapters (especially see Chapter 8). Some exclusions (e.g., excluding losses caused by pets), reduce the insurer's exposure to events that depend largely on the homeowner's actions and therefore are subject to moral hazard. Other exclusions eliminate coverage for events that have a high probability of occurrence and little uncertainty (normal wear and tear) and therefore would be too costly to insure once claims processing costs are considered. Homeowners policies also have exclusions that reduce an insurer's exposure to correlated losses. For example, losses from changes in laws, earthquakes, floods, nuclear accidents, and war are excluded. Box 22–1 illustrates how the exclusion for losses arising from laws can in some circumstances cause people to be significantly underinsured. Consumers can purchase coverage for some of these excluded perils through endorsements or separate coverage (e.g., earthquake coverage) or through special government programs (e.g., flood coverage). We describe some of these coverages later in the chapter.

Property Loss Settlement

Property losses under homeowners insurance are covered above a per occurrence deductible. A common deductible would be $250. Higher and lower deductibles usually are available for an adjustment in the premium. The actual amount of coverage provided above the deductible is complicated because different types of property are valued in different ways for the purpose of settling losses and because policies differ in their valuation methods. In addition, the co-insurance (insurance-to-value) provision limits coverage in some instances (see Chapter 8 for a general discussion of the co-insurance provision). Table 22–3 summarizes the different loss settlement provisions.

---

[2] Note, however, that liability for bodily injury or property damage caused by pets is covered under personal liability coverage.

Box 22–1

Exclusions for Losses Caused by Ordinance or Law

Following the Oakland Hills fire in California in 1993 and Hurricane Andrew in Florida in 1992, many people found themselves to be underinsured because of the ordinance and law exclusion in their HO policies. As a result of this exclusion, losses that occur as a result of laws or ordinances (e.g., building codes) are not covered.

Many of the homes damaged by the Oakland Hills fire were built prior to the enactment of building codes designed to reduce losses from earthquakes. The difference between the cost of rebuilding according to code and the cost of rebuilding using the original type of construction materials and building techniques often was not covered because of the ordinance and law exclusion in the HO policy.

Similarly, many coastal areas, including those in Florida, require that new homes and homes that are more than 50 percent destroyed be built a certain number of feet above ground level. Following Hurricane Andrew, the additional cost of rebuilding according to this requirement was not covered under some people's homeowners policies because of the ordinance and law exclusion.

Dwellings and Other Structures.   Under most homeowners policies, dwellings and other structures are insured up to their **like-kind replacement cost,** which means that the insurer will pay the cost for "like construction," provided the coverage chosen by the policyholder exceeds 80 percent of the building's full replacement cost prior to the loss (i.e., provided the co-insurance provision is met). Thus, if the minimum insurance requirement is met and the policy limit is adequate, replacement cost coverage will allow the insured to replace damaged property with new property: There is no deduction for depreciation of the damaged property prior to the loss. Exceptions are made for certain types of property covered under dwelling coverage, such as outdoor antennas, which are insured up to their actual cash value. The **actual cash value** generally is defined as the replacement cost minus depreciation. As discussed further below, personal property also is sometimes insured for its actual cash value.

In most cases, homeowners policies are issued only if the property is insured for at least 80 percent of the replacement cost, which implies that the co-insurance provision usually is satisfied. However, situations sometimes arise where the property is not insured up to 80 percent of the full replacement cost, in which case the insurer will pay less than the replacement cost even if the replacement cost is less than the amount of coverage. In particular, if coverage equals x percent of the full replacement cost, then the insurer will pay $(x/80)$ percent of the loss or the actual cash value, whichever is greater. In no case, however, will the insurer pay more than the coverage limits chosen by the policyholder.

Instead of like-kind replacement cost coverage with a co-insurance provision, homeowners can purchase **guaranteed replacement cost** coverage for the dwelling and other structures. This coverage will pay the like-kind replacement

TABLE 22–3   Typical Methods for Loss Settlement for Different Coverages

Policy Form	A and B Dwelling and Other Structures Coverage	C Personal Property Coverage
HO8	Functional replacement cost or actual cash value	Actual cash value
HO1	Like-kind replacement cost*	Actual cash value
HO2	Like-kind replacement cost*	Actual cash value or like-kind replacement cost
HO3	Like-kind replacement cost* or guaranteed replacement cost	Actual cash value or like-kind replacement cost
HO4 (Renter)	NA	Actual cash value or like-kind replacement cost with an endorsement
HO6 (Condominium owner)	Actual cash value $1,000 limit (can be increased)	Actual cash value or like-kind replacement cost

*Provided coverage exceeds 80 percent of replacement cost; if not, then settlement equals maximum of actual cash value and x percent of the loss, where x = (actual coverage/replacement cost)/0.8. Also, endorsements for guaranteed replacement cost coverage are available.

cost even if it turns out to exceed the policy limit. Some insurers, however, cap reimbursement at 125 or 150 percent of the limit under guaranteed replacement cost coverage. In addition to paying a higher premium for this type of coverage, most guaranteed replacement cost policies require that the insured purchase coverage equal to 100 percent of the originally estimated replacement cost and to increase the coverage with inflation and improvements in the property.

An alternative method of loss settlement that is used for dwellings and other structures under the HO8 policy and variations sold by some insurers is to pay the **functional replacement cost,** which is the cost of replacement of damaged property using materials that serve the same function as the original materials but are not necessarily the same. (In some states, HO8 or similar policies are required to pay actual cash value.) For example, with functional replacement cost coverage, the replacement cost could be calculated assuming that repairs/replacements are made with carpeting over plywood instead of hardwood, sheetrock instead of plaster, and linoleum instead of marble. To illustrate one common situation where functional replacement cost is likely to be used, consider an older home with unique features (e.g., wood floors, marble bathrooms, crown moldings) but a relatively low market value because of its location. The replacement cost of the home could greatly exceed the market value of the home, because of the cost of the materials and the craftspeople that would be needed for their installation. Another situation where either functional replacement cost or actual cash value coverage is sometimes used is for old, lower valued homes that have experienced substantial depreciation over time so that the market value or actual cash value is small compared to the like-kind replacement cost.

Insuring these types of homes for 80 percent or more of their like-kind replacement cost generally would cause the policy limit to exceed the market value of the home. This outcome might require a higher premium than many owners of such property would be willing to pay. Like-kind replacement cost coverage with a limit substantially in excess of the home's market value also could increase moral hazard because the homeowner could be better off financially after a loss (e.g., he or she could replace the home with a new home that would be worth substantially more than the existing home prior to the loss). By settling losses using functional replacement cost or actual cash value instead of using replacement cost with like-kind materials, the homeowner can purchase lower limits and the moral hazard problem can be reduced. Thus, the use of either functional replacement cost or actual cash value coverage instead of "like-kind" replacement cost can increase the availability and the affordability of coverage in depressed neighborhoods with older homes.[3]

Personal Property.   The standard homeowners forms generally cover personal property on an actual cash value basis (above the deductible).[4] However, like-kind replacement cost coverage is available through an endorsement to the leading forms for an additional premium. A majority of homeowners purchase this replacement cost endorsement, thus avoiding a reduction in the indemnity paid to reflect depreciation.

Pricing Homeowners Policies

Homeowners insurance premiums are set using two basic components. One component is the insured value of the property (e.g., the replacement cost) and the other is the rate per dollar of insured value. The premium is found by multiplying the two components. For example, if a home with a replacement cost of $220,000 is insured for this amount and the insurer charges a rate equal to 0.003, then the annual premium would equal $660 (plus the charge for liability and medical expense coverage).

Policies generally are initially issued with a dwelling limit equal to 100 percent of the dwelling's estimated replacement cost. Insurers use various methods to estimate replacement cost. One method can be explained with the aid of Table 22–4, which lists the characteristics used by some insurers to estimate a dwelling's replacement cost. Insurers use tables that provide an estimate of the replacement cost per square foot for each combination of the factors listed in the

---

[3] If the policyholder does not replace the home following a loss, the HO8 policy will pay the minimum of the market value, actual cash value, or functional replacement cost. This provision also helps reduce moral hazard. Some insurers offer a hybrid coverage on homes with low market value compared to replacement cost that pays functional replacement cost up to the market value of the home.

[4] Note that if dwellings and personal property are damaged in one occurrence, the deductible is applied only once.

TABLE 22–4   Characteristics of Homes Commonly Used by Insurers to Estimate Replacement Costs

Ground Floor Square Footage	Dwelling Type	Construction Grade and Quality	Construction Materials
Less than 1,000	Ranch	Economy	Frame
1,000–1,200	Cape Cod	Standard	Masonry
1,200–1,300	Colonial	Custom	Masonry
.	Victorian	Luxury	Veneer
.	Town house		
.	Contemporary		
Greater than 3,500	Split level		

table—ground floor square footage, dwelling type, construction grade, and construction materials. The replacement cost per square foot is multiplied by the home's square footage to find a base *replacement cost,* which is then multiplied by a location modifier to arrive at the replacement cost used for establishing premiums. The *location modifier* adjusts the base replacement cost for the variation across locations in construction costs.

To illustrate the estimation of replacement cost, suppose that an all-brick, custom ranch has 2,300 square feet and the insurer's table of replacement costs indicates that the cost per square foot to replace the home is $75. Then the base replacement cost equals 2,300 × $75 = $172,500. Assuming that the location modifier equals 1.1, the replacement cost is estimated to be $189,750 ($172,500 × 1.1). Although this procedure for calculating replacement costs is reasonably accurate for standard homes, it can result in considerable errors for high-priced, custom-built homes, which are becoming more common. Consequently, some insurers have moved to more sophisticated methods of calculating replacement costs, especially for pricing guaranteed replacement cost coverage.

The rates per dollar of replacement cost charged for homeowners insurance can vary with a number of factors (see Box 22–2). The home's location is one important factor, because it determines the home's exposure to weather-related perils (hurricanes, earthquakes, tornadoes, hail, etc.), its exposure to crime, and its proximity to fire protection. Rates also depend on the construction materials, such as wood versus brick.

22.2 Personal Umbrella Policies

Wealthier individuals often find the liability coverage limits available with their homeowners policy to be inadequate given their potential exposure. A common way to insure against large liability losses is through a personal umbrella policy, which usually provides excess coverage of at least $1 million for liability losses that could arise from multiple sources. The umbrella policy usually requires that

Box 22–2

Underwriting Based on Credit History of Homeowners and Allegations of Redlining

Some insurers employ the controversial practice of underwriting and basing rates for homeowners policies on the homeowner's credit history. There is statistical evidence that without higher rates the profitability of homeowners policies is lower, on average, for homeowners that have low credit ratings. This relationship might be explained by the reasoning that people with low credit ratings are (1) less likely to pay premiums on time, (2) more likely to fail to renew policies, (3) more likely to have claims, and (4) more likely to submit fraudulent claims. Critics of the practice of using credit information for insurance underwriting and pricing decisions sometimes allege that the practice predominantly affects lower-income individuals who disproportionately are minorities and therefore that the practice amounts to racial discrimination.

The specific allegation that insurers use credit histories to racially discriminate is an example of a more general allegation that insurers engage in the racially discriminatory practice of **redlining.** The term redlining refers to a practice of drawing red lines on a map to indicate areas that insurers (or other financial insti-

tutions) will not serve. While explicit drawing of lines on a map is unlikely today, insurers nevertheless are alleged to practice redlining by providing lower quality service (e.g., fewer offices) and charging higher prices in areas predominately populated by minorities. Insurers respond that they do not base business decisions on a person's race and that any differences in average quality and prices reflect cost differences, not racial discrimination.

Statistical analyses of the profitability of homeowners (and auto) insurance in different regions generally do not provide evidence of a relationship with percent minority population. While a detailed examination of this evidence is beyond the scope of this book, this evidence is inconsistent with discrimination at the market level. It also is worth noting that racial discrimination that had a substantive effect on the price charged or the service quality provided by insurers would imply unexploited profitable investment opportunities. It would thus require pervasive prejudice and significant entry barriers for potential nonprejudiced entrants.

the consumer have other liability coverage, such as homeowners and automobile liability. If losses exceed the limits on these other "primary" coverages, then the umbrella policy will pay losses up to its limit. Most umbrella policies also provide some coverage for liability exposures not covered under the insured's primary policies (e.g., libel or slander) subject to a self-insured retention that operates like a deductible.

To illustrate the basic coverage provided by an umbrella policy, suppose that a homeowner has the following liability coverages and limits:

Auto liability	$ 300,000
Homeowners	$ 100,000
Umbrella	$ 1,000,000

If the homeowner has a liability claim of $500,000 as a result of an automobile accident, then the auto insurer will pay $300,000 and the umbrella insurer will pay $200,000.

The premium required for $1 million of umbrella coverage commonly falls within the $150 to $250 range. The additional premium required for an additional $1 million (producing total coverage of $2 million) is smaller than the amount for the first $1 million. As a result, people with significant assets to protect against liability claims generally can purchase substantial coverage at a relatively modest cost.

22.3 Coverage of High Risk/Catastrophic Perils

This section provides an overview of insurance arrangements for high risk/catastrophic perils, including (1) private market earthquake coverage, (2) the National Flood Insurance Program, and (3) state residual market plans for urban property insurance and windstorm exposures. Section 22.4 then provides a detailed discussion of the impact of recent catastrophes on the private market and public sector programs.

Earthquake Coverage

Although earthquake coverage is excluded from the basic homeowners policy, most insurers offer earthquake coverage as an endorsement (or sometimes as a separate policy). Losses generally are covered above a deductible that is expressed as a percentage of the property's pre-loss value (e.g., 15 percent). California is the only state that requires homeowner insurers to offer earthquake coverage along with homeowners coverage. This requirement has been in effect since 1985. As we discuss in section 22.4, the inability of California insurers to deny earthquake coverage to homeowners policyholders has led some insurers to stop selling homeowners policies in the state and thus, ironically, has reduced the availability of coverage from the private market in general.

National Flood Insurance

As mentioned earlier, homeowners policies exclude coverage for damage caused by floods. Flood risk generally is viewed as being uninsurable privately because of the high correlation in losses and potential adverse selection and moral hazard. Homeowners who live in areas that have adopted zoning and building codes to reduce losses from floods can purchase coverage against flood losses through the **National Flood Insurance Program (NFIP).** The flood insurance program, however, excludes some coastal areas that Congress has sought to protect from development for environmental reasons. Flood insurance from the NFIP can be purchased through many private insurance companies. Although these companies service the policy, the risk is borne by the federal government. The program does not receive general tax revenue, but it has an ability to borrow from the Treasury if premiums are insufficient to pay claims in a particular year.

Structures that were built prior to 1978, which was when flood hazard areas were officially identified by the NFIP, are insured by the NFIP using a flat rate, regardless of construction and location. Structures that were built subsequent to 1978, however, pay premiums that reflect differences in expected claim costs.[5] People with pre-1978 built structures, however, can receive the post-1978 built rate. These features of the NFIP imply that many NFIP policyholders (mostly owners of structures built prior to 1978) pay rates that are below fair premiums; many policies are subsidized.

Subsidized rates often are criticized because they encourage people to develop property in some flood plains beyond the point that is justified if one were trying to minimize the cost of risk. That is, because of subsidized flood insurance, people who develop property in flood plain areas do not pay the full costs associated with their development. Consequently, an ex ante moral hazard problem develops—too much of the risky activity (building in flood plains) takes place. Since the subsidy mostly applies to properties built prior to 1978, the moral hazard problem associated with excessive development might not be severe. However, the subsidy still might encourage excessive redevelopment of properties damaged by floods. The designers of the NFIP have recognized the moral hazard problem and in recent years have increased efforts to discourage excessive development. For example, to be eligible to participate in the NFIP, a community must satisfy certain loss control requirements. In effect, the insurance is only available to residents of communities that have taken appropriate safety precautions that help to reduce expected losses.

One justification for subsidized flood insurance is that there are many low-income people who would not purchase flood insurance if it were fairly priced. These people, however, would obtain disaster relief following a flood and thus they ultimately might in effect obtain insurance at no cost. Taxpayers, in general, would pay the full cost of the insurance (disaster relief). Thus, it might be better to subsidize the insurance so that less disaster relief would be needed and, more importantly, so that people would incorporate at least part of the expected cost of floods when making decisions about where to live. This justification for the subsidy does not imply, however, that the subsidy would be based on when the structure was built; instead, it would imply that the subsidy would be based on income or wealth.

The pricing of NFIP policies also is criticized for not taking into consideration the differences in expected claim costs across potential policyholders. Consequently, adverse selection results—the people with the highest expected losses are more likely to purchase flood insurance. In an effort to reduce an extreme form of adverse selection, Congress passed a bill in 1994 (The National Flood In-

---

[5] For example, coverage for a single-family home with no basement built prior to 1978 in South Carolina costs $0.68 per $100 of coverage, up to $135,000 of coverage. The corresponding rates for structures built after 1978 range from $0.18 to $1.16, depending upon construction and location.

surance Reform Act) which extends the waiting period for an NFIP policy to become effective from 5 days to 30 days. This change reduces the likelihood that people will buy flood insurance when they think a flood is imminent (e.g., when the house of their friend who lives upstream floats by).

Despite often being priced below fair premium levels, many eligible residents fail to purchase insurance from the NFIP. One explanation is that they underestimate the expected losses from floods and therefore view the price as excessive despite the subsidy. Many low-income people simply may be unable to afford flood insurance even though it is subsidized. Also, as mentioned above, the incentive to purchase flood insurance may be reduced because of the disaster relief that often is available following major floods. In 1994, however, Congress passed legislation that limited disaster relief for people who do not participate in the NFIP.

Residual Market Plans

Insurers may view some areas as having high expected losses and high correlation in losses apart from the risk of earthquakes and floods. Insurers therefore will either not offer coverage or only offer coverage at very high premiums in these areas. States have responded to problems associated with insuring these other high risk or catastrophic perils by creating insurance arrangements for people who cannot obtain coverage in the private market at "affordable" prices. The basic structure and consequences of these plans are similar to the residual market plans used for automobile insurance that were discussed in the previous chapter.

FAIR Plans.   Following large losses caused by urban riots in 1967 and 1968, many insurers either withdrew or raised premiums substantially for property coverage in some urban areas. A number of states created **FAIR plans** to provide coverage for urban residents and businesses. (FAIR stands for "fair access to insurance requirements.") FAIR plans provide insurance coverage typically at rates below what private insurers would charge. It is not surprising therefore that FAIR plans typically receive less in premiums than they pay out in claim and administrative costs. Assessing property insurers operating in the state in proportion to their premium revenue makes up the shortfall. Thus, FAIR plans typically cause a subsidy from policyholders who purchase coverage in the private market to participants in FAIR plans. In 1996, 28 states, Puerto Rico, and the District of Columbia had FAIR plans.

Some states have expanded their FAIR plans beyond the original purpose of ensuring availability in the presence of potentially large (and correlated) losses from civil unrest, crime, and the like. California's experience in this regard is noteworthy, because it illustrates the problems that can develop when a state attempts to make insurance coverage available at below-market prices (below fair premiums) for all or a large part of its residents. Prior to May of 1996, the California FAIR plan was open to residents in nonurban areas under the reasoning that all consumers in California needed access to earthquake insurance. Following the

Northridge earthquake in 1994, however, some insurers refused to write earthquake coverage and many insurers raised premiums for earthquake coverage (see section 22.4). As a result, a number of homeowners applied for insurance through the FAIR plan. The number of policies in the California FAIR plan tripled. Given that premiums in the FAIR plan typically were less than a fair market price, there was a high likelihood that the FAIR plan would not be able to pay all of its claims if a major earthquake occurred. In May of 1996, the commissioner limited access to the FAIR plan to property in areas exposed to brush fires and in "underserved" (i.e., urban) zip codes, thus returning the FAIR plan to the more narrowly defined market segment for which it was originally intended.

Beach and Windstorm Plans.   Seven states on the East and Gulf coasts of the United States have special insurance programs called **beach and windstorm insurance plans.** These plans cover property owners who live in specified coastal regions that may find coverage "unavailable" in the private market due to the risk of large losses from hurricanes. Like other residual market plans, the underwriting results of beach and windstorm plans are shared across all property insurers in the state in proportion to market share, and there generally is some subsidy from policyholders in the private market to those in the beach and windstorm plan. Figure 22–1 provides information about the number of policies in the beach and windstorm plans for each of the seven states for 1995. Florida has by far the largest exposure. In addition, approximately one-half of the policies in Florida in 1995 were new policies as opposed to renewal policies. This is the result of the turmoil in the Florida coastal property insurance market following Hurricane Andrew in 1992, which we discuss in more detail in section 22.4.[6]

FIGURE 22–1

Number of policies for beach and windstorm plans in 1995

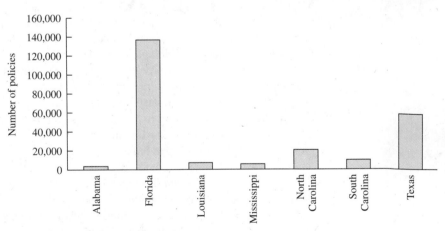

Source: *1997 Fact Book on Property and Casualty Insurance,* Insurance Information Institute.

---

[6] In 1996, Florida's beach and windstorm plan had 293,000 policies.

Concept Check

1. What would you expect to happen to the number of policies in residual market plans (such as FAIR and beach and windstorm plans) if state insurance commissioners froze property insurance rates for five years?

22.4 Impact of Catastrophes on Property Insurance

During the 1990s, US homeowners insurers experienced extremely poor operating results. One factor that caused the low profitability for many insurers was the frequency and severity of losses from catastrophes. Hurricane Andrew in 1992 ($16.3 billion in insured losses), the Northridge earthquake in 1994 ($12.5 billion), Hurricane Hugo in 1989 ($4.9 billion), and the Oakland Hills fire in 1991 ($1.8 billion) caused unusually high losses for homeowners insurers.

We begin our discussion of the impact of catastrophes by describing how two states, Florida and California, have responded to large catastrophe losses in recent years. These are interesting stories in their own right but, more importantly, they illustrate (1) the problems that arise from insuring losses with a large correlated component, (2) private market responses to large catastrophe losses, and (3) additional government efforts to satisfy residents' demand for affordable property insurance. We then briefly discuss two phenomena that have emerged in the wake of the large catastrophe losses to help finance future catastrophe losses. The first method is the creation of government-sponsored reinsurance programs; the second method is an expanded menu of capital market instruments to enable insurers to write coverage at a lower total cost.

Florida and Hurricane Andrew

The majority of the $16 billion of damage caused by Hurricane Andrew occurred in southern Dade County. The losses from Andrew could have been much worse. If, instead of hitting south of Miami, Andrew had gone through the heart of Miami, losses would have likely been over $50 billion. As it was, the losses caused 11 small insurers to become insolvent and disrupted the Florida property insurance market for a number of years as insurers tried to reduce their exposure to future hurricanes and raise rates. In addition, the state of Florida attempted to ensure that its citizens could purchase affordable property insurance.

Before describing the events following Hurricane Andrew, it is worth considering why Andrew would have caused as much disruption as it did. After all, could insurers have failed to anticipate that such a large hurricane was possible? Did the failure of some insurers to hold sufficient capital produce the significant disruption in the market? Why was the risk associated with hurricanes not reinsured more fully so that the impact of such an event would have been spread relatively thinly across many people/insurers all over the world? The costs of capital and reinsurance provide at least a partial answer, if not the full answer to these questions. It is possible that the events following Andrew were not surprising.

That is, some smaller insurers may have knowingly accepted the risk (given the cost of reducing the risk) that they would become insolvent if a large hurricane hit. Other insurers may have figured they could withstand one major hurricane, but after one hit they would reduce their future exposure. Alternatively, the magnitude of the losses from Andrew, especially the severity of losses per damaged home, may have taken some insurers by surprise, which caused them to increase their forecasts of expected future claim costs and to reevaluate how to deal with catastrophe exposures.

As noted above, a number of insurers decided to reduce their exposure in Florida following Hurricane Andrew and seek rate increases on future business. For example, Allstate, the largest homeowners insurer in Florida, announced that it would drop about one-third (300,000) of its Florida homeowners policies and that it would seek a 41 percent rate increase.[7] The Florida legislature responded to possible reductions in the supply of coverage by restricting insurers' ability to stop selling policies for three years. Insurers were not permitted to cancel or fail to renew more than 5 percent of their residential policies in one year or 10 percent in a single county. (These restrictions were extended in 1996.) In addition, the law required insurers that were expanding in Florida to write at least 20 percent of their new policies in Dade, Broward, and Palm Beach counties. While the Florida insurance commissioner granted rate increases, the increases were less than the amounts sought by insurers.

Despite the restrictions on insurers, a large number of homeowners found that their policies were canceled or not renewed. In response to the demand for homeowners insurance, Florida created the Residential Property and Casualty Joint Underwriting Association (JUA) in 1993 as an insurer of last resort. By 1996, the JUA had become the second largest homeowners insurer in the state. The JUA operated at a loss through 1995 and imposed assessments on private insurers to make up its shortfall ($22.8 million in 1995).

Florida already had in place a residual market mechanism for providing insurance against windstorm and hail losses. In particular, the Florida Windstorm Underwriting Association (FWUA) is one of the beach and windstorm plans discussed earlier. Its purpose is to sell windstorm and hail insurance policies in counties that may not be adequately served by the voluntary market. It originally wrote in one county, but by 1996, it wrote in 27 of 35 coastal counties. The FWUA's exposure increased significantly following Hurricane Andrew (see Figure 22–1).

FWUA and JUA rates generally are lower than what private insurers would charge for similar coverage, which in large part explains the FWUA's and JUA's relatively high market share. If it were not for restrictions on cancellations and nonrenewals, the market shares of the FWUA and JUA would have been even greater following Andrew. By 1996, the state took steps to provide incentives for the voluntary market to take out policies from the FWUA and JUA. For example,

---

[7] Allstate also announced plans to reorganize its Florida business by establishing new subsidiaries that would serve Florida policyholders. In essence, the reorganization would "wall off" Florida losses from the rest of the company's assets (see Chapter 17).

insurers who sold policies to people who previously were insured by the JUA were granted an exemption from JUA assessments. In addition, bonuses up to $100 were paid for each policy that was removed from the JUA.

In 1993, Florida took another step to deal with its property insurance problems when it created the Hurricane Catastrophe Fund (CAT Fund) to reinsure private insurance companies operating in the state. A controversial aspect of the CAT Fund is that all insurers operating in the state are required to purchase its reinsurance. In addition to receiving premiums from insurers, the CAT Fund has the authority to borrow up to $5 billion and to assess insurers up to 2 percent of premiums written from property and liability policies (excluding workers' compensation). The IRS granted the CAT Fund special tax status, which allows it to avoid paying tax on investment earnings. Recall from Chapter 4 and other discussions throughout the book that the tax on investment income is one of the costs to insurers of holding the capital that makes their promises to pay claims credible when losses are positively correlated. Thus, the special tax status of the CAT Fund has the potential to reduce the cost of reinsurance to Florida insurers.

California and the Northridge Earthquake

Following the Northridge earthquake in 1994, which caused over $12.5 billion in insured losses, the California homeowners insurance market experienced problems similar to those of the Florida market following Hurricane Andrew.[8] A few relatively small insurers became insolvent, many others tried to reduce their exposure to future earthquake losses, and the state developed a program to provide affordable earthquake insurance to its residents.

As discussed earlier, California is the only state that requires insurers to offer earthquake coverage with homeowners insurance. Following the Northridge quake, however, the requirement that earthquake coverage be offered with homeowners coverage led some insurers to reduce their supply of homeowners coverage. Similar to Florida, the California legislature responded in two ways. First, it limited the ability of insurers to cancel or fail to renew homeowners policies. Second, it created the California Earthquake Authority (CEA) to reduce insurers' exposure to earthquake risk.

The CEA is a state-run, privately financed plan for insuring earthquake risk. An insurer can satisfy its requirement to offer earthquake insurance with homeowners insurance by offering a CEA earthquake policy, which covers the primary residence with a 15 percent deductible, $5,000 of contents coverage, and $1,500 of living expense coverage. In essence, each participating insurer can write CEA earthquake policies, keep a portion of the premium for administrative expenses, and have the risk borne by the CEA. As summarized in Figure 22–2, the CEA can obtain up to $10.5 billion from various sources to pay claims (in addition to the

---

[8] Potential earthquake losses in California could be much greater than those inflicted by the Northridge quake. Loss estimates from an earthquake of the same intensity as the 1906 San Francisco quake are higher than $50 billion.

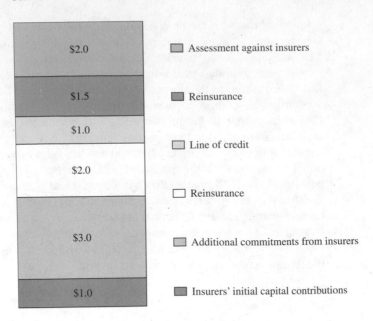

FIGURE 22–2

Source of funds for the California Earthquake Authority (CEA) (in billions of dollars)

premium revenue from CEA earthquake policies). Given its capital sources, the CEA can be viewed as a pooling arrangement among participating insurers.

Rationale for Government-sponsored Reinsurance Arrangements

As discussed above, both Florida and California have adopted reinsurance arrangements to finance future catastrophe losses. Hawaii also has adopted a program to finance hurricane losses, and there have been proposals for a federal catastrophe reinsurance program. These reinsurance arrangements provide two potential advantages relative to private catastrophe reinsurance arrangements. First, assuming that they obtain preferential tax treatment on investment earnings, they reduce the cost of maintaining a pool of capital to pay future catastrophe losses compared with private reinsurance arrangements. Of course, the government could alter the tax treatment to private insurers and reinsurers and obtain a similar effect.[9]

Second, the arrangements can facilitate risk pooling over time. Both the Florida CAT Fund and the CEA have the authority to borrow money to pay current catastrophe losses. The participants in the reinsurance arrangement have to pay back the funds that are borrowed so, in essence, the ability to borrow allows the participating insurers to pool catastrophe risk across years. To the extent that

---

[9] An argument could be made that extending the tax treatment to private insurers would entail additional monitoring costs to ensure that private insurers do not overestimate expected future losses.

catastrophe risk cannot be diversified across insurers within a given time period because of the high correlation in losses, pooling over time is the only feasible method of pooling.

The question remains: Why does a government entity have an advantage relative to private contracts in pooling risk over time? The answer may be that governments can mitigate problems associated with enforcing intertemporal pooling contracts. To illustrate, suppose that a $20 billion catastrophe will occur sometime over the next 20 years, but nobody knows which year. Ignoring the time value of money, an arrangement could be established whereby insurers privately agree to contribute $1 billion each year for 20 years to pay the losses. One problem with this arrangement is that the catastrophe could occur early on, when insufficient funds have been accumulated to pay all the losses. The insurers as a group would have to borrow the funds, but there is a chance that some insurers would not fulfill their promise to repay their portion of the loan. As a result, private borrowing would entail monitoring costs as well as the payment of risk premiums to the lenders. A government, however, may largely avoid these costs because its ability to tax people in the future reduces the default risk to the lenders.

While government reinsurance arrangements could potentially lower the cost of dealing with catastrophe risk, they have several problems that could undermine their effectiveness. One problem relates to inadequate pricing. If a program like the California Earthquake Authority charges premiums that are less than expected losses, then the program will discourage the private supply of insurance and promote the development of catastrophe-prone areas beyond the level that would minimize society's cost of risk. Another potential problem is political in nature. If large amounts of funds are built up over time for the purpose of paying catastrophe losses, political pressure may emerge to use those funds for other purposes.

New Capital Market Instruments for Financing Catastrophe Losses

In recent years, some interesting and innovative approaches for helping insurers finance catastrophe losses have been introduced by the private capital market. Recall again that insurers bond their promises to pay claims by holding capital. When claim costs are highly correlated due to the possibility of a catastrophe, insurers need to hold relatively large amounts of capital to make their promises to pay claims credible. The costs of holding capital, such as taxes and agency costs, cause insurers to charge high premiums for coverage or to not offer coverage at all. The new capital market instruments provide an alternative method of bonding promises to pay claims. Instead of the insurer holding capital until a catastrophe occurs, these instruments arrange for investors to provide funds to the insurer only if the insurer needs the funds to pay claims (i.e., following a catastrophe).

An example of one these new capital market instruments is *contingent equity*, whereby investors precommit to purchasing new common stock from an insurer at agreed upon prices if a certain contingency occurs, such as an earthquake. Also, several insurers have issued *cat bonds* (catastrophe-linked bonds) to raise capital to pay potential catastrophe losses. With these transactions, an insurer issues bonds for which the required payments of interest and principal are contingent on the occurrence of a catastrophe. For example, if a catastrophe occurs, the insurer may not have to pay interest (coupons) on the bonds, or the insurer may be able to delay the repayment of principal for many years.

Another innovation is the development of *catastrophe options,* which started trading at the Chicago Board of Trade in 1994. The payoffs on these option contracts are based on estimates of insured losses from catastrophes in certain geographical areas over a specified period of time. As an example of how these contracts could be used, a Florida insurer could purchase option contracts that provide a positive payoff to the insurer whenever insured catastrophe losses in Florida fall between $10 billion and $15 billion during the third quarter (hurricane season) of a particular year. Of course, the insurer would have to pay a premium for the options (see Chapter 13), which would depend on the market's assessment of expected hurricane losses. Provided the insurer has hurricane losses that are highly correlated with the losses experienced throughout the state, the option contracts will provide the insurer with funds exactly when the insurer needs them—following a major hurricane.

Only time will tell whether these new capital market instruments will ultimately be successful. Their success depends on whether they provide a lower cost method than holding capital for insurers to bond their promises to pay claims. One potential advantage of the instruments is that since insurers do not hold as much capital, the tax costs associated with insurers bonding promises to pay claims is reduced. Another potential advantage is that investors do not have to incur the agency costs associated with giving insurance company managers access to funds that are not immediately needed. While these new mechanisms for providing capital to insurers after a loss also may involve both tax and agency costs, these costs could be lower than with traditional capital arrangements.

Another reason catastrophe options could potentially provide a lower cost method of bonding insurers' promises is that the payoffs from the options depend on indexes of catastrophe losses that are largely outside of the control of insurers. Consequently, the moral hazard and adverse selection costs that arise with traditional reinsurance arrangements, which depend on the losses of the ceding insurer's book of business, may be largely avoided.

22.5 Summary

- Homeowners policies generally are standardized policies that provide property and liability coverage against a broad range of perils.
- Loss settlement for homeowners policies varies depending on the type of policy and whether the loss is part of structure or personal property.

The most common types of loss settlement methods are like-kind replacement cost, guaranteed replacement cost, and actual cash value.

- Rates for homeowners policies are based on the type of construction, the size of the home, and the location of the home.

- Personal umbrella policies provide liability coverage with high limits (typically $1 million or higher) above liability coverage provided by homeowners and automobile liability coverage.
- Losses arising from earthquakes and floods are excluded in the homeowners policy. Earthquake coverage can be purchased from private insurers as an endorsement to an HO policy or as a separate policy. Coverage for floods is available from the National Flood Insurance Program.
- Residual market plans for urban property (FAIR plans) and for coastal property (beach and windstorm plans) exist in a number of states.
- Catastrophes in the early 1990s disrupted property insurance markets in Florida and California. These catastrophes led to state provision of reinsurance as well as innovative private capital market instruments for financing catastrophe losses.

Key Terms

named peril policy   572
open peril policy   572
all risk policy   572
HO3 policy   572
dwelling coverage   574
other structures coverage   574
unscheduled personal property coverage   574
loss of use coverage   574
personal liability coverage   574

coverage for medical payments to others   575
like-kind replacement cost   576
actual cash value   576
guaranteed replacement cost   576
functional replacement cost   577
redlining   580
National Flood Insurance Program (NFIP)   581
FAIR plans   583
beach and windstorm insurance plans   584

Questions and Problems

1. Assuming that the loss is covered, how much would be paid for the following losses under a standard HO3 policy with dwelling coverage of $100,000? Assume no endorsements have been purchased.
   - (a) The homeowner's dog bites a child and $5,000 of medical expenses are needed.
   - (b) A fire in the yard causes the following damage: $2,000 to a picket fence, $10,000 to an in-ground swimming pool, and $2,500 to a tool shed.
   - (c) A social guest trips over a tricycle, smashes her head, and obtains a judgment of $75,000.

2. Suppose a policy provides like-kind replacement cost coverage for the dwelling and that $80,000 of coverage is purchased. How much will the insurer pay under each of

the following scenarios (ignoring any deductible):

Loss	Replacement Cost for the Dwelling at Time of Loss
$20,000	$100,000
80,000	100,000
20,000	130,000
80,000	130,000

3. If the base replacement cost equals $100,000, the location modifier equals 1.2, and the rate per dollar of replacement cost equals $0.005, what is the homeowner's premium for property insurance coverage?

4. While homeowners policies generally cover personal property losses (contents) only up to

their actual cash value but cover dwellings up to their replacement cost, a majority of policies are endorsed to provide replacement cost coverage on contents. Explain how replacement cost coverage on contents will lead to moral hazard. Given this problem, why is such replacement cost coverage provided?

5. If you were a manager of an insurance company and evidence came to your attention that other insurers operating in a particular urban area with a large proportion of minorities were charging premiums well above fair premiums because of their bigotry, what would you do if you were trying to maximize firm value?

6. Describe a proposal for changing the NFIP to eliminate subsidized policies. What are the advantages and disadvantages of your proposal?

7. Subsidized coverage under state beach and windstorm plans sometimes is justified as desirable to promote the tourist industry, which can then be taxed to benefit citizens who live outside of the subsidized areas. What is a counterargument to these subsidies?

8. Develop arguments for and against eliminating income taxes on insurer investment income on capital as a method of enhancing the availability and affordability of catastrophe coverage.

References

Harrington, Scott; Steven Mann; and Greg Niehaus. "Insurer Capital Structure Decisions and the Viability of Insurance Derivatives." *Journal of Risk and Insurance,* September 1995. (*Analyzes alternative ways that insurers can finance catastrophe losses, including catastrophe options.*)

Homeowners Insurance: Threats from Without, Weakness Within. Insurance Services Office, 1996.

(*Analyzes a number of issues facing homeowners insurers, including a brief discussion of new capital market instruments.*)

Richardson, Diane. *Insuring to Value.* Cincinnati, OH: The National Underwriter, 1996. (*Provides a detailed description of homeowners policies and issues associated with fully insuring a home.*)

Answer to Concept Check

1. Freezing homeowners insurance rates would not allow premiums to increase with the value of property being insured, which would lead insurers to reduce the amount of coverage that they would voluntarily sell to homeowners. This would likely lead to an enormous increase in the number of policies in residual markets.

CHAPTER 23

Life Insurance and Annuities

Chapter Objectives

- Provide a brief overview of major life insurance and annuity products.
- Describe the key features and uses of term, endowment, and whole life insurance policies.
- Describe the key features and uses of universal and variable life insurance policies and how these contracts compare to traditional whole life.
- Describe the key features and uses of annuity products.
- Discuss the tax benefits of life insurance and annuity products.
- Analyze the pricing of basic life insurance policies and annuities.
- Describe methods for comparing the cost of life insurance policies across insurers.

23.1 Life Insurance Product Overview

Table 23–1 summarizes the major types of individual life insurance. There are two broad types of life insurance: term and cash value policies. **Term insurance** simply provides death protection: If the insured dies during the policy period, the beneficiaries receive the amount of coverage purchased. In contrast, **cash value policies** bundle death protection and savings accumulation. When purchasing a cash value life insurance policy, a person essentially is both purchasing death protection and saving money with the insurance company. The amount of savings accumulated is called the policy's **cash value.** As discussed further below, policyholders can withdraw or alter the savings accumulations from cash value life insurance policies in various ways.

The most common types of cash value policies are whole life, universal life, and variable life. With whole life policies, the schedule of cash values over time is fixed at the time the policy is purchased. Implicit in this schedule of cash val-

TABLE 23–1 Overview of Types of Life Insurance Policies

	Term Insurance	Cash Value Life Insurance		
		Whole Life	Universal Life	Variable Life
Death benefit	Level death benefit equal to face amount over fixed number of years; decreasing term has a declining schedule of death benefits	Death benefit equal to the face amount is usually level over entire life; if policyholder survives to age 100, then receives death benefit; can purchase more coverage using policyholder dividends	Policyholder chooses between a level death benefit that equals face amount or a death benefit that equals face amount plus cash value	Guaranteed minimum death benefit plus a death benefit that varies with cash value
Typical premium schedules	Annual or five-year level	Single premium; level premium over fixed number of years or until death or surrender	First year required premium but flexible thereafter; sometimes subject to minimum and maximum	Same as whole life
Lapse or surrender	Fail to make premium payment	Fail to make scheduled premium payment, or cash value minus loan value equals zero	Cash value is less than cost of coverage for the period	Fail to make scheduled premium payment or cash value minus loan value equals zero
Cash value	None	Yes, follows a fixed schedule	Yes, varies over time depending on premium payments, charges, and credited interest	Yes, varies over time depending on investment returns
Return on savings accumulation	Not applicable	Implicit in fixed cash value schedule	Varies with interest rates, usually short term rates	Varies with returns on investments chosen by policyholder
Flexibility	Little; most have option to convert to cash value coverage	Limited flexibility; can borrow against cash value	Flexible premium and death benefits; often can borrow against cash value	Same as whole life
Risk borne by policyholder	Amount of dividends with participating policies; insurer insolvency risk	Amount of dividends with participating policies; insurer insolvency risk	Credited interest rate charges; mortality charges; insurer insolvency risk	Investment returns; insurer insolvency risk
Percentage of face amount of coverage sold in US in 1995	44%	20%	13%	2%
Percentage of policies sold in US in 1995	25%	45%	11%	1%

Note: Variable-universal life, which combines the flexible features of universal life and those of variable life, accounted for 11 percent of the face amount of coverage and 8 percent of the policies sold in 1995. Percentages do not sum to 100% because various specialty and combination policies also are not shown.

Source: *1997 Life Insurance Fact Book*, American Council of Life Insurance.

ues are returns earned on the savings that are accumulated within the policy. The implicit returns on a whole life policy generally are not reported to the policyholder, and no attempt is made to unbundle the death protection from the savings accumulation. Under modern variations of cash value life insurance (universal life and variable life), however, the separation of the death protection and savings accumulation are made more transparent to the policyholder. Also, instead of having a fixed schedule of cash values, the cash values can vary (depending on the type of policy) with current interest rates, the return earned on the insurer's entire asset portfolio, or the return on specific portfolios of investments, such as stock mutual funds. As a result, universal and variable life often are called investment sensitive contracts.

Policyholders are entitled to at least a portion of a policy's cash value if they **surrender** (terminate) the policy. Early policy surrenders are called **lapses.** With universal life and variable life policies, a surrender charge often is applied, which causes the amount of money that the policyholder can withdraw—the **cash surrender value**—to be less than the cash value. The surrender charges typically decrease with the number of years that the policy is in force. With whole life, explicit surrender charges are not used, and (assuming that no policy loan has been taken, see below) the policy's cash surrender value each year equals the predetermined cash value. However, the predetermined schedule of cash values reflects implicit surrender charges during the early years of the policy, which makes the implicit return earned on the policy's savings low if the policy is surrendered after only several years.

Why would a person wish to bundle death protection coverage with savings accumulation in a life insurance contract? One reason is that people desire permanent (i.e., lifelong) life insurance protection and, for budgeting purposes, they prefer to pay for this protection using a level premium over time. As will become clearer later, paying for permanent death protection with a level premium automatically gives rise to a cash value that increases over time. In other words, the savings accumulation is a byproduct of a fundamental desire for permanent life insurance and level premiums. Perhaps a more important reason for bundling death protection and savings accumulation is that there are tax advantages of saving with a life insurance policy, which we will analyze below. One disadvantage of saving through life insurance for some persons is that death protection also must be purchased to achieve these tax advantages. In addition, the transactions costs (including surrender charges) included in cash value policies often are comparatively large. These costs can offset the tax benefits from cash value policies, especially if the savings are withdrawn early. In some cases, tax penalties also can be applied if the policy is surrendered early.

When discussing life insurance policies, several terms can cause confusion. The **death benefit** is the amount of money that the beneficiaries receive from the insurer when the insured dies. As previously described, the cash value is the amount of savings accumulation from the policy. For term insurance, whole life insurance, and some types of universal life insurance, the death benefit equals the policy's **face amount,** which is the stated amount of coverage purchased by the policyholder. However, for some types of universal life policies, the death benefit equals the face amount plus the cash value. **Death protection** is the amount of pure death protection coverage provided by the policy. The amount of death protection equals the death benefit minus the cash value (i.e., death protection equals the total amount the policy would pay upon death of the insured compared to the amount that the insured could receive if the policy was surrendered).

23.2 Traditional Products: Term, Endowment, and Whole Life

Term Insurance

About one quarter of the life insurance policies sold in the United States in 1995 were term policies, but these policies represented 44 percent of the amount of death protection purchased (*1997 Life Insurance Fact Book*). A term policy provides a death benefit over a fixed term, usually one year or five years. Term insurance typically provides pure death protection; there is no savings feature and therefore no cash surrender value.

Almost all term policies are **guaranteed renewable,** which means that the policy can be renewed at a predetermined premium at the end of the term without proving insurability (e.g., by taking a physical exam) up to an advanced age, such as 65 or 70. To illustrate, suppose that you purchase a one-year renewable term policy with a $100,000 death benefit. At the end of the year, you can renew the policy for another year with a $100,000 death benefit at a predetermined premium without proving insurability. Also, again without showing proof of insurability, many term policies can be converted to a cash value policy.

The premium for yearly renewable term policies typically increases at the end of each year. For policies that extend over several years, such as a five-year renewable term policy, premiums can increase annually or they can be constant for the term (e.g., five years) and then increased upon renewal. Term insurance premiums increase as the policyholder ages because the probability of a person dying generally increases with age (see section 23.6). Compared to cash value life insurance (see below), the initial premium per $1,000 of face amount is much lower for term insurance, thus allowing a person to buy substantially more coverage for a given premium outlay.

Endowment Insurance

Although the market for endowment insurance in the United States is very small, endowment insurance is common in other countries. A basic understanding of endowment policies also will help you understand more common types of policies. For example, the whole life policy described next is just an endowment policy with a very long term. An **endowment policy** pays the face amount of the policy if the insured dies, but it also pays the face amount of the policy if the insured survives the policy term. For example, if Mr. Cox purchases a five-year endowment policy with a face amount equal to $100,000, the insurer will pay $100,000 to the beneficiaries if he dies in the subsequent five years. If he survives the five-year period, he would be paid the $100,000 at the end of this period. As you might expect, this policy would require a relatively large premium because the insurer will have to pay $100,000 regardless of whether Mr. Cox dies. The main source of uncertainty with an endowment policy is when the benefit payment will occur. Since either Mr. Cox or his beneficiaries will receive $100,000 sometime in the future, an endowment policy has similarities to a savings account.

The insight that endowment policies are largely savings vehicles helps to explain why endowment insurance has declined in importance in the United States but not in other countries. At one time, savings accumulation through endowment policies in the United States received tax advantages. People could save through endowment policies and not pay tax on part of the implicit returns that they earned. Unlike some other countries, the United States no longer grants this favorable tax treatment to endowment policies unless they have a very long duration, such as whole life insurance.

Whole Life Insurance

As the name suggests, the contract length of a **whole life policy** is, in effect, the policyholder's entire life. The death benefit equals the policy's face amount, which generally is fixed for the insured's entire life. For example, a $100,000 face amount whole life policy will pay the beneficiaries $100,000 regardless of when the policyholder dies. If the policyholder survives to age 100 and has paid all the required premiums, the policyholder is paid the $100,000 face amount at that time. Thus, most whole life policies are endowment policies to age 100.

Some whole life policies allow death benefits to be reduced over the course of the contract, and some policies have death benefits that are indexed to inflation. Some whole life contracts are sold with an option, known as the *guaranteed insurability option,* for the policyholder to purchase additional amounts of coverage at specified times and premium rates without proving insurability. Limits on the additional amounts of coverage and the times at which additional coverage can be purchased help reduce adverse selection.

Premium Payment.   Whole life insurance policies commonly use a level premium schedule over a fixed number of years. With a *single premium whole life* policy, the buyer pays the entire premium in a lump sum when the policy is issued. Alternatively, a level premium may be payable for a 10-year or 20-year period; these policies are called *limited pay whole life* (e.g., 10-pay life). However, a substantial majority of whole life policies sold in the United States have level premiums that continue until the policyholder dies, surrenders the policy, or reaches the age of 100—whichever comes first. These contracts are known as *continuous premium whole life.*

The key feature of the premium payment methods for whole life policies is that the premium generally does not increase over time in conjunction with the increased probability of dying. This feature contrasts with most term insurance policies, where the premium generally increases over time to reflect the higher probability of dying. Comparing premiums for yearly renewable term insurance and level premium whole life insurance issued at a given age, the term premium starts off much lower than the level whole life premium, but the term premium eventually exceeds the whole life premium. In the early years of a whole life contract, the level whole life insurance premium must exceed the term insurance premium for an insured at the same age in order to fund benefits in the future when the level premium is less than the annual cost of coverage.

Savings Accumulation.   In essence, when purchasing a whole life contract, you prepay part of the costs of life insurance for future years. That is, you pay more than the true cost of death protection in the early years of the contract and, assuming that you survive, you pay less than the true cost of death protection in the later years. As a result, with whole life and other cash value policies, policyholders are entitled to a return of their prepayments if they decide to surrender the policy. Policyholders can surrender the policy and, in effect, receive at least a portion of their prepayments back—in the form of the policy's cash surrender value. As mentioned above, the cash surrender value is the amount of money that the policyholder can receive if the policy is surrendered. Thus, the savings accumulate under whole life insurance policies because the premium payment schedule requires the policyholder to prepay the expected costs of future death protection. If the policy stays in force, the insurer needs these funds to cover future expected mortality costs (claim costs) when future premiums are insufficient to cover these costs. If the policy is surrendered, the insurer no longer needs these funds to cover future mortality costs associated with the policy. Therefore, the insurer can refund the cash value to the policyholder.

   Note that with whole life policies the beneficiaries do not receive the cash value in addition to the face amount if the insured dies. The beneficiaries receive the face amount only (which generally is fixed). If the policy has a face amount of $100,000, for example, the beneficiaries receive $100,000 regardless of the cash value. This $100,000 payment, however, can be viewed as consisting of a return of cash value plus an amount of pure death protection. If, at the time the insured dies, the cash value is $25,000, then the beneficiaries *in effect* receive the $25,000 cash value plus $75,000 in death protection for a total death benefit of $100,000 (the face amount). From this perspective, the effective or "net" amount of death protection with a whole life policy is less than the policy's face amount (death benefit) whenever the cash value is greater than zero. Stated differently, the amount of death protection varies inversely with the policy's cash value. We can summarize this fundamental aspect of a whole life policy as follows:

$$\text{Death protection}_t = \text{Death benefit} - \text{Cash value}_t = \text{Face amount} - \text{Cash value}_t$$

where the subscript t indicates a particular point in time.

   Traditional whole life policies are structured so that the policy's cash value grows each year and the amount of death protection declines. Figure 23–1 illus-

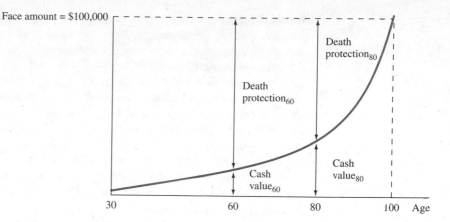

Face amount = $100,000

Death protection$_{80}$

Death protection$_{60}$

Cash value$_{60}$

Cash value$_{80}$

30   60   80   100   Age

trates this pattern for a level-premium whole life policy with a level death benefit (face amount equal to $100,000). It is important to note, however, that the division of the face amount of the policy into death protection and cash value is not explicit in a whole life policy. That is, the death protection and the savings accumulation aspects of the policy are not unbundled. The contract simply promises payment of the face amount upon death or payment of the cash surrender value upon surrender.[1]

Participating Whole Life and Policy Dividends.   Most whole life policies (and many term policies) are **participating policies,** which means that the policy can and usually does pay annual dividends. All whole life and term policies sold by mutual insurers are participating policies. Some stock insurers also sell participating policies. Participating whole life insurance policy premiums are based on conservative assumptions. Because the insurer's actual operating experience is expected to result in lower costs or higher rates of return on assets than are assumed in the premium calculation, the insurer generally pays a portion of the profits to policyholders in the form of policyholder dividends. These dividends are treated as a return of premiums and therefore are not taxable to the policyholder. Insurers generally do not vary dividends with year-to-year fluctuations in operating experience; instead, policyholder dividend formulas are changed periodically based on long-term changes in interest rates, expenses, and mortality costs.

Thus, when pricing participating whole life policies, insurers typically use conservative assumptions with the anticipation that dividends will be positive. If insurers instead determined premiums using assumptions that were closer to what was actually expected, premiums and expected dividends would be lower. Why do insurers follow the conservative approach? One answer relates to our discussion of correlated risk in the earlier chapters. The main factors affecting policy-

---

[1] Additional details on the relationship between cash values and death protection are presented in the appendix.

holder dividends are changes in interest rates and aggregate mortality experience. Because these factors cause profits on individual policies to be highly correlated, the uncertainty associated with these factors is costly, if not impossible, to diversify away. The use of conservative assumptions along with paying policyholder dividends shifts some of this correlated risk to policyholders. For example, if a highly contagious and deadly disease occurred or if returns on insurer investments declined substantially and remained at low levels over long periods, insurers could reduce policyholder dividends. The alternative would be for insurers to bear more of this correlated risk. The problem is that insurers then would need to hold much more capital to achieve the same level of insolvency risk. The costs of holding this capital would increase expected prices for life insurance. In summary, policyholder dividends are one method of allowing insurers and policyholders to share correlated risk.

Policies usually provide several options for the use of dividends. For example, whole life policyholders often have a choice as to whether dividends are used to increase the policy's face amount (known as paid-up additions) or pay part of the next premium due. When selling whole life insurance policies, agents present a table of illustrated dividends, net premiums (premiums minus illustrated dividends) if the policyholder uses the dividends to reduce future premiums, and illustrated death benefits if dividends are used to increase the policy's face amount. **Illustrated dividends** usually reflect what the insurer is currently paying on comparable policies. It is important to note, however, that these illustrations are not guaranteed (see Box 23–1). Illustrated dividends typically increase over time. The main reason for this increase is that most insurer dividend formulas reflect a credit for greater than assumed investment returns that is approximately proportional to the policy's cash value. As the guaranteed cash value grows over time, so does the illustrated dividend.

Surrender Options.   As mentioned above, a whole life policy can be surrendered for its cash surrender value. Most whole life policies provide two other sur-

---

Box 23–1

Interest Rates and Insurer Legal Problems

Universal life policies were introduced in 1979 when interest rates were at a very high level. Insurers marketed these policies by advertising that the cash value of the policy would vary directly with interest rates. Policy illustrations based on current interest rates at the time created the impression that the cash values of universal life policies would grow to enormous sums. Because interest rates fell in the late 1980s and early 1990s, many illustrations did not materialize. As a result, a number of policyholders filed suit against and obtained settlements from insurers, alleging that the insurers and their agents misled policyholders. Some participating whole life insurers similarly were sued by their policyholders when they reduced dividends below illustrated levels due to declining interest rates.

render options (technically known as nonforfeiture options): paid-up insurance and extended term insurance. With **paid-up insurance,** the cash surrender value is used as a single premium to purchase a paid-up whole life policy. For example, suppose that a 55-year-old person has a policy with face amount of $100,000 and cash surrender value of $30,000. The policy can be surrendered and the cash value can be used as a single premium to purchase life insurance for the remainder of the insured's life. If $30,000 is the single premium for a $75,000 face amount policy, then $75,000 is the amount of paid-up insurance. With **extended term insurance,** the cash value is used as a single premium to purchase a paid-up term policy with the same face amount as the original policy (e.g., $100,000). For example, if $30,000 is the single premium for a 15-year term policy with a $100,000 face amount, the policyholder could surrender the policy and receive the 15-year term policy. Whole life policy illustrations generally include a schedule of paid-up insurance and extended term insurance amounts available at various ages in addition to the schedule of cash values.

Policy Loans. Most whole life policies also allow the policyholder to obtain a large portion of the cash value of the policy without surrendering the policy by borrowing against the cash value in the form of a **policy loan.** To illustrate how a policy loan works, suppose that a $100,000 face amount policy has cash value of $30,000 and the policyholder borrows $10,000. Premiums still need to be paid after the loan is taken (unless more loans are used to pay the premium, see below), and the policy's cash value grows as originally scheduled. However, the policyholder owes the principal and interest on the loan. If the insured dies prior to paying back the loan, the loan balance reduces the death benefit. If the insured in this example died immediately after taking out the loan, the death benefit would be reduced to $90,000 ($100,000 face amount minus $10,000 loan amount). Similarly, the cash value available upon surrender would only be $20,000 ($30,000 cash value minus $10,000 loan amount). Some whole life policies have provisions whereby if a policyholder fails to make a premium payment, a loan against the cash value is automatically taken out in an amount equal to the missed premium (assuming that the cash value exceeds the premium).

Until the late 1970s and early 1980s, the interest rate on policy loans usually was fixed in the contract at the time the policy was issued. Periods of high interest rates during the 1970s and early 1980s led many policyholders to take loans in order to invest the loan principal in higher yielding securities. The resulting larger than expected cash withdrawals, known as disintermediation, caused insurers to reduce dividends on participating policies. As a result of their experience during these periods, many insurers moved to variable loan rates on whole life policies, and some insurers began paying lower dividends on policies that have loans outstanding.

Expense Loadings. Life insurance premiums must cover the insurer's underwriting, marketing, and claims processing costs, as well as other administrative costs (see Chapter 6 for a general discussion of these costs). The issue of how and when to recover these expenses is particularly important for life insurers because of the long-term nature of the policies and because a large part of the insurer's expenses are incurred at the time the policy is issued, such as expenses for marketing, underwriting, and sales commissions.

Whole life (and term) insurers generally front-end load expense charges. With a whole life policy, the front-end loading of expenses is accomplished by having a relatively low accumulation of cash value in the early years of the policy. Even with this front-end loading, insurers generally experience a net loss on policies that lapse within a few years of issue. The alternative of spreading expense charges more evenly over the life of the contract would imply that the insurer would recover even less of its costs from policies that were surrendered early.

The front-end loading of expense charges causes the implicit return earned on the savings accumulation portion of the policy to be relatively low until the contract has been in force for a number of years. In addition, insurers with higher early lapse rates need to charge higher rates, holding other factors constant, to recover all of their costs over time. The higher rates further reduce the implicit return available on their policies. Thus, there are two implications that you should be aware of: (1) Implicit returns on savings accumulated through life insurance will be low or even negative if the policy is dropped early, and (2) insurers with lower lapse rates can offer policies with higher returns.

Concept Checks

1. Assume that the face amount of a whole life policy equals $100,000 and that the cash value equals $20,000. What is the death benefit (total amount paid upon death)? What is the amount of death protection?

2. Show graphically how the cash value and death benefit change over time for a nonparticipating whole life policy with a face amount of $50,000.

23.3 Product Innovation: Universal and Variable Life

Universal Life

The period of high interest rates in the late 1970s led to the introduction in 1979 of **universal life policies** (see Box 23–1). Like traditional whole life policies, these policies provide permanent death protection and savings accumulation. However, universal life policies differ in that (1) they offer greater flexibility with respect to premium payments, and (2) the cash value varies explicitly over time based on premium payments, expense and mortality charges, and credited interest.

Premium Flexibility.   A fixed premium schedule is not used with universal life. The policyholder instead has flexibility in the payment of premiums, sometimes subject to annual minimum and maximum amounts. A scheduled premium payment generally can be skipped without surrendering the policy or taking a policy loan. Premium flexibility is one reason that the cash value of a universal life policy is not fixed in advance like a whole life policy. If the policyholder exercises the option to pay more or less in premiums, then the cash value of the policy will be adjusted accordingly. Lower premium payments imply lower cash values, all else being equal.

Cash Value Accumulation.   The cash value for a universal life policy varies over time, depending on the interest rate the insurer uses to credit the policy's cash value and on the explicit expense and mortality cost charges used to debit the policy's cash value. Implicit in a whole life policy is a predetermined interest rate credited to the policy's cash value, which, along with predetermined mortality and expense charges, determines the schedule of cash values. With universal life policies, the interest rate credits to the policy's cash value can vary monthly, depending on current market interest rates. For example, if market interest rates increase, the insurer will likely increase the interest rate credited to cash values, and then cash values will grow at a faster rate.

Given these explicit credits and charges (debits), the death protection and the savings accumulation portions of the policy are essentially unbundled with a universal life policy. The policyholder is given an explicit statement showing how the policy's cash value changes from period to period, depending on premium payments, interest rates, and expense and mortality charges. Figure 23–2 shows the important relationships.

Additional premium payments or higher interest credits cause the cash value to increase, holding mortality and expense charges constant. The annual mortal-

FIGURE 23–2

Main factors affecting cash value of a universal life policy

Cash value
at beginning of period

+

Premium payments
at beginning of period

−

Mortality charge
at beginning of period

−

Expense charge
at beginning of period

+

Interest credited
at end of period

=

Cash value
at end of period

ity charge generally reflects the insurer's expected claim costs for death protection. The insurer can modify the mortality charge per $1,000 of death protection for a given age, but this charge cannot exceed a maximum amount for each age that is specified in the contract. Expense charges commonly equal a percent of premiums, with a higher percent charge for the initial premium. This front-end loading of expense charges will cause the cash value to grow at a lower rate in the early years of the policy, all else being equal. The same is true for whole life policies, but the relationships are not made explicit. Most universal life policies also include a stipulated schedule of surrender charges.

The formula in Figure 23–2 makes it clear that the savings accumulation with a universal life policy explicitly depends on the insurer's charges, which can be expected to change over time in relation to its operating experience. The policyholder explicitly bears the risk associated with credited interest rates and mortality charges. In contrast, with nonparticipating whole life policies, the insurer's operating experience does not affect the policyholder (ignoring the risk of insolvency); that is, the schedule of cash values is guaranteed at the time the policy is purchased. With participating whole life policies, the effect of the insurer's operating experience on a policyholder is less immediate and direct than with universal life policies, because dividends generally change only slowly compared to those illustrated at the time of purchase. That is, dividends on whole life policies are based on longer term trends in interest rates, mortality charges, and other expenses, whereas cash value changes with universal life generally depend on short-term changes in interest rates (and sometimes mortality).

Universal life policies usually guarantee a minimum interest rate that will be credited to the cash value. Interest credits above the guaranteed rate are determined in various ways. One method is to explicitly link the interest credited to a short-term interest rate (e.g., the rate paid on specified US Treasury securities). Another method is for the insurer to choose a crediting rate for the coming year in view of the interest it can earn on new investments or on the expected return it will earn on its entire portfolio of investments.

When selling universal life policies, agents present projections of future premiums and cash values. The projections, by definition, are based on assumptions about crediting interest rates, mortality charges, expense charges, and other factors. Agents often have made projections using a current market interest rate as the crediting rate over the course of the entire policy. When interest rates were at historically high levels, projections based on current interest rate levels assumed that high interest rates would continue to prevail into the foreseeable future. The use of a high crediting interest rate will imply that the policy's cash value will grow at a fast rate and can suggest that premiums will vanish (no longer need to be paid) at some date, because the cash value will grow to a level that is sufficient to cover future charges.[2] If, however, interest rates do not stay at the high level that was assumed in the projections, cash values will not grow as rapidly and

---

[2] This also can (and did) occur for participating whole life policies during prolonged periods of high long-term interest rates.

premiums will not vanish as projected. Box 23–1 describes the legal problems some insurers experienced after universal life policies did not meet projections, in part because of falling interest rates.

Death Benefit Options.   With a universal life policy, the policyholder generally has a choice between two death benefit options. One option is to have the total death benefit (the amount paid upon the insured's death) equal to a level amount over time, as is true for a whole life policy. The other option is to have the death benefit increase as the cash value of the policy increases. That is, unlike whole life, the total death benefit at a point in time equals the initial face amount plus the cash value at that time. With the second option, the amount of death protection equals the face amount of the policy at all times (i.e., Death protection = Total death benefit – Cash value).

Under the level death benefit option, the amount of death protection decreases as the cash value increases, just as in a whole life policy. However, because the cash value is uncertain under a universal life policy, it is possible under the level death benefit option that the cash value could increase above the face amount of the policy. If this occurred, there would be no death protection and the policy's savings accumulation would not qualify for preferential tax treatment. For this reason, if the level death benefit option is chosen, the death benefit is automatically increased if the cash value approaches the policy's face amount so that a gap is always maintained between the death benefit and the cash value. This gap allows the policy to meet the complex rules (concerning the minimum amount of death protection in relation to savings accumulation) required to qualify for tax treatment as life insurance. Figure 23–3 illustrates how the death benefit and death protection vary if the cash value increases over time under each of the death benefit options.

FIGURE 23–3

Death benefit options for a universal life policy

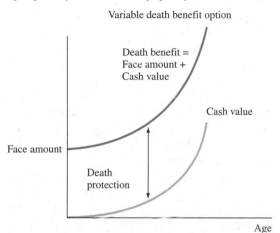

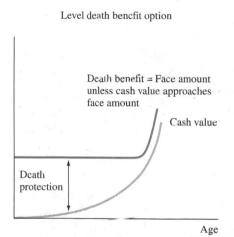

Loans and Partial Surrenders.   As with traditional whole life policies, policy-holders can take out loans on some universal life policies. Any unpaid interest on the loan is automatically deducted from the policy's cash value. In some cases, a lower interest rate is credited to the portion of the policy's cash value that is borrowed. For example, an insurer might credit 8 percent on unborrowed cash values and 6 percent on any amount borrowed. One reason for this provision is that if the loan rate (the interest rate paid by the policyholder) is fixed up front (e.g., at 6 percent), then the lower rate paid on the cash value helps prevent disintermediation by policyholders. That is, it reduces the extent to which policyholders take out loans at lower than market rates and still receive interest credited at market rates. Instead of loan provisions, some universal life policies allow partial surrenders. The policyholder can simply remove a portion of the cash value without terminating the policy. In these cases, no interest is credited (or no loan interest is due) on the portion of the cash value that is surrendered.

Concept Check

3. Other things being equal, explain how each of the following would be likely to affect the growth of a universal life policy's cash value.
   (*a*) The policyholder reduces the annual premium payment by 50 percent after five years.
   (*b*) Market interest rates are stable for five years and then decline sharply and remain at the lower level.
   (*c*) Researchers discover a cure for cancer five years after the policy is issued.

Variable Life

With a **variable life policy,** the growth in the cash value of a policy depends directly on the return earned on a portfolio of assets chosen by the policyholder. Recall that with universal life, credited interest rates are expected to vary in relation to current yields available to the insurer on new investments, its overall portfolio, or, in some cases, market interest rates. For variable life policies, however, the growth in cash value varies directly with the return earned on a portfolio of stocks and bonds that is chosen by the policyholder. If the return on the portfolio is negative, the cash value can decline with variable life. This contrasts with universal life policies, which specify a minimum rate of return that will be credited to cash values. Since the purchaser of a variable life policy is in effect investing in a mutual fund with an insurance wrapper, agents selling variable life policies are required to have a securities license. The policyholder also must be given a prospectus, as is required for sales of other securities.

The death benefit on a variable life policy varies with the policy's cash value, but a minimum death benefit is guaranteed. Thus, one can view the death benefit on a variable life policy as consisting of a level guaranteed death benefit plus an additional death benefit if the rates of return on the investments selected by the policyholder exceed some minimum threshold. In the latter case, the additional funds generated from the high returns are automatically used to purchase additional death benefits. If the rates of return on the investments selected by the policyholder fall short of the threshold, then previously purchased additional death benefits are surrendered.

Variable life policies, like whole life policies, generally have fixed and level premiums. Policy loans can be taken, with some policies offering a fixed loan rate and others offering a variable loan rate. Some policies have automatic loans to pay missed premiums. Absent this provision, failure to pay a premium due will produce a lapse or surrender. Not surprisingly, insurers have merged the variable life idea, where the rate of return on the policy's cash value varies with rates of return on portfolios of stocks and bonds chosen by the policyholder, with the universal life idea of flexibility in premium payments and death benefits. The result commonly is called **variable-universal life.**

23.4 Tax Benefits from Life Insurance Policies

Cash value life insurance policies are an income tax–advantaged method of saving. The tax advantages arise from the interaction of the following aspects of the tax code:

1. Death benefits are not taxable as income. (They may be subject to estate taxes.)
2. No income tax is paid on the annual increase in cash value while the policy is in force.
3. If the policy is surrendered, the policyholder pays income tax on the difference between the cash surrender value and the sum of all premiums less policyholder dividends.

The first and second features of the tax code in effect imply that the implicit returns on life insurance policy savings accumulation escape income taxation if the insured dies. In contrast, if an equivalent amount of funds were saved for the insured's beneficiaries in a nontax-advantaged account, then the nontax-exempt interest and dividends on those funds would have been taxed as they were paid and the capital gains would have been taxed as they were realized.

If the insured does not die, the second and third features imply that returns earned on life insurance policy savings are tax deferred until the policy is surrendered and are only partially taxed upon surrender. In some countries, the premiums paid for life insurance also are tax deductible. The combination of premium deductibility and tax deferment of investment earnings causes the tax benefits from life insurance in these countries to be equivalent to the tax benefits of qualified retirement plans in the United States (discussed in Chapter 19). Life insurance premiums are not tax deductible in the United States.[3] Thus, the tax benefits are similar to retirement accounts with tax deferral of investment income, but no deductibility of contributions.

---

[3] An exception is that the premiums on the first $50,000 of employer-provided life insurance are not taxable to the employee.

Since Chapter 19 provides a detailed analysis of the benefits of tax-deferred savings plans, we provide only a simple example here to illustrate this tax benefit. Suppose that the annual before-tax rate of return on taxable securities is 10 percent. Then an investor with a 28 percent marginal tax rate would earn 7.2 percent in a nontax-deferred account. Saving $1 in this way would yield $1.072 after one year and $1.072^{20} = 4.02 after 20 years. If, instead, the investor earned 10 percent on $1 for 20 years through a tax-deferred account (as cash value life insurance policies are), the investor would have $1.1^{20} = 6.73 before paying tax and $6.73 - 0.28 \times ($6.73 - $1.00) = 5.13 after paying tax at the end of 20 years. The difference between $5.13 and $4.02 is the benefit of tax-deferred savings in this example.

The actual benefit from tax deferral of investment earnings from life insurance is greater than what we just calculated, because the third feature of the tax code listed above overstates the "tax basis" (the amount deducted from the gross amount received to determine taxable income) compared to a nonlife insurance tax-deferred savings account. A higher tax basis implies that less tax is paid when the policy is surrendered. To illustrate, recall that the premium payments on a cash value policy can be viewed as consisting of two parts: (1) an amount needed to cover the cost of death protection (face amount minus the cash value in the case of whole life), and (2) an amount saved through the insurer. By allowing the total premium to be used as the tax basis, the tax basis allows a deduction for the cost of death protection in addition to the implicit savings contributions by the policyholder. Consequently, the tax paid once the policy is surrendered is less than what would be paid on an otherwise identical tax deferred savings account.

In summary, life insurance policies with cash values allow investors to (1) escape income taxes on the returns earned on the savings invested with the insurer if the insured dies, (2) defer income taxes on the returns earned on the savings invested with the insurer if the policy is surrendered, and (3) pay lower taxes when the policy is surrendered, compared to other tax-deferred savings accounts that allow tax deferral of investment income but no up-front deductibility of contributions. This tax treatment significantly increases the demand for cash value life insurance.

23.5 Annuity Contracts

Annuity contracts are an important and growing source of business for life insurers and tax-deferred savings for annuity policyholders. In 1995, US life insurers received $159 billion in annuity premiums, which was 47 percent of their total premiums for life insurance, health insurance, and annuities. Moreover, the percentage of premiums from annuities increased dramatically over the past 25 years. Annuity premiums represented only 17 percent of all life insurance company premiums in 1975.

A useful starting point for understanding annuities is to recognize that two periods are associated with any annuity: (1) the period when the policyholder pays premiums to the insurer, known as the **accumulation period,** and (2) the pe-

TABLE 23–2   **Overview of Annuity Contracts**

Characteristic	Variations
Premium payments	(a) Single premium
	(b) Fixed period, level premium up to an advanced age
	(c) Flexible premium over time
Annuity benefits begin	(a) Immediately
	(b) Deferred
Annuity benefits end	(a) Fixed number of years
	(b) Death of one or more individuals
	(c) Combination of (a) and (b)
Insurer payments	(a) Fixed
	(b) Vary with interest rates, with guaranteed minimum
	(c) Vary with returns on stock and bond funds chosen by policyholder

riod when the insurer makes payments to the policyholder, known as the **payout period.** The nature of payments during both the accumulation period and the payout period can take many forms. Table 23–2 summarizes the most common variations.

During the payout period, annuities pay a specified amount of money at given time intervals (e.g., monthly) over a specified length of time.[4] An annuity that only pays until the annuitant dies is called a **straight life annuity.** An annuity that pays over a fixed period of time regardless of death is called an *annuity certain.* These basic types of annuities can be combined, as well. For example, a life annuity, period-certain pays for a fixed number of years regardless of death, after which payments end when one or more people die. Joint and last survivor annuities are structured so that the insurer's payments end only after the death of two people (e.g., a husband and wife). Annuity contracts also can be purchased where payments are reduced, but not eliminated, when one person dies, but not the other.

Uses of Annuities

From a risk management perspective, the primary role of annuities during the payout period is to protect a person or persons from outliving their financial resources. For example, a retiree can pay an insurer a fixed amount of money (a portion of preretirement savings) and in exchange receive a monthly payment from the insurer for as long as the person lives. This would be an example of a single-premium life annuity with immediate payments. In contrast, a person who attempts to spread retirement savings over his or her remaining life without an annuity faces the risk that the savings fund will be exhausted prior to death (the person lives

---

[4] Annuities were discussed in Chapter 19 in the context of defined benefit pension plans that pay monthly benefits until death.

longer than expected). Alternatively, the person might die sooner than expected with money left in the bank (to the benefit of strangers or obnoxious heirs). Thus, annuities can be used to reduce the risk that savings are exhausted before the annuitant dies or vice versa. In effect, the funds of annuitants that die earlier are used by the insurer to fund payments for annuitants that die later.

As the previous example illustrated, a retiree can use a portion of preretirement savings to purchase a single premium annuity at retirement. In essence, the person accumulates funds while working and then spreads the funds over retirement using the annuity contract. An alternative approach is to purchase, prior to retirement, annuity contracts with deferred payments. **Deferred annuities,** which represent about 95 percent of all annuity purchases, essentially combine the preretirement accumulation of savings and the postretirement distribution of savings in one contract. The main reason for combining these two steps is the tax advantages of saving through deferred annuities: The returns implicitly earned from these contracts are not taxed until the insurer distributes them. Thus, like cash value life insurance policies, deferred annuity contracts are a tax-deferred savings vehicle.

While deferred annuities and cash value life insurance policies serve a similar purpose with respect to deferring tax on investment income, expense charges typically are lower with an annuity contract. Consequently, annuities often are the preferred method of savings. If death protection (pure insurance) and/or greater liquidity (see below) also are desired, there may be advantages of purchasing cash value life insurance rather than or in addition to annuities.

Specific Savings Features

The accumulation of savings through an annuity contract follows a pattern similar to other savings plans. Premium payments (contributions) and the return credited on past accumulations cause the savings accumulation to grow and expense charges reduce the growth rate. With **fixed annuities,** the return credited to an annuity contract in a given period usually varies with current interest rates, but the insurer guarantees a minimum rate of return (often 3 or 4 percent). With **variable annuities,** the return credited to the contract varies with the return on stock and bond funds that the policyholder chooses; there is no minimum rate of return. Thus, variable annuities are very similar to mutual fund investments. As is true for variable life insurance contracts, the agent selling variable annuities must be licensed to sell securities. Expense charges typically are a percentage (e.g., 2 percent) of the value of the accumulated funds. Some annuities have higher expense charges in the initial year than in later years; that is, there is a front-end load.

Deferred annuities have two basic types of premium payment methods. Single premium deferred annuities (SPDAs) are purchased with a single premium. Of course, multiple SPDAs can be purchased over time and in varying amounts. A flexible premium deferred annuity (FPDA) gives the purchaser flexibility as to the timing and amount of premium payments. A natural question is, Why distinguish SPDAs and FPDAs when both products allow the purchaser to make the same sequence of payments? One difference between the two contracts is in the nature of the guarantee provided by the insurer with respect to the rates of interest credited on the savings accumulations. SPDAs often will guarantee that interest will be credited on the savings accumulations using the current specified interest rate for several years. FPDAs typically do not provide such a guarantee.

When evaluating a deferred annuity it is important not only to consider the rate at which savings accumulate, but also the rate that is used to annuitize the savings accumulations. The benefit of a comparatively high interest rate used for crediting savings during the accumulation phase might be mitigated by a comparatively low interest rate used for distributing the savings accumulations over the payout phase.

Deferred annuities, however, do not have to be and often are not annuitized; that is, the purchaser can withdraw the accumulated funds prior to the payout period by surrendering the policy. Depending on the length of time that the contract has been in force, surrender charges may be applied. Insurers typically recover a large portion of their expenses associated with selling and administering annuity contracts that are surrendered early through surrender charges (i.e., most annuities have backend loads). Surrender charges generally are a percentage of the funds accumulated and decline over time. As a result, the return on these annuity contracts is higher, all else being equal, the longer that the contract is held prior to surrender.

There also are tax penalties if people withdraw their savings from annuity contracts prior to retirement. For example, if a person withdraws savings from an annuity contract prior to age 59½, then a 10 percent penalty on the returns from the savings generally is applied unless the funds are rolled into another annuity contract. Thus, although there is a tax advantage of saving through annuity contracts, the savings are illiquid in that they cannot be used for purposes other than retirement without paying a significant penalty. In contrast, loan provisions in most cash value life insurance policies allow access to savings without surrender charges or tax penalties.

Concept Checks

4. Explain how annuities are a form of insurance against living too long.
5. Explain how annuities are a tax-advantaged savings vehicle.

23.6 Life Insurance Pricing

A greater understanding of how life insurance works can be obtained by studying basic aspects of pricing. In this section, we start by pricing a sequence of one-year term life insurance policies. We then consider the pricing of a two-year term policy under two assumptions about the payment of premiums. A comparison of a two-year term policy with a sequence of one-year term policies provides many of the insights necessary for understanding whole life insurance policies. We then move on to the pricing of basic annuities and whole life insurance. Our discussion of pricing focuses on mortality costs and ignores expense loadings; that is, we examine what normally are called **net premiums.**

One-year Term Insurance

To price life insurance and annuity products, an insurer needs to estimate the probability of a person dying at different ages. For example, suppose that Mr. Babbel, a 40-year-old, purchases a one-year term life insurance policy with a face amount of $100,000. This policy will pay the beneficiaries of the policy (Mr. Babbel's family) $100,000 if Mr. Babbel dies. Assume that the insurer uses an estimate of the probability that Mr. Babbel will die during the coming year from a **mortality table** like Table 23–3 (also see Box 23–2). The column labeled "Probability of Dying" in the mortality table gives the probability of a male dying at the age of x given that he has lived x years. The other columns of the mortality table will be discussed as we proceed.

Table 23–3 indicates that the probability of a male who has lived to his 40th birthday dying at the age of 40 (before his 41st birthday) is 0.00302. Thus, the claim cost distribution for this one-year term policy is:

$$\text{Loss} = \begin{array}{ll} \$0 & \text{with probability } 0.99698 \\ \$100,000 & \text{with probability } 0.00302 \end{array}$$

The expected claim cost equals $302. From Chapter 6, you know that the expected claim cost is one of the fundamental factors affecting fair insurance premiums.

Box 23–2

Mortality Tables

According to the mortality table (Table 23–3), the probability of a 99-year-old person dying during the coming year equals 1. Of course, not all 99-year-olds will die by their 100th birthday. The assumption that everyone dies before the age of 100 is not restrictive for two reasons. First, term insurance is rarely sold to people beyond the age of 70, so that the probabilities during the older ages are not relevant to most term insurance policies. Second, most whole life policies are equivalent to endowment policies to age 100; that is, if the policyholder survives to be 100, he or she receives the face amount of the policy.

Many mortality tables exist; Table 23–3 is simply one example. Since the mortality risk of females and males differs, insurers typically use different mortality tables for males and females (if the law allows it). Insurers also use different mortality tables for smokers and nonsmokers. As discussed in Chapter 6, competition among insurers would be expected to lead insurers to identify and use low-cost information that helps predict the probability of a person dying.

Although we will not do so in this chapter, insurers use different mortality tables for life insurance products than for annuities. One reason is that the selection of people who purchase life insurance policies differs from the selection of people who typically buy annuities. Other things being equal, people who have a lower than average probability of dying are more likely to buy life annuities and less likely to buy life insurance.

TABLE 23–3   **1980 Standard Mortality Table for Males**

Age	Probability of Dying	Number of People	Number of Deaths	Age	Probability of Dying	Number of People	Number of Deaths
0	0.00418	1000000	4180				
1	0.00107	995820	1066	51	0.00730	890645	6502
2	0.00099	994754	985	52	0.00796	884144	7038
3	0.00098	993770	974	53	0.00871	877106	7640
4	0.00095	992796	943	54	0.00956	869466	8312
5	0.00090	991853	893	55	0.01047	861154	9016
6	0.00086	990960	852	56	0.01146	852138	9766
7	0.00080	990108	792	57	0.01249	842372	10521
8	0.00076	989316	752	58	0.01359	831851	11305
9	0.00074	988564	732	59	0.01477	820546	12119
10	0.00073	987832	721	60	0.01608	808427	13000
11	0.00077	987111	760	61	0.01754	795427	13952
12	0.00085	986351	838	62	0.01919	781476	14997
13	0.00099	985513	976	63	0.02106	766479	16142
14	0.00115	984537	1132	64	0.02314	750337	17363
15	0.00133	983405	1308	65	0.02542	732974	18632
16	0.00151	982097	1483	66	0.02785	714342	19894
17	0.00167	980614	1638	67	0.03044	694448	21139
18	0.00178	978976	1743	68	0.03319	673309	22347
19	0.00186	977234	1818	69	0.03617	650962	23545
20	0.00190	975416	1853	70	0.03951	627416	24789
21	0.00191	973563	1860	71	0.04330	602627	26094
22	0.00189	971703	1837	72	0.04765	576533	27472
23	0.00186	969867	1804	73	0.05264	549061	28903
24	0.00182	968063	1762	74	0.05819	520159	30268
25	0.00177	966301	1710	75	0.06419	489891	31446
26	0.00173	964591	1669	76	0.07053	458445	32334
27	0.00171	962922	1647	77	0.07712	426111	32862
28	0.00170	961275	1634	78	0.08390	393249	32994
29	0.00171	959641	1641	79	0.09105	360255	32801
30	0.00173	958000	1657	80	0.09884	327454	32366
31	0.00178	956343	1702	81	0.10748	295089	31716
32	0.00183	954640	1747	82	0.11725	263372	30880
33	0.00191	952893	1820	83	0.12826	232492	29819
34	0.00200	951073	1902	84	0.14025	202673	28425
35	0.00211	949171	2003	85	0.15295	174248	26651
36	0.00224	947168	2122	86	0.16609	147597	24514
37	0.00240	945047	2268	87	0.17955	123082	22099
38	0.00258	942779	2432	88	0.19327	100983	19517
39	0.00279	940346	2624	89	0.20729	81466	16887
40	0.00302	937723	2832	90	0.22177	64579	14322
41	0.00329	934891	3076	91	0.23698	50257	11910
42	0.00356	931815	3317	92	0.25345	38347	9719
43	0.00387	928498	3593	93	0.27211	28628	7790
44	0.00419	924905	3875	94	0.29590	20838	6166
45	0.00455	921029	4191	95	0.32996	14672	4841
46	0.00492	916838	4511	96	0.38455	9831	3780
47	0.00532	912328	4854	97	0.48020	6050	2905
48	0.00574	907474	5209	98	0.65798	3145	2069
49	0.00621	902265	5603	99	1.00000	1076	1076
50	0.00671	896662	6017	100		0	

Another factor affecting fair premiums is the time value of money. Therefore, we must consider the time between the receipt of premiums and the payment of claims, as well as the interest rate. To focus on the main points, we will assume that people purchase life insurance on the insured's birthday and that if they die during the year, the insurer pays the beneficiaries of the policy on the eve of what would have been the insured's next birthday. The other factors affecting fair premiums— expense loadings and profit loadings—will be ignored for simplicity.

To find the present value of expected claim costs on Mr. Babbel's one-year term policy, assume that the one-year interest rate equals 10 percent. Then the present value of expected claim costs equals $302/1.1 = $275; that is, the insurer would need to charge Mr. Babbel $275 in order to cover its expected claim costs. Ignoring insurer nonclaim costs, the fair premium for this one-year term policy would be $275.

Suppose that Mr. Babbel is lucky enough to survive his 40th year and decides to purchase another one-year term policy with a $100,000 death benefit for his 41st year. What is the fair premium (ignoring expense and profit loadings)? From the mortality table, the probability that Mr. Babbel dies in his 41st year is 0.00329, slightly higher than the previous year. The undiscounted expected claim costs therefore equal $329. Assuming the interest rate is still 10 percent, the present value of expected claim costs equals $299 ($329/1.1). The important point to notice is that the premium for one-year term insurance is higher than in the previous year. This premium increase is simply a reflection of the higher probability of dying as Mr. Babbel ages, as all other factors (e.g., interest rates, expense loadings) have been held constant.[5] If Mr. Babbel continued to purchase one-year term policies, the premium per $1,000 of coverage would continue to rise as depicted in Figure 23–4.

Concept Check

6. Assuming an interest rate of 8 percent, and using Table 23–3, calculate the present value of expected claim costs for a one-year term policy with a $1,000 death benefit for (*a*) a 50-year-old, and (*b*) a 95-year-old.

FIGURE 23–4

Expected claim costs on a one-year term policy with a $1,000 death benefit from age 35 to 99

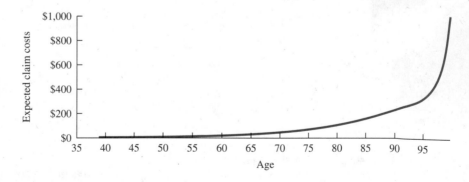

---

[5] Over a brief period in a person's twenties, the probability of dying declines with age, because of fewer accidental deaths (largely due to drunk driving) and suicides. After this period, the probability of dying increases with age.

Two-year Term Insurance

Now let's return to the situation where Mr. Babbel is 40 years old and suppose that, instead of purchasing a one-year term policy, he decides to purchase a two-year $100,000 term insurance policy. We will find the premium (ignoring expense and profit loadings) for this policy under two alternative methods of payment: a single premium and a level premium.

Single Premium.   A single premium policy requires Mr. Babbel to pay one premium at the initiation of the policy and no premiums thereafter. Since we are ignoring expense and profit loadings, the fair single premium equals the present value of expected claim costs. As in any present value problem, the best way to proceed is to identify all the expected cash flows and the timing of these cash flows. Table 23–4 summarizes the timing of possible claim costs and their expected values.

If Mr. Babbel dies in the first year, then the insurer will pay $100,000 one year after the contract is initiated. The probability that this will occur is 0.00302. Thus, the expected claim cost at the end of one year is $302. Assuming an interest rate of 10 percent, the present value of this expected cash outflow equals $275 = $302/1.1. This calculation is the same as was done earlier for the one-year term policy at age 40.

Now comes the more difficult part. If Mr. Babbel does not die in the first year of the policy, it is possible that he will die in the second year. The probability of dying at age 41 that is listed in the mortality table is the probability of dying conditional on the person living up to his 41st birthday. To find the expected claim costs, however, the insurer needs to know a different probability. Since the insurer is pricing the policy when Mr. Babbel is 40 years old, the insurer needs to know the probability that a person who just turned 40 will die at age 41 (in his 42nd year). For a 40-year-old male to die in his 42nd year, he must first live through his 41st year and then die in his 42nd year.

To calculate the relevant probability, we will use columns labeled "Number of People" and "Number of Deaths" in the mortality table. The mortality table starts with an arbitrary number of people at age zero; in Table 23–3, the initial number of people is 1,000,000. This imaginary group of people is then followed

TABLE 23–4   Insurer's Expected Claim Costs for a Two-year $100,000 Term Policy for a 40-year-old Male

Time	Claim Cost	Probability of Dying Given Alive at Contract Initiation	Expected Claim Cost	Present Value of Expected Claim Cost
End of year 1	$100,000	0.00302	$302	$302/1.1 = $275
End of year 2	100,000	0.00328	328	$328/1.1^2 =$ 271
Total				546

through time, assuming that the listed probabilities of death occur. Since the probability of death in a person's first year is 0.00418, then 4,180 of the 1,000,000 people who started the year are expected to be dead after one year. This leaves 995,820 people alive after one year. The table continues to track the expected deaths each year. At age 99, there are only 1,076 people left alive and by assumption they all depart before they reach the age of 100.

These columns can be used to calculate the probability of a 40-year-old male dying in his 42nd year. The table indicates that there are 937,723 people who will be expected to reach the age of 40. Of those people, 3,076 are expected to die in their 42nd year. Thus, the probability that a 40-year-old male dies in his 42nd year equals $3,076/937,723 = 0.00328$. In general, the probability of an x-year-old person dying when he or she is $x + y$ years old equals the number of people dying in year $x + y$ divided by the number of people alive at year x.

Returning to the calculation of the single premium for the two-year term policy, since the probability of Mr. Babbel dying in his 42nd year is 0.00328, expected claim costs at the end of the second year equal $328 (see Table 23–4). Adding the present values of expected claim costs for each year, we find that the single premium is $546 = $275 + $271.

A useful exercise for gaining insight into the pricing of multiple year life insurance policies is to track the cash flows received and paid by the insurer through time under the assumption that everything happens as expected. With Mr. Babbel's two-year, single premium term policy, the insurer would receive $546 when the contract is initiated. This money would be invested and after earning 10 percent interest for one year would grow to $546 \times 1.1 = $600.60. However, at the end of the year, the insurer would expect claim costs of $302 (see Table 23–4), leaving $298.60. This amount would again be invested and after earning 10 percent interest for another year would grow to $298.60 \times 1.1 = $328.46, which is the expected claim cost in the second year (plus some change due to rounding).

Concept Checks

7. Calculate the probability that a 35-year-old male dies when he is 55 years old.

8. Calculate the single premium for a two-year $100,000 term policy issued to a 50-year-old if the interest rate is 8 percent.

Level Premiums.   With a level premium payment schedule, the policyholder pays the same premium for a fixed number of years. In our two-year example, the level premium will be paid once at the initiation of the policy and then again at the beginning of the second year (or equivalently at the end of the first year) if the person survives to pay the second year's premium. The cash flows to the insurer from the two-year term policy with level premiums are summarized as follows:

	Contract Initiation	*End of Year 1*	*End of Year 2*
Inflows:	Premium payment	Possible premium payment	$0
Outflows:	$0	Possible claim payment	Possible claim payment

TABLE 23–5   Insurer's Cash Inflows with a Level Premium Schedule for a Two-year Term Policy for a 40-Year-Old

Time	Premium Payments	Probability	Expected Premium	Present Value of Expected Premium
Contract initiation	P	1	P	P
End of year 1	P	0.99698	$0.99698P$	$\dfrac{0.99698P}{1.1} = 0.906345P$
End of year 2	0	0	0	0

Notice that in the description of the cash flows, we wrote "possible premium payment" at the end of year 1, because the premium payment at the end of year 1 will occur only if the policyholder survives the first year (we are ignoring lapses).

The level premium is the amount that equates the present value of expected cash inflows to the present value of expected cash outflows. The present value of cash outflows is the same as with the single premium policy—$546; indeed, the single premium equals the present value of expected cash outflows at the time the policy is sold. Table 23–5 summarizes the cash inflows. Since we do not yet know the value of the premium (it is what we are trying to find), we denote the premium as P in Table 23–5. The insurer will receive a premium payment at the initiation of the policy with probability 1 (otherwise, the insurer would not issue the policy). If Mr. Babbel lives through the first year, the insurer will receive another premium payment, P, at the beginning of the second year. The probability that the insurer receives the second payment equals 0.99698, the probability of Mr. Babbel's survival (1 − Probability of death = 1 − 0.00302). The expected cash inflow at the beginning of the second year is therefore 0.99698 × P. The present value of expected cash inflows for the life insurer therefore equals

$$P + \frac{0.99698 \times P}{1.1} = P\left[1 + \frac{0.99698}{1.1}\right] = 1.906P$$

Setting the present value of expected cash inflows equal to the present value of expected cash outflows yields the following equation:

$$1.906\,P = \$546$$

Solving for P, we find that the level premium equals $286.41. Note that the level premium is not simply one-half of the single premium. This is because (1) there is a chance that the second premium payment will not be made, and (2) if the second premium payment is made, it occurs one year later, which reduces its present value.

Comparison

One of the important insights needed for understanding cash value life insurance can be obtained by comparing the three payment methods that Mr. Babbel can use to obtain life insurance coverage over his 41st and 42nd years. The first method is to purchase successive one-year term policies, paying $275 at the beginning of his 41st year and paying $299 at the beginning of his 42nd year if he survives. The second method is to purchase a single premium two-year term policy for a premium of $546. The third method is to purchase a two-year term policy using level premiums of $286 per year. The present value of expected premium payments is the same for all three methods, but the timing of cash flows differs. Table 23–6 summarizes these differences.[6]

Before comparing the three payment methods, it is important to note that the annual premiums for successive one-year term insurance policies reflect the annual costs of insuring someone over each successive year for a fixed amount of coverage. The premiums for successive one-year term policies—$275 and $298 respectively—therefore give the cost of insuring Mr. Babbel over time. With both the single premium and the level premium, the policyholder thus pays more in the first year than the cost of providing the insurance for the first year and pays less in the second year than the cost of providing insurance in the second year. The single premium of $546 greatly exceeds the cost of providing insurance in the first year ($275) and there are no future premium payments. With the level premium payment plan, the difference between the payments and the cost of providing the insurance is comparatively small ($286 versus $275). Of course, this does not imply that the policyholder is worse off by buying the two-year policy with a single or level premium. As we mentioned above, the present value of expected premium payments is the same for all three payment methods.

In summary, the cost of providing insurance increases over time because the probability of dying increases over time. Whenever premium payments are leveled over time or pushed toward the beginning of the contract period, the policyholder pays more than the cost of coverage in the early part of the coverage period and less than the cost of coverage during the latter part of the coverage period. This point is central to an understanding of cash value life insurance, where the magnitude of timing differences between premium payments and cost of coverage is much greater than in the two-year example.

TABLE 23–6   Timing Differences in Expected Premium Payments for Alternative Payment Methods (Mr. Babbel buys coverage for his 41st and 42nd years; interest rate = 10 percent)

	Beginning of 1st Year	Beginning of 2nd Year	Present Value
Successive one-year term policies	$275	$299 × 0.99698 = $298	$546
Level premium two-year term policy	286	$286 × 0.99698 = $285	546
Single premium two-year term policy	546	$0	546

---

[6] You can verify that the present values are the same using the cash flows in this table.

Pricing Immediate Annuities

Before analyzing the pricing of whole life insurance policies, we first will consider the pricing of simple immediate annuity contracts. Annuity pricing is of interest in its own right, and the method used also plays a role in the derivation of level premiums for whole life insurance. Recall that a straight life annuity pays a given amount of money every year until the person dies. To price a life annuity with a constant annual payment by the insurer, we will use the standard mortality table given in Table 23–3 that assumes a person dies by the age of 100. Recall, however, that mortality experience is lower for annuity purchasers than for life insurance purchasers (see Box 23–2).

Assume that the annuity purchaser is a 96-year-old male. The annuity will pay $5,000 at the end of each year, unless the person dies during the year. (In practice, most annuities make monthly payments.) Table 23–7 summarizes the expected cash outflows for the insurer. At the end of the first year, the insurer will pay $5,000 if the person survives, which occurs with probability 0.61545 (6,050/9,831). The expected cash flow therefore is $3,077, which has a present value of $2,797. The insurer will make another $5,000 payment at the end of the second year, provided the person survives the first two years. From the mortality table (Table 23–3), the probability of a 96-year-old male surviving two years equals the number of people at the beginning of year 98 divided by the number of people at the beginning of year 96. This ratio is 3,145/9,831, which equals 0.31991. The insurer will make a third payment with probability 0.10941, which is the number of people at year 99 divided by the number of people at year 96 (1,076/9,831). Since the probability of a 99-year-old male surviving one year is assumed to be zero, the insurer will not have to make a fourth payment. The present value of the insurer's expected cash outflows equals $4,530. Thus, ignoring expense loadings, the 96-year-old would have to pay $4,530 for a $5,000 life annuity.

TABLE 23–7   **Insurer's Annuity Payments for a $5,000 Life Annuity for a 96-year-old Male (the first payment occurs at the end of the person's 96th year)**

Age	Probability of 96-year-old Male Living to Specified Age	Expected Annuity Payment ($5,000 × Probability)	Present Value of Expected Annuity Payment
97	6,050/9,831 = 0.61545	$3,077	$3,077/1.1 = $2,797
98	3,145/9,831 = 0.31991	1,600	$1,600/1.1^2 =$ 1,322
99	1,076/9,831 = 0.10941	547	$547/1.1^3 =$ 411
100	0/9,831 = 0	0	0
Total			$4,530

Pricing Whole Life Insurance

The basic procedure for pricing whole life insurance is the same as for pricing term insurance. The only difference is that we must forecast cash flows until the policyholder reaches the age of 100.

Single Premium.   Suppose that at the age of 40 Mr. Babbel decides to purchase a whole life policy with a face amount of $100,000. Table 23–8 summarizes the calculation of expected claim costs using a 5 percent interest rate. The first step is to find the probability that a 40-year-old dies at each age between 40 and 99. This is done using the mortality table by taking the number of deaths at each age divided by the number of people at age 40. For example, the probability that Mr. Babbel dies at age 44 is 3,875/937,723 = 0.00413, and the probability that he dies at age 98 is 2,069/937,723 = 0.002207. By multiplying the probability of death at each age times $100,000, we find the expected claim cost at the end of each year. We then discount the expected claim cost to the present using the 5 percent rate of return. The sum of the individual present value calculations is the present value of expected claim costs. In this case, the present value of Mr. Babbel's expected claim costs equals $22,373. Ignoring expense and profit loadings, the present value of expected claim costs is the *single premium* (or net single premium).

Continuous Level Premium.   Now let's find the *continuous level premium* for this policy, which is the amount that Mr. Babbel would have to pay each year that he is alive. Notice that the continuous level premium is a life annuity (Mr. Babbel makes a payment each year until his death). Applying the general principle that the present value of expected premium payments must equal the single premium

TABLE 23–8   Calculation of Expected Claim Costs for a Whole Life Policy for a 40-Year-Old

Age	Probability of 40 Year Old Dying at Specified Age	Expected Claim Costs	Present Value of Expected Claim Costs	
40	0.003020	$302.00	$302.00/1.05	= $288
41	0.003280	328.00	$328.00/1.05^2$	= 298
42	0.003538	353.80	$353.80/1.05^3$	= 306
43	0.003832	383.20	$383.20/1.05^4$	= 315
44	0.004133	413.30	$413.30/1.05^5$	= 324
45				
.	.	.	.	
.	.	.	.	
.	.	.	.	
96	0.004032	403.20	$403.20/1.05^{57}$ =	25
97	0.003098	309.80	$309.80/1.05^{58}$ =	18
98	0.002207	220.70	$220.70/1.05^{59}$ =	12
99	0.001147	114.70	$114.7/1.05^{60}$ =	6
Total				$22,373

(which in turn equals the present value of expected claim costs), we need to find the life annuity payment amount that has a present value of $22,373 for a 40-year-old.

The first step in finding the life annuity payment amount is to find the probability that Mr. Babbel will be alive at each age between 41 and 99, because these probabilities determine the likelihood that Mr. Babbel will make a particular premium payment. The probability that Mr. Babbel is alive on his 41st birthday and thus makes the second premium payment is calculated from the mortality table by dividing the number of people alive at age 41 by the number of people alive at age 40, which equals 934,891/937,723 = 0.99698. The probability that he is alive on his 42nd birthday and thus makes the third premium payment is the number of people alive at age 42 divided by the number of people alive at age 40, which is 931,815/937,723 = 0.99370. Table 23–9 shows similar calculations for several of the years. Each of the probabilities is multiplied by the variable P, the symbol for the level premium that we are trying to calculate.

The next step is to calculate the present value of the expected premium payments using a 5 percent interest rate. The last column lists the present value of each expected premium payment. The final step is to sum the individual present value calculations to find the present value of all the expected premium payments. The last row of Table 23–9 indicates that the present value of paying P until he dies equals $16.30 × P. We want to find the value of P that makes paying P until Mr. Babbel dies equal to the present value of expected claim costs. Thus, we solve the following equation for P:

$$\$16.30 \times P = \$22,373$$

TABLE 23–9   Calculation of the Level Premium for a Whole Life Policy for a 40-Year-Old

Age	Probability of 40-Year-Old Living until Specified Age	Expected Premium Payment	Present Value of Expected Claim Costs	
39	1	$1 \times P$		P
40	0.996980	$0.996980 \times P$	$(0.996980 \times P)/1.05$ =	$0.9524P$
42	0.993700	$0.993700 \times P$	$(0.993700 \times P)/1.05^2$ =	$0.9013P$
43	0.990162	$0.990162 \times P$	$(0.990162 \times P)/1.05^3$ =	$0.8553P$
44	0.986330	$0.986330 \times P$	$(0.986330 \times P)/1.05^4$ =	$0.8115P$
.	.	.	.	.
.	.	.	.	.
.	.	.	.	.
96	0.010484	$0.010484 \times P$	$(0.010484 \times P)/1.05^{56}$ =	$0.0007P$
97	0.006452	$0.006452 \times P$	$(0.006452 \times P)/1.05^{57}$ =	$0.0004P$
98	0.003354	$0.003354 \times P$	$(0.003354 \times P)/1.05^{58}$ =	$0.0002P$
99	0.001147	$0.001147 \times P$	$(0.001147 \times P)/1.05^{59}$ =	$0.0001P$
Total				$\$16.30P$

This calculation produces a level premium for this whole life policy of $P =$ $1,372.58. Mr. Babbel could either pay $22,373 at the time the policy is initiated or pay $1,373.58 each year until he dies (again we are ignoring surrenders).

Limited Payment Whole Life Premiums.   Another premium schedule for whole life insurance is *limited payment,* whereby the policyholder pays a level premium for a fixed (limited) number of years, such as 20 years, provided that he or she is still alive. To find the 20-year level premium, we calculate the value of P such that the present value of receiving $$P$ each year for 20 years if Mr. Babbel is alive equals the present value of expected claim costs ($22,373). As before, we have to take into consideration that Mr. Babbel might die before making all of his premium payments. Following the same procedure as above, we solve the following equation for P (12.58 is the present value of paying $1 each year for 20 years or until death):

$$12.58 \times P = \$22,373$$

so that $P = \$1,778.45.$

To summarize, we analyzed three possible payment schedules for Mr. Babbel's whole life policy:

Pay $22,373 up front for a single premium whole life policy.

Pay $1,778 each year for 20 years for a 20-pay whole life policy.

Pay $1,373 each year for life for a continuous premium whole life policy.

With each payment schedule, Mr. Babbel pays more in the first years of the contract than the cost of death protection under annual term insurance. For example, not until Mr. Babbel reaches the age of 59 does the cost of $100,000 of term insurance under these assumptions exceed the level payment of $1,373. Conversely, in the later years of the contract period, Mr. Babbel pays less than what $100,000 of term insurance would cost. Thus, each of these premium schedules involves prepayment of Mr. Babbel's future expected claim costs and thus each causes the accumulation of cash values. The growth in cash values with a whole life policy depends on the premium payment pattern (e.g., single premium, continuous premium, etc.). Figure 23–5 illustrates how cash values will grow under the three options analyzed here.

23.7 Life Insurance Cost Comparisons

Background

Buying life insurance involves choosing a type of policy and an insurer. While buyers should consider insolvency risk and service when selecting an insurer, a particularly important issue for many buyers is how to compare the cost (or value) of different life insurance policies across insurers. Substantial evidence indicates significant variation in the cost of comparable policies among insurers due to dif-

FIGURE 23–5

Accumulation of cash value on a traditional whole life policy under three premium payment methods

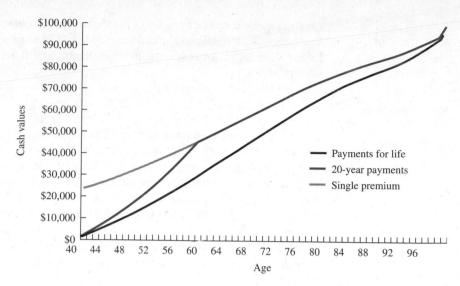

ferences in expense loadings, lapse and surrender rates, and other factors. Cost comparisons are complicated because life insurance policy cash flows occur over many years and are subject to uncertainty from various sources, such as whether the person dies, the effect of changes in interest rates on participating life policy cash values and universal life credited interest rates, and so on.

Commonly used cost comparison methods attempt to produce a single measure or index that can be used to compare policies of the same general type (e.g., two term policies offered by different insurers) with the same face amount. Given fundamental differences in contract design and risk to policyholders, these methods usually are less applicable, if at all, for comparing different types of policies (e.g., whole life to universal life or term insurance). While some cost comparison methods can provide broad guidance as to whether the buyer might prefer either cash value insurance or term insurance with noninsurance savings, it usually is preferable for a buyer to decide on a broad type of contract before conducting detailed comparisons of costs across insurers.

When making decisions about which type of coverage to buy, it is important to recognize that a given initial premium outlay will allow the purchase of a much larger face amount of term insurance than whole life or some other form of cash value insurance. As discussed earlier, although the term premium will increase over time, for many years it will remain lower than the level premium that would have to be paid if whole life were purchased. As a result, persons or families with a large need for death protection and limited funds for premiums often are advised (e.g., by consumer advisory organizations) to buy term insurance. In general, people need to consider several questions when deciding which type of policy to buy: (1) Am I able to afford to save through cash value insurance and still meet my need for death protection? (2) If so, do I want to save through cash value insurance as opposed to buying term insurance and investing elsewhere?

(3) Among the different types of cash value insurance policies, which is most attractive given my goals and attitude toward risk? Given this background, we now briefly describe major cost comparison methods for different types of life insurance products.

Term Insurance

The most common method of comparing the cost of term insurance across insurers is to use the **interest adjusted cost index.** Almost all states require insurers to disclose this index in their sales solicitations, and a number of publications contain interest adjusted costs for policies issued by many insurers. The interest adjusted cost per $1,000 of face amount commonly is calculated assuming that the policy will be held for 20 years and assuming a 5 percent interest rate. The cost index is derived in two steps. In the first step, the accumulated value or cost of scheduled premiums less any illustrated dividends for participating insurance over the 20-year period is calculated. The second step annualizes this accumulated cost.

The 20-year accumulated cost (AC_{20}) from the first step (assuming annual premiums and that all values are per $1,000 of face amount) is given by

$$AC_{20} = \sum_{t=1}^{20} P_t (1.05)^{20-t+1} - \sum_{t=1}^{20} D_t (1.05)^{20-t}$$

where P_t equals the annual premium payable at the *beginning of year t* and D_t equals the illustrated annual dividend to be paid at the *end of year t.* This amount (AC_{20}) has a simple interpretation. It represents the amount of money that the person could have accumulated at a 5 percent interest rate (after-tax) after 20 years if, instead of buying the policy, the person had invested an amount equal to the required premium less any dividend at the beginning of each year. It thus provides a simple measure of cost that considers the magnitude and timing of cash flows assuming that (1) the person survives to pay premiums and receive dividends for 20 years, and (2) dividends are paid as illustrated.

The interest adjusted cost index (IAC_{20}) is obtained in the second step as follows:

$$IAC_{20} = AC_{20} / \sum_{t=1}^{20} 1.05^t$$

The denominator is the accumulated value of $1 paid at the beginning of each year for 20 years at 5 percent interest. This value equals 34.7. The interested adjusted cost index is the level annual payment that would accumulate to AC_{20} over 20 years at 5 percent. It equals the accumulated difference between premiums and illustrated dividends divided by 34.7. While dividing the accumulated difference by 34.7 annualizes the cost measure, it does not affect the ranking of policies. That is, policies will be ranked identically using AC_{20} or IAC_{20}. In addition, the same ranking would be obtained if the policies were ranked based on the difference between the present value of future premiums and illustrated dividends.

The interest adjusted cost index does not consider the probability of surviving to pay premiums. Studies suggest, however, that incorporating this refinement produces a cost measure that is highly correlated with the interest adjusted cost index. Comparison of the interest adjusted cost index for a shorter assumed holding period, such as 10 years, can provide insight into whether cost rankings are sensitive to the assumed holding period of the policy. However, 10- and 20-year interest adjusted cost indexes generally are highly correlated across insurers.

Whole Life Insurance

The interest adjusted cost index also is commonly used to compare whole life insurance policy costs across insurers, and its disclosure by insurers to buyers again is usually required by law. For whole life insurance, one important change is made in the calculation of the index: The policy's cash value at the end of 20 years (CV_{20}) is deducted in the first step. Thus, the formula for the 20-year interest adjusted cost index becomes:

$$IAC_{20} = (AC_{20} - CV_{20})/\sum_{t=1}^{20} 1.05^t$$

The numerator of this formula again has a simple interpretation. It represents the difference between (1) the funds that would be available at 5 percent interest (after-tax) after 20 years if, instead of buying the policy, the person invested an amount equal to the required premium less the illustrated dividend at the beginning of each year (AC_{20}), and (2) the cash available from purchasing the policy and surrendering it for the cash value after 20 years (CV_{20}). (The formula ignores possible taxes that could be due upon surrender.) Comparison of interest adjusted cost indexes for a shorter horizon, such as 10 years, can give some insight into how cost rankings are affected by earlier surrender due to the impact of differences in expenses and lapse experience across insurers on premiums, dividends, and the cash value schedule.

Whole life insurance policy costs also can be compared using the estimated **implicit rate of return** on the portion of premiums that can be viewed as a contribution to a savings fund. The calculation of implicit returns is complicated, and there is no standard set of assumptions used. In addition, insurers are not required to disclose implicit rates of return.

The calculation of the implicit rate of return on a whole life policy involves dividing the whole life premium, net of any illustrated dividend, into two parts: (1) a contribution to savings, and (2) a term insurance premium to pay for death protection in a given year (defined as the policy's face amount less the value of the calculated savings accumulation to date). A computer program is then used to solve for the annual investment return needed on the savings fund to duplicate the policy's guaranteed cash value at a given point in time. This return is the estimated implicit rate of return on savings for the policy. Varying the assumed holding period produces implicit rates of return for different holding periods.

Although some insurers provide prospective buyers with an estimated implicit rate of return, the lack of standard assumptions suggests caution in using these figures. In particular, a critical input into the calculation is the assumed cost per $1,000 of death protection each year (that is, the assumed one-year term rates). A high assumed cost of term insurance reduces the assumed contribution to savings and drives up the calculated rate of return needed for the savings fund to equal the policy's cash value. The outcome is that a particular policy—or whole life insurance in general—may look artificially attractive.

Some organizations, such as Consumers Union (publisher of the magazine *Consumer Reports*), periodically calculate implicit rates of return for many policies using uniform assumptions. Assuming at least a 20-year holding period, the results generally indicate that insurers with higher return (lower cost) policies have attractive implicit rates of return compared to returns available on government and high-grade corporate bonds, especially in view of the tax deferral available with life insurance. Implicit returns generally decline substantially for holding periods of 10 years or less (and often are negative for holding periods under 5 years) due to the adverse effects of front-end expense loadings and early lapses on policy values.

Universal Life Insurance and Other Investment-Sensitive Products

Possible variation in future interest rates that will be credited to universal life insurance policy cash values considerably complicates the process of cost comparison. One approach is to calculate an interest adjusted cost index (or, less commonly, an implicit rate of return) using the cash value that would arise under an assumed premium payment pattern and the interest rate that currently is being credited by the insurer. However, in addition to uncertainty about future credited interest rates, differences in investment strategy and associated risk-related differences in credited rates reduce the comparability of policies issued by different companies. This problem is more pronounced for universal life comparisons than for participating whole life policy comparisons given the greater sensitivity of universal life policy values to short-term changes in interest rates and investment performance. A similar problem complicates cost comparisons for variable life and variable-universal life policies.

An alternative approach to comparing costs and values for these investment-sensitive products is to compare similar policy types across insurers on two dimensions: (1) the cost of expense, mortality, and surrender charges, and (2) investment strategy and credited investment rates. One method of comparing expense, mortality, and surrender charges is to assume a fixed premium schedule and then compare the cash values (after any surrender charges) that would be available for different insurers' policies (assuming comparable death benefit options) after a period such as 20 years at one or more assumed interest rates.[7] Policies with higher and/or earlier expense charges, higher mortality charges, and higher surrender charges will produce lower cash values. Thus, this method isolates differences in investment strategy and interest credits and allows policies to be ranked instead on the basis of other factors that affect cost or value. This in-

---

[7] For a given interest rate, the same ranking would be produced by calculating the present value of expense and mortality charges.

formation can then be used, along with information about the insurer's investment strategy and policy for crediting interest rates, to make an informed choice among insurers. A number of more elaborate methods also have been suggested for comparing costs for these contracts. There is no consensus, however, on which of these methods is likely to be most useful.

23.8 Summary

- There are two broad types of life insurance policies: term insurance and cash value policies. Term insurance provides pure death protection coverage. Cash value policies bundle death protection and savings accumulation. The main types of cash value policies are whole life, universal life, variable life, and variable-universal life.

- With a typical whole life insurance policy, level premiums are paid over a fixed number of years or until death. The policy provides a level death benefit and the sequence of cash values grows according to a fixed schedule over time. Most whole life policies are participating; that is, they pay annual policy dividends.

- With a typical universal life policy, the policyholder has considerable flexibility in the payment of premiums. The policy provides either a level death benefit or one that increases with the cash value of the policy. The cash value of the policy grows at an uncertain rate that depends on premium payments, expense and mortality charges, and interest rates credited over the course of the policy period.

- With a typical variable life policy, the policyholder pays premiums according to a fixed schedule. The policy provides a death benefit equal to a minimum amount plus the cash value of the policy. The cash value grows at an uncertain rate that depends on the rate of return earned on a pool of assets (mutual funds) chosen by the policyholder.

- Cash value policies provide a tax-advantaged method of saving, including income tax deferral on savings accumulations.

- Annuity contracts provide insurance coverage against living beyond a person's financial resources as well as a tax-deferred savings vehicle.

- A common method of comparing the cost of alternative life insurance policies of the same type is the interest adjusted cost method. In addition, implicit rates of return can be compared for whole life policies.

Key Terms

term insurance   593
cash value policies   593
cash value   593
surrender   595
lapses   595
cash surrender value   595
death benefit   595
face amount   595
death protection   596
guaranteed renewable   596
endowment policy   596

whole life policy   597
participating policies   599
illustrated dividends   600
paid-up insurance   601
extended term insurance   601
policy loan   601
universal life policies   602
variable life policy   606
variable-universal life   607
accumulation period   608
payout period   609

Questions and Problems

1. Jane is divorced with two small children. Her salary is $40,000 per year, and she has no group life insurance. Should Jane buy any life insurance? If so, should she buy term or whole life? Explain.

2. Suppose the following graph depicts the cash value of a universal life policy over the future years if all variables affecting the cash value take their expected value.

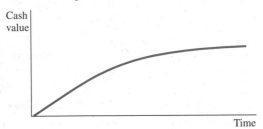

How would the cash value change if interest rates turned out to be lower than expected?

3. The following table provides information about a universal life policy. Fill in the table.

	Year 1	Year 2	Year 3
Cash value at beginning of year	$10,000		
Premium payments made at beginning of year	1,000	1,000	1,500
Mortality cost	550	600	675
Expense cost	100	50	50
Interest rate used for crediting cash value	6.0%	5.0%	5.0%
Credited interest			
Cash value at end of year			

4. Explain why death rates for life insurance buyers generally are higher than for people who buy annuities.

5. What is the sequence of net premiums for one-year term policies with face amounts equal to $1,000 for a male for the ages 50 through 52, assuming an interest rate of 6 percent?

6. What is the net single premium for a $1,000 face amount three-year term policy for a 50-year-old male, assuming an interest rate of 6 percent?

7. What is the net level premium for a $1,000 face amount three-year term policy for a 50-year-old male, assuming an interest rate of 6 percent?

8. Using Table 23–3, calculate the net level premium for a two-year endowment policy for a 50-year-old with an interest rate of 5 percent. Show that this premium is just sufficient to fund benefits over the two years at the assumed interest and mortality rates. Ignoring expenses, what would the policy's cash value equal after one year? If the policyholder surrendered the policy for this cash value after one year, would the insurer still have enough funds (given assumed interest and mortality) to pay off the other policyholders at the end of the second year?

9. Should the interest adjusted cost method be used to compare the cost of a term policy to the cost of a whole life policy? Explain.

10. Insurer testing for HIV provides a good example of how the cost of gathering information about mortality risk can sometimes cause insurers not to gather information. Insurers commonly use blood tests to identify HIV (if permitted by law).

However, since blood tests are not free, insurers only use blood tests if the expected costs of misclassification exceed the cost of the test. Suppose that the cost of the blood test is $100 and the probabilities of death for HIV-infected males is 20 times the probability listed in Table 23–3.

(*a*) What are the expected claim costs for a 30-year-old male applying for $100,000

of one-year term insurance if he is HIV negative? HIV positive?

(*b*) Suppose that 1,000 30-year-old males apply for insurance. The insurer knows that 2 percent of them are HIV positive but needs the blood test to identify those specific applicants. Should the insurer give all applicants a blood test?

References

Black, Kenneth; and Harold Skipper. *Life Insurance.* 12th ed. Englewood Cliffs, NJ: Prentice-Hall, 1994. (*Provides additional detail on the topics covered in this chapter.*)

Gustavson, Sandra; and Robert I. Mehr. *Life Insurance: Theory and Practice.* 4th ed. Plano, TX: Business Publications, 1987. (*Provides additional detail on the topics covered in this chapter.*)

Life Insurance Fact Book. Washington DC: American Council of Life Insurance. (*Provides data and other information on the life insurance industry.*)

Answers to Concept Checks

1. The death benefit would equal $100,000 and the amount of death protection would equal $80,000.

2.
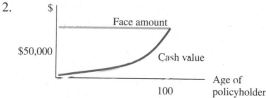

3. (*a*) The cash value would grow more slowly or decline if the policyholder reduced premium payments.

   (*b*) The cash value would grow more slowly or decline if interest rates declined.

   (*c*) The cash value would grow more rapidly if the cure for cancer caused mortality charges to decline.

4. A retiree with a fixed amount of retirement savings faces the risk that the savings will be depleted before the person dies. Annuities provide insurance against this risk; that is, annuities provide insurance coverage against the risk of outliving a person's resources.

5. With deferred annuities, a person pays an annuity premium to an insurer, who in turn invests this premium (net of expenses) until the payout period begins. The returns earned on the annuity are not taxed as they are earned. Consequently, annuities provide a tax-advantaged method of savings.

6. (*a*) Using Table 23–3, the expected claim costs = $1,000 × 0.00671 = $6.71. The present value of expected claim costs = $6.71/1.08 = $6.21.

   (*b*) The expected claim costs = $1,000 × 0.32996 = $329.96. The present value of expected claim costs = $329.96/1.08 = $305.52.

7. The probability that a 35-year-old dies when he is 55 = 9,016/949,171 = 0.00949.

8. The expected claim costs in the first year = $100,000 (0.00671) = $6.71. The expected claim costs in the second year = $100,000 (6,502/896,662) = $7.25. The present value of expected claim costs = $6.71/1.08 + $7.25/1.08^2 = $6.21 + $6.22 = $12.43.

APPENDIX 23A

RETROSPECTIVE ANALYSIS OF CASH VALUE ACCUMULATION

One of the most difficult concepts associated with cash value life insurance contracts is how the cash values accumulate over time. This appendix provides a framework for understanding the factors affecting cash value accumulation. While the actual calculations of cash values differ from the approach presented here, our objective is to provide some insight as to how cash values change over time within a framework that is capable of explaining many of the variations of cash value life insurance.[8] For simplicity, we continue to ignore nonclaim costs in this discussion.

As previously discussed, cash value life insurance involves prepayments of expected future claim costs. While neither technically nor legally accurate, a useful way of thinking about cash value life insurance is to view the insurer as placing the policyholder's prepayments into a fund. Each year, the fund grows as a result of additional premium payments made by the policyholder and interest earned on these additional premiums and the previous period's fund balance, and each year the insurer removes a portion of the fund to "pay" the policyholder's expected claim costs (and expenses). You can think of this fund as the policy's cash value. From this retrospective perspective, the policy's cash value moves over time according to the following formula:

Cash value $_t$
$$= \text{Cash value}_{t-1} + \text{Premium}_t - \text{Mortality cost}_t + \text{Interest credited to cash value}_t$$

The interest credited to the cash value over a given period can be viewed as some rate of return for the period times the amount of funds at the beginning of the period. Assuming premiums are paid at the beginning of the period and mortality costs are paid at the end of the period, the amount of funds at the beginning of the period equals the initial cash value plus any additional premium payments. Therefore, the interest credited to the cash value during the period equals

Interest credited to cash value $_t$
$$= \text{Rate of return}_t \times (\text{Cash value}_{t-1} + \text{Premium}_t)$$

Each period's mortality cost equals the expected claim cost, which equals the probability of dying times the amount of death protection for the period:

Mortality cost $_t$
$$= \text{Probability of dying}_t \times \text{Amount of death protection}_t$$

The equation for mortality cost illustrates that the mortality cost may vary over time for two reasons: (1) the probability of dying increases as a person ages, and (2) the amount of death protection may vary over time (depending on the policy). For example, with a whole life policy the death benefit equals the face amount minus the cash value. Consequently, the amount of death protection is less than the face amount of the policy; in particular,

Amount of death protection $_t$
$$= \text{Policy's face amount}_t - \text{Cash value}_t$$

The last two equations help answer a question about whole life policies that often is asked by students: How can the cash value grow over time when we know that the cost per dollar of death protection increases over time? The answer is that the increased cost per dollar of death protection as a person ages is offset in a whole life policy by a declining amount of death protection over time.

The equations above can be used to find how the cash value of a policy accumulates over time for a given set of assumptions. In particular, you would need to know (1) the expected cost per dollar of death protection from a mortality table; (2) a sequence of annual rates of return; (3) a schedule of premium payments; and (4) how the death benefit changes over time (i.e., whether it is fixed or varies directly with cash values). Given this information, you could find the sequence of cash values and the amount of death protection at each point in time by plug-

---

[8] We focus exclusively on a retrospective view of cash value accumulation as opposed to the mathematically equivalent (for given assumptions) prospective view that derives the cash value as the present value of expected future benefits minus the present value of expected future premiums. The retrospective approach to cash values is easier to follow and more useful for our purpose.

ging into the above equations.[9] Figure 23A–1 summarizes these relationships.

With whole life, the dynamics described above are hidden from the policyholder. That is, no attempt is made to explicitly partition the change in the cash value from one period to the next into premium payments, interest credits, and mortality cost components. Nevertheless, the equations are a useful way of thinking about how whole life policies work. In particular, the mortality costs, premium payments, interest credits, and death benefits are all fixed for the entire contract based on assumptions at the time the policy is issued. As a result, the schedule of cash values (and decline in death protection) over time is completely predetermined. Absent insurer insolvency and ignoring policyholder dividends, all the benefits from a whole life policy are guaranteed in advance, so that the policyholder bears no risk. In addition, because the cash value accumulates based on the same assumptions used to calculate the premiums, the cash value automatically grows to equal the face amount at age 100. The premium calculation produces a cash value, which, along with future premiums, is sufficient to fund future benefits at any point in time. Except for the ability to take out loans against cash values, whole life policyholders have limited flexibility with regard to premium payments or adjustments in death benefits.

The key point is that with a whole life policy the factors affecting cash values (the "inputs") generally are preset and equivalent to the assumptions used to calculate the premium. The modern variations of cash value life insurance, however, allow one or more of the inputs to vary over the course of the contract from the assumptions used in premium calculation. The precise variation is unknown at the time the contract is initiated. In some cases, policyholders have the flexibility to change the inputs over time; that is, policyholders can change the amount of premium paid and death benefits. In other cases, mortality costs and credited rates of return are varied in view of current experience or market conditions. Consequently, more of the risk of unexpected changes in mortality costs or rates of return is placed on the policyholder.

Specifically, with a universal life insurance policy, the mortality costs and credited rates of return can vary from year to year, depending on the insurer's experience and competitive pressure. The main risk borne by policyholders with universal life policies is that the credited return can vary over time depending on interest rates. Flexibility with respect to premium payments implies that cash values can grow or decline over time depending upon the amount of premiums paid. Universal life policies also provide the flexibility to increase death benefits as cash values grow. In contrast, premium payments on a variable life policy are fixed in advanced like a whole life policy. The credited return on savings, however, varies directly with the return earned on a portfolio of stocks and bonds chosen by the policyholder, and the amount of death protection varies with cash values.

FIGURE 23A–1

Summary of variables affecting cash values

Inputs	Outputs
Expected cost per dollar of death protection	
Rates of return each period	Amount of death protection each period
Premium payment each period	Cash value each period
Is death benefit level or does it vary with cash value?	

---

[9] You may notice that the amount of death protection at time t depends on the cash value at time t and vice versa. Therefore, the sequence of cash values must be solved simultaneously with the sequence of insurance coverage.

PART VII

Government Regulation of Insurance Markets

CHAPTER 24

Insurance Regulation

Chapter Objectives

- Briefly describe state insurance regulation and summarize major activities that are regulated.
- Explain the historical evolution of state regulation and arguments for and against state regulation compared with federal regulation.
- Discuss the normative view that regulation should serve the public interest by mitigating market imperfections and illustrate the application of this view to the problem of costly and imperfect information concerning the quality of insurance coverage.
- Discuss how political pressure may cause the practice of regulation to deviate from the public interest view.

24.1 Scope and Operation of State Insurance Regulation

The insurance business is heavily regulated in the United States and most other developed countries. We begin this chapter with a broad summary of the major activities that are regulated by the states to supplement our discussion in earlier chapters of solvency regulation, price regulation, residual markets, compulsory insurance requirements, and several other major types of government regulation affecting the purchase and sale of insurance.

Each state has a **state insurance department** (or commission) which implements state legislation governing the purchase and sale of insurance that is set forth in the state's *state insurance code*. In addition to mandates specified in the state insurance code, the insurance department has the authority to establish rules and procedures in order to implement legislative directives. The head of the state insurance department usually is called the **state insurance commissioner.** The state governor appoints the insurance commissioner in a significant majority of states.

Regulated Activities

When viewed broadly, insurance regulation includes the state insurance code, its implementation by the state insurance department, and other legislation related to insurance (such as compulsory insurance requirements) governing the purchase, sale, or enforcement of insurance contracts. In addition to regulation, the courts have a significant effect on contractual relations between insurers and policyholders through the interpretation and enforcement of contract provisions. The major activities that are regulated are discussed briefly below and summarized in Table 24–1. This table also shows the chapter of this text, if any, in which additional discussion is provided for a particular form of regulation.

• Licensing of insurers and agents/brokers: State insurance departments grant and renew licenses to conduct business in the state to insurers, agents, and brokers, and they have the power to revoke licenses. Regulation also stipulates conditions under which unlicensed insurers may conduct business through the nonadmitted market.

• Solvency: State solvency regulation includes solvency monitoring by state insurance departments, risk-based capital requirements, financial reporting requirements, direct controls on behavior (e.g., investment regulations), and the establishment of guaranty funds to pay claims against insolvent insurers.

• Rates: Many states require insurers to obtain prior regulatory approval of rate changes and rate differentials for different consumers from the state insurance department for certain types of voluntary market coverage. Rate regulation is most prevalent for workers' compensation insurance, automobile insurance, homeowners insurance, and individual health insurance.

• Residual markets: State law requires insurers to supply certain types of coverage through a residual market mechanism, such as an assigned risk plan, at a regulated rate to applicants who have difficulty obtaining coverage voluntarily. Residual markets are most prevalent for workers' compensation insurance, automobile insurance, urban and coastal property insurance, and individual health insurance.

• Content of policy forms: All state insurance departments regulate most contract language by requiring certain contract provisions and prohibiting other provisions, including regulation of insurance policy language that restricts the ability of insurers to cancel policies within the coverage period or to deny renewal at the end of a coverage period. Prior regulatory approval of policy forms usually is required except for customized policies sold to large businesses.

• Contract interpretation and enforcement: State insurance departments enforce legislation dealing with market conduct and unfair trade practices, such as provisions related to unfair claim settlement practices. Insurance contract provisions also are interpreted and enforced by the courts through resolution of litigation between insurers and customers.

TABLE 24-1 Overview of Regulated Activities

Activity	Description	Principal Types of Coverage and Prevalence across States
Licensing of insurers and agents/brokers	Granting, renewal, and revocation of license to conduct business by state insurance departments (see Chapter 10)	All types of coverage and states
Insurer solvency	Solvency monitoring by state insurance departments, capital and financial reporting requirements, investment regulations, and guaranty funds (see Chapters 4 and 5)	All types of coverage and states
Rates	Prior approval of rate changes and regulation of rate differentials across consumers by state insurance departments for the voluntary market (see Chapters 6, 16, and 21)	• Workers' compensation rates in about 80 percent of the states • Personal auto, homeowners, and other business property-liability insurance rates in about half of the states • Individual health insurance in some states • Credit life and health insurance in some states
Residual markets	Industry must supply coverage through residual market at a regulated rate to applicants who have difficulty obtaining it voluntarily, such as through an assigned risk plan or joint underwriting association (see Chapters 6, 16, 21, and 22)	• Personal automobile in all states • Workers' compensation in all states • Urban and coastal property insurance in some states • Individual health insurance in some states
Content of policy forms	Regulation of contract language (including provisions governing cancellation and nonrenewal, see Chapter 21) and approval of forms by state insurance departments	Most types of coverage in all states
Contract interpretation and enforcement	State insurance department enforcement of legislation dealing with market conduct and unfair trade practices (see Chapter 8)	Most types of coverage in all states
Insurer sales practices and information disclosure	Regulation of sales practices through state insurance department enforcement of market conduct/unfair trade practices legislation; required disclosure of price information; production and dissemination of information about prices and quality by regulators	Mainly for personal insurance in most states
Compulsory purchase of coverage	Compulsory insurance laws and their enforcement by the states (see Chapters 16 and 21)	• Personal auto liability in almost all states • Automobile personal injury protection coverage in most no-fault states • Workers' compensation insurance • Some types of professional liability insurance (e.g., medical malpractice insurance) and environmental liability insurance in most states

• Insurer sales practices and information disclosure: State insurance departments regulate potentially deceptive sales practices by insurers and agents through enforcement of market conduct and unfair trade practices legislation. Allegations of deceptive or misleading sales practices also are subject to litigation and resolution by the courts. Most states require the disclosure of specified price information in the sale of life insurance. Some states produce summary information on personal insurance rates charged by different insurers and/or the frequency of consumer complaints against different insurers. This information usually is provided to consumers on request.

• Compulsory purchase of coverage: State law generally mandates the purchase of certain types of coverage (e.g., auto liability and workers' compensation insurance). A variety of methods and state agencies are used to enforce these laws.

National Association of Insurance Commissioners

Insurance regulation is complex because of the scope of activities that are regulated and differences in regulation across states. However, a number of major activities are regulated in most or all states using the same broad type of regulation, such as solvency regulation and regulation of policy forms. These similarities are not surprising given that the problems that give rise to these regulations (see below) exist in all states.

Additional uniformity, cooperation, and coordination of state insurance regulation are achieved by the activities of the **National Association of Insurance Commissioners (NAIC).** The NAIC is a voluntary organization of all state insurance commissioners that holds regular meetings to discuss insurance regulatory issues and develop **model laws.** These model laws, or laws that are very similar to the model, often are adopted by many states. In addition to state insurance commissioners and insurance department staff, NAIC meetings are widely attended by representatives of the insurance industry and consumer groups. Industry and consumer group representatives also serve on the NAIC committees that develop model laws.[1]

An important example of efforts to coordinate state regulation exists in the area of solvency regulation (see Chapter 5). Some coordination of state solvency regulation has been achieved by having the state insurance department in which the insurer is domiciled (chartered) play a leading role in certain aspects of solvency oversight, such as conducting and preparing reports based on on-site financial examinations. The NAIC plays a major role in promoting uniform financial reporting and risk-based capital requirements across states. In addition, the NAIC oversees the coordination of financial examinations of insurance companies by state regulators.

Changes in solvency regulation in the early 1990s in response to earlier increases in the frequency and severity of insurance company insolvencies provide

---

[1] The NAIC has a central office in Kansas City, Missouri.

an important illustration of the coordination and cooperation of state regulators through the NAIC. Risk-based capital requirements (see Chapter 5), for example, were developed by the NAIC. In addition, the NAIC established a solvency regulation accreditation program in 1991 that specifies minimum standards for state solvency regulation. States that adopt specified model laws related to solvency regulation and meet minimum standards for solvency monitoring are accredited by the NAIC. States that are not accredited face some risk of increased monitoring or regulation of their home (i.e., domestic) insurers by other states' insurance departments and of being known for weak regulation. A significant majority of states were accredited by 1997; many of these states adopted or amended their laws and procedures to qualify for accreditation.

24.2 History and Efficacy of State Regulation

This section deals with two related issues: (1) how state regulation came about, and (2) the pros and cons of state regulation versus federal regulation. The description of how state regulation came about provides additional insight into rate regulation, the activities of insurance advisory organizations, and the insurance industry's limited exemption from federal antitrust law.[2] While we have our own opinions, we make no attempt to resolve the debate about state versus federal regulation. Instead, we have the more modest objective of summarizing the main arguments that favor state regulation and those that favor the replacement of much or even most state regulation with federal regulation.

History of State Regulation

State regulation of insurance companies and agents began to develop in the early part of the nineteenth century. The primary sources of regulation were restrictions and limitations concerning insurer operations contained in state charters issued to insurers and allowing them to conduct business. Domestic insurers were required to file annual reports as early as 1818, beginning in Massachusetts. The first state insurance department (commission) was established in New Hampshire in 1851, and other states soon followed.

Bills that would have created a federal agency to regulate insurance were introduced in the US Congress in 1866 and 1868, but they were not enacted. The Commerce Clause of the United States Constitution gives the federal government explicit authority to regulate *interstate commerce*. In addition, Article 10 of the Constitution states that powers that are not expressly given to the federal government are reserved for the states. In the twentieth century the US Supreme Court has interpreted Article 10 and other provisions to allow federal legislation and

---

[2] Much of our discussion of state regulation's history is based on Robert I. Mehr and Emerson Cammack, *Principles of Insurance,* 6th ed. (Homewood, IL: Richard D. Irwin, 1976), chapter 28, "Regulation of the Insurance Business: Objectives, Methods, and History."

regulation to go beyond specific powers stated in the Constitution. However, this broad interpretation of federal powers was not the case during the formative years of insurance regulation. Thus, to the extent that the insurance business was considered to be "local" in nature (i.e., conducted within a state) rather than interstate commerce, it could be argued that the Constitution permitted state regulation and prohibited federal regulation.

Paul v. Virginia.   The question of whether states had the power to regulate insurance was addressed in 1868 by the United States Supreme Court in the celebrated case of **Paul v. Virginia.** Mr. Paul was an agent for a group of New York fire insurers. Virginia law required out-of-state insurers and their agents to be licensed by the state. Mr. Paul refused to pay the security deposit that was required to obtain a license, kept selling policies, and subsequently was arrested, fined, and hanged. Actually, he was fined $50, which was a lot of money back then. Mr. Paul and the New York insurers challenged the conviction, arguing in part that the sale of insurance across borders was interstate commerce and thus that the Virginia law was unconstitutional because it interfered with interstate commerce. The US Supreme Court reached an interesting conclusion concerning this issue. It held that insurance was not commerce and therefore was not subject to laws affecting interstate commerce. Since insurance was not commerce, Virginia's law was not unconstitutional (see Box 24–1). Thus, Paul v. Virginia implied that states had the power to regulate insurance and that the federal government did not. This decision was upheld for approximately 75 years in many other cases that argued that insurance constituted interstate commerce.

Southeastern Underwriters Association Case.   During the 1870s, numerous insurance companies became insolvent as a result of major fires in Boston and Chicago. These events helped spur the development of *insurance rating bureaus,* precursor organizations to modern insurance *advisory organizations* (such as the Insurance Services Office). The rating bureaus set property insurance rates that would be charged by most companies, in principle to ensure adequate prices and therefore reduce insolvency risk. Many states either permitted or encouraged the development of rating bureaus, and some states began to regulate their activities. Regulators in a few states determined the rates that had to be charged by all insurance companies.

In response to a request from the Missouri attorney general in 1942, the antitrust division of the US Department of Justice began an investigation into the activities of a large rating bureau known as the Southeastern Underwriters Association. This association was subsequently indicted by the US attorney general for alleged violations of the federal Sherman Antitrust Act (which prohibits price fixing and related noncompetitive activities). The charges included restraining and monopolizing commerce, fixing prices and agents' commissions, attempting to force buyers to buy from member insurers, denying nonmember insurers access to reinsurance from member insurers, and refusing to do business with agents who represented nonmember insurers.

Box 24–1

Is Insurance Commerce? The Supreme Court Opines

In Paul v. Virginia, 75 US 168 (1868), the United States Supreme Court concluded that insurance was not commerce in the sense used by the constitution and thus that the interstate commerce clause could not be used to prohibit state laws regulating insurance. The Court's reasoning is reproduced in part below:

> Issuing a policy of insurance is not a transaction of commerce. The contracts are simple contracts of indemnity against loss by fire, entered into between the corporations and the insured, for a consideration paid by the latter. These contracts are not articles of commerce in any proper meaning of the word. They are not subjects of trade or barter offered in the market as something having an existence and value independent of the parties to them. They are not commodities to be shipped or forwarded from one state to another and then put up for sale. They are like other personal contracts between parties, which are completed by their signature and the transfer of consideration. Such transactions are not interstate transactions, though the parties may be domiciled in different states. The policies do not take effect—are not executed contracts—until delivered by the agent

in Virginia. They are, then, local transactions, and are governed by local law. They do not constitute a part of the commerce between States any more than a contract for the purchase and sale of goods in Virginia by a citizen of New York whilst in Virginia would constitute a portion of such commerce.

This ruling was overturned in United States v. Southeastern Underwriters Association et al., 51 F. Supp. 712 (1943). The majority opinion stated:

> Our basic responsibility in interpreting the Commerce Clause is to make certain that the power to govern intercourse among the states remains where the Constitution placed it . . . No commercial enterprise of any kind which conducts its activities across state lines has been held to be wholly beyond the regulatory power of the Congress under the Commerce Clause. We cannot make an exception for the business of insurance.

The court went on to say, however, that the opinion only affected state regulation that was inconsistent with federal law. The power of the states to regulate insurance was not overturned by this decision.

The Southeastern Underwriters Association suggested that many of these practices were beneficial given the nature of insurance. But its defense against this legal action was that the Sherman Antitrust Act did not apply to insurance because insurance was not commerce according to Paul v. Virginia. A federal district court upheld this view and dismissed the case. The US attorney general appealed to the Supreme Court.

The Supreme Court did not decide on the merit of the charges, but in the **Southeastern Underwriters Association decision** in 1943 it overturned Paul v. Virginia (by a four to three vote with two justices not voting). The court basically ruled that insurance is commerce, that it is interstate commerce when it takes place across state lines, that Congress therefore could regulate insurance, and that the Sherman Antitrust Act applied to insurance (see Box 24–1). The decision did not prohibit state regulation, but it held that state laws that were contrary to federal law were invalid. Nonetheless, the decision led to considerable uncertainty about the allowable scope of state regulation and the taxation of insurers. It also created considerable uncertainty about the legality of industry operating procedures, especially the use of rating bureaus.

The McCarran-Ferguson Act.   Given the uncertainty created by the Southeastern Underwriters Association decision, representatives of both the insurance industry and state insurance regulation sought legislation to clarify regulatory and taxation issues related to insurance. In response, the Congress enacted the **McCarran-Ferguson Act** in 1945.[3] This law states (1) that the continued regulation and taxation of insurance by the states is in the public interest, and (2) that the insurance business is exempt from federal antitrust law, provided that the relevant activities are subject to state regulation and do not involve "any agreement to boycott, coerce, or intimidate, or act of boycott, coercion, or intimidation." The implications of this legislation were clear. First, states would continue to have primary authority for insurance regulation, although the federal government could enact legislation regulating insurance if state regulation were found to be deficient. Second, many of the activities of rating bureaus would not be subject to federal antitrust law provided that they were regulated by the states and did not involve boycott, coercion, or intimidation.

Following the enactment of the McCarran-Ferguson Act, many states revised their regulatory systems to provide greater oversight of rating bureau activities. The most common approach was to make property-liability insurance rates developed by rating bureaus subject to regulatory prior approval. The laws generally either required or strongly encouraged all insurers to use bureau rates. Beginning in the late 1950s, most states began to permit or make it easier for insurers to charge rates that differed from bureau rates, and the large direct writers generally obtained approval to charge lower rates. Beginning in the mid-1960s, a significant number of states ultimately eliminated prior approval regulation, replacing their prior approval laws with competitive rating laws. As mentioned in earlier chapters, insurance advisory organizations now commonly file prospective loss costs with state regulators (as opposed to final rates) that can be used by insurers in their own rate filings. State oversight of these activities has been sufficient to keep them from being subject to federal antitrust law.

Challenges to McCarran-Ferguson.   During the mid-1980s and early 1990s, significant support for modifying or eliminating the McCarran-Ferguson Act arose in conjunction with rapid increases in property-liability insurance rates. While pressure for significant change in the act has since waned, some observers argue that the insurance industry's limited exemption from antitrust law facilitates collusion among insurers to increase prices. There are two main counterargu-

---

[3] This act is named after the two principal senators who sponsored the legislation. After attending a number of staff and insurance industry meetings where the McCarran-Ferguson Act was mentioned, a newly appointed insurance commissioner (in a state that will remain anonymous) is reported to have asked one of his staff, "Who is this Karen Ferguson, anyway?"

ments. First, unless prevented by price regulation, property-liability insurance markets are characterized by substantial heterogeneity in prices and underwriting standards. This heterogeneity is inconsistent with price fixing. Second, advisory organizations in principle can help promote healthy competition and thereby benefit consumers by providing insurers with valuable, low-cost information concerning projected loss costs. Specifically, the availability of loss forecasts based on aggregate industry data at low cost, when combined with an insurer's own data analysis, helps insurers obtain more accurate forecasts, thus reducing insurer risk and the need for capital. It also reduces the cost of rate-making and entry into a particular market or line of business.

A second challenge to state regulation and to the endorsement of state regulation contained in the McCarran-Ferguson Act occurred in the early 1990s in response to increases in the frequency and severity of insurance company insolvencies. Legislation was introduced in the Congress that would have allowed insurers to choose federal solvency regulation instead of state solvency regulation. This bill would have created a new federal agency with broad powers to regulate insurer activities that could affect solvency. Support for this proposal declined in conjunction with improved insolvency experience and changes in state solvency regulation following the early 1990s, such as the development of risk-based capital requirements and the NAIC's solvency regulation accreditation program.

As a practical matter, the US Congress can put substantial pressure on state regulators to change regulatory practices by threatening to adopt some form of federal regulation. While it is sometimes difficult to determine the extent to which changes in state regulation are undertaken to deter federal regulation, many observers believe that state regulators are influenced materially by the threat of federal intervention.

Concept Check

1. What is the economic rationale for allowing the activities of rating bureaus (advisory organizations) to have a limited exemption from federal antitrust law? In what ways is the exemption limited?

State versus Federal Regulation

The preceding discussion illustrates the long debate over whether the primary responsibility for insurance regulation should lie with the states or the federal government. This debate is one example of the general debate in political philosophy and economics over the advantages and disadvantages of centralization of government power versus decentralization. As a result, people that favor decentralization of power tend to view state regulation more kindly than do those who favor greater centralization of power in Washington.

Economists generally focus on the comparative efficiency of state versus federal regulation, but uncertainty about the magnitude of the costs and benefits associated with each system leads to diversity of opinion. The subject can become quite complicated given that the arguments for and against either type of regulation can vary across specific types of regulation (e.g., solvency regulation versus price regulation). The optimal system of regulation in theory also might involve some combination of state and federal regulation. As a practical matter, the enactment of any significant form of federal insurance regulation probably would leave some material role for state regulation. Thus, some form of *dual regulation* would be likely as opposed to the complete replacement of state regulation by federal regulation. We do not attempt to resolve the debate concerning state versus federal regulation. Instead, we simply summarize the most common arguments.

Arguments in favor of replacing a large part of or most state regulation with federal regulation can be summarized as follows:

• The lack of uniformity in state regulation across states increases costs to insurers (and therefore to consumers) of complying with regulation, and it is confusing and undesirable to consumers in view of the large mobility of the population.

• Federal regulation could achieve possible economies of scale and avoid costly duplication of regulatory activities.

• Cost savings from efficiencies in federal regulation would free up funds to improve regulation, for example, for attracting a greater number of talented people (or people with greater talent) to careers in insurance regulation.

• The quality of state regulation varies significantly across states and is inadequate in some states.

• Weak regulation in a given state can adversely affect people and insurers in other states. For example, inadequate solvency monitoring by regulators in an insurer's state of domicile might harm the insurer's policyholders in other states.

• State regulators may have an incentive to "free-ride" on the regulatory efforts of other states, which might reduce the average quality of regulation.

Arguments in favor of state regulation include:

• State regulation is tailored to reflect local needs, which vary across states in relation to the average income and other characteristics of a state's population.

• State regulation facilitates regional experimentation to determine what works and what fails, and the consequences of regulatory mistakes are localized.

• The NAIC reduces costly duplication, encourages desirable uniformity, and reduces free-rider problems.

• Significant federal regulation probably will duplicate some state regulation.

• The state system is known, whereas federal regulation would involve substantial start-up costs and uncertainty. ("The devil you know is better than the one that you don't know.")

• The track record of federal regulation of depository institutions does not inspire confidence. Federal regulation did not prevent and probably aggravated massive insolvency problems in the savings and loan industry due to congressional pressure for regulatory forbearance (i.e., for allowing weak or insolvent institutions to continue operating).

On average, the insurance industry traditionally has favored state regulation. Smaller insurers have been especially supportive, perhaps because they often have to deal with fewer state insurance departments. They also might fear that federal regulation would be accompanied by repeal of the industry's limited antitrust exemption, which in turn might have a greater adverse effect on small insurers if the activities of rating bureaus are curtailed. However, state rate regulation, which has constrained rate increases in the presence of rising claim costs and produced large residual markets in some states in recent years, has reduced insurer support for state regulation. In particular, it has caused some insurers to explore whether some form of federal regulation might allow them a partial or complete exemption from price regulation.

24.3 Objectives of Regulation: The Public Interest View

Serving the Public Interest by Mitigating Market Imperfections

The classical, normative view of economic regulation is that its objective should be to mitigate the impact of significant market imperfections (or market "failures") compared to the ideal of a perfectly competitive market. According to this view, which is commonly known as the **public interest view of regulation,** the decision to regulate is based on whether characteristics of the market differ significantly from those of a competitive market characterized by: (1) large numbers of sellers with relatively low market shares and low cost entry by new firms; (2) low cost information to firms concerning the cost of production and to consumers concerning prices and quality; and (3) an absence of spillovers (i.e., all costs are internalized to sellers or buyers).[4]

Desirable conduct and performance will characterize markets with these structural characteristics. Markets that significantly deviate from these characteristics and also exhibit conduct and performance that differ significantly from a competitive market are candidates for regulation to mitigate these imperfections and move the market's structure, conduct, and performance toward the competitive ideal. A well-known example, which most business students learn about at some point in their studies, is that firms may be able to exercise market power and raise prices above marginal costs if the market has only a few large firms and large entry barriers. If so, the consequences include reduced output, excess profits, and an overall reduction in welfare. As a result, markets with these characteristics may be candidates for antitrust enforcement, to increase the number and

---

[4] The public interest view of regulation also is sometimes called the *consumer protection view.* We don't like this description because it is potentially misleading. Some "consumer protection" groups argue for regulation that goes well beyond mitigation of market failure.

limit the size of firms, or for rate of return regulation (e.g., in the case of a so-called natural monopoly).[5]

According to the public interest view, the costs and limitations of regulation should be considered when deciding when and how to regulate. Regulatory tools are necessarily imperfect. Regulation always involves costs, and it entails the risk of unintended consequences. These problems suggest a two-pronged test before regulating a given market. First, there should be demonstrable market imperfections that lead to a significant deviation between market performance and the competitive market ideal. Second, there should be substantial evidence that the benefits from using the regulatory tool being contemplated will exceed the costs of regulation. Otherwise, regulation that is intended to mitigate market failure will make matters worse rather than better (i.e., the cure will be worse than the disease).[6]

The view that regulation should be used cautiously, while perhaps the most widely held view among informed, objective, and dispassionate observers (like us), is not held by everyone. Opinions vary substantially concerning how well particular markets perform and whether regulation is likely to be effective in any given case. At one extreme (even ignoring socialists), some people believe that very few markets work well without regulation, and they are confident in the ability of government experts to improve on market outcomes. At the other extreme, some people think that almost all markets work reasonably well in conjunction with contract enforcement by the courts, and they doubt that regulation will be effective for markets that do not.

An Example of the Public Interest View: Dealing with Costly and Imperfect Information

Although it does not imply that insurance regulation by and large minimizes the cost of risk in practice (see below), many of the regulatory tools summarized in Table 24–1 are related to imperfections in insurance markets. In particular, insurance markets often are characterized by imperfect and costly information. Con-

---

[5] As one example of using antitrust policy, the two largest vendors of office supplies in 1997 (Office Max and Office Depot) dropped their plans for merger after the antitrust division of the US Department of Justice announced that it would seek to block the merger. Critics of antitrust enforcement often argue that it sometimes prevents economically efficient mergers that would benefit both producers and consumers. Electric utilities have traditionally been subject to rate regulation that is designed to limit their rates of return to fair levels. In recent years there have been a number of attempts to create competition in the provision of electricity, which could reduce the prevalence of rate of return regulation.

[6] Recall from earlier chapters that from a normative perspective the appropriate societal goal for risk management and legal rules that affect the cost of risk is to attempt to minimize the total cost of risk in society and thereby maximize the value of societal resources and activities. In general, insurance regulation that focuses on cost-effective mitigation of insurance market imperfections can help reduce the cost of risk. Thus, the public interest view of insurance regulation might be restated as: *Regulation should be designed and implemented to minimize the total cost of risk.* At an abstract level, achieving this goal requires that the benefits from regulation (moving market conduct/performance closer to the competitive ideal) be weighed against the costs of regulation.

sumers are not fully informed about product quality and becoming better informed is costly. Much insurance regulation is related to these information problems, including, for example, licensing of insurers and agents, solvency regulation, regulation of contract language, regulation of deceptive sales and unfair claims practices, and information disclosure rules.[7]

The court system can address some problems related to imperfect information, such as litigation that alleges misrepresentation by an insurer in its sales practices or improper refusals to settle claims. However, reliance on the courts to settle disputes ex post often will not be an effective or efficient means of mitigating information-based problems, so that regulation may be desirable. If, for example, costly and imperfect information causes people to inadvertently buy coverage from a financially weak insurer that later fails, litigation following insolvency will be unable to compensate policyholders for their losses because the defendant will be insolvent. Moreover, the threat of such litigation obviously will not deter excessively risky behavior by insurers prior to failure. Costly and imperfect information also may lead to comparatively small harms to many people that might be more efficiently addressed by regulation than litigation.

Why Some Unregulated Markets May Not Provide Adequate Information.
Obtaining information about the quality of insurance is costly to consumers (it requires time and effort). Information that is available to consumers usually will be imperfect, which increases the risk that some consumers will inadvertently buy coverage from a company with lower quality than the consumer is willing to pay for. Incentives for insurers or other parties to provide useful information are reduced by the cost of producing the information and several additional factors, including:

• In an unregulated environment with imperfect information, it may be difficult or impossible for high quality insurers to develop accurate measures to demonstrate their quality that can be readily understood by most consumers.

• If high quality insurers advertise their quality, in some cases it might reduce overall consumer confidence in the industry by highlighting that quality might be low for other companies.

• Lower quality insurers might be able to provide false or misleading information and thus fool some unsophisticated consumers and perhaps some sophisticated consumers, at least for a time.

• Incentives for outside parties, such as the A. M. Best Company (see Chapter 5), to invest in the development and marketing of information about insurer quality are reduced (1) by the cost and difficulty of obtaining useful and accurate measures of quality, and (2) because the information produced might be obtained by many buyers without their paying for it.

---

[7] Residual market mechanisms might be justified based on the rationale that adverse selection might prevent viable markets for some customers. As we discussed in Chapter 21, compulsory insurance laws may reduce spillovers that arise when persons with few assets at risk drive without insurance.

Insurers might be able to cooperate to provide information about quality. For example, insurers with prompt and fair claim settlement, or with very low insolvency risk, might form an association that establishes minimum standards for membership and then advertises membership to the public. One limitation of this approach, in addition to the direct costs of forming the association and monitoring compliance, is that an insurer's proprietary information might have to be revealed to competitors. In addition, insurers who are denied membership might argue that the standards are too high and that the organization represents a noncompetitive restraint of trade that might involve "boycott, threat, or intimidation" and thus not be exempt from antitrust law.

The Potential Role for Regulation.   As a result of the limitations of private actions to reduce information problems, some degree of regulation to mitigate information problems may improve market performance and reduce the cost of risk. Moreover, most insurers will likely support some degree of regulation to prevent harm to the reputation of the entire industry. For example, many if not most insurers have an incentive to support solvency regulation and regulatory monitoring and oversight of unfair trade practices. Most insurers also have an incentive to support regulation of contract language to prevent industrywide reputation damage that would be likely if some insurers sold excessively restrictive coverage to unwitting consumers. While some standardization of contract language can be achieved from voluntary arrangements among insurers, regulation can facilitate this process by making it more costly or illegal for insurers to deviate from suitable contract terms. As suggested above, voluntary arrangements also might be challenged as noncompetitive agreements that harm firms that do not comply.

This discussion also suggests, however, that regulation can create a type of moral hazard problem. If people are protected by regulation, they may expend less effort in locating a high-quality insurer (e.g., guaranty funds reduce the incentive to purchase coverage from a financially strong insurer; see Chapter 5). In addition, insurers, agents, and other parties have less incentive to provide consumers with information about quality. If regulation does not effectively replace or substitute for these reduced incentives, it might increase the number of people that buy products from insurers that they would have avoided with less regulation, thus reducing the advantages (increasing the costs) of regulation.

Information Disclosure and Minimum Standards.   Assuming that information problems are severe enough to justify government action, there are two broad approaches to regulation: (1) information disclosure, and (2) establishing minimum standards and monitoring compliance with these standards. These approaches are not mutually exclusive.

Information disclosure, either in the form of mandatory disclosure of information by insurers or regulatory dissemination of information, has the appeal of going to the heart of the problem. The idea is this: If imperfect and costly information creates significant problems, then let's provide consumers with better information and let the market work! Unfortunately, as we suggested above, it is often difficult or impossible to develop accurate and easily understood measures of quality that will not be misleading or subject to misuse by many consumers (or insurers). If regulators disseminate insolvency risk ratings, for example, two types of mistakes will be common. Some insurers will be rated too high compared to the true but unobservable risk; others will be rated too low. The over-rated companies will tend to be rewarded by increased sales and profits; the under-rated companies will be punished and perhaps pushed toward insolvency. If regulators instead disseminate complex but more accurate information, the information will be unintelligible to many consumers, especially those who might need the most help.

As another illustration of practical problems that arise with disclosure, consider the case of regulators making available information about complaints against insurers. A few states publish complaint ratios, that is, the number of consumer complaints against an insurer divided by its premium volume or number of customers. For a given level of quality, such as promptness and fairness of claims settlement, complaint ratios will tend to be higher for companies with higher risk policyholders. The reason is that high-risk insureds generate more claims. Holding average quality per claim constant, a greater number of claims will tend to produce more complaints.[8] In addition, complaint ratios could vary substantially across smaller companies and over time due to random variation in claim frequency, thus reducing the information's accuracy with potentially undesirable distortions in consumer decisions.

Problems with the disclosure approach to dealing with costly and imperfect information encourage greater use of minimum quality standards, whether through formal rules or informal benchmarks, and monitoring of compliance with standards by regulatory experts. This approach is used in solvency regulation and in regulation of unfair claims practices and deceptive sales practices. As suggested above, a limitation of minimum standards is that those standards might not be accurate. They might misclassify and unfairly penalize and/or increase costs for some high-quality firms and fail to catch low-quality firms. These limitations bring us back to an earlier point: Because regulation will be costly and imperfect, it probably should be used only when people are fairly confident that the benefits will exceed the costs.

24.4 Regulation and Political Pressure

Regulators as Agents of the Public

You may be convinced that regulation *should* serve the public interest by attempting to minimize the cost of risk through the cost-effective mitigation of significant market imperfections. Then the question arises: Will regulation generally attempt to achieve this goal?

---

[8] To illustrate, if two auto insurers both have a 0.01 probability that a claim will result in a complaint, an auto insurer with policyholders with an average accident rate of 0.06 per year will on average have a 50 percent larger ratio of complaints to policyholders than an auto insurer for which the average accident rate is 0.04 per year.

While many of the types of regulation summarized in Table 24–1 are plausibly related to material imperfections in insurance markets, some regulations are more difficult to reconcile with the classical goal of mitigating market imperfections. As our discussion in several earlier chapters implied, for example, regulation of voluntary market rates, restrictions on rate classification, and residual market rate regulation have produced large residual markets and cross-subsidies for some types of business in some states. These policies arguably create distortions beyond any that previously existed. Given that many sellers with comparatively small market shares and low entry barriers generally characterize insurance markets, competition can be expected to prevent excessive prices and profits. Until the 1960s, some observers argued that rate regulation was needed to prevent inadequate prices and too many insolvencies. Even if this argument had merit at the time, it cannot explain the focus of modern price regulation on restraining rates.[9]

Instead of asking how regulation *should* be designed and implemented to achieve some normative goal, such as the mitigation of market failure, much economic analysis of regulation instead focuses on how regulation *will* be designed and implemented if legislators and regulators seek their own interest. Analogous to our discussion in Chapter 2 of whether managers seek to maximize firm value, regulators (and legislators) can be viewed as agents of the "public." As with all principal-agent relations, agents may seek their own interests to the detriment of the principal. Thus, regulators might attempt to minimize conflict, ensure generous campaign contributions to the governor (or, if elected, to their own campaigns), and/or obtain high-paying positions in the regulated industry after they leave office (see Box 24–2).

As a result, regulation generally involves agency costs: Regulators need to be monitored, and they sometimes deviate from seeking the public interest. Also, the agency problem that arises with regulation may be especially severe because the principal (the public) consists of a large number of people with heterogeneous objectives and goals. In contrast, stockholders usually share the objective of wanting the stock price to be as high as possible.

The Economic Theory of Regulation

A major alternative to the public interest view posits that regulators seek their own interest by maximizing political support (or, equivalently, minimizing opposition).[10] Known as the **theory of economic regulation,** this analysis predicts that

---

[9] It might be argued that some forms of price regulation (e.g., restrictions on rate classification) increase fairness, as opposed to being a rational response to some form of traditional market failure. In principle, the traditional view could be expanded to include fairness; then, benefits of possible increased fairness from regulatory policies designed to deviate from the results that would arise with competition could be weighed against the costs.

[10] Political support is broadly defined to include contributions of time and money, intensity of support, and the like. Several University of Chicago economists have played leading roles in the development of this theory, including George Stigler, Gary Becker, and Sam Peltzman. Stigler and Becker are both recipients of the Nobel Prize in economics. Stigler's prize was based in part on his work on the theory of economic regulation.

Box 24–2

Appointed versus Elected Commissioners and the Revolving Door

The governor appoints the insurance commissioner in a majority of states. The commissioner is elected in most other states. Whether one approach is more efficient than the other is uncertain in theory and practice.

An argument for having the governor appoint the insurance commissioner is that it helps insulate the commissioner from political pressure in support of inefficient market intervention (such as price controls). Short-sighted and uninformed consumers might press for lower rates even if rate reductions will produce an inefficient reduction in the supply and quality of coverage. Self-interested groups of consumers might press for lower rates even if other consumers have to pay more in order to finance the subsidy. Many of these people, however, will not be exclusively influenced by insurance regulatory policy when voting in gubernatorial and legislative elections; that is, they are unlikely to be "single issue" voters with respect to insurance. As a result, governors and their appointed commissioners may be less vulnerable to pressure of this sort. The counterargument is that appointed commissioners might favor the industry to the detriment of consumers because they are less "accountable to the public" and therefore more readily influenced by insurance companies and agents.

A related issue concerns the background and qualifications of commissioners. People with prior experience in the insurance industry often are appointed, and many insurance commissioners accept employment in the industry following their tenure in office. Critics argue that this "revolving door" constitutes obvious evidence of capture by the industry. They argue that electing rather than appointing the insurance commissioner will make this outcome less likely. If people without substantial background in insurance are appointed, the process is criticized for leading to the appointment of incompetent, political hacks.

Although these criticisms often play well and are not implausible, an alternative perspective is that extensive background in insurance makes for more knowledgeable and effective commissioners. In addition, the expertise developed by regulating competitive insurance markets efficiently makes talented commissioners attractive employees in the industry when they leave office, especially in government affairs. As a result, the best regulators, from the perspective of both the industry and the average consumer, will be most likely to obtain attractive industry positions following their tenure as commissioner. If serving as an effective regulator enhances future employment prospects, agency costs will decline because commissioners will have more incentive to regulate efficiently. If so, the labor market for former commissioners may reduce the agency problem in insurance regulation, just as the managerial labor market helps reduce agency costs associated with possible conflicts between managers and shareholders (see Chapter 2).

---

the maximization of political support often will lead regulators to redistribute income between producers and consumers or between different groups of consumers, as opposed to pursuing the public interest by efficiently mitigating market failures. Groups that can more effectively generate political support (or pressure) will likely be favored by regulation at the expense of groups that are less effective in generating support.

One prediction from this theory is that relatively small groups that have large per capita stakes in the outcome of regulation have a significant incentive to become informed about regulation and organize to influence regulation. As a result, these groups are likely to benefit at the expense of larger groups for which the per capita stakes are small. This possible comparative advantage in generating political support for small groups with large per capita stakes might frequently cause regulators to be captured by the regulated industry. In other words, regulators will adopt policies that increase profits for the regulated industry at the expense of the public interest (large numbers of uninformed consumers with low per capita stakes in the regulatory outcome). The prediction that regulation often will benefit the regulated industry at the expense of consumers is accordingly known as the **capture theory,** or perhaps more accurately, the *capture hypothesis* or *producer protection hypothesis.*

Some observers suggest that strict prior approval regulation of property-liability insurance rates up until the late 1950s and 1960s, which made it difficult for insurers to charge rates lower than those developed by insurance rating bureaus, is consistent with the capture hypothesis (also see Box 24–2). Regardless of the extent to which this is historically accurate, the capture of regulators is inconsistent with the modern emphasis of rate regulation in many states on limiting rate increases to make coverage more affordable or on promoting large cross-subsidies between groups of insurance buyers. It appears instead that rapidly rising costs produce effective political pressure for policies that slow the growth in premiums, even if this reduces the supply and quality of coverage and causes insurers to suffer losses—the opposite of what would be expected if regulators are captured by insurers.

Cross-subsidies that have occurred from lower to higher risk consumers (e.g., in some auto and workers' compensation insurance markets) also might suggest that higher risk buyers may be able to exert more pressure for lower rates than lower risk buyers. This might occur, for example, if high-risk buyers have greater incentive to become informed about and influence regulation, to be single issue voters, or simply to complain to the insurance department or legislators. In addition to diffuse pressure by relatively large groups of consumers, some organized consumer groups actively fight insurance rate increases and support regulatory policies that produce cross-subsidies and large residual markets.

24.5 Summary

- State insurance codes and insurance departments regulate (1) the licensing of insurers, agents, and brokers; (2) solvency; (3) premium rates in many lines and states; (4) residual markets; (5) the content of policy forms; and (6) insurer sales practices and information disclosure. The National Association of Insurance Commissioners helps to coordinate state regulation.

- The McCarran-Ferguson Act of 1945 endorses state regulation of insurance and provides the insurance industry with a limited exemption from federal antitrust law. This exemption allows insurers to cooperate in ways that otherwise would be illegal. In particular, the exemption facilitates joint analysis of data, including the development of claim cost forecasts using industrywide data.

- State regulation is criticized for its lack of uniformity, unnecessary duplication, and differences in quality across states. On the other hand, state regulation is more readily tailored to local needs, it facilitates cautious experimentation, and the effects of regulatory mistakes are localized.
- The public interest view of regulation holds that

regulation should be designed to alleviate significant market imperfections, such as problems that arise due to costly and imperfect information in insurance markets. In practice, political pressure sometimes causes regulatory policies to deviate from this objective, responding instead in ways that benefit particular groups at the expense of others.

Key Terms

state insurance department   635
state insurance commissioner   635
National Association of Insurance Commissioners
  (NAIC)   638
model laws   638
Paul v. Virginia   640

Southeastern Underwriters Association
  decision   641
McCarran-Ferguson Act   642
public interest view of regulation   645
theory of economic regulation   650
capture theory   652

Questions and Problems

1. Briefly describe the historical evolution of state insurance regulation including the effects of Paul v. Virginia, the Southeastern Underwriters Association decision, and the McCarran-Ferguson Act.

2. Summarize the main arguments that favor federal insurance regulation and the main arguments that favor state regulation. Based on the discussion in the text and your own views concerning centralization versus decentralization of government power, which type of insurance regulation do you believe is better?

3. Contrast the public interest view of regulation with the economic theory of regulation.

4. Are problems associated with costly and imperfect information concerning product quality likely to be more severe in insurance markets than for: (*a*) commercial banking, (*b*) the market for personal computers, and (*c*) the market for sterco equipment? Explain. (Note: We did not address this specific

question in the chapter. You should be able to come up with a reasonable response given your knowledge of insurance and your knowledge and experience with these other markets.)

5. Why might establishing and monitoring compliance with minimum quality standards be preferable in some cases to disclosure of more information as a method of addressing the problem of costly and imperfect information?

6. Some state insurance departments develop summaries of auto insurance rates charged by different insurers for a benchmark set of coverages and driver characteristics and make this available to consumers on request. Briefly describe the possible benefits and costs of this form of disclosure, including the usefulness of the information. (Hint: Also consider the possible impact of differences in underwriting standards across insurers on the information's utility to buyers.)

7. The development of the Internet has made the transmission of information to large numbers of people much cheaper than in the past. Does this reduce the case for using regulation to deal with costly and imperfect information in insurance markets?

8. If insurance price regulation suppresses rates below the cost of providing coverage, explain why this outcome is inconsistent with the public interest view of regulation. Answer the same question for price regulation that leads to cross-subsidies among insurance consumers.

References

Breyer, Stephen. *Regulation and Its Reform.* Cambridge, MA: Harvard University Press, 1982. (*Detailed discussion of the public interest view of regulation, the limitations of regulation, and major types of economic regulation that have been used in the United States for a variety of industries.*)

Danzon, Patricia. "The McCarran-Ferguson Act: Anticompetitive or Procompetitive?" *Regulation: Cato Review of Business and Government* 15 (1992), pp. 38–47. (*Detailed discussion of the effects of the limited antitrust exemption.*)

Harrington, Scott. "Should the Feds Regulate Insurance?" *Regulation: Cato Review of Business and Government* 14 (1991). (*Detailed discussion of state versus federal regulation of solvency.*)

Harrington, Scott; and Helen Doerpinghaus. "The Economics and Politics of Automobile Insurance Rate Classification." *Journal of Risk and Insurance* 60 (1993). (*Discussion of how interest group pressure may affect auto insurance rate classification.*)

Joskow, Paul. "Cartels, Competition, and Regulation in the US Property-Liability Insurance Industry." *Bell Journal of Economics and Management Science* 4 (1973), pp. 375–427. (*A classic economic analysis of property-liability insurance market structure, conduct, and regulation.*)

Lilly, Claude. "A History of Insurance Regulation in the United States." *CPCU Annals* 29 (1976), pp. 99–115. (*Detailed discussion of the history of insurance regulation.*)

Mehr, Robert I.; and Emerson Cammack. *Principles of Insurance.* 6th ed. Chapter 28. Homewood, IL: Richard D. Irwin, 1976. (*Discusses the history of insurance regulation.*)

Stigler, George. "The Theory of Economic Regulation." *Bell Journal of Economics and Management Science* 2 (1971), pp. 3–21. (*A classic article on the economic theory of regulation and capture theory by a Nobel Prize–winning economist.*)

Answer to Concept Check

1. The limited antitrust exemption increases the accuracy of claim cost forecasts, thus reducing the amount of capital that many insurers need to hold to achieve a high probability of solvency. It also lowers insurers' costs of rate-making. The exemption is limited in two main ways: (1) an activity must be subject to state regulatory oversight in order to be exempt, and (2) any activity involving boycott, coercion, or intimidation is not exempt.

Index